Reformation without end

D1595820

MANCHESTER 1824

Manchester University Press

Politics, culture and society in early modern Britain

General Editors

This important series publishes monographs that take a fresh and challenging look at the interactions between politics, culture and society in Britain between 1500 and the mid-eighteenth century. It counteracts the fragmentation of current historiography through encouraging a variety of approaches which attempt to redefine the political, social and cultural worlds, and to explore their interconnection in a flexible and creative fashion. All the volumes in the series question and transcend traditional interdisciplinary boundaries, such as those between political history and literary studies, social history and divinity, urban history and anthropology. They thus contribute to a broader understanding of crucial developments in early modern Britain.

Recently published in the series

Chaplains in early modern England: Patronage, literature and religion
HUGH ADLINGTON, TOM LOCKWOOD AND GILLIAN WRIGHT (eds)

The Cooke sisters: Education, piety and patronage in early modern England GEMMA ALLEN

Black Bartholomew's Day DAVID J. APPLEBY

Insular Christianity ROBERT ARMSTRONG AND TADHG Ó HANNRACHAIN (eds)

Reading and politics in early modern England GEOFF BAKER

'No historie so meete' JAN BROADWAY

Republican learning JUSTIN CHAMPION

News and rumour in Jacobean England: Information, court politics and diplomacy, 1618–25 DAVID COAST

This England PATRICK COLLINSON

Sir Robert Filmer (1588–1653) and the patriotic monarch CESARE CUTTICA

Doubtful and dangerous: The question of succession in late Elizabethan England
SUSAN DORAN AND PAULINA KEWES (eds)

Brave community JOHN GURNEY

'Black Tom' ANDREW HOPPER

Royalists and Royalism during the Interregnum JASON MCELLIGOTT AND DAVID L. SMITH

Laudian and Royalist polemic in Stuart England ANTHONY MILTON

The crisis of British Protestantism: Church power in the Puritan Revolution, 1638–44
HUNTER POWELL

The gentlewoman's remembrance: Patriarchy, piety, and singlehood in early Stuart England ISAAC STEPHENS

Exploring Russia in the Elizabethan Commonwealth: The Muscovy Company and Giles Fletcher, the elder (1546–1611) FELICITY JANE STOUT

Full details of the series are available at www.manchesteruniversitypress.co.uk.

Reformation without end

Religion, politics and the past in post-revolutionary England

ROBERT G. INGRAM

Manchester University Press

Published by Manchester University Press
Altrincham Street, Manchester M1 7JA, UK
www.manchesteruniversitypress.co.uk

British Library Cataloguing-in-Publication Data is available

ISBN 978 1 5261 2694 8 *hardback*
ISBN 978 1 5261 4357 0 *paperback*

First published by Manchester University Press in hardback 2018

This edition first published 2019

Typeset by Servis Filmsetting Ltd, Stockport, Cheshire

I give it to you not that you may remember time, but that you might forget it now and then for a moment and not spend all your breath trying to conquer it. Because no battle is ever won he said. They are not even fought. The field only reveals to man his own folly and despair, and victory is an illusion of philosophers and fools.

William Faulkner, *The Sound and the Fury*

Had someone said: 'All differences are theological differences?'

Evelyn Waugh, *Unconditional Surrender*

Contents

Part III: Neither Jacobite, nor republican, Presbyterian, nor papist: Zachary Grey

Part IV: The abuses of fanaticism: William Warburton

List of illustrations

Preface

The Parallel: or, Laud & C-d-x compared. Being true Pictures of those Celebrated High Priests, shewing the great Resemblance between them, both in principles and practice appeared in 1736. Britannia sat next to the royal shield and pointed at twinned images of Charles I's archbishop of Canterbury William Laud (1573–1645) – who, the print noted, was 'beheaded on Tower Hill' – and Edmund Gibson (1669–1748), bishop of London and author of *Codex Juris Ecclesiae Anglicanae* (1713). Above their portraits ran a warning: 'Britons beware! Mark them which cause divisions and offences, they serve not our Lord Jesus Christ, but their own belly'. It also reminded readers that 'as Englishmen and Protestants, they ought to be subject to Principalities and Powers, and to obey the Civil Magistrates'. Beneath the portraits ran a litany of Laud's offences; 'So is C-d-x' followed each one. Laud, we learn, 'was for Usurping a dominion over the Faith & Consciences of the Laity, terming all Enthusiasts or Hereticks, who did not believe his Impositions; & persecuting such as would not Submit to his Discipline'. Furthermore, he used the church courts against the laity and even subverted the royal supremacy. 'Tho' Sworn to acknowledge ye King as Supreme in all Matters as well Ecclesiastical as Civil', Laud instead 'was for making the Church independent of the State, and exempting the Clergy from the Jurisdiction of the Secular Magistrate'. Moreover, he was a crypto-papist who 'introduced many popish Rites into the Church'. These policies proved bloody: 'Laud by creating jealousies between ye King & his Subjects, set ye whole Nation in a flame which at last ended in a Civil War'. On *The Parallel*'s reading, the civil wars of the mid-seventeenth century were wars of religion caused by a high priest whose thoughts on theology, liturgy, ecclesiology and Church–state relations had destabilized the civil order. Furthermore, while the English were Protestants they were, more fundamentally, subjects, subordinate to the 'Secular Magistrate'.

The Parallel was the not the only work during the 1730s to liken Gibson to Laud. Indeed, it was a commonplace move for eighteenth-century anticlericals to accuse the Church of England's leaders of being latter-day Lauds,

Figure 1 The Parallel: or, Laud & C-d-x compared, 1736

just as Laud had been accused of being a latter-day Thomas Cardinal Wolsey (*c.* 1474–1530).[1] But was this polemical move in *The Parallel* a vestigial tic or a sign of the seventeenth century's continued relevance into the eighteenth century? Most historians would say the former since most historians also locate the 1630s and the 1730s on opposite sides of an historiographical continental divide located somewhere at or around 1688. West of that divide, the historical waters pooled into the Sea of Early Modernity. East of it, the historical waters flowed swiftly and ineluctably into the large Ocean of Modernity. In each body of water swam wholly different species. That was not how the eighteenth-century English saw it. For most living during the 1730s, William Laud's world a century earlier remained recognizable and instructive. This book explains why.

That explanation requires acknowledging two things about eighteenth-century England. Firstly, it was a post-revolutionary society. The mid-seventeenth century civil wars killed off nearly 4 per cent of the English and 7.5 per cent of all Britons; it also gave the nation its only stretch of republican government. The Glorious Revolution three decades later was no 'bloodless' conflict, but a violent revolution whose aftermath saw fundamental changes to the nation's constitution. Out of these revolutions emerged a new religious and political order. Historians looking back see that post-revolutionary order as durable: it lasted for almost a century and a half. But the eighteenth-century English living in the near-aftermath of the seventeenth-century revolutions worried that what had caused them had not been finally sorted and they feared that the new order built in the revolutions' stead was dangerously unstable.

Secondly, eighteenth-century England was also a world awash in print. More so than ever before, there was printed material available and more people able to read it. The number of works published during the 1760s was more than twice that of the 1660s, while literacy rates had more than doubled in the intervening century. There existed a steadily expanding print culture, one which simultaneously reflected the existence and catalysed the further creation of multiple audiences which authors tried to mobilize for support. Among the prevailing concerns of eighteenth-century English print culture were what had caused the seventeenth-century revolutions; what had had been done to resolve those revolutions; and whether the post-revolutionary order was sustainable.

This book is about the ways that the eighteenth-century English debated the causes and consequences of their seventeenth-century revolutions. More specifically, it is about the ways that polemical divines debated the causes and consequences of those revolutions. The book argues two things. Firstly, those living in post-revolutionary England paradoxically conceived of themselves as still living in the midst of the very thing which they reckoned had caused the seventeenth-century revolutions: the Reformation. And that Reformation had not yet ended. Secondly, the book argues that the reasons for and the legacy of the Reformation remained hotly debated in post-revolutionary England precisely because the religious and political issues generated by it remained unresolved and because that lack of resolution continued to cause problems for the post-revolutionary English. Not surprisingly, a plurality of everything published during the first half of the eighteenth century concerned religion in general and religious history more particularly. Among the chief producers of published work on religion were polemical divines.

To understand fully what those eighteenth-century English polemical divines were trying to achieve in their printed works requires looking beyond their printed works. It requires reading those printed works in the light of all other evidence – marginalia, rough drafts, correspondence and the like – to gauge what audiences they aimed to reach; how they pitched their arguments to reach them; and what even constituted a work of polemical divinity. As importantly, it requires identifying what polemical divines and their contemporaries thought constituted victory in public debate and how far they were willing to go to win. This book tries to do these things by surveying the intertwined lives and careers of four of eighteenth-century England's most prominent polemical divines: Daniel Waterland, Conyers Middleton, Zachary Grey and William Warburton. Their polemical careers illustrate why both they and many of their contemporaries feared that they lived in a Reformation without end. In their world, William Laud and the civil wars he watched begin – or perhaps even caused – remained sources of debate, instruction and warning.

NOTE

1 [Anonymous], *A true description, or rather a parallel between Cardinall Wolsey, Arch-bishop of York, and William Laud, Arch-Bishop of Canterbury* (1641: R23148). F. Peck, *New memoirs of ... John Milton* (1740: T097527), pp. 430–7, attributed *A true description* to John Milton. Modern Milton scholars do not accept that attribution: D. Wolfe (ed.), *Complete Prose Works of John Milton. Volume I, 1624–1642* (New Haven, 1953), p. 581, n. 35. Cf. *The Parallel Reformers, the Renowned Wickliffe and the Reverend Mr. Whitefield Compared* (1740), National Portrait Gallery, London, D43261.

Acknowledgements

Many thanks to those who made this book possible. I have tried out bits of it on various seminar and conference audiences, and parts of it have appeared in print, for which Bill Gibson, Tony Claydon, William Altman, Don Yerxa and Jeremy Gregory gave excellent editorial advice. Thanks too to the two anonymous readers for Manchester University Press.

The Historical Society of the Episcopal Church, the Ohio University Humanities Research Fund and the Ohio University Research Council provided the resources which allowed me to research in Britain, where the staff at Queen Mary's Mile End dormitories are always welcoming. Thanks to all the archivists who let me into their libraries and helped me work in their collections: I particularly appreciate the Church Commissioners and the Bishop of Worcester for allowing me to quote from materials in the Hurd Library. The Earhart Foundation and the John Templeton Foundation's Religion and Innovation in Human Affairs Program freed up unbroken stretches of time to write in my Alden Library bolt hole. Durham University's Institute of Advanced Studies provided an idyllic setting for uninterrupted work during a glorious spring term. Thanks to Ingrid Gregg, Don Yerxa and Stephen Taylor for their support of this project and to Alex Barber for the daily Durham company. Thanks too to MRS for helping in Durham and for putting her shoulder to the plough in other ways.

At Ohio University, I have had hyper-competent department heads, including Norm Goda, Patrick Barr-Melej and Katherine Jellison. They rightly recognize that research, writing and teaching are complementary activities and allocate resources accordingly. Running the George Washington Forum made me to see this book more clearly. Norm, Patrick and Katherine let me alone with the GWF, against some people's wishes, while Ben Ogles, Howard Dewald, Susan Downard and Matt Roberts helped me keep it going. I appreciate their support, especially when they might have thought I was hanging out past where the bus lines run. Thanks to Mike Andrews and Pamela Edwards for having made it possible at all and to Patrick Peel, Chris Barker and Tim

Lehmann for their good fellowship. The students who have come through the GWF continue to delight. I particularly thank Casey Arnold, Emily Hawley Riley, Wen Zhang, Amrit Saini, Evan Ecos, Joseph Gattermeyer, Tanner Ogle, Precious Oluwasanya and Michael Gerber for their research help. Brian Schoen, Paul Milazzo, Bruce Steiner, Rich Vedder, Mark LeBar, Eric LeMay, Josh Hill, Sarah Kinkel and Jess Roney tolerated me and let me vent my spleen. Sam Venable and Joe Pauwels ensured that I was less splenetic, if debilitatingly sore, and reminded me that faculty are not the only people at universities who are bonkers.

Paul Halliday, Bill Gibson and Pat Griffin are mentors, now friends, who wrote for my grant applications, sometimes, I suspect, with bemusement at my choice of topics but always with good cheer, unstinting encouragement and unquestioning support. I still owe them a debt I cannot repay. Bill read the whole manuscript and (finally) convinced me that there is no such thing as a 40,000-word chapter. Pat saw from 40,000 feet how the project could fit into the landscape below and encouraged me to do so too. Mike Ashby, Jim Bradley, Justin Champion, Jonathan Clark, Tony Claydon, Tom Cogswell, Brian Cowan, Rose Dixon, Sarah Ellenzweig, Stephen Fallon, Brad Gregory, Elish Gregory, Jeremy Gregory, Bill Jacob, Jamie Latham, Paul Lim, Simon Lewis, Scott Mandelbrote, Anton Matytsin, Noah McCormack, Noah Millstone, Ken Owen, Chris Penney, Steve Pincus, Nick Popper, Joan-Pau Rubiés, Nigel Sharp, Brent Sirota, Max Skjönsberg, Ralph Stevens, Tim Stuart-Buttle, Scott Taylor, Andrew Thompson, James Vaughn, David Womersley, David Wykes and Sam Zeitlin all clarified my thinking, pointed me down fruitful paths, passed along references or provided other help. Behind this book lies the quiet, unintended influence of Charles Perry.

Jason Peacey and Peter Lake run the Skinners Arms seminar, from which I've learned much. I appreciate Jason and Peter's willingness to think that a book on eighteenth-century stuff rightly fits into a series on early modern stuff. Bill Bulman, Alex Barber and Karl Gunther introduced me to the Skinners Arms group and have provided equal measures of encouragement, reassurance and sober correction. I had originally envisaged this book as something very different and very short; it turned into something much longer and much different because of them. They bear no responsibility for the errors or infelicities, which are mine alone, and this is decidedly not the book any of them would have written. But I hope that they like it and accept it as a token of thanks and of friendship.

I dedicate the book to my wife, our daughters and my father. Jill once explained to me why she doesn't read what I write: 'I love you, not your work'. Also, 'your prose makes my head hurt'. Claire and Lucy are less charitable about my work or my prose. (As you and that plain-speaking Yorkshireman George Whitebread would say, Lucy, 'No offence!') But they love me enough to let me get on with research and writing, even when that means putting up with my absences, irritability, obsessiveness and preoccupation. I remember too well what my life was like without the three of them in it, and I never forget the light they bring in that keeps the darkness at bay. That I made it this far owes everything to Dad. He knows how. Thanks is insufficient for him or for Jill, Claire and Lucy. But thanks anyway. And all my love.

Athens, Ohio
Feast day of Blessed Anthony Turner 2017

Abbreviations

AC	J. Venn and J.A. Venn, *Alumni Cantabrigienses ... Part I. From the Earliest Times to 1751*, 4 vols. (Cambridge, 1922)
Add.	Additional
AEH	*Anglican and Episcopal History*
Annals	C. Cooper, *Annals of Cambridge* (Cambridge, 1852), IV
BCP	D. MacCulloch (ed.), *Book of Common Prayer* (1999)
Beinecke	Beinecke Rare Book and Manuscript Library, New Haven, CT
BJHS	*British Journal for the History of Science*
BL	British Library, London
Bodleian	Bodleian Library, Oxford
CCED	*Clergy of the Church of England Database* [www.theclergy-database.org.uk]
CUL	Cambridge University Library
ECS	*Eighteenth-Century Studies*
Egmont	*Manuscripts of the Earl of Egmont. Diary of Viscount Percival afterwards first Earl of Egmont*, 3 vols. (1920–23)
Harley	Edward Harley, second earl of Oxford
Hervey, *Memoirs*	J. Hervey, *Some Materials towards Memoirs of the Reign of King George II*, ed. R. Sedgwick, 3 vols. (1931)
HJ	*Historical Journal*
HL	Hurd Library, Hartlebury
HMC	Historical Manuscript Commission
HRC	Harry Ransom Research Center, Austin, TX
Huntington	Huntington Library, San Marino, CA
JBS	*Journal of British Studies*
JHI	*Journal of the History of Ideas*
JMEMS	*Journal of Medieval and Early Modern Studies*
JRULM	John Rylands University Library, Manchester
JWCI	*Journal of the Warburg and Courtauld Institutes*

Kilvert	F. Kilvert (ed.), *A Selection of the Unpublished Papers of … William Warburton* (1841)
LA	J. Nichols, *Literary Anecdotes of the Eighteenth Century*, 9 vols. (1816)
LI	J. Nichols, *Illustrations of the Literary History of the Eighteenth Century*, 8 vols. (1822)
LLEP	*Letters from a Late Eminent Prelate to one of his friends* (1809)
LPL	Lambeth Palace Library
LWCY	*Letters from the Reverend Dr. Warburton, Bishop of Gloucester, to the Hon. Charles Yorke, from 1752 to 1770* (1812)
MCC/MR	Magdalene College Library, Cambridge, Master's Records C/DW/I
MWCM	*Miscellaneous Works of Conyers Middleton*, 4 vols. (1752: T126587)
NP	*Newton Project* [www.newtonproject.sussex.ac.uk]
ODNB	H. Matthew and B. Harrison (eds.), *Oxford Dictionary of National Biography*, 60 vols. (Oxford, 2004)
OW	*Old Whig; or Consistent Protestant*
PH	*Parliamentary History*
P&P	*Past and Present*
SAL	University of St Andrews Library
SCH	*Studies in Church History*
SJCC	St John's College Library, Cambridge
SRO	Suffolk Record Office, Bury St. Edmunds
TCC	Trinity College Library, Cambridge
TNA	The National Archives, Kew
TRHS	*Transactions of the Royal Historical Society*
WAM	Westminster Abbey Library and Muniment Room, London
WC	W.S. Lewis *et al.* (eds.), *The Yale Edition of Horace Walpole's Correspondence*, 48 vols. (New Haven, CT, 1937–83)
WDW	Daniel Waterland, *Works of… Daniel Waterland*, ed. W. Van Mildert, 6 vols. (Oxford, 1823)
WM	*Weekly Miscellany*
WNC	'William Warburton's Notes on Lord Clarendon's History of the Rebellion', in Edward Hyde, *History of the Rebellion and Civil Wars* (Oxford, 1849), VI, pp. 475–600
WNDN	'William Warburton's marginal notes to Daniel Neal's *History of the Puritans*, 3 vols. (1732: T133485), *c.* 1754, Durham Cathedral Library, Shelfmark E IV.B.30–32
WWW	R. Hurd (ed.), *Works of … William Warburton*, 12 vols. (1811)

ZGMSSB	Zachary Grey Manuscript Sermons, 1729–58 (Beinecke, Osborn C88)
ZGMSSC	Zachary Grey Manuscript Sermons, 1727–39 (CUL, Add. MS 8516)

All dates before 1752 are given in British 'Old Style' (Julian calendar), which was eleven days behind the Continental 'New Style' (Gregorian calendar). The year is taken to begin on 1 January. Spelling in quotations has been modernized. Titles of pre-1800 works in the notes are abbreviated, but include the English Short-Title Catalogue reference number. Where an archival source is cited in the notes, it is implied, unless otherwise noted, to be a manuscript. The place of publication is London, unless otherwise noted.

Chapter 1

Why then are we still reforming?

WHAT THE GOLDEN KING BEGAN

This account of the past's hold on post-revolutionary England opens with the stories of two doubting Thomases – Thomas Woolston and Thomas Rundle. One questioned Christ's miracles, the other, Christ's divinity. They rehashed heresies from antiquity and both suffered when their doubts became public. The fates of these two doubting Thomases remind us of salient features of eighteenth-century England that most have forgotten. They remind us that the eighteenth-century English obsessed about the past and debated furiously what guidance it should have for the present. They remind us of the places where and the ways in which the eighteenth-century English fought their positions. They remind us of the character of the post-revolutionary politics of religion. They remind us of the role of restraint – official and unofficial, overt and unspoken – in shaping and managing public debate. And they remind us of the central role played in those public debates by clerics. Those eighteenth-century English polemical divines tried to use Renaissance tools to solve Reformation problems that had caused seventeenth-century religious wars. When they failed to solve those problems, the English state did. In the end, Leviathan won.

Both the Woolston and Rundle controversies were fights about the past. The controversy centring on Thomas Woolston (1668–1733) erupted during the late 1720s, almost three centuries after the English Reformation had begun; but the Reformation was the framework within which many located it. Just after Christmas 1728, for instance, Edmund Gibson, bishop of London, received a pseudonymous letter from Christodulus. '[B]y the very same Sophistry wherewith you Protestants a Century or two ago unfortunately explained away the points of Holy writ, the authority of the church and the real presence ... one of your brotherhood has explained away the whole and the same foul breath that raised your Bubble of a church has blown it into nothing', Christodulus charged. '...[Y]our first step over the brink of heaven naturally landed to hell, the first step you took with your Back to the

Catholic Church naturally led you to Deism and Bold Woolston has but ended what the Golden king began, our unhappy Henry the Eight'.[1] Christodulus referred to Thomas Woolston's recent work on Christ's miracles. Woolston argued that 'the literal history of many of the miracles of Jesus as recorded by the Evangelists, does imply Absurdities, Improbabilities and Incredibilities, consequently they, either in whole or in part, were never wrought, as they are commonly believed now-a-days, but are only related as prophetical and parabolical Narratives of what would be mysteriously and wonderfully done by him'. Jesus, Woolston acknowledged, was the Messiah, but prophecy, not miracles, proved it. Woolston promised 'not [to] confine myself only to Reason, but also the express Authority of the Fathers, those holy, venerable and learned Preachers of the Gospel in the first Ages of the Church, who took our Religion from the Hands of the Apostles and of apostolical Men, who died, some of them and suffered for the Doctrines they taught, who professedly and confessedly were endued with divine and extraordinary Gifts of the Spirit'.[2] Woolston's six discourses (1727–29) denied the literal truth of Christ's miracles, caused a furore and sold nearly twenty thousand copies. The Roman Catholic Christodulus saw in Woolston's denial of miracles the natural terminus of Protestant logic. Leading figures in the Protestant English church-state judged differently, reckoning Woolston a 'fool and madman' whose works caused 'mischief'.[3] Woolston, an idiosyncratic figure with no powerful patron, got punished as a cautionary example. Many of the established Church's leading figures rebutted him in print and the state brought the royal justice to bear against him.

Woolston's 1729 trial for blasphemy took place at the Court of King's Bench.[4] There the crown's prosecutors argued that Woolston's view of Christ's miracles was illegal. '[T]his was the most Blasphemous Book that ever was Published in any Age whatsoever', claimed Attorney-General Philip Yorke. In it 'our Saviour is compared to a Conjurer, Magician and Imposter and the Holy Gospel, as wrote by the Blessed Evangelists, turned into Ridicule and Ludicrous Banter, the Literal Scope and Meaning wrested and the Whole represented as idle Romance and Fiction'. Woolston's writings, Yorke warned, threatened to cause 'the truth of the Holy Scriptures to be denied and to weaken their authority and thereupon to spread among the king's subjects irreligious and diabolical opinions'.[5] Yorke had made an analogous argument in *Rex* v. *Curll* (1727). There Yorke had contended that by publishing an obscene book Edmund Curll had committed an 'offence at common law, as it tends to corrupt the morals of the King's subjects and is against the peace of the King. Peace includes good order and government and that may be broken in many instances without an actual force. 1. If it be an act against the constitution or civil government; 2. If it be against religion: and, 3. If against morality'.[6] Theological heterodoxy threatened the state because it could disrupt the peace.

Woolston countered that he had not aimed 'to bring Our Religion into

Contempt, but to put Our Religion upon a better Footing and shew, That the Miracles of our Saviour were to be understood in a Metaphorical Sense and not as they were Literally Written'.[7] When denying Christ's transfiguration or healing miracles, Woolston protested that he had followed primitive precedent. 'I do profess here before God and the World that I am a Christian', he pleaded, 'for if I am not a Christian, not even the Fathers themselves are Christians since they believed exactly as I do'. In fact, he continued, 'the Fathers say Christianity in the Allegorical Sense of the Scriptures' and no less than St Jerome had argued 'that the literal sense is contrary to Christianity'.[8] His discourses aimed only 'to establish the Christian Religion upon the Foundation of the Fathers and to interpret the Scriptures as they did'.[9] Woolston's defence failed to sway the jury, which convicted him of blasphemy. Neither were the judges lenient: they punitively fined him and jailed him in the King's Bench prison in Southwark, where he remained on and off for the next four years before influenza killed him. Woolston's supporters claimed he had 'dyed under Persecution for Religion'.[10] Leaders of the English church-state, by contrast, thought they were protecting truth and ensuring civil peace. Either way, there was no denying that the church-state had sent an unmistakeable message to heterodox polemical divines through Woolston's exemplary punishment.

The message that heterodoxy harmed clerical careers likewise got sent in the case of Thomas Rundle (1687–1743).[11] Nearly a year after Woolston's death, Lord Chancellor Charles Talbot put forward his domestic chaplain, Rundle, for the vacant see of Gloucester. Queen Caroline also supported Rundle. Yet, from the outset, Edmund Gibson, whom some called Robert Walpole's 'pope', sought to scupper Rundle's candidacy. The nomination, Gibson reported, had 'given very great offence to the clergy; and I may truly add, that the uneasiness is general, among the Whig as well as the Tory part of them'.[12] There were longstanding rumours that Rundle was an Arian, something neither Rundle nor his supporters publicly denied and something to which his friendships with heterodox figures lent credibility.[13] Moreover, Richard Venn, a hyper-orthodox and politically well-connected London priest, recounted to Gibson a long-ago conversation in which Rundle had argued that Abraham's almost-sacrifice of Isaac was 'an action unjust and unnatural, that it was the remains of his Idolatrous Education and proceeded from a vain affection of exceeding other Nations, that had indeed been guilty of human sacrifice ...; that in order to justify and heighten his character in the esteem of his friends, he pretended a Revelation from God, commissioning him to enter upon this bloody affair'. Venn charged that Rundle had 'falsely accused the Father of the Faith, or else I am sure the whole Christian Religion must be false itself'.[14] Others provided corroborating evidence. Charles Lamotte, a Northamptonshire clergyman, wrote unbidden to Gibson, informing him that years earlier Rundle had been 'very free with his speech and very loose in his Religion; talking sometimes like an Arian, sometimes like a Socinian'.[15]

The prospect of a Christologically heterodox new bishop who had also questioned the Bible's historical accuracy was too much for Gibson and most clergy. '[T]he general sense of the Bishops and Clergy, will not permit me to concur or acquiesce in it', Gibson informed Walpole, before adding that the episcopate's obeisance to the state had earned it the right to have its wishes heeded on Church matters: 'The Bishops, on account of their dutiful behaviour to the Court, might hope for some regard to their inclination and good liking in the choice of every new member of the Bench'.[16]

In the end, Walpole withdrew Rundle's nomination.[17] Contemporaries got the message. '[T]he case of Dr Rundel admonishes me, as indeed my own case had done before, of the danger of touching the third & most important article above, Religion. For the Informer against the Dr is not watchful only over the Episcopate, but extends his care to the lowest order of the Clergy', the talented and ambitious Cambridge cleric Conyers Middleton observed. 'Thus they guard the gate of Paradise, as it was of old, with a flaming sword; & treat freethinking or any thinking different from their own, as the sin against the Holy Ghost; never to be remitted, either in this life or the next.'[18] Where Middleton read the Rundle affair as a sign of the Church's power, some orthodox bishops actually feared that it had exposed the Church's weakness. '[W]hat has passed with [Rundle], shews too strongly, how vain an attempt it will be to endeavour to exclude others, against whom there shall be no other objection, but a want of Orthodoxy, in some certain points', Francis Hare, bishop of Chichester, lamented to Gibson.[19] Hare feared that the Church could not always expect the support and forbearance that its senior partner, the state, had recently shown. He was right.

The government scuttled Thomas Rundle's episcopal nomination and prosecuted Thomas Woolston for blasphemy not simply because of clerical lobbying but also because polemical divines successfully used print to shape opinions and to mobilize support. In the public debates over both Rundle and Woolston, participants returned regularly to contested patches of the Christian and English past. Woolston's opponents argued that he and his supporters had perverted ancient Christian truths.[20] The 'Primitive Martyrs and the Reformers ... gave us Truth', Daniel Waterland insisted; those who advocated prosecuting Woolston acted 'from a true Christian and Apostolical Spirit'.[21] Richard Smalbroke likewise accused Woolston's supporters of perverting primitive Christianity. 'Persons, ... under the specious Colour of Liberty are employing all their Artifices to reduce us again to a State of Heathenism and the Religion of Nature', he fretted. Tellingly, he contended 'that the Present Licentiousness bears too near a Resemblance to that which was Previous to the Public Confusions in the Age of our Forefathers; Confusions, that ended in the Ruin of the Constitution of both Church and State'.[22] Woolston's supporters also hearkened to the previous century. They countered that Smalbroke's arguments for 'persecution' called to mind Judge George Jeffreys (1645–89) and that '[a] proceeding like this would have incurred an Impeachment in former Times and Arch-Bishop Laud was brought to the Scaffold, for Offences much less injurious to his Country'.[23]

Thomas Rundle's proposed promotion to Gloucester similarly got related to England's past.[24] *The Weekly Miscellany*, a Gibsonite newspaper edited by the acidulous William Webster, savaged Rundle's candidacy in a way that implicitly connected the present with the past. '[T]here is not an Infidel, Deist, or modern Freethinker in the Kingdom, who is not zealous for [Rundle's] Promotion', Webster's newspaper pronounced. Conversely, Rundle's heterodoxy rankled the orthodox. Indeed, the *Miscellany* argued, the putatively Arian Rundle was a heretic, since both Elizabethan and Williamite statues had unambiguously hereticated Arianism. Furthermore, Rundle's opponents were moderates, ones who recognized that there was a 'Medium between no Toleration and an absolute, unlimited Toleration': by implication, some things – like Christological heterodoxy – were intolerable.[25] *The Old Whig: or, the Consistent Protestant*, a pro-Rundle newspaper, judged differently but similarly recalled older debates. It not so subtly warned its readers that the fight over Rundle's candidacy signalled the revival of the previous century's religio-political battles. 'The nation is on all Hands alarmed with the Growth of Popery', it fretted. Worse than the papists themselves were the papist wolves in Protestant clothing. '[T]here are not wanting Men amongst ourselves, who, though Protestants by Profession, yet retain and inculcate the most dangerous Principles of Popery', the *Old Whig* claimed. But, unlike the seventeenth century, when the English monarchs had been crypto-popery's most powerful proponents, in the mid-1730s it was the Church of England's leaders who sought to subvert English liberties. The established Church's priests were 'Advocate[s] for the Inquisitorial Power and for the Subjection of the Crown itself to the Lordly Claims of the more sacred Priesthood!' Lest those with longer historical memories retort that Whigs had spearheaded the last successful plot to overthrow an English monarch, the *Old Whig* editorialist reassured its readers that he 'brings with him no more of Republican than he doth of Slavish Principles, is a hearty Friend to the present Constitution and an Enemy to none but those who are Enemies to the Religion and Liberties of his Country'.[26]

The fundamental problem evinced by both the Rundle and Wolston affairs was how to manage religious difference, especially when unmanaged religious difference had so recently torn apart England's civil order. That the seemingly arcane theological views of two doubting Thomases worried leaders of Church and state during the 1720s and 1730s suggests that grave concerns about the post-revolutionary settlement's stability remained. Those worries stemmed from the inability definitively to solve epistemological, theological, ecclesiological and political problems unleashed by the Reformation. What magnified these problems was that all were subject to intensive public debate long after the seventeenth-century wars were done. For some, religious polemic was a way to manage religious difference, one which offered the prospect of defeating one's ideological foes publicly and finally. In practice, public polemic was a style of conflict management that tended to roil waters, not calm them.

Among the many changes catalysed in England by the seventeenth-century revolutionary wars and the Reformation that spawned them was an explosion of printed material, which even until the mid-eighteenth century mostly concerned religion. This book gives an account of both the content and content-producers of English polemical divinity in the third of a century or so after the Hanoverian succession of 1714.[27] That stretch of time comprises a significant chunk of that thing we now call England's Enlightenment.[28] This book tries to think about the world of eighteenth-century polemical divinity as those at the time thought about it. None of them thought they were living during the Enlightenment. Instead, eighteenth-century English polemical divines had a common metaphor to describe the character and to identify the stakes of their efforts – *warfare*. Daniel Waterland, one of Woolston's opponents, disagreed with those who argued that 'all polemics were unbecoming our calling as Christians and our profession as divines'. Rather, he countered, 'The Church is militant and such soldiery is our profession and business and such warfare our proper employment'.[29] Or, as his contemporary William Warburton later put it, '[my] life is a warfare upon earth (that is to say with bigots and libertines, against whom I have denounced eternal war, like Hannibal against Rome at the Altar)'.[30] This metaphor of intellectual combat recurred in contemporary analyses of the age. But what was that 'warfare' all about? Where did it begin? And how did contemporaries think that it could be won?

What follows is the story of that polemical war told from four proximate, yet distinct, vantages, the intertwined lives and careers of Daniel Waterland (1683–1740), Conyers Middleton (1683–1750), Zachary Grey (1688–1766) and William Warburton (1698–1779). Each was an influential polemical divine during the mid-eighteenth century and each instigated or contributed to charged public debates in ancient and modern history, philosophy, literary scholarship and theology. Their contemporaries recognized them as some of the most important producers of polemical divinity. Daniel Waterland, who wrote mostly about primitive Christianity, was orthodoxy's paragon; Conyers Middleton was not, for, while he matched Waterland's erudition, he reached far different – far more heterodox – theological conclusions than his hated Cambridge contemporary. Zachary Grey likewise knew much about Christianity's early history, but he knew far more about sixteenth- and seventeenth-century English history: in defending orthodoxy, he brought to bear that deep knowledge of England's internecine religious wars. William Warburton too claimed to have read everything published in England during the 1640s and 1650s; indeed, he seems to have known a lot about most everything. In this idiosyncratic polymath was to be seen both the apotheosis and the futility of the 'warfare upon earth'.

That war was not just about methods and sources. It was about individual authors, too. The humanness of those involved in eighteenth-century polemical divinity is all too often missed, which means that much about its character and course are also missed. Waterland, Middleton, Grey and Warburton were human beings in the round, each with his own idiosyncratic aversions, affinities and associations. Each not only had arguments that he made but also had reasons why he made those arguments, reasons which often had more to do with the vagaries of contingent circumstance than with working out a line of thought's logic to its ineluctable conclusion. This means that the story on offer in this book tries to convey the eighteenth century as those living at the time saw it and to show how and where they fought over truth.[31]

This approach – covering much the same ground from four different points of view and often in fine-grained ways – yields a story that widens the scope of inquiry beyond the usual Enlightenment pantheon. Locke, Newton, Hume and Gibbon, for instance, each wrote works whose importance was recognized by contemporaries and which ultimately transcended the particular era in which they were composed. Yet the print culture into which Locke, Newton, Hume and Gibbon launched their works was religion-suffused, filled as it was by polemical divinity. Locke, Newton, Hume and Gibbon, put another way, were but soldiers – and not the only ones, or, at times, even the most important ones – in the 'warfare upon earth'.

In addition, the book elucidates not just what polemical divines argued but why they argued what they argued and why they chose particular moments and media to convey their arguments. Printed sources are the obvious place to begin when studying polemical divinity, for they reveal much – though not all – of *what* was argued. But they can be maddeningly elusive at illuminating *why* authors argued what they argued. Manuscript sources, though, shed light on the reasons for composition and publication. They also can reveal the business of polemical divinity, helping us grasp what sorts of polemical works were and were not financially viable and, by implication, which were and were not publicly appealing. All of this together identifies the terrain upon and tactics by which the 'warfare upon earth' was fought.

Finally and perhaps most importantly, the book's approach shows what the 'warfare upon earth' was all about. Jettisoning stadial and supercessionist accounts of historical development, especially those which draw sharp distinctions between a premodern religiously infused past and an increasingly secular modern one, it rejects the notion that the primary tension within eighteenth-century English intellectual life was between an enlightened, secularizing modernity and its unenlightened, sacralised opposite.[32] It questions, in other words, the liberation narrative in which the liberating – and liberal – forces of enlightenment battled with and ultimately triumphed over, the benighted 'kingdom of darkness'.[33] That morality tale is a reductive lumper's tale, one which reduces eighteenth-century English intellectual life to a contest between the religious and the a-religious.

This, instead, is a splitter's book. Locating polemical divines in their political, cultural, social, religious and intellectual contexts, it reveals the complexities, contradictions and, at times, the incoherencies of the period. For rarely, if ever, are there clean breaks between one epoch and the next and this certainly was the case for eighteenth-century England. There were, instead, a set of interrelated questions which had animated English political, religious and intellectual life from the Reformation's outset. But the English tried to answer those questions in constantly changing circumstances which themselves changed the sorts of answers that were plausible or workable. At no point did the Reformation-generated questions get answered definitively: some merely seemed more urgent than others at one or another time. Indeed, the very process of trying to answer the Reformation-spawned questions about religion and politics itself generated other, eventually more urgent, questions.

PROMOTING TRUE RELIGION

The English Reformation spurred a long conversation, one which was fundamentally about what constituted truth. That conversation proved inconclusive, leading some to suggest that '[r]eligious and political diversity ... meant a state of relativism, in which good and truth were subjective and defining the motives of an individual or party became a fraught affair as the sincerity of anyone became a matter of partisan conjecture'.[34] The eighteenth-century English living in the grey dawn of modernity would have thought that postmodern hand-wringing about the very possibility of making non-scientific truth claims was wrong.[35] Truth, perhaps ineffable, was ultimately identifiable. Among the most prominent early eighteenth-century voices in the conversation about what constituted truth were the idiosyncratic nonjuror Henry Dodwell (1641–1711) and the Boyle Lecturer and heterodox churchman Samuel Clarke. In 1706, Dodwell published *An Epistolary Discourse*, which argued for mortalism, adducing evidence not just from the Bible but also from patristic writings.[36] For Dodwell, both scripture and Church history proved that the human soul was 'naturally mortal'; that only the Holy Spirit could grant the soul immortality; and that only an episcopal church whose clergy held office by apostolic succession could confer the gifts of the Holy Spirit by way of the sacrament of baptism. These arguments were characteristic digs by a nonjuror at what he took to be the not-apostolic Church of England. Yet Dodwell's was also an unexpected take from someone who combatted freethinking materialism and the theologically heterodox: to advocate for mortalism was to advocate for heresy. Not unsurprisingly, Dodwell's *Epistolary Discourse* elicited rejoinders, including from Samuel Clarke, whose retort pointed up Dodwell's philosophical and scholarly errors. What especially galled Clarke was the encouragement he thought Dodwell's discourse gave to the era's 'libertines'. In particular, Clarke fretted that *An Epistolary Discourse* removed the fear of a future state of rewards and punishments. As he explained privately to Dodwell, 'this last Book of yours, was judged by all serious men of all parties and particularly by those, whose judgEment your Opinions in some other matters should make you value most, to be of dangerous consequences; and in the event it appeared notoriously, that the loose and profane people about the Town and elsewhere embraced your notion with greediness and boasted of it with great pleasure in all companies'. Worse still, 'Loose men' had taken some of Dodwell's 'Quotations out of the Fathers, particularly your long one out of Tertullian' and had used them 'to Ridicule you and the Fathers, & indeed Religion itself'.[37]

The Clarke–Dodwell exchange illustrates that, for the eighteenth-century English, ideas had consequences; that some ideas were right, others wrong; and that properly reading the past was crucial to the task of distinguishing correct from incorrect ideas. At its heart, the 'warfare upon earth' was about Truth: or, as Clarke put it to Dodwell, it was about 'true Religion'.[38] Polemical divines like Clarke and Dodwell contested 'true Religion' along two connected fronts, the one concerning ideas, the other politics. The intellectual front concerned the ways Truth could be ascertained and defined, the political one, the ways Truth could best be promulgated and defended: the former was about scholarship, the latter, about anything and everything that touched upon the relation of Church to state.[39] Both were necessary because the eighteenth-century English disagreed vigorously about what actually constituted the truth and they aired those disagreements publicly and politically. That 'sincerity' was floated as one possible potential litmus test of truth did not mean that the eighteenth-century English were relativists.[40] To their way of thinking, their public sphere swirled not with a welter of truth-claims but with a welter of truths and untruths. This is why the literature of the period abounded with accusations of stupidity and imposture: Truth was Truth and those who denied it either were too thick-headed to ascertain it or else they were liars. Ferreting out liars was one of the polemical divine's chief tasks. The fixedness and immutability of the truth also explains why most thought that restraint and coercion were not just acceptable but morally necessary. The only questions were whom it was acceptable to restrain or to coerce and how to go about restraining or coercing them.

The origins of the eighteenth-century 'warfare upon earth' lay in the sixteenth century, in the Reformation, a religious movement meant to ground truth on something solid, irrefutable and irrefragable: *sola scriptura*. Rather than revealing or recovering truth, though, the Reformation unexpectedly and wholly unintentionally generated competing truth-claims. In the name of truth, it disturbed the peace, pitting man against man, Church against Church, nation against nation in violent struggle over what was the truth or, perhaps more accurately, over who or what had the power to determine or to assert the truth. In mid- and late seventeenth-century England, an intra-Protestant war and a political revolution erupted over these issues and, in their wakes, people sought again to establish truth on something firm and permanent. A few proposed rationalistic metaphysics as that foundation.[41] Most did not, not least because that rationalistic metaphysics only catalysed the production of more and more truth-claims. Instead, far more tried to ground truth on history, since it was something which existed not in the mind's eye but in the actual, documented historical record. The past had happened and, presumably, was recoverable. Eighteenth-century English intellectual life was primarily about trying to recover or recreate a golden past, a state of primitive purity before things had gone badly wrong.[42] Where that golden past lay and precisely what constituted it formed the crux of English intellectual debate in the century after the revolutions. The past – its meanings, its guidance, its hold in the present – was terrain to be seized and secured in the 'warfare upon earth'.

In short, the eighteenth-century English were a revolution-haunted people. They, to borrow John Pocock's evocative description, 'lived with the memory of the civil wars as a nightmare from which [they were] struggling to awake, or, if you prefer, to go to sleep again'.[43] What made that nightmare doubly terrifying was that the debates which the Reformation had spawned and which the religious wars of the seventeenth century had sought to resolve were themselves unresolved. The eighteenth-century, then, was a chapter in the Reformation which had not yet ended, its story, the middle part of a longer one, rather than an early scene in a new one. In the age of enlightenment, English polemical divines engaged primarily in what they conceived of as a restorative project – the reformation of the Reformation. However, that restorative project – like the Reformation – also proved enormously creative. That creativity itself threatened to destabilize civil society unless it could be channelled, controlled or squelched.

AN INSTRUMENT OF CONVINCING SOME MEN'S MINDS

The English Reformation had succeeded through coercion and persuasion. English Protestants, no less than their Continental counterparts, needed the state's support – and its coercive powers – to ensure that religious reform could survive.[44] But the Reformation's survival also depended on the success of those who jockeyed publicly to convince the English people that the Church of Rome posted the greatest threat to true religion and to their liberties. The English had to believe in Protestantism for it to survive and thrive. Yet precisely because the arguments being publicly debated were contentious, they had sometimes to be made anonymously lest the state might decide to punish those who, even unwittingly, disturbed the civil order.

This held true even after the Glorious Revolution. The post-revolution settlement's success required the state's support and required most people to believe in it. Yet making the case for that settlement meant reconciling it with a variety of Christian and English pasts. At times, it meant being discreet to avoid being coerced by the state. John Jackson (1686–1763) was one of those still trying to come to grips with those pasts; and he was one whose polemical career also bears witness to the persistent need for discretion.[45] In 1714, he began his career as a polemical divine anonymously defending Samuel Clarke's Christologically heterodox *Scripture-Doctrine of the Trinity*. In the ensuing years, Jackson turned his fire not just on the orthodox but also on other heterodox figures, including the prominent Socinian Stephen Nye (1647–1719).[46] In early 1715, Jackson wrestled with whether to affix his name to the title-page of his forthcoming anti-Nye piece. Clarke counselled him to remain anonymous, not least because it might stall Jackson's clerical career. Jackson recognized that publicly embracing Clarke's Christology might damage him: 'I have an increasing Family and for their sakes would not expose myself to more Danger than I believed to be absolutely necessary, knowing that their Calamities would make my sufferings the more grievous'. Notwithstanding this, he still wanted publicly to claim authorship and for reasons which are illustrative. To begin with, Nye might be more likely to defend his own position publicly if Jackson acknowledged his authorship; 'but if I were Anonymous, He might with some pretence neglect or despise me'. More importantly, though, if Jackson's identity were known, it might mobilize support to his and Clarke's theological position regarding Christ's nature. Firstly, if York clergy knew that Jackson had published a book, they would be more apt to read it and to rally around Jackson because in the diocese he was 'generally beloved'. Secondly, Jackson reckoned that he might 'be an Instrument of convincing some men's minds and possibly stir up some other men able and eminent in the Church openly to defend this Cause'. Finally, he reckoned that he might actually be able to avoid official punishment, especially in light of a recent deal which Clarke had struck with the bishops: 'I am apt to think that our Convocation will do nothing, unless yours proceed further; so that, I may be sheltered under your Wing'.[47]

Though a rural Yorkshire cleric, John Jackson displayed a careful shrewdness common to eighteenth-century polemical divines, who were thoughtful and skilled craftsmen. Moreover, Jackson's letter to Samuel Clarke reminds us that the whole point of polemical divinity was to convince others and to mobilize opinion. Print was the primary venue in which arguments were to be made. Eighteenth-century England itself was awash in printed material. The figures are striking. Before the English Civil War, around 850 individual imprints appeared from English presses each year; by the end of the century, that number had doubled to around 1670 imprints; and by the mid eighteenth century, that number had itself increased by half again to around 2500 titles.[48] These figures only count for single-title imprints, not variants or editions. Nor do they account for the expansion of newsprint during the eighteenth century. Simultaneously a cause and effect of this massive uptick in printed material was that people publicly made – indeed increasingly *had* publicly to make – their arguments in order to persuade and mobilize opinion.[49]

While many have noted the explosion of printed material, fewer have noted the degree to which eighteenth-century English print culture abounded with religious material: indeed, it was hard to open any popular periodical from the period without being struck not just by its presence there, but also by the sorts of subject and arguments on offer. A reader of the January 1736 issue of the popular *Gentleman's Magazine*, for instance, would have found it opening with a short defence of 'particular providence' by 'W.J.' from Oxford. The letter writer wrote to rebut a *Grub Street Journal* contributor – a 'Mr. Prompter' – who '[b]y the Discovery of Reason ... acknowledges the Existence of a Supreme Being, governing by general Laws and a general Providence', but who nevertheless denied God's particular providence. To W.J.'s way of thinking, Mr. Prompter was 'a very ignorant Philosopher, if he cannot by the light of Reason, how imperfect so ever it is, discover the Necessity of a particular Providence'. Rather than being one of the 'Inventions of human Pride' that have 'defaced [Christianity's] primitive Beauty', the belief in God's particular providence was entirely consonant with 'the sacred Writings'.[50] Having opened with this full-throated defence of providence and of the contemporary Church of England's primitive purity, the rest of the issue of the *Gentleman's Magazine* abounded with stories touching on religion, from a dissection of the papacy's claims to depose secular authorities to accounts of Henry II and John's 'scandalously submit[ting] to the Pope's extravagant Authority' to a paean to the colony of Georgia – 'a Charitable Benefaction of Heaven' – to a set of queries regarding Edmund Gibson's *Codex Juris Ecclesiastici*.

Near the back of the magazine appeared a register of thirty-five works which had been published that month. Twelve publications – works like William Warburton's *Alliance between church and state*; an English translation of Abbot Aelfric of Eynsham's *Testimony of antiquity concerning the sacramental body and blood of Christ*; and a selection of 'Athanasian Forgeries' drawn from William Whiston's writings by a pseudonymous 'Lover of Truth' – dealt explicitly with religious subjects. Yet at least six other works printed during the first month of 1736 touched upon religion. Two pieces on spirituous liquors addressed not just the physical and economic effects of the 'gin craze' but also its moral causes and effects, while Voltaire's *Tragedy of Zara* contained biting criticisms of both Muslims and Christians. Still other publications hearkened back to the internecine religio-political English conflicts of the seventeenth century, including a treatise on current party politics and a poem entitled *Britain: being the fourth part of Liberty*, in which the poet credited the Tudors before the Stuarts ruined things by abandoning Reformation political and religious principles.[51]

The *Gentleman's Magazine* was not anomalous – polemical divinity dominated eighteenth-century booksellers' catalogues, with between one-quarter and one-third of all titles, most narrowly conceived, being 'religious' ones. That percentage goes up steeply when we account for the fact that some titles which might not seem religious (historical, philosophical or political works for example) were centrally concerned with religious issues.[52] Moreover, booksellers were not operating public charities, but were instead bottom-line-minded businessmen who printed what they thought they could sell. Some were likely willing to publish loss-leaders, but, for most booksellers, the line between profit and penury was thin.[53] There was, in other words, a vibrant market for polemical divinity: and there was a vibrant market because the issues which animated polemical divinity continued to matter.

Eighteenth-century English booksellers got their polemical divinity from authors who hailed from broadly similar backgrounds. Not all who wrote polemical divinity were themselves clerics – John Toland, Anthony Collins and Matthew Tindal, for instance – but, for the most part, those who did were clergymen. A few were Dissenters, but the vast majority, like the vast majority of the English nation itself, were members of the Church of England. This included even some of the most heterodox divines of the period, including Woolston. The Dissenters had usually gone to English Dissenting academics and sometimes to Scottish or Dutch universities, while the established churchmen had almost always spent time in the clerical factories at Oxford and Cambridge.[54] Some remained as college fellows there, but most dispersed to the four corners of the land to one or another of their ecclesiastical livings. From there, they kept abreast of new books and pamphlets primarily by way of newspapers, whose pages teemed with advertisements and recommendations of new titles and by way of extensive clerical correspondence networks. Like the rest of the nation, the clergy were politically divided, with Tories outnumbering Whigs early in the century, a numerical advantage that dwindled significantly as the Walpolean Whigs gradually and successfully convinced Tories that they too could safeguard the established Church's rights and privileges.[55] A great deal of polemical divinity produced dealt with those political divisions in Church and state and with the relationship between the Church and the state, though a shorthand definition of polemical divinity would be any published work that dealt either directly or implicitly with religious matters. Sermons, catechisms, biblical exegeses and church histories count among their number, but could also include works on politics, philosophy, literature, natural science or even works of hack journalism. To distinguish between dispassionate works of scholarship and of putatively raw polemic or between pastoral works and polemical ones, is mostly to make an artificial distinction.[56] The whole range of works of polemical divinity got published mainly by London-based presses or by ones in either of the university towns.[57]

Eighteenth-century English polemical divines were either *orthodox* or not. Affixing labels to the participants in eighteenth-century polemical divinity or to the positions they held is a fraught matter, not the least because the century itself was almost as awash in labels as it was in print.[58] Contemporaries employed *orthodox, heterodox, high church, low church, dogmatic, latitudinarian, papist, popish, deist, atheist, infidel* and other labels simultaneously as terms of description and of abuse, no less than those in the previous century had bandied about *Puritanism*: eighteenth-century labels were at once substantive and contested categories.[59] Yet, perhaps surprisingly, *orthodoxy* was the most substantive and least contested of contemporary categories during the early and mid-eighteenth century. In general, contemporaries reckoned that *orthodoxy* entailed belief in the Nicene and Athanasian Creeds; the episcopal ecclesiology of the Church of England; and the necessity of the church's legal establishment, an establishment safeguarded by penal laws. Where contemporaries disagreed was over whether or not *orthodoxy* was a good or a bad thing, whether it contained the sum of all true doctrine and thus promoted moral and social order or whether it betrayed 'true religion' and was punitive and persecutory. Debates over *orthodoxy* tended to be about its value rather the about its content. By contrast, virtually every other label employed in eighteenth-century English polemical divinity was hotly contested.

To locate the line between orthodoxy and not-orthodoxy, eighteenth-century English polemical divines employed methods of argument that bore striking similarities to the methods employed by English polemical divines since the 1530s. The binary languages of *anti-popery* and *anti-puritanism* still proved enormously useful during the eighteenth century, as did that of *moderation*, with all of its implications regarding restraint and coercion.[60] So too did the apologetical triumvirate of *faith, reason* and *tradition* also continue to be invoked, though in the eighteenth century *tradition*, whose truths were discerned by the application of reason to the historical record, was the chief figure in that trinity.[61]

REFORMATION IS GOOD, WHEN REFORMATION IS WANTING

If some of the methods of argument which characterized sixteenth- and seventeenth-century English intellectual life continued on into the eighteenth century, the circumstances in which they were employed had altered significantly. Revolutions have effects; multiple revolutions have profound effects. Eighteenth-century polemical divinity both reflected the changes to English society wrought by the seventeenth-century revolutions *and* was a debate about the character and nature of those revolutionary outcomes.

There are a few basic stories which historians tend to tell about what happened to England in the wake of the seventeenth-century religio-political wars. The predominant story is one of discontinuity in which issues of religion, the constitution, the succession and foreign policy imbricate seamlessly. On this reading, the revolution of 1688–89 provoked an 'Anglican crisis' which played out for the next quarter-century.[62] That crisis turned on the relationship between the established Church of England and the English state; and it at once overlay and informed the period's turbulent party politics. For many Church of England clergymen and their Tory supporters, the post-revolutionary settlement had betrayed the established Church. William of Orange's ascension to the throne forced the clergy to reconcile the new political realities with their post-Civil War public teaching about indefeasible hereditary right and the duty of loyalty and obedience to God's providentially chosen, divinely anointed monarch: another option, of course, was nonjuring and deprivation of one's livings. It was an attractive choice for few. That the new Dutch Calvinist king seemed initially that he might actively be trying to provoke the established Church by pursuing alliances with Protestant nonconformists; that the Toleration Act rendered the Church of England functionally a voluntary body; and that the state seemed unwilling to do anything to stem the rise of what many clergy saw as 'blasphemy' and 'irreligion' only made matters worse. The Church was 'in danger'. Clerical resentment over the post-revolutionary religio-political order soured steadily through the Convocation crisis of the late 1690s – which saw the archbishop of Canterbury marshalling the talents of rising clerical stars like Edmund Gibson and William Wake to make the (accurate) historical case that the Convocation sat at the king's pleasure – until matters finally came to a head during the Sacheverell crisis of 1709–10. The subsequent passage of the Occasional Conformity Act (1711) and the Schism Act (1714) were not, as it turned out, irreversible moments of high church triumph but high-water marks of Tory influence, for after the Hanoverian succession in 1714, the Whigs 'took their revenge and the Church of England went under the iron hand of patronage'.[63] First under the avowedly anticlerical Stanhope–Sunderland ministry and then under the slightly less confrontational Walpolean regime, Whigs brought the Church of England to heel so that religion would not rend the nation asunder as it had during the seventeenth century and as it had threatened to do during the first decade of the eighteenth.

Standing opposed to this story of the growth of secular politics and of its concomitant, political stability, in the wake of the post-revolutionary, religiously fuelled 'rage of party' is a second story, one which emphasizes continuities and highlights the continued importance of religion in the nation's politics and political thought. In this counter-narrative, the stretch of time between 1660 and 1832 is a coherent entity – the 'long eighteenth century' – an era inaugurated by the Restoration of the Stuarts in 1660.[64] Far from restoring the old order, the Restoration settlement actually attempted to reconcile new realities with older assumptions and practices. In particular, providentialist ideas of hierarchy found their instantiation and validation in the monarchy, while the Church of England was restored without some of its important prerogatives. Perhaps most significantly, 'the ideal of a church of all the English was, in practice if not in theory abandoned: now, a hegemonic established Church was to be the church of nine out of ten of the population', even as the 10 per cent of the populace who were religious dissidents were left to form their own uncomprehended churches while being 'accorded freedom of worship'. This new religio-political order would survive, not unchallenged, until 1832, when the passage of the Great Reform Act marked an own-goal, the entirely voluntary 'end of the Protestant constitution'.[65]

This book synthesizes these two stories, giving due weight both to the continuities and to the discontinuities of the period. It begins by recognizing that, while the Restoration was a moment of disjuncture in English history, it was a disjuncture that itself resulted from England's distinctive Reformation: the civil war which the Restoration followed had erupted because the English Reformation had produced a particular set of intellectual and political problems. Furthermore, the book recognizes that the Restoration decidedly did not provide solutions to those Reformation-spawned intellectual and political problems, problems with which the eighteenth-century English continued to grapple. By the same token, this book appreciates the contradictory effects of the seventeenth-century revolutions. Much, admittedly, had not changed after them. The nation emerged from the seventeenth century retaining its monarchy and its parliament, while the established Church retained its episcopal ecclesiology and its articles of religion. But other changes were profound. After the Glorious Revolution, the Church was functionally, though not theoretically, the state's subordinate partner. That disconnect between theory and practice at once underlay, informed and fuelled religious debates during the eighteenth century.[66] Most fundamentally, what had changed since the seventeenth century were the revolutions themselves, the memories of which were debated and contested throughout the eighteenth century. The ease and frequency with which contemporaries invoked the Glorious Revolution might seem testimony to its widespread acceptance by the nation. The fact that the abdicated king had been a papist and his successors both relatives and Protestants surely helped to make the regime change easier to accept.[67] But the Glorious Revolution had been bloody and the religio-political order built in its stead proved fully satisfactory neither to many religious minorities, who thought the Toleration Act had not gone far enough, nor to many within the Church of England, who thought that the Toleration Act had gone too far.[68] The contorted and tortured logic which characterized the annual 30 January and 29 May sermons during the eighteenth century, though, more glaringly testified to the degree to which the causes and implications of those wars continued to disturb the nation long after their purportedly glorious resolution in the decade after 1688.[69] And this unease, this fear that things might relapse into a state of chaos and bloodshed, underlay the eighteenth-century cult of personal restraint through moderation, politeness and civility.[70]

Fear of relapse into anarchy also helps to explain some characteristic features of eighteenth-century English polemical divinity. The first was the common lament by the established Church of England's leadership that the spectre of the sixteenth and seventeenth centuries made restraint more difficult. 'This is our misfortune; we are so afraid of the least tendency to persecution, that we cannot bear the least restraint', Archbishop William Wake lamented in the run-up to the Woolston trial. 'It is a sad case that we cannot keep in the middle way and allow what is fit to be published, or may be read without reproach, but at the same time both restrain and punish what is openly blasphemous and tends to the ruin of all religion and indeed of all respect for everything that is either pious or serious.'[71] The second notable feature of eighteenth-century polemical divinity was the palpable frustration among polemical divines that they might have found themselves at an intellectual dead-end. Paradoxically, historical research – the process of making documentable, and hence presumably verifiable, historical claims that all could recognize as both legitimate and true – itself sometimes seemed to undermine truth. History did not resolve the debates between competing camps, it multiplied the fights and, unwittingly and unintentionally, helped to secularize thought, as Samuel Johnson and his contemporaries would have understood it: it took religion and made it 'worldly'.[72] This, from the perspective of eighteenth-century polemical divines was a tragedy glimpsed, if not always grasped. But it was, in retrospect, an almost inescapable tragedy because another of the Reformation's legacies was a univocal God, one who existed within and thus in relation to his creation rather than transcendentally to it.[73] He was, then, subject to its rules and the evidences for his existence subject to the same standards of proof as anything else in nature. When the rules of historical evidence were incapable of proving definitively God's existence, much less illuminating his providential design for his creation, a notable feature of the modern world emerged, the state's functional monopoly on the truth. For when even history could not reconcile or arbitrate between competing truth-claims, into the breach stepped Leviathan. Thus, when Edmund Gibson admonished the clergy of London that one of the best ways to combat infidelity was 'to express a dutiful Behaviour to the Government and a Desire to promote Peace and Quietness in our several Stations', he was tacitly acknowledging what many at the time feared, that they were living through a Reformation without end.[74] Or, as Daniel Waterland exasperatedly put it, 'Reformation is good, when reformation is wanting: but to be always reforming is no reforming at all: it is behaving as children tossed to and fro with every wind of doctrine. All errors of any moment have been purged off long ago, by the care of our Reformers and why then are we still reforming?'[75]

NOTES

1 Christodulus to Gibson, 31 December 1728 (BL, Sloane 4050, fol. 27). Cf. P. Rogers, '*God's Judgment upon Hereticks*: A "Lost" Satire on Thomas Woolston and Edmund Gibson', *Review of English Studies* 65 (2014), pp. 78–98.

2 T. Woolston, *Discourse of the miracles* (1727: T077543), pp. 4, 5.

3 Waterland to Thomas Bishop, 1 January 1730 (MCC/MR).

4 D. Manning, 'Blasphemy in England, c. 1660–1730' (Ph.D. thesis, University of

Cambridge, 2008), pp. 283–329; W. Trapnall, *Thomas Woolston* (Bristol, 1994), pp. 50–79, 133–67. The decision to prosecute Woolston in King's Bench rather than in the ecclesiastical courts is notable: a conviction in the royal courts would ensure a harsher penalty. I thank Bill Gibson for this point.

5 [T. Woolston], *Tryal of Thomas Woolston* (1729: N013667), p. 2; Trapnell, *Thomas Woolston*, p. 61.

6 J. Strange, *Reports of adjudged cases* (1795: N012814), p. 789. Cf. [E. Curll], *Life of Mr. Woolston* (1733: T077528), p. 15.

7 [Woolston], *Tryal*, p. 3.

8 Woolston's speech at his trial for blasphemy, 1729 (BL, Add. 35886, fol. 26; TNA, SP 46/143/1, fol. 384). J. Whiston, *Historical memoirs* (1730: T036320), I, p. 198 traced Woolston's heterodox theological method to his study of 'Origen's allegorical works'. J. Hunt, *Religious Thought in England* (1870), III, p. 383, reckoned that 'Exclusive study of the Fathers made Woolston a maniac'.

9 Woolston's response to charges of blasphemy, 1729 (BL, Add. 35880, fol. 12).

10 [Curll], *Life of ... Woolston*, p. 31.

11 N. Sykes, *Edmund Gibson* (Oxford, 1926), pp. 155–61; T. Kendrick, 'Sir Robert Walpole, the old Whigs and the Bishops, 1733–1736', *HJ* 11 (1968), pp. 426–8; S. Taylor, 'Queen Caroline and the Church', in S. Taylor, C. Jones and R. Connor (eds), *Hanoverian Britain and Empire* (Woodbridge, 1998), pp. 99–100.

12 Gibson to Walpole, [December 1733] (SAL, Gibson 5285a).

13 Chubb to Cox Macro, 18 July 1719 (BL, Add. 32556, fol. 140).

14 Venn to Gibson, 27 December 1733 (SAL, Gibson 5293). See also Egmont, II, pp. 2, 23, 39, 49.

15 Lamotte to Gibson, 26 October 1734 (SAL, Gibson 5289).

16 Gibson to Walpole, 18 December 1733 (CUL, Cholmondeley Ch (H) 2106). Cf. Hervey, *Memoirs*, II, pp. 399–405; Egmont, II, pp. 136–7. More generally, see S. Taylor, '"Dr. Codex" and the Whig "Pope": Edmund Gibson, Bishop of Lincoln and London, 1716–1748', in R. Davis (ed.), *Lords of Parliament* (Stanford, 1995), pp. 9–27; S. Taylor, 'The Bishops at Westminster in the Mid-Eighteenth Century', in C. Jones (ed.), *A Pillar of the Constitution* (1989), pp. 137–63.

17 Bishops unsuccessfully opposed Rundle's subsequent appointment as bishop of Derry: R. Mant, *Church of Ireland* (1840), II, pp. 537–43.

18 Middleton to Hervey, 12 March 1734 (SRO, 941/47/8).

19 Hare to Gibson, 4 August 1736 (SAL, Gibson 5311).

20 M. Suarez, '"The most Blasphemous Book that ever was Publish'd": Ridicule, Reception and Censorship in Eighteenth-Century England', in W. Kirsop (ed.), *The Commonwealth of Books* (Melbourne, 2007), pp. 48–77; R. Lund, 'Irony as Subversion: Thomas Woolston and the Crime of Wit', in R. Lund (ed.), *Margins of Orthodoxy* (Cambridge, 1995), pp. 170–94.

21 [D. Waterland], *Defence of the lord bishop* (1730: T141508), pp. 20, 32.

22 R. Smalbroke, *Vindication of the miracles* (1731: T105058), I, dedication.

23 J. Jones, *Instructions* (1729: T115803), p. 11.

24 Cf. C. Gerrard, *The Patriot Opposition to Walpole* (Oxford, 1994), pp. 27–34.

25 *WM* (7 December 1734), p. 1.

26 *OW* (13 March 1735), pp. 1, 2. See also A. Thompson, 'Popery, Politics and Private Judgment in Early Hanoverian Britain', *HJ* 45 (2002), pp. 333–56.

27 The eighteenth-century polemical divine is not an over-studied type, but see B. Young, *Religion and Enlightenment in Eighteenth-Century England* (Oxford, 1998); B. Young, 'Theological Books from *The Naked Gospel* to *Nemesis of Faith*', in I. Rivers (ed.), *Books and Their Readers in Eighteenth-Century England: New Essays* (London, 2001), pp. 79–104.

28 W. Bulman, 'Enlightenment for the Culture Wars', in W. Bulman and R. Ingram (eds), *God in the Enlightenment* (Oxford, 2016), pp. 1–41; J. Robertson, *The Enlightenment* (Oxford, 2015). On religion and the English Enlightenment, see Young, *Religion and Enlightenment*; J. Pocock, *Barbarism and Religion*, 6 vols (Cambridge, 1999–2016); J. Pocock, 'Post-Puritan England and the Problem of Enlightenment', in P. Zagorin (ed.), *Culture and Politics from Puritanism to the Enlightenment* (Berkeley, 1980), pp. 91–112; J. Pocock, 'Clergy and Commerce: The Conservative Enlightenment in England', in R. Ajello and F. Venturi (eds), *L'eta dei Lumi* (Naples, 1985), pp. 525–62.

29 Waterland to Bishop, 11 December 1733 (MCC/MR).

30 Warburton to Richard Hurd, 25 May 1763 (*LLEP*, pp. 346–7). Alexander Pope surely coined this phrase. 'The life of a Wit is a warfare upon earth; and the present spirit of the world is such, that to attempt to serve it (anyway) one must have the constancy of a martyr and a resolution to suffer for its sake': A. Pope, *Works* (1717: T005388), I, preface. Warburton was Pope's literary executor.

31 B. Gregory, 'Can We "See Things Their Way"? Should We Try?', in A. Chapman, J. Coffey and B. Gregory (eds), *Seeing Things Their Way* (Notre Dame, IN, 2009) pp. 24–45.

32 B. Gregory, *The Unintended Reformation* (Cambridge, MA, 2012), pp. 1–24; A. Walsham, 'Migrations of the Holy: Explaining Religious Change in Medieval and Early Modern Europe', *JMEMS* 44 (2014), pp. 241–80.

33 A. Pagden, *The Enlightenment* (2013); J. Israel, *A Revolution of the Mind: Radical Enlightenment and the Origins of Modern Democracy* (Princeton, 2011).

34 M. Knights, *The Devil in Disguise: Deception, Delusion and Fanaticism in the Early English Enlightenment* (Oxford, 2011), p. 5. See also M. Knights, 'Public Politics in England, c. 1675–c. 1715', in N. Tyacke (ed.), *The English Revolution, c. 1590–1720* (Manchester, 2007), pp. 169–84.

35 Early modern scepticism and postmodern relativism differ in kind, not degree: R. Popkin and M. Goldie, 'Scepticism, Priestcraft and Toleration', in M. Goldie and R. Wokler (eds), *Cambridge History of Eighteenth-Century Political Thought* (Cambridge, 2006), esp. pp. 79–92; P. Graham, 'The Relativist Response to Radical Skepticism', in J. Greco (ed.), *Oxford Handbook of Skepticism* (Oxford, 2008), pp. 392–414.

36 B. Young, '"The Soul-Sleeping System": Politics and Heresy in Eighteenth-Century England', *JEH* 45 (1994), pp. 76–9; Wigelsworth, 'Samuel Clarke's Newtonian Soul', *JHI* 70 (2009), pp. 54–8. Cf. J.-L. Quantin, *The Church of England and Christian Antiquity* (Oxford, 2009), pp. 366–95.

37 Clarke to Dodwell, [1706] (BL, Add. 4370, fol. 2).

38 Ibid.

39 W. Bulman, *Anglican Enlightenment: Orientalism, Religion and Politics in England and Its Empire, 1648–1715* (Cambridge, 2015); D. Levitin, 'From Sacred History to the History of Religion: Paganism, Judaism and Christianity in European

Historiography from the Reformation to 'Enlightenment', *HJ* 55 (2012), pp. 1117–60.

40 M. Knights, 'Occasional Conformity and the Representation of Dissent: Hypocrisy, Sincerity, Moderation and Zeal', *PH* 24 (2005), pp. 41–57.

41 J. Henry, 'The Reception of Cartesianism', in P. Antsey (ed.), *Oxford Handbook of British Philosophy in the Seventeenth Century* (Oxford, 2013), pp. 116–43; A. Milton, 'Authority and Reason: The Seventeenth Century', in A. Hastings and A. Mason (eds), *Christian Thought: A Brief History* (Oxford, 2002), pp. 108–12.

42 Quantin, *Church of England* provides indispensable background. Cf. G. Bennett, 'Patristic Authority in the Age of Reason', *Oecumenica* (1971/2), pp. 72–87.

43 J. Pocock, 'Within the Margins: The Definitions of Orthodoxy', in R. Lund (ed.), *Margins of Orthodoxy* (Cambridge, 1995), p. 38.

44 E. Duffy, *The Stripping of the Altars* (New Haven, 1992), pp. 377–593; E. Shagan, 'The Emergence of the Church of England, c. 1520–1553', in A. Milton (ed.), *Oxford History of Anglicanism. Volume I* (Oxford, 2017), pp. 28–44.

45 B. Young, 'Newtonianism and the Enthusiasm of Enlightenment', *Studies in History and Philosophy of Science: Part A* 35 (2004), pp. 645–63.

46 Unless otherwise noted, all quotations in this paragraph draw from Jackson to Clarke, 30 April 1715 (CUL, 7113). See also P. Lim, 'The Platonic Captivity of Primitive Christianity and the Enlightening of Augustine', in W. Bulman and R. Ingram (eds), *God in the Enlightenment* (Oxford, 2016), pp. 136–56.

47 Jackson eventually affixed his name to the title-page of J. Jackson, *Examination of Mr. Nye's explication* (1715: T096861).

48 J. Barnard and M. Bell, 'Appendix 1', in J. Barnard and D. McKenzie (eds), *Cambridge History of the Book, Vol. IV: 1557–1695* (Cambridge, 2002), pp. 783–4; M. Suarez, 'Towards a Bibliometric Analysis of the Surviving Record, 1701–1800', in M. Suarez and M. Turner (eds), *Cambridge History of the Book, Vol. V: 1695–1830* (Cambridge, 2009), pp. 42–4.

49 J. Peacey, *Print and Public Politics in the English Revolution* (Cambridge, 2013), provides essential background. Most early modern English historians have rejected Jürgen Habermas's definition of the bourgeois public sphere; his explanation for its emergence and transformation; and his chronology of its appearance and disappearance. They have, though, opted for a less technically specific, more capacious understanding of a practical public sphere – roughly, what people did publicly when trying to convince others to do what they wanted them to do: P. Lake, 'Post-Reformation Politics or, on Not Looking for the Long-Term Consequences of the English Civil War', in M. Braddick (ed.), *Oxford Handbook of the English Revolution* (Oxford, 2015), pp. 21–42.

50 *GM* (January 1736), pp. 3–4.

51 [J. Thomson], *Britain* (1736: T029680).

52 Suarez, 'Towards a Bibliometric Analysis'; J. Feather, 'British Publishing in the Eighteenth Century: A Preliminary Subject Analysis', *The Library*, sixth series, 8 (1986), pp. 32–46; I. Rivers, 'Religious Publishing', in M. Suarez and M. Turner (eds), *Cambridge History of the Book, Vol. 5: 1695–1830* (Cambridge, 2009), pp. 579–600. For an earlier period, Patrick Collinson, Arnold Hunt and Alexandra Walsham, 'Religious Publishing in England, 1557–1640', in J. Barnard and D. McKenzie (eds), *Cambridge History of the Book, Vol. IV: 1557–1695* (Cambridge,

2002), pp. 29–66. For sermons, easily the most popular form of polemical divinity, R. Dixon, 'Sermons in Print, 1660–1700', in P. McCullough, H. Adlington and E. Rhatigan (eds), *Oxford Handbook of the Early Modern Sermon* (Oxford, 2011), pp. 460–79; W. Gibson, 'The British Sermon, 1689–1901: Quantities, Performance, Culture', in W. Gibson and K. Francis (eds), *Oxford Handbook of the Modern British Sermon, 1689–1901* (Oxford, 2012), pp. 3–30. Jamie Latham's forthcoming Cambridge Ph.D. thesis ('The Clergy and Print in Eighteenth-Century England, c. 1714–1750') will be indispensable for scholars of print culture.

53 J. Raven, *The Business of Books: Booksellers and the English Book Trade* (New Haven, 2007).

54 H. McLachlan, *English Education under the Test Acts* (Manchester, 1931); J. Gascoigne, *Cambridge in the Age of Enlightenment* (Cambridge, 1989); W. Ward, *Georgian Oxford: University Politics in the Eighteenth Century* (Oxford, 1958).

55 J. Chamberlain, *Accommodating High Churchmen: The Clergy of Sussex, 1700–1745* (Urbana, 1997); S. Taylor, 'Church and State in the Mid-Eighteenth Century: The Newcastle Years, 1742–62' (Ph.D. thesis, University of Cambridge, 1987); Sykes, *Edmund Gibson.*

56 Cf. D. Levitin, *Ancient Wisdom in the Age of the New Science: Histories of Philosophy in England, c. 1640–1700* (Cambridge, 2015); I. Green, *Print and Protestantism in Early Modern England* (Oxford, 2000).

57 J. Raven, 'London and the Central Sites of the English Book Trade', in M. Suarez and M. Turner (eds), *Cambridge History of the Book, Vol. V: 1695–1830* (Cambridge, 2009), pp. 293–308; I. Gadd (ed.), *The History of Oxford University Press* (Oxford, 2013), I; D. McKitterick, *A History of Cambridge University Press* (Cambridge, 1998), II.

58 S. Taylor, 'Church and State', pp. 215–16.

59 P. Lake, 'The Historiography of Puritanism', in P. Lim and J. Coffey (eds), *Cambridge Companion to Puritanism* (Cambridge, 2008), pp. 346–71; P. Lake, *Boxmaker's Revenge: 'Orthodoxy', 'Heterodoxy' and the Politics of the Parish in Early Stuart London* (Stanford, 2001).

60 For an earlier period, P. Lake, 'Antipopery: The Structure of a Prejudice', in R. Cust and A. Hughes (eds), *Conflict in Early Stuart England* (1989), pp. 72–106; P. Lake, 'Anti-Puritanism: The Structure of a Prejudice', in P. Lake and K. Fincham (eds), *Religious Politics in Post-Reformation England* (Woodbridge, 2006), pp. 80–97; E. Shagan, *The Rule of Moderation: Violence, Religion and the Politics of Restraint in Early Modern England* (Cambridge, 2011).

61 J. Champion, *The Pillars of Priestcraft Shaken: The Church of England and Its Enemies, 1660–1730* (Cambridge, 1992); R. Ingram, 'Nature, History and the Search for Order: The Boyle Lectures, 1730–1785', *SCH* 46 (2010), pp. 276–92.

62 D. Hayton, *The House of Commons, 1690–1715* (2002), I, pp. 28–35, reliably surveys the historiography. R. Ingram, 'The Church of England, 1714–1783', in J. Gregory (ed.), *Oxford History of Anglicanism. Volume II* (Oxford, 2017), pp. 49–67, surveys post-revolutionary ecclesiastical politics. Cf. C. Dudley, 'The Decline of Religion in British Politics, 1710–1734', *British Scholar* 3 (2010), pp. 43–60.

63 G. Bennett, 'Conflict in the Church', in G. Holmes (ed.), *Britain after the Glorious Revolution, 1689–1714* (1968), p. 174.

64 J. Clark, *English Society, 1660–1832: Religion, Ideology and Politics during the Ancien*

Regime (Cambridge, 2000). Clark's work has buttressed important research on religious institutions and belief in eighteenth-century England: M. Goldie, 'Voluntary Anglicans', *HJ* 46 (2003), pp. 977–90. S. Taylor, 'Un Etat confessionel? L'Eglise d'Angleterre, la constitution et la vie politique au XVIIIe siècle', in A. Joblin and J. Sys (eds), *L'identité anglicane* (Arras, 2004), pp. 141–54; J. Gregory, *Restoration, Reformation and Reform, 1660–1832* (Oxford, 2000); Champion, *Pillars*, offer trenchant criticisms of Clark's thesis.

65 Clark, *English Society, 1660–1832*, pp. 63–4.

66 G. Bennett, *The Tory Crisis in Church and State, 1688–1730* (Oxford, 1975); N. Sykes, *From Sheldon to /Secker: Aspects of English Church History, 1660–1768* (Cambridge, 1959), pp. 36–67; N. Sykes, *Church and State in England in the XVIIIth Century* (Cambridge, 1934), pp. 284–331.

67 G. Glickman, 'Political Conflict and the Memory of the Revolution, 1689–1745', in S. Taylor and T. Harris (eds), *The Final Crisis of the Stuart Monarchy* (Woodbridge, 2013), pp. 243–72.

68 R. Stevens, 'Anglican Responses to the Toleration Act, 1689–1714' (Ph.D. thesis, University of Cambridge, 2014).

69 S. Connolly, 'The Church of Ireland and the Royal Martyr: Regicide and Revolution in Anglican Political Thought, c. 1660–c. 1745', *JEH* 54 (2003), pp. 484–506; J. Caudle, 'Measures of Allegiance: Sermon Culture and the Creation of a Public Discourse of Obedience and Resistance in Georgian Britain, 1714–1760' (Ph.D. dissertation, Yale University, 1995), pp. 235–61.

70 M. Peltonen, 'Politeness and Whiggism, 1688–1732', *HJ* 48 (2005), pp. 391–414.

71 Wake to Turrentini, 28 November 1728, quoted in N. Sykes, *William Wake* (Cambridge, 1957), II, 170–1.

72 S. Johnson, *Dictionary of the English Language* (1799: T116650), II, unpaginated. 'To make worldly' was Johnson's second definition of *secularize*; his first was 'to convert from spiritual appropriations to common use'. See also B. Young, 'Religious History and the Eighteenth-Century Historian', *HJ* 43 (2000), pp. 849–68; B. Young, '"Knock-Kneed Giants": Victorian Representations of Eighteenth-Century Thought', in J. Garnett and C. Matthew (eds), *Revival and Religion since 1700* (1993), pp. 79–93. I. Hunter, 'Secularization: The Birth of a Modern Combat Concept', *Modern Intellectual History* 12 (2015), pp. 1–32, is especially perceptive. A. Walsham, 'The Reformation and "the Disenchantment of the World" Reassessed', *HJ* 51 (2008), pp. 497–528, highlights some of the analytical flaws of K. Thomas, *Religion and the Decline of Magic* (1971), a work whose premises and conclusions still exert scholarly influence.

73 B. Gregory, 'The Reformation Origins of the Enlightenment's God', in W. Bulman and R. Ingram (eds), *God in the Enlightenment* (Oxford, 2016), pp. 201–14. See also J.-L. Marion, 'The Idea of God', in D. Garber and M. Ayers (eds), *Cambridge History of Seventeenth-Century Philosophy* (Cambridge, 1998), I, pp. 265–304; M. Buckley, *Denying and Disclosing God: The Ambiguous Progress of Modern Atheism* (New Haven, 2004), pp. 1–24. Cf. P. Lim, 'Not *Solely Sola Scriptura* or, a Rejoinder to Brad S. Gregory's *The Unintended Reformation*', *JMEMS* 46 (2016), pp. 603–28.

74 E. Gibson, *Charge of … 28th day of May, 1730* (1731: T068116), p. 28.

75 [D. Waterland], *Remarks upon Doctor Clarke's Exposition* (1730: T046863), p. 94.

Part I

Purity of faith and worship against corruptions: Daniel Waterland

Chapter 2

Truth is always the same

'I am' very sorry to hear the ill news from Caius, which is got to Town ... & alarms many good Men there', Daniel Waterland wrote to Zachary Grey in early 1739.[1] The news from Gonville and Caius College in Cambridge concerned one of its junior fellows, Tinkler Ducket (*c.* 1711–74),[2] soon to face trial in the vice-chancellor's court on charges of 'entertaining atheistical Notions' and of 'endeavouring to seduce others into the same'.[3] The trial stemmed from the recent discovery of a 1734 letter in which Ducket had extolled the virtues of Samuel Strutt's *Philosophical enquiry into the physical springs of human actions* (1732). Strutt had rejected immateriality, an 'unphilosophical Notion': 'we have no Reason to conclude, that any part of the human Composition consists of Immaterial Substance; because we have no Ideas of any other Substance than Matter, and because there is nothing (that we know of) in the Nature of Matter, which is incompatible with Thinking'. By implication, to speak of immaterial entities, such as the soul or God, was to speak non-sense.[4] Strutt's materialist argument convinced Ducket, who unwisely confided to his friend, Stephen Gibbs, that in 'further Progress in Atheism' he had 'arrived at the Top, the *ne plus ultra*, before I enjoyed the Beatific Vision ... being fixed & immoveable in the Knowledge to the Truth, to which I attained by Means of that infallible Guide, the *Philosophical enquiry*'.[5] Unfortunately for Duckett, his letter to Gibbs became public.

The letter roused anger in Cambridge and beyond. The fellows of Caius presented it to the university's vice-chancellor, who then consulted the archbishop of Canterbury and a handful of bishops. Some worried that Cambridge's 'public statutes [had] not specifically made provisions for the case of Atheism'; but Thomas Baker – a Jacobite who had resigned his St John's College fellowship, rather than take the 1717 abjuration oath – found 'a precedent of a parson degraded & expelled from the university in the reign of Charles II for maintaining Hobbism & Atheism'.[6] That Hobbist was Daniel Scargill (1647–1721). Like Scargill, Ducket stood accused not just of heresy but of immorality.[7]

Figure 2 'Daniel Waterland', after 1717, by John Faber Jr, after Richard Phillips

Ducket offered a peculiar defence against the charges of atheism. Though he recanted the atheistic materialism of his 1734 letter, he pled his right to have thought errantly. He insisted 'on the Right & Obligations of private Judgement, the indispensable duty of making Reason our Guide with or without Revelation' and of following that guide 'wheresoever she leads'. Furthermore, he asserted that 'if Reason leads to Atheism, there is as much Virtue in that as in the contrary persuasion, provided there has been the same Impartiality in the Inquiry'.[8] Ducket implied that there was no fixed and constant truth, that what mattered was the intellectual traveller's sincerity not his final destination. This might have been the only defence that Ducket could have made under the circumstances, but it was bound not to be persuasive in an intellectual climate which took for granted that some things were true and others were not. What constituted truth was debatable; truth's existence was not.

After quick deliberation, the vice-chancellor's court convicted Ducket and voted to expel him from the university and to strip him of his degrees. University graces confirming expulsion followed.[9] Edmund Gibson, Ducket's diocesan, suspended him from his Essex curacy.[10] There would be no Church of England career for Ducket, who ended his days in Constantinople as a secretary to British diplomats, long after those who had publicly punished him had gone to their graves.[11] A point, though, had been made: religious heterodoxy could kill a clerical career.

Tinkler Ducket had the personal misfortune to have had his privately held heterodoxy made public at a time when anticlericalism waxed precipitously.[12] His materialism would never have gone down well in the universities, but it went down especially poorly during the 1730s, when the Church of England's clergy faced bitter criticism. For the most part, the formal assaults in Parliament on the established Church's legal privileges went nowhere.[13] Nonetheless, anticlerical sentiment unsettled the Church's leaders, who directly correlated anticlericalism's rise with what they perceived to be a spike in theological heterodoxy: private error, in their view, necessarily had public consequences. Thus, Tinkler Ducket had to be punished.

Daniel Waterland, situated just down the road from Caius in the master's lodge at Magdalene College, certainly saw things this way. What Waterland thought about the subject mattered because friend and foe alike thought him orthodoxy's apotheosis. Some mocked him as the 'Master of Maudlin'; but he articulated orthodoxy in its most clarified and robust form.[14] Mark Pattison signalled Waterland's importance when he jibed that '[t]he genuine Anglican', when 'constructing his *Catena Patrum* ... closes his list with Waterland or Brett, and leaps at once to 1833, when the *Tracts for the Times* commenced'.[15] The late nineteenth-century agnostic Leslie Stephen judged him 'the most learned of the contemporary divines' and 'the greatest living champion of orthodoxy' during the mid-eighteenth century.[16] Indeed, even in Stephens's own lifetime, Waterland's hermeneutics and conclusions remained influential and highly praised.[17] Daniel Waterland was, then, a figure of consequence, one whose life and career provide an obvious point of entry into the eighteenth-century orthodox mind.

Part I offers a sense of eighteenth-century orthodoxy's doctrinal content and its modes of argument. It does so by focusing on Daniel Waterland's polemical divinity. This introductory chapter (Chapter 2) sketches the lineaments of Waterland's theological approach. It begins by considering Waterland's 1710 *Advice to a young student*, a compulsory educational manual for eighteenth-century Magdalene College students. The bulk of the chapter anatomizes the arguments in a set of archidiaconal visitation charges. During the 1730s, Waterland surveyed the intellectual landscape for his Middlesex archdeaconry's clergy and identified for them the pastoral threats they faced.[18] His message to them was clear: truth is constant; some doctrines are fundamental to Christianity; and those fundamentals are to be found in the primitive sources of the Christian past rightly interpreted.

The next three chapters in Part I drill down more deeply into Waterland's polemical divinity to consider three theological questions. What sort of god was God? How could God be known? And, how, if at all, did God effect an individual's salvation? The next three chapters anatomize Waterland's answers to those questions by considering particular polemical debates which sharpened his thinking about them. Chapter 3 concerns the Christian God's nature: it focuses on Christology. Chapter 4 concerns the sources of that triune God's revealed truth about himself and his creation: it focuses on 'deism'. Chapter 5 concerns the ways in which the Christian God effected an individual's salvation: it focuses on the Eucharist. Waterland understood the eighteenth-century debates over these issues as continuations of earlier ones: they were eighteenth-century debates over ancient issues refracted through sixteenth- and seventeenth-century English religious and political history. His peers reckoned that, in those eighteenth-century debates, Waterland most formidably defended orthodoxy.

Daniel Waterland (1683–1740) wrote primarily from Cambridge, the centre of his universe after he entered Magdalene College as a sizar in 1699.[19] The product of a Lincolnshire clerical family, he received his early education in the Lincoln free school.[20] He was the third generation of Waterlands to attend Magdalene. His father, Henry was a student at Magdalene during the last four years of the Interregnum. Apparently the college's 'godly' ethos during the 1650s rubbed off on Henry Waterland.[21]

Daniel Waterland's Magdalene tutor, Samuel Barker, likely directed him through the typical bachelor of arts degree course.[22] He ascended steadily through the college and university ranks. He earned his A.B. in 1702 and in 1704 the Magdalene fellows elected him to their membership.[23] For the rest of his life, Waterland taught the bulk of the college's students.[24] He remained a 'pupil-monger' even after becoming Magdalene's master during the last years of Queen Anne's reign, a post he got thanks to the college visitor's patronage.[25] Waterland led Magdalene until his death in 1740, and also held a variety of other positions within and without the university. Within Cambridge, he was the university's vice-chancellor in 1715, when political tensions ran high in the Jacobite rising's aftermath. Outside of Cambridge, he was a royal chaplain in 1717 and held a number of clerical livings, including rectories in London and Twickenham; a prebend of Windsor; the chancellorship of York; and the archdeaconry of Middlesex.[26] Surprisingly for a man of acknowledged intellectual distinction, Waterland became neither a bishop nor a chaired professor.[27] His permanent perch in Cambridge, though, gave him access to some of England's best libraries, including the University Library, Magdalene's Pepys Library and Wimpole's Harleian Library.[28]

Daniel Waterland did more than anyone during the mid-eighteenth century, other than his ally, Edmund Gibson, to convince the Church of England's clergy that the Whigs could be trusted to protect the established Church.[29] Waterland and Gibson shared an inveterate commitment both to the Whig party and to theological orthodoxy, a twin commitment characteristic of the Church of England during the half-century or so from Walpole's assumption of power.[30] The Walpolean Church–Whig alliance was a complicated one, especially because anticlericalism underpinned Whiggism and because the Stanhope–Sunderland ministry had been especially deeply anticlerical.[31] The alliance had consciously and concertedly to be forged. Gibson focused on Church patronage, while Waterland produced polemical divinity which demonstrated that Tories were not orthodoxy's lone defenders. In his published work, he confronted head-on many of the heterodox assaults on orthodox doctrine, combining both the exactitude of a scholar and the acerbity of a polemical hack. As Leslie Stephen put it, Waterland 'illustrated the truth that wide learning and elegant scholarship may be combined with controversial brutality'.[32] Thomas Babington Macaulay, another Victorian anticlerical, was moreblunt: 'Waterland [is] an ass'.[33] Suffice it to say that Waterland was a relentlessly serious man whose work was his life.[34] The Newtonian antiquary William Stukeley, Waterland's admirer and friend, described him as a 'very hard stud[en]t' and noted that he 'had an extraordinary zeal for religion'.[35] That zeal manifested itself mostly as seriousness; one searches in vain even in Waterland's private correspondence for the faintest glimpses of humour. One finds there, instead, what one finds in his printed work: an unstinting focus on the content and defence of Christian fundamentals.

At times, Waterland despaired of what he could achieve through polemical divinity because he feared he had been insufficiently combative. 'I often think, we are rather too civil towards these wretches, in reasoning with them', he lamented to a friend. 'They were never brought into their loose principles by reasoning, nor will ever be reasoned out of them. They love to be called Deists, freethinkers, Infidels, or perhaps even Atheists, rather than whoremasters, procurers, Panderers, and perjured villains.'[36] Despite occasional despair, he published a largely uninterrupted flow of work which blended a commitment to Hanoverian Whiggery and to theological orthodoxy.

Unlike many of his Cambridge contemporaries, Waterland never flirted with Toryism. He was, instead, a resolute Whig throughout his career. Despite his enormous published output, Waterland committed little to print before 1719, when he was thirty-six years old. The handful of sermons he published before then, though, illuminate his political sentiments.[37] In them he emphasized the duty to live 'peaceably' and pointed up the dangers of division to the nation. Yet he also stressed the necessity of orthodoxy. Protestantism, for instance, was an 'act of charity' because 'it is for the Good of Mankind Here and Hereafter, that Truth be defended against Error; Purity of Faith and Worship against Corruptions; True and Undefiled Religion against Idolatry and Superstition'. Indeed, though one should aspire to abide in a state of peace, one is also obligated to defend truth. 'What concerns us as private Men is, to defend our Religion, and to maintain the true faith and Worship, by Discourse or Writing, as not to lose our Charity', he warned. 'Religion is a

Cause that deserves our Zeal; and if many will be offended with us for telling them the Truth, and not complying with such Errors as would lead both to their and our Destruction, the Fault is their own.'[38]

Insufficiently defending truth publicly resulted in events like the 1715 Jacobite rebellion which erupted not long after Waterland took office as Cambridge's vice-chancellor. While Cambridge was not the hotbed of Jacobitism that Oxford was, it nonetheless saw open displays of anti-Hanoverianism on, for instance, George I's and the Pretender's birthdays.[39] Waterland entered office at a time, then, when Cambridge political tensions ran high. His deftness in managing those tensions was evident in his and Richard Bentley's success in helping to pass an April 1716 grace congratulating the king on putting down the Jacobite rebellion, despite veto threats in the university's Caput.[40] Waterland's exact Cambridge contemporary, future polemical opponent and then-Tory, Conyers Middleton, explained that he and others had opposed the grace less out of political principle than out of personal pique: they thought the address was a bald bid by Waterland to get a plum ecclesiastical living and by Bentley to get even more control over Trinity College.[41] Bentley complained that '[t]he fury of the whole disaffected and Jacobite party here against me and Mr Waterland is unexpressible: one would think that the late Address had given them a mortal blow, by the desperate rage they are in. I suppose you have seen a virulent lying paper printed at London about the Address, wherein Mr Waterland and I are described as objects of universal hatred'.[42] Eventually, the enmity many had for Bentley waxed precipitously while theirs for Waterland subsided. That Waterland turned on Bentley during the early 1720s raised his Cambridge peers' estimation of him.[43] Waterland's even-handed performance of his duties as vice-chancellor – including his help in the university's receipt from George I of Bishop John Moore's massive library, itself a gift intended to strengthen the ties between the Church and the Whigs – also helped his cause.[44]

Waterland subsequently became known for his resolutely orthodox polemical divinity. In the absence either of published work or private correspondence before the late 1710s, it is difficult to gauge the formation of his theological sentiments. A few sources offer suggestive glimpses. The most important piece of evidence is Waterland's *Advice to a young student*, written around 1710 for private use by Magdalene's students, though published only much later.[45] Students at Waterland's Magdalene had to transcribe a fair copy of the *Advice* before beginning their studies.[46] In that work Waterland laid out a programme of study, one capaciously conceived. Students preparing for a clerical career (the majority of eighteenth-century Oxbridge students) should study philosophy, classics and divinity. Philosophy and classical studies together, Waterland advised, 'are the Foundation, without which a Man can hardly be a judicious, 'tis certain he cannot be a learned Divine'.[47] Within *philosophy*, he comprehended mathematics, geography, astronomy, chronology, physics, logic, ethics and metaphysics, while he included within *classical studies*, languages, oratory, history and poetry.[48] The range of 'philosophical' authors whose works he advised studying was broad, including the ancient Greek geometer Euclid (*c.* 330–260 BC), the Italian ecclesiastical historian and metaphysician Caesare Baronius (1538–1607), the Dutch logician Franco Burgersdijk (1590–1635), the Dutch jurist Hugo Grotius (1583–1645), the German natural lawyer Samuel Pufendorf (1632–94), the English natural philosopher Thomas Burnet (1635–1715), the English natural philosopher William Whiston (1667–1752), the Scottish mathematician James Keill (1671–1721), the Scottish physician George Cheyne (1671–1743), the French mathematician Jacques Rohault (1618–72), the French astronomer Philippe de la Hire (1640–1718) and the Scottish astronomer David Gregory (1659–1708). Sir Isaac Newton's work on trigonometry and optics was also essential, as was John Locke's work, especially his *Essay concerning Human Understanding*, a 'Book so much (and I add so justly) valued, however faulty the Author may have been in his other Writings'.[49] Equipped with knowledge of philosophy and classical studies, students were then to study divinity. Divinity preparation involved learning the Bible – Waterland recommended reading in it at least an hour each day – and studying closely exemplary English sermons by everyone from Benjamin Hoadly and Nicholas Clagett to Robert South and Francis Atterbury, from Thomas Sharpe and John Norris to Samuel Clarke and Edward Stillingfleet. John Tillotson (1639–94), in particular, had given sermons which were models of the art form, Waterland reckoned, though '[t]here is one or two Points of Doctrine, particularly that of Hell-Torments, justly exceptionable'.[50] Waterland stressed that mastering tools of historical scholarship was essential to studying divinity. 'Chronology is a necessary Part of Learning, and ought to be well understood', he insisted at one point, while advising at another that '[i]t would be very convenient for you to have a Map before you, and chronological tables, when you read any History'.[51]

It becomes clear why Waterland might have advised his students closely and concertedly to study the past when we survey his own 1713–14 correspondence regarding lay baptism. When defending the nonjuror Roger Laurence's position on the invalidity of non-episcopally sanctioned baptisms, Waterland adduced evidence primarily from Scripture and from the history and practice of the primitive Church.[52] He also deployed historical arguments when defending Nicene Christology, the first public case for which he made in his 1714 B.D. divinity act over the question of whether Arian subscription was lawful. In a 'theological disputation [which] excited an uncommon sensation, not confined to the University', Waterland debated the question with Thomas Sherlock, then the master of St Catharine's College. Henry James, the regius professor of divinity, moderated the set-piece debate and, at one point, himself challenged Waterland's case for Arian subscription's invalidity. Waterland's eulogist reckoned that Waterland had so 'unravelled the Professor's Fallacies, reinforced his own Reasonings, and shewed himself so perfect a Master of the Language, the Subject, and Himself; that all agreed, No one ever appeared to greater Advantage'. A number of Oxford visitors present at the act later 'remember[ed] the great Applause he received, and the uncommon Satisfaction which he gave'.[53]

Though his contemporaries judged that Waterland had distinguished himself in his 1714 divinity act, what precisely he argued for during that public debate is not known. It is, however, possible fully to reconstruct Waterland's mature thought on this subject and much else because he produced a body of published work which runs to well over three dozen titles and which, together with the responses of his opponents, highlights many of the core concerns of polemical divines in eighteenth-century England.

As Daniel Waterland described it in his Middlesex visitation charges (1731–39), the contemporary debate between Christians and 'Infidels' was 'in Substance much the same with what the ancient Jews and Christians were employed in against the Infidels of their Times'.[54] His was a world in which the early Church fathers and their opponents remained relevant figures: the former had got things right, the latter had not. Since 'Truth is always the same', those who agreed with the early Church fathers had still to be right and those who disagreed, still wrong.[55] Waterland's point was not that the patristic fathers had a monopoly on truth, but that they had first discerned important Christian truths which should not be jettisoned. Admittedly, the circumstances in which the ancient and modern debates played out differed significantly, which meant, in turn, that they had different political, cultural and social valences. But for Waterland, the core contentious issues themselves remained much as they had ever been.

What one thought about the Trinity mattered because everything else hinged on it, Waterland admonished the Middlesex clergy. Most importantly, Christology determined how one viewed the nature of Christ's sacrifice and, consequently, the path to salvation. 'Low Notions of the Person of Christ are apt to bring in low Notions of his Merit and Satisfaction, and of the Use and Value of the Christian Sacraments, which represent and apply them', Waterland reckoned. Degrading Christ's divinity could lead one either to popery or to natural religion, which itself was the final way station on the road to atheism. '[W]hen Faith in Christ's Blood is once depreciated or frustrated, it is natural to set up Works, not only as the conditional, but as the efficacious, or even meritorious Cause of Salvation', a clear warning that the putative Roman Catholic doctrine of salvation by works alone flowed naturally from a suspect Christology. Depreciating the person of Christ might also lead one 'to exalt Morality in Opposition to Faith, and mere Morality in Opposition to instituted Religion; which again prepares the way for looking upon all revealed Religion as needless, or useless, which comes to the same Thing with denying its Truth, because an all-wise God can do nothing in vain'.[56] Whether one ended up on the road to Rome or the one to natural religion and, from thence, to atheism, the final destination – eternal damnation – was the same.

If the Christian God's precise nature mattered, how to grasp that nature posed epistemological challenges. Very few during Waterland's day – '[t]hese Men we call Deists, a Name of their own choosing to avoid a worse' – argued that reason alone provided a sufficient guide to the truth.[57] The ancient Jews and primitive Christians, though, had, Waterland insisted, rebutted these very same claims. They had proved instead 'that their boasted Wisdom was, for the most Part, human Folly; and that whatever they really knew, or taught, deserving any Praise, they had mostly borrowed it from divine Revelation, while they meanly and ungratefully disowned it; but that it was very wrong in them, to drink only of the polluted Streams, instead of coming directly to the Fountain-Head, and Madness to prefer the faint Reflections of a Cloud, before the open Sunshine'.[58] Most during the early eighteenth century saw the claims of natural and revealed religion as complementary, compatible, overlapping. Waterland accepted their complementarity, with reservations. There had been English divines, such as John Wilkins (1614–72), Richard Cumberland (1632–1718) and William Wollaston (1659–1724), who had developed 'several good Systems of Natural Religion' which 'took a rational and consistent way, and such as must inevitably terminate, when properly pursued, in a serious Belief of divine Revelation'. 'Deism', by contrast, rejected divine revelation and, thus, 'must as inevitably terminate, if consistently pursued, in downright Atheism'.[59] What exactly constituted *reason* was, during the mid-eighteenth century, mostly implied. It seems to have meant something like thinking deductively, thinking without recourse to concrete facts. Samuel Johnson defined it as '[t]he power by which man deduces one proposition from another, or proceeds from premises to consequences'.[60] Reason could let you know that God exists and even let you know what some of God's qualities were. But reason was not itself a sufficient guide to truth. This meant that historical scholarship, for instance, could be reasonable – it could make sense – but not be the product of reason. Reason, rightly understood, confirmed revealed truth; but, it could neither supplant nor alter the truths of revealed religion.[61]

To access and assess God's revelation required closely engaging with the sources of Judaeo-Christian history, especially the Scriptures in which that history had been recorded. The stakes were significant: as Waterland succinctly put it, 'the Christian Religion is most evidently true ... if any ancient Facts whatever can be proved to be true'.[62] That interpretative task was difficult. Some, for instance, argued that the Jews were an unlearned people wholly unfit to have spread God's message. Others contended that the Jews had borrowed many of their characteristic beliefs and rituals from the Egyptians.[63] These were significant challenges since Christians had long conceived of their history as a providential one in which the Jews played a crucial early role as God's chosen people, the initial recipients of revealed truth.

Furthermore, the providential Christian historical narrative did not always overlie neatly atop the chronologies of ancient Greek or Roman history.[64] Nor did it help that the early Church fathers sometimes disagreed amongst themselves about fundamental Christian doctrines.

Sorting through these and other questions related to the Christian past involved addressing a perennial Protestant hermeneutical challenge – interpreting the written record of God's revealed truth, the Bible. The mainstream of eighteenth-century English intellectual life was Protestant and nearly all mainstream English Protestants agreed with the Chillingworthian mantra that 'the Bible, I say the Bible only, is the religion of Protestants!'[65] But how to interpret the Bible always posed a challenge for Protestants. Were the Scriptures literally true? Or should they be read beyond the literal written word? Should they, as Waterland put it at one point, 'admit of some Latitude of Construction'?[66] The patristic fathers (whom Waterland revered) and the Roman Catholic Church (which he loathed) adopted a capacious interpretative method, one which allowed for possible allegorical, tropological and anagogical readings of the Scriptures in addition to the literal one.[67] Its advantages included an interpretative flexibility when confronting seemingly contradictory biblical passages; its chief disadvantage, in some Protestants' eyes, was that it led to corrupt and fanciful interpretations of pure Scripture truth. Indeed, Protestants privileged biblical literalism, since the Bible had literally to be true because it was God's divinely inspired Word. That could, as Protestants had always realized, sometimes place them in a hermeneutical straitjacket from which it was difficult to escape without recourse to purportedly popish interpretative methods. For nearly everyone during the eighteenth century, then, interpreting the Bible correctly and consistently was of paramount importance. Protestants thought that Catholics employed undue interpretative latitude which led them into error. Catholics retorted that Protestants' commitment to literalism was easier said than done, without betraying Protestant hermeneutical first principles.[68]

These Christological, epistemological and hermeneutical issues were not new to eighteenth-century England. As Waterland acknowledged, they had been debated from Christianity's onset. The circumstances in which they were addressed and the actors addressing them had changed, though. Most obviously, more than one and three-quarters of a millennum separated Waterland's world from that of the earliest Christian Church. At some point during that intervening stretch of time, both Waterland and nearly all of his non-papist theological opponents would have agreed, the Church's original doctrinal and ecclesiological purity had been corrupted. The instantiation of that corruption was the Church of Rome. Protestants contended that the Reformation aimed to reclaim the Church's primitive purity, to return it once again to its original, golden age by removing the Roman stain.

There intra-Protestant agreement stopped, though, for the Reformation, an event which Waterland rarely addressed directly in his work, had spawned as many problems as it had solved.[69] Its effects were fissiparous, catalysing epistemological confusion and rending the 'holy catholic and apostolic Church' over a whole host of issues, separating not just Protestant from papist but some Protestants from other Protestants. Furthermore, in response to the Reformation's evident hermeneutical failures, other options emerged to compete with the papist and various Protestant ones on offer. Waterland lumped together most of these options under the penumbra of *infidelity*. In so far as post-Reformation English 'Infidelity' was concerned, he located the origins of 'these licentious Principles' on the Continent. They came to England through Thomas Hobbes (1588–1679) – 'reputed the first or principal Man that introduced them here, or ... that openly and glaringly espoused them' – who 'it is not unlikely ... imbibed his loose Principles in France and Italy, as he also composed his famed Pieces while residing in foreign Parts'. As for the most prominent of infidels in his own day – the 'Deists' – Waterland followed Pierre Bayle (1647–1706) in pinpointing their beginnings on the Continent and to the mid-1560s.[70] Infidelity, like popery, was an imported intellectual disease. Like popery, it threatened the intellectual, social and political order because it could subvert and destroy 'true religion'. As for what constituted *infidelity*, that, like the content of its only slightly less malign relative, *heterodoxy*, was mostly in the eye of the beholder. For the orthodox, an infidel's identity was self-evident; those tagged as infidels, though, did not adopt that label for themselves. Thus, the boundaries of *infidelity* were sites of significant polemical contestation.

Whatever *infidelity*'s precise definition, properly to confront it required recognizing it for what it was, a dogmatic irreligion. 'It cannot be pretended that [infidels] believe less than we, since our Creeds reversed ... are as long Creeds as before', Waterland advised the Middlesex clergy. '... He that believes, for instance that there is no Heaven, no Hell, no future State, no Providence, no God, is as much a Believer, in his way, as the most Religious Men can be in theirs'. Indeed, they 'appear to be zealous Bigots to their Systems, to their Creeds, to their Paradoxes, to their Party; all which they adhere to, as pertinaciously as we can do to our Bible'.[71] Nor were modern infidels advocating new ideas, but recycling older pagan or heretical ones. Hobbes, for instance, 'was little more than a disciple of Epicurus, in his system of Religion, or Irreligion', while 'modern Deism' was 'little else but revived Epicureism, Sadducism and Zendichism'.[72] Furthermore, infidels lied. Rather than lay out their doctrines in the plain light of day, modern infidels hid them, implicitly acknowledging their inherent unpopularity. Waterland was probably right in this regard, but his accusations of heterodox imposture were also polemically savvy, since anti-trinitarianism – a persistent feature of not-orthodox thought – pointedly was not protected under the Toleration Act.

The theologically heterodox deployed ridicule to fight their way out of this corner. As one of Waterland's friends later put it, 'The Design of the Deists, Arians, Socinians & other Enemies to Christianity and the Established

Church, were then preparing for … [was] to overturn the Church of England, & to introduce into its Place all Sorts of Confusion & Disorder. The Way to do this was by Ridicule, as it could not be done by Argument.'[73] Secondly, the heterodox pushed back against the orthodox by employing an interconnected series of keywords, especially *credulity, superstition, enthusiasm, statecraft, priestcraft* and *imposture*. The gist of their argument was that the orthodox were exceedingly credulous, holding beliefs that were the product of superstition and enthusiasm. The orthodox espoused these views with a bigoted zeal and protected them through an unholy alliance with the coercive state (statecraft) and a clerical caste which perpetrated systemic fraud in the name of true religion (priestcraft).[74] In response to these charges, Waterland advised the orthodox to articulate their fundamental beliefs as clearly as possible.

With regard to Christianity, a *fundamental* was something 'so Necessary to its Being, or at least to its well-being, that it could not subsist, or not maintain itself tolerably without it'.[75] Waterland's search was deductive, rather than inductive, proceeding as it did from clear notions of what a Christian fundamental must entail. '… [S]uch Doctrines are found to be Intrinsical and Essential to the Christian Covenant, are Fundamental Truths, and such as are plainly and directly subversive of it, are Fundamental Errors', he reasoned. God's covenant with man, then, was the starting point of Waterland's examination of Christian fundamentals, not its end. And that covenant contained seven core principles: '1. A Founder and principal Covenanter. 2. A Subject capable of being covenanted with. 3. A Charter of Foundation. 4. A Mediator. 5. Conditions to be performed. 6. Aids or means to enable to performance. 7. Sanctions also, to bind the Covenant, and to secure obedience.'[76] In practice, this meant that Christians had to believe in God as 'Creator, Preserver and likewise Inspector of our Thoughts, Words and Actions'; in the doctrine of free will and of the distinction between good and evil; in Scripture's divine inspiration; in a fully divine and consubstantial Jesus Christ who atoned for mankind's sins; in the doctrine of repentance; in the sacraments as a means of grace; in a state of future rewards and punishments; and in Christ's final judgement of all.[77]

Having first established what were Christian fundamentals, Waterland next laid out rules for distinguishing them from non-fundamentals. He approached the issue apophatically, detailing what did *not* constitute proper rules for uncovering Christian fundamentals. It was wrong to argue that a particular doctrine was fundamental simply because the Church said so: the Church of Rome, after all, claimed as much for its own false doctrines. Neither did the literalist *sola scriputralism* favoured by some Protestants unfailingly lead one to the truth. To be sure, 'God's plainly revealing any Doctrine, carries in it a Force of a strict Command to assent to it as true, whenever we think of it as revealed'. But to insist that the Bible contains everything fundamental related to the Christian covenant 'is faulty in defect, as narrowing the Foundation more than is just or proper'.[78] If Christian fundamentals were not confined solely to the Bible, certainly they were not confined to a single scriptural passage. Samuel Clarke, for instance, had insisted that Hebrews 6:1–2 contained the whole of Christian fundamentals, a proposition which Waterland rejected not least because in those verses 'no express mention is made of the Doctrine of Christ Crucified, which the Apostle elsewhere lays a very particular stress upon; no mention of justification by the Merits and Death of Christ, in opposition to justification by mere Works, though an essential of the Gospel in St. Paul's account; no express mention of any Thing more than whatsoever Heretics condemned by St. Paul as such'.[79] Though Waterland was eighteenth-century England's fiercest and most prolific defender of Nicene Christology, he nevertheless insisted that the Nicene Creed was itself incomplete as 'the rule & Sample of Fundamentals' since both papists and various anti-Trinitarian Protestants – Arians, Socinians, Sabellians – assented to that creed. Even less satisfactory was John Locke's argument in *The Reasonableness of Christianity* (1695) that accepting Jesus as the Messiah constituted the lone Christian fundamental. Least sufficient of all were the notions that Christian fundamentals were confined to those things upon which all Christians could agree; to those things upon which all had agreed through all ages; or merely to living 'a good life'.[80]

In taking up the issue of Christian fundamentals and the ways in which they could be known, Waterland trod a delicate path, trying to avoid what he saw as the hermeneutical errors of popery, with its blind appeal to tradition; of Protestant nonconformity, with its literalist *sola scripturalism*; and of infidelity, with its excessive rationalism. His was an approach which, with its emphasis on the guiding importance of primitive Christian thought and practice, opened up Waterland to charges that he himself was a crypto-papist, with the attendant implications not just that he was wrong (and perhaps intentionally and wilfully so) but also that he also was persecutory.

Accusations of persecution were to be expected, though, because establishing what were Christian fundamentals meant articulating a principle of exclusion. If some things were right, their opposite had necessarily to be wrong. And those who were wrong should be excluded from communion with the Church. It had been that way in the primitive Church, in which 'Unity in the fundamental Articles of Faith was always strictly insisted upon, as one necessary Condition of Church-membership'. Waterland thought it should remain so during the eighteenth century because salvation was at stake. Excluding the not-orthodox from church communion, Waterland insisted, helped 'preserving Others from going astray, and keeping ourselves pure and undefiled, and the maintaining Truth and Godliness in the Face of the World'.[81] Furthermore, because church communion remained a legal requirement for full participation in eighteenth-century English political life, the search for truth was necessarily freighted with political significance. The theological was political; the political, theological; and both, hotly disputed.

Daniel Waterland engaged in those eighteenth-century debates over religion and politics arguing the orthodox case. He spent the bulk of his career using history to defend the primitive purity and, hence, the truth of Christianity. Most importantly for him, he spent a great deal of effort defending the primitive purity and, hence, the truth of Nicene Christology. For accepting the understanding of Christ as spelled out in the fourth-century ecumenical councils was, Waterland insisted, 'the Sum of Christianity: On this Foundation were the Apostles to erect a Church all the World over'.[82] Others, including another prominent Cambridge-educated polemical divine, Samuel Clarke, disagreed. For them, the fourth-century creeds were man-made formulae which contained in them fundamental errors about the Christian God's nature.

NOTES

1 Waterland to Grey, 31 January 1739 (BL, Add. 5831, fol. 175).

2 J. Stephens, 'Tinkler Ducket (c. 1711–c. 1774)', in A. Grayling (ed.), *Continuum Encyclopedia of British Philosophy* (2006), I, p. 899.

3 Account of Tinkler Ducket's trial, n.d. (BL, Add. 35202, fol. 80). See also BL, Add. 5822, fols 90–4; CUL, Mm.I.51, fols 38–9; CUL, Ee.VI.43, fols 4–14; JRULM, GB 133 Eng 1169, fols 1–9.

4 [S. Strutt], *Philosophical enquiry* (1732: T027267), pp. 2, 3. See also J. Yolton, *Thinking Matter: Materialism in Eighteenth-Century Britain* (Minneapolis, 1983), pp. 137–42.

5 William Cole's account of Tinkler Ducket's trial, n.d. (BL, Add. 5822, fol. 90).

6 James Tunstall to Harley, 23 January 1739; 3 February 1739 (BL, Add. 4253, fols 86, 87–8).

7 J. Parkin, *Taming the Leviathan: The Reception of the Political and Religious Ideas of Thomas Hobbes in England, 1640–1700* (Cambridge, 2007), pp. 244–52, covers the Scargill case. Officials had accused Scargill of consorting with young women in town and of gaming; Ducket was accused of trying to seduce a widow, Mary Richards. But whereas the testimony about Scargill's improper conduct was largely hearsay, the evidence against Ducket came both from a letter that he wrote to Richards and from her testimony about how he 'importuned her, to grant him the favour, which he explained by being his pretty little mistress'. This request 'she understood [to be] lying with her ... and that upon asking her the favour, in her Bed-chamber, he added, that was the time to make him happy'. Copy of letter from Ducket to Mary Richards, [*c.* 1736–37] (BL, Add. 4253, fols 91–2; CUL, Ee.VI.43, fol. 7). For the analogous case of Nicholas Stevens's ejection from Oxford in 1729, Ward, *Georgian Oxford*, pp. 145–6; Chancellor's court papers for a case of blasphemy regarding Nicholas Stevens, of Trinity College, Oxford, October 1728 (Bodleian, CC Papers 1728/101:1–3); Court Act Book regarding Nicholas Stevens of Trinity College, Oxford, October 1728 (Bodleian, Hyp/A/57, fol. 107); Robert Clavering to Gibson, 8 November 1728; Thomas Tanner to Gibson, 26 November 1728 (SAL, Gibson 5240, 5248).

8 Tunstall to Harley, 11 March 1739 (BL, Add. 4253, fols 89–92).

9 Tunstall to Harley, 24 March 1739, [April] 1739 (ibid., fols 94–5).

10 Tunstall to Harley, 6 May 1739 (ibid., fols 96–7). Gibson had earlier ordained Ducket into the diaconate and priesthood and had confirmed him into his Essex curacy: LPL, Fulham XLII, fols 4, 20.

11 D. Horn (ed.), *British Diplomatic Representatives, 1689–1789* (London, 1932), pp. 114, 143, 154.

12 N. Sykes, *Edmund Gibson* (Oxford, 1926), pp. 241–332; S. Taylor, 'Whigs, Tories and Anticlericalism: Ecclesiastical Courts Legislation in 1733', *PH* 19 (2000), pp. 329–55. For background, M. Goldie, 'Priestcraft and the Birth of Whiggism', in N. Phillipson and Q. Skinner (eds), *Political Discourse in Early Modern Britain* (Cambridge, 1993), pp. 209–31; J. Champion, '"Religion's Safe, with Priestcraft is the War": Augustan Anticlericalism and the Legacy of the English Revolution, 1660–1720', *European Legacy* 5 (2000), pp. 547–61.

13 A. Thompson, 'Contesting the Test Acts: Dissent, Parliament and the Public in the 1730s', *PH* 24 (2005), pp. 58–70; J. Bradley, 'The Public, Parliament and the Protestant Dissenting Deputies, 1732–1740', *PH* 24 (2005), pp. 71–90; R. Barlow, *Citizenship and Conscience: A Study in the Theory and Practice of Religious Toleration during the Eighteenth Century* (Philadelphia, 1963), pp. 80–93; N. Crowther-Hunt, *Two Political Associations: The Quakers and the Dissenting Deputies in the Age of Sir Robert Walpole* (Oxford, 1961), pp. 118–62.

14 Satirical poem, n.d. (BL, Add. 5832, fols 142–4).

15 M. Pattison, 'Tendencies of Religious Thought in England, 1688–1750', in H. Nettleship (ed.), *Essays by ... Mark Pattison* (Oxford, 1889), II, p. 43.

16 L. Stephen, *History of English Thought in the Eighteenth Century* (1902), pp. 86, 257. E. Duffy, 'Pudding Time, 1713–1781', in P. Cunich, E. Duffy, D. Hoyle and R. Hyam (eds), *A History of Magdalene, College Cambridge, 1428–1988* (Cambridge, 1994), p. 160 ranks Waterland's erudition alongside that of his sometime friend and colleague, the great classicist Richard Bentley.

17 C. Abbey and J. Overton, *The English Church in the Eighteenth Century* (1906), pp. 1, 205–15; C. Dugmore, *Eucharistic Doctrine in England from Hooker to Waterland* (1942), pp. 169–83; P. Nockles, *The Oxford Movement in Context: Anglican High Churchmanship, 1760–1857* (Cambridge, 1994), pp. 4, 235–8. See also B. Young, '"Knock-Kneed Giants": Victorian Representations of Eighteenth-Century Thought', in J. Garnett and C. Matthew (eds), *Revival and Religion since 1700* (1993), pp. 86, 87, 91; B. Young, *The Victorian Eighteenth Century* (Oxford, 2007), pp. 103–47. Waterland's works were also being reprinted well into the nineteenth century: in addition to *WDW* (1823, first edition; 1856, third edition), D. Waterland, *Critical History of the Athanasian Creed* (1850) and D. Waterland, *Review of the Doctrine of the Eucharist*, ed. W. Van Mildert (Oxford, 1896), which was reissued so that it would be accessible 'especially [to] candidates for Holy Orders' (preface).

18 Waterland's visitation charges and sermons became eighteenth-century standards of the genre: W. Gibson, '"This Itching Ear'd Age": Visitation Sermons and Charges in the Eighteenth Century', in W. Gibson and K. Francis (eds), *Oxford Handbook of the Modern British Sermon* (Oxford, 2012), p. 295.

19 B. Young, 'Daniel Waterland (1683–1740)', *ODNB*; R. Holtby, *Daniel Waterland* (Carlisle, 1966); W. Van Mildert, 'Life', in *WDW*, I, pp. 1–266; *Biographia Britannica* (1766), VI, part II, pp. 4161–72.

20 For the Waterland family tree, *Publications of the Harleian Society* 39 (1869), pp. 875–6. Waterland's older brother, Theodore (d. 1764), also attended Cambridge (Clare College) and for three decades helped Daniel run Magdalene College. *CCED*; *AC*, IV, p. 345.

21 *CCED*; *AC*, IV, p. 415, 416; Duffy, 'Pudding Time', p. 160.

22 D. Winstanley, *Unreformed Cambridge* (Cambridge, 1935), pp. 41–57.

23 He also earned his B.D. in 1714 and his D.D. in October 1717: BL, Add. 33491, fols 18–19; *AC*, IV, p. 345.

24 Duffy, 'Pudding Time', pp. 160–1, notes that he taught 64 of the 74 Magdalene undergraduates admitted, 1708–17.

25 Henry Howard, sixth earl of Suffolk (1670–1718), was Magdalene's visitor. Waterland had taught his son, Charles Howard, the future seventh earl of Suffolk (1693–1722), who had matriculated at Magdalene in 1711: *AC*, II, p. 415. For Waterland's correspondence regarding the Magdalene student Thomas Whichcote, later an MP for Lincolnshire, see Lincolnshire Archives, Aswarby 10/15/1–13.

26 *CCED*; *AC*, IV, p. 345.

27 Edmund Gibson assured Waterland that Queen Caroline had not, as rumoured, blocked Waterland's nomination to the see of Bristol: Waterland to Gibson, 15, 16 September 1734 (LPL, 1741, fols 96, 98). There were rumours that Waterland had hoped to get the Lady Margaret Professorship when it came open in 1727. Waterland to Bishop, 10 May 1727 (MCC/MR): 'As to the Regius Professorship, which you mention, I have long declared against it, as too much trouble for me, and not consistent with such Residence as I intend in London. The other [Lady Margaret] Professorship is easy, and consistent with everything.'

28 For Peyps Library books which Waterland lightly annotated, C. Knighton (ed.), *Catalogue of the Pepys Library at Magdalene College, Cambridge. Supplementary Series. Volume I: Census of Printed Books* (Woodbridge, 2004). For Waterland's use of the Harleian Library, C. Wright and R. Wright (eds), *The Diary of Humfrey Wanley, 1715–1726* (1966), II, pp. 221, 290. For Waterland's own substantial private library, *Catalogue of … Daniel Waterland* (1742: T187372).

29 Gibson helped to promote Waterland's career by recommending him for prestigious preferments in the crown's gift: [Thomas Rogers] to Gibson, [19] September 1724 (TNA, SP 35/52 fol. 95).

30 Sykes, *Edmund Gibson*, pp. 83–182; Taylor, 'Church and State'; Chamberlain, *Accommodating High Churchmen*.

31 M. Goldie, 'Priestcraft and the Birth of Whiggism', in N. Phillipson and Q. Skinner (eds), *Political Discourse in Early Modern Britain* (Cambridge, 1993), pp. 209–31; A. Starkie, *The Church of England and the Bangorian Controversy, 1716–1721* (Woodbridge, 2007), pp. 19–48. Robert Walpole had been a Whig manager in Henry Sacheverell's trial, and most recognized the lasting effect that debacle had both on him and on Whigs of his stripe. In 1750, for instance, William Warburton explained to Philip Doddridge the Whig church policy and its origins: 'The present Ministers were bred up under and act entirely on the maxims of the last. And one of the principal of his was *not to stir what is at rest*. He took a medicine for the Stone that killed him. And on his death-bed he said he fell by the neglect of his own maxim. Those at the head of affairs, find it as much as they can do to govern

things as they are and they will never venture to set one part of the Clergy ag[ain]st another' (Huntington, HM 20438). Emphasis in the original.

32 Stephen, *History*, I, p. 253.

33 Macaulay's annotated edition of *MWCM* (1755), quoted in H. Trevor-Roper, *History and the Enlightenment* (New Haven, 2010), p. 81.

34 Waterland married Jane Tregonwell (d. 1761), of Anderton, Dorset; their marriage produced no children. Will of Daniel Waterland, 1740 (TNA, PROB 11/708, fol. 109); Will of Jane Waterland, 1761 (TNA, PROB 11/871, fols 329–31).

35 *Family Memoirs of … William Stukeley* (Durham, 1882–87), I, p. 127. Stukeley also provides one of the few descriptions of Waterland's human qualities, noting that he was 'a great smoker, which did him much prejudice: exhausting his vital spirits by losing much saliva' (ibid.).

36 Waterland to Bishop, 15 April 1735 (MCC/MR).

37 D. Waterland, 'Duty of Doing Good. Sermon … November 2, 1712', *WDW*, V, pp. 299–312; D. Waterland, *Sermon preach'd … July 21. 1713* (Cambridge, 1713: N022806); D. Waterland, *Sermon preached … 7th of June, 1716* (Cambridge, 1716: T049135). No pre-1717 correspondence of Waterland's is now extant, save for synopses of 1715–16 letters on Christ's nature published by John Jackson without Waterland's consent: [J. Jackson], *Collection of queries* (1716: T103684).

38 Waterland, *Sermon preached … July 21. 1713*, pp. 5, 17.

39 *Annals*, pp. 137–8; A. Starkie, 'William Law and Cambridge Jacobitism, 1713–16', *Historical Research* 75 (2002), pp. 448–67.

40 *Annals*, pp. 142–5; Van Mildert, 'Life', pp. 13–16; J. Gascoigne, *Cambridge in the Age of Enlightenment* (Cambridge, 1989), p. 91.

41 Van Mildert, 'Life', pp. 16–17.

42 Bentley to Clarke, 18 November 1716 (C. Wordsworth (ed.), *Correspondence of Richard Bentley* (1842), II, p. 52).

43 Censure against Richard Bentley, 27 February 1721 (BL, Add. 22908, fol. 116); J. Monk, *Life of Richard Bentley* (1842), II, pp. 139–40, 206; Van Mildert, 'Life', pp. 20–3.

44 Van Mildert, 'Life', pp. 11–13; J. Ringrose, 'The Royal Library: John Moore and His Books', in P. Fox (ed.), *Cambridge University Library: The Great Collections* (Cambridge, 1998), pp. 78–89.

45 D. Waterland, *Advice to a young student* (1730: T067473), sig A2. Waterland to Gibson, 29 December 1730 (LPL, 1741, fols 78–9), discusses how to reform Cambridge's clerical education. See also J. Gascoigne, *Science, Philosophy and Religion in the Age of the Enlightenment* (Aldershot, 2010), pp. 1–65.

46 Newcomen Wallis's 1715 fair copy of Waterland's *Advice* (MCC, C/DW/II/1); M. Hughes, *The Pepys Library and the Historical Collections of Magdalene College Cambridge* (Cambridge, 2015), p. 56.

47 Waterland, *Advice*, p. 12.

48 Ibid., p. 7.

49 Ibid., pp. 18–29.

50 Ibid., p. 24. See also P. Davies, 'The Debate on Eternal Punishment in Late Seventeenth- and Eighteenth-Century English Literature', *ECS* 4 (1971), pp. 257–76.

51 Waterland, *Advice*, pp. 11, 26.

52 D. Waterland, 'Letters on Lay Baptism', in *WDW*, VI, pp. 85–223. See also B. Sirota, *The Christian Monitors: The Church of England and the Age of Benevolence, 1680–1730* (New Haven, 2014), pp. 178–84; Holtby, *Daniel Waterland*, pp. 118–22. Waterland took an unusual position for a Whig, especially in 1713–14, since it implied invalidating German Lutheran baptisms. The Hanoverians were German Lutherans. See also R. Stevens, '"King George's Religion": Lutheranism and the Religious Politics of the Hanoverian Succession', *Journal of Religious History, Literature and Culture* 2 (2016), pp. 84–104.
53 Monk, *Richard Bentley*, I, pp. 371–2; J. Seed, *Happiness of the good* (1741: T107357), p. 21; Winstanley, *Unreformed Cambridge*, pp. 64–5, 105.
54 D. Waterland, *Charge ... May 19, 1731* (1731: T060325), p. 5.
55 D. Waterland, *Eight sermons* (1721: T116445), p. 104.
56 Ibid., p. 4.
57 Waterland, *Christianity vindicated* (1732: T070169), p. 62.
58 Waterland, *Charge ... May 19, 1731*, pp. 6, 45–9.
59 Waterland, *Christianity vindicated*, pp. 76–7. Cf. S. Mandelbrote, 'Early Modern Natural Theologies', in R. Manning (ed.), *Oxford Handbook of Natural Theology* (Oxford, 2013), pp. 74–99.
60 Johnson, *Dictionary*, II, unpaginated.
61 Cf. C. Taylor, *Dilemmas and Connections* (Cambridge, MA, 2011), pp. 326–46.
62 Waterland, *Charge ... May 19, 1731*, p. 33.
63 Ibid., pp. 17–44, 54–5. Cf. J. Gascoigne, 'The Wisdom of the Egyptians and the Secularisation of History in the Age of Newton', in S. Gaukroger (ed.), *The Uses of Antiquity* (Dordrecht, 1991), pp. 171–212; D. Levitin, 'John Spencer's *De legibus Hebraeorum* (1683–5) and "Enlightened" Sacred History: A New Interpretation', *JWCI* 76 (2013), pp. 49–92.
64 S. Mandelbrote, '"The Doors shall fly open": Chronology and Biblical Interpretation in England, c. 1630–c. 1730', in K. Kileen, H. Smith and r. Wilie (eds), *Oxford Handbook of the Bible in Early Modern England, 1530–1700* (Oxford, 2015), pp. 176–95.
65 W. Chillingworth, *Religion of protestants* (Oxford, 1638: S2558), p. 375.
66 Waterland, *Eight sermons*, p. 127.
67 P. Harrison, *The Bible, Protestantism and the Rise of Natural Science* (Cambridge, 2001), pp. 11–27; A. McGrath, *The Intellectual Origins of the European Reformation* (Oxford, 2004), pp. 148–53; J. Kelly, *Early Christian Doctrines* (1960), pp. 64–79.
68 S. Schreiner, *Are You Alone Wise? The Search for Certainty in the Early Modern Era* (Oxford, 2011), pp. 79–129, 420–30; N. Sykes, 'The Religion of Protestants', in S. Greenslade (ed.), *Cambridge History of the Bible: The West from the Reformation to the Present Day* (Cambridge, 1963), pp. 178–82.
69 B. Gregory, *The Unintended Reformation* (Cambridge, MA, 2012).
70 D. Waterland, *Christianity vindicated*, pp. 4, 6.
71 Ibid., pp. 21, 29, 75.
72 Ibid., pp. 29–30, 75. See also J. Sheehan, 'Thomas Hobbes, D.D.: Theology, Orthodoxy and History', *Journal of Modern History* 88 (2016), pp. 249–74; J. Collins, 'Thomas Hobbes, "Father of Atheists"', in W. Hudson, D. Lucci and J. Wigelsworth (eds), *Atheism and Deism Revalued: Religious Identities in Britain, 1650–1800* (Aldershot, 2014), 25–44.

73 William Cole on Waterland, n.d. (BL, Add. 5836, fol. 26). More generally, J. Spurr, 'Style, Wit and Religion in Restoration England', in S. Taylor and G. Tapsell (eds), *The Nature of the English Revolution Revisited* (Woodbridge, 2013), pp. 233–59.
74 Champion, *Pillars.*
75 D. Waterland, *Discourse of fundamentals* (Cambridge, 1735: N008822), p. 4.
76 Ibid., pp. 14, 15.
77 Ibid., pp. 15–23.
78 Ibid., pp. 23–40, at p. 39.
79 Ibid., p. 45.
80 Ibid., pp. 51–8.
81 Ibid., pp. 6, 62.
82 Waterland, *Eight sermons*, p. 287.

Chapter 3

Philosophy-lectures or the Sermon on the Mount: Samuel Clarke and the Trinity

Christianity differentiates itself from other Western monotheisms in holding that God took human form and died to atone for human sins. Belief in Jesus Christ's atoning sacrifice is essential to salvation: 'He that believeth on him is not condemned: but he that believeth not is condemned already, because he hath not believed in the name of the only begotten Son of God' (John 3:18). Yet precisely what it meant to be 'the only begotten Son of God' was a question which consumed much of the theological energy of the early Church.[1] At the Council of Nicea (AD 325), questions over God's nature dominated proceedings. The council hereticated the claim that Christ was divine but subordinate to the Father, a view propounded most prominently by the Alexandrian priest Arius (d. AD 336) and his followers, known as Arians. The subsequent Council of Constantinople (381) confirmed the Nicene Council's conclusions, formalizing them in the Niceno-Constantinopolitan Creed, referred to in the Thirty-Nine Articles simply as the Nicene Creed. That creed insisted on Christ's eternal consubstantiality with the Father: 'I believe ... in one Lord, Jesus Christ, the only-begotten Son of God, Begotten of his Father before all worlds, God of God, Light of Light, Very God of very God, Begotten, not made, Being of one substance with the Father'.[2] Christ, on this view, was no creature but a fully divine, eternal being of the same substance as the Father. On the whole, these fourth-century councils settled the debate over the Trinity for the next millennium. Anti-trinitarianism would not revive again in a significant way until the late sixteenth century, most notably in the person of Fausto Sozzini (1539–1604) and his intellectual heirs, known collectively as the Socinians, who held that Christ was merely human and did not atone for human sins with his death on the Cross.[3]

Socinianism and allied forms of anti-trinitarian thought gained some traction in England during the mid-seventeenth century, at around the same time that the nation's religio-political order was collapsing.[4] Arianism revived later, in the Glorious Revolution's wake.[5] Because of the Church of England's official self-conception – as expressed, for instance, in the Thirty-

Nine Articles and in the Book of Common Prayer – the re-emergence of anti-trinitarianism cut to the core of the institution's identity.[6] For the English Church styled itself simultaneously as a church established by law and as an apostolic church.[7] It was, to begin with, the nation's legally established church, the product of a series of Erastian religious settlements dating back to the 1530s. While the monarch lacked authority to administer sacraments, '[t]he King's Majesty hath the chief power in this Realm of England and other his Dominions, unto whom the chief Government of all Estates of this Realm, whether they be Ecclesiastical or Civil, in all causes doth appertain'. Indeed, God enjoined 'all godly Princes' to 'rule all estates and degrees committed to their charge by God, whether they be Ecclesiastical or Temporal and restrain with the civil sword the stubborn and evil-doers'.[8] The English monarch's government, then, had an obligation to defend the truth as taught by the Church over which he had dominion: not doing so would have meant undermining that dominion. Yet the Church of England's Erastian origins did not, its formularies held, diminish the fact that it was also an apostolic church, one which retained its primitive purity. Unlike the churches of Jerusalem, Alexandria, Antioch and Rome, the Church of England was part of the 'visible Church of Christ ... a congregation of faithful men, in which the pure Word of God is preached and the Sacraments be duly ministered according to Christ's ordinance in all those things that of necessity are requisite to the same'.[9] Furthermore, the Church of England explicitly confirmed its commitment to what it held to be the apostolic understanding of God's nature, Nicene Christology. The first of its articles of religion proclaimed that there 'is but one living and true God, everlasting, without body, parts or passions; of infinite power, wisdom and goodness; the Maker and Preserver of all things both visible and invisible. And in unity of this Godhead there be three Persons, of one substance, power and eternity; the Father, the Son and the Holy Ghost.'[10] Furthermore, the eighth article of religion enjoined that '[t]he Three Creeds, the Nicene Creed, Athanasius's Creed and that which is commonly called the Apostles' Creed, ought thoroughly to be received and believed: for they may be proved by most certain warrants of holy Scripture'.[11] Including the Athanasian Creed – with its explicit anathemas regarding those who questioned Christ's consubstantiality with the Father – into both the Thirty-Nine Articles and into the liturgy unmistakably signalled the Church of England's commitment to an unambiguous Christological vision.

At least five things flowed from that commitment. The Church of England's dual commitment to apostolicity and to Nicene Christology necessarily implied that Nicene Christology was apostolic.[12] Some inevitably demurred, so that, secondly, debates about toleration, liberty and enlightenment in early modern England were fundamentally debates about the latitude with which one could understand Christ's divinity and, more particularly, about the Nicene articulation of Christ's nature.[13] Thirdly, contention over God's precise nature meant that Nicene Christology's defenders had to prove

Christ's consubstantiality with the Father to justify or, at the least, to reaffirm the Nicene and Athanasian Creeds' truth-claims. Fourthly, that historically contingent and era-specific process of definition and rationalization of what was a supra-rational mystery risked demystifying it: the particular eighteenth-century English orthodox defence of God unintentionally risked robbing God of his transcendence, as he became an actor – albeit an exceptionally powerful one – in the unfolding story of his Creation. Finally, the early modern English state was bound by its alliance with the established Church legally to privilege Nicene orthodoxy. It was no surprise, then, to find the Toleration Act (1689) specifically excluding from its protections any clergyman who 'shall deny in his preaching or writing the doctrine of the blessed Trinity, as it is declared in the aforesaid articles of religion'.[14] So too did the Blasphemy Act (1698) ban anyone 'by writing, printing, preaching, teaching or advised speaking, [to] deny any one of the persons of the Holy Trinity to be God; or shall assert or maintain there are more Gods than one'.[15]

The need to defend Nicene Christology itself emerged during the Reformation and most likely flowed straight from it, as particular metaphysical assumptions about the ways in which God existed in relation to his Creation supplanted older ones which presumed His radical transcendence.[16] English historians who have been interested in Christology have paid attention primarily to seventeenth-century discussions of the subject.[17] For the period after 1700, though, the issue recedes almost entirely from historiographical importance, save perhaps for its relation to the origins of political radicalism.[18] Yet the issue remained important both to orthodox apologists like Waterland and to his polemical opponents because all thought that most everything else flowed from one's stance on Christ's divinity.[19]

This chapter reconstructs those mid-eighteenth-century Christological debates.[20] It focuses especially on the Christological debates between Daniel Waterland and his era's most influential Christologically heterodox polemical divine, Samuel Clarke. Firstly, it examines how Newtonianism or Lockeanism could produce different conceptions of God. Secondly, it anatomizes the competing historical narratives which demonstrated how and why the ancient, primitively pure of Christian thinking about God got perverted. Finally, it explains why charges of imposture were so prevalent in eighteenth-century English polemical divinity.

What provoked Daniel Waterland – 'the famous Defender of the Faith against the Arians' – to produce the most sustained orthodox defence of Nicene Christology during the eighteenth century were the effects he thought he saw from the anti-trinitarian work of the eminent polemical divine Samuel Clarke and his surrogates.[21] 'The Papists make their harvest out of the Bangorian and Arian distractions', Waterland complained to a friend in late 1721. 'About ten days ago 24 at a time were admitted into popish communion, renouncing the protestant Religion.'[22] Waterland blamed Clarke for having helped to create these distractions. Waterland thought that anti-trinitarianism of the sort taught by Clarke was an existential threat to true religion: it needed to be confronted head-on. Christological debates between Waterland and Clarke followed in the immediate wake of the Trinitarian controversies of the 1690s.[23] At bottom, the Waterland–Clarke debates were ones about epistemology and hermeneutics: how could one know the truth and how should one interpret the various sources that revealed truth? More particularly, it was a debate about which primitive Christian sources mattered most and how they should be interpreted. Their Christological exchange burned most intensely during the late 1710s and early to mid-1720s. Waterland's *A Vindication of Christ's Divinity* (1719) – itself a belated response to Samuel Clarke's *Scripture-Doctrine of the Trinity* (1712) and to John Jackson's *A Collection of Queries* (1716) – launched the debate in earnest. From there, more than two dozen pamphlets and books appeared in print in the next decade.

Samuel Clarke (1675–1729) was a Cambridge-educated divine, eight years Daniel Waterland's senior.[24] Like Waterland, he distinguished himself in the public acts for his university degrees. Like Waterland, he was recognized by his contemporaries, both friend and foe, for his wide learning, for his deep intelligence and for his published works of undoubted intellectual distinction. And, like Waterland, he never held the high ecclesiastical office that his evident talents and powerful political connections seemed destined to ensure. But where Waterland's failure to ascend to the top of the ecclesiastical ladder of preferment was hard to explain, Clarke's failure was understandable: he held theological views that disqualified him from promotion, despite being one of Queen Caroline's favourite clerics.[25] Particularly disqualifying were his views on God's nature. These were heterodox, even heretical.

The dispute between Waterland and the Clarkeans was not one between religious believers and atheistic freethinkers but between two different sorts of Christians. It was also a dispute between two intellectual traditions – Newtonianism and Lockeanism – that most would now finger as quintessentially 'Enlightenment' traditions and which many, furthermore, would conflate.[26] The point is not that Lockeanism put one on the path to orthodoxy, while Newtonianism set one down the path to heterodoxy: John Locke, after all, was probably a Socinian and certainly an anti-trinitarian.[27] It is, though, to note that eighteenth-century English polemical divines often thought in ways we might not expect them to have thought and that we need to be alive to those differences. Neither was the Waterland–Clarke debate one between relativists but between two sides who were convinced that they alone were right. Finally, the Waterland–Clarke debate was not just a debate about the epistemological, hermeneutical and metaphysical paths to truth but also a rawly polemical one over labelling: winning the dispute had more to do with successfully affixing one or another pejorative label to your opponent than it did with propositional logic. The primary way by which polemical divines tried to stick those pejorative labels on to one another was by creating the most convincing narratives of the past. The key to polemical victory – properly understood as the defence of truth – was to write good history.

The first glimmers of Clarke's not-orthodox Christology were on display in his 1704–5 Boyle Lectures. Just before his death in July 1691, the natural philosopher Robert Boyle (1627–91) added a codicil to his will to endow an annual lecture 'for proving the Christian religion against notorious infidels, viz. Atheists, Theists, Pagans, Jews and Mahometans, not descending lower to any controversies that are among Christians themselves'.[28] Boyle thought that Christian virtuosi were ideally suited to bring experimental knowledge to bear in Christianity's defence. The very early Boyle lectures bore the influence of England's most eminent Christian virtuoso, Isaac Newton, who assured Richard Bentley, the inaugural lecturer, '[w]hen I wrote my Treatise about our System, I had an Eye upon such Principles as might work with considering Men, for Belief in a Deity and nothing can rejoice me more than to find it useful for that Purpose'.[29] Samuel Clarke was an avowed Newtonian and his distinguished Boyle Lectures employed Newtonian natural philosophy to prove God's existence.[30]

That proof had potentially heterodox implications, especially for a Lockean like Daniel Waterland, who responded most systematically to Clarke's *a priori* defence of God in an unsigned appendix to Edmund Law's *Enquiry into the ideas of space, time, immensity and eternity* (1734).[31] That Clarke was trying to rebut Hobbesians and Spinozists who denied God's existence mattered less to Waterland than the fact that Clarke's defence was, he thought, perversely wrong-headed. Waterland objected first to Clarke's mode of reasoning. In particular, he objected to Clarke's *a priori* argument, an approach which seemed to Waterland both unnecessarily to discount or to devalue certain kinds of evidence for God's existence and nature and artificially to limit God to his Creation. On the one hand, Waterland rejected the Newtonian insistence that God was knowable by unaided reason. Clarke had sought to prove in his Boyle Lectures that God 'must be Self-existent, that is, Necessarily-Existing' and he insisted that only *a priori* reasoning could prove as much to the satisfaction of Hobbesian or Spinozist atheists, who would not accept ephemeral phenomena as evidence.[32] Newton likewise had argued in his *Principia Mathematica* that 'the supreme God exists necessarily; and by the same necessity he exists always and everywhere'.[33] Waterland countered that the *a priori* approach which yielded these arguments about God's necessary existence had repeatedly been tried and proved inadequate across the last 1500 years. It was, as such, dangerous to 'rest any important and unquestionable Truth upon precarious Principles, too weak to support it'.[34] Only *a posteriori* reasoning, he countered, offered sound proofs of God's existence, citing John Locke's pointed rejoinder to Cartesians as evidence:

> It is an ill way of establishing this Truth and silencing Atheists, to lay the whole stress of so important a Point upon that sole Foundation ... and out of an over-

> fondness for that Darling Invention, cashier or at least endeavour to invalidate all other Arguments and forbid us to hearken to those proofs, as being weak or fallacious, which our own Existence and the sensible parts of the Universe, offer so clearly and cogently to our Thoughts, that I deem it impossible for a considering Man to withstand them.[35]

To Waterland, the record of human history provided concrete evidence of God's existence, of his works and of his nature. Or, as he scribbled curtly in the margins of one defence of Clarke's thought, the fundamental issue was '[w]hether philosophy-Lectures or the Sermon on the Mount have most divine wisdom in them'.[36]

If Clarke's Newton-inspired mode of reasoning bothered the Lockean Waterland, Clarke's conclusions about God upset him even more. Most, it should be noted, seem to have found Newtonian natural philosophy perfectly consonant with orthodox Christian doctrine, arguing that the order which Newton had uncovered in nature and the providential role of God in maintaining that order applied equally to human history.[37] Yet others, like Waterland, worried that Newtonian theology could be dangerously heterodox. For Clarke's Boyle Lectures, like Newton's *Principia*, implied an anti-trinitarian views of God. To be sure, both Newton and Clarke insisted that God was ultimately unknowable. 'We have ideas of his attributes, but what the real substance of anything is we know not', Newton noted of God, while Clarke acknowledged that 'the Substance or Essence of the Self-Existent Being, is itself absolutely Incomprehensible to us'.[38] By Newton's reckoning, God was God because he had 'dominion', he was 'Lord God Pantokrator or Universal Ruler'. His dominion extended to the natural world. Indeed, Newton insisted that the universe itself necessarily required the hand of God to guide and maintain it. In this, he distinguished himself from those whose mechanical philosophy presumed that God did not involve himself in the workings of his creation: Newton's God of dominion was anything but inactive. Yet the God of Newton's *Principia* – and still more of his private theological reflections – was also a decidedly not-trinitarian one; so too was the God of Samuel Clarke's Boyle Lectures. Furthermore, the God of Newton's *Principia* seemed, despite his incomprehensibility, to be bounded by his Creation. 'He is not Eternity and Infinity, but Eternal and Infinite; he is not Duration and Space, but he endures and is present. He endures forever and is everywhere present; and, by existing always and everywhere, he constitutes Duration and Space', Newton contended. 'Since every particle of Space is always and every indivisible moment of Duration is everywhere, certainly the Maker and Lord of all things cannot be never and nowhere.'[39] One could easily have taken from this that God somehow at once consisted and was confined to and by the universe which he had created. Since the universal mechanics could explain the operations of that universe, God's actions should, by implication, be explicable. Though Newton and the Newtonians insisted upon God's unknowableness, their natural philosophical assumptions robbed him, at least implicitly, of his transcendence.[40] Waterland understood this, remarking in his rejoinder to Clarke's Boyle Lectures that 'Space and Time are advanced, as amounting to the same with Infinity and Eternity and are supposed really to exist *ad extra* and as certainly as that twice two makes four: Whereupon they are exalted into Modes or Attributes or Properties of the divine Substance and God himself is imagined to be the Substratum of both'.[41] Waterland reckoned instead that God was radically, unknowably transcendent. '… [T]hough an uncaused Being is an unfathomable Abyss and we can scarce forbear asking childishly, how and why or for what Reason it exists and must exist?', he acknowledged, 'yet our recollected Thoughts must tell us, that such Questions are improper and impertinent and resolve only into a fond Conception or contradictory notion of something still higher than the highest and prior to the first'.[42] God could be known, but was not knowable.

Daniel Waterland drafted his critique of Samuel Clarke's Newtonian-infused theologizing about God's attributes three decades after Clarke had originally delivered his Boyle Lectures and with a retrospective sense of Clarke's mature Christological thought. In his *Scripture-Doctrine of the Trinity* (1712), Clarke fleshed out his views more far fully, robustly and controversially than he had in his Boyle Lectures, in which he had only intimated his thoughts on Christ's divinity. It was a turn not just in subject but in style for him, as he moved from the metaphysical argumentation of his Boyle Lectures to a careful engagement with the sources of the Christian past. Prominent figures in Church and state pleaded with Clarke not to publish *Scripture-Doctrine*, recognizing that it would anger those who thought the Church of England's greatest threat was the enemy within, the people Tory firebrand Henry Sacheverell had recently impugned as 'false brethren'. In 1712, the earl of Godolphin implored Clarke on behalf of the Whigs that 'the Affairs of the Public were with Difficulty then kept in the Hands of those that were all for Liberty; that it was therefore an unreasonable Time for the Publication of a Book that would make a great Noise and Disturbance; and that therefore they desired him to forbear, till a fitter Opportunity should offer itself'.[43] Clarke ignored Godolphin's advice.

Three parts comprised Samuel Clarke's *Scripture-Doctrine*. Part one assembled 1251 texts from the New Testament, subdivided into three sections concerning the three persons of the Trinity. The book's second part made 55 propositions which together contained the book's core argument. One learned there that God was unitary, a 'simple, uncompounded, undivided, intelligent Being or Person'. The Father has always existed, as has the Son and the Holy Spirit. But, the 'Father (or First Person) Alone, is Self-existent, Underived, Unoriginated, Independent; made of None, begotten of None, Proceeding from None'. The Son, by contrast, 'is not Self-evident, but derives his Being or Essence and All his Attributes, from the Father, as from the Supreme Cause', though in 'what Particular Metaphysical Manner' the Son derives from the Father is unknown. As such, the Son 'is evidently Subordinate to the Father' and 'acts in all things according to the Will and by the Mission or Authority of the Father'.[44] In the book's third section, Clarke assembled passages from the Book of Common Prayer to show how they expressed the understanding of God which he had just propounded in the book's second part.

Clarke's *Scripture-Doctrine* riled up the orthodox. While Clarke doggedly refused to align himself with a particular Christological camp and, indeed, rejected outright the appellation *Arian*, nearly all of his contemporaries and subsequent historians reckoned that his views embodied the Arian Christological position.[45] Arianism, though, was heretical and wholly unprotected by the Toleration Act, which explicitly endorsed the Christological dogmas expressed in the Nicene and Athanasian Creeds. Facing prosecution from Convocation's lower house, Clarke accepted a settlement negotiated by some Whig bishops that allowed him to retract what he had earlier argued regarding Christ's subordinate nature in return for never again publicly discussing or writing about the subject.[46] Clarke mostly kept to the letter of his end of the bargain, while violating its spirit by actively aiding surrogates, especially John Jackson (1686–1763) and Arthur Ashley Sykes (1684–1756). In their string of responses to Daniel Waterland's defences of Nicene Christology, Jackson and Sykes amplified Clarke's original arguments about Christ's non-consubstantiality with the Father.[47] They evidently felt freer to write about these matters following Convocation's post-1717 emasculation by the Hanoverian monarchs and their ministers.[48]

In his Christological conclusions, no less than in his metaphysical assumptions, Samuel Clarke shared much with Isaac Newton. He also shared Newton's historical explanation for those Christological conclusions.[49] In the *Scripture-Doctrine*, Clarke told a story of primitive Christianity's perversion, of the loss of a pure understanding of God's nature. Christianity was uncorrupted at its outset. 'As in Matters of Speculation and Philosophical Inquiry, the only Judge of what is right or wrong, is Reason and experience; so in Matters either of humane Testimony or divine Revelation, the only Rule of Truth is the Testimony of the Revelation itself', Clarke insisted. By that standard, whatever Christ had taught was 'infallibly True and to us (in matters of Religion) the Rule of Truth'. Likewise, whatever the Apostles preached or wrote was also 'a part of the Rule of Truth'. During the apostolic age, 'Christianity was perfect and continued for some Ages, in a tolerable Simplicity'.[50] As time wore on, though, piety waned, contention waxed and unscriptural accretions infested the Church. In particular, the proliferation of creeds undermined 'pure' Christianity. As Clarke explained it,

> the several Churches ... inlarged their Creeds and Confessions of Faith; and grew more minute, in determining unnecessary Controversies; and made more and more things explicitly necessary to be understood: and (under pretence of

> explaining authoritatively,) imposed things much harder to be understood than the Scripture itself; and became more uncharitable in their Censures; and the farther they departed from the Fountain of Catholic Unity, the Apostolical form of sound words, the more uncertain and unintelligible their Definitions grew; and good men found nowhere to rest the Sole of their Foot, but in having recourse to the original words of Christ himself and of the Spirit of Truth, in which the Wisdom of God had thought fit to express itself.[51]

For Clarke, the Councils of Nicea and Constantinople marked not the moment when the Christian Church's leaders gathered together to clarify God's nature but a moment of unnecessary obfuscation and wilful corruption. Furthermore, they signalled a persecutory turn, as the Church – with the state's aid – thereafter defended man-made creeds. Error and coercion together catalysed Christianity's rot. Across the Middle Ages, religion decayed 'till at last (according the Predictions of the Apostles) it was swallowed up in the great Apostasy, Out of Which it began to recover at the Reformation; when the Doctrine of Christ and his Apostles was again declared to be the only Rule of Truth'. Though Protestants would agree that the Bible was 'the only Rule of Truth', intra-Protestant divisions emerged because some did not adhere to the Bible's original meaning, which all could recover and all should follow.[52]

Those divisions were especially stark over how to comprehend and articulate God's nature. Samuel Clarke posited that understanding properly 'the distinct Powers and Offices of each of the Three Persons' is important because it constitutes 'the great Foundation and the main Economy of the Christian Religion; the Doctrine, in to which we are baptized'.[53] Christology was, for Clarke, not a matter of adiaphora. By his count there had been four Christological heresies, all of which had 'puzzled the plain and practical Doctrine of Scripture': Tritheism, Sabellianism, Arianism and Socinianism. Each, in its own way, had perverted biblical teaching; and only by prioritizing 'Scriptural authority' over 'Humane Authority' could these four Christological perversions be proved wrong.[54] Apprehending and then following 'true religion' meant prioritizing and properly interpreting the Scriptures: the truth lay within the Bible's pages, unchanging but waiting to be recovered.

Daniel Waterland agreed, while at the same time reaching wholly different conclusions about God's nature from the Bible. Waterland assailed the biblical interpretation of Samuel Clarke and his surrogates. In tandem, he tried to offer a more plausible, more convincing counter-narrative. He started this in *A vindication of Christ's divinity* (1719), followed closely by his Lady Moyer Lectures (1721) and then another ten works over the next dozen or so years, culminating in his summative *The Importance of the Doctrine of the Trinity* (1735).[55] All of these works – save for the Lady Moyer lectures and *The Importance of the Trinity* – were animadversions, a literary form still favoured by many at the time but also one which soon become increasingly rare.[56] Animadversions generally had two parts. The first was a short preface in which the author declared his 'impartiality'. The second part, the works' main body, consisted of citations or quotations from the offending text followed by retorts. Produced by less delicate hands animadversions could degenerate quickly into *ad hominem* attacks. Waterland managed the form relatively skilfully, countering what he took to be specious arguments while simultaneously arranging the pieces from which a larger narrative could be built. A clear argument connected Waterland's various Christological writings, whatever their style. He amplified that argument through the years, but the lineaments remained the same from the start.

Like Samuel Clarke, Daniel Waterland told a story of primitive Christianity's perversion, of the loss of an originally pure understanding of God's nature. But Waterland told a story in which the reasons for and the character of primitive Christianity's perversion differed markedly from those identified by Samuel Clarke. To Waterland, the Bible revealed truth, while tradition and reason affirmed it. He aimed 'to show, that we follow not mere Human Decisions or Words of Men, as hath been slanderously reported, but the infallible Word of God'.[57] Yet, Waterland argued, reliance on the Bible alone had not yielded consensus about the truth. 'Men's Wits are so various, that several Interpretations may be invented of the same Texts; and perhaps none of them so manifestly absurd, but that They possibly may be true; nor so manifestly right, but that They possibly may be wrong', he reckoned. 'You bring your Scripture-Proofs; and I produce Mine"[58] Part of the problem was the ambiguity of language, part was human nature. Together, they ensured that a strict *sola scriptura* approach confused as much as it clarified. Compounding that confusion, some biblical texts seemingly contradicted other biblical texts. What was needed was a rule both to discriminate between various sorts of evidence and to identify the most important evidence. That task of discrimination was best done by gauging the value of a particular biblical doctrine 'by the Relation or Connexion which [it] is conceived to have with Christian Practice or Worship or with the whole Economy of Man's Salvation by Christ; or by its being plainly, frequently or strongly inculcated in holy Scripture'.[59] Even applying that rule of thumb, though, left many biblical passages difficult to interpret.

For Samuel Clarke and his surrogates, this was no problem, since everything that was true in the Bible must necessarily also be reasonable. What Clarke called *reason*, Waterland called *metaphysics*; and metaphysics, he contended, led inevitably to scepticism because it provided a necessarily incomplete account of truth. As Waterland put it, 'Metaphysics take in only part of the Idea, consider the Nature abstracted from the Relation, leaving the relative Part out'.[60] Reason alone, for instance, could not 'demonstrate that there must be some eternal God, in the metaphysical Sense'; indeed, '[i]t would be ridiculous to talk of proving from Reason only, without Revelation, that the Person whom we call the Father, the God of Jews and Christians, is the Eternal God'.[61] There were limits to reason, then, and people had sometimes to rely on 'moral Probabilities' which can have in themselves 'an irresistible Strength, little short of the strictest Demonstration'.[62]

Tradition offered even more conclusive proofs than those moral probabilities. Or, as Waterland put it at one point, 'Antiquity ought to Attend as a Handmaid to Scripture, to wait upon her as her Mistress and to observe Her; to keep off Intruders from making bold with her and to discourage Strangers from misrepresenting Her'.[63] Clarke placed no probative value on tradition, but Waterland insisted that it was crucial to the hermeneutical task of interpreting the Bible, whose interpretation sometimes had necessarily to be probabilistic since the Scriptures' literal meaning was often unclear. Tradition stood ready to clarify the unclear, to bring some certainty to uncertainty, for 'if what appears but probably to be taught in Scripture itself, appears certainly to have been taught by the Primitive and Catholic Church; such probability so confirmed and strengthened, carries with it the force of Demonstration'.[64] Indeed, tradition could protect true religion from the innovations which unchecked reason inevitably introduced. 'It is a sufficient Demonstration of our Doctrine, that we have a Tradition coming down to us from our Fathers; a Kind of Inheritance successively conveyed to us by the primitive Saints from the Apostles Themselves', Waterland contended. 'They that have changed those Doctrines for the present Novelty, will have very great need of the Succours of Reason and Argumentation'.[65] And if *sola ratio* sent one off down the path toward untruth, so too could reason as applied to Scripture also lead one astray. After all, the Bible's language, like all language, consisted of 'Words and ... Words are but Signs and that common Usage and Acceptation is what must settle their Meaning. And when any thing comes down to us in a dead Language, as Scripture now does, the customary Use of Words in that Language, at the time when they were spoken or written, must be the Rule and Measure of Interpretation'. A knowledge of the history and traditions of primitive Christianity, then, helped both to recover the original meaning of the Scripture *and* to prevent its perversion by those, like the Socinians and 'Romanists', who were guilty of 'torturing plain Words' to render errant interpretations. Waterland concluded that 'Scripture and Antiquity (under the Conduct of right Reason) are what we ought to abide by, for the settling Points of Doctrine'.[66]

Regarding Christological doctrine, Waterland insisted that the Bible taught and tradition confirmed Nicene Christology. Like Clarke, Waterland identified four Christological options. Both he and Clarke agreed that Sabellianism, Socinianism and Arianism were live Christological heresies. Sabellianism was a revived form of the third-century heresy sometimes known as Monarchianism, which argued for the unity of God by contending that the different 'persons' of the Trinity were really just different modes or operations.[67] Socinianism, too, had its origins in primitive Christological heresies. Though its modern origins lay in the thought of the sixteenth-century Italian, Fausto Sozzini, Socinianism was really, for Waterland, the logical refinement of ancient Sabellianism and its cousin heresy, Photinianism.[68] Yet while the modern Sabellians and their descendants, the Socinians, might have been wrong, they were also thin on the ground. Arians, by contrast, were more numerous and more influential during the early eighteenth century. Like Sabellianism and Socinianism, Arianism traced its roots back to the early Church. The Arians' misinterpretation of Christ's nature, on Waterland's reading, stemmed from their over-reliance on 'Metaphysics in great Plenty, sufficient, one may think, to furnish out an ordinary School-man'. Their metaphysics, in conjunction with their own reading of the Bible, led them to conclude that Christ had been 'generated', a determination which itself led to a number of others about Christ's nature.

> That Generation implies Division and necessary Generation, outward Coaction; that Generation must be an Act and every act must mean Choice; that necessary Agents are no Agents and necessary Causes no Causes; that nothing individual can be communicated; that Three Persons must be Three intelligent Agents and Three intelligent Agents, reciprocally, Three Persons; that Three Agents cannot be One Being, One Substance, One Lord or One God; that there can be no Medium between Being and not Being; that inseparable Union, without identical Life, will not suffice to make Two Persons One God; and that if there be identical Life, then They are no longer Two Persons; nor can there be any Equality or Subordination; that the same living God necessarily signifies the same individual intelligent Agent or person; that God the Son must be either the same identical whole Substance or an homogenous undivided Part of the infinite Substance, upon my Principles; and that He can be neither; and therefore not one and the same God with the Father.[69]

This, for Waterland, was the obverse of the Nicene Christology, both in its verdict about Christ's nature and in the ways in which it reached that verdict.

The Nicene Christological position he described as the 'Catholic' one. Clarke dubbed it 'Tritheism' and deemed it heretical. Nicene Christology was, though, a position which Waterland claimed had biblical warrant and primitive confirmation. As he explained to the anti-trinitarian clergyman Daniel Whitby (1637–1726), 'The Catholics ... down from the fourth (I may say from the first) Century, have believed that there is no Disparity of Nature, no Division of Substance, no Difference in any Perfection between Father and Son; but that They are equally Wise, equally Infinite, equally Perfect in all Respects; differing only in that, that the one is a Father and the other a Son, one Unbegotten, the other Begotten, as a Third is proceeding'. Moreover, he continued, 'these three different Manners or Modes, of Existence distinguish the Persons one from another, perfectly alike and equal in all other respects'.[70] There was nothing exceptional in this synopsis of 'Catholic' Christology: it was, after all, just restated Nicene Christology. But Waterland freely admitted that this 'Catholic' Christology was mysterious. How, after all, could three be one? What did it mean to be omnipresent? How was Christ incarnated but not created? What is eternity? What is self-existence? All of these divine attributes and much else about God were mysteries, but these supra-rational mysteries of 'Catholic' Christology did not make them wrong. Indeed, error always creeps in when humans try fully to grasp or to explain that which is necessarily mysterious about a radically transcendent God. 'Many have been prying and inquisitive into this Matter, hoping to know something more particularly of it, till they have come to doubt even of the Thing it self and so have fallen into Heresy', Waterland argued. 'And Catholics have sometimes exceeded in this way, endeavouring to explain beyond their Ideas; which is nothing else but multiplying Words.'[71] This insistence that there were limits to what reason can reveal, that humans cannot completely wrap our minds around God, failed to satisfy those at the time who thought that Christianity should not be mysterious, that *mystery* connoted *popery*. For Waterland, by contrast, the sorts of objections posed by modern Arians like Samuel Clarke were '*difficiles nugae*, mostly verbal or vain Inquiries; and do not concern common Christians, any farther than to be upon their Guard, that they be not imposed on by these Subtleties, invented to puzzle and perplex a plain Scripture Truth, which is easily perceived and understood in the general, that is, as far as is required to be believed'.[72]

Waterland's insistence that the Nicene Christological position was 'plain Scripture Truth' points to a signal feature of early modern English polemical divinity – the conviction that one's opponent must have been lying when he held different views. Claims of imposture were, indeed, sure signs that polemical divines during the eighteenth century were neither actual nor functional relativists: they believed that truth was absolute and that their opponent's failure to acknowledge that absolute truth was the product of invincible ignorance, at best, or mendacity, at worst.[73] This accounts for the ubiquity of insult in eighteenth-century English polemical divinity. Opponents were regularly denounced as thick-headed, 'brutishly stupid' 'Fools and Idiots'. Hence, too, the conviction that truth was absolute helps to account for the pervasive accusations of imposture in the era's polemical divinity. It is widely acknowledged that the eighteenth-century heterodox routinely accused their orthodox opponents of imposture and, indeed, some went so far as to produce histories of religion which accused Moses and Jesus of having been impostors: on this view, the history of religion *was* a history of imposture.[74] Yet it was also the case that the orthodox had a theory of imposture which itself served in the cause of absolute truth.[75] On this view, for instance, Samuel Clarke and his surrogates were guilty not of error but of lying, so that Waterland's task lay 'in detecting Sophistry, laying open Disguises, exposing Misreports, Misquotations, Misconstructions or any other Engines of Deceit'.[76] In one of his rejoinders to Clarke, Waterland spelled out just how Clarke and his supporters had gone about hiding the Bible's plain truth about Christ's nature. First, 'they ... ransack'd the Socinian Stores for the eluding and frustrating the Catholic Interpretation of Scripture-Texts' and then they went 'to [the] Fathers: and whatever they could there, by wresting and straining, by mangling, by misinterpreting, by false rendering and the like, they have done their utmost to make them all Arians'. Afterwards, they 'attempted the same Thing upon the ancient Creeds and even upon modern Confessions; upon the very Articles and Liturgy of the Church of England'. In their purposefully deceitful scholarship, they 'spared no Pains or Art, to disguise and colour over their wretched Tenets and to give them the best Face and Gloss that they possibly could bear'.[77] Waterland implied here that the Clarkeans employed traditional forms of historical proof not as proof so much as cover for their conclusions which they had reached via 'Metaphysics'.

Not only did modern Arians lie about their Christological beliefs, they counselled others to subscribe casuistically to the English articles of religion which propounded Nicene Christology.[78] For Waterland, the Clarkean admonition that people should subscribe to the articles as they understood them undermined subscription's purpose.[79] Where Clarke contended that it was 'plain that every person may reasonably agree to such Forms, whenever he can in any sense at all reconcile them with Scripture', Waterland saw deceit.[80] For it was not for the individual to decide what the articles meant but to follow the meaning of the 'compilers' and 'imposers' of those religious articles; instead, he should follow the meaning as propounded by the Church of England. Waterland went so far as to declare that 'Subscribers must believe it True in That particular Sense which the Church intended'.[81] And lest anyone doubt how the Church interpreted the creeds, Waterland produced a handful of works which demonstrated that both the compilers and the imposers of the Nicene and Athanasian Creeds understood Christ to be eternally begotten of the Father and consubstantial with him.[82] This issue mattered not just to the established Church's reputation as the teacher and defender of truth but also to the security of the state, because 'There can be no Security against Men's putting their own private Senses upon the Public Laws, Oaths, Injunctions, &c in contradiction to the Imposers, if These Principles about Church Subscription should ever prevail amongst us'.[83]

When lobbying against Samuel Clarke's elevation to the episcopate, Edmund Gibson explained to Walpole that promoting Clarke 'would be condemned by the whole body of the clergy, Whig as well as Tory; a very few excepted'.[84] Not even Queen Caroline's active support could overcome such clerical opposition. Yet two things must be noted of Clarke. Despite his heterodox views on some important theological matters, he remained socially acceptable, retaining, for instance, the queen's favour.[85] Moreover, Clarke never denied that Christ was at least partially divine. Neither of these things could be said of Matthew Tindal, author of *Christianity as Old as the Creation* (1730), a book dubbed 'the Bible of all Deistical readers' and one that had among its many targets Samuel Clarke.[86]

NOTES

1 R. Wilken, *The Spirit of Early Christian Thought* (New Haven, 2003), pp. 80–135; H. Chadwick, *The Early Church* (London, 1993), pp. 125–51; J. Kelly, *Early Christian Doctrines* (1960), pp. 83–162, 223–421.
2 *BCP*, p. 249. Cf. J. Pelikan and V. Hotchkiss (eds), *Creeds and Confessions of Faith in the Christian Tradition* (New Haven, 2003), I, pp. 162–3. See also J. Kelly, *Early Christian Creeds* (London, 1972), pp. 205–331.
3 S. Mortimer, *Reason and Religion in the English Revolution: The Challenge of Socinianism* (Cambridge, 2010), pp. 13–38.
4 P. Lim, *Mystery Unveiled: The Crisis of the Trinity in Early Modern England* (Oxford, 2012).
5 M. Wiles, *Archetypal Heresy: Arianism Through the Centuries* (Oxford, 1996), pp. 62–134.
6 D. MacCulloch, *Thomas Cranmer* (New Haven, 1996), pp. 503–4, 527–9, 536–8, details the compromises that went into the composition and parliamentary acceptance of the Forty-Two Articles and, later, the Thirty-Nine Articles.
7 J. Pocock, 'Within the Margins: The Definitions Of Orthodoxy', in R. Lund (ed.), *The Margins of Orthodoxy: Heterodox Writing and Cultural Response, 1660–1750* (Cambridge, 1995), pp. 33–53.
8 *BCP*, p. 564 [Article XXXVII]. See also the post-1689 English coronation oath, in which the monarchs pledged to 'maintain the laws of God, the true profession of the gospel and the protestant reformed religion established by law' and to protect the 'rights and privileges' of the bishops and clergy: B. Williams, *The Eighteenth-Century Constitution* (Cambridge, 1960), p. 38.
9 *BCP*, p. 558 [Article XIX].
10 Ibid., p. 552 [Article I].
11 Ibid., p. 554 [Article VIII].
12 J. Pocock, *Barbarism and Religion: Volume 5. Religion: The First Triumph* (Cambridge, 2015).
13 Pocock, 'Within the Margins', pp. 48–50.
14 Williams, *Eighteenth-Century Constitution*, p. 46.
15 *The Thirty-Nine articles and the constitutions and canons of the Church of England* (1739: T102476), p. 120.
16 B. Gregory, 'The Reformation Origins of the Enlightenment's God', in W. Bulman and R. Ingram (eds), *God in the Enlightenment* (Oxford, 2016), pp. 201–14. On univocity, see B. Gregory, *The Unintended Reformation* (Cambridge, MA, 2012), pp. 25–73; J.-L. Marion, 'The Idea of God', in D. Garber and M. Ayers (eds), *Cambridge History of Seventeenth-Century Philosophy* (Cambridge, 1998), I, pp. 265–304; A. Funkenstein, *Theology and the Scientific Imagination from the Middle Ages to the Seventeenth Century* (Princeton, 1986), pp. 23–116. Cf. P. Lim, 'Not Sola Scriptura or, a Rejoinder to Brad S. Gregory's *The Unintended Reformation*', *JMEMS* 46 (2016), pp. 603–28. On testimony and proofs, see R. Serjeantson, 'Testimony: The Artless Proof', in S. Adamson, G. Alexander and K. Ettenhuber (eds), *Renaissance Figures of Speech* (Cambridge, 2007), pp. 179–94; J. Levine, 'Matter of Fact in the English Revolution', *JHI* 64 (2003), pp. 317–35.
17 B. Sirota, 'The Trinitarian Crisis in Church and State: Religious Controversy

and the Making of the Post-Revolutionary Church of England, 1687–1701', *JBS* 52 (2013), pp. 26–54; Lim, *Mystery Unveiled*; Mortimer, *Reason and Religion*; H. McLachlan, *Socinianism in Seventeenth-Century England* (Oxford, 1951); J. Hunt, *Religious Thought in England* (1870), III, pp. 201–22.

18 The best overview of the subject remains Abbey and Overton, *English Church*, pp. 197–219. See also K. Haugen, 'Transformations of the Trinity Doctrine in English Scholarship: From the History of Beliefs to the History of Texts', *Archiv für Religionsgeschichte* 3 (2001), pp. 149–68; J. Clark, *English Society, 1660–1832: Religion, Ideology and Politics during the Ancien Régime* (Cambridge, 2000), pp. 318–422. The sizeable literature on eighteenth-century deism says little about Christology. Scholars of Newtonianism, by contrast, have focused more concertedly on the subject: S. Snobelen, 'Isaac Newton, Socinianism and the "One Supreme God"', in M. Mulsow and J. Rohls (eds), *Socinianism and Cultural Exchange* (Leiden, 2005), pp. 241–93; R. Iliffe, 'Prosecuting Athenasius: Protestant Forensics and the Mirrors of Persecution', in J. Force and S. Hutton (eds), *Newton and Newtonianism* (Dordrecht, 2004), pp. 113–54.

19 A. Waterman, *Political Economy and Christian Theology since the Enlightenment* (2004), pp. 31–54. Cf. J. Bradley, 'The Religious Origins of Radical Politics in England, Scotland and Ireland, 1662–1800', in J. Bradley and D. Van Kley (eds), *Religion and Politics in Enlightenment Europe* (Notre Dame, 2001), pp. 187–253.

20 Cf. R. Holtby, *Daniel Waterland* (Carlisle, 1966), pp. 12–49, 105–17.

21 *Biographia Britannica* (1766), VI, part II, p. 4161. *The Present State of the Republick of Letters* XII (1733), pp. 371–2, commends Waterland for having 'exerted his Zeal, and displayed his Erudition to great Advantage in favour of the Catholic Doctrine of the holy Trinity'. The most thorough, though contradictory, examinations of Clarke's Christology are T. Pfizenmaier, *The Trinitarian Theology of Dr. Samuel Clarke (1675–1729)* (Leiden, 1997); J. Ferguson, *Dr. Samuel Clarke: An Eighteenth-Century Heretic* (Kineton, 1976), pp. 47–105, 119–95.

22 Waterland to Bishop, 21 November 1721 (MCC/MR). See also E. Duffy, '"Poor Protestant Flies": Conversions to Catholicism in Early Eighteenth Century England', *SCH* 15 (1978), pp. 289–304.

23 W. Bulman, *Anglican Enlightenment: Orientalism, Religion and Politics in England and Its Empire, 1648–1715* (Cambridge, 2015), pp. 262–76.

24 J. Gascoigne, 'Samuel Clarke (1675–1729)', *ODNB*; Ferguson, *Samuel Clarke*. Clarke had been educated at school in Norwich by Benjamin Hoadly's father. I thank Bill Gibson for this point.

25 S. Taylor, 'Queen Caroline and the Church', in S. Taylor, C. Jones and R. Connor (eds), *Hanoverian Britain and Empire* (Woodbridge, 1998), pp. 86–7.

26 B. Young, *Religion and Enlightenment in Eighteenth-Century England* (Oxford, 1998), pp. 83–119; B. Young, 'Newtonianism and the Enthusiasm of Enlightenment', *Studies in History and Philosophy of Science: Part A* 35 (2004). Cf. L. Stewart, 'The Trouble with Newton in the Eighteenth Century', in J. Force and S. Hutton (eds), *Newton and Newtonianism* (Dordrecht, 2004), pp. 221–38; J. Israel, *Radical Enlightenment: Philosophy and the Making of Modernity, 1650–1750* (Oxford, 2001), pp. 515–27; Gascoigne, *Cambridge*; M. Jacob, *The Newtonians and the English Revolution, 1689–1720* (Ithaca, NY, 1976).

27 J. Marshall, *John Locke: Resistance, Religion and Responsibility* (Cambridge, 1994).

28 R. Maddison, *The life of … Robert Boyle* (London, 1969), pp. 257–82. See also R. Ingram, 'Nature, History and the Search for Order: The Boyle Lectures, 1730–1785', *SCH* 46 (2010); Jacob, *Newtonians*, pp. 162–200.
29 Newton to Bentley, 10 December 1692 (I. Newton, *Four letters* (1756: T040093), p. 1).
30 B. Hoadly, 'Preface', in J. Clarke (ed.), *Sermons* (1731: T155510), I, pp. ii–v, charts Clarke's rejection of the Cartesianism of his tutor, John Ellis, for Newtonianism, which he thought was 'Real and Substantial'.
31 Waterland's appendix to Law's *Enquiry* was entitled *A dissertation upon the argument a priori for proving the existence of a first cause*, signed by 'a Learned Hand'. Waterland had remarked unfavourably on Clarke's commitment to *a priori* reasoning in a number of his works during the 1720s, but his appendix to Law's *Enquiry* was his most sustained treatment of the matter. Waterland to Thomas Bishop, 27 February 1734 (MCC/MR): Edmund Law and Joseph Clarke 'are preparing something against' John Jackson and Samuel Clarke 'upon the subject to Time and Space and the famed Argument a priori. I am persuaded, that they will go near to put an end to that controversy; which has subsisted hitherto upon nothing else but equivocation.' On the unlikely Waterland–Law friendship, Young, 'Newtonianism', p. 652; J. Stephens, 'Edmund Law and His Circle at Cambridge: Some Philosophical Activity of the 1730s', in G. Rogers and S. Tomaselli (eds), *The Philosophical Canon of the 17th and 18th Centuries* (Rochester, 1996), pp. 163–74; W. Van Mildert, 'A Review of the Author's Life and Writings', in *WDW*, I, p. 113. See also Holtby, *Daniel Waterland*, pp. 105–17.
32 S. Clarke, *Demonstration of … God* (1705: T116144), p. 27.
33 I. Newton, *Mathematical principles*, trans. A. Motte (1729: T142590), II, pp. 390–1.
34 [D. Waterland], *Dissertation upon … a priori*, in E. Law, *Enquiry into the ideas of space, time, immensity and eternity* (1734: T087827), p. 86.
35 Ibid., p. 91, quoting J. Locke, *Essay Concerning Human Understanding*, ed. P. Nidditch (Oxford, 1975), p. 622.
36 Waterland's annotations of Henry Stebbing's *Defence*, n.d. (Bodleian 8⁰ Rawl 437, p. 5).
37 Ingram, 'Nature, History and the Search for Order'; R. Ingram, '"The trembling earth is God's Herald': Earthquakes, Religion and Public Life in Britain during the 1750s', in T. Braun and J. Radner (eds), *The Lisbon Earthquake of 1755* (Oxford, 2005), pp. 97–115.
38 Newton, *Mathematical principles*, II, p. 391; Clarke, *Demonstration of … God*, p. 81.
39 Newton, *Mathematical principles*, II, p. 390.
40 For the relationship between Newton's conception of God and his natural philosophy, see S. Snobelen, 'The Theology of Isaac Newton's *Principia Mathematica*: A Preliminary Survey', *Neue Zeitschrift für Systematische Theologie und Religionsphilosophie* 52 (2010), pp. 377–412; S. Snobelen, '"God of Gods and Lord of Lords": The Theology of Isaac Newton's General Scholium to the *Principia*', *Osiris* 16 (2001), pp. 169–208; Buckley, *Denying and Disclosing God*, pp. 18–24; M. Buckley, 'The Newtonian Settlement and the Origins of Atheism', in R. Russell and C. Coyne (eds), *Physics, Philosophy and Theology* (Notre Dame, 1988), pp. 81–102. Cf. D. Levitin, 'Newton and Scholastic Philosophy', *BJHS* 49 (2016), pp. 53–77.

41 [Waterland], *Dissertation*, p. 92.
42 Ibid., p. 82.
43 Whiston, *Historical memoirs*, p. 25.
44 Clarke, *Scripture-doctrine*, pp. 241, 243, 270–6, 304, 322.
45 See, for instance, M. Wiles, *Archetypal Heresy: Arianism Through the Centuries* (Oxford, 1996), pp. 110–34. Cf. Pfizenmaier, *Trinitarian Theology;* T. Pfizenmaier, 'Why the Third Fell Out: Trinitarian Dissent', in W. Gibson and R. Cornwall (eds), *Religion, Politics and Dissent* (Aldershot, 2010), pp. 17–34.
46 Ferguson, *Samuel Clarke*, pp. 83–97; G. Bray (ed.), *Records of Convocation* (Woodbridge, 2005), XI, pp. 62–3, 70–2, 75–9. Clarke contended that he was merely clarifying what he had written in *Scripture-Doctrine* not retracting what he had written in his declaration to Convocation that 'Concerning the eternity of the Son and Holy Spirit, my opinion is that the Son of God was eternally begotten by the eternal, incomprehensible power and will of the Father and that the Holy Spirit was likewise eternally derived from the Father by or through the Son, according to the eternal, incomprehensible power and will of the Father'. Clarke was one of the few not to have taken this as a retraction: William Wake to Samuel Clarke; William Fleetwood and George Smalridge to Clarke, 4 July 1714 (BL, Add. 4370, fols 5, 7).
47 Jackson's close association with Clarke and his unauthorized publication of correspondence with Waterland in [Jackson], *Collection of queries*, could not but have soured Waterland personally upon both Clarke and his protégé. For the correspondence which details Clarke's active engagement and close collaboration with Jackson, CUL, Add. 7113; J. Sutton, *Memoirs ... of John Jackson* (1764: T071594), pp. 13–14, 16, 23–30. For Jackson's self-defence, [J. Jackson], *Memoirs of ... Waterland* (1736: T039144), pp. 17–19. For Clarke's fairly obvious breach of his agreement with the 1714 Convocation, [S. Clarke], *Modest plea &c. continued* ((1720): T145668) and [S. Clarke], *Observations on Dr. Waterland's second defense* (1724: T026796). See also J. Stephens, 'Arthur Ashley Sykes (c. 1684–1756)', *ODNB*; B. Young, 'John Jackson (1686–1763)', *ODNB*; Arthur Ashley Sykes's commentary on a sermon by Daniel Waterland, *c.* 1730 (Emory University Library, 021/1/3).
48 N. Sykes, *Church and State in England in the XVIIIth Century* (Cambridge, 1934), pp. 312–14; P. Langford, 'Convocation and the Tory Clergy, 1717–61', in E. Cruickshanks and J. Black (eds), *The Jacobite Challenge* (Edinburgh, 1988), pp. 107–22.
49 S. Mandelbrote, '"Than this nothing can be plainer": Isaac Newton Reads the Fathers', in G. Frank, T. Leinkauf and M. Wriedt (eds), *Die Patristik in der Frühen Neuzeit* (Stuttgart, 2006), pp. 277–97; S. Mandelbrote, 'Newton and Eighteenth-Century Christianity', in I. Cohen (ed.), *Cambridge Companion to Newton* (Cambridge, 2002), pp. 409–30; Iliffe, 'Prosecuting Athanasius'.
50 S. Clarke, *Scripture-Doctrine of the Trinity* (1712: T115758), pp. i, iv, viii.
51 Ibid., pp. vii–viii.
52 Ibid., pp. ix, xix.
53 Ibid., pp. xxvi, xxvii.
54 Ibid., pp. xxix–xxx.
55 S. Mandelbrote, 'Eighteenth-Century Reactions to Newton's Anti-Trinitarianism', in J. Force and S. Hutton (eds), *Newton and Newtonianism* (Dordrecht, 2004), pp.

101–2.
56 J. Champion, *The Pillars of Priestcraft Shaken: The Church of England and Its Enemies, 1660–1730* (Cambridge, 1992), pp. 29–52; J. Raymond, *Pamphlets and Pamphleteering in Early Modern Britain* (2006), pp. 210–14. Cf. K. O'Brien, 'History and Literature, 1660–1780', in J. Richetti (ed.), *Cambridge History of English Literature, 1660–1780* (Cambridge, 2005), pp. 363–90; K. O'Brien, 'History and the Novel in Eighteenth-Century Britain', *HLQ* 68 (2005), pp. 397–413.
57 Waterland, *Eight sermons*, dedication.
58 Waterland, *Vindication of Christ's divinity* (1719: T117074), pp. 454, 455.
59 Waterland, *Importance of the doctrine of the Holy Trinity* (1734: T117012), p. 8.
60 Waterland, *Vindication*, p. 53.
61 Ibid., p. 116.
62 Waterland, *Eight sermons*, p. 83.
63 Waterland, *Importance*, p. 361.
64 Waterland, *Eight sermons*, p. iv.
65 Waterland, *Second vindication of Christ's divinity* (1723: T146641), p. xii.
66 Waterland, *Importance*, pp. 361, 363, 465.
67 Chadwick, *Early Church*, pp. 87–8; Kelly, *Early Christian Doctrines*, pp. 119–23.
68 Waterland, *Eight sermons*, p. 9, insisted that Jean Le Clerc (1657–1736) had 'openly espoused this Photinian Notion in part; distinguish it a little under the Name *Reason*'. Photinus was a fourth-century bishop of Sirmium and espoused a Christology closely aligned to Sabellianism: Kelly, *Early Christian Doctrines*, pp. 241–2.
69 Waterland, *Second vindication*, p. 4.
70 Waterland, *Answer to Dr. Whtiby's reply* (1720: T22010), 8. Despite Waterland's assertions of primitive unity regarding Christ's nature, his repeated proofs of that unity (especially Origen) suggest that many during his day doubted that unity: Waterland, *Importance*, pp. 222–354; Waterland, *Vindication*, pp. 197, 379–89; Waterland, *Eight sermons*, dedication, pp. 19–21, 37, 65, 139, 243–5, 287; Waterland, *Second vindication*, pp. v–xii, xiii–xxiv, 71–126, 163–4.
71 Waterland, *Vindication*, pp. 313–21, at p. 321.
72 Ibid., p. 322.
73 Karl Gunther's forthcoming book (*Wrong! Confronting Error in Reformation England*) will treat this subject more fully.
74 J. Champion, 'Legislators, Impostors and the Politic Origins of Religion: English Theories of "Imposture" from Stubbe to Toland', in S. Berti, F. Charles-Daubert and R. Popkin (eds), *Heterodoxy, Spinozism and Free Thought in Early-Eighteenth-Century Europe* (Dordrecht, 1996), pp. 333–56; R. Iliffe, 'Lying Wonders and Juggling Tricks: Religion, Nature and Imposture in Early Modern England', in J. Force and D. Katz (eds), *Everything Connects* (Leiden, 1999), pp. 211–40.
75 Bulman, *Anglican Enlightenment*.
76 Waterland, *Answer to Dr. Whitby*, p. 82.
77 D. Waterland, *Farther vindication of Christ's divinity* (1724: T084971), pp. 128–9.
78 Young, *Religion and Enlightenment*, pp. 45–79.
79 Waterland to Daniel Finch, earl of Nottingham, 4 July 1721 (Leicestershire Record Office, DG7, Bundle 27). I thank Noah McCormack for this reference.
80 Clarke, *Scripture-doctrine*, pp. xx–xxi.

81 D. Waterland, *Case of Arian-subscription* (1721: T116447), p. 67.
82 Ibid.; D. Waterland, *Supplement to the case of the Arian subscription* (1722: T116444); D. Waterland, *Critical history of the Athanasian Creed* (1727: T145279).
83 Waterland, *Case of the Arian-subscription*, p. 7.
84 Gibson to Walpole, n.d. (SAL, Gibson 5201).
85 Ferguson, *Samuel Clarke*, pp. 222–4.
86 P. Skelton, *Deism revealed* (1751: T101682), II, p. 265.

Chapter 4

Has not reason been abused as well as religion? Matthew Tindal and the Scriptures

Christianity as Old as the Creation (1730), like everything Matthew Tindal (1657–1733) wrote, provoked his contemporaries.[1] His friend Edmund Curll noted, Tindal fought 'a continual Warfare in the Republic of Letters for the space of above forty Years'.[2] If *Christianity as Old as the Creation* lacked the intellectual heft and polemical bite of earlier works like the *Rights of the Christian Church* (1706), it nevertheless elicited responses from some of the most important clerical polemicists of the day. Daniel Waterland entitled his three-part anti-Tindal retort *Scripture Vindicated* (1730–32).[3] As the trilogy's title suggests, Waterland's exchange with Tindal turned on the Bible's authority as a historical source. Tindal had deep reservations about the Bible's usefulness; Waterland had deep reservations about Tindal.

This chapter anatomizes the Tindal–Waterland debate.[4] While it addressed many of the same concerns as the Clarke–Waterland debate, it did so more starkly, especially concerning God's nature. At its heart, the Tindal–Waterland debate was not just about how God could be known; it was also about God's relation to and scope of action within his creation. In Waterland's defence of the Bible's truth, he argued for a radically transcendent God, one who could do whatever he wanted; whenever and wherever he wanted; and for reasons wholly inscrutable to human beings. To Tindal, this was an irrational – and, hence, an immoral – argument. This chapter explains why Tindal and Waterland argued as they did. Locating their dispute within eighteenth-century debates over *deism*, it also shows how Waterland worked out his thinking about Tindal's *Christianity as Old as the Creation* in the margins of his own copy of the work. His initial objections focused on the threat Tindal's work posed to the nation's morality. In *Scripture Vindicated*, though, Waterland focused on Tindal's hermeneutical challenges.

Many during the eighteenth century described Matthew Tindal as a *deist*. He was, Elisha Smith argued, one of the 'oracles of Deism'. The Irish Presbyterian John Leland contended that Tindal had espoused 'the Religion of a Deist'; in

Leland's later retrospective and influential genealogy of deism, Tindal was one of its leading lights, a verdict shared by most historians since.[5] Some at the time, mostly anti-deists, thought deism was a discernible set of beliefs. Leland, for instance, characterized a deist as one who had decided 'to set aside revelation, and to substitute mere natural religion, or, which seems to have been the intention of some of them, no religion at all in its room'.[6] The encylopaediast Ephraim Chambers denied that deists were a-religious, simply noting that they 'reject all Revelation as an Imposition, and believe no more than what natural Light discovers to them; as that there is a God, a Providence, a future State, with Rewards and Punishments, for the Good and the Bad; That God must be honoured; and his Will, so far as we can learn it, performed; but that each Person is to do this after his own Manner, and as his own Conscience suggests'.[7] But, how did deism in practice correlate with deism in definition? Was *deism* a set of identifiable and stable characteristics straight the way from Charles Blount's emergence in the 1670s to Matthew Tindal's twilight in the early 1730s?[8] Or was it instead from its very origins in the mid-sixteenth-century confessional crises an unmistakably pejorative and intentionally vague label, one polemically employed to marginalize one's opponent rather than accurately to describe his position?[9] Did the inverse proportion of accused deists to self-proclaimed ones mean that *deism* was little more than a 'myth'?[10]

Samuel Clarke's second set of Boyle Lectures – which Tindal addressed at length in *Christianity as Old as the Creation* – identified what he held to be the deistic threat.[11] Clarke's first set of Boyle Lectures concerned God's existence and the divine attributes; the second set aimed to prove 'the unalterable obligations of Natural Religion, and the certainty of Divine Revelation'.[12] Clarke's story mirrored stories in his later Christological writings: it was a declension narrative in which a primitive state of purity gave way to a degenerate state of corruption. On his reading, the unquestioned failure of the 'wise and brave and good men' of antiquity 'to reform the World, with any considerably great and universal Success' demonstrated the necessity of a divine revelation 'to recover Mankind out of their universally degenerate Estate, into a State suitable to the original Excellency of their Nature'.[13] The only religion which rightfully could claim this was Christianity, which 'in its primitive simplicity, and as taught in the Holy Scriptures' was 'actually and truly a Divine Revelation'.[14] Clarke, though, recognized that some (primarily those whom he called 'deists') rejected such claims, objecting to Christianity on 'Matters of Fact'.[15] The defence of Christianity's truth required, Clarke thought, a historically minded reasoning.

Clarke identified four kinds of deists. The first sort believed in a clockmaker God, one who had created the universe and set it in motion before stepping back once and for all from his creation. Yet for Clarke a non-providential God was not God because the universe required him not just for its existence but for its maintenance, as the Newtonian laws of motion and gravitation proved.[16] A second type of deist accepted that God providentially managed the physical universe while rejecting the notion that he distinguished good from evil. This too was nonsense, Clarke insisted, because God's natural attributes cannot be separated from his moral ones. These two kinds of deists united in their implicit commitment to 'down-right Atheism' and in their 'Profane and debauched' behaviour.[17] Clarke did not impute immorality to the other two sorts of deists, however. The third sort acknowledged God's providential management of his creation and the distinction between moral good and evil; they parted paths with Christians, though, in denying the human soul's immortality and, hence, of any judgement in the afterlife. The fourth and final sort, by contrast, accepted the soul's immortality; a future state of rewards and punishments; and providence. However, they rejected any proofs from revelation. These last were, in Clarke's words, the only 'true Deists', and were, he concluded, the only ones susceptible to being convinced of Christianity's truth.[18]

While much of Samuel Clarke's description of deism applied to Matthew Tindal, Tindal did not self-identify as a deist. Rather he defined himself in terms of what he was not – a persecutory, bigoted, orthodox churchman. An account of Tindal's final days by his physician provides a useful point of entry into the character and content of his thought.[19] His chief regret as he lay dying was that he had not completed the second volume of *Christianity as Old as the Creation*, which targeted the orthodox notion of 'the Eternity of Hell Torments'.[20] As to what lay beyond death, he reckoned that 'if there was a God He was sure that He should go to a merciful one not a cruel & revengeful one, such an One as He is described to be & always shews himself in Scripture'. That God, if he existed at all, would surely not to be the God of the Nicene and Athanasian Creeds: the portrait of Jesus on the Cross which hung in his room led Tindal to remark incredulously, 'How is it possible ... that I should ever believe that fellow to be the Son of God?' The question of Jesus's nature dogged him until the very end, for, with only a few hours left to live, Tindal called for his literary executor, Eustace Budgell, to inform him of two things that he had forgotten to address in *Christianity as Old as the Creation*'s unfinished second volume. Lazarus's raising from the dead, he noted to Budgell, 'was mentioned only by St. John, & not by any others of the Evangelists'. Moreover, 'all the Miracles which were said to be wrought were none of them wrought in Jerusalem, where there were persons of Sense & Discernment, who were capable of seeing them, & who might have detected him, but in some obscure paltry villages & corners, where there was nothing but a parcel of mean, ignorant people & his own illiterate followers, who might easily be cheated & imposed upon'. Jesus, by implication, was an imposter, a charlatan who had gulled the credulous into believing made-up stuff: in this regard he was, for someone like Tindal, the prototypical Christian priest. Tindal's obvious rejection of orthodox Christian doctrine, though, did not make him a relativist. For him, some things were wrong, others were not. In his work of revealing the truth, Tindal proceeded apophatically – his method was to strip away the layers of error which obscured truth rather than to build up some new philosophical or theological system. He had supreme confidence that public debate in print best allowed him to expose those errors and to recover truth in its primitive purity. Furthermore, that public debate would necessarily centre on the Christianity's historical record.[21]

Matthew Tindal brought to his polemical divinity an apostate's zeal and a lawyer's mind.[22] A native of Devon, he studied at Lincoln College, Oxford, during the early 1670s, when George Hickes (later a leading nonjuror) taught him. All Souls College elected Tindal to its fellowship in 1678, a position he kept for the rest of his life, splitting his time between Oxford and Gray's Inn, where he kept rooms and based his legal practice. The security and stability afforded by his All Souls fellowship did not immunize Tindal from the turbulent religious politics of the late seventeenth century. For a time during James II's reign, he was a practising Roman Catholic before conforming to the Church of England in late 1688. Having turned his back on Rome, he subsequently turned it on James II, taking to print to defend the Glorious Revolution and, presumably, to testify publicly to his anti-papist *bona fides*. His contemporaries thought that Tindal had twice traversed the Tiber 'either bribed by his Hopes, or awed by his Fears'.[23] Whether his back-to-back-to-back conversions emerged from conviction or from more *politique* considerations, they undoubtedly gave him practical experience in the two Christian churches – of Rome and of England – which he excoriated during his polemical career.

Edmund Gibson's pastoral letters to the inhabitants of London, themselves written in response to Thomas Woolston's 1728 blasphemy trial, provoked Tindal to draft *Christianity as Old as the Creation*.[24] Concerned with what he perceived to be the growing number of works which promoted 'Atheism and Infidelity', Gibson did not pretend to offer an original defence of Christianity. Instead he synopsized arguments from the most important recent works on the subject.[25] His first letter identified ten prophylaxes against infidelity, ranging from maintaining a sincere desire to know God's will to revering sacred things to combating religious indifference. At the heart of Gibson's advice, though, was an examination of the evidences of Christianity, both natural and revealed. The problem with natural religion, Gibson argued, was that it had produced little more than 'the endless and irreconcilable differences among the ancient Philosophers, not only in Speculative Opinions, but in the great Rules of the Duty, as to what is right and wrong, lawful or unlawful; and even in the chief End or Good which man ought to propose to himself in order to his Happiness'.[26] If reason was such a sure guide to truth, why had ancient philosophers reached no consensus about it? One explanation concerned the ends to which reason got put, for on Gibson's reading, natural religion in antiquity had been primarily about the 'Government of Appetites'. Moreover, ancient natural religion almost always argued for the soul's immortality and for a future state of rewards and punishments and, furthermore, granted that human knowledge had its limits.[27] Modern natural religion, by contrast, had none of this. Its proponents employed ridicule in their works 'not to inform the Understanding, but to corrupt the Heart' and to subject even the most sacred subjects 'into Jest and Ridicule; and by being so turned may be made to appear mean and despicable'.[28] In the face of such contempt, people needed to focus on the unquestionable historical evidences of Christianity's truth including, 'types', prophecies, 'facts', the consequences of those facts, miracles, predictions that have been fulfilled, and the propagation of the Gospel itself. In all of this, the Bible was crucial, constituting as it did a 'Message from God to Men'. The Bible, in other words, was a divinely inspired work of history: Christ's miracles were 'Historical Truths'.[29]

Tindal's initial, anonymous response to Gibson appeared within a month of the first pastoral letter's publication.[30] Its central argument was that priests had corrupted 'true religion'.[31] No less than Gibson or Waterland, Tindal argued for truth's constancy: 'Truth is the same by whomsoever delivered, 'tis What is said, and not Who says it'.[32] Yet priests had distorted and hidden the truth. The trouble began when Christian priests came to power under Constantine the Great during the fourth century, and 'the Clergy in all Churches ever since, when undermost, have pleaded for Toleration from the New Testament; and when uppermost, for Persecution from the Old'. Indeed, popery itself had emerged as 'the Consequence of the Magistrate's using Force at the Direction of the Priests, to keep out what they called Profaneness, Irreligion, Schism, Heresy, Impiety, Infidelity, Blasphemy &c and that Force thus directed, produced a Superstition'. Even at the Reformation, Protestant priests had acted like the papist ones whose abuses they had sought to reform. '[D]id not the Priests, both Here and Abroad, claim the same impious Power they exclaimed against in the Papists; and like the true Inquisitors, condemn Heretics to the Flames?', Tindal asked rhetorically. 'And if we could not Then meet with Sincerity in the Priests, when are we to expect it?'[33] The danger to English society was real, for, if someone like Henry Sacheverell came to power, he might topple the post-revolutionary settlement.

> Should a Man of such Principles, and of a violent Temper, and who did not want Cunning to contrive, or Boldness to execute any hazardous Attempt, be placed at the Head of the Clergy, to what a Height might he not carry Church-Power, when backed by a High-Church Clergy, having the Mob at their Devotion, and ready to come into any measures, to destroy that hated Liberty, which men of all Persuasions now enjoy; and to get that Independency they have so long aimed at.[34]

Tindal concluded that persecuting clergy deserved death, and he lamented that Edmund Bonner (d. 1569), Queen Mary's bishop of London – a man who 'outdid all the Popish Bishops in Cruelty, and took a savage Delight in insulting, as well as tormenting Protestants' – had not been 'cooped up with the less savage animals, Lyons and Tigers'.[35] Perhaps, by implication, the current bishop of London, Edmund Gibson, deserved the same fate?

The only way to combat clericalism, Tindal advised, was to allow free inquiry; to follow reason; and to engage in ridicule. 'Liberty of Inquiry', he claimed, was the most effective antidote to the 'Hatred and Cruelty' which exist when men were hindered 'from thinking freely themselves'.[36] He had beaten this particular drum since the 1690s, a time when free inquiry had, he believed, produced salutary results in public theological debates.[37] 'In former Ages, the Sword, which carried with it Infallibility, determined the Fate of the Trinitarian Doctrine; and the Councils always declared those Orthodox who had the Power to persecute', he contended. 'But now since Men, without any such Danger, are suffered to debate this Point, different Opinions have occasioned no more Prejudice to the Public, or Breach of Charity amongst private Persons, than the Disputes about Predestination; which once caused great Disturbances,'[38] In addition to advocating free inquiry's efficacy in combating clericalism, Tindal counselled that reason must be truth's sole touchstone: '[a]re not the Dictates of Reason, the Dictates of God himself?' Revelation, by contrast, was unneeded to distinguish truth from untruth because an infinitely good and just God must necessarily want what is good and just for his creatures. To this end, 'God gave them Reason to distinguish Good from Evil, useful from useless Things; Or, in other Words has made them moral Agents capable of discerning the Relations they stand in to God and one another'; and those relations are ones which of necessity 'must at all Times, and in all Places alike be immutable'. The dictates of 'external Revelation' did not, to Tindal's mind, meet that test.[39] Finally, if liberty of inquiry and the guiding hand of reason did not together vanquish persecutory clergy and extirpate the 'Maxims' they preached which ruined religion, ridicule was available for 'a Man ... out of Charity to his Neighbour, [to] expose the Folly of his Opinion by ridiculing it as it deserves'.[40] Far from being a solvent of true religion, ridicule was, to Tindal's mind, a tool for defending it.

Tindal merely fleshed out this argument in *Christianity as Old as the Creation*, a work he published anonymously and one which, for all the contemporary furore it stirred up, was nonetheless a jumbled, bloated mess. Published in April 1730, its argument was straightforward. 'I desire no more than to be allowed, That there's a Religion of Nature and Reason written in the Hearts of every one of us from the first Creation; by which all Mankind must judge of the Truth of any instituted Religion whatever', Tindal synopsized his own argument, 'and if it varies from the Religion of Nature and Reason in any one Particular, nay, in the minutest Circumstance, That alone is an Argument, which makes all Things else that can be said for its Support totally ineffectual'.[41] Tindal concluded that 'traditionary religions' like Christianity are false where they do not accord perfectly with natural religion and that the Christian priest had, since the Council of Nicea, taken on the role of 'a sovereign Interpreter of Laws' and had taught the people 'to renounce both Natural and Revealed Religion; and become Priest worshippers, and to have a divine Faith in their Dictates'. By implication, all priests (either popish or

Protestant) were power-hungry frauds. In consequence, Tindal insisted that priests were wholly unnecessary because 'True Religion, can't but be plain, simple and natural' since it is 'designed for all Mankind, adapted to every Capacity, and suited to every Condition and Circumstance of Life'.[42] This was not an argument bound to win widespread clerical support.

Polemical divines of all stripes and ranks – 'too many even to name', Tindal boasted – responded to *Christianity as Old as the Creation*, with more than six dozen works appearing in print.[43] In the face of this onslaught, Tindal pledged that '[r]ather than quit the Field, thoough attacked by a Host of Adversaries, he resolves to die, Soldier-like, *La Plume à la Main*'.[44] He never completed his riposte before dying in 1733, but in the prospectus for it he singled out John Jackson, James Foster and John Conybeare ('the First a Low Church-man, the Other a Dissenter, and the Third a High Church-man') as formidable foes.[45] Jackson, Waterland's old Christological opponent, had differentiated Samuel Clarke's brand of natural religion from Tindal's. Tindal had argued for natural religion's complete sufficiency and had aspersed Clarke's defence of revelation in the final, lengthiest, chapter of *Christianity as Old as the Creation*. Jackson animadverted Tindal's evidence and reasserted Clarke's positions that the Fall made revelation necessary; that God had intended the Mosaic law to draw man away from 'idolatry' and 'impiety'; and that God's revealed truth was entirely consonant with natural religion.[46] From a different flank, John Conybeare (1692–1755), lobbed his *Defence of Revealed Religion* (1732), an orthodox, Edmund Gibson-orchestrated book which assailed Tindal. Its structure roughly followed Tindal's *Christianity as Old as the Creation*, tackling in sequence what Conybeare took to be Tindal's eight central propositions. Like Jackson, Conybeare defended the necessity of revelation, though he correlated natural and revealed religion less closely than had Jackson. The crux of Conybeare's argument was that 'if human Reason is not absolutely perfect, neither can that Religion be so, which reaches no farther than human Reason can carry us'.[47] Since, Conybeare argued, human history amply testified to reason's imperfections, God had necessarily to reveal himself to humans.

Daniel Waterland would have disagreed with little of John Conybeare's argument, especially Conybeare's qualms about human reason.[48] Where some at the time sullied revealed religion as an accreted perversion of the originally pure religion of nature, Waterland prioritized revelation, arguing 'that natural Religion never did subsist without Revealed. I believe it to be true universally.'[49] The historical evidence he offered for this assertion was the ubiquity of the idea of a future state of rewards and punishments, something which neither he nor Tindal believed natural religion taught. One ascertained the dictates of natural religion purely by reason, Tindal argued; but in response to those *sola ratio* claims, Waterland retorted, 'Has not Reason been abused as well as Religion? By Fools ... madmen, Deists, Atheists?'[50]

'If Scripture must be charged and impeached as often as Men may reason ill from it, then may also the first Principles of Natural Religion ... be in like manner impeached, because foolish or partial Men may wrest and pervert it to ill Purposes', Waterland reckoned. 'If there be any thing in the Argument, it points directly against the Use of Reason; as Reason is liable to Abuse, and human Faculties are imperfect, or depraved.'[51] Yet Waterland did not wholly reject reason's efficacy, arguing rather that reason naturally complemented revelation. The 'Light of Reason', properly employed, taught man 'Modesty' when thinking about 'the Depths of the divine Counsels and Government': reason might point the way towards belief in God, but only revelation could flesh out God's nature and purposes. Moreover, reason confirmed many, though not all, of revelation's truths. On this account, Waterland held that 'Natural Religion, justly so called, is bound up in Revealed, is supported, cherished, and kept alive by it; cannot so much as subsist in any Vigour without it'.[52] His opposition to Tindal's *sola ratio* arguments notwithstanding, Waterland left it to John Conybeare to rebut them.

Waterland's own contribution to the anti-Tindal orthodox counter-offensive took a different line and adopted a distinctive format, one which itself pointed up what especially worried Waterland about *Christianity as Old as the Creation*. Waterland devoted both energy and zeal to writing *Scripture Vindicated*. 'I am in the offensive way with those men, and I mean to continue it', he admitted to Edmund Gibson right after he had committed *Scripture Vindicated*'s second instalment to press in late 1730. 'There is no end of being upon the defensive only, and letting them pelt us: They shall be pelted in their turns, that we may see how they can stand the Infamy.' Yet, Waterland conceded, the eighteenth-century orthodox had at their disposal fewer weapons than past generations had possessed, for Tindal and his allies 'are in no fear now of legal correction'. Without state coercion, Waterland had to employ 'another kind of correction', one which would expose Tindal and the like-minded 'to the popular odium and contempt'.[53]

Waterland's marginal notes in his personal copy of *Christianity as Old as the Creation* cast stark light on his animus. It was not simply Tindal's argument which bothered Waterland but also what he took to be Tindal's motives in making that argument. Just as the heterodox believed that the orthodox were guilty of imposture, so too did the orthodox believe that the heterodox were liars and cheats who tricked people into unbelief.[54] 'There is more of impious Fraud in infidels, than pious Fraud in Christians, Protestants especially, who are not chargeable with anything of that kind', Waterland scribbled in the margins next to Tindal's insinuation that the Church of England's clergy were like 'Persecuting Papists' who deceived the laity. 'It is impious Fraud in this writer', Waterland continued, '1. To pretend a zeal for morality, when he is slyly undermining it. 2. To pretend a zeal against superstition only, when his design is against all Revelation'.[55] Elsewhere he reckoned that '[w]here there is religion and piety, there will be some religious, or pious Fraud': nonetheless, a world without religion would be even worse, for 'where there is no Religion, there will be more impious Fraud of all kinds'.[56]

Embedded in Waterland's criticisms of Tindal's imposture were two related complaints. Firstly, Tindal and his allies were 'infidels' bent upon destroying religion. Tindal may have pretended reverence for God, yet, Waterland argued, he simultaneously equated religion with superstition and pointed out what he held to be religion's historical abuses: in so doing, Tindal merely aped the ancient Epicurean schemes to destroy religion.[57] Where, for instance, Tindal ridiculed the popish sacrament of extreme unction, with its use of oil to anoint the sick, Waterland countered that 'the Infidels have built a much worse practice upon that: which is to blaspheme God, and throw off all Religion, because some have not made so good a use of Religion as they might have done'.[58] Secondly, Waterland charged that Tindal and his allies aimed to set themselves up as 'Infidel, pagan Priests', who would lead the laity astray. 'Infidel Priests, God be thanked, never yet have been tried', Waterland bemoaned. 'But five such men as a writer, if attended to, would do more mischief in the world, than 500 of the worst Christian priests. Bad Christian priests may corrupt Religion: but these Priests of Belial would destroy all Religion, and all Morality.'[59] This turned Tindal's anticlerical arguments on their head, countering that it was Tindal and his allies who really sought to set up themselves as a persecutory caste.[60]

This putative infidel priest-caste threatened the nation's moral order. It is telling that Waterland opened up *Scripture Vindicated* with a discussion of Tindal's moral aims and their likely consequences if achieved. For what had led Tindal into error, Waterland proposed, had been not a failure of logic but a wilful surrender to disordered desires. 'Lust and Malice are very strong and impetuous Passions', Waterland insisted, 'and where they take any deep Root, will of course incline Men to Principles of Infidelity'.[61] Infidels were infidels because they had freely succumbed to those baser passions. As a result, '[t]hey love darkness rather than light, because their Affections are corrupt, because their deeds are evil'.[62] They aimed, moreover, to drag down the rest of the nation, chiefly by convincing people that there would be no future state of rewards and punishments. For most in eighteenth-century England, belief in an afterlife in which virtue would be rewarded and unrepentant vice punished was a linchpin of societal order. It was certainly an orthodox commonplace that one who did not believe in Heaven and Hell had no incentives in the here and now to be virtuous. Waterland insisted that Tindal's scheme was 'but the old Epicurean Game plaid over again, with some slight refinements'. For like the ancient Epicureans, Tindal and his allies 'aimed to remove the fear of future Penalties, and, particularly, of the Eternity of them'.[63] Absent the moral deterrence which a future state of rewards and punishments offered, anarchy loomed.[64] This was one reason why Tindal frightened Waterland more than Clarke: despite Clarke's own heretical acceptance of mortalism, at least he believed that there was a future state of rewards and punishments.[65] For Waterland, proving both the necessity and historical reality of revealed religion, then, was no purely academic exercise: it was a project both about the here (societal order) and the hereafter (salvation).

Waterland defended revealed religion in *Scripture Vindicated.* Rather than follow *Christianity as Old as the Creation*'s structure, Waterland structured *Scripture Vindicated* like the Bible, starting with the verses Tindal had addressed in Genesis and proceeding book by book through the Old Testament.[66] Since the early Church, it had been a commonplace that the Book of Nature contained essential truths about God, and by the 1730s, there was a well-developed tradition of English natural theology.[67] But what did the Book of Nature have to do with the Book of Scripture? The Thirty-Nine Articles were unambiguous that 'Holy Scripture containeth all things necessary to salvation: so that whatsoever is not read therein, nor may be proved thereby, is not to be required of any man, that it should be believed as an article of the Faith, or be thought necessary to salvation'.[68] Daniel Waterland organized *Scripture Vindicated* in such a way both visually to demonstrate the Bible's reliability as a historical source of revealed truth and substantively to unfold a narrative of human history different from the one offered in *Christianity as Old as the Creation.* In the process, he tried to show not just the relevance of the Book of Scripture to the Book of Nature, but the subsummation of the Book of Nature within the Book of Scripture.

In a general preface to *Scripture Vindicated*'s 1734 third edition, Waterland spelled out his hermeneutical method. By the time he sat down to draft it, he had already been aspersed from at least three different directions, so that he wrote the preface with his polemical opponents firmly in mind. Firstly, there were those Protestants who had objected to his inclusion of non-literalist interpretations in *Scripture Vindicated.* Protestant biblical exegesis – with its commitment to a literalist hermeneutics – had always been a fraught matter because the letter of the text at times strained credulity. Developments in biblical scholarship during the seventeenth century, especially the increasing sophistication of antiquarian scholarship, made that task neither easier nor less urgent.[69] Indeed, a signal feature of eighteenth-century freethinking was its employment of biblical criticism and antiquarian scholarship to chip away at the Bible's integrity as a reliable historical source. Secondly, then, Waterland anatomized his biblical hermeneutics with freethinkers like Tindal and his allies in mind. Finally, allied to the freethinkers (at least in the minds of Waterland and his orthodox allies) were Protestants like Conyers Middleton, who had objected to what they reckoned was Waterland's strict literalism. When Waterland wrote his general preface in 1734, then, he was doing so for at least three different audiences, ones which had sometimes contradictory complaints about *Scripture Vindicated.*

Waterland's general preface explained how to interpret the Bible for readers who 'often confounded' the various interpretative modes.[70] In that explication, he premised that the Bible has one meaning, rendered in various ways. Some had pilloried what they took to be his strict literalism. Waterland clarified that, while the Bible was true, it was not always literally so. Where critics like Conyers Middleton had argued that allegorical interpretations of the Bible were necessary, Waterland concurred. Waterland's hermeneutical method, he freely acknowledged, owed much to the Lutheran biblical scholar Salomon Glassius's *Philologia Sacra* (1623). Waterland contended that there were three different ways to interpret the Bible: literally, figuratively and mystically. The literal interpretation was that which 'the Words properly and grammatically bear, or require, without any Trope, Metaphor or Figure, and abstracting from any mystic Meaning': some literal meanings concerned history, while others concerned doctrine.[71] If the literal interpretation was relatively straightforward, the figurative and mystical ones, by contrast, needed more explication. Waterland defined the figurative interpretation as one which required interpreting text 'not by what the Words would in themselves most strictly and properly import, but what they really intend under a Figure'.[72] So, for instance, when Isaiah 11:6 prophesied that 'The wolf shall dwell with the lamb', the text's literal meaning would, as Waterland acknowledged, 'be absurd': in such cases, the meaning was clearly figurative. Yet Waterland bristled at the suggestion that countenancing a figurative meaning meant likewise countenancing – as he claimed 'Romanists' did – different meanings of the same words. Rather, Waterland contended that 'the text has but one true sense', which was to say that it has only one true meaning.[73] Even more challenging for some than a figurative reading of the Bible was a 'Mystical' one, which Waterland defined as the interpretation required 'when the Words of Scripture, over and above their literal and immediate Meaning, have also a more remote Signification, a sublime or spiritual Sense'.[74] So, for instance, when Jonah 1:17 recounts that 'Jonah was in the belly of the fish three days and three nights', it was simultaneously a 'real Fact' *and* a signification that Christ would himself spend three days and nights in the belly of the Earth.

For Waterland, these careful hermeneutical distinctions and the interpretations which flowed from them were evident. But he recognized that others found biblical interpretation difficult. '[N]o one thing requires more Thought or Judgment, than to be able to discern in particular Passages which of these kinds of Interpretation ought to take place', he acknowledged.[75] Yet it was Waterland's application of his own interpretative method to the Bible in *Scripture Vindicated* which so roiled up many polemicists during the early 1730s. Tindal surprised no one when he rejected Waterland's method and his conclusions. But Conyers Middleton's anti-Waterland work most clarified some of the intra-Protestant divisions regarding the Bible. In particular, Middleton and other not-orthodox Protestant readers objected to Waterland's insistence that certain parts of the Old Testament – the Fall, for instance – were not allegorically true, but were historical facts.[76]

In the first edition of *Scripture Vindicated*, Waterland had accepted the account of The Fall in Genesis 2–3 as a matter of historical fact. Tindal had complained in *Christianity as Old as the Creation* that it would have been impossible for the serpent to have spoken to Eve, firstly, because language would not then have existed and, secondly, because serpents cannot speak. Waterland retorted that God had created language, after which he named some things, while leaving it to Adam – using 'that Faculty of Reason, and of speech, which God had endowed him with' – to name others: 'thus Language began'.[77] Eve picked up language from Adam, while the Devil had both sufficient time and ability to learn it. Once possessed of language, the Devil tempted Eve, working through a serpent. Tindal had jibed that 'Christians are now ashamed of the literal Interpretation of this Story'; Waterland was not the least embarrassed. For him, the testimonies of Moses and St Paul were sufficient proofs of the matter, ones which reason only confirmed. 'That Serpent, as we have abundant Reason to assert, was the Devil possessing and actuating a real Serpent', he insisted. 'A wicked Spirit was the inward Agent, and a Serpent the outward Organ ... There was a real Serpent actuated, and there was also Satan actuating.'[78] In response to Tindal's objection that a serpent would have been unable to speak with a human voice, Waterland brushed it aside as but 'the mean Objection of the Apostate Julian [which] has already been obviated' by others.[79] Once again, Waterland cast Tindal as a renovator of error.

As Waterland explained in his 1734 general preface, Tindal's assaults on the literal interpretation of the Bible were little more than the rehashed arguments of earlier heretics and freethinkers. In so far as the Fall was concerned, for instance, Tindal wrote in the tradition of literalist-deniers like Thomas Burnet (1635–1715) and Charles Blount (1654–93), who had argued – disingenuously, Waterland thought – for an allegorical understanding. Their interpretation was not itself actually allegorical, Waterland continued, but was instead 'parabolical or fabulous, because it excludes the literal and historical Meaning, resolving the whole into ingenious Device or Fiction'. While he granted that there were indeed parables and other 'prophetic Schemes' in Scripture, 'the Account of the Fall of Man is certainly true History, and ought not to be resolved into any such prophetic Scheme, or well-devised Parable; much less into Egyptian Fable or Hieroglyphic, as others more profanely have insinuated'.[80] By way of explanation, he argued that if a historical account 'so circumstanced as that is' is turned into a mere fable or parable, 'no History whatsoever can stand secure, but a wide Door will be opened to all the Rovings of sportive Wit, or wanton Fancy'. More importantly, though, treating the Fall as an allegory 'would undermine the Doctrine of our Redemption as laid down in the New Testament'.[81] At stake were the historical proofs of revealed religion and, concomitantly, the path to – or perhaps even the necessity of – salvation.

Also at stake was how to understand God's nature. Presuming that God existed, was he a hands-off deity who gave humans reason to understand the world and to determine his moral obligations? Or, was he a deity with no limits on his scope of action nor with any inherent need for his actions to be scrutable by human reason? Was God generally or particularly providential? Did he set up the world only to step back and watch human history unfold? Or, did he intervene regularly in human affairs? Was the Bible a historical record of that active intervention in human affairs from the Creation until the end of the century after Christ's birth? If God was providential, to what temporal and eternal ends? Matthew Tindal believed that, if there were answers to these questions, reason would illuminate them; Daniel Waterland, by contrast, countered that both God's being and reasons were ultimately incomprehensible to human beings.

Other polemical divines at the time – Joseph Butler, George Berkeley and William Law, most notably – joined Waterland's assault on deism and deists. By any fair estimation, they won the contemporary debate; or, as Mark Pattison memorably put it, by the 1750s 'the Deists had ceased to be'.[82] But why did the anti-deists win? Part of the answer is that the deism was primarily destructive, that deists were more intent on puncturing holes in orthodoxy's logic than in building up something that could itself one day be a new orthodoxy. Or perhaps, to put it more pointedly, Tindal and the deists lost because theirs was a posture rather than an agenda, a sensibility rather than coherent intellectual programme, one which could not deliver what it promised – the unquestionable truth. Deists vowed to solve the problem of the truth-claim cell division set in motion by the Reformation. But they succeeded only in producing yet more truth-claims, ones not self-evidently true to anyone but deists themselves. In part, deists lost the field because they had lost the argument.

Deists also lost because they were outmanned and outgunned.[83] Matthew Tindal would surely have been among the most socially distinguished of the deists. But even he, who had the lifetime security of an All Souls fellowship, published *Christianity as Old as the Creation* anonymously. Neither did he affix his name to any of his earlier incendiary works but one. Even he thought there was nothing to be gained and potentially much to be lost by formally acknowledging his authorship. As much as someone like Waterland might have wrung his hands over deism's threat to orthodoxy, it was a threat from outside of the Church establishment that was seen off during Waterland's lifetime.

But what about those who criticized orthodoxy from *within* the Church establishment? There the ability to punish or coerce which came with orthodoxy's political clout and social cache was sometimes less evident and hence the intra-Church polemical fights between the orthodox and their enemies were even more bilious. Few episodes better illustrate this than the contemporary furore which attended the publication of Benjamin Hoadly's *Plain Account of the nature and end of the sacrament of the Lord's Supper* (1735), a work some contemporaries reckoned had not been written by a 'true Christian'.[84]

NOTES

1 B. Young, 'Matthew Tindal (1657–1733)', *ODNB*.

2 [E. Curll], *Memoirs of... Matthew Tindal* (1733: T72148), p. 1.

3 *Scripture Vindicated* appeared in three instalments across three years, which allowed Waterland to gauge and address critical responses to one instalment in the subsequent one. Like Tindal's *Christianity as Old as the Creation, Scripture Vindicated* appeared anonymously, though everyone seems to have known that Waterland wrote it, just as everyone seems to have known that Tindal wrote *Christianity as Old as the Creation*.

4 Cf. R. Holtby, *Daniel Waterland* (Carlisle, 1966), pp. 73–104.

5 [E. Smith], *Cure of deism* (1736: T098223); J. Leland, *Answer* (1733: T136971); J. Leland, *View of the principal deistical writers* (1755: T140688). L. Stephen, *History of English Thought in the Eighteenth Century* (1902), I, 134–63, argued that Tindal's *Christianity as old as the Creation* brought 'out with great distinctness the most essential position of the deists'. For treatments of Tindal's 'deism', J. Wigelsworth, *Deism in Enlightenment England* (Manchester, 2009); W. Hudson, *The English Deists* (2009), pp. 106–11; W. Hudson, *Enlightenment and Modernity: The English Deists and Reform* (2009), pp. 34–46; D. Lucci, *Scripture and Deism: The Biblical Criticism of the Eighteenth-Century British Deists* (Bern, 2008), pp. 169–87. P. Gay, *Deism* (Princeton, 1968) ranks John Toland, Anthony Collins, Thomas Woolston and Matthew Tindal as the major English deist writers. Cf. A. Barber, '"The Voice of the People, no Voice of God": A Political, Religious and Social History of the Transmission of Ideas in England, 1690–1715' (Ph.D. thesis, University of London, 2010); D. Levitin, 'Matthew Tindal's *Rights of the Christian Church* (1706) and the Church–State Relationship', *HJ* 55 (2012), pp. 717–40.

6 Leland, *View*, I, p. v. See also Leland, *Answer*, I, p. 347.

7 E. Chambers, *Cyclopedia* (1728: T114002), I, pp. 179–80.

8 W. Hudson, 'Atheism and Deism Demythologized', in W. Hudson, D. Lucci and J. Wigelsworth(eds), *Atheism and Deism Revalued: Religious Identities in Britain, 1650–1800* (Aldershot, 2014), pp. 13–24; Hudson, *English Deists*, pp. 1–40; and Hudson, *Enlightenment and Modernity*, pp. 1–23, argue for 'multiple deisms' rather than for a unitary deistical doctrinal position. Hudson posits, furthermore, that we should conceive of English deists as 'constellational writers' who adopted 'multiple personae'. Hudson nevertheless treats *deism* as a positive stance with stable characteristics. Wigelsworth, *Deism*; Lucci, *Scripture and Deism*; B. Garrish, 'Natural and Revealed Religion', in K. Haakonssen (ed.), *Cambridge History of Eighteenth-Century Philosophy* (Cambridge, 2006), II, pp. 641–65; M. Stewart, 'Revealed Religion', in ibid., pp. 688–95; and J. Israel, *Radical Enlightenment: Philosophy and the Making of Modernity, 1650–1750* (Oxford, 2001), pp. 599–627, express greater certainty about deism's doctrinal coherence. For older treatments, see R. Stromberg, *Religious Liberalism in Eighteenth-Century England* (Oxford, 1954), pp. 52–87; N. Torrey, *Voltaire and the English Deists* (New Haven, 1930); Stephen, *History*, I, pp. 74–277.

9 J. Champion, 'Deism', in R. Popkin (ed.), *Columbia History of Western Philosophy* (New York, 1999), pp. 437–45.
10 S. Barnett, *The Enlightenment and Religion: The Myths of Modernity* (Manchester, 2002), pp. 11–44; I. Rivers, *Reason, Grace and Sentiment: A Study of the Language of Religion and Ethics in England, 1660–1780* (Cambridge, 2000), II, pp. 7–84; J. Clark, *English Society, 1660–1832: Religion, Ideology and Politics during the Ancien Régime* (Cambridge, 2000), pp. 324–35; R. Popkin, 'The Deist Challenge', in O. Grell, J. Israel and N. Tyacke (eds), *From Persecution to Toleration: The Glorious Revolution in England* (Oxford, 1991), pp. 195–215; J. Sullivan, *John Toland and the Deist Controversy* (Cambridge, MA, 1982), pp. 205–34.
11 Clarke, *Discourse concerning ... natural religion* (1706: T116093).
12 Ibid., p. 4.
13 Ibid., pp. 11–12.
14 Ibid., p. 13.
15 Ibid., p. 18.
16 Ibid., pp. 19–20. Cf. J. Force, 'Samuel Clarke's Four Categories of Deism, Isaac Newton and the Bible', in R. Popkin (ed.), *Scepticism in the History of Philosophy* (Dordrecht, 1996), pp. 53–74. For Newton's 'God of Dominion', see S. Snobelen, '"God of Gods and Lord of Lords": The Theology of Isaac Newton's General Scholium to the *Principia*', *Osiris* 16 (2001), pp. 169–208.
17 Clarke, *Discourse concerning ... natural religion* pp. 28–30. Many contemporaries held *licentiousness* to be a signal feature of *deism*.
18 Ibid., p. 37.
19 Unless otherwise noted, quotations in this paragraph are drawn from Peirce Dod to unknown, 9 September 1733 (BL, Egerton 2618, fols 229, 230). Dod (1683–1754) was an All Souls fellow and a London physician.
20 Cf. D. Berman and S. Lalor, 'The Suppression of *Christianity as Old as the Creation, Vol. II*', *Notes & Queries* 31 (1984), pp. 3–6.
21 Champion, 'Deism', p. 441.
22 Many at the time might have said that he also bought a debauchee's taste to polemical divinity: [A. Evans], *The Apparition* (1710: T058886); [T. Newcomb], *Blasphemy as old as the creation* (1730: T053397); *Daily Post* (20 August 1733), p. 1; Anonymous, *Religious, rational and moral conduct of Matthew Tindal* (1735: T100270); *Biographia Britannica* (1766), VI, part 1, p. 3960. Cf. [Curll], *Memoirs*, pp. 8–10.
23 Anonymous, *Religious, rational and moral conduct*, p. 16.
24 N. Sykes, *Edmund Gibson* (Oxford, 1926), p. 249; N. Sykes, *William Wake, Archbishop of Canterbury, 1657–1737* (Cambridge, 1957), II, p. 171.
25 See [Thomas Rogers] to Gibson, September 1724 (TNA, SP 35/52 fol. 95) for the emphasis Gibson placed on intellectual distinction for preferment; clerics needed not just to be loyal, but they needed to be able to defend the faith.
26 Gibson, *Bishop of London's pastoral letter* (1728: T087814), p. 9.
27 Ibid., pp. 10–11.
28 Ibid., pp. 8, 27.
29 Ibid., p. 27.
30 [M. Tindal], *Address to the inhabitants ... of London and Westminster* (1728: T020445).

31 R. Popkin and M. Goldie, 'Scepticism, Priestcraft and Toleration', in M. Goldie and R. Wokler (eds), *Cambridge History of Eighteenth-Century Political Thought* (Cambridge, 2006), esp. pp. 79–92; J. Champion, *The Pillars of Priestcraft Shaken: The Church of England and Its Enemies, 1660–1730* (Cambridge, 1992).
32 [Tindal], *Address*, pp. 37–8.
33 Ibid., pp. 23, 26–7.
34 Ibid., pp. 16–17.
35 Ibid., p. 27.
36 Ibid., p. 3. See also A. Barber, '"Why don't those lazy priests answer the book?" Matthew Tindal, Censorship, Freedom of the Press and Religious Debate in Early Eighteenth-Century England', *History* 99 (2014), pp. 1–28.
37 P. Miller, '"Freethinking" and "Freedom of Thought" in Eighteenth-Century Britain', *HJ* 36 (1993), pp. 599–617; J. Dunn, 'The Claim to Freedom of Conscience: Freedom of Speech, Freedom of Thought, Freedom of Worship?', in O. Grell, J. Israel and N. Tyacke (eds), *From Persecution to Toleration: The Glorious Revolution in England* (Oxford, 1991), pp. 171–95.
38 [Tindal], *Address*, p. 70.
39 Ibid., pp. 53–4.
40 Ibid., p. 28.
41 [M. Tindal], *Christianity as old as the creation* (1730: T101189), pp. 50–1.
42 Ibid., pp. 216, 217.
43 S. Lalor, *Matthew Tindal, Freethinker* (2006), pp. 111–40.
44 [M. Tindal], *Introduction* (1732: T103576), p. i.
45 Ibid., p. iv. There were unfounded rumours at the time that Edmund Gibson had destroyed the second volume of *Christianity as Old as the Creation*: Young, 'Matthew Tindal'.
46 [J. Jackson], *Remarks* (1731: T005269). Jackson also insisted that the Bible, properly read, proved the subordination of the Son to the Father in the Trinity: ibid., p. 54.
47 J. Conybeare, *Defence of reveal'd religion* (1732: N000497), dedication, p. 73.
48 Waterland was eager for Conybeare's work to appear and prodded Conybeare to finish up his response to *Christianity as Old as the Creation* more quickly. Waterland to Gibson, 22, 29 December 1730, 21 January 1731 (LPL, 1741, fols 76–80).
49 Waterland to Gibson, 22 November 1730 (LPL, 1741, fol. 81).
50 Waterland's annotations to Tindal's *Christianity as Old as the Creation*, n.d. (Bodleian, 4^0 Rawlinson 92, p. 99).
51 [D. Waterland], *Scripture vindicated ... Part I* (1730: T070867), pp. 84–5.
52 Ibid., p. 18.
53 Waterland to Gibson, 22 November 1730 (LPL, 1741, fol. 80).
54 D. Berman, 'Deism, Immorality and the Art of Theological Lying', in L. Lemay (ed.), *Deism, Masonry and the Enlightenment* (Toronto, 1987), pp. 61–78, argues that Tindal and other prominent deists were indeed atheists who lied openly to hide their true beliefs. Cf. Wigelsworth, *Deism*, which accepts Tindal's theism at face value.
55 Waterland's annotations to *Christianity as Old as the Creation*, n.d. (Bodleian, 4° Rawlinson 92, p. 157).

56 Ibid., p. 162.
57 [Waterland], *Scripture vindicated ... Part II*, pp. 131–4.
58 Waterland's annotations to *Christianity as Old as the Creation*, n.d. (p. 118).
59 Ibid., pp. 93, 108.
60 N. Aston, 'Anglican Responses to Anticlericalism in the "Long" Eighteenth Century, c. 1689–1800', in N. Aston and M. Cragoe (eds), *Anticlericalism in Britain, c. 1500–1914* (Stroud, 2000), pp. 115–37.
61 [Waterland], *Scripture vindicated ... Part I*, p. 7.
62 Ibid., p. 5.
63 [Waterland], *Scripture vindicated ... Part II*, p. 130.
64 Ibid., p. 134. Cf. P. Almond, *Heaven and Hell in Enlightenment England* (Cambridge, 1994); D. Walker, *The Decline of Hell: Seventeenth-Century Discussion of Eternal Torment* (Chicago, 1964). There is no sustained treatment of the doctrine of future rewards and punishments for eighteenth-century England, though see T. Ahnert, 'Religion and Morality', in J. Harris (ed.), *Oxford Handbook of British Philosophy in the Eighteenth Century* (Oxford, 2013), pp. 638–58; G. Sholtz, 'Anglicanism in the Age of Johnson: The Doctrine of Conditional Salvation', *ECS* 22 (1988/9), pp. 182–207; D. Greene, 'How "Degraded" was Eighteenth-Century Anglicanism?', *ECS* 24 (1990), pp. 93–108.
65 Wigelsworth, 'Samuel Clarke's Newtonian Soul'. See also B. Young '"The Soul-Sleeping System": Politics and Heresy in Eighteenth-Century England', *JEH* 45 (1994), pp. 64–81.
66 [Waterland], *Scripture vindicated ... Part I*, p. 9. Waterland never published a reply to Tindal regarding New Testament biblical texts, but see Portions of Daniel Waterland's notes for his book *Scripture Vindicated*, which deals with the New Testament, n.d. (Bodleian, Rawl.D.1264).
67 Mandelbrote, 'Early Modern Natural Theologies'.
68 *BCP*, p. 553 [Article VI].
69 S. Mandelbrote, 'Early Modern Biblical Interpretation and the Emergence of Science', *Science and Christian Belief* 23 (2011), pp. 99–113; S. Mandelbrote, 'Origen against Jerome in Early Modern Europe', in S. Bergjan and K. Pillman (eds), *Patristic Tradition and Intellectual Paradigms in the 17th Century* (Tübingen, 2010), pp. 105–13; S. Mandelbrote, 'Isaac Newton and Thomas Burnet: Biblical Criticism and the Crisis of Late Seventeenth-Century England', in R. Popkin and J. Force (eds), *The Books of Nature and Scripture* (Dordrecht, 1994), pp. 149–78; J. Champion, 'Père Richard Simon and English Biblical Criticism, 1680–1700', in J. Force and D. Katz (eds), *Everything Connects* (Leiden, 1999), pp. 39–61.
70 Waterland to Zachary Pearce, 12 July 1734 (WAM 64814); [Waterland], *Scripture vindicated ... Part I. Third edition*, p. i.
71 [Waterland], *Scripture vindicated ... Part I. Third edition*, pp. ii–iii.
72 Ibid., p. iii.
73 Ibid., p. iv.
74 Ibid., p. vi. There were four kinds of mystical interpretation: the parabolical, the symbolical, the typical and the allegorical.
75 Ibid., p. xxvi.
76 I. McFarland, 'The Fall and Sin', in J. Webster, K. Tanner and I Torrance (eds), *Oxford Handbook of Systematic Theology* (Oxford, 2007), pp. 140–59; P. Harrison,

The Fall of Man and the Foundations of Modern Science (Cambridge, 2007); P. Almond, *Adam and Eve in Seventeenth-Century Thought* (Cambridge, 1997), pp. 173–214.

77 [Waterland], *Scripture vindicated ... Part I*, pp. 10–11.

78 Ibid., pp. 12, 15.

79 Ibid., p. 14.

80 [Waterland], *Scripture vindicated ... Part I. Third edition*, p. xix.

81 Ibid., pp. xx, xxi.

82 W. Law, *Case of reason* (1731: T73537); G. Berkeley, *Alciphron* (1732: T86055); J.Butler, *Analogy of religion* (1736: T67971); Pattison, 'Tendencies', p. 49.

83 Stephen, *History*, I, pp. 86–7.

84 [D. Tovey], *Winchester converts* (1735: T052549), p. 24.

Chapter 5

The sacrament Socinianized: Benjamin Hoadly and the Eucharist

The Eucharist long exerted centripetal and centrifugal forces on Christianity, and the Church of England's formularies captured why that was the case. The Thirty-Nine Articles declared that the sacraments were 'ordained of Christ' and were 'not only badges or tokens of Christian men's profession, but rather ... certain sure witnesses, and effectual signs of grace, and God's good will towards us, by which he doth work invisibly in us, and doth not only quicken, but also strengthen and confirm our Faith in him'. The eighteenth-century Church of England, like all Protestant churches, recognized only two sacraments, 'Baptism and the Supper of our Lord'. It held that those two sacraments 'were not ordained of Christ to be gazed upon, or to be carried about, but that we should duly use them'; yet only those who 'worthily receive' the sacraments could expect to have 'a wholesome effect or operation: but they that receive them unworthily purchase to themselves damnation'. In so far as the Eucharist was concerned, the Church of England's articles of religion held that it was simultaneously 'a Sacrament of our Redemption by Christ's death' and 'a sign of the love that Christians ought to have among themselves one to another'. While denying outright the doctrine of transubstantiation, the Church's religious articles noted that 'the Bread which we break is a partaking of the Body of Christ; and likewise the Cup of Blessing is a partaking of the Blood of Christ'.[1] This formulation raised as many questions as it resolved. If the sacraments were signs of grace through which God works invisibly on us, are the sacraments themselves necessary for salvation? If so, what does it mean worthily to receive the Eucharist? Who is to judge if a communicant is a worthy recipient? Furthermore, since worthy reception of the Eucharist is, at the very least, closely related to salvation, could reception also be a litmus test for other things in society? If the elements (the bread and the wine) must be sanctified to make them sacramental, does that make the priestly sanctifiers a group with special powers or privileges? Moreover, what actually happens to the Eucharistic elements if they are not transubstantiated? How can one partake of Christ's body and blood if neither is actually there to be consumed? These were soteriological, philosophical and political questions which had almost always characterized debates about the Eucharist and which were at the heart of the Eucharistic debates in which Benjamin Hoadly and Daniel Waterland themselves engaged during the 1730s.[2]

This chapter reconstructs the Hoadly–Waterland Eucharistic debates.[3] It locates those debates within wider ones during the 1730s about whether or not to repeal the Test and Corporation Acts. It shows how those sacramental debates got refracted through the memory of the seventeenth century which had produced the Test and Corporation Acts. Finally, it demonstrates why Waterland thought that when responding to Hoadly he was but reiterating Thomas Cranmer's sacramental theology, which itself had reiterated the pure sacramental theology of the primitive Church. Both Waterland and Hoadly thought that theirs was a replay of older debates in a new, post-revolutionary setting.

For the orthodox like Waterland, Benjamin Hoadly (1676–1761) epitomized the enemy within, and they feared that more like him lurked amongst the clerical ranks.[4] Hoadly had been promoted to the episcopal bench in 1716, during the Stanhope–Sunderland ministry, which did not favour orthodoxy of the sort propounded by Waterland and Edmund Gibson. His political allegiances were reliably Whig; his theology, reliably heterodox. Since early in Anne's reign, he had been a Tory and high church scourge.[5] Yet Hoadly's theological heterodoxy did not block his ascent up the clerical ladder of preferment, thanks mostly to Queen Caroline's political support.[6] By the time he published his *Plain Account of the Nature and End of the Sacrament of the Lord's-Supper* in 1735, Hoadly had risen to the bishopric of Winchester, a post to which he had been named the previous year and in which he would remain until his death three decades later. His mere presence on the episcopal bench offended the orthodox.

Daniel Waterland ranked among Hoadly's more formidable orthodox opponents, and his Eucharistic debates with Hoadly during the 1730s marked the latter's return to polemical prominence after a decade of quietude. Hoadly's *Plain Account* offended many contemporaries because the eighteenth-century English especially valued the sacraments.[7] But its arguments also touched on sensitive political issues of the day: the *Plain Account*'s salience came from the ways it got refracted through the memory of the seventeenth-century English religio-political wars and in which it then got related to contemporary political concerns.

Hoadly was an anti-sacerdotalist churchman. The product of a seventeenth-century Puritan family, he formed his views on the proper function of the priesthood within the context of the previous century's religio-political 'troubles'. He had set out these views in his controversial sermon on *The Nature of the Kingdom, or Church, of Christ* (1717), the piece which sparked the Bangorian controversy. Taking John 18:36 as its starting point, that sermon at the royal court fleshed out the logic of his *Preservative against the Principles and Practices of Nonjurors* (1716), a work which itself had also drawn the ire not just of high churchmen but of many other less altitudinarian clergy besides.[8] The posthumous publication of George Hickes's *The Constitution of the Catholick Church* (1716) had spurred Hoadly to pen the *Preservative*, but the spectre of the failed Jacobite rebellion of 1715 also informed it. The nonjuror Hickes had argued that William of Orange had unlawfully usurped the English throne in 1689 and that his subsequent deprivation of the nonjuring bishops was therefore illegal. He also held that the Church stood wholly independent from the state. The 'incorporate Body of Christians', the Church was 'by its Constitution a Holy Royal or Regal Priesthood', firstly because Christ, its head, was 'a Sacerdotal Sovereign or Regal Priest' and, secondly, because 'this Sacerdotal Sovereign has committed the Government and administration of his Kingdom to Ministerial Priests'.[9] The real schismatics were the Church of England's clergy, not the nonjurors.

Hoadly countered Hickes by crafting alternative Christian and English histories. In 1688, 'the whole Nation of Protestants ... universally and equally, felt and saw themselves on the Brink of Destruction' because of James II's popish tyranny. Fearing the nation's ruin, 'the Chief Men amongst us (not the Greatest Churchmen excepted)' sought Dutch assistance, after which James abdicated his throne. The nonjurors subsequently refused to 'give the common Security of Faithfulness and Allegiance' to the lawful new government, which rightfully deprived them of their offices.[10] While Hoadly's was a mainstream reading of the Glorious Revolution's causes and outcomes, his understanding of the Church of England's position was not. For he denied that Christ had enjoined any particular ecclesiology or that there was any primitive theological doctrine distinctively preserved by the Church of England. He also denied wholly the apostolic succession of priests either of the Church of England or of the nonjuring Church. This meant that the priestly order had no salvific function: instead, God gave humans the power over their own 'Salvation, and Happiness'.[11] In Hoadly's view, the Church of England was not independent. It was, instead, a subordinate partner to the English state, something which both ecclesiastical and English history proved. This was justly so, since in any contest between the civil and religious powers, '[t]he Civil Power, properly so called, must quickly be swallowed up by the Other. It is natural to expect it, and true in Experience'.[12] Most of Hoadly's fellow clergy rejected the *Preservative*'s arguments. A committee of Convocation's Lower House charged him with drawing 'contempt on a regular succession of the ministry', while even Whig bishops fretted that Hoadly's work had done more damage to the Church of England than the nonjurors whom he retorted.[13]

Undeterred, Hoadly only deepened his commitment to his religio-political interpretation in the ensuing decades. It was on full display in his *Plain Account*, a work which spurred Waterland to compose *A Review of the Doctrine of the Eucharist* (1737). Waterland's *Review* formulated the Church of England's semi-official position on the Eucharist for the next two centuries.[14] Some later claimed that it 'had little of the aspect of a polemical work, although so large a portion of it may be applied as a corrective, or a preservative of error'.[15] The *Review*'s prose is indeed measured; the vantage, Olympian; the method, rigorously historical. Both its structure and its scholarly apparatus aimed to convey authority and to elicit assent. The work opened with a consideration of the names used for the Holy Communion before proceeding to consider in turn the biblical institution of the sacrament, its various purposes and how properly to prepare for it. It was a work of immense erudition. As Waterland's antagonist Conyers Middleton noted, Waterland aimed 'to give a genuine account of [the Eucharist] from Antiquity, without any particular reference to the late controversy'.[16] Put the *Review* in the context of its time, though, and it is evident that it was a concerted polemic, written to rebut Hoadly and those who shared his historical understanding; his mode of reasoning; and his heterodox conclusions. Waterland certainly thought it his responsibility to offer his own orthodox rejoinder to *The Plain Account*: 'I am afraid the labour of considering what concerns the Sacrament must at length fall upon me'.[17]

Benjamin Hoadly first took a sustained interest in the Eucharist during the 1730s, just after Samuel Clarke's death and within the context of contemporary debates over the Test and Corporation Acts. He drafted the *Plain Account* a few years before publishing it in June 1735, that is to say a few years before he was promoted to the see of Winchester.[18] The early 1730s witnessed fresh debates over the fate of the Test Act (1673) (which enjoined all crown officials to 'receive the sacrament of the Lord's Supper, according to the usage of the Church of England') and of the Corporation Act (1661) (which required all municipal officials annually to take 'the Sacrament of the Lords Supper according to the Rites of the Church of England'). The Eucharist was central to these acts, which aimed to bar Roman Catholics and Protestant Dissenters from holding public office.[19] Edmund Gibson led the orthodox opposition to repeal, insisting that successive post-revolutionary parliaments had purposefully maintained these legal prohibitions, the 1719 repeal of the Occasional Conformity Act notwithstanding.[20] For one thing, the Test and Corporation Acts buttressed the Church establishment: '[t]his Caution therefore of making one established Faith, seems to be universal, and founded upon the strongest Reasons; the mistaken or affected Zeal of Obstinacy, and Enthusiasm having produced such a Number of horrible, destructive Events, throughout all Christendom'. Without a legally established Church, hyper-pluralism would reign, with competing religious groups trying to convince people of their rightness, which itself would lead inevitably to civil unrest. 'This was the very Case of England, during the Fanatic Times', Gibson pled. 'And against all this, there seems to be no Defence, but that of supporting one established Form of Doctrine and Discipline, leaving the rest to a bare Liberty of Conscience; but without any Maintenance or Encouragement from the Public'[21] For orthodox churchmen like Gibson, sacramental tests ensured civil peace.

Hoadly rejected Gibson's analysis. Firstly, he noted that Britons always retained their right to petition Parliament and that Parliament always retained its right (as evidenced by the Occasional Conformity Act's repeal) to reconsider bad legislation. No parliamentary statute, not even the Toleration Act, was 'an eternal unalterable barrier'.[22] Secondly, Hoadly rejected Gibson's reading of recent English history. Where Gibson saw Protestant Dissent as a destabilizing force in seventeenth-century England, Hoadly blamed 'the most zealous Church-men possessing such Power and Interest, as to enable them to carry on politick Schemes of Oppression and Hardship on their Fellow Subjects'.[23] Finally, where Gibson saw the Test and Corporation Acts as barriers to a rising Dissenting tide which might destroy the established Church, Hoadly saw them as obstacles to liberty, ones which angered Dissenters and promoted tyranny. 'If pinching Men a little has not Effect enough, then cutting and lancing must be applied; supposing that this distant Danger to a Church ought to be warded off by secular Methods', he jibed. 'If a Toleration itself is to be treated of as a Matter of Favour, and a Thing which political Reasons only are to govern; the Inquisition and Rack are better at first, than last.' Lest his readers miss his point, Hoadly concluded, '[t]hus the Church of Rome proceeded from one Step to another, till they found the true and only effectual Way of keeping all things quiet, and secure from the Attempts of such as either liked another Way better than theirs, or would not in all things comply with what was settled for them by their Superiors'.[24] For a heterodox churchman like Hoadly, clerical severity during the seventeenth century had produced revolution, while tolerance had produced peace. Sacramental tests of the sort legally enshrined in the Test and Corporation Acts would produce civil unrest.

Just as the renewed push to repeal these Restoration-era acts ramped up, Samuel Clarke died in May 1729. His death and the posthumous publication of his *Exposition of the Church Catechism* prompted Hoadly to think afresh about the Test and Corporation Acts and about the Eucharist. Hoadly and Clarke's friendship dated to their Cambridge student days, and Hoadly's admiration for his friend did not dim with the passing years. Neither did he distance himself from Clarke's theological conclusions.[25] In a laudatory 1731 life of Clarke, Hoadly highlighted Clarke's aversion to Cartesianism, which even as a Cambridge student he had considered to have been 'no more than the Inventions of a very Ingenious and Luxuriant Fancy; and having no Foundation in the Reality of Things, nor any Correspondency to the Certainty of Facts'. Instead, Clarke had adopted Newtonian natural philosophy, which he took to be 'Real and Substantial'.[26] Clarke's primary interests, though, lay not in natural philosophy but in divinity, where 'his great Aim [was] to settle beyond all Contradiction what must be the support of True Religion'.[27] This meant providing *a priori* proofs of God's existence and *a posteriori* proofs of his nature; or, as Hoadly put it, '[t]he necessary Existence of One only God, and the Impossibility of the Existence of More Than One'.[28] This characterization, as Hoadly surely knew, did not clarify the matter, because most contemporaries thought Clarke's Newtonian God of Dominion was not the God of the Nicene or Athanasian Creeds. Hoadly pointedly refused to judge of the matter. He simply noted that Clarke's Christological conclusions never wavered and that Clarke's 'Method' in reaching those conclusions had been unquestionably 'Christian'. Hoadly's take on Clarke's Christology was significant because most rejoinders to the *Plain Account* charged that Hoadly was Christologically heterodox.

Samuel Clarke's Christology informed his sacramental theology. In an interleaved 1724 edition of the Book of Common Prayer, Clarke had emended the liturgy, including sections within the prayer book concerning the sacraments, in a way that exalted God the Father over God the Son. In the section on Communion, for instance, Clarke struck out the Nicene Creed and replaced a passage which praised 'the only begotten son Jesus Christ; O Lord God, Lamb of God, Son of the Father, that takest away the sins of the world' with one which emphasized the Father's dominion:

> We bless thee for sending thy only-begotten Son Jesus Christ our Lord, to be the True Lamb that taketh away the Sins of the world. We bless thee for exalting him to thy right hand in Heaven, there to intercede for us until his Second Coming. We bless thee for the Hope of eternal Life, and for all the Gifts and Graces of thy Holy Spirit, which thou hast given up in our Saviour Jesus Christ.[29]

Here and elsewhere in the prayer book, Clarke proposed language changes that derogated, however subtly, the Son's divinity.

Daniel Waterland would not have known about Clarke's revised Book of Common Prayer; but he was aware of Clarke's *Exposition of the Church Catechism* (1729), which revealed the logic behind his private prayer book emendations. Originally lectures at St James's, Westminster, the *Exposition* returned to Christology, the subject Clarke had sworn off publicly discussing after his 1714 run-in with Convocation. Clarke's lectures on the catechism, like others in the genre, explicated the meaning of the prescribed catechetical questions and answers, the Apostles' Creed, the Ten Commandments, the Lord's Prayer and the sacraments. Clarke closely attended to Christ's nature when considering the Apostles' Creed, not surprisingly emphasizing the Son's subordination to the Father. Equally unsurprisingly, when explicating the Lord's Supper, he de-emphasized Christ's atonement for human sin. In the Lord's Supper, 'we declare our Continuance' as Christians and 'live in constant Communion both with Christ the Head, and with all the Members of his Spiritual Body'. Through it, we also 'perpetually repeat and ratify, confirm and renew' our vows of obedience to God's commands and 'lay afresh upon ourselves the most solemn Obligations, to indeavour constantly with God's assistance to perform it'.[30] As against those who saw some connection between worthy reception of the Lord's Supper and salvation, Clarke countered that '[t]here is no Superstition whatsoever more mischievous and destructive of True Religion; than men's imagining, that, in a Sacrament, the inward and spiritual Benefit is necessarily and in course connected with the outward Performance'.[31] To argue otherwise, Clarke insisted, was to commit popish error.

Daniel Waterland's sacramental theology likewise flowed from his conception of God's nature. Waterland identified two salient problems with Clarke's *Exposition*: 'the subject of positive and moral duties and the true use and value of the Sacraments'.[32] He took up the second subject in the first of his three anonymous replies to the *Exposition*.[33] A liturgy, Waterland argued, 'should be so contrived, as effectually to point out the Object of Worship'.[34] Clarke, by contrast, aimed 'to leave out the real Divinity of the Son', something which, he claimed, went even farther than the Arians or Socinians had proposed.[35] Indeed, Clarke intimated that Nicene Christianity itself involved the worship of 'Idol Gods' and that clergy who professed the Nicene Creed were sacerdotalist 'Idol-Mediators'.[36] Waterland retorted that the Christian liturgy's proper end was worship of the God who had become incarnate and who had died on the Cross to atone for sin. That made the Eucharist the liturgy's single most important part. For where Clarke understood the Eucharist as a mere memorial, Waterland reckoned that Christ's death was 'a Method of Expiation' for sin and that 'the Scriptures seem to lay a particular Stress and Emphasis upon the Propitiation made by the Blood of Christ, as if there were some intrinsic Merit, both real and great in it'.[37] This gave the Eucharist particular meaning, for '[t]he eating his Flesh, and drinking his Blood ... mean having a Part in that Atonement, being Partakers of the Benefit of Christ's Death and Satisfaction. By this and this only we live; without it we die.'[38] Being a member of the true Church of Christ and receiving the Eucharist worthily opened up one to salvation.

Clarke would have disagreed with Waterland's assessment of the Eucharist's nature and importance not just because he conceived of the path to salvation differently but also because he thought the sacraments were 'positive' rather than 'moral' duties. In the *Exposition*, Clarke had distinguished between 'positive Institutions' and 'Moral Virtues': the former could never 'be of any Use or Benefit without' the moral virtues and could not 'be in any degree Equivalents for the Want of them'.[39] By this, Waterland understood Clarke to have meant that positive duties 'are always of slighter Obligation than moral' and that those institutions are themselves but 'instrumental only to moral Virtue, and is not moral Virtue'. Furthermore, Waterland understood Clarke to have meant that 'the two Christian Sacraments, are merely positive Institutions' and that 'Obedience to Christ's Law concerning them, or the Use of the Sacraments, is not moral Virtue'.[40] Thus, taking part in the sacraments was less important than moral virtue itself.

Waterland, however, distinguished fundamentally not between positive and moral duties but between 'natural' and 'supernatural' ones, with the natural ones being 'those discoverable by the bare Light of Nature' and the supernatural ones being 'those that are discovered by Revelation'. Furthermore, he identified two types of supernatural duties: 'constant'/'moral' ones, which 'are of eternal and immutable Obligation' and 'occasional'/'positive' ones, which 'are temporary, or changeable'. In Waterland's hierarchy of obligations, then, constant/moral duties held pride of place. Among those constant/moral duties were 'the Precepts concerning the two Christian Sacraments, which shall continue as long as the Christian Church, or as the World shall continue'.[41] God had instructed humans what to do; not to follow those divine instructions would be an act of gross disobedience, since natural and supernatural duties 'are alike obligatory, as enjoined by the same Authority, and inforced by the same Sanctions'.[42] For this reason Waterland insisted that '[a]ny habitual wilful Neglect or Disuse of the Holy Communion may be as bad or worse than neglecting to feed the Hungry, or clothe the Naked'.[43]

So what *had* God instructed regarding the Eucharist and how was that sacrament to be understood? Waterland stressed its sacrificial nature. The sacraments were the 'ordinary standing Means by which the salutary Influences of Christ's Passion are conveyed. They are the Channels of Remission and Pardon'.[44] Thus, when worthy communicants participate in the Eucharist, they 'spiritually eat Christ's Flesh, and drink Christ's Blood. They eat them and drink them in such a Sense as that can be done; that is to say, their Souls or Spirits receive ... all the spiritual Advantages and Comforts arising from the all-sufficient Atonement made by Christ upon the Cross'.[45] The Eucharist was no mere commemorative rite, but one through which eternal salvation was to be achieved, since 'the blood of Christ and his merits have a proper efficacy towards procuring the salvation of man [that] nothing else has'.[46] Given the Eucharist's crucial salvific role, the role of the priests who administered that sacrament was necessarily up for debate, especially during a period when anticlericalism waxed.

In his *Plain Account*, Hoadly hammered away at the sacerdotalism inherent in orthodox sacramental theology like Waterland's.[47] His work simultaneously amplified and simplified Samuel Clarke's arguments regarding the Eucharist. The New Testament, he explained at the *Plain Account*'s outset, was the only source regarding the Eucharist to be trusted because '[t]he Passages ... which relate to this Duty, and they alone, are the Original Accounts of the Nature and End of this Institution' and its authors had either been 'Witnesses to the Institution itself, or instructed by Those who were so; or, as afterwards receiving what They taught from Christ himself'.[48] The New Testament rightly claimed the mantle of the most primitive (hence, the purest) source regarding Christian truth. By contrast, the apostolic and patristic fathers had corrupted, even if inadvertently, the primitively pure truths conveyed in the New Testament. 'A very few Years make a great alteration in Men's Notions, and Language, about such Points of Religion', Hoadly insisted. 'And the distance of Many Years makes a still greater Alteration; whilst Men of Various Opinions, and Strong Imaginations, are continually going to comment and enlarge upon such Subjects.'

For Hoadly, the New Testament clearly treated the Eucharist as 'the Memorial of [Christ's] Body broken; and ... the Memorial of his Blood shed'.[49] The 'absurd' Roman Catholic doctrine of transubstantiation 'and other Dark and Unintelligible Notions' contravened scriptural teachings, but so too did the nonjuring and orthodox teaching that the Eucharist was some kind of sacrifice.[50] Instead, the Eucharist was, as Hoadly had earlier explained in a 1730 royal sermon, nothing more than 'a Remembrance of that Master who taught us the absolute Necessity of Morality, or Virtue, to our Happiness; and particularly, the Remembrance of his Death, which was the greatest example of the many Virtues to be practiced by us in this imperfect and afflicted State'. Christ instituted it not as a means to salvation but as a means to 'our Improvement in all Morality'.[51] In the *Plain Account*, Hoadly reiterated his memorialist interpretation. St Paul, for instance, never used the language of sacrifice when discussing the Eucharist, though he warned repeatedly against idolatry. Furthermore, the table at which Christ and his disciples took the Lord's Supper 'having never been declared or called an Altar; nor appointed to serve any One particular purpose of an Altar, ought to retain its One and only Original Name' and not be referred to as an altar at which a sacrifice is offered up to God.[52] Only Christ's death was a genuine sacrifice and it was, furthermore, a self-sufficient one: '[t]he only thing in the Christian Dispensation which answers to any of the Legal Sacrifices ... is the Death of Christ', so that 'the very cross upon which Christ died' is the only real Christian altar.[53] As such, the Eucharist had, on Hoadly's reading, no relation to the forgiveness of sins: the sacrament's benefits are moral, not soteriological. Hence it mattered not whether communicants received the Lord's Supper worthily or not, frequently or not.

Contemporary response to Hoadly's *Plain Account* was overwhelmingly hostile, with most sharing the bishop of Chichester's 'great contempt for his Lordship's writings'.[54] Some, like the future archbishop of Canterbury Thomas Herring, could 'see no reason for such a prodigious outcry upon "The Plain account" &c. I really think it a good book, as orthodox as archbishop Tillotson'.[55] Herring was among the very few, though, who somehow missed the provocation of the *Plain Account*'s argument. Even those who privately applauded Hoadly acknowledged that 'by throwing down the shrines and altars of the Church', he had courted censure.[56]

The print debate over the *Plain Account* drew in leading polemical divines and elicited dozens of pamphlets, books and newspaper articles. Those arrayed against Hoadly included an alliance of orthodox churchmen, nonjurors and Roman Catholics, including, most notably, Henry Stebbing, William Whiston, Charles Wheatly, William Law and Thomas Brett. In general, the anti-Hoadlyites rejected Hoadly's claims to primitive purity; denied his adherence to Reformation principles; and objected to the *Plain Account*'s memorialism, explaining the last away by Hoadly's putative Christological heresy, which appealed to 'the Favourers of Socinus and his Polonian, Dutch or English Brethren'.[57] Those who supported Hoadly drew from the ranks of nonconformity and heterodoxy, including Thomas Chubb and Strickland Gough. It was a roster of supporters not bound to help Hoadly's cause with mainstream churchmen. In general, Hoadly's defenders stressed his sola scripturalism; his sacramental theology's similarity with that of the English Zwinglian John Hales (1584–1656); and the value that he had placed on Christ's merits. Hoadly kept quiet after the *Plain Account*'s publication, save for one anonymous pamphlet and another sermon in which he likened his opponents to seventeenth-century Laudians and Arminians who unduly elevated the Eucharist's salvific efficacy.[58]

Waterland objected to the *Plain Account* because he thought that Hoadly had dropped 'the meritorious sacrifice of Christ, and the supernatural grace of the Holy Spirit'.[59] Or, as he put it more bluntly elsewhere, Hoadly's 'scheme is nothing else but the doctrine of the Sacrament Socinianized; ours is the Trinitarian doctrine of the Sacrament'.[60] Initially, Waterland did not think he had the time to respond to the *Plain Account*, and he was heartened to hear that Henry Stebbing and Thomas Sherlock planned to join William Webster's *Weekly Miscellany* in making the orthodox case against Hoadly.[61] Yet Stebbing dithered and Sherlock backed out, leaving William Whiston as the most prominent anti-Hoadlyite author in the wings. Waterland, however, fretted that the wholly idiosyncratic and openly Arian Whiston would 'both over-do and under-do, and is no fit man to rest such a cause upon', not the least because '[t]here are many by-question which must be cleared in the course of such a work: and to do it thoroughly cannot take up less than four or five hundred pages in octavo'.[62] Though he subsequently assisted and approved of Richard Warren's long three-part response to Hoadly, Waterland judged that he himself was the only person properly able to rebut the bishop of Winchester.[63] By March 1736, he had begun to amass materials for the project, and by the end of the year he had completed a draft of the *Review*.[64]

Hoadly preoccupied Waterland when he researched and wrote the *Review* and its companion pieces, but so too did the Eucharistic writings of eighteenth-century nonjurors and their orthodox sympathizers command his attention. For in spelling out precisely how Hoadly had got the Eucharist wrong, Waterland had also to position himself in relation to those whom Hoadly had in mind when drafting the *Plain Account*. Waterland's extensive annotations of John Johnson's *Unbloody Sacrifice* (1714) and Thomas Brett's *Discourse concerning the necessity of discerning the Lord's body in the Holy Communion* (1720) highlight the issues through which he worked. The Kentish churchman John Johnson (1662–1725) remained a juring clergyman until his death, but his Eucharistic works influenced nonjurors.[65] Johnson argued in *The*

Unbloody Sacrifice that the Eucharist was a material sacrifice in which the consecrated elements became, through the suprarational operations of the Holy Spirit, the virtual body and blood of Christ. While stopping short of transubstantiation, Johnson nevertheless argued that God conveyed his grace (and, hence, salvation) through the Eucharist. Reception of the Eucharist, then, should be frequent and prefaced by critical self-examination. Johnson grounded these arguments on what he took to be the thought and practice of the primitive Church and the imprimatur given them by seventeenth-century English divines like Lancelot Andrewes (1555–1626), John Overall (1561–1619), Edward Stephens (d. 1706) and Jeremy Taylor (1613–67).[66]

Waterland's personal copy of *The Unbloody Sacrifice* – 'Johnson's Romance', he dubbed it on the title-page – is the most heavily annotated of his extant books, and slight changes of hand in the marginal notes suggest that he returned to the work again and again through the years.[67] Waterland focused particularly on the portions of Johnson's argument regarding the nature of Christ's sacrifice and its relation to the Eucharist. While agreeing with Johnson that the Eucharist was a sacrifice, Waterland parted ways with him over the particular nature of that sacrifice. 'Who doubts but that the Eucharist is a sacrifice?', he scribbled at one point. 'It is a combination of Sacrifices, and all of the Spiritual kind. In short, it is a Christian and evangelical Sacrifice, not a legal, or Jewish one; that is, not a material one'.[68] By this, he meant to distinguish the 'spiritual' sacrifice from the 'popish sacrifice' (which was 'absurd, profane') and from Johnson's 'material sacrifice' – which Waterland took to be 'a Jewish Sacrifice, or a meaner than Jewish' one. Waterland's spiritual sacrifice, by contrast, 'impli[ed] right Faith, pure worship, and Holy Life: the sacrifice our selves'. Indeed, it alone was 'the true and ancient, and scriptural notion of it', and furthermore, '[a]ll our divines (some few only excepted since Mr. Mede's Time) have disowned all material sacrifice, have admitted none but spiritual'.[69]

Thomas Brett's work also engaged Waterland when he thought through his stance on the Eucharist. Brett (1667–1744), unlike Johnson, was a Cambridge-educated nonjuror, one who broke from the established Church after George I's accession to the throne in 1714.[70] Soon after his withdrawal from the Church of England, Brett became a nonjuring bishop and that church's leading liturgist. Brett's 1720 *Discourse* on the Eucharist, in which he, like Johnson, argued for the sacrament as a material sacrifice got Waterland's repeated attention. In his personal copy of Brett's *Discourse*, Waterland not only reiterated his commitment to the Eucharist as a spiritual sacrifice but insisted that the English Church had rejected the material sacrifice since the sixteenth century. On the flyleaf at the beginning of the Brett's *Discourse*, for instance, Waterland transcribed part of Thomas Cranmer's *Answer to Gardiner* (1551) in which Cranmer had spelled out the nature of the sacrifice: '[M]y meaning is, that the Force, the Grace, and the Virtue and Benefit of Christ's body that was sacrificed for us, and of his Blood that was shed for us, be really and effectually present with all them that duly receive the Sacraments'.[71] Nor did Waterland accept Brett's contention that Cranmer's understanding had subsequently been supplanted as official doctrine by that of Peter Martyr (1499–1562) and Martin Bucer (1491–1551), whom Brett characterized as 'zealous Calvinists'. Waterland, by contrast, reckoned that '[u] nder the names of Bucer and Martyr, [Brett] lashes Cranmer, Jewel and Hooker and all our best divines' and that '[t]he pretended change of doctrine, is all fiction and dream'.[72] On Waterland's reading, Cranmer had articulated an orthodox English Protestant position on the Eucharist which had remained correct and predominant, if not unchallenged, down to the eighteenth century.

Waterland fleshed out his thinking on the Eucharist in full detail in his *Review*, published in April 1737, and in four subsequent archidiaconal charges on the subject. For those who had read his earlier responses to Samuel Clarke's *Exposition*, the argument was familiar. What was new was the barrage of evidence – drawn from antiquity to contemporary continental European scholarship – to support that argument. By the time Waterland wrote the final charge in 1740, he admitted that he had gone on 'perhaps even to a degree of Tediousness'. Nonetheless, he continued, 'considering the great Importance of the Subject, I am not unwilling to dismiss it, when I see room left for throwing in any farther light on it'.[73] In the *Review* and the charges, he sought to position himself between what he defined as the extremes of the Hoadleian and nonjuring Eucharistic schemes. He recognized that the biggest descriptive challenge concerned 'the Thing Signified' in the Eucharist. 'The Lutherans have stated it most wretchedly; the Calvinists have not hit off clear: our divines have done best; and yet they are often confused, and have been various at various times', he explained to a friend. 'Cranmer, Latimer and Ridley, in my judgment, performed better upon that argument, than those who came after; because they took their ideas from Antiquity, and not from modern divines in Germany or Switzerland.'[74] As with every other theological issue Waterland faced, primitive precedent – not the individual's conscience or sincerity – were the touchstones of truth.

Waterland focused especially on who instituted the Eucharist and the nature of the thing instituted. The New Testament mentions the Eucharist four times, which he thought was 'an Argument of the great Weight and Importance of it'.[75] Most 'Learned' Christians agreed that the Eucharist had 'succeeded in the place of the Jewish Passover'.[76] Most similarly agreed about what it was *not*: it was not – as Hoadly would have had it – a mere commemoration of Christ. 'It is not sufficient to remember Christ merely as a very great and good man, a wise Instructor, and an admirable Teacher … [since] all this comes vastly short of what sacred Write declares of Him', Waterland contended.[77] Neither would it do simply to remember him as 'an eminent Prophet' or as 'our Head, Lord, and Master' or even 'as higher than the Angels or older than the System of the World'.[78] It was not, in sum, 'sufficient to commemorate the Death of Christ without considering what his Death means, what were the moving Reasons for it, and what its Ends, and Uses' were. And Christ's death, the Bible taught, was 'a true and proper Expiatory Sacrifice for the Sins of Mankind'. The Eucharist memorialized this sacrifice at the Lord's Table.[79] Thus, participating in the Eucharist was crucial to achieving eternal salvation.

In the *Review*, Waterland anatomized the four causes of salvation and identified the Eucharist's role in the salvific process. The possibility of eternal salvation owed everything to the 'primary, or principal Cause' of salvation, which was '[t]he Divine Philanthropy'. But, Waterland argued, God's grace was not nearly the final step to being saved from damnation. Any person's salvation had a 'conditional Cause', which was '[o]ur performing the Duties required, Faith and Repentance, by the Aid of Divine Grace'. Neither faith nor repentance alone, though, was sufficient to secure salvation because fallen creatures cannot earn their salvation. Instead, there was a 'meritorious Cause' to salvation, which was the 'Sacrifice of Christ's death, recommending and rendering acceptable our imperfect Performances'. Finally, the sacraments of baptism and the Eucharist are 'the instrumental Causes, in and by which God applies to Men fitly disposed, the Virtue of that Sacrifice' of Christ's death.[80] Given Waterland's understanding of salvation's causes and processes, his insistence that the Eucharist was a sacrifice and that the Christ who sacrificed himself on the cross must be understood in the Nicene formulation makes more sense: only a fully divine and fully human Christ could properly atone for human sins. For this reason, Waterland believed that the sacraments, properly understood, bolstered Christian orthodox doctrine.[81]

At issue was the Eucharistic sacrifice's nature. Waterland reckoned that there were eight different kinds of sacrifice comprehended within the Eucharist, including the sacrifices 'of Prayer'; 'of Praise and Thanksgiving'; 'of a penitent and contrite Heart'; 'of ourselves'; of 'the mystical Body of Christ, that is, his Church'; 'of True Converts, or sincere Penitents to God'; and 'of Faith and Hope, and Self-humiliation, in commemorating the grand Sacrifice'.[82] The problem Waterland and those like him faced, though, was distinguishing the Eucharistic sacrifice he envisioned from the Eucharistic sacrifice of the Roman Catholic Mass. The problem, in other words, was distinguishing between the true religion of the Church of England and that idolatrous false religion, popery. To distinguish between the two, Waterland offered a story of the Eucharist whose central features included the origins, corruption, recovery and eventual misunderstanding of a primitively pure doctrine. From the very beginning, Waterland argued, both the apostles and the primitive fathers conceived of the Eucharist as a 'spiritual sacrifice', with Augustine of Hippo describing it most succinctly in the *City of God*: 'A true Sacrifice is any Work done to keep up our League of Amity with God, referred to Him as our Sovereign Good in whom we may enjoy true Felicity'.[83] The

Eucharist was precisely this kind of sacrifice, but, crucially, it was a 'spiritual' sacrifice rather than the 'material' one supposedly practised in the Catholic Mass. For the primitive fathers, spiritual sacrifices were 'true sacrifices', while material ones were idolatrous; and, until at least the sixth century, the fathers 'will all be found constant and uniform in one Tenor of Doctrine, rejecting all material, corporeal, terrene, sensible Sacrifices, and admitting none but Spiritual'.[84] Somehow, though, this original distinction had got lost, so that 'Moderns generally have reckoned all the Spiritual Sacrifices among the nominal, improper, metaphorical Sacrifices; whereas the Ancients judged them to be the truest Sacrifices of any, yea and infinitely more excellent than the other'.[85] Put another way, Waterland's contemporaries judged *his* conception of the Eucharist as a spiritual sacrifice to be no less misguided than the Roman Catholic conception of it as a material sacrifice.

The origins of this confusion over kinds of sacrifice lay in the Reformation. As Waterland explained it, Roman Catholic theologians until 1556 accepted the Eucharist as a spiritual sacrifice, but Reformation-era polemical exigencies led them to abandon this doctrine. 'The Romanists, wanting Arguments to support their Mass-Sacrifice, thought of this Pretence, among others, that either their Mass must be the Sacrifice of the Church, or the Church had really none', Waterland contended. 'And so if the Protestants resolved to throw off the Mass, they would be left without a Sacrifice, without an Altar, without a Priesthood, and no longer a Church,'[86] To distinguish themselves from the Protestants, Roman Catholics jettisoned the doctrine of the Eucharist that had been orthodoxy for a millennium and a half. In turn, many Protestants – mistakenly, in Waterland's view – rejected the notion of the Eucharist as a sacrifice. A notable exception, of course, was Thomas Cranmer, whose Eucharistic theology Waterland thought most reflected the primitive consensus. 'Cranmer's Single Preface to His Answer to Gardiner is to me more instructive, for settling the true notion of the Sacrament, than whole volumes of other moderns', he explained to a friend. 'He there interprets the real Presence, as imparting the merit of Christ's death and Benefit of his passion, conveyed to the worthy receiver by Christ Spiritually present in his divine nature or by the Holy Ghost. This I take to be the true and the old notion.'[87] In the *Review*, Waterland quoted at length from Cranmer's *Answer to Gardiner* to demonstrate what was the proper Protestant understanding of the Eucharist.[88]

After Cranmer, Protestants splintered into three distinct groups regarding the Eucharist. One group correctly understood the Eucharist as a sacrifice in pre-Tridentine terms. Included in this group 'that adhered to the old Language, and still continued to call the Eucharist a true or proper Sacrifice, but of the spiritual kind' were Continental Calvinists like Amandus Polanus (1561–1610) and Johannes Scharpius (1572–1648), as well as a number of early seventeenth-century Arminian bishops, including Lancelot Andrewes, John Buckeridge (d. 1631), James Montague (1568–1618) and, above all, William Laud (1573–1645), whom Waterland referred to as '[t]his great Man'.[89] Restoration divines like Jeremy Taylor, John Bramhall (1594–1663), Benjamin Lany (1591–1675) and Daniel Brevint (1616–95) also adhered to the older understandings of the Eucharist. Two other groups of English divines, though, disagreed with this primtivist camp. One group, whose number included Richard Hooker (1554–1600), conceived of the Eucharist in a way that did not accord with pre-Tridentine understandings of the Eucharist; instead they denied that the Eucharist was 'a true, real or proper Sacrifice'.[90] Though Waterland only discussed Hooker, Francis White (1563–1638), Robert Abbot (1559–1618), John Davenant (1572–1641), Richard Crakanthorpe (1568–1624) and Thomas Morton (1564–1659) among this group, he implied that they represented the mainstream of English thinking on the matter. Almost equally misguided were a third group of English divines, who tried to reconcile ancient and modern understandings of the Eucharist. As Waterland explained it, 'some serious Men perceiving how much the ancient and modern Language differed in this article, and that by means of the now prevailing Definitions, they were likely to lose their sacrifice ... thought of reconciling the Eucharistic Sacrifice with the new Definitions, by making it a material Sacrifice'.[91] Chief among these were Joseph Mede (1586–1638); the nonjurors George Hickes and Henry Dodwell; and John Johnson, author of *Unbloody Sacrifice*. To rectify matters people needed to recover the primitive understandings of the Eucharist: 'Return we but to the ancient Ideas of spiritual Sacrifice, and then all will be clear, just and uniform'.[92] That, as Waterland synopsized at the end of the *Review*, was a Eucharist which had crucial soteriological importance. It was not 'a bare Memorial, a Memorial of an absent Friend, Master, or chief Martyr'; instead it was a 'Sacramental memorial ... of Christ God-Man, who died a willing Sacrifice for the Sins of Mankind' and 'a real and present Exhibition of the Graces, Comforts, or Blessings accruing therefrom, to every worthy Receiver'.[93]

The *Review* and the accompanying archidiaconal charges mostly met with approval and its reputation steadily grew. Those at the time who griped about it did so for predictable reasons.[94] One group which found its arguments objectionable were the nonjurors, especially Thomas Brett, who condemned Waterland in print for everything from errantly interpreting primitive Christian sources to being 'strangely prejudiced in Favour of that great and illustrious Reformer John Calvin' to acting like a Socinian or Deist.[95] Privately Brett was even more scathing. 'Dr Waterland being not willing to put himself out of the way of preferment studied for colourable arguments to support Calvinistic doctrines so long that he believed them himself', he groused to his son.[96] Other nonjurors goaded Brett to respond, on the view that Waterland's 'name, his authority alone will with many, with most be thought a sufficient force to weigh down the notion of a material sacrifice'.[97] Thomas Bowyer even went so far as implausibly to insist that Hoadly and Waterland had made much the same arguments in their Eucharistical works.[98]

Yet if some nonjurors got exercised by Waterland's take on the nature of the Eucharistic sacrifice, others sympathetic to the nonjuring cause recognized the damage that might be done by such public wrangling. Charles Wheatly (1686–1742), friend to both Brett and Waterland, repeatedly urged Brett to tone down his public criticism of Waterland, lest 'Enemies of Religion ... take advantage of the Disagreement between two such great Men ... even to ridicule and insult (as they are too apt to do already) the Institution of the Sacrament'.[99] In the end, Wheatly's admonitions had no effect.[100] Waterland, for his part, pitied his old friend. 'Brett, poor man! Has again drawn upon me. Scolds most vehemently, says anything that first comes into his distempered head, and almost raves', he confided to John Lewis. '... I have a true commiseration for him, and am too much affected at such melancholy instances to take any handle for insulting and exposing a weak man'.[101]

Waterland shared no such sympathy for Hoadly, who never responded to the *Review*. The question, though, was what to do to him besides rebut his arguments in print? In an unpublished tract in response to Matthew Tindal, Waterland had fleshed out his thoughts on the distinction between prosecution and persecution, rejecting Tindal's conflation of the two. In *Christianity as Old as the Creation*, Tindal had pointed to Christ's enjoiner in Matthew 5:43–4 to love one's enemies as evidence against punishing someone for his views. Waterland read the passage differently. 'To bring wicked men, in some cases to condign Punishments, provided it be done in a proper manner, and before a proper Tribunal, is no contradiction to the Rule of loving enemies', he insisted. 'An Informer may prosecute, a witness accuse, a jury bring in guilty, a judge condemn, and an executioner dispatch a criminal, without any malevolence or Hatred at all, wishing well to the criminal and doing Him good all the time (so far as He is capable in his circumstances) but so as not to be cruel to others, or negligent of the public welfare'.[102] To prosecute error *was* to love one's neighbour, not to persecute him. But how practicably to do this to Benjamin Hoadly during the mid-1730s proved unclear to orthodox churchmen. Unlike Thomas Rundle, who also enjoyed Queen Caroline's favour, Hoadly was already a bishop when he ran afoul of the orthodox establishment during the 1730s; and even Rundle ended up getting an Irish bishopric after being blocked for Gloucester. In the end, it proved impossible decisively to punish a heterodox figure like Hoadly beyond, perhaps, depriving him of another episcopal see he particularly coveted.[103] There were, though, instances in which coercion *was* employed against the heterodox, especially against those who lacked the protection of high office that Hoadly possessed. The story of Waterland's Cambridge contemporary Conyers Middleton is especially instructive in this regard. Indeed, few cases testify more clearly how heterodox views presented a barrier to ecclesiastical preferment.

NOTES

1 *BCP*, pp. 559–61 [Articles XXV, XXVIII].

2 D. Sheerin, 'Eucharistic Theology', in S. Harvey and D. Hunter (eds), *Oxford*

Handbook of Early Christian Studies (Oxford, 2008), pp. 711–43; A. McGrath, *Reformation Thought* (London, 1993), pp. 159–87; E. Duffy, *The Stripping of the Altars* (New Haven, 1992), pp. 89–130; C. Dugmore, *Eucharistic Doctrine in England from Hooker to Waterland* (1942).

3 Cf. R. Holtby, *Daniel Waterland* (Carlisle, 1966), pp. 144–95; B. Douglas, *A Companion to Anglican Eucharistic Theology. Volume 1: The Reformation to the Nineteenth Century* (Leiden, 2012), pp. 408–21.

4 S. Taylor, 'Benjamin Hoadly (1676–1761)', *ODNB*; N. Sykes, 'Benjamin Hoadly, Bishop of Bangor', in F. Hearnshaw (ed.), *The Social and Political Ideas of Some English Thinkers of the Augustan Age, 1650–1750* (1928), pp. 112–55; W. Gibson, *Enlightenment Prelate: Benjamin Hoadly, 1676–1761* (Cambridge, 2004).

5 Cf. G. Sanna, 'How Heterodox Was Benjamin Hoadly?', in W. Gibson and R. Ingram (eds), *Religious Identities in Britain, 1660–1832* (Aldershot, 2005), pp. 61–80

6 S. Taylor, 'Queen Caroline and the Church', in S. Taylor, C. Jones and R. Connor (eds), *Hanoverian Britain and Empire* (Woodbridge, 1998), pp. 82–101; N. Sykes, 'Queen Caroline and the Church', History 11 (1927), pp. 333–9; Hervey to Middleton, 20 August 1734 (SRO, 941/47/7).

7 F. Mather, 'Georgian Churchmanship Reconsidered: Some Variations in Anglican Public Worship, 1714–1830', *JEH* 36 (1985), pp. 255–83; P. Doll, *After the Primitive Christians: The Eighteenth-Century Anglican Eucharist in Its Architectural Setting* (Cambridge, 1997); A. Hunt, 'The Lord's Supper in Early Modern England', *P&P* 161 (1998), pp. 39–83.

8 Gibson, *Enlightenment Prelate*, pp. 139–98; A. Starkie, *The Church of England and the Bangorian Controversy, 1716–1721* (Woodbridge, 2007); Hoadly to Charlotte Clayton, 27 September 1715 (Beinecke, Osborn FC110, fols 19–20).

9 G. Hickes, *Constitution* (1716: T088125), p. 66.

10 B. Hoadly, *Preservative* (1716: T018256), pp. 6, 73.

11 Ibid., p. 78.

12 Ibid., p. 63.

13 Gibson, *Enlightenment Prelate*, pp. 144–5.

14 P. Nockles, *The Oxford Movement in Context: Anglican High Churchmanship, 1760–1857* (Cambridge, 1994), pp. 237–8; R. Sharp, 'New Perspectives on the High Church Tradition: Historical Background, 1730–1780', in G. Rowell (ed.), *Tradition Renewed* (Allison Park, 1986), pp. 11–12; Dugmore, *Eucharistic Doctrine*, pp. 169–83; D. Stone, *A History of the Doctrine of the Holy Eucharist* (1909), II, pp. 501–9; J. Jackson, 'Preface', in Waterland, *Review ... of the Eucharist*, ed. W. Van Mildert (Oxford, 1896), pp. v–vii.

15 W. Van Mildert, 'A Review of the Author's Life and Writings', in *WDW*, I, p. 188.

16 Middleton to Warburton, 31 March 1737 (BL, Add. 32457, fol. 118).

17 Waterland to Loveday, 18 September 1735 (*WDW*, VI, p. 421).

18 Hervey, *Memoirs*, II, pp. 498–500, records George II's acid response to Hoadly's publishing the *Plain Account* only *after* his translation to Winchester.

19 J. Kenyon, *The Stuart Constitution* (Cambridge, 1966), pp. 376–8, 461–2.

20 B. Sirota, 'Occasional Conformity Controversy, Moderation and the Anglican Critique of Modernity, 1700–1714', *HJ* 57 (2014), pp. 81–105; G. Townend,

'Religious Radicalism and Conservatism in the Whig Party under George I: The Repeal of the Occasional Conformity and Schism Acts', *PH* 7 (1988), pp. 24–44.

21 E. Gibson, *Dispute adjusted* (Dublin, 1733: T075446), pp. 15, 16.

22 [B. Hoadly], *Objections against the repeal* (1739: T104017), pp. 12, 15. Hoadly wrote this pamphlet (first published in 1736) during 1732–33 in direct response to Gibson's *Dispute adjusted* (1732): Taylor, 'Benjamin Hoadly'.

23 [Hoadly], *Objections against the repeal*, p. 38.

24 Ibid., 25, 26.

25 Waterland characterized Hoadly's putative inscription to Clarke's 1729 *Exposition of the Catechism* as 'fulsome and vile, and ... an affront and insult upon all friends of our Church and Establishment': Waterland to Bishop, 1 January 1730 (MCC/MR).

26 Hoadly, 'Preface', pp. ii–iv.

27 Ibid., p. xxxv.

28 Ibid., pp. xxxv–xxvi.

29 Clarke's interleaved and annotated *Book of Common Prayer*, n.d., unpaginated (BL, shelfmark C. 24 b. 21).

30 S. Clarke, *Exposition of the church-catechism* (1729: T074270), pp. 279–80.

31 Ibid., pp. 288–9.

32 Waterland to Bishop, 28 February 1730 (MCC/MR). See also Waterland to Gibson, 10 January 1731 (LPL, 1741, fols 72–3).

33 'I do not set my name to it, because the Author I write against is dead, besides other prudential reasons: But everybody will know whose it is, being printed for the two Crownfield's ... And I do not myself design to make any great secret of it': Waterland to Bishop, 1 January 1730 (MCC/MR). See also J. Ferguson, *Dr. Samuel Clarke: An 18th Century Heretic* (Kineton, 1976), pp. 162–78.

34 [Waterland], *Remarks upon ... Exposition*, p. 20.

35 Ibid., pp. 29, 21.

36 Ibid., pp. 4–6.

37 Ibid., pp. 76, 77.

38 Ibid., p. 80.

39 Clarke, *Exposition*, p. 282. See also D. Norton and M. Kuehn, 'The Foundations of Morality', in Haakonssen (ed.), *Cambridge History of Eighteenth-Century Philosophy*, I, pp. 949–51; J. Ferguson, *The Philosophy of Samuel Clarke and Its Critics* (New York, 1974), pp. 170–242.

40 [D. Waterland], *Nature, obligation and efficacy of the Christian sacraments* (1730: T153595), pp. 5, 6.

41 Ibid., pp. 10–12.

42 [D. Waterland], *Supplement to the treatise* (1730: T060370), p. 17.

43 [Waterland], *Nature, obligation and efficacy*, p. 76.

44 Ibid., p. 58.

45 Ibid., p. 62.

46 Ibid., p. 65.

47 N. Sykes, 'Benjamin Hoadly', bishop of Bangor', in F. Hearnshaw (ed.), *The Social and Political Ideas of Some Thinkers of the Augustan Age, 1650–1750* (Oxford, 1928), p. 50.

48 [B. Hoadly], *Plain account* (1735: T018286), p. 7. Cf. W. Bulman, *Anglican*

Enlightenment: Orientalism, Religion and Politics in England and Its Empire, 1648–1715 (Cambridge, 2015), pp. 132–40, 180–6, for seventeenth-century work on Jewish and pagan traditions and the Eucharist. See also S. Rutherford, 'Benjamin Hoadly: Sacramental Tests and Eucharistic Thought in Early Eighteenth-Century England', *AEH* 71 (2002), pp. 473–97; Gibson, *Enlightenment Prelate*, pp. 233–47.

49 [Hoadly], *Plain account*, pp. 23–4. Stone, *History*, p. 489, and Rutherford, 'Benjamin Hoadly', characterize Hoadly's Eucharistic theology as 'Zwinglian', while Dugmore, *Eucharistic Doctrine*, pp. 158–9, describes it as the product of 'orthodox rationalism'. B. Spinks, *Do This in Remembrance of Me: The Eucharist from the Early Church to the Present Day* (London, 2013), pp. 341, 342, reckons that Hoadly's view of the Eucharist was 'an expression of Lockean theology' and 'an extreme example of symbolic memorialism'. Douglas, *Companion*, pp. 345–7, characterizes it as 'nominalist, with a separation of sign and signified'.

50 [Hoadly], p. 100.

51 B. Hoadly, 'Sermon ... February 15, 1729/30', in Hoadly, *Works*, III, pp. 737–8.

52 [Hoadly], *Plain account*, pp. 40, 47–50, 55.

53 Ibid., pp. 53–4.

54 [Francis Hare] to Gibson, 29 July 1735 (LPL, 1741, fol. 118); Gibson, *Enlightenment Prelate*, pp. 233–47.

55 Herring to William Duncombe, 9 November 1735 (T. Herring, *Letters ... to William Duncombe* (1777: T130272), p. 28).

56 Middleton to Hervey, 27 July 1735 (BL, Add. 32458, fol. 187). See also Hervey to Middleton, 29 November 1735 (SRO, 941/47/4, fols 93–4).

57 T. Brett, *True scripture account of ... the Holy Eucharist* (1735: T051924), p. 44.

58 [B. Hoadly], *Apologetical defence* (1735: T018333); B. Hoadly, *Plain account ... a sermon on I Cor. Xi.24* (1736: T203528). Cf. Rutherford, 'Benjamin Hoadly', p. 82, which denies Hoadly's authorship of the *Apologetical defence*.

59 Waterland to Bishop, 24 June 1735 (MCC/MR). See also Waterland to Loveday, 6 July 1735 (*MWDW*, VI, p. 418), in which he identified the chief issues as 'the doctrine of the Atonement and Divine Grace'.

60 Waterland to Loveday, 15 July 1735 (*MWDW*, VI, p. 420). See also Waterland to Zachary Grey, 17 March 1736 (*LI*, IV, p. 388).

61 Ibid.; *WM* (12 July 1735), pp. 1–2; (16 July 1735), p. 1.

62 Waterland to Loveday, 18 September 1735 (*MWDW*, VI, p. 421). Cf. W. Whiston, *Primitive Eucharist reviv'd* (1736: T044314). See also P. Gilliam, 'William Whiston: No Longer an Arian', *JEH* 66 (2015), pp. 755–71; M. Feingold, 'A Rake's Progress: William Whiston Reads Josephus', *ECS* 49 (2015), pp. 17–30.

63 Richard Warren to Thomas Brett, 6 December 1735 (Bodleian, Eng.th.c.33, fol. 283); R. Warren, *Answer to ... A plain account* (Cambridge, 1735: T063132); Warren, *Appendix to the answer*.

64 Waterland to Grey, 17 March 1736 (BL, Add. 5831, fols. 173–4); Waterland to Loveday, January 1737 (*MWDW*, VI, pp. 423–5).

65 R. Cornwall, *Visible and Apostolic: The Constitution of the Church in High Church and Non-Juror Thought* (Newark, 1993), pp. 120–2, 126–9, 136, 141.

66 W. Grisbrooke, *Anglican Liturgies of the Seventeenth and Eighteenth Centuries* (London, 1958), pp. 71–88.

67 Waterland's annotations of Johnson's *The Unbloody Sacrifice*, n.d. (Bodleian, Rawl. 8⁰ 418). See also, Charles Wheatly to Brett, 17 September 1737 (Bodleian, Eng.th.c.34, fols 25–7).
68 Waterland's annotations of Johnson's *The Unbloody Sacrifice*, p. 78.
69 Ibid., p. iv.
70 R. Cornwall, 'Thomas Brett (1667–1744)', *ODNB*; H. Broxap, *The Later Nonjurors* (Oxford, 1924); W. Grisbrooke, *Anglican Liturgies of the Seventeenth and Eighteenth Centuries* (1958), pp. 88–112.
71 Waterland's annotations of Brett's *Discourse concerning the … Holy Communion*, n.d., flyleaf (Bodleian, Rawl. 8⁰ 405). See also Waterland to Bishop, 26 July 1735 (MCC/MR). Cf. P. Brooks, *Thomas Cranmer's Doctrine of the Eucharist: An Essay in Historical Development* (Houndmills, 1992).
72 Ibid., pp. iv, v.
73 D. Waterland, *Distinctions of sacrifice* (1740: T185171), p. 1.
74 Waterland to Bishop, 26 July 1735 (MCC/MR).
75 D. Waterland, *Review of … the Eucharist* (1737: T103628), p. 58.
76 Ibid., p. 64.
77 Ibid., pp. 75–6.
78 Ibid., pp. 77–8.
79 Ibid., pp. 95, 96.
80 Ibid., p. 105.
81 D. Waterland, *Doctrinal uses of the Christian sacraments* (1736: T034787).
82 Waterland, *Review*, pp. 475–6.
83 Ibid., p. 471.
84 Ibid., p. 521.
85 Ibid., pp. 473–4.
86 D. Waterland, *Christian sacrifice explained* (1738: T117449), pp. 7, 8.
87 Waterland to Bishop, 26 July 1735 (MCC/MR).
88 Waterland, *Review*, pp. 192, 252–3.
89 Waterland, *Christian sacrifice*, pp. 26–32.
90 Ibid., pp. 32–7. Waterland's understanding of Hooker clearly had evolved since the early 1730s. Where he had praised Hooker's Eucharistic thought in the anti-Clarke pieces, he noted of Hooker's Eucharistic formulation, 'But I commend not the Use of such new Language, be the Meaning ever so right: The Fathers never used it' (ibid., p. 33).
91 Ibid., p. 37.
92 Ibid., p. 45.
93 Waterland, *Review*, p. 600.
94 Middleton to Warburton, 22 September 1737, 5 July 1750 (*MWCM*, II, pp. 472–3; BL, Add. 32457, fol. 100).
95 Brett, *Some remarks on Dr. Waterland's review*, p. 208; Brett, *Supplement to the Remarks*, pp. 20, 24. See also Charles Wheatly to Brett, 13 December 1737 (Bodleian, Eng.th.c.34, fols 385–7).
96 Brett to Nicholas Brett, 10 May 1741 (Bodleian, Eng.th.c.35, fol. 290).
97 Thomas Bowyer to Brett, 6 September 1739 (Bodleian, Eng th.c.34, fol. 21). See also Robert Gourdon to Brett, 27 February 1739, 29 March 1737 (ibid., fols 407, 421–3); Thomas Wagstaffe to Brett, 7 January 1739 (ibid., fol. 397).

98 Bowyer to Brett, 14 November 1737 (ibid., fols 95–6).
99 Wheatly to Brett, 11 October 1737 (ibid., fol. 25). See also Brett to [Robert Gourdon], 2 March 1739 (LPL, 2219, fol. 4). Cf. Daniel Waterland's annotations to Charles Wheatly's *Rational Illustration of the Book of Common Prayer*, n.d. (St John's College, Oxford, Archiv.a.17).
100 Brett to [Gourdon], 2 March 1739 (LPL, 2219, fol. 4).
101 Waterland to Lewis, 17 September 1738 (Bodleian, Clar. Press c.18, fol. 293).
102 Waterland's notes for *Scripture Vindicated* dealing with the New Testament, n.d., p. 11 (Bodleian, Raw. D. 1264).
103 Hoadly had long desired to be the bishop of Durham, a post to which he was denied translation in 1730 on account of his heterodoxy: Gibson, *Enlightenment Prelate*, pp. 228–30. When Winchester opened up in 1734, Lord Hervey pointedly advised him, 'Remember how you failed of Durham – at least, that from silence you were told you failed. Write therefore now, come, speak, dun, and behave, not as your laziness inclines you, but as your interest directs, as common prudence dictates, as your friends advise, and as what you owe to yourself and your family requires': Hervey, *Memoirs*, II, p. 396.

Part II

The history of the Church be fabulous: Conyers Middleton

Chapter 6

I know not what to make of the author

Daniel Waterland initially had no idea who had written *A Letter to Dr. Waterland* (1731), but he did not like what he read. 'I have seen the Letter written to me by name, which was not fair but against Rule', he complained to Edmund Gibson in late December 1730, less than two weeks after the anonymous pamphlet's appearance. 'I know not what to make of the Author. The letter seems to me to be Sneer: And if so, He is a thorough-paced deist. But if it be serious, He is a semi-deist.'[1] To another friend Waterland described the piece as 'very superficial, and indeed a childish performance'.[2] Yet, the margins of Waterland's own copy of the *Letter* reveal his substantive concerns. 'So this pretended Believer and real infidel, gives up the Inspiration of the Scripture at once in a fit of rage, and madness', he scribbled at one point, before noting on the next page, 'this whole piece is written without regard to Truth, and is everywhere full of ... falsehood'. Elsewhere, he worried that to the *Letter* writer 'it seems Religion is a human invention: And this great defender undertakes to justify the inventing it, by his wise Argument'; near the end of the pamphlet, Waterland lamented that the author 'does not yet, not once assert the truth and reality of revealed Religion'.[3]

The unsigned broadside to which Waterland took such objection had aspersed him for Waterland's own rebuttal of Matthew Tindal's *Christianity as Old as the Creation*. The anonymous *Letter* writer accused Waterland of 'not reasoning but railing' and contended that Waterland's anti-Tindal argument was 'built upon a wrong Principle, and proceeds upon a system, that cannot be maintained viz. that every single passage of the Scriptures, we call Canonical, must needs be received, as the very word and as the voice of God himself'. Furthermore, the *Letter* writer continued, '[t]his notion, which you everywhere inculcate, as 'tis false in itself, so must necessarily lead you into error and absurdity, and expose you to contempt and ridicule of all rational men, who can never embrace an Hypothesis, however confidently asserted, which they see contrary to fact and the plain conviction of their senses'.[4]

Waterland, the *Letter* writer implied, was a bad historian and, hence, a mistaken theologian.

The anonymous *Letter to Dr. Waterland* provoked the orthodox, a number of whom rushed into print to defend the master of Magdalene. First out of the gate was Zachary Pearce, royal chaplain and a former Trinity College, Cambridge, fellow. 'My present Business with you, Sir, is ... to set before you and expostulate with you, about the many Falsehoods which your Letter abounds with, both in the Quotations and Historical Facts insisted upon by You', Pearce began. '... [Y]ou have hardly made one original Quotation of an Author in this True Sense, very often in the sense most opposite to his True one; and represented not only Passages but Facts too in so wrong a Light, that whatever you searched for, it is plain you have miss'd of Truth'.[5] Waterland thought that Pearce had fought ably on the *Letter* writer's own turf and had blown apart his argument. 'I think myself obliged to you, as the public also is, for chastising that noisy conceited man', he complimented Pearce. '... He was in hopes of, by throwing a bone in my way, to take me off from pursuing their high Leader ... But I am very glad you have taken this Amalekite off my hands. I believe you have demolished him at once, and he will scarce be able to rally any more'.[6] Waterland was wrong: the arguments put forward by the anonymous letter writer had not been demolished. However, the letter writer's career prospects had been torched. For to question Waterland's form of primitivism was to question orthodoxy's foundation, method and content. To assail the apotheosis of orthodoxy and one of Cambridge's most respected figures was also to commit career suicide if one hoped for high preferment within the Church of England.

Yet there was something odd about the orthodox response to the *Letter* writer because few of his arguments were new and, indeed, many of them had been employed by some of the established Church's most ardent defenders during the seventeenth century. Those ideas, though, had a different valence during the 1730s than they had during the previous century. What accounted for that change had primarily to do with the politics of religion. Put another way, if orthodoxy's core content remained constant, its borders fluctuated and what shifts occurred at the margins of orthodoxy were more the product of politics than of theology or of propositional logic. The career of the *Letter to Dr. Waterland*'s author, Conyers Middleton, especially evinces this.

Part II of this book tells the story of Conyers Middleton (1683–1750) and his stunted ecclesiastical career.[7] This introductory chapter (Chapter 6) anatomizes the orthodox Tory Middleton's feud with the Whig classicist Richard Bentley. That feud set the tone for Middleton's future polemical divinity while also providing the occasion for him to rethink his earliest religious and political commitments. Chapter 7 turns to Middleton's *Letter to Dr. Waterland* (1730) and the fallout from its publication, especially the breakdown of the relationship with his patron, Edward Harley. Chapter 8 focuses on Middleton's subsequent patron–client relationship with John

Figure 3 'Conyers Middleton', *c.* 1751, by John Faber Jr, after John Giles Eccardt

Hervey and their effort to salvage Middleton's career prospects with a life of Cicero. Part II concludes with Chapter 9, which shows how Middleton's life of Cicero failed to remove orthodox doubts about his theological soundness. That failure deepened his theological heterodoxy. Together the chapters in Part II highlight the career price to be paid by heterodox polemical divines for their not-orthodoxy and the ways that their polemical divinity often reflected the pressure brought to bear upon them. This introductory chapter sets the scene for this story by considering the Middleton–Bentley feud and its implications for Middleton's later career.

That Conyers Middleton wrote the *Letter to Dr. Waterland* surprised most at the time, not least because his was not the profile of a heterodox anticlerical. He had been a staunch Tory; a longtime scourge of Cambridge's most prominent Whig; and an ally and a friend to some of Cambridge's most avant-garde orthodox for nearly two decades. Nor was he naturally acerbic: by all accounts, he was eminently sociable. William Cole, who knew him well, thought him 'one of the most sober, well-bred, easy & companionable Men

I ever conversed with'. If in the twilight of Middleton's life he was 'bitter & severe [in] his sarcasms and reflections ... in his writings against the Fathers and the Miracles of the primitive Ages', Cole subsequently recollected, '... during the many years of uninterrupted Friendship & Converse with him, I never in my Life heard the least indecent or unbecoming Reflection in Conversation, or any Thing in the least tending to depreciate or under-value the Establishment of the Church'.[8] Waterland, Middleton's exact contemporary though no close friend, expressed surprise to find himself laid into by such an unlikely antagonist. 'They are strange pieces he has written, and his manner is strange ... I wish him a better mind', Waterland lamented, concluding with evident bewilderment that Middleton 'is a man of my year, wears a gown, writes D.D., has learning and Parts'.[9]

Nearly all agreed that Conyers Middleton's attack on Waterland came from an unexpected quarter. Many also soon concurred that Middleton was 'the most acute controvertist of the Age'.[10] Few knew better how to play with polemical short knives, how to assess an intellectual enemy's weaknesses or how to attack them more elegantly and more devastatingly. Few at the time poked more sharply at the weaknesses in orthodoxy's primitivist armament than did Middleton. After his death those sympathetic to him could reckon that he had 'left very few behind him of equal talents & Abilities' and that he 'will certainly be considered for Ages to come as one of the first & standard writers of this age'.[11] That Middleton so agitated some of orthodoxy's most vocal and consistent defenders also suggests that his polemical enemies took his ideas seriously.

History has largely forgotten Conyers Middleton, his reputation having subsequently been overshadowed by those of both David Hume and Edward Gibbon. Yet both of these famous religious sceptics acknowledged Middleton's importance. Hume rightly recognized that Middleton's *Free Inquiry into the miraculous powers* (1749) had touched a more sensitive nerve than his *Enquiry concerning Human Understanding* (1748): 'I had the mortification to find all England in a ferment on account of Dr. Middleton's Free Enquiry; while my performance was entirely overlooked and neglected', he groused.[12] For his part, Gibbon's first encounter with Middleton's work in 1753 drove him into the arms of the Roman Catholic Church. 'The name of Middleton was unpopular; and his proscription very naturally led me to peruse his writings, and those of his antagonists', Gibbon recollected. From that reading, he developed unsettling doubts about the authenticity of the post-apostolic Christian miracles. 'I still revered the character, or rather the names, of the saints and fathers whom Dr. Middleton exposes; nor could he destroy my implicit belief that the gifts of miraculous powers were continued in the church, during the first four or five centuries of Christianity', Gibbon recalled. 'But I was unable to resist the weight of historical evidence, that within the same period most of the leading doctrines of popery were already introduced in theory and practice: nor was my conclusion absurd, that miracles are the test of truth, and that the church must be orthodox and pure, which was so often approved by the visible interposition of the Deity.' The sixteen-year-old Gibbon resolved this conflict between 'implicit belief' and 'the weight of historical evidence' by converting to Roman Catholicism.[13] Years later Gibbon again found inspiration in Middleton. 'This man was endowed with penetration and accuracy', he noted after re-reading the *Free Inquiry*. 'He saw where his principles led; but he did not think proper to draw the consequences'.[14] Gibbon, or so he thought, followed them to the end of the line in his *Decline and Fall of the Roman Empire* (1776). A continent away and four decades later, Thomas Jefferson likewise acknowledged Middleton's instruction and inspiration. 'Middleton's writings, especially his letters from Rome, and to Waterland, [serve] as the basis of my own faith', he explained. '[T]hese writings have never been answered, nor can be answered, by quoting historical proofs, as they have done. [F]or these facts therefore I cling to their learning, so much superior to my own.'[15] Even someone like John Henry Newman paid close attention to Middleton's arguments against miracles, going so far as to chalk up 'some flippant language against the Fathers' that he had employed in an 1825–26 article to his having 'read Middleton on the Miracles of the early Church, [having] imbibed a portion of his spirit'.[16]

If Conyers Middleton was a more important figure in his own time than is now remembered, he has proved a difficult figure to situate historically.[17] It is best to think about Middleton in the ways that he and his contemporaries thought about him. He and they would have identified a few salient points. Firstly, Middleton's body of work points up primitivism's potentially *anti*-coagulative effect on theological orthodoxy. Middleton, no less than Waterland, was a primitivist, but his hermeneutics differed from Waterland's and his scholarly conclusions unnerved many of his contemporaries. As William Cole noted in the margins of his own copy of Middleton's *Free Inquiry*, 'This is certainly right Argumentation: but where will it lead us? Either into Popery or Infidelity. For if we come to question the Miracles of the Age immediately following that of the Apostles, it is but too much to be feared that Enquires of a free Nature will not stop there. It has proved to be so.'[18] In addition to highlighting primitivism's potentially destabilizing role in religious apologetics, Middleton's polemical career illustrates concretely the coercive side of eighteenth-century polemical divinity and the price to be paid for orthodox apostasy. The bishop of Chichester nicely captured the Church establishment's thinking when he contended in 1737, 'I truly think no one thing can hurt the King and his Government more than distinguishing by his favours men marked for heterodoxy or infidelity. Nothing more has alienated the minds of the University, Clergy, and serious Christians, than the jealousies that have long entertained of this kind.' Conyers Middleton got punished for this. 'And this is the single reason for which I should be against Dr. M[iddleton]'s promotion by the Crown; who is certainly a very ingenious man, and has a fine pen', the bishops declared.[19] Even association with Middleton could potentially damage one's career prospects, as William Warburton discovered. Warburton published his correspondence with Middleton as a way to set the record straight about their relationship. 'You know my acquaintance with him has been looked upon with an evil eye, & objected to me with an evil tongue by the Bigots', he lamented to a friend. 'I was not averse to have the public know the whole of our connection & the nature of it: ... And throughout the whole you will find that the use I made of my interest with him was to induce him to think better of Religion, & to make a less ambiguous profession of what he pretended to me to believe.'[20] Lastly, and perhaps most importantly, Middleton's career offers clear evidence of the ways in which such coercion could reshape or accelerate certain themes in an author's thought. From early 1731 onwards, there was a steep acceleration in all that was best and worst in Middleton's polemical divinity: his prose became clearer; his style, more lively; his arguments, more trenchant; his heterodoxy, more evident; his vitriol, more caustic; his frustrations, more evident. To his chagrin, nearly everything that he published after the *Letter to Dr. Waterland* lost Middleton influential friends; gained him influential enemies; and knocked him out of the running for plum preferments. Stung by his inability to gain ecclesiastical posts commensurate with his evident talents, Middleton returned to polemical divinity during the early 1740s after a brief self-imposed period of quiet and he did so with little restraint. 'No man ever had more Ambition to be at the Helm of the Church than poor Dr Middleton', Cole adjudged, '& it is no Sort of Doubt, nor ever was, but that the Disappointments of his view of this Kind, flung him upon writings of this restive Strain'.[21] Middleton's heterodoxy and his disappointment over an unfulfilled career existed in direct proportion to one another.

Conyers Middleton hailed from Yorkshire, where his father served as a non-resident rector in the North Riding.[22] Born in 1683 and brought up in York, he received 'School Learning' (especially Latin and Greek) in the local grammar school.[23] 'The scene of it is laid in a place and age, which are familiar to us from our childhood', Middleton recollected, 'we learn the names of the chief actors at school, and choose our several favourites according to our tempers or fancies; and when we are least able to judge the merit of them, form distinct characters of each, which we frequently retain throughout life'.[24] As his abiding love of the classics endured for the rest of his life, so did his 'Yorkshire dialect very strong in many words', though he returned to his native county only once after his father's death in 1714.[25] Middleton's world, like Waterland's, centred on Cambridge, where he went up in 1699 as a pensioner of Trinity College.[26]

Middleton entered Trinity in the same year that Richard Bentley (1662–1742) moved into the Master's Lodge. The government had appointed Bentley to shake up things in a college whose prestige had plummeted. 'I found the College filled (for the most part) with ignorant, drunken, lewd Fellows and Scholars', Bentley later recalled, 'but in the course of about nine years (wherein I had chosen forty new Fellows, and had quite a new race of scholars), were grown to that deserved fame for discipline, learning, numbers of gentry, improvements of revenue, of public buildings ... that we became the envy, not only of our own, but of the other University'.[27] Many contemporaries and most of posterity reckoned differently.[28] Middleton was one of those forty new fellows chosen by Bentley during his first decade as master. We know little about the education that he received in Bentley's Trinity, though it is unlikely that the reforms in natural philosophy which the new master instituted were complete by the time Middleton took his B.A. in 1703 and his M.A. in 1706. Instead, he would have taken the regular course of studies and examinations pursued by graduates of arts.[29]

The Conyers Middleton who entered into the fellowship of Trinity College in 1705 was a resolute and vocal Tory at a time when 'Church in danger' cries inflamed the nation's politics. Early on, Middleton publicly sided with the Tories against the Whigs, sometimes obnoxiously so. In early July 1710, for instance, Richard Laughton, the militantly Whig senior proctor for Cambridge, walked into The Rose tavern late one evening only to encounter 'a Company of University Men', who, he subsequently reported, 'insulted, & affronted me & the Fellow commoners, & scholars that were with me in a most abusive manner'. Rather than being awed by Laughton when he reminded them of 'the execution of [his] office', the group harangued him and his accompanying 'Myrmidions' and, to taunt them further, toasted to Henry Sacheverell's health. Realizing that he had stumbled on to a scene beyond his control, Laughton prudently retreated. Yet, he reported, 'when we were gone down into the Courtyard there was a Chamber-pot thrown out of their window at us, or Something of that nature. And loud laughing in their Chamber when it was done.' Insulted but undeterred, Laughton that night returned twice to the tavern to instruct the members of the group to return to their colleges, only to be 'treated in a very rude and abusive manner'.[30] The group of young Tories Laughton had come upon at the Rose included future politicians and current Cambridge dons, especially the sarcastic and somewhat threatening Conyers Middleton.[31]

Laughton counted Richard Bentley among his friends, and, just a few months later, Middleton joined with a number of other Trinity College fellows in what would eventually become a two-decade feud with Bentley, who had been brought in to Trinity not just to reform the college but also to help turn around the university's resolutely Tory political culture.[32] During that long-running quarrel, Middleton cut his teeth as a polemicist. His anti-Bentleian performances foreshadowed his later polemical fights, from the perils of publishing anonymously to the risks of hunting overly powerful quarry and of going a bridge too far in pursuit of them. When Middleton defended what he took to be truth, it hurt his career.

Richard Bentley's attempted deprivation of Edmund Miller from his college fellowship served as the proximate cause of the hostilities' commencement. Bentley was eighteenth-century England's greatest classicist and he vigorously promoted natural philosophy at Cambridge. Yet he was a disastrous administrator, at turns vengeful, rapacious, petty and arrogant. He brooked no dissent, gave no quarter, and kept his college in fear. As Miller memorably, if self-servingly, described it, 'when [Bentley] came to College, it was easy to perceive in their Countenances how most of the Fellows were terrified, as well as dissatisfied with what they thought [he] was doing; they scarce spoke to one another, but looked like so many Prisoners which were uncertain whether to expect military Execution, or the favour of Decimation'.[33] In late 1709, Bentley pursued a novel plan to redistribute the college's dividends; the college fellowship, advised by Miller, appealed for help to the college's visitor. Their petition, which Middleton signed, argued that the college fellows had lived in peace before Bentley; after his arrival, though, 'the peace ... was soon disturbed, by his demanding and taking ... several unusual and great sums of money, which he applied to his own use' and by subsequent arrogations of power and college money to himself, including his recent 'alteration ... in their dividends and dues, whereby they are maintained'.[34] Even before the petition, Bentley threatened the fellows who opposed his redistributive plans: 'From henceforward, farewell peace to Trinity College'. He did everything in his power to make that a reality. Once joined officially, the fight between the Bentley and the Miller camps dragged on into the late 1710s, by way of the formal visitorial process and a series of competing, accusatory pamphlets. Middleton dropped away from this initial phase of the fight with Bentley because his 1710 marriage to Sarah Drake required that he resign his fellowship.[35]

In 1717, though, Middleton opened up a new front in the war. Bentley, by then regius professor of divinity, required Middleton and all the other D.D. candidates that year to pay him a four guinea fee. Middleton objected, turning over the money only after Bentley had agreed to refund it if it turned out that the king had not authorized the fee. Since George I had not in fact approved the fee beforehand and since Bentley refused to return Middleton's four guineas, Middleton had Bentley arrested for debt in October 1718. The vice-chancellor's court (led by the Middleton's old friend, the then-resolute Tory Thomas Gooch) subsequently deprived Bentley of his degrees, a ruling which a 'very full' Caput confirmed.[36]

The fight spilled quickly over into print when Arthur Ashley Sykes published a series of pieces in the *St. James's Post* defending Bentley.[37] An Essex rector, Thomas Sherlock's opponent in the Bangorian controversy and a protégé to both Benjamin Hoadly and Samuel Clarke, Sykes focused on procedure and politics in his pro-Bentley letters. Bentley, he argued, had been denied due process by his opponents, who colluded to strip him of his offices. 'The Inquisition abroad, and our Star-Chamber at Home, were never the Instruments of so much Violence, as to Condemn and Punish any Person unheard', he contended, employing the language of persecution common among his theological *confrères*.[38] That Bentley's Cambridge enemies persecuted hardly surprised Sykes since many of them, especially Gooch, held decidedly suspect – that is, Tory – political views. 'But tho' the Majority, which voted the Degradation, was considerable', Sykes suggested, '[Bentley] had the Honour to have for his Friends All that are remarkable for their steady Affections to this Government'.[39] Such provocative charges invited response. Thomas Sherlock, master of St Catharine's College, immediately penned a short pamphlet emphasizing Cambridge's right to self-governance and Bentley's wilful defiance of the university's self-governance. The vice-chancellor's court had justly punished him for that defiance.[40] But Middleton's anonymous contribution to the debate – *A full and impartial account of the late proceedings in the University of Cambridge against Dr. Bentley* – accelerated matters.

Nearly thirty-five years old when he wrote *A full and impartial account*, Middleton began his polemical career with a confident authorial voice, one in which vitriol and elegance existed in easy equipoise. During the next year, he followed up his inaugural performance with three more anonymous anti-Bentley pamphlets, each of which pressed matters farther until at last he went too far and opened himself up to charges that he had disparaged the king's government, charges which the government made him answer at the King's Bench. In these pamphlets, Middleton repeated Sherlock's arguments. But where Sherlock's pamphlet read like a legal indictment, Middleton's read like a character assassination. Bentley, on Middleton's telling, was a disingenuous hypocrite who expected to be treated better than he treated his own subordinates. While Bentley, for instance, bridled at the vice-chancellor's deprivation of his degrees, he had earlier treated Edmund Miller unjustly and had once even expelled a young man from his Trinity fellowship, 'which was at that time the only Subsistence and Income he had in the World, without any previous Notice or Summons, or the least appearance of any Evidence against him, upon the sole Pretence of a common Fame'.[41] Furthermore, Middleton recounted, Bentley insulted his social superiors, even the university's chancellor, the duke of Somerset.[42] 'We may strip [Bentley] of his Titles, but we can never, we see, of his Insolence; he has ceased to be Doctor, and may cease to be Professor, but he can never cease to be Bentley', Middleton concluded. 'There he will triumph over the University to the last; all its Learning being unable to polish, its Manners to soften, or its Discipline to tame the superior Obstinacy of his Genius.'[43]

Middleton got into trouble with the government not because he insulted Bentley but because of his treatment of sensitive political subjects. For one thing, he aggressively defended Cambridge's Tories. Middleton bridled at Sykes's insinuation that Bentley's opponents did not support the Hanoverian regime. Where was the evidence of Cambridge Tory disloyalty, he wondered? Why, if their loyalties were so suspect, did those very same Tories welcome a royal visitation of the university on whatever terms that George I and his ministers desired?[44] Middleton even defended the controversial doctrine of passive obedience. 'It is now one of [Bentley's] Threats to us, that the Passive Obedience of the University will soon be put to the Trial', he contended. '.... Whatever has been condemned as extravagant and ridiculous in that Principle of the Tories, is a tame Submission to our Princes, when acting contrary to the Laws and Constitution of the Realm; a legal Obedience is, I hope, a Duty of Whigs as well as Tories.'[45] This inhabited dangerous polemical ground.

Middleton's ardent and aggressive defence of Cambridge's rights and prerogatives, though, crossed into dangerous legal territory. Middleton overlay his account of the English universities on to the story of post-Reformation English religion and politics. Universities, Middleton claimed, in 'all civilized Nations ... have always been cherished and encouraged by special Favours and Immunities, and distinguished by peculiar Privileges, from all other Corporations whatsoever'. As a result, those universities were not, 'like the Monkish Societies, a Nest of Drones, but have often been compared to a Nest of Hornets, provided with Stings for Such B–ntl–ys as would violate their Privileges, and disturb their Repose'. Even Henry VIII ('so resolute and arbitrary a Monarch, and so impatient of Contradiction') had trodden lightly with Oxford and Cambridge to get them to accept his reforming plans. When Elizabeth I redrafted the universities' statutes during the 1570s, she aimed merely to eliminate popish abuses and to harness the universities' support of the Reformation. Thus, she allowed Oxford and Cambridge near-absolute autonomy to govern themselves. Oliver Cromwell had challenged that self-governance in the 1650s, when his government expelled loyalists from their posts at Cambridge. James II had likewise forced the universities to defend their rights and privileges. After the Glorious Revolution, though, the Williamite government had left the old Elizabethan statutes in force, unchallenged and unchanged.[46] Why, then, would Arthur Ashley Sykes recommend that George I refuse to leave 'us to the quiet Enjoyment of our Charters and Immunities', but instead to 'blow up Church and University in an instant'?[47]

Insinuating that George I might even possibly behave like Oliver Cromwell or James II was ill-advised, but Middleton crossed a clear legal line in *A true account of the present state of Trinity College*, which appeared anonymously in November 1719. That pamphlet focused closely on Bentley's tyrannical management of Trinity College, and it abounded with details known only to an insider. The pamphlet was rife with what Bentley and his supporters deemed to have been 'wicked calumnies, tending to the detriment and dishonour of this flourishing Society'; Bentley reckoned the whole thing 'a false, and malicious, and scandalous libel'.[48] Two paragraphs in which Middleton questioned the administration of justice by the king's government doomed him. 'While the Liberty of an Englishman is so much the Envy of other Nations, and the Boast of our own, that the meanest Peasant knows where to find

Redress for the last Grievance he has to complain of', Middleton claimed, 'it is hardly credible, that a Body of learned and worthy Men, oppressed and injured daily, in everything dear and valuable to them, should not be able to find any proper Court of Justice in the Kingdom that will receive their complaints'.[49] This was enough for Bentley to try to haul up *A true account*'s author before the King's Bench; but it was unclear initially who had written the pamphlet. So, Bentley threatened *A true account*'s bookseller, Thomas Bickerton, with a suit for libel.[50] Middleton initially thought Bentley was bluffing, before soon realizing that he needed to admit his authorship to spare Bickerton, who seemed 'to be a little uneasy at the threatened prosecution'.[51] In early February 1720, Middleton published a letter formally acknowledging his authorship, though, even for some time after that public confession, Bentley pressed his suit against Bickerton.[52] The subsequent legal proceedings against Middleton dragged on for nearly two more years, until in November 1721, a jury found Middleton guilty of libel. While Lord Chief Justice Pratt forced him and Bickerton to pay Bentley's legal costs, Pratt handed down no sentence and scolded Bentley in court. Middleton considered this outcome 'more reputable to me than a fine, [though it] will be also more heavy & expensive'. In the end, he conceded, 'there was no remedy for me, & the Lawyers think it a Triumph to me to have come off as I have done, considering the Scrape I was in'.[53]

While the libel case against him languished in King's Bench, Middleton came at Bentley from another flank. In October 1720, Bentley had published proposals for an edition of the New Testament in Greek and Latin. Bentley had been interested in the project for some time, having noted to William Wake in 1716 that the 'Various Lections' in the extant manuscripts of the Greek New Testament had proved a polemical boon to the Church of England's religious enemies. 'The Papists have made a great use of them against the Protestants, and the Atheists against them both', he assured the new archbishop of Canterbury. Bentley's aim was to 'peruse many of the oldest MSS of the Greek Testament and of the Latin too of St Jerom[e]' in order 'to give an edition as it was in the best exemplars at the time of the Council of Nice[a]'.[54] When he finally came to publish his proposals in late 1720, Bentley fleshed out the method he had originally proposed to Wake four years earlier, though promising that he was 'very sensible, that in the Sacred Writings there's no place for Conjectures or Emendations. Diligence and Fidelity, with some Judgment and Experience, are the Characters here requisite'. His aim, he concluded, was to produce a work '[s]o that the Reader has under one View what the first Ages of the Church knew of the Text; and what has crept into any Copies since, is of no Value or Authority'.[55] Bentley cast his work as a restorative project, one which preserved the original Bible against true Christianity's enemies.[56]

With Bentley's suit against him still at the King's Bench, Middleton could not resist pillorying Bentley's published proposals. Middleton's anonymous pamphlet was part invective, part substantive critique of Bentley's plans. He protested disingenuously that he wrote not from 'Personal Spleen, or Envy of the Author of the Proposals, but by a Serious Conviction that he has neither Talents nor Materials proper for the Work he has undertaken, and that religion is much more likely to receive Detriment than Service from it'. Then he accused Bentley of failing properly to acknowledge the researches of his friend John Walker (1692/3–1741); of trashing the reputation of all previous editors of the Bible, including that of John Mill (1644–1705); and of having a 'slovenly and suspicious Way of quoting Manuscripts'.[57] But Middleton also pointed to serious substantive problems with Bentley's proposals. He argued, for instance, that Origen (*c.* 185–*c.* 254) was not the model of learning amongst the primitive fathers; instead he had produced a text of the New Testament that was riddled with errors, as even his own contemporaries recognized. That was a problem, Middleton pointed out, because Bentley had contended that Origen's New Testament 'was the Standard to the most Learned of the Fathers, at the time of the Council of Nice[a] and two Centuries after.' Furthermore, Middleton continued, Bentley's suggestion that Jerome's Latin Vulgate and the original Greek manuscript of the Bible 'would still be found to agree both in Words and Order of Words' struck him as absurd since he 'could shew from twenty Places of St Jerome, that he never in the least dreamt of confining himself to the Order of Words in any of his Versions'.[58] Likewise, where Bentley thought his critical method could clear up the 'Labyrinth of Thirty Thousand Various Readings, that crowd the Pages of our present Best Editions', Middleton saw something markedly different. 'The Popish Writers indeed say in Defence of [Jerome's Vulgate], that being made in the earliest Ages of Christianity, from the pure Exemplars of those Times, and having continued ever since in the constant Use and Service of the Latin Church, it must needs be of equal Authority to any Greek Copies now extant', Middleton countered. 'And is not our Author here saying and doing much the same thing which we justly condemn in the Church of Rome; undervaluing the Credit of all the Greek Copies; advancing and authorizing the Vulgar Latin, and proving it to be the best means we can use of finding out the true Exemplars of the Ancients?'[59] Bentley's critical method, Middleton intimated, led down a road not to an authentically Protestant Bible but to popery itself.

An infuriated Bentley vitriolically responded to Middleton's anonymous pamphlet with an anonymous piece of his own. In it he fingered a long-disgruntled Trinity College fellow, John Colbatch (1665–1748), as the author of the *Remarks, paragraph by paragraph*, and he insulted Colbatch gratuitously and repeatedly. 'The highest Reputation in Letters, acquired by repeated Proofs, for the space of above Thirty Years, like Jonas's Gourd, is in one Day to be blasted by an Insect', Bentley inveighed. 'Let no body confide or be secure in his Good Name: A Worm, a Maggot without a Name can demolish it in a trice.'[60] Colbatch, though, had not written *Remarks, paragraph by paragraph*, something which gave Middleton and Colbatch an opening to strike back at Bentley.[61] Middleton quickly produced a long, elegant, understated and pointed riposte to Bentley, one which affixed his own name to the title-page and one which contained a declaration from Colbatch that he had not authored *Remarks, paragraph by paragraph*. Middleton's signed reply criticized Bentley's initial proposals and his subsequent defence of them. In addition to fleshing out his previous observations regarding the deficiencies of Bentley's critical method, he added a new line of attack, questioning Bentley's theological orthodoxy. For someone whose professed aim was to defend the Protestant Bible against papists and atheists, Bentley had some dodgy theological views. In particular, Middleton reminded readers of Bentley's 1717 probationary lecture, given upon assuming the regius professorship of divinity. By all accounts, Bentley had dealt in his unpublished *praelectio* with the so-called Trinity proof-text or Johannine comma. He had dealt with it for heterodox ends. 'He has already, we know determined against the Genuineness of the famous Passage of St. John, 1 Epist. v. 7, a Reading, by far the most important of all the thirty thousand; supported by good Authorities, and consonant and agreeable to the Doctrine of the Apostle', Middleton pointed out. 'For what Reason then has he condemned it as spurious? Why because some Manuscripts and some Fathers have omitted it.'[62] Here Middleton simultaneously wrapped himself in orthodoxy's banner and called into question Bentley's theological credibility, a tactic Middleton's own polemical opponents later employed against Middleton.[63]

If Middleton's embrace of Christological orthodoxy in 1721 casts his later heterodoxy in a somewhat different light, so too did his eagerness to use the law to coerce Bentley make the Middleton of the 1730s seem less the virtuous victim than the luckless loser in polemical warfare. Though everyone at the time knew that Bentley had written the anonymous response to *Remarks, paragraph by paragraph*, he had not affixed his name to the title-page, so that his authorship had to be proved. In late February 1721, Laurence Echard reported back to Colbatch that his inquiries suggested that Jacob Tonson, rather than John Knapton, had actually printed the piece and that the manuscript had been 'brought in and managed by a near Relation of B[entley] and of his own Names'.[64] By late March, Middleton had confirmed as much himself, by talking with a few of the major London printers. 'Most people think it proper to get some Evidence against Knapton in order to move for an Information against him next Term', he informed Colbatch, 'but such a Process will perhaps be too chargeable to make it worthwhile'.[65] The difficulties of proceeding against Knapton notwithstanding, Middleton confronted him in person and 'threatened him with an Information, but [could] get nothing from him'. Given Knapton's refusal to buckle before the threat of an information and to admit that Bentley had in fact written the libellous pamphlet, Middleton reckoned that 'it may perhaps be worthwhile to move for an Information against him *in order to fright him & make him squeak if we can*'.[66]

In the end, Middleton dropped the matter, but his private correspondence reveals him as someone no less willing than his polemical opponents to use the law to bully.

Richard Bentley never produced the Greek and Latin New Testament. Whether he abandoned the project because of the Middleton's trenchant critique is unclear.[67] For Conyers Middleton, his inaugural polemical quarrel with Bentley marked a turning pointin his life. He earned a lifetime post as a result of it. In December 1721, Cambridge's anti-Bentley senate installed him in the newly created office of *protobibliothecarius*, a reward in the wake of his recent defeat at the King's Bench. The office, which he held and whose duties he performed mostly desultorily for the rest of his life, carried an income of £50 per annum, provided him unobstructed access to a world-class library and allowed him the leisure to read and write.[68] It also gave him the time to think of how he might retaliate against Bentley. In early 1723, he insinuated in a tract on the university library's organization that Bentley had removed some of the library's most valuable manuscripts to his own lodgings; even more unwisely, he took a thinly veiled swipe at the Court of King's Bench, which had consistently sided with Bentley in his fights with the university.[69] Once again, Bentley pursued Middleton for seditious libel and once again Middleton lost. In June 1723, he got dragged before the King's Bench, briefly imprisoned and forced to pay a £50 fine.[70] Shortly thereafter, Middleton applied to the University for a leave of absence to travel abroad 'for the Recovery of his health & for the viewing of foreign libraries'.[71] In August 1723, he left for the Continent and spent much of the next eight months in Rome, a stay which catalysed changes in the way he looked at the world, changes whose first public inklings were apparent in his *Letter from Rome*, a work published a half-decade after his return to England. That change of worldview doomed his future career prospects and radicalized his thought.

NOTES

1 Waterland to Gibson, 29 December 1730 (LPL, 1741, fol. 78).
2 Waterland to Thomas Bishop, [early 1731] (MCC/MR).
3 Waterland's annotations of *Letter to Dr. Waterland*, n.d. (Bodleian, 8⁰ Rawl. 431 (1), pp. 44, 45, 49, 62).
4 [C. Middleton], *Letter to Dr. Waterland* ((1731): T220974), pp. 5, 45.
5 [Pearce], *Reply to the Letter*, pp. 6, 7.
6 Waterland to Pearce, 21 January 1731 (WAM 64807).
7 J. Dussinger, 'Conyers Middleton (1683–1750)', *ODNB*; H. Trevor-Roper, *History and the Enlightenment* (New Haven, 2010), pp. 71–119; M. Lawrence, 'Conyers Middleton: Polemic Historian' (unpublished Ph.D. thesis, Columbia University, 1970); M. Clarke, 'Conyers Middleton' (TCC, Add. A 298). The most perceptive treatments of Middleton's thought are B. Young, 'Conyers Middleton: The Historical Consequences of Heterodoxy', in J. Robertson and S. Mortimer (eds),

The Intellectual Consequences of Religious Heterodoxy, 1600–1750 (Leiden, 2012), pp. 235–65; T. Stuart-Buttle, 'Classicism, Christianity, and Ciceronian Academic Scepticism from Locke to Hume, c. 1660–c.1760' (D.Phil. thesis, University of Oxford, 2013), pp. 179–218.

8 Cole's account of Conyers Middleton, n.d. (BL, Add. 5933, fols 229, 233; *WC*, XV, p. 315).

9 Waterland to Thomas Bishop, [*c.* 1731] (MCC/MR).

10 Hurd to John Potter, 27 January 1743 (S. Brewer (ed.), *Early Letters of Bishop Richard Hurd, 1739–1762* (Woodbridge, 1995), p. 95).

11 John Green to William Heberden, 28 July 1750 (BL, Add. 32457, fol. 187). See also Warburton to Hurd, 1 September 1750 (*LLEP*, p. 57), which lamented 'the real value of that loss to the Republic of letters ... sustained by Dr. Middleton's death'.

12 J. Grieg (ed.), *Letters of David Hume* (Oxford, 1932), I, p. 3. Cf. I. Rivers, 'Responses to Hume on Religion by Anglicans and Dissenters', *JEH* 52 (2001), pp. 675–95.

13 G. Birckbeck Hill (ed.), *Memoirs of ... Edward Gibbon* (1900), p. 68. Cf. D. Womersley, *Gibbon and the 'Watchmen of the Holy City': The Historian and His Reputation, 1776–1815* (Oxford, 2002), pp. 309–13; J. Pocock, *Barbarism and Religion: Volume 5. Religion: The First Triumph* (Cambridge, 2015), pp. 219–30; B. Young, '"Scepticism in Excess": Gibbon and Eighteenth-Century Christianity', *HJ* 41 (1998), pp. 182–5. B. Young, 'Preludes and Postludes to Gibbon: Variations on an Impromptu by J.G.A. Pocock', *History of European Ideas* 35 (2009), p. 422, rightly warns of the dangers of 'allow[ing] Gibbon to overshadow Middleton, whose significance is not contained by the peculiar effect of his work on one, decidedly atypical, Oxford undergraduate'.

14 E. Gibbon, *Miscellaneous works* (1796: T079697), III, p. 45.

15 Jefferson to John Adams, 22 August 1813 (J. Looney (ed.), *Papers of Thomas Jefferson. Retirement Series* (Princeton, 2010), VI, p. 440).

16 J. Newman, *Apologia Pro Vita Sua and Six Sermons*, ed. F. Turner (New Haven, 2008), p. 144.

17 W. Hudson, *Enlightenment and Modernity: The English Deists and Reform* (2009), pp. 61–71; Trevor-Roper, *History and the Enlightenment*, pp. 71–119; L. Stephen, *History of English Thought in the Eighteenth Century* (1902), pp. 253–73; N. Torrey, *Voltaire and the English Deists* (New Haven, 1930), pp. 154–74, characterize him as a 'deist'. Cf. G. Roberts, 'Historical Argument in the Writings of the English Deists' (Ph.D. thesis, University of Oxford, 2014), pp. 213–15; J. Robertson, 'Hugh Trevor-Roper, Intellectual History and "The Religious Origins of the Enlightenment"', *EHR* 124 (2009), pp. 1389–421; J. van den Berg, 'Should Conyers Middleton (1683–1750), Principal Librarian in Cambridge, Be Regarded as a Deist?', *Notes and Queries* 56 (2009), pp. 255–7; Young, 'Conyers Middleton'; B. Young, *The Victorian Eighteenth Century: An Intellectual History* (Oxford, 2007), pp. 103–47. J.-L. Quantin, *The Church of England and Christian Antiquity* (Oxford, 2009), pp. 2, 26, 380, 408 labels him a 'freethinker'.

18 Cole's annotated copy of Middleton's *Free Inquiry* (BL, shelfmark 4535.h.7, p. v).

19 Francis Hare to Warburton, 9 March 1737 (Kilvert, p. 102).

20 Warburton to Thomas Balguy, 11 February 1752 (HRC, William Warburton II, no. 10).

21 Cole's annotated copy of Middleton's *Free Inquiry*, [*c.* 1779] (BL, shelfmark 4535.h.7, vii).
22 William Middleton (d. 1714) was a pensioner at Clare College, Cambridge (1663–67) and served as rector of Hinderwell (1670–1714) throughout the rest of his career. His first marriage produced one son, William, while his second, to Barbara Place, produced three sons, of whom Conyers Middleton was the oldest. His own tastes and the expense of his children's education left William Middleton impoverished in his last years: *LA*, V, pp. 405–6; *CCED*.
23 William Cole's account of Conyers Middleton (BL, Add. 5833, fol. 232); *AC*, III, p. 184.
24 C. Middleton, *History of Marcus Tullius Cicero* (1741: T125479), I, p. xvi.
25 Cf. Middleton to Elizabeth Montagu, 4 October 1742 (Princeton University Library, Elizabeth Montagu Correspondence, Box 1, Folder 28).
26 Cole's account of Middleton (BL, Add. 5833, fol. 230); *AC*, III, p. 184; *CCED*; Clarke, 'Conyers Middleton', pp. 1–2.
27 Bentley to Thomas Bateman, [1712] (Wordsworth (ed.), *Correspondence*, II, p. 448).
28 G. Trevelyan, *Trinity College: An Historical Sketch* (Cambridge, 1943), p. 56.
29 D. Winstanley, *Unreformed Cambridge* (Cambridge, 1935), pp. 41–57.
30 Laughton's account, n.d. (BL, Add. 32459, fol. 12). See also [S. Thirlby], *University of Cambridge vindicated* (1710: T050500), pp. 21–33; D. Hayton (ed.), *The House of Commons, 1690–1715* (Cambridge, 2002), II, p. 56.
31 'Upon this Mr. M-d-ton of Trinity College, as he is a very Gentile, well bred Man, drew him a Chair and desired him to sit down, telling him, since he intended to honour 'em with his company, and stay as long as they did, he might probably be tired with standing': [Thirlby], *University of Cambridge*, pp. 25–6. Laughton himself recorded that Middleton 'called one of the Scholars that were with me Coxcomb & told him in a threatening manner, that he would take care of him': Laughton's account (BL, Add. 32459, fol. 12). Others there included Cambridge dons – Thomas Gooch, Thomas Paske, Thomas Sherwell, John Chapman (d. 1731) – and Robert Tillotson, along with Tory MPs for Cambridge – Arthur Annesley, Dixie Windsor and John Hynde Cotton.
32 J. Gascoigne, *Cambridge in the Age of Enlightenment* (Cambridge, 1989), pp. 71–114.
33 E. Miller, *Some remarks upon ... Trinity College* (1710: T049385), p. 85.
34 Monk, *Richard Bentley*, I, pp. 251–2. The petition was dated 6 February 1710. Monk recounts Bentley's vendetta against Miller in forensic detail in ibid., I, pp. 241–65, 281–9, 297–306, 256–371, 392–6, 408–20; II, pp. 81–8. In the end, Miller dropped the case in return for having his legal costs of £528 covered. Bentley scandalously had the college pay both Miller's and his own legal costs.
35 Sarah Drake (*c.* 1673–1731), who hailed from Kent and was the widow of Robert Drake (d. 1702), brought into her marriage with the twenty-eight-year-old Middleton 'a large Jointure & good separate Fortune'. Edward Rud, a fellow of Trinity at the time, intimated that Middleton had hid the fact of his marriage so that he could, against college regulations, keep his fellowship for a few months longer. The Middletons lived in a house abutting Gonville and Caius College. Three years after his first wife's death, Conyers Middleton married Mary Place (*c.* 1705–45), a much younger cousin. She was, William Cole reported, 'as odd a

woman as ever existed, except his 1ST [wife] who I don't remember, both of which had pretty strong Claims to a Stall in Bedlam'. Middleton, though, was disconsolate on her death. In 1747, he married Anne Wilkins (d. 1760), widow of an impoverished Bristol bookseller. Cole suggested that perhaps Anne was not wholly faithful to her husband: 'I believe it is much certain, that some young Gentleman of her former Acquaintance, 2 in Particular, whom I remember, came down on a visit, & used very innocently to play at Shuttle-Cock with the Lady in the Dining Room, close to the Theatre, while the good Doctor was writing against the Fathers & Miracles in the Study over Head: little suspecting that without any Miracle he was Danger of being made a Father, without his Participation'. Middleton and his wives were buried in St Michael's Church, Cambridge. Dussinger, 'Conyers Middleton'; Cole's account of Middleton (BL, Add. 5833, fol. 230); William Cole's notes on Conyers Middleton and family, 1745 (BL, Add. 5809, fols 80–3; *WC*, XV, pp. 301–11); E. Luard (ed.), *The Diary (1709–1720) of Edward Rud* (London, 1860), p. 3. For Middleton's thoughts on marriage, see Middleton to Elizabeth Montagu, 17 August 1742 (Huntington Library, MS 1551); same to same, 4 October 1742 (Princeton University Library, Elizabeth Montagu Correspondence, Box 1, Folder 28).

36 Luard (ed.), *Diary*, p. 23.

37 Sykes's letters were dated 12 October, 21 October, 20 November and 27 November 1718. Sykes assembled them together in [Sykes], *Case ... truly stated.* See also J. Stephens, 'Arthur Ashley Sykes (c. 1684–1756)', *ODNB*. A. Starkie, *The Church of England and the Bangorian Controversy, 1716–1721* (Woodbridge, 2007), pp. 53–4, 58, 79–81, 102; E. Carpenter, *Thomas Sherlock, 1678–1761* (London, 1936), pp. 98–100 considers the Sykes–Sherlock debate.

38 [A. Sykes], *Case of Dr. Bentley* (1719: T020014), p. 6.

39 Ibid., p. 9.

40 [T. Sherlock], *Proceedings* ((1719): T109098). Cf. Monk, *Richard Bentley*, II, pp. 66–7, which, uncharacteristically for Monk, slightly mischaracterizes Sherlock's argument.

41 [C. Middleton], *Full and impartial account* (1718: T040294), pp. 26, 27–9.

42 Ibid., p. 30.

43 Ibid., p. 42.

44 Cf. J. Gascoigne, 'Church and State Allied: The Failure of Parliamentary Reform of the Universities, 1688–1800', in A. Beier, D. Cannadine and J. Rosenheim (eds), *The First Modern Society* (Cambridge, 1989), pp. 413–18.

45 [Middleton], *Second part of the full and impartial account* ((1719): T47341), pp. 13–18, 27.

46 Ibid., pp. 18, 19–24.

47 [Middleton], *Some remarks upon a pamphlet*, pp. 10, 11.

48 Bentley's complaint against the anonymous author of *A true account*, co-signed by six other Trinity senior fellows, is reprinted in Monk, *Richard Bentley*, II, pp. 93–4.

49 [Middleton], *True account*, p. 5.

50 J. Feather, 'The English Book Trade and the Law, 1695–1799', *Publishing History* 12 (1982), pp. 59–63; C. Kropf, 'Libel and Satire in the Eighteenth Century', *ECS* 8 (1974–5), pp. 153–68.

51 Middleton to John Colbatch, 13 December 1719 (TCC, B.17.15).
52 Middleton's formal declaration is reprinted in Monk, *Richard Bentley*, II, pp. 95–6; Middleton to Colbatch, 14 May 1720 (TCC, B.17.15).
53 Middleton to Colbatch, 25 November 1721 (TCC, B.17.15).
54 Bentley to Wake, 15 April 1716 (Wordsworth (ed.), *Correspondence*, II, p. 503).
55 [R. Bentley], *Dr. Bentley's proposals* (1721: T086196), p. 4.
56 K. Haugen, *Richard Bentley: Poetry and Enlightenment* (Cambridge, MA, 2011), pp. 187–210; J. Sheehan, *The Enlightenment Bible: Translation, Scholarship, Culture* (Princeton, 2005), pp. 46–9; D. Katz, *God's Last Words: Reading the English Bible from the Reformation to Fundamentalism* (New Haven, 2004), pp. 185–204.
57 [C. Middleton], *Remarks, paragraph by paragraph* (1720: T086622), pp. 3, 4–6, 15.
58 Ibid., 9; [Bentley], *Dr. Bentley's proposals*, pp. 3, 4.
59 [Middleton], *Remarks, paragraph by paragraph*, p. 12.
60 [Bentley], *Dr. Bentley's proposals*, p. 10.
61 Some thought Bentley knew full well that Colbatch had not written *Remarks, paragraph by paragraph* but had aspersed him nonetheless: 'I was misled, viz., that Bentley had mistaken his adversary, and fallen foul on Dr. Colebatch [*sic*]: whereas, that varlet did – not mistake him, but – knowingly and wittingly take an opportunity to fall foul on the Doctor with the most scurrilous and abusive language Bentley himself, the master of ribaldry, could invent': Thomas Tudway to Matthew Prior, 29 January 1721 (HMC, *Calendar of the Manuscripts of the Marquis of Bath, ... at Longleat, Wiltshire. Vol. III*, p. 496). See also [Middleton], *Remarks, paragraph by paragraph*, preface.
62 C. Middleton, *Some farther remarks, paragraph by paragraph* (1721: T086204), p. 15. See also Katz, *God's Last Words*, pp. 193–4; Haugen, *Richard Bentley*, pp. 194–205; R. Iliffe, 'Friendly Criticism: Richard Simon, John Locke, Isaac Newton and the *Johannine Comma*', in A. Hessayon and N. Keene (eds), *Scripture and Scholarship in Early Modern England* (Aldershot, 2006), pp. 137–57; J. Levine, *The Autonomy of History: Truth and Method from Erasmus to Gibbon* (Chicago, 1999), pp. 157–240.
63 Edmund Gibson thought highly of Middleton's *Remarks, paragraph by paragraph*: Laurence Echard to John Colbatch, 25 February 1721 (BL, Add. 22908, fol. 121).
64 Ibid. [Bentley], *Dr. Bentley's proposals*, title-page states that it was 'Printed for J. Knapton at the Crown in St. Paul's Church-Yard'.
65 Middleton to Colbatch, 30 March 1721 (TCC, B.17.15). An *information* was a legal move, distinguished from an indictment, by which one party identified another as having breached a penal law or statute: G. Jacob, *New law-dictionary* (1729: T137460), unpaginated ('Information').
66 Middleton to Colbatch, April 1721 (TCC, B.17.15). Emphasis mine.
67 D. Katz, *God's Last Words: Reading the English Bible from the Reformation to* Fundamentalism (New Haven, 2004), p. 200.
68 D. McKitterick, *A History of Cambridge University Press* (Cambridge, 1992), II, pp. 168–86.
69 C. Middleton, *Bibliothecæ Cantabrigiensis* (1723: T021630). See also Monk, *Richard Bentley*, II, pp. 199–202.

70 J. Monk, *The Life of Richard Bentley* (1833), II, pp. 201–2; Middleton to Colbatch, 15 June 1723 (TCC, B.17.16).

71 Quoted in D. McKitterick, *Cambridge University Library: A History. The Eighteenth and Nineteenth Centuries* (Cambridge, 1986), p. 174.

Chapter 7

Conversing … with the ancients: Rome and the Bible

'Much Leisure, with an infirm State of Health, was the Cause of my Journey to Italy', Middleton informed the readers of his *Letter from Rome* (1729).[1] The Grand Tour was an established part of the English gentleman's education for life.[2] While in Italy, Middleton met prominent Italian antiquarians, including Francesco Bianchini (1662–1729) and Giusto Fontanini (1666–1736), as well as local dealers in antiquities, including Francesco de' Ficoroni (1664–1747), who obtained objects for Middleton, which he much later sold to Horace Walpole.[3] He also had Giovanni Pozzi (1670–1752) produce for him a classically inspired medallion, with his own image on the front and a library with the bust of Minerva on the reverse.[4] During his time abroad Middleton broadened the scope of his scholarly vision and contacted Italian scholars with whom he corresponded after his return to England.[5] During his travels he also developed a view of Christian antiquity at odds with the mainstream orthodox one.

This chapter details the evolution of Middleton's views and the consequences of that evolution. It anatomizes the arguments of his *Letter from Rome*, highlighting their latently heterodox implications. It shows how the *Letter from Rome*'s latent heterodoxy became manifest in Middleton's *Letter to Dr. Waterland* (1730). Finally, it details the ways that his attacks on Daniel Waterland destroyed his relationship with his patron (Edward Harley, second earl of Oxford) and permanently damaged his career prospects.

Middleton explained that he had planned, while in Rome, 'to visit the genuine Remains of venerable Relics of Pagan Rome; the authentic Monuments of Antiquity that demonstrate the Certainty of those Histories, which are the Entertainment, as well as the Instruction of our Younger Years'. Yet despite his 'original Intention of conversing solely or chiefly with the Ancients', the striking similarities between pagan and Roman Catholic rites struck Middleton profoundly. Indeed, he argued, the Catholic Church had baldly appropriated 'the Rituals of Primitive Paganism, as if handed down by an uninterrupted Succession from the Priests of Old to the Priests of the New Rome'.[6] Middleton proposed to trace for his readers 'the true Spring and Source of those Impostures, which, under the Name of Religion, have been forged ... for no other Purpose, than to oppress the Liberty, as well as engross the Property of Mankind'. What particularly distinguished Middleton's analysis, he argued, was that he had 'grounded [it] on Facts, which I have been the Witness to myself, and which others, perhaps, had not the Opportunity of examining personally, or considering so particularly as I have done'. Furthermore, he had, 'for each Article charged on the Church of Rome ... generally produced such Vouchers, as they themselves will allow to be authentic'.[7] He conjoined his travel narrative with a historical one about the primitive Church.

In his *Letter from Rome*, Middleton detailed precisely what the Church of Rome had got from ancient pagan religions. Almost no Protestant could have objected to most of his examples of popish appropriations from paganism – the use of incense, holy water, lamps, candles and offerings, for instance.[8] But in at least four areas of his *Letter*, Middleton dealt with slippery subjects. Firstly, while he declaimed the worship of idols ('Images of the Dead'), he ran the antiquarian risk of reducing all religious rites merely to functional, political acts devoid of any independent spiritual worth or efficacy.[9] Secondly, while he enumerated the 'pretended Miracles, and pious Frauds of the Church of Rome' and traced 'them all to the same Source of Paganism', his analysis invited the question whether other – perhaps even *all* – Christian miracles might have been faked.[10] Thirdly, his conception of the priesthood implicitly questioned the Church of England's official doctrine regarding its priesthood's nature and organization.

> In their very Priesthood they [i.e., the Church of Rome] have contrived ... to keep up as near a Resemblance as they could to that of Pagan Rome. And the Sovereign Pontiff, instead of deriving his Succession from St. Peter ... may with more Reason and much better Plea for the Power he enjoys, style himself the Successor of the Pontifex Maximus, or Chief Priest of old Rome; whose Authority and Dignity was the greatest in the Republic; and who was looked upon as the Arbiter or Judge of all things, Civil as well as Sacred, Human as well as Divine.[11]

Protestants agreed that the bishop of Rome's claims to temporal and spiritual authority were bogus. But the Church of England – like the Church of Rome – had an episcopal ecclesiology: was that too borrowed from pagan Roman practice? Or, at the very least, did English priests conceive of their roles in much the same way as had pagan priests? Was the Church of England a proponent not of true religion but of priestcraft?[12] Finally, Middleton pointedly refused to offer a chronology of Christian corruption.

> I shall not trouble myself with inquiring at what time, and in what manner these several Corruptions were introduced into the Church, whether they were contrived by the intrigues and Avarice of Priests, who found their Advantage in reviving and propagating Impostures which had been of old so profitable to their Predecessors:

> or whether the Genius of Rome was so strongly turned to Fanaticism and Superstition that they were forced, in Condescension to the Humour of the People, to accommodate and dress up their new Religion to the Modes and Fopperies of the old one.[13]

This, again, raised questions. Had the rot that Middleton had identified in the Church of Rome set in during the first few centuries of the primitive Church? And if so, did that itself not suggest that the Church of England's claims to primitive purity were perversely claims to primitive impurity? Middleton's take on these questions became clearer during the 1730s, but readers at the time mostly applauded the *Letter from Rome*'s exposure of Roman Catholic imposture, idolatry and priestcraft.[14] The anonymous reviewer in the *Present State of the Republick of Letters* judged it 'much the best book that has yet appeared on this subject; wrote in so exact and judicious a manner, and in so elegant and fine a taste, as may justly discourage others from copying or writing after him upon this argument'.[15]

Almost immediately after returning from Rome, Middleton started raising money for a trip back. He sold manuscripts that he had collected there to Edward Harley, second earl of Oxford (1689–1741).[16] Harley was Robert Harley's (1661–1724) only son and heir both to his fortune and to his library. By 1715, the library contained 3000 books, 13,000 charters and 1000 rolls. By 1721, the collection had grown to 6000 books and 14,000 manuscripts. By Edward Harley's death in 1742, the Harleian library included 50,000 books, 350,000 pamphlets and 41,000 prints. After his father's death, Edward Harley housed the books at Wimpole Hall (a dozen miles south-west of Cambridge) and the manuscripts in London (at the family's Dover Street residence). He owned England's largest private library at the time, with a collection spanning from antiquity to the present. Edward Harley had less taste for public affairs than his father. Instead, he poured his energy into building up the library's collections and to patronizing artists, architects and authors.[17] Given its proximity to the university, Wimpole became a gathering place for Cambridge antiquarians.[18]

Thomas Baker (1656–1740) was one of the antiquarians who frequented Wimpole.[19] Middleton, part of Baker's circle, later recollected that he and his friends ('learned Men') used also regularly to gather together at the university library ('my Library') 'to pass the Evening ..., according to Custom, as well in familiar as learned Discourses'. The nonjuring Baker 'used not only to be present at these our Assemblies, but even to preside, on Account of that Knowledge of Antiquity, in which he transcends all others'.[20] Baker was also Harley's close scholarly confidant, and by 1726 Middleton was ferrying letters and packages of books and manuscripts for him out to Wimpole.[21] It signalled his own entry into the ranks of Harley's friends and clients.

Middleton had angled for admission into the Harley circle for nearly a decade. It was a natural fit, since his and Harley's political sympathies and intellectual interests aligned closely.[22] Yet Middleton's pursuit of Harley was sometimes painfully awkward. By 1721 he was sending copies of his published work to him, while, just before his trip to Rome in 1723, Harley's librarian, Humfrey Wanley, recorded in his diary, 'Dr Mid[d]leton came & tarried above two Hours in talking about Library-affairs; and renewing his Offer to serve my Lord in his Travels'.[23] In late 1724, when Middleton was again trying to drum up funds to get back to Rome, he promised Harley, 'I shall look upon myself only as a kind of Agent of yours, since next to the advantage I hope for to my health I shall have no pleasure so great as that of collecting such Curiosities as may be found worthy of a place in your Lordship's Cabinet'.[24] Middleton never returned to Rome, but from the mid-1720s he regularly visited Wimpole, dining with the family; selling Harley manuscripts and other antiquities; trading political and academic gossip; and using the Harleian library. In Wimpole's library he wrote the work that won him the orthodox's enmity and lost him Harley's friendship.

Middleton had used the Harleian library before, most notably for research on medicine in ancient Rome. The resulting pamphlets assailed Richard Bentley's close friend, the eminent physician Richard Mead (1673–1754). In 1723, Mead had used the occasion of his annual Harveian Lecture to the Royal College of Physicians to brag that physicians had been esteemed in ancient Greece and Rome.[25] Middleton countered that doctors in ancient Rome had been slaves and that 'the Art of Physic was not only less cultivated in the Times of the old Romans, but even unknown'.[26] Middleton had the better of the argument, one which he continued to prosecute until Harley arranged a peaceful truce between him and Mead at Wimpole.[27] No one, alas for Middleton, later mediated between him and Harley after his authorship of the *Letter to Dr. Waterland* became public knowledge.

Before publishing his *Letter to Dr. Waterland*, Middleton had dealt in print either with entirely secular matters (like ancient medicine or Richard Bentley's tyrannical mastership) or with seemingly innocuous religious ones (like pagano-papism). In attacking Waterland, Middleton traded safe polemical turf for parlous ground, something he clearly recognized. 'I send you the papers Your Lordship observed me so busied about in Your Library', he wrote to Harley in late November 1730, '& take the liberty to beg your perusal of them & opinion whether it will be advisable for me to print them, as I have an inclination to do, without my name, in the expectation of lying effectually concealed; but in this as in all other cases shall be glad to determine myself by your judgment'.[28] Evidently Harley did not advise halting publication, and the *Letter* appeared in print in late December 1730. That Harley did not counsel Middleton to scuttle its publication altogether surprises since nearly everything about the *Letter* seemed calculated to upset the orthodox, from its interpretative method to its denigration of ancient Jewish learning to its take on civil religion to its derision of dogmatism and orthodoxy. The latent heterodoxy of Middleton's *Letter from Rome* became glaringly obvious to most contemporaries in the *Letter to Dr. Waterland*, a pamphlet occasioned by the September 1730 appearance of Waterland's anti-Tindal *Scripture Vindicated*.

Fully to appreciate the *Letter to Dr. Waterland* and Middleton's three sequel pamphlets requires understanding what Middleton thought he was doing in them; what he actually did in them; and how his contemporaries interpreted what he did in them. Middleton's *Letter to Dr. Waterland* was the product of a stridently Protestant Erasmian, a Christian sceptic, one for whom the conjoined twins of orthodoxy and dogmatism were anathema, but one who never saw himself as anything other than a believing Christian.[29] Most of Middleton's contemporaries either ignored or discounted his Christian scepticism, though. The *Letter to Dr. Waterland* fell into two parts. The first focused on Waterland's reasoning; the second spelled out how Waterland might more effectively have responded to Matthew Tindal's *Christianity as Old as the Creation*. Middleton's critical treatment of Waterland and of orthodox apologetics more generally took up the bulk of the pamphlet. Not unnaturally his contemporaries placed the greatest weight on that part of the work, largely ignoring his concluding criticisms of Tindal's 'blunders of history'; 'his inconsistency with himself'; his 'malice to the Clergy'; and his 'obstinate perseverance in errors'. Yet what drove Middleton to excoriate Waterland's method of reasoning was his frustration with Waterland's ineffective rebuttal of Tindal. On his own telling, Middleton unequivocally rejected Tindal's argument that 'the Christian Religion is nothing else but a Republication of the Law of Nature, and cannot be true and obligatory any farther, than as it corresponds entirely with that original Law'. In Waterland's *Scripture Vindicated*, Middleton had hoped to find one of the Church of England's most prominent theologians exposing the fundamental flaws of Tindal's reasoning. Instead he thought Waterland had mischaracterized Tindal's work – 'Such a disingenuous way of forming an indictment must needs appear odious not only to the enemies, but much more to the true friends of a Religion' – and had employed a method of reasoning which weakened belief in the Bible. The results, Middleton insisted, crippled the cause of true religion. For if Waterland's *Scripture Vindicated* failed in its apologetical aims, it would 'expose the Scripture itself to contempt; give a real triumph to its enemies; confirm them in their infidelity; and inject probably new scruples where none had been entertained before'.[30]

Middleton's dispute with Waterland centred on how properly to interpret Christianity's foundational and most primitive source, the Bible. The Middleton–Waterland hermeneutical contretemps distinguished itself from the Tindal–Waterland one: the latter dealt fundamentally with God's nature, the former, with how to interpret God's instructions to humankind. Waterland, Middleton argued, had misunderstood the Bible for two reasons. Firstly, he had argued only from external evidences. Even worse, Waterland had interpreted the Bible's contents literally, focusing solely upon 'the external evidence of the fact' rather than correlating the historical record with 'the internal merit of its doctrines'. This, Middleton contended, was 'beginning at the wrong end; since 'tis allowed on all hands, that if any narration can be shewn to be false; any doctrine irrational or immoral; tis not all the external evidence in the world that can or ought to convince us, that such a doctrine comes from God'.[31] Waterland would have protested that he was not a strict literalist. But Middleton targeted examples of Waterland's literalism in *Scripture Vindicated.* In particular, Middleton subjected the biblical accounts of the Fall, circumcision and Babel to close scrutiny and asked if they made literal sense. Where Waterland treated the biblical account of the Fall literally, for instance, Middleton countered 'that all Commentators whatsoever are forced in some measure to desert the letter, in order to make the story rational and credible'.[32] Even Waterland had to. The Bible, after all, makes no mention of the Devil, yet Waterland had posited that 'the Deceiver was a real Serpent, actuated by the Devil'. Furthermore, Middleton continued, it would have made no sense for the Devil to assume the form of a snake since it is 'natural to be jealous and on guard against the counsels, to distrust all offers of kindness of the subtle and malicious: so that an Ass or a Dove must needs have been a fitter engine for Satan, under the disguise of folly or innocence, to have insinuated his poison by'. The difficulties with the biblical account of the Fall did not end there, for even if the Devil had tried to tempt Eve, why did God not 'interpos[e], in so unequal a conflict'? No literal answer readily offered itself. Middleton suggested, however, that recourse should be made to allegory, with Adam representing 'reason of the mind of man; ... Eve, the flesh or outward senses; [and] the Serpent, lust or pleasure'. The 'true causes of man's fall and degeneracy' then become evident: '... as his mind, through the weakness and treachery of his senses, became captivated and seduced by the allurements of lust and pleasure, he was driven by God out of Paradise; that is, lost and forfeited the happiness and prosperity which he had enjoyed in his innocence'. All of this, Middleton concluded, made the story of the Fall 'intelligible and rational; agreeable not only to the common notions and tradition of history, but to the constant and established method of God's Providence'.[33] In this, Middleton assured his readers, he followed the interpretative lead of 'several of the Ancients', including Augustine of Hippo.

Middleton likewise tried to demonstrate that the biblical accounts of circumcision and of Babel strained credulity. To prove this he cited as his authorities not just reason but patristic sources. The divine injunction to circumcise, for instance, contravened both scholarship and probability. All authorities 'that can be called unprejudiced, and whose credibility cannot be liable to suspicion either of malice or partiality in the case' (from Herodotus to Strabo, from Diodorus Siculus to Josephus, from John Marsham to John Spencer) agreed that the Egyptians had circumcised long before the Mosaic injunction. Reason buttressed these scholarly authorities. Were not the Jews 'an obscure contemptible people, famed for no kind of literature; scarce known to the polite world, till the Roman Empire dispersed them; and then the more despised for being known'? Were not the Egyptians, by contrast, a remarkably learned people? Why would the Egyptians 'valuing themselves so much on their wisdom, ... borrow so remarkable a custom from a Nation they always hated and despised'? Or was it not more reasonable to reckon 'that the Lawgiver of a petty infant State should copy that, as well as many other of his constitutions, from the practice of a great and flourish [*sic*] Kingdom?' Just as the biblical account of circumcision's institution seemed implausible to Middleton, so too did the literal biblical account of Babel contravene the scholarly consensus on the origin of languages, which located the cause 'in reason and nature; in the necessary mutability of human things; the rise and fall of States and Empires; change of modes and customs, which necessarily introduce a proportionable change in language'. What gave particular credibility to those scholarly arguments regarding the profusion of languages was that they were 'grounded on fact, and the testimony of history'.[34]

In addition to highlighting the inadequacies of literalist biblical hermeneutics, Middleton argued for civil religion's necessity. Natural religion, he noted, had never been sufficient in ancient societies to serve as a nation's moral guide: 'there never was a nation in the world, whose public Religion was formed upon the plan of Nature, and instituted on the principles of mere Reason: but that all Religions have ever derived their Authority from the pretence of a Divine Original, and a Revelation from Heaven'. Indeed, he continued, even when the 'Moralists of the Heathen World ... clearly saw the cheat and forgery of the established Religion', they nevertheless 'always persuade and recommend a submission to it; well knowing what mischief must needs befall the State by the subversion of constitutions so greatly reverenced by the people'. The truth of a civil religion mattered not; that it was a civil religion was what counted.[35] An irritated Waterland later accused Middleton of having argued for a 'practical Hobbism ... He could be an Episcopalian in England, a Presbyterian in North Britain, a Calvinist at Geneva, a Lutheran at Leipsic, a Papist at Rome, a Mahometan at Constantinople'.[36]

Middleton concluded his *Letter to Dr. Waterland* as he had begun it, chastising both the orthodox and Daniel Waterland. He admitted that he had 'used expressions of sharpness and severity', protesting that he did so not out of envy of Waterland but out of 'an indignation raised in me to see you dictate so arbitrarily, and decide so dogmatically in points of the utmost difficulty and uncertainty; and in questions where hardly two Commentators have ever agreed in the same solution, condemn all objections as slight and trivial'. The 'right orthodox Divine', he contended, embraced difficult solutions rather than clean, reasonable answers to theological conundrums: 'nothing easy will go down with him; nothing but the marvelous and the improbable will please him; and the good old principle *credo quia impossible*, is with him the only touchstone of a true saving Faith'.[37] This, though, was not the sneer of the atheistic freethinker but the frustration of one Christian with another.

All he aimed to do in his *Letter*, he insisted, was to strengthen Christianity against its foes:

> 'Tis not my design to destroy or weaken any thing but those senseless systems and prejudices, which some stiff and cloudy Divines will needs fasten to the body of Religion, as necessary and essential to the support of it. For in this age of Scepticism, where Christianity is so vigorously attacked, and as it were closely besieged, the true way of defending it, is not to enlarge the compass of its fortifications, and make more help necessary to its defence, than it can readily furnish; but like skilful Engineers, to demolish its weak outworks, that serve only for shelter and lodgment to the enemy, whence to batter it the more effectually, and draw it within the compass of its firm and natural entrenchments, which will be found in the end impregnable.[38]

Middleton surely intended to deflect the increasingly intense criticism of him. Yet he seemed genuinely bewildered, since he thought that he had defended Christianity, not undermined it.

Responses to the *Letter to Dr. Waterland* were uniformly negative, even before people discovered Middleton had written it.[39] Almost no one at the time sided with the *Letter* writer, so that Middleton fended off all-comers without the support from allies.[40] Waterland distilled Middleton's 'hypothesis' to three points: '1. That all traditional religion is mere invention. 2. That the invention came from Egypt. 3. That nevertheless it is necessary to have some traditional religion, that the world may be kept in order.'[41] Waterland framed the ensuing debate, perhaps not least because Waterland advised some of Middleton's disputants. He also identified some important orthodox anxieties regarding the nature of Christianity's most primitive source (the Bible) and the intentions of its first author, Moses.[42] The stakes were significant: as William Berriman (1688–1750) noted, 'The Revelation of Moses was that system of religion, under which the Jewish state was erected and continued. It was under the influence and persuasion of its divine authority, that the Prophetick writings of the Old Testament were constantly delivered. It is attested and appealed to in the New Testament, as the undoubted Word of God.'[43] Yet Middleton's 'hypothesis' destabilized this Mosaic revelation. Had Moses, for instance, been divinely inspired when writing the book of Genesis? Did all that he included in Genesis come straight from God? Or did he borrow from the Egyptians? Or had he even invented things for the good of his people? The first task of the orthodox was to re-establish Moses' divine inspiration and his historical accuracy.[44] As Berriman explained, 'Nor can we maintain [Moses'] Inspiration as a Lawgiver, without asserting it first as an Historian, since it is upon the Credit of his History, that the Divine Authority of his Laws must be established'. Others, like Philip Williams, defended the proposition that the Pentateuch was 'written either by the immediate suggestions of the Spirit of God, or guarded by his divine superintendence from all errors and mistakes either of facts, reasoning, or doctrine'.[45]

Middleton explicitly embraced a 'general belief of the Divine Origin and Inspiration of the Books of the Old and New Testament: a Doctrine too clearly delivered in the Scriptures, to be doubted of and called in question by any one, who lays claim to that title [of Christian]'.[46] Though he conceded that he was 'far from thinking every Tittle in the Holy Scriptures to be inspired', he acknowledged that it was 'a Point fundamental and necessary to be believed by all Christians, that whilst a Man is under the actual Influence and Direction of the Holy Ghost, he must at the same time be infallible and superior to all Error; or else Christianity cannot be defended'.[47] This did not mean that *all* of the Bible was divinely inspired.[48] Nor did it mean that Moses was always under the Holy Ghost's direction and influence when writing. When arguing this, Middleton claimed to follow the ancient Jewish historian Josephus (b. AD 37), who had contended that Moses was a wise lawgiver, in the manner of Minos or Lycurgus, not a consistently divinely inspired lawgiver. '[W]hereas the modern Advocates of Christianity insist, that every word of the Mosaic writings must be received as divinely inspired; every act of Moses as miraculously directed from heaven', Middleton posited, 'my opinion is, that with the notion of general Inspiration, which I readily allow, we are obliged by fact and the history itself, to admit a distinction and exception, in some particular passages of the Law; some particular acts of its Founder.'[49]

This idea of partial or general inspiration raised another thorny question: how should one read the Bible? Waterland recognized that the answer to this question mattered, since Protestantism's central doctrine of *sola scriptura* was impossible without a stable and agreed-upon hermeneutic. The controversy over *Christianity as Old as the Creation* had exposed the faultlines between 'deists' and the orthodox regarding biblical hermeneutics. When Tindal had argued that parts of the Bible contravened natural religion and, hence, were untrue, Waterland had countered in *Scripture Vindicated* that the Bible truthfully recorded history. Reason, reckoned Waterland, might be able to take us some way towards the truth, but only the Bible articulated the revealed Christian doctrine necessary for salvation. Furthermore, historical proofs showed that God's revelations were true. In his *Letter to Dr. Waterland*, Middleton waded into this battle on the side of neither combatant. Instead, he offered a third way, one which accepted Christian revelation but one which argued that the Bible must not be read as a literal account of the historical record because its history was often incomplete, contradictory or, at times, even irrational. An avowed, if sceptical, Christian like Middleton posed a greater threat to orthodoxy than the 'deist' Tindal, since he wrote from within the establishment. Waterland articulated the problem succinctly to Edmund Gibson: 'They that most scrupulously adhere to the literal construction, argue thus: that if we prefer an Allegorical Sense from a seeming indecency of Action, or acting below character, the Adversary may push it farther, and turn it against the Part which the Son of God acted in the Redemption: whereas the justifying such a dispensation towards the Prophets before, might be a sort of preparatory Apology for the Humiliation of God the Son'. However, he realized that 'if we adhere too Scrupulously, in such cases, to the Letter, The danger is of the Adversary's turning it to ridicule, and playing it in so lively and forcible a manner, that it may be hard to withstand it'.[50] Orthodox polemical divines had to defend a literalist hermeneutics while acknowledging that there were complementary ways of reading the scriptures. Edward Underhill, for instance, conceded that many ancient writers 'did, by way of allegory, and in a figurative Manner, make use of real Facts, the better to illustrate moral Truths'; but, he continued, they 'never intended anything to the Prejudice of real Facts, nor by their allegorical Use of them, do anything that might be of the Detriment to the Letter'. Similarly, Philip Williams contended that it did not alter the Bible's truth if some primitive writers 'in order to vindicate scripture, thought it necessary, in some cases, to recur to allegory'. Another respondent awkwardly tried to turn Augustine against Middleton, cherry-picking a quotation from the bishop of Hippo's *Against the Epistle of Manichaeus* in which Augustine merely had not foreclosed the possibility of an authentic, historically accurate literal reading of the whole of the Bible.[51]

Middleton retorted that, if the Bible is to be Protestantism's bedrock, a standard, consistently applicable interpretative method is needed. 'Now is it not more rational to follow one uniform, consistent way of Interpretation, than to jump at every step so arbitrarily from Letter to Allegory: and if the Letter be found in fact contradictory to Reason and the notions we have of God, what is there left us but to recur to Allegory?', he asked rhetorically, 'for which we have the authority of the Primitive Fathers, and the best Jewish Writers: and the allegorical way of expounding was so far from giving scandal in former ages of the Church, that on the contrary, to fight it was looked upon as heretical and full of dangerous consequences'.[52] Reading the Bible in this way made it more rational because it was not the case, as orthodox polemical divines had argued, 'that the truth of the Gospels stands on the same bottom with every other historical truth in the world'.[53] That literalist interpretative method worked only if the Bible is 'of the same class and species with other histories; a narration of facts by credible persons, who knew them to be true, and related what they knew of them'. But the Scriptures were at the very least the partially inspired Word of God, not straightforward histories, something which only added to the interpretative difficulty. To make sense of the Bible one needed not just to read it in different registers but to read it with a view to what was reasonable, for, as Cicero had proved long ago, 'our belief or opinion of things ought not to depend on Testimony or Authority, but on the weight and moment of Reasons'.[54] This view echoed John Locke's on the relationship of reason to revelation. In his *Essay Concerning Human Understanding* (1689), a copy of which Middleton owned, Locke argued that 'Credibility' is conferred either by 'Common Observation in like cases' or 'particular Testimonies in that particular instance'. Neither source, of course, is infallible and at times 'Testimonies contradict common Experience, and the reports of History and Witnesses contradict the ordinary course of Nature, or with one another'. In such an event, the contradiction may be resolved by 'nicely weighing every particular Circumstance'.[55] When faced with the Genesis descriptions of the Fall, the profusion of languages after the fall of the tower of Babel and the divine institution of circumcision, Middleton reckoned that only allegory made them reasonable. An orthodox task when rebutting Middleton's *Letter* was to show that a literalist reading of the Fall, Babel and circumcision was both true and sufficient.

The literal interpretation of the Fall, Middleton later noted, 'has been a perpetual source of doubts and difficulties to the best Commentators; and of raillery and ridicule to the enemies of revealed religion in all ages'.[56] His opponents sought to make it literally explicable, though. Zachary Pearce acknowledged that, while many had imputed 'a mystical Meaning' to the serpent's deception of Eve, 'still the Story itself in all the Parts of it lies open and plain; still it is Literally true, that such a Sentence was pronounced by God'. The fact that the Devil acted through the serpent did not render the literal story false, nor did the fact that many of the primitive fathers interpreted the Fall allegorically undermine the Genesis account's literal truth.[57] Others, likewise, tried to prove that the Devil worked through the snake to deceive Eve. 'For the Serpent considered as a Beast only, could know nothing of God's Command concerning the eating the forbidden Fruit, neither could he reason with Eve about it', one anonymous author argued. 'Nor could the Devil himself have done so, but under some visible Shape; it being impossible for any Spiritual or Invisible Being, any Angels, either good or bad, to converse with Men, without assuming, or clothing themselves with something that shall be visible.' This, he assured his readers, is both evident in the Scriptures and 'what our Reason and the Nature of Things convince us, that they must necessarily do'.[58]

Middleton's take on the Genesis account of the profusion of languages after the Tower of Babel's fall also got picked at by his orthodox critics. Where Middleton argued that natural causes adequately accounted for the variegations of human languages, his orthodox opponents countered that those variegations had miraculous origins.[59] Zachary Pearce asserted that the multiplicity of languages proved that they were divinely produced and he instanced a number of common words 'which have not the least Affinity with one another, no not so much as in one Radical Letter'. The English word *bread*, for example, was *lechen* in Hebrew, *artos* in Greek and *panis* in Latin. Examples like this led Pearce to conclude that natural causation insufficiently explained the profusion of human languages, since 'Natural Causes could only have produced at most some Alteration of the Sounds, not entirely new Sounds: For what could tempt Men to create New Words, when they had Old ones before for the very same purpose?'[60] John Chapman dealt with the issue of language in his anti-Middleton pamphlet, arguing that while the 'three last Denominations and Kinds may admit of a certain Date, and Historical Deduction of Men of Letters, yet the first sort, the Ancient and Primitive Language of Italy and the Parts adjacent, stands still unoriginated without any particular Era, Cause, and Account fix'd to it'. Indeed, he continued, it is only relatively modern languages or their variants which can be accounted for by natural causes and which 'subsisted in the Room of others more Ancient and pure'. Those pure languages of the greatest antiquity miraculously emerged straight from God.[61]

Middleton's critics similarly charged him with misreading the historical record regarding circumcision's origins. He contended that the Jews had got circumcision from the Egyptians and that it was not, in consequence, a divinely ordained practice. This called into question the Mosaic laws' divine origin. Admittedly, seventeenth-century authors, such as John Spencer (1630–93) and John Marsham (1602–85), had argued that God had worked through natural causes – including through the assimilation of Egyptian practices – to achieve his providential purposes with the Jews.[62] But figures as disparate as Isaac Newton and Daniel Waterland rejected this as wrong-headed: Newton believed that Egyptian influence had corrupted true religion, while Waterland held that God had divinely instituted signal Jewish religious practices, circumcision included. Those who came to Waterland's defence in the aftermath of the *Letter* followed his lead. Moses Marcus (b. 1701), a Jewish convert to Christianity, made the most sustained case. In his rejoinder, Marcus latched on to what he took to be Middleton's ignorance of the Talmud and Jewish traditions, accusing him of relying overly much on the seventeenth-century scholarship of Spencer and John Lightfoot (1602–75) rather than 'searching the Originals, which, if look'd into, might have prevented your Misconceptions, and set you to Rights'.[63] Spencer's argument that circumcision was too painful for God to have ordained it ran counter to the scholarly judgments of Maimonides (1135–1204). Lightfoot's assertion that the first- and second-century Rabbis Nathan and Eliezer ben Hyrcanus were 'Israelites in all Respects, Priests in all Respects' despite their being uncircumcised also ignored Jewish scholarly consensus.[64] Other Waterland defenders echoed Marcus, while also driving home the point that the Jews far surpassed the Egyptians in learning and culture during Moses' lifetime.[65] Jewish religious practices were not derivative.

In retrospect, Conyers Middleton's self-appointed task of rebutting Matthew Tindal while simultaneously criticizing Daniel Waterland was a fool's errand, not least because it was hard for others to tell whether he was friend or foe.[66] Philip Williams (an orthodox Cambridge divine who called for Middleton's anti-Waterland pieces 'to be burned, and the Author of them Banished') reckoned that Middleton had attacked both 'Infidelity and Orthodoxy'.[67] By the same token, Middleton had it on good authority 'that Tindal and his club are writing against the latter part of the Letter', a rumour which also reached Daniel Waterland.[68] Hardly anyone approved of Middleton's efforts. Certainly Middleton's reputation (including in the eyes of his would-be patron, Edward Harley) did not survive the *Letter to Dr. Waterland* controversy intact. The unraveling of that particular relationship offers a case study of the burden borne by heterodox thinkers during the first half of the eighteenth century and the effects of that pressure on their subsequent careers. Middleton did not, like Thomas Woolston, go to jail for his thought. But he, like others at the time, nonetheless paid for his heterodoxy. The pressure placed upon him was both overt and subtle, brazen and understated. Above all, it was effective in marginalizing, if not finally silencing, him; indeed, it catalysed the process by which his thought became ever more heterodox.

Middleton's friendship with Harley was complicated. Middleton was not a man without friends, but he had no influential patrons: Harley, he hoped, would be that patron. Yet their friendship yielded little tangible by way of ecclesiastical preferment, perhaps not least because Harley (a Tory) had little access to or influence over ecclesiastical patronage. Middleton spent the latter part of the 1720s as he would spend much of the rest of his life, angling for recently or soon-to-be vacant livings. The one prominent office that he did obtain – the Woodwardian Professorship of Geology in 1731 – he got thanks to his longstanding friendship with Dixie Windsor, a sometime Tory MP for Cambridge and one of the Woodwardian trustees.[69] Furthermore, that position required of him 'a course of study wholly new to me' and, even more problematically, forbade marriage, John Woodward (*c.* 1665–1728), the position's benefactor, having 'so unlike his own Antediluvian Worthies, ... made [the position] incompatible with a wife'.[70] Middleton took it because nothing else was on offer.

Yet if Harley had not delivered preferments in the 1720s, there was always the possibility that he *might* be able to do so in the future. So, Middleton continued to cultivate the friendship. After his return from Rome in 1724, he wrote regularly to the bibliophilic earl and visited him both in London and at Wimpole. They even traveled together to Oxford, where they met with local antiquarians.[71] In the Wimpole library he drafted his *Letter to Dr. Waterland*, a work which he clearly knew would be contentious since he asked Harley's opinion of the manuscript.[72] Middleton certainly thought that he had Harley's approval: as he reminded him a few years later, '[b]efore its publication I had the pleasure of your Lordship's approbation of it; & as long afterwards as the Author continued unknown, that of hearing it commended by your Lordship, as oft as mentioned at your Table'. Indeed, Middleton continued, he had 'had the Authority of your Lordship's judgment entirely along with me' because he had 'submitted the other [anti-Waterland] pamphlets in the same manner to your Lordship; who made no other exception to them, but what your kindness to me suggested, of the hurt which they might possibly do to myself in the University, & of the sharpness of some expressions, which by your Lordship's direction I readily corrected'.[73] By the time Middleton wrote this reminder to Harley, his relationship with the earl had turned cold, something he did not foresee in mid-December 1730 when he sent off the *Letter* to press in London.

Middleton preserved his anonymity for over a year; but by late 1731 word had begun to spread that he had penned the *Letter*. 'It is hard surely to know, and not very safe to publish the names of the Author's in the controversy you mention', Thomas Baker wrote to Richard Rawlinson. '[Y]ou know Dr Middleton's case, and how dear it cost him.'[74] By early 1732, the consequences of authorship were becoming even clearer. The *Letter* 'makes a great deal of Noise in London', Harley fretted to Middleton in late January 1732. 'I had yesterday two letters from two persons who have a very great esteem for you. They expressed their concern that you should be named the author of those two pamphlets and hoped it was false'.[75] The response in Cambridge was pointed and direct, as some among the 'younger part of the University' drafted a grace which purported that Middleton's Woodwardian Professorship interfered with his duties as university librarian and that he should be stripped of his professorship.[76] Faced with such opposition, Middleton hoped that 'the heats of the University will evaporate at least in smoke, especially if the Vicechancellor throws cold water on them', though he acknowledged freely, 'I am sensible on what slippery ground I stand, & shall for that reason be very cautious of the next step I take, nor suffer any violence to push me down the precipice I see before me'. His hope was 'to make as reputable a retreat as I can into the Quarters of Orthodoxy' and 'to silence all clamour by slipping as quietly as I can out of the squabble'.[77]

Retreat proved difficult. His post-*Letter* correspondence with Harley aimed to project the *status quo ante*, filled as it was with much the same scholarly, political and gossipy banter that had filled up their earlier correspondence. But things were decidedly not normal for Middleton, especially in the Cambridge that had been his home for over three decades. The original grace to deprive him from holding his university library position morphed into a grace entirely to abolish the position of *protobibliothecarius*, a move short-circuited only by the successful intervention of Thomas Gooch, bishop of Ely and the university's vice-chancellor, and Francis Dickins, the regius professor of civil law.[78] While his opponents failed to debar him from his university offices, they permanently damaged his reputation. His old foe, Richard Bentley, went about declaiming the 'Pagan Middleton', while others in private and print insisted that he was an *infidel*.[79] That 'stain of infidelity' as Middleton would later mockingly refer to it, ended his friendship with Edward Harley.[80] Harley's decision to return to Middleton a harpsichord which Middleton had earlier given to him brought matters to a head. Upon receiving the instrument, Middleton vented his spleen to the earl.

> I have diligently attended & observed your Lordship for many years past with no other prospect & for no other reward, but the honor of your friendship & yet when I stood the most in need of that friendship, & had the most reason to depend upon it, I found myself disappointed of it, & deserted by your Lordship: & it is with concern that I am forced to say, at taking leave, that your Lordship has not treated me with that justice & generosity, which is agreeable to the character, that I shall always wish you to sustain, of a Great man & a Great Lord.[81]

There was no saving the friendship. Despite Lord Hervey's attempts to bring about a rapprochement, Middleton's heart did not seem in it.[82] The breach, though, presented a practical problem for Middleton: to whom should he look for patronage? He cast about, trying to secure Arthur Onslow (1691–1768), the anticlerical speaker of the House of Commons, and Thomas Townshend (1701–80), MP for Cambridge, as patrons.[83] Eventually, Lord Hervey accepted him as a client and offered him the best prospects for career advancement.

NOTES

1 For complementary analyses of the *Letter from Rome*, B. Young, 'Conyers Middleton: The Historical Consequences of Heterodoxy', in J. Robertson and S. Mortimer (eds), *The Intellectual Consequences of Religious Heterodoxy, 1600–1750* (Leiden, 2012), pp. 240–7; B. Young, 'Preludes and Postludes to Gibbon: Variations on an Impromptu by J.G.A. Pocock', *History of European Ideas* 35 (2009), pp. 422–4; M. Snow, 'Conyers Middleton: Polemic Historian' (Ph.D. thesis, Columbia University, 1970), pp. 24–88. Cf. H. Trevor-Roper, *History and the Enlightenment* (New Haven, 2010), pp. 79–80.

2 R. Sweet, 'The Changing View of Rome in the Long Eighteenth Century', *Journal for Eighteenth-Century Studies* 33 (2010), pp. 145–64; J. Ingamells, 'Discovering Italy: British Travellers in the Eighteenth Century', in A. Wilton and I. Bignamini (eds), *Grand Tour: The Lure of Italy in the Eighteenth Century* (London, 1996), pp. 21–30; J. Black, *Italy and the Grand Tour* (New Haven, 2003); T. Claydon, *Europe and the Making of England, 1660–1760* (Cambridge, 2007), pp. 13–66; C. Haynes, *Pictures and Popery: Art and Religion in England, 1660–1760* (Aldershot, 2006), pp. 14–45.

3 J. Spier and J. Kagan, 'Sir Charles Frederick and the Forgery of Ancient Coins in Eighteenth-Century Rome' *Journal of the History of Collections* 12 (2001), pp. 40, 44; M. Clarke, 'Conyers Middleton' (TCC, Add. A 298), p. 2; J. Spier, 'Conyers Middleton's Gems', in M. Henig and D. Plantzos (eds), *Classicism to Neo-Classicism* (Oxford, 1999), pp. 204–15; Walpole to Middleton, 21 April 1743 (*WC*, XV, pp. 18–20).

4 M. Baker, C. Harrison and A. Laing, 'Bouchardon's British Sitters: Sculptural Portraiture in Rome and the Classicising Bust around 1730', *Burlington Magazine* 142 (2000), pp. 759–61; C. Middleton, *Germana quædam antiquitatis* (1745: T125483), title-page.

5 Middleton to Harley, 5 December 1724 (BL, Add. 70410); Middleton to Ficoroni, 16 August 1726 (BL, Add. 32457, fol. 89); Bernardo Sterbini to Middleton, 4 July

1733 (BL, Add. 32457, fols 45–8); J. Ingamells (ed.), *Dictionary of British and Irish Travellers in Italy, 1701–1800* (New Haven, 1997), pp. 658–9.
6 C. Middleton, *Letter from Rome* (1729: T121512), preface, pp. 11, 13.
7 Ibid., preface.
8 Ibid., pp. 15–28. Cf. O. Ormerod, *Picture of a papist* (1606: S113457); J. Stopford, *Pagano-papismus* (1675: R20561); T. Gale, *The court of the Gentiles: Part 1* (1669: R202248).
9 Ibid., pp. 29–36. See also J. Sheehan, 'Temple and Tabernacle: The Place of Religion in Early Modern England', in P. Smith and B. Schmidt (eds), *Making Knowledge in Early Modern Europe: Practices, Objects and Texts, 1400–1800* (Chicago, 2007), pp. 248–72; J. Sheehan, 'The Altars of the Idols: Religion, Sacrifice and the Early Modern Polity', *JHI* 67 (2006), pp. 649–73; J. Sheehan, 'Sacred and Profane: Idolatry, Antiquarianism and the Polemics of Distinction in the Seventeenth Century', *P&P* 192 (2006), pp. 35–66.
10 Ibid., p. 52. Cf. J. Champion, 'Legislators, Impostors and the Politic Origins of Religion: English Theories of "Imposture" from Stubbe to Toland', in S. Berti, F. Charles-Daubert and R. Popkin (eds), *Heterodoxy, Spinozism and Free Thought in Early-Eighteenth-Century Europe* (Dordrecht, 1996), pp. 333–56.
11 Ibid., pp. 65–6.
12 J. Champion, '"My Kingdom is not of this world": The Politics of Religion after the Revolution', in N. Tyacke (ed.), *The English Revolution, c. 1590–1720 (Manchester, 2007)*, pp. 185–202; J. Champion, '"To Govern is to Make Subjects Believe": Anticlericalism, Politics and Power, c. 1680–1717', in N. Aston and M. Cragoe (eds), *Anticlericalism in Britain, c. 1500–1914* (Stroud, 2000), pp. 67–92; J. Champion, '"Religion's Safe, with Priestcraft is the War": Augustan Anticlericalism and the Legacy of the English Revolution, 1660–1720', *European Legacy* 5 (2000), pp. 547–61.
13 Middleton, *Letter from Rome*, pp. 67–8.
14 E.g., A. Young, *Historical dissertation on idolatrous corruptions* (1734: T078093), p. 258.
15 *Present State of the Republick of Letters* (1729), p. 437.
16 Middleton to Harley, 3 November 1724 (BL, Add. 70410); C. Wright and R. Wright (eds), *The Diary of Humfrey Wanley, 1715–1726* (1966), pp. 323, 341–5.
17 C. Wright, 'Portrait of a Bibliophile VIII: Edward Harley, 2nd Earl of Oxford, 1689–1741', *Book Collector* 11 (1962), pp. 158–74; C. Wright, 'Humfrey Wanley: Saxonist and Library Keeper', *Proceedings of the British Academy* 46 (1960), pp. 99–129; A. Turberville, *History of Welbeck Abbey and Its Owners ... 1539–1755* (1938), pp. 361–87; W. Speck, 'Robert Harley, First Earl of Oxford and Mortimer (1661–1724)', *ODNB*.
18 D. Adshead, '"A Noble Musaeum of Books": A View of the Interior of the Harleian Library at Wimpole Hall', *Library History* 18 (2002), pp. 191–206.
19 F. Korsten, 'Thomas Baker (1656–1740)', *ODNB*.
20 C. Middleton, *Dissertation on the state of physicians* (1734: N007583), pp. i, iv. Baker defended his friend even after Harley had fallen out with Middleton. 'Though Dr. Middleton may seem to have changed his Principles, yet he has a Principle of Honor': Baker to Richard Rawlinson, 22 May 1734 (Bodleian, Rawl.lett.30, fol. 106).

21 BL, Add. 70422 attests to the depth of the Baker–Harley relationship.
22 Middleton to John Audley, 15 November 1718 (Beinecke, Osborn c.195/128); Middleton voted for Harley in the 1722 election: *Copy of the poll ... Cambridge, March the 29th, 1722* (1722: T185206), p. 7.
23 Middleton to John Colbatch, 16 May 1721 (BL, Add. 22908, fol. 122); Wright and Wright (eds), *Diary*, p. 249.
24 Middleton to Harley, 1 December 1724 (BL, Add. 70410).
25 R. Mead, *Oratio anniversaria harveiana* (1724: T043311).
26 Middleton, *Dissertation on the state of physicians*, p. 5. This pamphlet had originally appeared in Latin in 1727: Middleton, *Dissertationis de medicorum Romæ*. See also V. Nutton, 'Murders and Miracles: Lay Attitudes towards Medicine in Classical Antiquity', in R. Porter (ed.), *Patients and Practitioners* (Cambridge, 1986), pp. 23–4.
27 Thomas Birch to Philip Yorke, second earl of Hardwicke, 4 August 1750 (BL, Add. 35397, fols 269–70); Trevor-Roper, *History*, pp. 77–9. After his peace accord with Mead, Middleton gave Harley the manuscript copy of an 'Appendix' that he had written against Mead. William Heberden, Middleton's executor, published it in the 1760s, after all the parties in the agreement were dead and after the Harleian library had been subsumed within the British Library: Middleton, *Dissertationis de servili medicorum*.
28 Middleton to Harley, 20 November 1730 (BL, Add. 70410).
29 Young, 'Conyers Middleton', p. 244; B. Young, '"Scepticism in Excess": Gibbon and Eighteenth-Century Christianity', *HJ* 41 (1998), pp. 184–5; T. Stuart-Buttle, 'Classicism, Christianity, and Ciceronian Academic Scepticism from Locke to Hume, c. 1660–c.1760' (D.Phil thesis, University of Oxford, 2013), pp. 185–93. Cf. Trevor-Roper, *History*, pp. 71–119.
30 [Middleton], *Letter to Dr. Waterland* ((1731): T220974), pp. 2, 7, 57, 64–6, 67.
31 Ibid., p. 46.
32 [Waterland], *Scripture vindicated ... Part I*, p. 15; [Middleton], *Letter to Dr. Waterland*, p. 13.
33 [Middleton], *Letter to Dr. Waterland*, pp. 14–21.
34 Ibid., pp. 24–6, 29–30, 38, 39.
35 Ibid., pp. 50, 52.
36 Waterland to Pearce, 19 December 1731 (WAM 64808).
37 [Middleton], *Letter to Dr. Waterland*, pp. 15, 47.
38 [Middleton], *Defence of the letter to Dr. Waterland*, pp. 2–3.
39 Initially, Zachary Pearce – the first into print to excoriate the *Letter to Dr. Waterland* – fingered a London physician as author: Harley to Middleton, 6 February 1731 (BL, Add. 32457, fol. 67).
40 Thomas Cooke's *The Comedian, or philosophical enquirer* II (May 1732), pp. 31–4, was a rare exception. It reckoned that Middleton 'proves Dr. Waterland to be rather a weak, and abusive, Railer, than an able, and sober, Reasoner'. It also hoped that 'the University of Cambridge had suffered too much in passed Times by laying Restraints on Men of Genius, Learning and Probity, to attempt the like again'.
41 Waterland to Pearce, 2 January 1732 (WAM 64809).
42 Waterland to Pearce, 19 December 1731, 2/9 January 1732 (WAM 64808–10).

43 Berriman, *Gradual revelation* (1733: T035779), I, p. xxxviii.
44 J. Gascoigne, 'The Wisdom of the Egyptians and the Secularisation of History in the Age of Newton', in S. Gaukroger (ed.), *The Uses of Antiquity* (Dordrecht, 1991); D. Stolzenberg, 'John Spencer and the Perils of Sacred Philology', *P&P* 214 (2012), pp. 129–63.
45 Berriman, *Gradual revelation*, p. xi; [P. Williams], *Some observations* (1733: T049310), p. 19. See also [Z. Pearce], *Reply to the defence of the letter* (1732: T012466), pp. 60–73; Anonymous, *Reflections on the letter to Dr. Waterland* (1732: T046566), pp. 27–34; [P. Williams], *Reply to remarks on some observations* (1734: T175971), pp. 42–4.
46 [C. Middleton], *Some remarks on a reply to the defence of the letter to Dr. Waterland* (1732: T012468), p. 68.
47 [Middleton], *Defence of the letter to Dr. Waterland* (1731: T032264), p. 72.
48 [Middleton], *Some remarks on a reply*, pp. 69–71.
49 [C. Middleton], *Remarks on some observations* (1733: T046788), p. 15.
50 Waterland to Gibson, 29 July 1731 (LPL, 1741, fol. 84).
51 E. Underhill, *Celsus triumphatus* (1732: 728979), p. 30; Anonymous, *Reflections on the letter to Dr. Waterland*, p. 4; [Williams], *Some observations*, p. 29.
52 [Middleton], *Defence of the letter to Dr. Waterland*, pp. 13, 15.
53 [C. Middleton], *Remarks on some observations* (1733: T046788), p. 20.
54 [Middleton], *Defence of the letter to Dr. Waterland*, p. 13.
55 J. Locke, *Essay Concerning Human Understanding*, ed. P. Nidditch (Oxford, 1975), p. 663; J. Whiston, *Catalogue of ... Conyers Middleton* (1751: T064471), p. 4.
56 C. Middleton, 'An Essay on the Allegorical and Literal Interpretation of the Creation and Fall of Man', *MWCM*, II, p. 125.
57 [Pearce], *Reply to the defence*, pp. 48–60. Waterland did not initially know, however, that it was Pearce who had written the first *Reply to the Letter to ... Waterland*: Waterland to Edmund Gibson, 21 January 1731 (LPL, 1741, fol. 76).
58 Anonymous, *Reflections on the letter to Dr. Waterland*, p. 6.
59 Cf. N. Hudson, 'Theories of Language', in H. Nisbet and C. Rawson (eds), *Cambridge History of Literary Criticism. Volume 4: The Eighteenth Century* (Cambridge, 1997), pp. 335–48.
60 [Pearce], *Reply to the letter*, pp. 52–4.
61 [Chapman], *Remarks on a letter*, pp. 24–6. Waterland to Pearce, 13 February 1732 (WAM 64812): 'I could have wished also that you had made some reference to Mr. Chapman's piece on Languages ... Did you never see Chapman's? It is an excellent piece.' Chapman had been one of Middleton's companions at the Rose Tavern in 1710: Richard Laughton's account, n.d. (BL, Add. 32459, fol. 12).
62 Gascoigne, 'Wisdom of the Egyptians'; Stolzenberg, 'John Spencer'; Sheehan, 'Sacred and Profane'.
63 [M. Marcus], *Answer to the letter to Dr. Waterland* (1731: T022065), pp. 4–9. See also Waterland to Pearce, 13 February 1732 (WAM 64812); D. Ruderman, *Connecting the Covenants: Judaism and the Search for Christian Identity in Eighteenth-Century England* (Philadelphia, 2007), pp. 20–76.
64 [Marcus], *Answer*, pp. 9–21.
65 [Pearce], *Reply to the defence*, pp. 15–20, 22–3; Anonymous, *Reflections on the letter*

to Dr. Waterland, pp. 12–27; E. Underhill, *Celsus triumphatus* (1732: 728979), , pp. 8–28, 36–47.
66 Waterland to Gibson, 29 December 1730 (LPL 1741, fols 78–9).
67 [P. Williams], *Some observations* (1733: T049310), title-page, p. 5.
68 Middleton to Harley, 25 January 1732 (BL, Add. 70410); Waterland to Pearce, 13 February 1732 (WAM 64812).
69 Middleton to Harley, 30 March 1731, 22 April 1731 (BL, Add. 70410). For Middleton's subsequent difficulty in voting against Windsor in the 1734 parliamentary election, Middleton to Hervey, 30 April 1734 (SRO, 941/47/8).
70 Middleton to Hervey, 27 December 1733 (SRO, 941/47/8). See also Middleton to Harley, 19 May 1728 (BL, Add. 70410).
71 T. Hearne, *Reliquiae Hernainae*, ed. P. Bliss (London, 1869), III, p. 58.
72 Middleton to Harley, 20 November 1730, 30 March 1731 (BL, Add. 70410).
73 Middleton to Harley, 10 June 1733 (BL, Add. 32457, fols 83–4).
74 Baker to Rawlinson, 21 September 1731 (Bodleian, Rawl.lett.30, fol. 89).
75 Harley to Middleton, 24 January 1732 (BL, Add. 32457, fol. 71).
76 Middleton to Harley, 24 January 1732 (BL, Add. 70410).
77 Middleton to Harley, 25, 29 January 1732 (ibid.).
78 Middleton to Harley, 21, 25 March 1732 (ibid.).
79 Waterland to Pearce, 9 January 1732 (WAM 64810); Warburton to Pearce, 4 March 1731 (WAM 64779); [Pearce], *Reply to the defence*, p. 61; Anonymous, *Reflections on the letter to Dr. Waterland*, pp. 3–5; Underhill, *Celsus triumphatus*, pp. 4–7.
80 Middleton to Hervey, 18 August 1734 (SRO, 941/48/8).
81 Middleton to Harley, January 1734 (BL, Add. 32457, fol. 93).
82 Middleton to Harley, 24 June 1733 (SRO, 941/47/8).
83 Onslow to Middleton, 6 July 1733 (BL, Add. 32457, fols 85–6); Middleton to Townshend, 10 August 1735 (TCC, R.1.88, fol. 1).

Chapter 8

Treating me worse, than I deserved: heterodoxy and the politics of patronage

The anticlerical John, Lord Hervey (1696–1743) differed markedly from Edward Harley. Though his flamboyance and sexual preferences opened him up to Alexander Pope's merciless abuse in the *Epistle to Arbuthnot* (1735), Hervey had what Harley had not: access to power. By the early 1730s, he was a member of the privy council, Queen Caroline's closest confidant and Robert Walpole's unswerving ally.[1] Middleton pursued him with a vigour and persistence that, even by the standards of the day, seemed unctuous. 'It is a singular pleasure to me & I embrace it as a lucky omen, that the first Letter your Lordship has honoured me with, should furnish a subject of writing of all the most agreeable, that of congratulating with your Lordship on your advancement in honour', he gushed in his first letter to Hervey, '& I easily foresee by the short acquaintance I have had with your Lordship that I shall oft be called upon hereafter to pay the same duty'.[2] Things got only slightly less saccharine thereafter.

How Middleton came to know Hervey is unclear. Perhaps they met during Hervey's own undergraduate days at Cambridge; perhaps they got acquainted during one of the times Hervey stopped through town on his way to his Suffolk estate of Ickworth; or perhaps Hervey was one of the many who frequented Middleton's house near Gonville and Caius.[3] Their correspondence began in earnest during the summer of 1733, when Middleton's friendship with Harley was in its death-throes. At the time, Middleton was a fifty-year-old university professor and librarian. All agreed he was too clever to have risen so low. Hervey, Middleton hoped, might change his fortunes in a way Harley had been unable to. From Middleton, Hervey got a sympathetic confidant as well as someone who allowed him to keep a foot in the world of scholarship. Hervey was a cultured man, one with some felicity in both Latin and French and someone who fancied himself more than a polemicist on behalf of the Walpolean regime. In Middleton, he had a client who was learned but no pedant, someone who had been abroad, someone who was cultured and urbane.

The Middleton Hervey took on as a client was a man conflicted. On the one hand, Middleton constantly sought after ecclesiastical preferment; on the other, he relentlessly disparaged the established Church's clerical leaders. On the one hand, he claimed after the Waterland controversy that he aimed simply to be quiet and not draw attention to himself; on the other, he produced deeply anticlerical and unmistakably heterodox pieces whose publication, had they not been scotched by Hervey, would have drawn even greater orthodox contempt down upon him. Though Hervey might not have been able to deliver the patronage that either he or Middleton had hoped for, he, more effectively than anyone else, restrained Middleton's worst instincts. Yet if Hervey could quiet Middleton for a while, he could not stop the corrosive effects of orthodox censure on his client. Orthodox criticism changed Middleton. Far from always being a closet deist or freethinker, he grew into – or, perhaps, was driven into – his mature heterodoxy. He was never likely to be a Waterland acolyte, but would he have been as heterodox as he was by the end of his life had a plum ecclesiastical living been found for him during the late 1720s, one which acknowledged his evident intellectual talents? Those who knew him best thought not.[4]

This chapter highlights the ways that eighteenth-century orthodox clergy tried to coerce or punish their fellow clergy whom they judged heterodox. It opens with a consideration of Middleton's unsuccessful attempts to secure plum preferments with Hervey's assistance. It then anatomizes the arguments in the heterodox works that Hervey convinced Middleton not to publish in order to better his chances for preferment. Middleton returned to these unpublished manuscripts during the 1740s when he wrote about miracles. The chapter concludes by detailing Middleton's failed effort during the late 1730s and early 1740s to redeem himself in the eyes of the orthodox by writing about Cicero. The process of bringing his life of Cicero to press also casts light onto the business of publishing with which Middleton and all other polemical divines had to deal.

Age did not diminish Middleton's ambition. In late 1733, less than a week after the death of Cambridge's regius professor of modern history, for instance, Middleton explained to Hervey that he had been 'told at the same time by my friends, that the University in general point me out for the Successor'.[5] The next day, he outlined how Hervey might surmount clerical objections to him assuming the regius professorship and the advantage to the government from him holding the post. '[I]n order to soften any opposition that may be made to my name, it will be necessary to represent, that it is no Ecclesiastical preferment, or such as can raise envy in the Clergy', Middleton advised, '& for the rest, Your Lordship may venture to insist, that such a mark of favour to me would in general be popular here, except to those who are utterly disaffected to the Court, & that I stand very fair in the opinion both of the Heads & Body of the Whig Party; who have shewn themselves disposed to give me proofs of their esteem'.[6] The threat of clerical opposition clearly worried him, so that he later counselled Hervey, 'if there be any cry against me on the part of the Bishops, I have reason to believe Dr [Thomas] Sherlock if appealed to would give a favourable opinion of me'.[7] Though Hervey lobbied both Robert Walpole and Queen Caroline, he could not prevent a scholarly nonentity from obtaining the position, leaving a dejected Middleton to bemoan, 'All the revenge I now meditate, for the perverseness, I have met with, is to double my diligence in the pursuit of virtue, & knowledge, & as far as I am able, to leave upon the World the reproach of treating me worse, than I deserved'.[8]

Despite such declarations, Middleton relentlessly pursued preferment. He worried particularly that Thomas Pelham-Holles, duke of Newcastle (1693–1768) (Walpole's point man for ecclesiastical patronage), might bar him from office. 'The D[uke] of Newcastle, who knew me personally at Cambridge may possibly retain some prejudices, not favourable to my character', he fretted to Thomas Townshend in early 1737, before asking Townshend 'whether it may not be of use to give me the credit of Your Testimonial likewise there; to clear our way the better from all obstructions'.[9] Townshend's interventions did little good because later that year Newcastle blocked Middleton obtaining the Charterhouse mastership. In August 1737, the Charterhouse's master of two decades died. Even before his death, Middleton had travelled to London to plump for the position because Robert Walpole and 'some other Great ones' had recommended him for the position.[10] Despite the sitting prime minister's backing, Middleton found Newcastle blocking his path to the master's post, something Townshend found remarkable: 'It is, as I believe, the first time the Duke of Newcastle's recommendation ever prevailed against Sir Robert Walpole's'.[11] Newcastle's intransigence owed less to his own theological predilections, than to the opposition of Edmund Gibson and Thomas Sherlock.[12]

Middleton suspected Sherlock's opposition, complaining that the bishop 'has not treated me with that candor & justice, which his outward carriage & old acquaintance with me had given me reason to expect'.[13] A few years later, he learned both the depth of Sherlock's opposition to him and the reasons for it when Robert Walpole, then out of office, invited Middleton to spend the day with him at Houghton Hall. Walpole apologized to Middleton for not having been able to deliver the Charterhouse mastership, but explained 'that Bishop Sherlock was the person that wholly obstructed it'.[14] Middleton had earlier suspected Sherlock's ambivalence. But learning that Sherlock inveterately opposed his promotion to any higher office surprised him, not least because 'he never went to London without paying his Respects to him, & always thought that he had been upon civil & friendly, if not upon the most intimate & very best terms with him'. Indeed, the two men went back some ways, with Sherlock having helped him during his earlier legal wranglings with Richard Bentley.[15] An irritated Middleton got Walpole's approval to discuss the matter with Sherlock. On his next trip to London, Middleton 'waited upon Bp Sherlock at the Temple, told him the Cause he had to think that he was very injuriously used by him'. Rather than deny his role in the matter, Sherlock was unapologetic and blunt.

> He put [Middleton] in Mind, how very obnoxious he had made himself to the whole Body of the Clergy by taking Part in the Cause of Infidelity, against Dr Waterland, who had wrote in Defence of Christianity: that He himself, & all the World knew that the King referred the Promotion of the Clergy to Bp Gibson & himself; that if one who had made himself so justly obnoxious to the clergy, & the believing Part of the Kingdom was to be promoted to such a Piece of Preferment in the City of London, the Odium thereof must necessarily fall on him: therefore he very fairly confessed to the Doctor, that he was so far obstructive of his Promotion, as far as this Representation of the Case to Sir Robert Walpole might be called so; adding, that when he made this Relation to Sir Robert, he also put him in Mind, that if he had an earnest Desire that Dr Middleton should succeed, it was only taking the Merit of it upon himself, & exonerating the 2 Bishops of having any Hand in it.

The irony was that the Charterhouse mastership went to an avowed Arian, Nicholas Mann (1680–1753). When making the rounds of the Charterhouse governors to thank them for choosing him, Mann purportedly said to John Potter, the archbishop of Canterbury, 'I suppose your Grace knows that you have made choice of an Arian'. Potter's retort? 'An Arian perhaps may be better than a Deist.'[16] Such was Middleton's reputation by the late 1730s that this probably apocryphal story seemed believable.

Yet the Charterhouse experience did not extinguish Middleton's ambition for higher office. When Richard Bentley seemed at death's door in 1738, Middleton aggressively self-recommended for the not-yet-vacant mastership of Trinity College.[17] Hervey promised to round up testimonials from heads of Cambridge colleges 'sufficient to answer any impertinent objections to your advancement that may be made by the uncharitable unforgiving Christians of the high Church Party who hold that every Man who dares to think truths they don't like deserves to be hanged & he who speaks them to be dam[ne]d'.[18] Middleton directly lobbied Newcastle, trying to convince him that Bentley's already-chosen successor, Robert Smith, had a legal impediment to assuming the college mastership.[19] Bentley, it turned out, lived nearly four more years. But even had Bentley died in 1738, Robert Walpole would not have broken his promise to Queen Caroline to promote Smith to the post. Nor would Newcastle, Gibson and Sherlock have countenanced Middleton's advancement even had Walpole been willing to break his pledge to the late Queen.

These serial career disappointments deepened Middleton's anticlericalism. Hervey viewed the established Church of England decidedly dimly, and Middleton played up anticlerical themes in his own responses.[20] '[I]t is my misfortune to have had so early a taste of Pagan sense, as to make me very squeamish in my Christian studies', he confided to Hervey early on in their friendship. A year later he complained, 'Sunday is my only day of rest, but not of liberty; for I am bound to a double attendance at Church, to wipe off the Stain of Infidelity. When I have recovered my credit, in which I make daily progress, I may use more freedom.'[21] Middleton never wrote anything like this to Edward Harley. Why? For one thing, Middleton clearly became increasingly embittered with the orthodox in the wake of the *Letter to Dr. Waterland* controversy. 'In primitive times Heretics were delivered over to Satan to be buffeted; but our Orthodox now take that province to themselves; as if they were as good at buffeting as he', he inveighed.[22] In particular, he hated the episcopate. 'For our modern Bishops I think all you say of them but too true' he groused to Hervey at one point, '& can never hold it good Policy in any Government to vest any set of men with more Power than is necessary to serve that Government; since the Moment it passes that Bound, it generally grows to the full as troublesome as the Disorder it was first employed to regulate'. A few months later, he contended that 'the Bench ... makes politics not principle the rule of conduct'.[23]

Despite Hervey's own anticlerical inclinations, he strongly counselled Middleton not to write publicly about contentious religious subjects, including any responses to Waterland. 'I heartily wish your Pen & Learning, capable of any Work, was imployed in one, less dangerous to your-self & more entertaining to your Readers', Hervey advised his client, '& that you would leave the Discussion of that clouded Subject to your clouded Antagonist, who could never be a match for you in a Dispute where your Hands are untied, & fights at too great an Advantage in one where every blow you give that will hurt him as an Author may, by recoiling, wound you as a Divine'.[24] For his own part, Middleton claimed to want to avoid controversy, and, indeed, researched and wrote up a short dissertation on printing, one which proved that William Caxton (1415–92) had established the first printing press in England. Lest Hervey worry that his client was 'sadly employed in turning over such rubbish' in producing such a recondite pamphlet, Middleton reassured him that 'it is just the reverse in the learned of what it is in the active world: the more obscure and trifling our pursuits are, the greater fame of learning is acquired by tempting them; & a few more performances of this kind may raise me to a rank of glory with the Great [Thomas] Hearne of Oxford'.[25] Similarly, Middleton used his Woodwardian lectures 'to demonstrate the reality of a Universal deluge from the proof of Woodward's Cockle Shells', an argument which might have earned him orthodox approbation.[26]

Despite these attempts to avoid writing pieces of polemical divinity, Middleton nevertheless produced in manuscript a string of deeply anticlerical, unmistakably heterodox pieces, nearly all of which Hervey convinced him not to print. But these unpublished pieces shine light on to Middleton's increasingly embittered mindset during the mid-1730s. Middleton fixated in particular on two of orthodoxy's leading lights: Edmund Gibson and Daniel Waterland. Gibson's role in blocking Thomas Rundle's translation to the see of Gloucester unnerved and upset him.[27] Middleton also blamed Gibson for mobilizing clerical and political opinion against him. The appearance in March 1734 of William Arnall's anonymous *Letter to Dr. Codex* – a work to which Hervey had first alerted him and one which Middleton reckoned was 'written with more vivacity, than good judgment' – nevertheless gave an opening to draft a piece defending Arnall's pointed criticism of Gibson.[28] Arnall had lambasted Gibson ('this Protestant Pontiff') for having tried to control ecclesiastical patronage. Arnall's criticism clearly had irked Gibson and his allies, one of whom, William Webster, used the pages of his hyper-orthodox *Weekly Miscellany* to defend Gibson. During its nine-year run, the *Miscellany* functioned as a semi-official organ of the orthodox wing of the established Church, one which had Gibson's active support.[29] Within a month of the appearance of Arnall's *Letter to Dr. Codex*, the *Miscellany* defended Gibson's behaviour in the Rundle affair and flatly denied that Gibson had tried to scuttle the 1733 appointment of Hervey's client Robert Butts to the see of Norwich.[30] Not a month after the *Miscellany*'s apology for Gibson, Middleton had written a rebuttal. If Middleton's dealings with Edward Harley had taught him anything it was to get his patron's pre-publication approval in writing, and he promised to send to Hervey for 'some advice ... in a kind of writing, which I have not been used to, & where shall never care to venture into public without Your Lordship's imprimatur'.[31] Hervey fretted that he 'should be sorry, if the thing you speak of be very hard on the Bishop, to have it known that you are the author of it'.[32] Hervey approved of Middleton's argument, yet he refused his imprimatur for publication. Eventually, Middleton concurred: 'I have smarted so much already for the iniquity of my former writings, that the point of prudence will for some time at least be the most prevailing principle with me.'[33]

Such prudence was well-founded, for in his manuscript Middleton had argued that the bishop of London and his orthodox allies were persecutory. The entire piece played on contemporary complaints that Gibson, who had thirty years before been 'a most virulent Jacobite', currently functioned like a latter-day Archbishop Laud, a point upon which Arnall and others regularly hit.[34] Middleton's piece rehearsed the familiar seventeenth-century arguments about the connection between popery and arbitrary government.[35] On the one hand were the vast majority of churchmen, those able 'to reconcile their principles of Religion to reason; their principles of loyalty to public liberty: they now taste the happy fruits of the Revolution and Protestant Succession, and are convinced, that the steady conduct of the Government is the only way of securing them to us: they are well affected to the Ministry'. These loyal churchmen, whom the orthodox nonetheless disfavoured, would be more 'zealous' to defend the Church if they were not 'turned over, as a turbulent and untractable order of men, to the Tribunal of an Inquisitor General; who by a dark scrutiny into their behaviour, managed by Spies and whisperers, and a charge of crimes by unknown witnesses, must often ruin the character and even fortunes of the most deserving'. The effects on the Church from this were grim. '[S]uch are the terrors of Orthodoxy; and such vengeance threatened to all, who deviate from it; that it destroys all trust and confidence among Ecclesiastics; and to impart scruples against an Established Government; your best friends will betray you, for the sake of their own safety.' This was predictable when the 'most favoured Divines', like Middleton's foe Daniel Waterland, argued 'that Apostasy and some kinds of heresy are greater crimes than Felony or Treason'. Furthermore, Middleton cautioned, Gibson posed a threat not just to the established Church but to the state, as well: 'to transfer the supremacy of the church, and dependence of the Clergy to any single Bishop, must make the Court dependent on him too; ... a subjection, that no wise ministry would willingly be reduced to: in the Church of Rome, all the Cardinals made by any Pope, are ever styled the Creatures of that Pope; and generally act as such towards Him and his family'. This, Middleton concluded, would be 'hurtful to Society'.

The next year Middleton felt sufficiently provoked to respond to another piece from the *Weekly Miscellany*. In its 15 February 1735 edition, the *Miscellany* ran a long unsigned editorial on its front page, which opened with advice about how to deal with the enemies of 'true Religion', counselling that '[w]e should ... pursue the Enemy, even after he has been routed and cut off all possible Retreats lest he should invade us again with more Success, when he is less expected'. It then turned immediately to assail an unnamed 'apostate Priest', one who had questioned the Bible's literal truth and one who, like 'the crafty Jesuit' he was, had changed the terms of the debate when his initial attack on the inspiration of the scriptures had been rebuffed.[36] If there was any doubt to whom the piece referred, Richard Venn (1691–1739) – an Edmund Gibson protégé; an informant against Thomas Rundle; and a frequent *Weekly Miscellany* contributor – confirmed it when he referred to Middleton by name as an 'Apostate Priest' in William Innys's London bookshop. Rather than respond to Venn's charges in print, Middleton wrote directly to Venn.[37] Middleton charged Venn with 'Calumniating' and challenged him, 'If your Religion prescribes, permits, or does not condemn, all such defamation as impious & detestable; you clear me at once of Apostasy: for that Religion was never mine: & I cannot be charged with deserting, what I had never professed'. Middleton accused Venn not only of doing nothing to convert people 'in this Sceptical age' but of playing into the papists' hands. What had been the origin of Venn's animosity to Middleton? Surely the same as that of his patron, Edmund Gibson, Middleton's *Letter from Rome*. 'As soon as it was published, that learned Divine, your Partner, happening to meet me in the Streets, told me, with a formal face and air of importance, that he had been in company with certain friends, who declared themselves offended at it', Middleton charged. To drive home the point that Gibson was a crypto-papist, Middleton followed up this story with a rumour he had heard that the sub-dean of the royal chapel, Edward Aspinwall (1678–1732) – 'a pretended Convert from Rome ... yet who lived all the while a Covert Papist & died, as I am told, a professed one' – also disliked the *Letter from Rome*. Middleton wrote his letter to Venn, he subsequently informed Hervey, 'in a Stile not likely to please him'.[38] Rather than respond directly to Middleton, Venn published it in the *Independent London Journal*, without Middleton's permission.[39]

If Middleton's antipathy towards Edmund Gibson and his acolytes at the *Weekly Miscellany* ran deep, his hatred for Daniel Waterland seemed fathomless. Though he published nothing about Waterland during the mid-1730s, the master of Magdalene College preoccupied Middleton. Middleton privately seethed at the damage done to his career by the *Letter to Dr. Waterland* and he blamed Waterland his troubles. When Waterland's *Importance of the Doctrine of the Holy Trinity* appeared in print in late 1733, it gave Middleton the opportunity to assail his nemesis. Waterland's book was, Middleton complained to Hervey, 'a surprising piece of nonsense & irreligion: the principle he professedly attacks is that of reconciling parties; not condemning the men, as well as their doctrines; not driving out of Society all who differ from him on that article; the preferring peace, to the true Christian Charity of saving men's Souls; or the not refusing them from eternal torments hereafter, by tormenting them charitably here'.[40] The pall cast by Waterland's book and by William Berriman's recent Boyle Lectures did not dissipate quickly, for a few weeks later Middleton reported to Hervey that his 'Studies have been much employed of late on Dr. Waterland & Berriman & in tracing their nonsense to its primitive source, of ancient Fathers & Doctors, more absurd, if possible, than they'.[41] These reports displeased Hervey: 'I do not approve of your tiring your attention with wading through Berriman's Phlegm, & Waterland's Enthusiasm; your answering them is the only way to make their names eminent, or their Works read'.[42]

His new patron's disapprobation notwithstanding, Middleton produced first a short piece which dealt with Waterland's and Berriman's use of the story of the Gnostic Cerinthus (fl. *c.* 100). In *Against the Heresies*, Irenaeus (130–202) recounted that St John shunned Cerinthus because of his heterodox views of the Creation and of Christ's divinity. On Irenaeus's telling, when John encountered Cerinthus in an Ephesian bathhouse, he 'leaped out of the bath without using it, adding, Let us fly, lest the very bath fall on us, where Cerinthus, the enemy of truth is'.[43] Both Waterland and Berriman took the stories of Cerinthus and an analogous one regarding Marcion (d. *c.* 160) as emblematic of how heretics should be treated. 'No matter what their Motives were in other Respects: They corrupted the Faith of Christ, and in effect, subverted the Gospel', Waterland insisted. 'That was enough to render them detestable in the Eye of all Men who sincerely loved and valued sound Faith.'[44] By implication, Waterland's heretical contemporaries should be treated similarly.

In his riposte, Middleton scrutinized the Cerinthus story, whose external and internal evidences led him to doubt its authenticity.[45] The story had dubious sources. Irenaeus was an unreliable reporter, for 'though he was a most diligent collector of Apostolic traditions, taken by himself as he affirms, from the report of those ancient men, who had conversed with the Apostles, yet in every single instance which he has particularly recorded & positively attested, he was either deluded himself, or has wilfully deluded others, by false & forged pretence of apostolic authority'. Irenaeus claimed, for instance, that Christ had lived until he was fifty years old, yet all other primitive fathers had agreed that Christ had died in his thirties. That Irenaeus argued farther than the evidence might have held was, to Middleton's way of thinking, understandable, since 'the Gospel was then only in a few hands & Apostolic tradition the shortest way of silencing those Heretics with whom Irenaeus was engaged'. Other evidential problems also arose. Some primitive fathers recounted something like the Cerinthus story, only with different names: how could one be certain that the version in Irenaeus was *the* authoritative account? Furthermore, the fact that Irenaeus got his account of Cerinthus from Polycarp (69–155), by way of some of Polycarp's followers, further vitiated the story's authenticity. At best, this was hearsay evidence. If the external evidence for Irenaeus's Cerinthus story was weak, so too was the internal evidence. John's behaviour, for instance, was unworthy of an apostle and, furthermore, ran counter to what Waterland had written regarding John's benevolence. Yet even if all of these evidential problems were to be surmounted and Irenaeus's Cerinthus story were stipulated as true, it was, Middleton concluded, nothing more than 'an extraordinary case, or ... the effect of that divine power, which resided in the Apostles, & enabled them to discern the hearts of men, & the secret springs & motives, which actuated those early corrupters of the Christian faith'. Cerinthus's case was a one-off, not a normative prescription for how to deal with heretics.[46]

Heterodoxy and the treatment of the heterodox were, for obvious reasons, subjects close to Middleton's heart in late 1733, as it had by then become clear to him that his career prospects suffered mightily because of his *Letter to Dr. Waterland*. The anger attending that recognition came through clearly as he inveighed against orthodox persecution:

> Every man's experience will furnish instances at this day of the wretched fruits of this zeal in some worthless, vicious, ignorant bigots, both of the clergy, & the Laity, who puffed with pride of an imaginary Orthodoxy, & detesting all free inquiry, as likely to disturb their ease, & to expose their ignorance, take a pleasure in defaming & insulting men of candor, probity & learning, who happen to be touched with any scruples, or charged with peculiar opinions, which they think fit to call Heretical.

Orthodox censures against 'heretics' were so damnable because those censures rested on claims of infallibility, substantively no different from popish ones, and on a perversion of the civil authority to enforce those censures: 'there is no difference between Protestant & Popish tyranny, if a liberty be not allowed to private judgement, in all speculative matters, without punishment or restraint, on any other account, than of being exerted intemperately or unseasonably to the disturbance of the state'. This analysis had been a popular Protestant one since the early days of the Reformation; and it frequently got employed during the eighteenth century.

Daniel Waterland continued to bedevil Conyers Middleton. Less than a year after finishing up his first brief rejoinder to Waterland's *Importance of the Doctrine of the Holy Trinity*, Middleton wrote to Hervey reporting that he had just finished a much longer response to Waterland's book, one which focused not on Trinitarian theology but on what Middleton described as Waterland's 'system of power'. This treatment, running to nearly 17,000 words, built upon Middleton's initial retort. It included his discussion of Cerinthus and his analysis of orthodox persecution; it amplified his arguments about the distinction between true Protestantism and crypto-papist orthodoxy.[47] Waterland's *Importance*, Middleton insisted, 'suggest[ed] the notion of some Jesuit, defending the furious spirit of Rome; or a Dominican, vindicating the discipline of the Inquisition'. He and the orthodox were 'the morose & supercilious; who give the law from their study, as the Monk from his Cell, to a world, that they know but little of'. Middleton, by contrast, wanted nothing more than 'to enforce the true principle of Protestants, the necessity of adhering to the Scriptures, as the only standard, & perfect rule of faith, exclusive of Tradition'. Only by founding Christianity on *sola scriptura* could it be 'plain, easy and rational' rather than 'difficult, uncertain, perplexed', signal features of 'traditionary' religion.

This longer anti-Waterland piece located orthodoxy within the story of the Protestant Reformation. Aping the 'Jewish Drs, [who], for the sake of authority & gain, first contrived to corrupt the Law of Moses by the invention of Traditions', papist clerics corrupted the Christian religion. As a result, 'the first step necessary to our Reformers was to clear Religion from the impure mixture, that had so long debased it'. In response to this Protestant purification, papists persecuted those whom they deemed to be heretics, so much so that heretic hunting became a kind of 'sport of the High Churchmen'. Yet, as Middleton recognized, an agreed-upon *sola scripturalism* did not itself make for Protestant unanimity. Indeed, he pointed out that since the Reformation many, such as the Huguenot Lady Margaret Professor of Divinity Peter Baro (1534–99), had once been persecuted for beliefs that later were held to be 'true & orthodox'.[48] Thus, enforced adherence to 'fundamental' doctrines was inherently wrongheaded. For Middleton, willfully seeking to destabilize the state should be heresy's sole litmus test. Quietly being heterodox should be acceptable.

Despite Middleton's assurances that his second go at Waterland was 'formed on a plan truly Theological, & such as may be espoused by the most Orthodox of the Clergy', Hervey wished that Middleton's 'Pen & Learning, capable of any Work, was imployed in one, less dangerous' to him and that he 'would leave the Discussion of that clouded subject to [his] clouded antagonist'.[49] Nevertheless, Hervey showed the piece to Benjamin Hoadly, an orthodox *bête noire*, and forwarded his own lengthy suggestions for improving the text. Indeed, he became sufficiently satisfied with Middleton's renewed attack on Waterland that he eventually *encouraged* publication. 'I should be very sorry after all the Pains you have taken with what I had the Pleasure of reading, that you should deny yourself the Credit & the World the Benefit of making it public; especially since you have taken care to guard it from any attacks your Enemies might be glad to make upon it on the side of Heterodoxy; & that I know, whatever you write, is invulnerable to any other Weapon of Criticism', he reassured Middleton. 'I therefore hope you will forward this Paper immediately to the Press.'[50] This contravened all else that Hervey had advised Middleton; in the end, his client decided that discretion was the better part of valour. He subsequently turned his near full attention to a project which Hervey had even more strongly prodded him to pursue: a life of Cicero.

Marcus Tullius Cicero (106–43 BC), or 'Tully' as he was often called, was an authoritative figure during the eighteenth century.[51] Freethinkers like John Toland and Anthony Collins found in him a kindred spirit, while others, like Herbert of Cherbury and Samuel Clarke, employed him as a tool against Hobbesian materialism.[52] Walpolean Whigs found Cicero's political vision an increasingly useful one to counter-balance the Catonic vision of the oppositional Whigs, and the 1720s and 1730s saw attempts to cast Walpole as a responsible Ciceronian leader.[53] For Middleton's part, Cicero had been the gold standard in his debates with Waterland regarding how to weigh testimony and authority when interpreting evidence from Christian history.[54] In the immediate aftermath of the *Letter to Dr. Waterland* controversy, Middleton dived more and more into reading ancient Greek and Latin authors, with 'Tully the Favourite above all; whose works are a treasure of all the knowledge & learning of those who lived before him. These are the companions I delight to converse with.'[55] By November 1734, he had decided to take up his new patron's advice and write up a life of Cicero, news which pleased Hervey.[56] It was a chance to step away from overt polemical divinity. Instead, Hervey hoped that Middleton might win over some orthodox supporters if he could forgo overt polemical divinity and produce a relatively apolitical life of Cicero, one which highlighted the quality of Middleton's scholarship and prose. Little did either Hervey or Middleton know that the life would not appear for another seven years.

In the intervening period, Hervey actively assisted his new client in producing the work. Organization was the first problem, for Middleton soon discovered that the material for the project seemed to expand exponentially. Two years into research and writing, he reported to Hervey that the book 'swells greatly under my hands, & I am continually enlarging it, by introducing all such Letters & Speeches, as give the best idea of the man, as well as of the other Great ones of those time'.[57] By the autumn of 1738, Middleton had completed the first section of what he projected would be an 800-page book in quarto.[58] By publication, the work had grown by another 50 per cent. Part of what expanded the work was Middleton's insistence on long quotations from Cicero's letters and orations, on the view that Cicero's 'own words would be more affecting to a reader, than any abstract of the substance of them from another hand'. Hervey did nothing to stem the expansion, insisting that his client should add an introductory 'Exordium of the whole' in which he surveyed the Rome of Cicero's time, 'with a little Deduction of the various transitions by which the Empire fell into that opulent, corrupt, fractious, formidable, & powerful situation in which your Hero found it'. Most importantly, advised Hervey, Middleton needed to highlight the 'conversion of a free Government into a despotic one'.[59] These additions swelled the work, so that, when it appeared in print in early 1741, it ran to 1200 pages in two quarto volumes, 1300 pages in three octavo ones.

The capacious scope of Middleton's plan partially accounts for the seven years that it took him to produce his life of Cicero, but so too did the continuing allure of polemical divinity, precisely the thing from which Hervey sought to divert him. When Richard Challoner's *Catholic Christian* appeared in 1737, for instance, Middleton felt compelled to respond, since Challoner's preface had dealt specifically with the *Letter from Rome*. '[S]ome friends have advised me to answer it, for the sake of healing my character with the Bishops', he ventured to Hervey, before concluding disingenuously, 'but I am loth to be drawn away from my present task, especially into a religious war; & to fight for a Church, which treats me as a rebel'.[60] Hervey responded unambiguously: 'I am against you meddling with the Church Dispute, because it will be read chiefly by churchmen, whom you cannot oblige'. Better, instead, it was to '[p]ursue & finish the classical work you are about, which will be read by every Body'.[61] Middleton heeded his patron's advice and refrained from entering into any print controversies over religious matters until after he completed his Cicero project. Even so, his work on Cicero was, by his own admission, slowed during the late winter and spring of 1738 on account of his concerted study of William Warburton's *Divine Legation of Moses*.[62] Hervey took it upon himself to hector Middleton back on to task during fallow stretches like these.

The greatest assistance that Hervey gave to Middleton in the Cicero project was in getting the work published. Even after Middleton had embarked upon the project, he could not settle on the method of publication. Perhaps surprisingly, the Society for the Encouragement of Learning, an organization with a decidedly orthodox disposition, encouraged Middleton to publish the volume under its auspices.[63] Middleton decided instead to publish by subscription, a method that removed the uncertainty of relying solely upon sales and one that, if the list of subscribers was large enough, might enrich an author.[64] For a time, he thought about going with the Cambridge publisher William

Thurlbourn because, he reasoned, Cambridge would 'be most convenient to me ... [because] we have a Syndicate on Foot to regulate the Press, and bring it again into Credit and Order'.[65] In the end, though, Middleton chose the London bookseller Richard Manby to produce his book.

Authors publishing by subscription had to line up subscribers. Without them, any project would be stillborn. Middleton's life of Cicero was one of only a handful of books during the eighteenth century to amass over one thousand subscribers. In Middleton's case, 1803 people or institutions subscribed to his Manby-published life of Cicero, while another 186 subscribed to the Irish octavo edition of the book.[66] Two advantages enabled Middleton to recruit so many subscribers. Firstly, his prominence and long history within Cambridge helped his subscription campaign, as it allowed him to tap not only into the university community but also into the wider, national family, patronage and other informal networks to which the members of that university community belonged.[67] So, for instance, right at two hundred of Middleton's subscribers were clerics of one rank or another, most of them with Cambridge connections; even more – over seven hundred subscribers – were lawyers, many of them who also had spent time at the university. Secondly, Middleton had both Lord Hervey and Thomas Townshend actively recruiting subscribers for the work.[68] Hervey doggedly lined up subscribers; he advised about how to pitch the printed subscription proposals and to price the various-sized editions; and he collected subscription money. Middleton's dedicatory preface to Hervey in his life of Cicero would later be mocked for its praise, hyperbolic and obsequious even by eighteenth-century standards. Yet he surely recognized that the project came off only because of Hervey's assistance. Thomas Townshend likewise lent a hand to the subscription campaign, drumming up subscribers in both England and Ireland, where he served as secretary to the lord lieutenant. By late March 1739, Middleton marvelled at 'what I may literally call a Royal list of Subscribers', and he did not exaggerate.[69] The final list of subscribers included six members of the royal family, dozens of the nobility and, perhaps surprisingly in Middleton's case, more than half of the episcopal bench. Among those bishops who did not subscribe, only one (Edmund Gibson) looks likely to have done so out of conviction. Otherwise, even some of Middleton's most inveterate critics (Thomas Sherlock and John Potter, for instance) subscribed to his Cicero project.

By the spring of 1739, they and many other subscribers were hoping to get their promised volumes. Hervey found that 'People are very impatient to have the Book come out' and he was disappointed that Middleton had not finished up the project by then.[70] Part of the not-finishing could be put down to a slow author, one who did not submit the book to press until October 1739, nearly five years after he had first begun to write on it.[71] But a year and a quarter's delay had to do with something entirely beyond Middleton's control: paper scarcity.[72] Hervey had insisted that given the subscribers' list, a project of this sort had to be produced to the highest standards. Paper was not always readily available, though. By April 1740, the indexing was done, but Manby had to wait for paper to arrive before he could finish printing the book. Things had not got any better three months later, when Middleton lamented to William Warburton that the 'impression of Tully is at a full stop for want of Genoa paper; with which we unluckily set out, without knowing what a scanty stock of it there was in England; a fresh cargo, that lately arrived, did not prove good enough, but we expect better every day'. In the event the new shipment was not up to quality, though, 'we have ordered some to be made at home of the same quality, as near as possible, and if that answers our purpose shall shortly be at work again, and depend still on publishing some time before Christmas'.[73] By September, Manby the bookseller had received 'a stock of paper at last from Genoa, sufficient for finishing the first volume, & have provided a quantity also of our own manufacture, which is the better of the two, for carrying on the second Volume at the same time'. Middleton still hoped, then, that 'we may be able still to publish both the volumes before Christmas'.[74] Hervey again implored him to finish it up quickly, 'for however just the Excuse might have been, I fear no Excuse for a new delay would have been very well received by your Subscribers; & as the month of February will be a time when the Business of Parliament will be pretty well over & the Business of Elections not begun it will be the best month for your book to make its Appearance'.[75] This was a deadline that Middleton and Manby could meet and the volumes finally appeared in print in mid-February 1741.

Their publication proved enormously successful for Middleton, going through several editions, also being translated into both French and Spanish. It allowed him to purchase a farm in Hildersham, ten miles out from Cambridge. It was, he assured Hervey, 'the pleasantest spot of the whole County ... Here I hope to enjoy a quiet & philosophical old age, neither meditating hurt to others, nor fearing any to myself, & without any concern for what the busy or ambitious part of the world may be projecting.'[76] These plans notwithstanding, Middleton clearly hoped that Hervey would be right that his life of Cicero would win him a reprieve from the orthodox and reopen the path to ecclesiastical preferment commensurate with his talents. It did not, and he was forced to take on a few private pupils, the father of one of whom, Sir John Frederick, presented him to the rectory of Hanscomb, Surrey, a living into which Benjamin Hoadly instituted him.[77] That, though, was not what either Middleton or Hervey had sought in 1735, when he started work on Cicero: they had sought Middleton's rehabilitation and the plum ecclesiastical preferment that would attend that rehabilitation. A furious Middleton dove back into polemical divinity, even before Hervey's death in August 1743, producing in the last years of his life works more troubling to his contemporaries than anything he had hitherto published.

NOTES

1 R. Halsband, *Lord Hervey, Eighteenth-Century Courtier* (Oxford, 1974); R. Browning, *Political and Constitutional Ideas of the Court Whigs* (Baton Rouge, LA, 1982), pp. 35–66. Parts of this chapter appeared in R. Ingram, 'Conyers Middleton's *Cicero*: Enlightenment, Scholarship and Polemic', in W. Altman (ed.), *Brill's Companion to the Reception of Cicero* (Leiden, 2015), pp. 94–123.

2 Middleton to Hervey, 14 June 1733 (SRO, 941/47/8).

3 Thomas Blackwell to Warburton, 25 June 1736 (Kilvert, pp. 154–5); Gray to Thomas Wharton, 9 August 1750 (E. Grosse (ed.), *Works of Thomas Gray* (New York, 1885), I, p. 199).

4 William Cole's account of Conyers Middleton (BL, Add. 5833, fol. 233).

5 Middleton to Hervey, 26 December 1733 (SRO, 941/47/8).

6 Middleton to Hervey, 27 December 1733 (ibid.).

7 Middleton to Hervey, 3 January 1734 (ibid.). Middleton had misread Sherlock's disposition towards him.

8 Middleton to Hervey, 31 January 1734 (ibid.). Shallet Turner, a fellow of Peterhouse, had the backing of Thomas Townshend and of Sir Henry Lidell, whom Turner had led on his grand tour. Turned proved to be a singularly undistinguished regius professor: D. Winstanley, *Unreformed Cambridge* (Cambridge, 1935), pp. 156–7.

9 Middleton to Townshend, 4, 6 January 1737 (*TCC*, R.1.88, fols 5, 6). See also S. Taylor, '"The Fac Totum in Ecclesiastical Affairs"? The Duke of Newcastle and the Crown's Ecclesiastical Patronage', *Albion* 24 (1992), pp. 409–33; N. Sykes, 'The Duke of Newcastle as Ecclesiastical Minister', *EHR* 62 (1942), pp. 59–84.

10 Warburton to Robert Taylor, 21 May 1738 (HRC, William Warburton I, p. 58); Middleton to Warburton, 22 September 1737 (*MWCM*, II, p. 472).

11 Townshend to Middleton, 21 August 1737 (BL, Add. 32457, fol. 122). See also Middleton to Townshend, 15 August 1737 (TCC, R.1.88, fol. 12).

12 Cole's copy of Middleton's *Free Inquiry*, [*c.* 1779] (BL, shelfmark 4535.h.7, fols v–vi).

13 Middleton to Hervey, 22 September 1737 (BL, Add. 32458, fol. 5).

14 Unless otherwise noted, all quotations in this paragraph are drawn from Cole's account of Conyers Middleton, n.d. (BL, Add. 5833, fol. 233). Sherlock later claimed that he 'did not oppose' Middleton nor 'interfered in it farer than being pressed hard by Sir Robert Walpole to give him his advice, whether it would be relished by the clergy or not: the bishop told him it would not': *Gentleman's Magazine* (September 1773), p. 542.

15 Middleton to Colbatch, 8 May 1722 (TCC, B.17.16); Alexander Clayton to Thomas Crosse 14 April 1722; Middleton to Crosse, 8 May 1722; Sherlock to Crosse, 10 May 1722 (BL, Add. 22908, fols 128–9, 134, 136).

16 T. Newton, *Works* (1782: T053426), I, pp. 20–1; [N. Mann], *Critical notes* ((1747): T034423).

17 Middleton to Hervey, 2 May 1738 (BL, Add. 32458, fol. 40).

18 Hervey to Middleton, 4 May 1738 (ibid., fol. 42).

19 Middleton to Newcastle, 7 May 1738 (BL, Add. 32691, fol. 133); Middleton to Hervey, 2 May 1738 (BL, Add. MS 32458, fol. 40).

20 Hervey to Middleton, 6 September 1733 (SRO, 941/47/7); Hervey, *Memoirs*, II, pp. 399–405.
21 Middleton to Hervey, 31 July 1733, 18 August 1734 (SRO, 941/47/8).
22 Middleton to Hervey, 19 September 1733 (ibid.).
23 Middleton to Hervey, [March] 1734, 18 August 1734 (ibid.).
24 Hervey to Middleton, 28 September 1734 (SRO, 941/47/7).
25 Middleton to Hervey, 18 August, 24 October 1734 (SRO, 941/47/8); Middleton, *Dissertation upon the origin of printing* (1735: T014359). Hervey to Middleton, 21 November 1734 (SRO, 941/47/7): 'I had almost forgot to tell you how glad I am to hear you have written something upon any Subject but Religion'.
26 Middleton to Hervey, 31 July, 25 August 1733 (SRO, 941/47/8).
27 Middleton to Hervey, 12 March 1734 (ibid.).
28 [W. Arnall], *Letter to ... Dr. Codex* (1734: T103584); Middleton to Hervey, [March] 1734, 2 April 1734 (SRO, 941/47/8).
29 Webster also courted Daniel Waterland's favourable opinion, sending him 30 copies of the *Miscellany*'s first issue: Webster to Zachary Grey, 14 December 1732 (BL, Add. 5143, fol. 100). See also Webster to Grey, 7 September 1732 (*LI*, IV, p. 392). For more on Gibson's relationship with Webster, see below, Chapter 11. Contemporaries certainly saw a close working connection between Gibson and Webster. See, for instance, C. Tracy (ed.), *The Poetical Works of Richard Savage* (Cambridge, 1962), pp. 189, 201.
30 *WM* (13 April 1733), pp. 1–2; Hervey, *Memoirs*, II, pp. 532–3.
31 Middleton to Hervey, 9 May 1734 (SRO, 941/47/8).
32 Hervey to Middleton, 20 May 1734 (SRO, 941/41/7).
33 Middleton to Hervey, 11 June 1734 (SRO, 941/47/8).
34 [Arnall], *Letter to...Dr. Codex*, pp. 11–14, 32; N. Sykes, *Edmund Gibson* (Oxford, 1926), p. 119; P. Langford, *Walpole and the Robinocracy* (Cambridge, 1986), plates 43–4.
35 Unless otherwise noted, all quotations in this paragraph are drawn from Middleton to the Author of the *Miscellany*, 9 May 1734 (BL, Add. 32457, fols 97–104).
36 *WM* (15 February 1735), pp. 1–2.
37 Unless otherwise noted, the quotations in this paragraph are drawn from Middleton to Venn, 23 February 1735. (BL, Add. 32457, fols 112–13). Innys published a number of Middleton's works, including his original *Letter from Rome* (1729); Innys also frequently published titles in conjunction with Richard Manby, someone who published many of Middleton's post-1735 works.
38 Middleton to Hervey, 9 March 1735 (SRO, 941/47/8); Middleton to Hervey, 13 April 1735 (SRO, 941/47/9).
39 *Independent London Journalist* (19 July 1735), p. 1. *MWCM*, II, pp. 496–500, reprints this letter. Venn redacted bits concerning Edward Aspinwall. See also Hervey to Middleton, 24 July 1735 (SRO, 941/47/7); Middleton to Thomas Townshend, 10 August 1735 (TCC, R.1.88, fol. 1).
40 Middleton to Hervey, 21 October 1733 (SRO, 941/47/8).
41 Middleton to Hervey, 8 November 1733 (ibid.). Berriman's Boyle Lectures for 1730–32 appeared in *Gradual revelation*.
42 Hervey to Middleton, 15 November 1733 (SRO, 941/47/7).

43 Irenaeus, *Five books of S. Irenaeus Bishop of Lyons Against the Heresies*, trans. J. Keble (Oxford, 1872), pp. 77, 208.
44 D. Waterland, *Importance...of the Holy Trinity* (1734: T117012), p. 128. See also W. Berriman, *Gradual revelation* (1733: T035779), II, pp. 345, 352.
45 Unless otherwise noted, all quotations in this paragraph and the next are drawn from Conyers Middleton's unpublished response to Daniel Waterland's *Importance ... of the Trinity*, November 1733 (BL, Add. 32459, fols 26–30).
46 For Middleton's more focused reflections on this story, 'Some short remarks on a story told by the Ancients, concerning St. John the Evangelist, and Cerinthus the Heretic', *MWCM*, II, pp. 107–20. Undated drafts of this are to be found in BL, Add. 32459, fols 26–30; Beinecke, GEN MSS vol. 93.
47 Unless otherwise noted, all quotations in this paragraph and the next are drawn from Expostulatory letter to the Revd. Dr. Waterland on the subject of certain principles advanced in ... *The Importance of the Doctrine of the Trinity*, September 1734 (BL, Add. 32459, fols 52–97).
48 Cf. P. Lake, *Moderate Puritans and the Elizabethan Church* (Cambridge, 1982), pp. 227–42.
49 Middleton to Hervey, 22 September 1734 (SRO, 941/47/8); Hervey to Middleton, 28 September 1734 (SRO, 941/47/7).
50 Hervey to Middleton, 3 December 1734 (SRO, 941/47/7). See also same to same, 15 October 1734, 19 November 1734 (ibid.).
51 T. Stuart-Buttle, 'Classicism, Christianity, and Ciceronian Academic Scepticism from Locke to Hume, c. 1660–c.1760' (D.Phil thesis, University of Oxford, 2013); G. Gawlick, 'Cicero and the Enlightenment', *SVEC* 25 (1965), pp. 657–82; M. Fox, 'Cicero during the Enlightenment', in C. Steel (ed.), *Cambridge Companion to Cicero* (Cambridge, 2013), pp. 318–36.
52 J. Champion, *Republican Learning: John Toland and the Crisis of Christian Culture, 1696–1722* (Manchester, 2003), pp. 51, 105, 110, 145–6, 158, 173, 175, 178, 191, 222; J. Champion, *The Pillars of Priestcraft Shaken: The Church of England and Its Enemies, 1660–1730* (Cambridge, 1992), pp. 183–6.
53 R. Browning, *Political and Constitutional Ideas of the Court Whigs* (Baton Rouge, LA, 1982), pp. 210–27; A. Ward, 'The Tory View of Roman History', *Studies in English Literature, 1500–1900* 4 (1964), pp. 413–56.
54 [C. Middleton], *Defence of the letter* (1731: T032264), p. 13; [C. Middleton], *Some remarks on a reply* (1732: T012468), pp. 15–16. See also C. Roberts, *Edward Gibbon and the Shape of History* (Oxford, 2014), pp. 24–5.
55 Middleton to Hervey, 31 July 1733 (SRO, 941/47/8).
56 Middleton to Hervey, 28 November 1734; Hervey to Middleton, 3 December 1734 (ibid.).
57 Middleton to Hervey, 25 December 1737 (BL, Add. 32458, fol. 19).
58 Middleton to Hervey, 9 November 1738 (ibid., fol. 53).
59 Hervey to Middleton, 11 November 1738 (ibid., fol. 60).
60 Middleton to Hervey, 29 January 1738 (ibid., fol. 21).
61 Hervey to Middleton, 4 February 1738 (ibid., fol. 24).
62 Middleton to Thomas Townshend, 23 April 1738 (TCC, R.1.88, fol. 15); Middleton to Hervey, 23 April 1738 (BL, Add. 32458, fol. 39).
63 Middleton to Warburton, 31 March 1737 (BL, Add. 32457, fol. 118); Alexander

Gordon to William Richardson, 8 December 1736 (*LA*, pp. 90–2). See also C. Atto, 'The Society for the Encouragement of Learning', *The Library* 19 (1938), pp. 263–88.

64 D. McKitterick, *A History of Cambridge University Press* (Cambridge, 1992), II, pp. 151–64; H. Amory, 'Virtual Readers: The Subscribers to Fielding's "Miscellanies" (1743)', *Studies in Bibliography* 48 (1995), pp. 94–112; W. Speck, 'Politicians, Peers and Publication by Subscription, 1700–50', in I. Rivers (eds), *Books and Their Readers in Eighteenth-Century England* (Leicester, 1982), pp. 47–68; P. Wallis, 'Book Subscription Lists', *The Library* 29 (1974), pp. 255–86.

65 Middleton to Warburton, 18 November 1738 (*MWCM*, II, p. 477).

66 See also Wallis, 'Book Subscription Lists', pp. 275–6; F. Robinson and P. Wallis, *Book Subscription Lists: A Revised Guide* (Newcastle, 1975), p. 23.

67 McKitterick, *History of Cambridge University Press*, II, p. 154.

68 Hervey to Middleton, 29 August 1738 (BL, Add. 32458, fol. 49).

69 Middleton to Hervey, 25 March 1739 (ibid., fol. 98). Other contemporaries similarly marvelled at Middleton's subscriber list: Samuel Knight to John Ward, 19 December 1739 (BL, Add. 6210, fol. 161).

70 Hervey to Middleton, 14 April 1739 (BL, Add. 32458, fol. 111).

71 Middleton to Warburton, 27 October 1739 (BL, Add. 32457, fols 143–4).

72 J. Bidwell, 'The Industrialization of the Paper Trade', in M. Suarez and M. Turner (eds), *The Cambridge History of the Book, Vol. V: 1695–1830* (Cambridge, 2009), pp. 200–17.

73 Middleton to Hervey, 27 April 1740 (BL, Add. 32458, fol. 147); Middleton to Warburton, 19 July 1740 (BL, Add. 32457, fol. 145); Middleton to Townshend, 29 July 1740 (TCC, R.1.88, fol. 41).

74 Middleton to Hervey, 4 September 1740 (BL, Add. 32458, fol. 164).

75 Hervey to Middleton, 27 December 1740 (ibid., fol. 174).

76 Middleton to Hervey, 21 October 1739 (ibid., fol. 129). See also Middleton to Townshend, 21 October 1739 (TCC, R.1.88, fol. 40). Despite unfounded accusations during the 1780s that Middleton had plagiarized from William Bellenden's *De Tribus Luminibus Romanorum* (1634), editions of Middleton's life of Cicero were produced in England until the mid-nineteenth century: H. Trevor-Roper, *History and the Enlightenment* (New Haven, 2010), pp. 99–100; M. Clarke, 'Conyers Middleton's Alleged Plagiarism', *Notes & Queries* 30 (1983), pp. 44–6.

77 Deed of institution for Conyers Middleton, 1747 (LPL, CM 25/2).

Chapter 9

Flood of resentment: assailing the primitive Church

Conyers Middleton's *History of the Life of Marcus Tullius Cicero* (1741) proved not to be a vehicle for personal and professional redemption. Its content rankled the orthodox so that the book failed to remove the heterodox stain to his reputation. While he profited financially from it, his ecclesiastical career remained stalled, his resentment metastasized and he returned again to overt polemical divinity. This chapter explores how orthodox coercion and punishment intensified and deepened one polemical divine's heterodoxy. Firstly, it explains what about an ostensibly theologically neutral work bothered the orthodox. It details next how Middleton, uninhibited by hopes of ecclesiastical promotion, returned to overt polemical divinity during the mid-1740s. Finally, it shows how his treatment of miracles focused on epistemological and hermeneutical problems that had long consumed him and whose origins Middleton explicitly traced to England's Reformation.

Middleton's take on Cicero's philosophical and religious positions implicitly commented on eighteenth-century English intellectual life.[1] In Cicero's Rome, three main philosophical 'sects' predominated: Stoics, Epicureans and Academics. The Stoics, of whom Cato (95–46 BC) was emblematic, sounded much like the eighteenth-century orthodox.[2] Middleton characterized them as 'bigots or enthusiasts in philosophy; who held none to be truly wise or good but themselves; placed perfect happiness in virtue, though stripped of every other good; affirmed all sins to be equal; all deviations from right equally wicked'. Furthermore, they held 'that a wise man could never forgive; never be moved by anger, favour or pity; never be deceived; never repent; never change his mind'.[3] At the other end of the philosophical spectrum stood the Epicureans, of whom Atticus (b. 110 BC) was the quintessence. Middleton characterized the Epicureans as the ancient analogue to modern freethinking materialists, for they 'held pleasure to be the chief good of man; death the extinction of his being; and placed their happiness consequently in the secure enjoyment of a pleasurable life: esteeming virtue on no other account, than as it was a handmaid to pleasure; and helped to ensure the possession of it, by preserving health and conciliating friends'. The typical Epicurean, following materialist logic, believed that he 'had no other duty, but to provide for his own ease; to decline all struggles; to retire from public affairs; and to imitate the life of their Gods; by passing his days in a calm, contemplative, undisturbed repose; in the midst of rural shades and pleasant gardens'.[4] The Academics, by contrast, offered a 'middle way' between the Stoics and the Epicureans. They rejected both the dogmatism of the Stoics (who 'embraced all their doctrines, as so many fixed and immutable truths') and the radical scepticism of the Epicureans (who 'observed a perfect neutrality towards all opinions; maintaining all of them to be equally uncertain'). Instead, the Academics tried to get towards the truth by distinguishing between what was 'probable' and 'improbable'. In that way, they 'kept the balance in an equal pose between the two extremes; making it their general principle, to observe a moderation in all their opinions'.[5]

Cicero was the quintessential Academic philosopher, one who adopted metaphysical positions based on probability.[6] Middleton had long admired Cicero's standards for evaluating evidence. During the Waterland controversy, he had praised Cicero for asserting 'that our belief or opinion of things ought not to depend on Testimony or Authority, but on the weight and moment of Reasons' and for declaring 'it unworthy of a Philosopher or Man of Sense to appeal to such Witnesses as may be suspected of having falsified, or feigned the Facts they relate: and to shew the argument of things by extraordinary Events instead of Arguments'.[7] Middleton later fleshed out this line of argument when detailing Cicero's religious views. These included belief in general and particular providence; in the soul's immortality; and in a future state of rewards and punishments. None of these were the positions of a modern freethinker: all could have been espoused by any orthodox churchman. Yet, there was a rub, for Cicero held those positions 'as probable only, and not certain: and as probability implies some mixture of doubt, and admits the degrees of more and less, so it admits also some variety into the stability of our persuasion'.[8] If Cicero held them only as probabilities, did Middleton also hold them only probably to be true? Nothing in Middleton's life of Cicero did anything to counter such potential orthodox objections.[9]

Yet even if that life of Cicero had been a model of orthodoxy, Middleton still faced the implacable and, as it turned out, insuperable opposition of another powerful ecclesiastical figure, John Potter (1673/4–1747), the archbishop of Canterbury. Shortly after Potter took up his new post in 1737, Middleton had complained to William Warburton about the support which the new archbishop gave to William Webster and Richard Venn. He worried a few years later that Potter had recommended Webster's *Weekly Miscellany* during his primary visitation to Canterbury.[10] Nonetheless, as he wound down his Cicero project, Middleton travelled to Lambeth Palace in June 1739 to supplicate with Potter. Their 'conference', he noted tersely, 'ended in no great satisfaction to either side'.[11] Unable to meet again with Potter in June,

Middleton conferred with John Chapman (*c.* 1705–84) (a polemical enemy and Potter's domestic chaplain) '& shewed him several passages from the book, which would enable me to make a better defence of it, than His Grace seemed disposed to allow'.[12] That overture also failed. Finally, in October 1740, Middleton wrote a long exculpatory letter. Hervey approved, acknowledging that 'softening [Potter] would certainly be an advantage' to Middleton. Nonetheless, he cautioned, 'in general I do not take [the archbishop's] opinions or Prejudices to be of a very waxen make'.[13]

Middleton both admitted error and defended his *Letter to Dr. Waterland.* During their initial conference at Lambeth, Potter referred repeatedly to Middleton's earlier anti-Waterland works, works which Middleton hoped 'had been forgotten by everybody'.[14] Potter had certainly not forgotten them and 'insisted with relation to them ... that there was nothing contained in them, from which one could infer the author's belief of the Christian religion'. In his letter to Potter, Middleton conceded that he had handled 'some things of great importance ... with a levity & wantonness of raillery, which may justly be thought indecent, & unbecoming the gravity of the subject'. He also contended that his subsequent silence signalled a retraction of his former views. '[T]en years are now past, since those books were published', he protested to Potter, 'during all which interval, the author, by dropping the pursuit of those principles in effect tacitly retracted them, & shewn a desire to be reconciled to those, whom he had offended, as far as it could be done without injury to his character; that is, without taking to himself a shame & guilt; from which he knows himself to be free, of a wilful design to weaken the authority either of the Jewish or the Christian religion'. Middleton was willing to concede defeat if he could save at least some face.

While Middleton acknowledged his errors, he also defended his *Letter to Dr. Waterland.* That defence contained little new. His *Letter,* he explained, made 'an argument of a positive kind' against natural religion shorn of revelation, an argument 'for a more effectual defence of revelation; than what had been offered by our other Apologists'. That positive argument was better suited to rebut the 'scepticism' he identified as 'the peculiar character of this age'. Could anyone deny that 'the Deists have never been able to make any reply' to it, he wondered. Moreover, his arguments (especially those regarding allegory and the divine inspiration of the Scriptures) were arguments made by the primitive fathers. Nonetheless, primitive precedent was not probative. This became clear from Middleton's own synopsis of the distinction between 'our religion itself' and 'the history or tradition of it, by which it has been handed down to us'. On the one hand, he claimed to approve of orthodox Christianity.

> I look upon our religion as a wonderful scheme of the divine wisdom & goodness, proposed & revealed in a miraculous manner, & at different times, as the exigencies of man required, from the beginning of the world, to the coming of Christ; in

order to secure us that happiness, for which we were originally created, by marking out the true road to it, & setting us right again, whenever we had lost it. I hold the substance of these revelations to be recorded in the Holy Scriptures so far as to make us wise unto Salvation; or to enable us to attain all the happiness both in this life & the next, or which our nature is capable, & am persuaded, that those sacred books carry with them such intrinsic proofs of their veracity & divine authority, as cannot reasonably be contradicted.

On the other hand, he qualified his putative orthodoxy in a way bound to disconcert his polemical opponents:

... but when all this is affirmed & believed, I do not see the necessity of maintaining every individual book, or narration of the Old & New Testament to be absolutely inspired, or dictated by God; which, instead of adding any new strength to our faith, would tend rather to distract it, by subjecting us to a multiplicity of questions, from which it might be difficult to extricate ourselves. But as these are points of a very important & delicate nature, so I am sensible, that it will always be imprudent, to make them the subject of a public controversy, & have never formed any settled opinion about them, without some distrust of my own judgement.

Where Middleton saw probability, though, his orthodox opponents saw absolute certainty; where he wrote to rebut 'scepticism', his orthodox opponents saw his work as aiding and abetting sceptics.

Not long after Middleton sent his letter to Potter, Hervey reported that he and Thomas Gooch, bishop of Ely, had 'resolved ... to take opportunities of softening the Archbishop upon your Chapter, & make him at least a neutral Power if we could get him no farther'.[15] Their efforts proved useless in the face of 'the stern Inflexibility of the Archbishop', who they nevertheless hoped would look upon Middleton's recently published life of Cicero 'as a Propitiation for your former sins, which were so like what he tells us was the original sins of our first Parents'.[16] News of Middleton's supplicating letter to Potter also circulated in Cambridge.[17] A stung Middleton groused about 'the dull bigotry of the ... Archbishop'.[18] More importantly, he re-entered the arena of polemical divinity after nearly a decade's self-imposed exile.

Richard Challoner's updated *The Catholic Christian*, whose 1737 preface addressed the *Letter from Rome*, occasioned Middleton's return to the polemical fray. The response was, he promised Archbishop Potter in late 1740, '[t]he only work of a controversial kind, which remains upon my hands', after which he would 'devote the remainders of my days to the quiet pursuit of my studies, without engaging myself in any dispute, or giving offence to any man; & whatever be my particular opinions, to content myself with the freedom of my own thoughts, without troubling the public about them'.[19] He broke this pledge. In the 1737 preface to *The Catholic Christian*, the Roman Catholic Challoner had accused Middleton of being a heretic. 'But fame may possibly apprehend, from the Way that the Doctor speaks of the martyrs of

Christ, that he is no greater Friend to Christianity in general than he is to Popery', Challoner jibed, likening Middleton to Julian the Apostate (331–63).[20] Middleton delayed responding until he had finished his life of Cicero. But once he had, he turned his attention to Challoner. The charge of heresy from a papist clearly touched a neuralgic spot, as Middleton included in his published response to Challoner a letter from a Cicero subscriber which had contended that Challoner's 'scandalous reproaches brought upon yourself, and also upon the Protestant Religion by your writings, make it incumbent on you, to wipe off these stains'. That letter writer furthermore had accused Middleton of having urged Edmund Gibson to throw Challoner's printer into prison, a charge Middleton denied vigorously, not least because his 'aversion to Popery is grounded, not only on its paganism and idolatry, but on its being calculated for the support of despotic power'.[21]

Middleton's 1741 published retort to Challoner contained little new substantively – he still focused on eight specific ways in which paganism and popery were in 'exact conformity' and he still argued that his interpretative method accorded with that of the primitive fathers. What was new about his long preface to the 1741 *Letter from Rome,* though, was the weight he gave to arguments about authority and miracles. There he made clear that while he rejected out of hand 'popish miracles' (those associated with St Thomas Becket's shrine in Canterbury, for instance) he fully accepted the miracles recounted in the Bible. 'I look upon miracles, when accompanied with all the circumstances proper to persuade us of the reality of the facts, said to be performed, and of the dignity of the end, for which they were performed, to be the most decisive proofs, that can be given, of the truth and divinity of any religion', he insisted. 'This was evidently the case of the Jewish and of the Christian miracles; wrought in such a manner, as could leave no doubt upon the senses of those, who were the witnesses to them; and for the noblest end, ... the universal good and salvation of man'.[22] He fleshed out these arguments more fully during the late 1740s.

In 1747, Middleton published *An Introductory Discourse to a larger work, designed hereafter to be published, concerning the miraculous powers*, the first of a handful of provocative works which culminated his theological development. It seemed to have come out of nowhere, unannounced even in his private correspondence. Why publish the *Introductory Discourse* when he did? In part, it may be put down to other publishing projects on ancient Rome which he undertook during those years.[23] Yet, it was also the case that, by 1747, he had turned a corner in his life and the conjunction of a few things during the period likely spurred him to produce his anti-orthodox treatments of miracles. Firstly, he had given up hopes of preferment. As late as 1742, Middleton pestered both Lord Hervey and Thomas Townshend to intervene with the duke of Newcastle to obtain for him a prebend of Canterbury cathedral.[24] In August 1743, though, Hervey died, robbing Middleton of a stalwart patron.[25] Secondly, Middleton's work on Cicero had attracted criticism from certain orthodox quarters that provoked him. In April 1742, James Tunstall (*c.* 1708–62), a fellow of St John's College, Cambridge, published his *Epistola ad virum eruditum Conyers Middleton*, a work which argued (wrongly, as it turned out) that the letters between Cicero and Brutus (correspondence which Middleton referenced in his life of Cicero) were forgeries.[26] 'I have been very busy lately upon Tunstall's Latin Epistle, in which my Life of Cicero is sifted with more ill nature & ill manners, than I had reason to expect from one, who has been obliged to me', Middleton complained shortly after the *Epistola* appeared in print.[27] He had a right to be surprised, as he and Tunstall had long been friends. Both were part of Thomas Baker's circle and both were members of the Old Maid Club, a small group of Cambridge men who regularly gathered at a coffeehouse in the evenings to discuss literary matters.[28] A year before publishing his *Epistola*, Tunstall had also 'in a very genteel way acquainted [Middleton] with his Intentions, and ... asked leave to address them to himself'.[29] Middleton considered the *Epistola* a personal betrayal; and the cordial tone of their private exchange did not carry over into their public squabble. Unsurprisingly, he started referring to Tunstall in much the same way he did to every other of his orthodox opponents. Tunstall's performance was 'an obscure, trifling piece of Sophistry, which it is my power to expose, as completely as I would wish', he bragged to Townshend.[30] After reading Middleton's published retort, Tunstall was off-put. As Warburton reported at the time, Tunstall 'is rather exasperated than dismayed with the stroke that he has received from Dr. M[iddleton]: therefore expect a bloody fight'.[31] Things only got worse when Tunstall included in his own subsequent anti-Middleton treatise an appendix by John Chapman, one of Archbishop Potter's chaplains and a polemical divine who, along with William Berriman, Henry Stebbing and Waterland, represented for Middleton all that was execrable in orthodoxy.[32]

The appearance in June 1746 of Chapman's archidiaconal charge to the clergy of Sudbury likely provoked Middleton to draft his *Introductory Discourse*. Chapman's charge was part of a deluge of anti-popish works which attended the Jacobite Rebellion of 1745. It distinguished itself from most of the rest of its type by arguing that there was afoot a secret popish intellectual plot driven by 'the zealot Court-Jesuits in the Popish Countries' who took their lead from the French Jesuit antiquarian Jean Hardouin (1646–1729). Hardouin and the Jesuits inspired by him, Chapman contended, sought to take away the Church of England's primitivist intellectual armament by finding forgeries everywhere in antiquity. They aimed ultimately 'to stab our Cause to the Heart with the admired Spirit of Incredulity and Free-thinking' and 'to establish the Vulgate Latin, as the only authentic Text of both Testaments, and to prop up, as far as possible, what they call their Apostolical Traditions'.[33] Not long after Chapman's charge appeared in print, Middleton started drafting his *Introductory Discourse*, a work which he intended as the prelude to his much longer *Free inquiry*. Both inspired dozens of responses, few of which supported Middleton's argument. David Hume was correct when he griped to his publisher that Middleton's critique of miracles overshadowed his own.[34] Middleton's was more incendiary because Middleton's mode of historical argument mattered to contemporaries more than Hume's mode of argument.

Hume's sceptical consideration of miracles in the tenth section of *An Enquiry concerning human understanding* (1748) is one of the most famous treatments of the subject in Western philosophy.[35] Hume defined a miracle as 'a violation of the laws of nature; and as a firm and unalterable experience has established these laws'. By his reckoning, no testimony of a miracle has ever amounted to a probability, much less to a proof, so that, in the end, 'a miracle can never be proved, so as to be the foundation of a system of religion'.[36] Middleton's treatment of miracles differed markedly from Hume's in that he allowed for God's immanence, while simultaneously denying particular reports of that immanence during the primitive era: put another way, Middleton, unlike Hume, believed that God could and did contravene nature's laws, yet he only trusted the New Testament reports of those contraventions of natural law.[37] Hume assailed miracles in general; Middleton assailed 'false' or 'popish' miracles.

Middleton's work on miracles, though, was not really about the miraculous as such.[38] Instead, he focused even more clearly on the hermeneutical issues with which he had dealt in the Waterland controversy and exposed what he saw as the inherent problem of orthodoxy – its uncritical reliance on tradition. It also gave him the best chance to put his orthodox enemies on the defence. That neither the *Introductory Discourse* nor the *Free Inquiry* was fundamentally about miracles is made clear not least by the fact that both built upon Middleton's 1733–34 unpublished responses to Daniel Waterland's *Importance of the Doctrine of the Trinity*. At the time that the *Introductory Discourse* appeared in April 1747, a Cambridge wit 'was heard to say [of it], that "The Doctor had erected a ladder against the steeple, and that he foresaw the Aspirants would be in such haste to climb, that they would expose themselves to the company below in very ludicrous attitudes"'.[39] Claiming to be motivated by the 'growth of popery' in England at the time, Middleton opened the work by arguing that some of the most eminent orthodox polemical divines (Charles Leslie, Henry Dodwell, Daniel Waterland, William Berriman and John Chapman among them) had unwittingly supported popery by using the primitive Church as the measure of doctrinal and liturgical purity. '[T]hese eminent Divines, pursuing their several systems, and ambitious of improving still upon each other's discoveries, seem unwarily to have betrayed the Protestant cause, by transferring the miraculous powers of the Church, the pretended signs of truth and orthodoxy, into the hands of its enemies', contended Middleton, who styled himself as the true Protestant.[40] Reprising nearly every argument and example that he had employed in *A Letter from Rome* two decades earlier, he argued that the 'chief corruptions of Popery' were introduced during the first centuries immediately after the apostolic age.

Miracles ranked among the most important of those corruptions. In his *Letter from Rome* Middleton had argued that '[i]f we examine the pretended Miracles, and pious Frauds of the Church of Rome, we shall be able to trace them all to the same Source of Paganism, and find that the Priests of Rome are not in the least degenerated from their Predecessors, in the Art of imposing upon their fellow Citizens, by the Forgery of these holy Impostures'.[41] Two decades later in the *Introductory Discourse*, he insisted that 'after the strictest attention to what both the ancients and the moderns also have delivered on this subject, I find great reason to be convinced, that the pretended miracles of the fourth century, were not only in general, and for the greatest part, but entirely and universally the effects of fraud and imposture'.[42]

To separate frauds and impostures from real miracles, Middleton applied the Lockean test of necessity. Only miracles of Christ and his apostles passed that test, for they were 'wrought ... for an end so great, so important, and so universally beneficial, as to be highly worthy of the interposition of the Deity; and wrought by the ministry of mean and simple men, in the open view of the people, as the testimonial of that divine mission, to which they pretended'. Furthermore, he continued, the miracles of Christ and his apostles were 'delivered to us by eyewitnesses, whose honest characters exclude the suspicion of fraud, and whose knowledge of the facts, which they relate, scarce admits the probability of a mistake'.[43] The miracles of the primitive Church, by contrast, were unnecessary and fraudulent. Middleton promised in his forthcoming *Free Enquiry* 'to evince by particular facts and testimonies ... that the pretended miracles of the primitive Church were all mere fictions; which the pious and zealous Fathers, partly from a weak credulity, and partly, from reasons of policy, believing some perhaps to be true, and knowing all of them to be useful, were induced to espouse and propagate, for the support of a righteous cause'.[44] The orthodox had not detected the fraud because they had failed 'to fix the religion of Protestants on its proper basis, that is, on the sacred Scriptures; not on the authority of weak and fallible men, the detection of whose errors, and the suspicion of whose frauds would necessarily give a wound to Christianity itself'.[45]

Perhaps, though, the problem ran even deeper, originating in the Church of England's very DNA. Middleton, for all his concerns about the uses and abuses of clerical power, was a man almost wholly uninterested in ecclesiology (an issue which had bedevilled the sixteenth- and seventeenth-century English) perhaps because he would gladly have accepted a seat on the episcopal bench if one had been offered to him. But he did see clearly the epistemological and hermeneutical problems thrown up by the English Reformation, whose story he told in his *Introductory Discourse*. Henry VIII had both enabled and obstructed the Reformation, for he was 'an arbitrary Prince, who would not suffer [the Reformers], to take the least step but by his immediate direction, and from his high conceit of his Theological learning, gave the law even to his Bishops, in all the religious disputes of those days and whose chief view after all was, to banish rather the power, than the religion of the Pope, out of his realm'. One of Henrician policy's effects was that the Reformers could not 'make such changes in the old worship, as put them under a necessity of discarding the authority of the primitive Fathers; but on the contrary, were obliged against their wills, to comply still with many rites and doctrines, which had no other foundation, but in that authority'. While at 'the same time reforming Bishops found themselves at liberty' during Edward VI's reign 'to carry on their work to its full perfection', they did not want overly to disturb the majority of the clergy, 'who still generally favoured the old forms'.[46] After the 'sad catastrophe' of Mary's reign, Elizabeth I 'finally established the Reformation'. Yet her approach to attracting papists to the Church of England itself undermined the Reformation cause by continuing to appeal to antiquity's authority.

> Her view was, to moderate the prejudices of the Popish clergy; and to reconcile them by degrees to the new settlement, by leaving in it an outward shew, and some resemblance of the old. From the same principle, a reverence was still kept up to Antiquity; and appeals made on both sides, to the primitive Fathers and ancient Councils, by the Professors of the new, as well as of the old doctrines: which practice has been followed ever since, by the greatest part of our leading Churchmen. But from the little success which it has had, or ever can have, in our controversies with the Papists, it is evident, that it cannot be considered in any other light, but as a vain ostentation of learning, and an impatient zeal, to repel that charge of ignorance and contempt of primitive Antiquity, with which the Protestant Churches are constantly reproached by the Romanists.[47]

Things degenerated during the early seventeenth century under James I and Charles I, when the 'popish interest' revived. Archbishop William Laud, in particular, 'from a compliance with the principles of the Court, and an abhorrence of those of the Puritans' tried to reconcile the Churches of England and Rome 'by giving such an interpretation to the doctrines and form to the discipline of our Church, as might invite all moderate Papists, to join with them in its communion'.[48] All that came of these efforts was a bloody civil war, which tore apart the nation. Yet at the Restoration, Stuart governments largely readopted Laud's policies and the spectre of Protestant separatism actually catalysed an increased reverence for the primitive Church, since warrant could be found in primitive practice for the Church of England's liturgy and discipline. Middleton thought this weakened Protestantism: 'by agreeing with the Romanists thus far, and joining with them in a common appeal to primitive antiquity, we allow all, which they can fairly draw from it, to be sound and orthodox; and though in the end, they may not perhaps gain everything, which they aim at, yet they will be sure always, to come off with great advantage'.[49] Put simply, Middleton viewed the English Reformation not just as incomplete but as inherently flawed. To be authentically Protestant (and hence authentically Christian), English churchmen needed to reject the epistemological and hermeneutical methods which the Church of England had, since its inception in the mid-sixteenth century, held to be orthodox. It was, at once, a provocative challenge and a hopeless wish.

In the *Free Inquiry into the miraculous powers, which are supposed to have subsisted in the Christian Church, from the earliest ages through several successive centuries* (1748), Middleton provided fuller evidence to support the indictment in the *Introductory Discourse.* Middleton promised to examine closely 'all the principal testimonies' to miracles in the primitive Church; to query 'the condition of the persons who are said to have been indued with [miraculous] gifts'; to illuminate 'the particular characters and opinions of the Fathers, who attest to those miracles'; to ask 'how far the credibility of [the primitive miracles] may reasonably be suspected'; and to refute 'some of those most plausible objections, which have hitherto been made by my antagonists'.[50] His argument, he reassured his readers, proceeded from 'plain reasoning grounded on plain facts'. The facts had led him to conclude that 'The History of the Gospel, I hope may be true, though the History of the Church be fabulous', a proposition he aimed to prove in the *Free Inquiry* by discrediting the primitive Church.[51] Why, Middleton wondered, did miracles cease after the apostolic age only to reappear by the end of the second century? Why should we believe in that revival of miracles? The orthodox insisted that the testimony of the primitive fathers was sufficiently persuasive to warrant assent; but Middleton, in relentless and systematic fashion, charged the early church fathers with being liars at worst, dupes at best. Polycarp, Justin Martyr, Irenaeus, Cyprian, Tertullian, Origen, Athanasius, Jerome, Basil and John Chrysostom all came under his withering glare, and some of the examples he adduced against them hailed from his earlier anti-Waterland manuscripts from the mid-1730s. Irenaeus (130–202), for instance, claimed that Christ had lived until he was nearly fifty years old, something which even no other primitive father contended.[52] Cyprian (d. 258), who was 'fond of power and Episcopal Authority', evoked visions when he wanted to assert that episcopal authority. Dionysius (d. 264), bishop of Alexandria, claimed to have seen visions in order to justify his flight from persecution.[53] On and on Middleton continued. When he was done, the primitive fathers' credibility seemed battered, as he had exposed what he saw to be the irrationalities, contradictions, silences and impossibilities in their testimony. His conclusion was unambiguous:

> I have shewn, by many indisputable facts, that the ancient Fathers, by whose authority that delusion was originally imposed, and has ever since been supported, were extremely credulous and superstitious; possessed with strong prejudices and an enthusiastic zeal, in favour, not only of Christianity in general, but of every particular doctrine, which a wild imagination could ingraft upon it; and scrupling no art or means, by which they might propagate the same principles. In short: that they were of a character, from which nothing could be expected, that was candid

> and impartial; nothing, but what a weak or crafty understanding could supply, towards confirming those prejudices, with which they happened to be possessed; especially where religion was the subject, which above all other motives, strengthens every bias, and inflames every passion of the human mind.[54]

Not just the primitive fathers but their modern orthodox defenders came in for rough treatment. John Chapman had relied on the work of the Roman Catholic French ecclesiastical historian Sébastien Le Nain de Tillemont (1637–98); and his defence of fifth-century miracles (which Middleton reckoned were 'impostures') invited ridicule.[55] Similarly, William Berriman's claim that the Arian Vandal king Huneric (*c.* 484) persecuted anti-Arian Trinitarians was likewise wildly improbable.[56] And, of course, Daniel Waterland came in for abuse, as Middleton pointed out that Waterland had relied unquestioningly on Gregory of Nyssa's account of the Athanasian Creed's Trinitarian claims when even Henry Dodwell had rejected some fourth-century miracle claims because Athanasius and Gregory of Nyssa proved unreliable witnesses.[57]

The orthodox response to Middleton was visceral. But, fuelled by a deep reservoir of resentment, he refused to soften his imprecations upon 'the quackery and imposture' of 'primitive wonder-workers' and the fraudulence of primitive miracles.[58] An appreciation of the depth and distorting power of that resentment was evident from an exchange he had with Thomas Gooch, bishop of Ely, in early 1749. Middleton had sent a copy of the *Free Inquiry* to Gooch, a decades-old friend and an ally who had only a few years earlier joined with Lord Hervey to lobby Archbishop Potter for Middleton. Gooch returned a warm note of thanks. 'I have read it', he explained, '& shall always read with pleasure, what comes from you, even though I should happen to differ in opinion with you, or should wish you had less to say on your side of the Question'.[59] Gooch's was not a long letter, but it was a kind note of acknowledgement sent by a busy administrator. Middleton expected more and got apoplectic. As he explained in a long, intemperate reply, '[t]he chief end of my writings, is not to please only, but to convince; and my subjects are chosen with that view, as proper to instruct, rather than to entertain; by recommending some important truth, or exposing some prevailing error'. If, then, Gooch only got pleasure from the *Free Inquiry*, Middleton had failed. But perhaps, he insinuated, Gooch was at fault, for '[a]n ingenious friend of mine of the Clergy, who is as well informed of the sentiments of the men of letters and judgment in London, as any one there, sends me word; that they are unanimous in their approbation, both of the matter and manner of my work; and declare without hesitation, that the argument is indisputably on my side'. Even within Cambridge, 'where objections are apt to be dispensed with much freedom', there had been no public complaints about the *Free Inquiry*. In addition to being wrong, Gooch had also, Middleton noted, been thoughtless. While knowing even before he sent the book to him that Gooch would not agree with his argument, 'I had reason to expect at the same time from a friend, with whom I have conversed and corresponded familiarly for forty years past' a fuller explanation of the nature of those disagreements along with 'some facts and testimonies overlooked or misapplied by me, which had induced him to dissent from me'. Had Middleton stopped there, it would have been awkward enough. But he continued, complaining not just about Henry Stebbing (a Thomas Sherlock protégé whom Gooch had recently granted a living) but also about Sherlock himself (Gooch's brother-in-law, who had chosen not 'to confute my opinions, by a fair & public examination of them' but instead 'to depress my character & fortunes, by private insinuations in the Cabinet of a Minister').[60] Gooch could only 'express my Surprise at finding such a flood of Resentment poured upon Me by One' to whom he had written in friendship and 'for whom I had all my Life long been endeavouring to do good Offices'.[61]

During the last years of Middleton's life, Thomas Gooch was not alone in finding himself overwhelmed by Middleton's 'flood of Resentment'. Responding to his critics, as Middleton freely admitted to a friend in April 1749, had become 'the chief business & delight of my life' and defending his 'duty' and his 'reputation' was, he reckoned, what he would spend his time doing 'for the remainder of my life'.[62] In the last year of his life, he widened the scope of his attack on orthodoxy to rebut Thomas Sherlock's *The Use and Intent of Prophecy*. It looked like a gratuitous attack, not the least since Sherlock's book had first been published a quarter century earlier. Middleton protested that he had not read it when it first appeared and that he had read it recently only because someone had recommended it to him.[63] The London bookseller John Whiston recalled things differently: 'Sherlock told me that he presented Dr. M. with his book when first published in 1725, and that he soon afterwards thanked him for it, and expressed his pleasure in the perusal'.[64] Whether or not Whiston remembered correctly, Middleton would have been familiar with Sherlock's argument, given the degree to which he kept abreast of the latest works of English polemical divinity. More likely, Sherlock's promotion to the bishopric of London in late 1748 prompted Middleton to begin his belated retort to Sherlock, while the appearance in June 1749 of Sherlock's *Appendix to the Second Dissertation being a further Inquiry into the Mosaic account of the Fall* lay behind the 'Cursory Animadversions' which Middleton appended to his anti-Sherlock book. The result was an uncharacteristically muddled, graceless piece of prose, a work which showed every sign of having been written in great haste.

Prophecy was an important proof of Christianity during this period, in some ways even more important than miracles, since it did not have to rely on the accuracy of historical reports but could, in the present, be observed unfolding.[65] Yet Middleton's writings about prophecy were less about prophecy than they were about epistemology and hermeneutics, in much the same way that his writings about miracles were not really about the miraculous as such. Sherlock had written his *Use and Intent of Prophecy* as a riposte to Anthony Collins's *Discourse on the Grounds and Reasons of the Christian Religion* (1724), in which Collins – following the lead of Grotius and LeClerc – had argued that the literal fulfilment of prophecies was impossible and, thus, that Jesus could not possibly be the literal fulfilment of the Old Testament prophecies. At stake was no less than the truth of Christianity.[66] Sherlock argued instead for a developmental understanding of biblical prophecy. It was an interpretative strategy acceptable both to biblical literalists, in that it acknowledged the truth of all biblical prophecies, and to those who read the Bible with slightly more latitude, in that it insisted that the individual prophecies made full sense only when understood as part of a larger scheme whose meaning was only gradually unfolded to man by God. Middleton, by contrast, reckoned that the only persuasive answer to Collins's freethinking objections was to acknowledge that those who wrote the Bible were not always divinely inspired and, thus, that mistakes could and did enter into the text. That concession alone, he insisted, would cut the feet out from under freethinking critics of prophecy, for the truth of particular prophecies, like the truth of miracles, could be ascertained by judging the credibility of the prophets themselves. Middleton, in other words, thought that some Old Testament prophecies were true, others not: the task of the reader was to discern the true from the false. This was an agenda entirely different from that of the freethinking Collins.[67]

One patch of ground on which Middleton and Sherlock fought concerned the Fall, a subject at the centre of Middleton's attacks on Waterland two decades earlier. In his *Appendix*, Sherlock had insisted that the Mosaic account of the Fall was not allegorical but literally true. For instance, with regard to the story of the serpent deceiving Eve, Moses 'relates this Fact as an Historian' and gives us 'the very Words of God'. Part of God's punishment after that deception was to condemn serpents to be accursed beasts who should for ever slither on their bellies and have enmity with Eve and her progeny: 'it shall bruise thy Head, and thou shalt bruise his Heel' (Genesis 3:14–15). By way of proof that the current condition of serpents proved the literal fulfilment of God's prophecy regarding man's victory over the serpent, Sherlock pointed out that 'Naturalists are agreed that the Head of a Serpent is the tenderest Part, and that Wounds there, if they are such as bruise or break the Head, are incurable. Upon this Ground the Scripture elsewhere representing great evil Powers under the Image of Dragons and Serpents, relates or foretells their certain Ruin by the same Figure of bruising or breaking their Heads'. For Sherlock, this was proof of literal prophetic fulfilment.[68] Middleton reckoned entirely differently, asking why the curse on the serpent would not be expected in the very nature of the animal and noting that the biblical account of the serpent speaking accorded with what one might expect from most ancient fables in which animals speak. All of this led Middleton to conclude that the account of the Fall had to be understood allegorically and, perhaps more importantly to him, that Sherlock had offered in his defence of its literalness more of 'the same slimy stuff; a fine-spun web of fantastical whims, and precarious suppositions worked up together into some resemblance of arguments, whence many surprising and recondite inferences are occasionally deduced by him'.[69]

As with his works on miracles, Middleton's anti-Sherlock work on prophecy inspired heated responses from some of the most prominent polemical divines of the day. 'You see how Middleton is paid off for meddling with the Bishop of London', William Warburton observed. 'Every week launches two or three thunderbolts at his head.'[70] Middleton, though, would not live to see to its conclusion the controversy which he had stirred up, for on 28 July 1750, he died at his farm in Hildersham, aged sixty-seven.[71] His widow asked William Heberden to go through her late husband's papers. Heberden found more anti-orthodox material awaiting publication.[72] Some made its way into Middleton's collected works in 1752; but some did not, including a Latin treatise on miracles (not published improbably upon the advice of the undoubtedly heterodox Bolingbroke) and a piece on the 'inefficacy of prayer', which purportedly got burned.[73] In death, as in life, few knew what to make of Middleton or his legacy.[74] Middleton's sometime friend, Warburton, reflected the uncertainty which most at the time felt. He had been informed that a few days before his death, Middleton had said that he could die 'with that composure of mind' which befit 'a sincere searcher after Truth' and that he only worried that he could not get all he had planned to write into print. For his part, Warburton thought that was all well and good, '[i]f this Truth be, that the Providence of God governs the moral as well as the natural world; and that, in compassion to human distresses, he has revealed his will to mankind, by which we are enabled to get the better of them, by a restoration to his favour'. On the other hand, 'if the Truth discovered be that we have no farther share in God than as we partake of his natural government of the Universe; or that all there is in his moral government is only the natural necessary effects of Virtue and Vice upon human agents here, and that all the pretended Revelations of an hereafter were begot by fools, and hurried up by knaves', then this was surely false comfort. In the end, Warburton hoped that death would finally bring his old friend peace. 'All that I hope and wish is, that the Scribblers will let his memory alone: for though (after the approbation of the good and wise) one cannot wish anything better for one's self, or one's friend, than to be heartily abused by them in this life, because it is as certain a sign of one's merit, as a dog barking at the Moon is of her brightness', he wrote to John Jortin. '[Y]et the veil that Death draws over us is so sacred, that the throwing dirt there has been esteemed at all times, and by all people, a profanation.'[75] Most of Middleton's contemporary polemical divines were less charitable, judging that it was Middleton's works which were the real profanation, a profanation, Middleton might have added, that owed much to his treatment at the hands of some of those very same polemical divines.

What both Middleton and his opponents shared, though, was a recent national and European past riven by religious and political faction and war. That past fuelled their efforts to recover truth; to fend off its enemies; and to secure it for posterity. In the polemical careers of divines like Zachary Grey and William Warburton, the hold of the sixteenth- and seventeenth-century past on the eighteenth century is even more evident.

NOTES

1 T. Stuart-Buttle, 'Classicism, Christianity, and Ciceronian Academic Scepticism from Locke to Hume, c. 1660–c.1760' (D.Phil. thesis, University of Oxford, 2013), pp. 179–218. Parts of this chapter appeared in R. Ingram, '"The Weight of Historical Evidence": Conyers Middleton and the Eighteenth-Century Miracles Debate', in R. Cornwall and W. Gibson (eds), *Religion, Politics and Dissent, 1660–1832* (Aldershot, 2010), pp. 85–109; R. Ingram, 'Conyers Middleton's *Cicero*: Enlightenment, Scholarship and Polemic', in W. Altman (ed.), *Brill's Companion to the Reception of Cicero* (Leiden, 2015), pp. 94–123.

2 R. Browning, *Political and Constitutional Ideas of the Court Whigs* (Baton Rouge, LA, 1982), pp. 211–27.

3 C. Middleton, *History of the life of Marcus Tullius Cicero* (1741: T125479), III, p. 360.

4 Ibid., p. 362.

5 Ibid., pp. 331–2.

6 L. Daston, 'Probability and Evidence', in D. Garber and M. Ayres (eds), *Cambridge History of Seventeenth-Century Philosophy* (Cambridge, 1998), II, pp. 1108–44; R. Serjeantson, 'Proof and Persuasion', in K. Park and L. Daston (eds), *Early Modern Science* (Cambridge, 2006), pp. 132–75.

7 [C. Middleton], *Defence of the letter* (1731: T032264), p. 13.

8 Middleton, *Cicero*, III, p. 356.

9 Cf. [T. Birch], review of Middleton's *Cicero*, *History of the Works of the Learned* (1741), I, pp. 152–60, 239–49.

10 Middleton to Warburton, 14 March 1737 (BL, Add. 32457, fol. 116); Middleton to Warburton, 4 September 1739 (Beinecke, Osborn Files Folder 10185).

11 Middleton to Warburton, 6 June 1739 (BL, Add. 32457, fol. 138).

12 Middleton to Townshend, 19 June 1739 (TCC, R.1.88, fol. 33). Potter's domestic chaplains would later include another Cambridge figure and Middleton polemical enemy, James Tunstall.

13 Hervey to Middleton, 20 September 1740. (BL, Add. 32458, fol. 168). See also Hervey to Middleton, 9 September 1740; Middleton to Hervey, 16 September 1740 (BL, Add. 32458, fols 165, 166).

14 Unless otherwise noted, all quotations in this paragraph and the next are drawn from Middleton to Potter [October] 1740 (BL, Add. 32457, fols 155–8).

15 Hervey to Middleton, 13 November 1740 (BL, Add. 32458, fol. 171).

16 Hervey to Middleton, 12 September 1741 (ibid., fol. 175).

17 Middleton to Warburton, 8 January 1741 (*MWCM*, II, p. 484).

18 Middleton to Birch, 19 November 1747 (BL, Add. 4314, fol. 24).
19 Middleton to Potter, October 1740 (BL, Add. 32457, fol. 157).
20 [R. Challoner], *Catholic Christian instructed* (1737: T072815), p. xiii; [R. Challoner], *Plain answer to Dr. Middleton's Letter* (1741: T011586), p. 11.
21 C. Middleton, *Letter from Rome* (1741: T087410), pp. cxiii–cxv. Middleton had threatened Richard Bentley's printer in 1721 with legal action: Middleton to Colbatch, April 1721 (TCC, B.17.15).
22 Ibid., p, lxxxv.
23 C. Middleton, *Germana quædam antiquitatis* (1745: T125483); Middleton, *Treatise on the Roman senate* (1747: T071115); T. Knowles (ed.), *Letters between Lord Hervey and Dr. Middleton* ((1778): T060921).
24 Middleton to Townshend, 20 October 1741, 12 May 1742 (TCC, R.1.88, fols 45, 47). At the time, Hervey's health was declining quickly: Hervey to Middleton, 22 May 1742 (BL, Add. 32458, fol. 178).
25 The death in April 1745 of Middleton's second wife, Mary, also delivered a 'cruel shock', the 'effects of which I shall ever feel through the rest of my declining life': Middleton to Townshend, 15 May 1745 (TCC, R.1.88, fol. 53).
26 J. Tunstall, *Epistola* (1741: T075098); J. Levine, '"Et Tu Brute?" History and Forgery in Eighteenth-Century England', in R. Myers and M. Harris (eds), *Fakes and Frauds* (Winchester, 1989), pp. 71–97.
27 Middleton to Townshend, 12 May 1742 (TCC, R.1.88, fol. 47).
28 R. Masters, *Memoirs of ... Thomas Baker* (1784: T073604), pp. 112–13, 114, 115; G. Dyer, *The Privileges of the University of Cambridge* (1824), II, pp. 136–7.
29 Charles Yorke to Philip Yorke, 2 June 1741 (BL, Add. 35360, fols 42–3). Cf. Charles Yorke to Birch, 29 May 1742 (BL, Add. 4325, fol. 44).
30 Middleton to Townshend, 12 May 1742 (TCC, R.1.88, fol. 47).
31 Warburton to Thomas Birch, 18 January 1743 (BL, Add. 4320, fol. 174); C. Middleton, *Epistles of ... Cicero to ... Brutus* (1742: T075405).
32 J. Tunstall, *Observations on the ... epistles between Cicero and M. Brutus* (1743: T081114). In 1744, Tunstall joined Chapman as one of Potter's chaplains. Chapman had once been one of Middleton's friends.
33 J. Chapman, *Popery the true bane of letters* (1746: T044070), pp. 3, 6. Cf. A. Grafton, 'Jean Hardouin: The Antiquary as Pariah', *JWCI* 62 (1999), pp. 241–64.
34 J. Greig (ed.), *The Letters of David Hume. Volume I: 1727–1765* (Oxford, 1932), p. 3.
35 R. Burns, *The Great Debate on Miracles: From Joseph Glanville to David Hume* (1981); J. Shaw, *Miracles in Enlightenment England* (New Haven, 2006).
36 D. Hume, *An Enquiry Concerning Human Understanding*, ed. T. Beauchamp (Oxford, 2006), pp. 85–6, 97.
37 B. Gregory, *The Unintended Reformation* (Cambridge, MA, 2012), pp. 60–2. See also J. Harris, *Hume: An Intellectual Biography* (Oxford, 2015), pp. 228–30.
38 B. Young, 'Preludes and Postludes to Gibbon: Variations on an Impromptu by J.G.A. Pocock', *History of European Ideas* 35 (2009), pp. 424–5; B. Young, 'Conyers Middleton: The Historical Consequences of Heterodoxy', in J. Robertson and S. Mortimer (eds), *The Intellectual Consequences of Religious Heterodoxy, 1600–1750* (Leiden, 2012), pp. 251–8; H. Trevor-Roper, *History and the Enlightenment* (New Haven, 2010), pp. 101–5.

39 F. Blackburne, *Occasional remarks upon ... The confessional. Part II* (1769: T004910), p. 2.
40 [C. Middleton], *Introductory discourse* in C. Middleton, *Free Inquiry* (1748: T086639), p. li.
41 Middleton, *Letter from Rome* (1729), p. 52.
42 [Middleton], *Introductory discourse*, p. lxxv.
43 Ibid., p. xciv. See also J. Locke, *Writings on Religion*, ed. V. Nuovo (Oxford, 2002), pp. 44–50.
44 [Middleton], *Introductory discourse*, p. xci.
45 Ibid., p. cxi.
46 Ibid., pp. ci, cii.
47 Ibid., pp. ciii–civ.
48 Ibid., p. cv.
49 Ibid., p. cix.
50 Middleton, *Free inquiry*, pp. 1–2.
51 Ibid., xxxi, p. 162.
52 Ibid., p, 45. Cf. Middleton's unpublished response to Waterland's *Importance*, November 1733 (BL, Add. 32459, fol. 27).
53 Ibid., pp. 101–4, 106.
54 Ibid., pp. xxxi–xxxii.
55 Ibid., pp. 164, 174–6.
56 Ibid., pp. 182–4.
57 Ibid., 146–9.
58 Ibid., p. 21.
59 Gooch to Middleton, 24 January 1749 (BL, Add. 32457, fol. 178).
60 Middleton to Gooch, 7 February 1749 (ibid., fols 175–8).
61 Gooch to Middleton 14 March 17 (ibid., fol. 1749). See also Warburton to Hurd, 13 January 1750 (*LLEP*, pp. 31–2). William Cole nicely encapsulates the vicissitudes of the Gooch–Middleton friendship. 'Dr. Gooch & Dr. Middleton had been great Friends; were both of a Party, & both changed it; yet it is my real Belief, that both their Hearts were with their old Friends: & though this does not seem to add much to their Character; neither does it in my Opinion take much away from it. They had made an Opposition, till they saw the utter Impossibility of doing any good by it; & seeing that the full Tide & Stream of Preferment was against them, they did wisely to swim with the Stream: the Misfortune was, Dr Middleton, by being in great an Hurry, was carried beyond his Depth; whereas Dr Gooch, by calmly watching Opportunities arrived at a good Harbour in the Isle of Ely': William Cole's account of Conyers Middleton, n.d. (BL, Add. 5833, fol. 236).
62 Middleton to Heberden, 3 April 1749 (BL, Add. 32457, fol. 184).
63 C. Middleton, *Examination of the Lord Bishop of London's discourses* (1749: T18295), pp. 1, 3.
64 A. Chalmers, *General Biographical Dictionary* (1815), XXII, p. 142. Middleton owned only the 1740 edition of Sherlock's *Use and Intent of Prophecy*: J. Whiston, *Catalogue of ... Conyers Middleton* (1751: T064471), p. 14.
65 P. Harrison, 'Prophecy, Early Modern Apologetics, and Hume's Arguments against Miracles', *JHI* 60 (1999), pp. 241–56; N. Sykes, *From Sheldon to Secker: Aspects of English Church History, 1660–1768* (Cambridge, 1959), pp. 171–2;

L. Stephen, *History of English Thought in the Eighteenth Century* (1902), II, pp. 212–27.

66 J. O'Higgins, *Anthony Collins* (The Hague, 1970), pp. 55–199.

67 Cf. Trevor-Roper, *History*, pp. 105–7.

68 T. Sherlock, *Appendix to the second dissertation* (1749: T093246), pp. 2–3, 17, 27.

69 Middleton, *Examination of the Lord Bishop of London's discourses*, pp. 123, 132.

70 Warburton to Nathaniel Forster, 3 April 1750 (BL, Add. 11275, fol. 198). Sherlock himself thought Rutherforth, *Defence of ... discourses* was especially effective: Sherlock to Rutherforth, 8 May 1750 (Beinecke, Osborn File Folder 13729).

71 John Green to Heberden, 28 July 1750; Robert Plumptre to Heberden, 29 July 1750 (BL, Add. 32457, fols 187, 189); Cole's account of Middleton (*WC*, XV, pp. 313–14).

72 John Robartes to William Heberden, 20 November 1750 (Beinecke, GEN 93, fol. 1).

73 Bolingbroke to Heberden, 11 September 1751 (BL, Add. 32457, fol. 198); Gray to Horace Walpole, 8 October 1751 (E. Gosse (ed.), *The Works of Thomas Gray* (New York, 1885), I, pp. 214–17).

74 Trevor-Roper, *History*, pp. 293 fn. 139, 294 fn. 174.

75 Warburton to Jortin, 30 July 1750 (*LI*, II, pp. 179–81). See also Warburton to Edward Littleton, 11 July 1750 (Staffordshire RO, D.1413/1); Thomas Birch to Philip Yorke, 10 August 1750 (BL, Add. 35397, fol. 275).

Part III

Neither Jacobite, nor republican, Presbyterian, nor papist: Zachary Grey

Chapter 10

Popery in its proper colours

Zachary Grey's *Popery in its proper colours* appeared in December 1745, one of hundreds of works responding to the Jacobite rebellion of 1745.[1] In retrospect, the rebellion was doomed to failure, but many at the time, especially leaders in Church and state, reckoned differently.[2] They worried that the nation was morally and physically weak and that the rebellion on the Stuarts' behalf would succeed. A restoration of Roman Catholicism and an overthrow of the post-revolution religious and political settlements would follow. This prospect terrified Protestant clerics, who preached and wrote against the putative popish menace at 'full drive'.[3]

The anti-Jacobite literature highlighted the lengths to which Catholics would go to make converts and thereafter to destroy English religious and political liberties. Zachary Grey explained how this would happen. '[T]he Factors of Rome' worked ceaselessly 'to gain one Proselyte', Grey argued, and never more so than 'when a Rebellion is actually afoot'. Papists employed subterfuge and imposture, so that it was the 'Duty of every true Briton ... to expose the Artifices with which lie in wait to deceive'. Grey thought this best done through rigorous historical argument, by 'producing incontestable Matters of Fact, in proof of the gross Corruptions and horrid Superstition of that Church ... and of the detestable Villainies made use of to support their Religion (otherwise indefensible)'.[4] In *Popery in its proper colours*, Grey strung together long quotations from presumably unimpeachably reliable English historians. The pamphlet opened with an extended excerpt from Gilbert Burnet's Swiss and Italian letters (1686) on the imposture of Johannes Jetzer and the Dominicans in 1507 Bern regarding Marian visitations. There followed selections from Henry Care's anti-popish *Weekly Pacquet* (1678–83) against saints, indulgences, clerical absolution and 'cursing with bell, book and candle'; from Henry Wharton's *Enthusiasm of the Church of Rome* (1688) on the implausibility of St Almachius (d. 391); and from William Wake's *Second Defence of the Exposition of the Doctrine of the Church of England* (1688) against the efficacy of saints' relics. The one eighteenth-century text quoted

Figure 4 'Zachary Grey', *c.* 1795, by Philip Audinet, after Silvester Harding

– Conyers Middleton's *Letter from Rome* – freely admitted its own indebtedness to seventeenth-century scholarship.[5]

Zachary Grey's anti-Jacobite *Popery in its proper colours*, like most of his nearly three dozen published works sprawling across over five thousand octavo pages, wrestled with eighteenth-century problems by way of sixteenth- and seventeenth-century texts.[6] Grey wrote them from comfortable, though not prestigious, ecclesiastical perches. While he wrote much, he wrote poorly, participating in print controversies rather than sparking them. Yet he won the support of Edmund Gibson, Daniel Waterland and other consequential orthodox churchmen because his blunt, artless scholarship had direct contemporary relevance during an era when Protestant nonconformists were agitating for a loosening (some thought a dissolution) of the legal ties between Church and state, ties that had emerged during the sixteenth century and that had been reaffirmed and cemented after the Restoration. Those nonconformists mostly couched their arguments in historical terms, so that defenders of the *status quo* had too to ground their defences in history, especially in English history. Grey's mastery of that particular historiographical terrain and his doggedness in defending it made him useful to the orthodox in their fight to assert the lessons and to claim the mantle of England's fragmented religious past.

Part III of this book concentrates on Zachary Grey (1688–1766).[7] Chapters 11 and 12 anatomize his explanations for and analysis of the intra-Protestant divisions spawned by the Reformation. It focuses especially on his anti-Puritan writings and on his scholarship concerning primitive Christianity. Chapter 13 reconstructs Grey's proposed solutions to the religious divisions which he thought still haunted eighteenth-century England. It looks closely at his unpublished sermons to congregations in Bedfordshire and in Cambridge. This introductory chapter (Chapter 10) suggests why Grey thought that history might solve those Reformation-spawned problems and points to the fate he predicted for England if the country did not solve them. It explains why intra-Protestant divisions so exercised him: the alternative to Protestantism properly understood was tyranny and slavery at the hands of Antichrist's agents. This chapter begins by showing how Zachary Grey's own family history emblematized the complicated legacy of England's Reformation. It turns next to consider his undergraduate reading notebooks, which foreshadow his mature thought regarding the English Church and state. It concludes with a close examination of his unpublished work on Islam and on the Portuguese Inquisition, which together reveal the lineaments of his anti-popery.

Zachary Grey's family history attested to the complicated legacies and unfinished nature of England's Reformation and reminds us that the seventeenth-century past was not ancient history for those living during the eighteenth century. Grey's political and religious allegiances sat uneasily against the backdrop of his family's history. The Greys hailed from County Durham, where Zachary's paternal great-grandfather, George Grey (d. 1661), fell afoul of the Caroline royalist Walter Balcanqhal, dean of Durham during the late 1630s.[8] Grey, a collier, had leased land from the Durham dean and chapter for nearly a decade. Balcanquhal and the chapter raised lease renewal fines, Grey joined with Anthony Smith in 1639 to petition Charles I and his council for relief.[9] When Grey and Smith presented their petition to the king's council when the North lived under the shadow of Scottish troops massing along England's border. Balcanquhal had recently helped to formulate the royal response to the growing covenanting challenge by ghost-writing

Charles I's *Large Declaration* (1639).[10] He saw connections between anticlericalism, religious nonconformity and political instability, as evidenced by his complaints about the help rendered to the covenanter army by Newcastle's 'known Puritans'.[11] Balcanquhal's response to Grey's petition explicitly linked Grey's land dispute with civil unrest in the North of England. When Balcanquhal's case came before the council, Laud personally urged the body to rule against the petitioners; encouraged the dean and chapter 'to proceed against them in the Star-Chamber'; and concluded that 'he was confident that [Grey's and Smith's petition] was a practice against the Church, and did believe there was some further design in that Business'. George Grey challenged Balcanquhal's prerogative at a time when ecclesiastical authorities felt intense pressure upon them. In Grey, the royalists Balcanquhal and Laud saw someone whose challenge to Church authority conjoined with a thinly veiled challenge to the king's authority. Balcanquhal won the first round in this legal dispute, with both Grey and Smith being imprisoned for over a year. But Balcanquhal's victory was fleeting. When the Scottish forces swarmed through the region, Balcanquhal fled, first to Oxford and then elsewhere, before dying destitute at Denbigh on Christmas Day 1645.

Walter Balcanqhal was just the sort of man George Grey's great-grandson, Zachary, would later extol – a resolute loyalist persecuted for his devotion to king and Church by anticlericals and religious radicals. What exactly Zachary Grey made of his anticlerical great-grandfather or indeed of his grandfather (a captain in the parliamentary army during the English Civil Wars) is unknown. Indeed, much about Grey is unknown since virtually nothing remains to document the first three decades of his life. He was born in Yorkshire in 1688, the second son and youngest child of the vicar George Grey (1652–1711) and his first wife, Elizabeth Cawdrey (1653–90).[12] Like Zachary Grey's father's family, his mother's line bore the marks of England's long Reformation. The Cawdreys were a clerical family with a decided streak of religious nonconformity. Elizabeth's grandfather had been ejected from his Rutland living for puritanical views on the liturgy and priesthood, despite having William Cecil as his patron. Her uncle, the fiercely anti-Laudian Presbyterian Daniel Cawdrey (1587/8–1664), likewise had lost his living in 1662, despite the earl of Clarendon's recommendation that he be given a bishopric. Even Elizabeth's father and Zachary Grey's namesake, Zachary Cawdrey (1618–84), had been deprived of his Cambridge college living during the 1640s, though for his royalism rather than for his Puritanism or Presbyterianism.[13] But, whereas Zachary Cawdrey tried, after the Restoration, to foster good relations between the worlds of moderate dissent and conformity, his grandson was an unyielding and unforgiving polemicist on behalf of the established Church of England.

Zachary Grey published nothing until 1720, when he was thirty-two years old, and had been a parish priest for nearly a decade. He likely had studied in the Burniston Latin school which his brother had attended.[14] Instead of following his older brother into the law, Zachary went up to Cambridge in 1704, being admitted a pensioner at Jesus College before migrating to become a scholar of Trinity Hall in 1707. It is unclear why he moved from the poor and undistinguished Jesus (headed by the Tory Charles Ashton) to the only slightly less poor and undistinguished Trinity Hall (headed by the zealous Whig George Oxendon), though the position of pensioner at Jesus was dying off during Ashton's mastership.[15] Whatever accounts for his move between colleges, after graduating with an Ll.B. in 1709 and after being ordained in 1711, Grey settled into a series of comfortable livings, the first of which was in Lincolnshire.[16] In 1720, the widower Grey married Susanna Hatton (*c.* 1690–1771), the daughter of the former innkeeper at Cambridge's Three Tuns tavern.[17] Susanna's own twice-widowed mother would marry thirdly to the high church Tory Robert Moss (*c.* 1666–1729), dean of Ely. Moss named Grey rector of Houghton Conquest, Bedfordshire, in 1726. Grey subsequently split his time between the nearby market town of Ampthill and Cambridge, where he also held livings.[18]

The country cleric became a prolific author with an especially rebarbative style. As with Conyers Middleton, the gap between Grey's polemical persona and his private personality yawned wide. Robert Masters, a friend of Grey's, reckoned that 'notwithstanding his great Application to his Studies, [Grey] always appeared lively and cheerful, and no Man delighted more in the Company of his Friends, or entertained them in a more hospitable and agreeable Manner. In short, he seemed to enjoy, all that Ease and Happiness, usually arising from a good Heart, and a contented Mind.'[19] Others concurred.[20] Grey's published work, by contrast, conveyed none of the personal qualities his friends admired; instead it oozed an acidic virulence remarkable even for the age.

Grey had a talent for friendship, pursuing his work with and among wide and overlapping circles of friends and scholars. The centre of his intellectual universe lay in Cambridge, 'where he usually resided for Half of the Year'.[21] This allowed him access to two great libraries. Grey often cited works (with their library shelfmarks) from Cambridge's university library, over which Conyers Middleton presided. He also worked in Wimpole's Harleian library, which he described as 'the best in England purchased at immense Expense, if we do consider the very large number of curious printed Books, & invaluable Collection of Manuscripts'. He privately recorded his 'most grateful Sense of Lord Oxford's Favours, who, long before his Death, had laid me under the highest Obligations'.[22] Grey's time in Cambridge also deepened his acquaintance with Daniel Waterland, who turned to Grey for scholarly assistance and who tapped him to respond to Isaac Newton's biblical scholarship during the mid-1730s.[23] By far the most important figure to Grey in Cambridge, though, was Thomas Baker. [24]

A fellow northerner, Thomas Baker was one of his era's most well-connected and learned antiquarian scholars.[25] He came to antiquarianism only in midlife, though, after his career in the established Church ground abruptly to a halt with the oath of allegiance's imposition in 1690. No slavish proponent of James II, Baker had lost his chance for preferment by refusing publicly to read James II's Declaration of Indulgence (1687). Yet Baker believed that oaths were sacred and could not be broken. His nonjuring required that he resign his Durham rectory in 1690. With the abjuration oath's imposition in 1717, he also lost his fellowship of St John's College, Cambridge, though he kept his college rooms, a small income and some privileges throughout his life. In Cambridge, Baker's closest circle included Francis Dickins, William Baker, Conyers Middleton, Philip Williams, William Heberden and Zachary Grey.

Grey thought highly of Baker, describing him in print as 'a person universally esteemed for his great Knowledge in almost all the Branches of Literature and who ... is the most knowing in our English History and Antiquities'.[26] Other contemporaries shared this estimation. 'He is said to have vast materials in the Historical Way', William Warburton explained to Thomas Birch in 1739. '... The people of St. John's almost adore the man; for, as there is in him much to esteem, much to pity, and nothing (but his virtue and learning) to envy; he has all the justice at present done him that few people of merit have till they are dead.'[27] Grey's primary debt to Baker was scholarly, for Baker ushered Grey into a wider circle of English antiquarians and opened the doors of important collections like the Harleian library.[28] Barred from the ecclesiastical establishment, Baker nevertheless had close ties to those in it, ranging from archbishops and bishops to Oxbridge fellows to notable antiquarians such as John Walker (1674–1747) and John Strype (1643–1737).[29] Baker garnered near universal admiration not just because of his unquestioned erudition but also because he was someone whose irenic temperament and unassuming personality won him lasting friendships and whose lack of bitterness was notable among nonjurors of the day.[30] He seemed also to have recognized that his friend Grey's politics were not irenic, noting to one Dissenting historian that Grey was 'a man of high Principles', while nevertheless hoping that '[s]uch little differences ought to make no break of Friendship'.[31]

Neither were Grey's 'high Principles' Baker's, since he was no nonjuror. William Cole nevertheless described him as being 'of the Most High Church' and suggested that Grey was 'of a contrary party', presumably the Tories.[32] Grey certainly had a deep and lasting affinity for Henry Sacheverell. Like his father-in-law, Robert Moss, and his then friend Conyers Middleton, Grey voted solely for Dixie Windsor in the 1727 parliamentary election, when the only way to signal that one was a dyed-in-the-wool Tory was to vote singly for Windsor.[33] Since no poll lists for Cambridge between 1727 and 1780 survive, it is impossible to know for whom Grey voted in the parliamentary elections. But there is little evidence that his political allegiances, unlike Middleton's, changed during the 1730s and 1740s.

Grey shared with Thomas Baker a fundamental scepticism about human learning and knowledge. Baker dealt with the subject in his *Reflections on learning* (1699), a work which aimed 'to shew the Insufficiency of Human Learning, [rather] than wholly to discredit its Use'.[34] Human learning, Baker argued, was a useful 'handmaid' to religion; but it could not supplant revelation, knowledge's only truly reliable source.[35] The *Reflections* is unsurprisingly shot through with a deep suspicion of the grand claims to infallibility of 'Natural Reason' in all things, including religion. Moreover, Baker had little confidence in history's ability reliably to ground knowledge, citing by way of example that, while most historians claimed to be 'true' historians, they nevertheless reached no consensus on the past. Moreover, he insisted that, while we can know 'Matters of Fact', the motives of peoples in the past are unknowable.[36] Despite these qualms, Baker reckoned that history provided the least fallible guide among the various modes of human knowledge. In particular, he placed great store in 'Ecclesiastical History, from which, next to Sacred Story, we have the greatest Assurance; and even from Profane History (notwithstanding all its Flaws) we have more Assurance than in most Sorts of Learning'.[37] Zachary Grey agreed. It fell to the historian accurately to recover and interpret the past.

Grey started wrestling with the Reformation, its history and its legacies during his Cambridge undergraduate days. The contents of a notebook from his time at Trinity Hall foreshadowed his mature intellectual project.[38] That notebook opened with a short discussion of the Swedish dimension of the Thirty Years War before closely synopsising Charles Leslie's *Second Part of the Wolf Stript of his Shepherds Cloathing* (1707), itself a pointed riposte to Matthew Tindal's *Rights of the Christian Church* (1706). Tindal's *Rights* had trashed, among other things, the clergy's sacerdotal nature; *jure divino* episcopacy; the Church's innate and inalienable independence; and the argument from primitivity.[39] Tindal intended to set off someone like Charles Leslie, whose confessional register stretched from nonjuring to high church Toryism.[40] In the *Second Part*, Leslie argued that Tindal's dismissal of a sacred priesthood ignored the indisputable fact that Christ himself had instituted the priesthood and had 'instate[d] the Apostles in the Possession of the Keys of Heaven'.[41] Leslie also criticized Tindal for not accepting the Church as a 'visible Society' which required a 'fixed and settled' government, one which was primitively episcopal. Grey summarized this argument in his notes. Especially suggestive, considering Grey's later writings, was Leslie's explicit association of early eighteenth-century anticlericals with seventeenth-century English rebels. Leslie contended that Tindal suffered from 'Enthusiasm': on his reading a 'Whig is a State Enthusiast, as a Dissenter is an Ecclesiastical'.[42] In an age that counted 'enthusiasm' a cardinal sin thanks to its association with the seventeenth-century wars of religion, these were serious charges.[43] On Leslie's reading, Tindal and his followers – a motley crew of deists, Whigs, 'Commonwealthsmen', Socinians and 'Libertines', all bound together by 'the Principles of Forty one' – were also Erastians, who, like the 1641 Irish Catholic rebels, meant to destroy the English church-state.[44] Did not both papists and Presbyterians deny the English king's political supremacy over the Church of England?[45] Did not Presbyterianism as put into practice in Scotland demonstrate conclusively that 'Presbyterians ... are gainers by Erastianism, how much soever they may pretend to hate it'? Did not Erastianism derive directly from popery? Did not Tindal make an argument against the English Church which papists themselves could also easily endorse? 'The *Rights of the Christian Church, &c* lays the main stress on the Act of Submission', Leslie reckoned, so that 'when, [Tindal] argues, that we have no Church, Priesthood or Sacraments; He means since the Reformation, by which he would lead us back again to Popery'.[46] Lastly, contended Leslie, in addition to sharing an Erastian view of Church–state relations with the papists, Tindal and his followers had, like the Church of Rome's adherents, broken from the true church. 'Now there is nothing required as a Condition of Communion in the Church of England but the Apostles Creed, and that is not so in the Church of Rome, and therefore though we had just cause to separate from the Church of Rome, yet our Dissenters had no manner of cause to separate from the Church of England', Leslie concluded. 'Therefore their separation is Schism; but not ours from the Church of Rome. For that Church is guilty of their separation who part from her for sinful Conditions of Communion imposed, and such separations are no Schism.'[47]

Grey synopsised Leslie's *Second part* during the febrile days of the 'Church in danger' controversy, a time when orthodox churchman like Charles Leslie thought the English church-state was under concerted and co-ordinated assault from religious nonconformists, anticlericals and freethinkers. It hardly surprises that Henry Sacheverell, the orthodox martyr-hero who warned of the 'perils of false brethren' from St Paul's Cathedral's pulpit on 5 November 1709, recurred sympathetically in works Grey wrote and published long after his trial. Neither in Grey's undergraduate notes nor in his subsequent work is there anything to suggest that he anything but wholeheartedly agreed with the hyper-orthodox Leslie about who had constituted (and who continued to constitute) the greatest danger to the established Church and societal order.

Charles Leslie's arguments, though, raised some problems for robust defenders of the Church of England's ecclesiology, liturgy and theology. His defence of the clergy's sacred nature invited derisive comment from the age's anticlericals (who complained about pervasive priestcraft) and opened up him up to charges that he himself was no more than a papist wolf in Protestant sheep's clothing. It is suggestive, then, that Grey's synopsis of Charles Leslie's tract is followed up immediately in his undergraduate notebook by a short consideration of priestly absolution. The issue had been at the centre of Reformation-era Protestant self-definition, as Protestants rejected the late medieval Roman Catholic penitential theology and practice which involved confessing sins to a priest before receiving his absolution. Priestly absolution had explicit biblical warrant, given Christ's post-resurrection proclamation to the Apostles, 'Whose soever sins ye remit, they are remitted unto them; and whose soever sins ye retain, they are retained' (John 20:23).[48] Unsurprisingly, then, Grey noted that '[m]inisterial absolution is allowed by all the Reformed Churches ... but some are more Liberal others more reserved in the Point'. In trying to show with how much liberality the point should, in fact, be treated, he situated himself in a position triangulated by Hobbes, Geneva and Rome. There were, he suggested, two especially influential (errant) Protestant positions on absolution. On the one hand were the 'Erastians [who] seeing that the Churchmen could not agree about Them, would deliver all into the hands of the Chief Magistrate'. Though unnamed by Grey, these surely were admirers of Thomas Hobbes, who had argued that all religious claims were nonsensical and only Leviathan had authority to assert what were or were not acceptable theological and ecclesiological positions.[49] On the other hand were the 'sour Democratical People' who would not commit the keys of absolution 'to the Chief Stewards but to all the Servants of the family alike'. Their approach, Grey reckoned, led necessarily to 'a disorderly House' since 'each in the Family had his Privy Key to all'. The adherents of this position were the 'Congregationals', Puritans and other Protestant nonconformists who would be the villains in nearly all of Grey's mature works and who, he argued, had misinterpreted Psalm 149:8 and placed power 'Radically in the People'. The Erastians, then, had denied that transcendent truth existed – and, concomitantly, that there were sins that needed absolving. They therefore advocated state control over the Church and its ministry in the name of societal peace. Protestant nonconformists, by contrast, believed in truth and sin; feared the agglomeration of power in the hands of a priestly caste; and placed no intermediary between man and God, who alone could absolve him of his sins.

The undergraduate Zachary Grey identified another way to think about the 'keys' of absolution, one which sounded much like that spelled out by the late-seventeenth-century high churchman William Sherlock (1639/40–1707).[50] As Grey understood it, Christ had indeed conferred upon his Apostles the power of 'Absolution Personal', but the 'power of forgiving sins is really in God alone and none can forgive sins but can God'. Properly understood, then, clergy lacked judicial power of absolution (which Grey argued was the hallmark of 'the Popish Doctrine') but possessed instead declarative power of absolution. That is to say, priests had the power to declare a sinner absolved of sin, but not to grant absolution by right of office. Thus, under Grey's scheme, when a priest absolved a sinner, he did so not as a judge who determined whether or not the sinner was truly penitent, but as a discerning messenger declaring God's absolution. 'Such is the absolution of an able minister which will be satisfactory to the true penitent and will be of no avail if he be not so', Grey concluded. This vision retained robust priestly authority while stopping well short of the popish doctrine of granting priests judicial authority. However, Grey and other orthodox churchmen had to distance themselves from that popish doctrine.

Though he published less on anti-popery than he did on the dangers of intra-Protestant divisions, Zachary Grey, like most of his contemporaries, was stridently anti-papist.[51] Though English Catholics got treated less poorly during the eighteenth century than they had previously, the seventeenth-century anti-popish logic would have been both recognizable to and applied by most in Georgian England.[52] Popery was an anti-religion to Protestantism. Popery was foreign, superstitious, man-made and fraudulent; Protestantism was English, rational, biblical and true. The pope and the clergy subordinate to him exercised a kind of spiritual tyranny, one enabled by the Catholic laity's ignorance and by those secular governors who claimed to rule by divine right. While much had changed since the worldview's formation during the late sixteenth and seventeenth centuries, it still provided a way for many eighteenth-century English men and women, and especially the Protestant clergy, to explain the world around them. Certainly this was true for Zachary Grey, as a few of his manuscript works illustrate.

Grey's unpublished *Mahometism and Popery compared*, for instance, argued that popery was the product of an even greater imposture than Islam.[53] It opened with a short life of the prophet Muhammad (*c.* 570–632), which prefixed a comparison of the two religions. The first half of *Mahometism and Popery compared* savaged Islam, the second half, popery itself: both were conventional Protestant polemical moves since the sixteenth century.[54] Grey drew his materials for his account of Muhammad mostly from Humphrey Prideaux's *True Nature of Imposture, fully displayed in the life of Mahomet* (1697).[55] Prideaux (1648–1724) wrote that work to defend the Church of England against deists. He had tried to show that while Islam was fraudulent, Christianity – and, by extension, the Church of England – was not. The influential *True Nature of Imposture* went through ten editions by 1722. Its influence owed less to the quality of its scholarship – which borrowed significantly from the pioneering earlier work of the seventeenth-century orientalist and Laud professor of Arabic studies at Oxford, Edward Pococke (*c.* 1648–1726) – than it did to the polemical uses to which Prideaux and others, like Zachary Grey, could put that scholarship.[56]

On Grey's accounting, Islam was not a divinely revealed religion but Muhammad's fraudulent creation. The prophet had been born into a wealthy family and got wealthier through hard work, ingenuity and a fortuitous marriage. Having by twenty-eight become 'equal with the wealthiest men of [Mecca], his ambitious mind spurred him on to the thoughts of possessing himself over the Sovereignty of it'. The best way to do this, he judged, was 'to make a more than ordinary shew of Religion which might in all probability gain his party many proselytes'. For this reason, he learned as much as he could about Judaism and Christianity, having recognized 'that they far excelled [the religion] of the Pagans, in which he had been bred'. At length, he 'approved of Christianity as the Best'; adopted its mores; led a solitary existence; and spoke in a manner that was 'grave and serious, and commonly attended with a solemn exhortation to a Holy life'. In this way, Muhammad impressed his contemporaries with his sanctity. Furthermore, he 'made use of a natural disorder, namely the Epilepsy, or Falling Sickness'. This gave cover for his imposture: 'whenever the fit was upon him, he pretended to be in a Trance, and that then the Angel Gabriel conveyed to him, and was sent from God with some new Revelation to him, the splendour of whose appearance, he not being able to bear, this caused him to fall into those Trances in which the Angel delivered to him'. Successfully fostering a reputation for exemplary piety and special revelation was insufficient for Muhammad, though. To build 'a mighty empire', he decided 'to strike out something new in Religion'. To do this, he enlisted the aid of Salman al-Farisi ('a learned Jew born in Persia, a Rabbin in his sect') and of Sergius ('a Nestorian Monk, and apostate, who was expelled [from] his monastery for his disorderly life'). From al-Farisi, the 'Illiterate' Muhammad got stories from the Old Testament, 'blended with Chimaeras, and Dreams from the Talmud', to which he added some marvellous tales of his own invention. From Sergius, he learned the New Testament and 'church discipline', all of which 'He changed and corrupted with Fables, which He borrowed from the Pseudo-Gospels and the Apocryphal Books'. Together this formed the content of the Qur'an, the collection of holy teachings which were the basis of Muhammad's 'new religion'.[57]

The prophet next seized power. Many 'Lovers of Novelty' flocked to his new religion, but others worried that it 'might in all probability be attended with a New Form of Civil Government'. War broke out; Muhammad's forces won. His response to victory, though, was – 'with a Counterfeit Holiness (under the Masque of which he intended to take his ease)' – to withdraw from public affairs and to let his subordinates run his new empire, which they did even after his death.[58]

These were the origins of 'Mahometism', a religion, on Prideaux's and Grey's telling, built by imposture and that aimed from the start for worldly power. Having established Islam's origins in imposture, Grey turned in the main body of his tract to compare it with popery. For evidence, Grey drew significantly from Prideaux's *The true nature of imposture*; from George Sales's 1734–35 English edition of the Qur'an; from Gilbert Burnet's 1678 account of the St Bartholomew's Day massacre; and, above all, from Henry Care's *Weekly Pacquet*, itself written in response to the Popish Plot of Charles II's reign.[59] Grey made two familiar claims. Firstly, popish beliefs were even more 'absurd' than those of the Mahometans. Secondly, papists were not Christians because they lacked 'the true Christian Spirit'.

The litany of popish absurdities Grey adduced would have been familiar to any seventeenth-century reader. The 'Turks' did not venerate 'the vain traditions of their People', whereas the papists did. The 'Turks' did not 'blaspheme' Christ and, indeed, punished 'most severely' those who did, whereas papists blasphemed him regularly, especially through the doctrine of transubstantiation, a doctrine 'so gross and absurd, that it gives a scandal to the Mahometans'. The 'Turks' did not postulate the existence of Purgatory nor worship images nor have mendicant friars, whereas the papists did. Most importantly, the 'Turks' had nothing like the bishop of Rome. Indeed, the papists were 'more slavish and miserable vassals than the Mahometans, and the Pope more proud and arrogant than the Mufti'.[60]

Grey's point about papal power fed directly into his second claim, that papists were not Christians because they lacked 'the true Christian spirit', particularly in their application of power. The Mahometan persecutory spirit was well-known 'to any that have travelled the Levant, or are by Books acquainted with their Laws and Customs, or rather the rigours of their tyranny'. Notwithstanding this, the papists treated 'sincere Christians' so badly that it was 'less grievous and dangerous for such to live in the dominions, and under the government of the Grand Seignior than in places where the Pope and his clergy have power'. Grey cited as evidence the two most familiar anti-Protestant atrocities to the English, the St Bartholomew's Day massacre of 1572 and the Irish rebellion of 1641.[61] Grey's point was obvious: papists had always persecuted Protestants, the only 'true' Christians.

In making the case about the popish abuse of power, Grey also invoked the example of the Spanish Inquisition, a body which he dealt with at length in another unpublished work, *The Horrid Barbarity of the Spanish Inquisition Exemplify'd*.[62] Grey's *Horrid Barbarity* recounted the Spanish Inquisition's treatment of the early seventeenth-century Scottish traveller William Lithgow. To this, Grey prefixed a short general history of the Spanish Inquisition, drawn mostly from Michael Geddes's account of the expulsion of the Moriscos from Spain in 1609.[63] Geddes (1647–1713) was a Scottish-born clergyman who served during the early 1680s as chaplain to the English factory in Lisbon before the Inquisition barred him from performing his official duties. He eventually returned to England where, with the encouragement of episcopal sponsors like Gilbert Burnet, he wrote a string of anti-popish works that analysed what Burnet described as 'a true nature of popery', that is 'a political combination, managed by falsehood and cruelty, to establish a temporal empire in the person of the popes'.[64]

Grey's account of the Spanish Inquisition's origins and its treatment of religious minorities purported to show that the clergy's power trumped that of the Iberian peninsula's secular rulers and that its 'barbarity [was] not exceeded by the greatest cruelties of the Heathen persecutors'.[65] Clerics were the chief villains in his story. In the thirteenth century, for instance, the Spanish clergy encouraged King James I of Aragon (1208–76) to banish the Moors (Muslims) from newly conquered Valencia. Fearing that mass expulsions might depopulate his kingdom, James ordered the clergy to learn Arabic so that they could convert the Moors to Christianity. Yet, 'either through their own impatience and misconduct in other respects, or the obstinacy of the Moors, their preaching proved very unsuccessful'. Afterwards not only did the clergy present the Moors as 'incorrigible Infidels, pretending that nothing but force would reduce them, upon whom so many miracles had been thrown away'. Moreover, Pope Clement IV also encouraged James to banish the recalcitrant Muslims from his kingdoms. Only the Cortes, his legislature, restrained James. It countered 'that it would be a wicked thing to expel them on account of their Religion' and that, if the clergy really did want to convert them, then they should redouble their pastoral efforts.[66] On Zachary Grey's telling, then, the medieval Spanish clergy were persecutory and the only thing that prevented the Moors from being expelled during the thirteenth century was the legislature's intervention.

Three centuries later, efforts ramped up again to get rid of the Moors. The chief villain this time was Cardinal Francisco Jiménez de Cisneros (1436–1517), 'a very crafty man, and one who was seldom baffled by anything he undertook'. The year 1492 witnessed both the expulsion of the Jews from Spain and the reconquest of Granada from the Moors. The formal capitulation terms for the Moors seemed lenient, nominally allowing them to retain their religion, customs, laws and property; but, in practice, efforts commenced to persuade those Granadan Moors who did not emigrate to North Africa to convert to Christianity. These initial missionary efforts failed, though, so that by 1499 King Ferdinand and Queen Isabella asked Cisneros what to do. The archbishop proposed a more coercive approach and for those Moors who 'refus[ed] compliance' he 'put off his appearance of mildness, nay, laying aside all humanity, he commanded them to be apprehended, and loaded with Irons, and to be thrown into dark and comfortless dungeons'. Soon afterwards, the monarchs compelled the Moors who chose to remain in Spain forcibly to be baptised and to convert to Christianity. By 1501, the government's operating assumption was that there were no more Moors in Granada; there were only Moriscos (Christian Muslims).[67]

This allowed the Spanish Inquisition (which had jurisdiction only over Christians) actively to persecute the Moriscos. Indeed, the body 'did exercise the utmost to their cruelty of all such Moors, as had been baptised, and revolved to the Mahometan Religion'. According to Grey, over the next four decades the Inquisition condemned more than a hundred thousand Moriscos, living and dead, burning four thousand along the way. Not until the end of the sixteenth century did a successful push to expel the Moriscos recommence. Juan de Ribera and Gaspar de Quiroga, the archbishops of Valencia and Toledo, spearheaded those efforts, strongly encouraging Philip III (1578–1621) to cast out the Moriscos, despite objections from many nobles. In particular, de Quiroga – 'by whom the King was at times absolutely governed' – was 'so zealous for the expulsion of the whole race of them, that when it was proposed to detain all their children under seven years of age, he affirmed that '[i]t was more advisable to cut the throats of all of them, men, women, and children, than to have any of their children left in Spain, to defile the Spanish with a mixture of Moor's blood'. Finally in 1609, convinced by the two archbishops and their allies among his royal advisers, Philip III expelled the Moriscos. Grey put the number ejected at between six hundred thousand and one million, and argued that Spain 'has not recovered that terrible blow to this day'. Indeed, he continued, Philip III soon regretted what he had done, after realizing that 'the ruinous state of the Kingdom' had been 'occasioned by the expulsion of so great a number of industrious and useful subjects'. He soon banished from court those clerics who had advised him to expel the Moriscos and had at least one of his secular advisers executed.[68] Grey's point was that, no matter if it took centuries to achieve its tyrannical goals, the popish clergy would achieve them and they would do so through lies and force. Popery and arbitrary government, the twin bogeymen of seventeenth-century English Protestants, remained threats. The only sure prophylaxis was true religion, Protestantism.

A decade after the Moriscos got expelled from Spain, the Protestant Scottish traveller William Lithgow (*c.* 1582–1645) suffered at the hands of the Spanish Inquisition.[69] Lithgow's autobiographical account of his capture and torture went through ten editions by the 1690s. Grey culled his materials for his abstract of Lithgow's encounter with the Spanish Inquisition from the tenth edition.

In 1619, Lithgow, a seasoned traveller, set out to find the Ethiopian dominions of Prester John, the legendary Eastern Christian ruler. In late 1620, he found himself awaiting passage to Egypt in the Spanish port of Malaga when an English fleet showed up in port, having been sent to the Mediterranean to harry Algerian pirates. The local inhabitants, though, feared that the English had arrived to attack Malaga. The Spanish governor arrested Lithgow as an English spy after the fleet departed. From that point in October 1620 until his release on Easter Sunday 1621, the Spanish government and then the Spanish Inquisition tortured Lithgow. While Lithgow's narrative contained inconsistencies and while he undoubtedly crafted it with Foxe's *Book of Martyrs* in mind, clearly he suffered greatly during his Spanish captivity. English Protestants mostly accepted it as gospel truth.

The part of Lithgow's story on which Grey focused especially in *The Horrid Barbarity* concerned the bigotry, secrecy and brutality of the Spanish government and the Inquisition. For the Malagan governor not only arrested Lithgow but stole his money; denied him access to the English factors in town; and had him secreted away 'to a Chamber in an unfrequented part of the palace, clapping bolts upon his legs of that monstrous size, that he could neither walk, stand, nor sit nor turn himself, being continually on his back: the irons being there as heavy as the weight of his body'. The only people to treat him with any human decency during his confinement were two non-

Europeans, a 'Turkish slave' and an Indian Negro woman servant. Lithgow's Spanish captors, by contrast, brutalized him, putting him repeatedly to the rack; breaking his bones; and knocking out his teeth. Even under intense torture, Lithgow refused to confess to being a spy, so that the Malagan governor eventually recognized that he had mistaken the Englishman's intentions. Yet rather than admit error and set Lithgow free, he 'could not forgive the person whom he had so highly injured, and therefore pursued his revenge in a different form': he subjected Lithgow to the cruelties of the Spanish Inquisition.[70]

The Inquisitor and four other priests who first interrogated Lithgow focused on 'whether he was a Roman Catholic and acknowledged the Pope's supremacy?' Their central concern had to do with priestly power and its sources. Lithgow denied he was a papist. He also pointed out to the Inquisitor that the Inquisition had no right, under recent Anglo-Spanish peace terms, to detain or question English citizens. The Inquisitors ignored this, giving Lithgow eight days to convert to Roman Catholicism or face death for heresy. When he later insisted to his tormenters that he was, in fact, a member of 'the Reformed Catholic Church' and 'that all their threatening of Fire, Death and Torments, should not make him shrink from the Truth of God's Word as set forth in the Sacred Scriptures', he was subjected to yet more torture and condemned to be transported to Granada 'to be burnt, Body and Bones unto Ashes, and the Ashes to be [blown] into the Air'. It was only when a Flemish servant alerted the English authorities to Lithgow's imprisonment and imminent fate that he got set free. He returned to England a broken – though fêted – man. Ferried to the house of the Spanish ambassador Gondomar, he was promised compensation for his treatment, compensation that never materialized.[71]

To Zachary Grey, the Lithgow affair's lessons were straightforward. Papists were both persecutory and treacherous. Furthermore, what the Inquisition had done to William Lithgow, it and its secular allies would surely do to Protestants everywhere if unchecked. Zachary Grey thought this was as true during the mid-eighteenth century as it had been during the mid-seventeenth century. Yet while it seemed axiomatic to him and his orthodox brethren that the legally established Church of England allied to a Protestant state was the surest prophylaxis against popish persecution of the English, not all English Protestants agreed. Many nonconformists had long seen the English Church not as unquestionably Protestant but, rather, as crypto-popish and, hence, as inherently persecutory. This leads back to Charles Leslie's *Second Part of the Wolf Stript of his Shepherds Cloathing*, the book which so interested Zachary Grey when he was a Cambridge student.

An implicit problem raised by Leslie's argument in *The Second Part* concerned English history. If it was true that the English state could be strong only when allied to a spiritually independent church and if it was furthermore true that Protestant nonconformists and their political allies had always opposed the Church of England and, hence, the English state, this charge needed to be proved historically. The orthodox challenge was to write the history of the Christian Church and of English religion and politics in a way that defended clericalism; that distinguished the English Church from the Roman one; that explained how the established Church of England and the state with which it was allied had always been beset by threats from Protestant nonconformists; that showed how the church-state had mostly managed to see off those threats; and yet that demonstrated those threats nonetheless still remained potent, if unrecognized or unacknowledged. Zachary Grey's core intellectual project was writing that history, part of which tried to demonstrate that Protestant nonconformists themselves had from the Reformation's beginnings shared more in common with their papist arch-enemies than either had been prepared to admit.

NOTES

1 J. Caudle, 'The Defence of Georgian Britain: The Anti-Jacobite Sermon, 1715–1746', in W. Gibson and K, Francis (eds), *Oxford Handbook of the British Sermon* (Oxford, 2012), pp. 245–60.

2 S. Taylor, 'Church and State in the Mid-Eighteenth Century: The Newcastle Years, 1742–62' (Ph.D. thesis, University of Cambridge, 1987), pp. 150–60; C. Haydon, *Anti-Catholicism in Eighteenth-Century England, c. 1714–80* (Manchester, 1993), pp. 129–63. See also George Grey to Zachary Grey, December 1745 (*LI*, IV, pp. 317–18).

3 Edmund Pyle to Thomas Birch, 20 October 1745 (BL, Add. 4317, fol. 65).

4 Z. Grey, *Popery in its proper colours* ((1745): T178347), pp. iii, v.

5 Ibid., pp. 23–8.

6 Henry Fielding referred to him as 'the laborious much-read doctor Zachary Grey': H. Fielding, *Journal of a voyage to Lisbon* (1755: T131334), p. iii. See also William Cole to Richard Gough, 29 June 1780 (BL, Add. 5834, fol. 106): 'The Number of his Publications was so numerous that Bishop Warburton insultingly abuses him upon that Account'.

7 There is no modern biography of Grey, but see S. Mandelbrote, 'Zachary Grey (1688–1766)', *ODNB*.

8 F. Raines, *The Fellows of the Collegiate Church of Manchester: Part I* (Manchester, 1891), pp. 95–104.

9 Unless otherwise noted, information in this paragraph is drawn from the family memoir written by George Grey (1681–1772) and which appears in R. Surtees, *History and antiquities of ... Durham* (Sunderland, 1908), II, pp. 77–84; J. Rushworth, *Historical collections* (1721: N033526), pp. 1051–2; HMC, *Fourth Report. Part I: Report and Appendix* (1874), pp. 26–7.

10 [W. Balcanquhal], *Large declaration concerning ... Scotland* (1639: 21906). See also M. Kishlansky, 'A Lesson in Loyalty: Charles I and the Short Parliament', in J. McElligott and D. Smith (eds), *Royalists and Royalism during the English Civil Wars* (Cambridge, 2007), pp. 23–5.

11 Balcanquhal to Laud, [30 January] 1640 (W. Hamilton (ed.), *Calendar of State Papers, Domestic Series, of the Reign of Charles I, 1639–40* (1877), pp. 401–2).
12 George Grey (1652–1711) graduated from Trinity College, Cambridge, with a B.A. (1672) and M.A. (1675) before going on to serve as rector of Lawton, Cheshire (1679–1682), and vicar of Burniston (1682–1711): *CCED*.
13 S. Guscott, 'Zachary Cawdrey (1618–1684)', *ODNB*; A. Matthews, *Walker Revised* (Oxford, 1988), pp. 89–90.
14 R. Surtees, *History and Antiquities of ... Durham* (Sunderland, 1908), II, p. 80: George Grey had praised his first Latin master, Samuel Hulm, but thought that Mr. Lindsey, who arrived in January 1694, 'was not equal to Mr. Hulm in his way of teaching'.
15 A. Gray, *Jesus College* (London, 1902), pp. 141–62; C. Crawley, *Trinity Hall* (1977), p. 116; D. Hayton (ed.), *House of Commons, 1690–1715* (Cambridge, 2002), V, pp. 50–2.
16 Grey served as rector of Hemingby, 1711–26. Leonard Smelt, a Yorkshire Whig MP who matriculated at Jesus College in 1700 and was one of Zachary Grey's relatives, was the living's patron: Hayton (ed.), *The House of Commons, 1690–1715*, V, p. 494; *CCED*; *LA*, VII, pp. 414–15.
17 It is unclear when Zachary Grey's first wife, Mary (née Tooley), died.
18 F.G. Stokes (ed.), *Blecheley Diary of ... William Cole ... 1765–67* (1931), p. 160; Cole to Gough, 29 June 1780 (BL, Add. 5843, fol. 106). See also Zachary Grey's *Life of Robert Moss*, n.d. (Corpus Christi College, Cambridge, 563).
19 Masters, *Memoirs*, p. 117.
20 Stokes (ed.), *Blecheley Diary*, p. 160; Cole to Gough, 29 June 1780 (BL, Add. 5843, fol. 106). See also Cole to Walpole, 29 January 1779 (*WC*, II, p. 360). William Warburton's nineteenth-century biographer likewise concluded that 'Grey appears to have been generally regarded as a man of honour and good faith': J. Watson, *Life of William Warburton* (1863), p. 339.
21 Cole to Gough, 29 June 1780 (BL, Add. 5834, fol. 106).
22 Zachary Grey's account of Edward Harley, second earl of Oxford, n.d. (BL, Add. 5344, fol. 163). Grey also worked through Conyers Middleton to win Harley's favour: Middleton to Harley, 5 January, 7 February, 7 December 1727 (BL, Add. 70410). In turn, Harley gave Grey 'many marks of friendship, particularly a present of a noble silver cup and ewer': *LA*, II, p. 534. See also Harley to Grey, 14 January 1734 (HL, Hurd 19, no. 14).
23 See, for instance, Baker to Grey, 15/28 July 1728 (Masters, *Memoirs*, pp. 62–4).
24 Grey would provide most of the materials for Robert Master's *Life of Thomas Baker*: Zachary Grey's collections for a life of Thomas Baker (SJCC, 0.54/55); BL, Stowe 1057, fols 2–51. See also Cole to Walpole, 4 October 1777, 8 July 1780 (*Walpole's Correspondence*, II, pp. 63–4, 231–2).
25 R. Masters, *Memoirs of ... Thomas Baker* (1784: T073604); J. Overton, *The Nonjurors* (1902), pp. 189–95; F. Korsten, *Catalogue of the Library of Thomas Baker* (Cambridge, 1990), pp. xi–xli.
26 Z. Grey, *Impartial examination of the second volume ... of Daniel Neal* (1736: T112825), p. 62n.
27 Warburton to Birch, 12 July 1739 (*LI*, II, pp. 106–7).
28 Baker to Humfrey Wanley, 9 March 1723: cited in Korsten, *Catalogue*, p. xxiv.

See also Wright and Wright (eds), *Diary*, II, p. 221: 'Dr Grey and Mr [Charles] Wheatley brought Hither Dr Waterland of Magdlene College in Cambridge & [blank space] to whom I shewed many of my Lord's Manuscripts for above two hours; to their great Satisfaction, as they said' [3 May 1723].

29 Korsten, *Catalogue*, pp. xix--xx; Overton, *Nonjurors*, pp. 190–1.

30 James Tunstall to Edward Harley, 5 July 1740 (BL, Add. 70396). See, in a similar vein, H. Walpole, *Works of Horatio Walpole* (1798: T149673), II, pp. 341–62.

31 Baker to Joseph Ward, 18 May 1735 (BL, Add. 6209, fol. 34): cited in Korsten, *Catalogue*, p. xx.

32 Cole to Horace Walpole, 29 January 1779 (*WC*, II, p. 360).

33 *Copy of the poll ... for the University of Cambridge, on Tuesday, August 22. 1727* (1727: T034154), p. 13; W. Gibson, 'The Tories and the Cambridge University Election of 1720', *PH* 22 (2003), pp. 308–14.

34 [T. Baker], *Reflections* (1708: T115163), sig. A2. The book went through eight editions and contemporaries recognized it as an important, if controversial, work: F. Korsten, 'Thomas Baker's *Reflections Upon Learning*', in G. Janssens and F. Aarts (eds), *Studies in Seventeenth-Century English Literature, History and Bibliography* (Amsterdam, 1984), pp. 133–48; J. Gascoigne, *Cambridge in the Age of Enlightenment* (Cambridge, 1989), pp. 165–6.

35 [Baker], *Reflections*, pp. 281–91.

36 Ibid., pp. 133–45, 147–8.

37 Ibid., p. 151. Cf. the lengthy exchange between Baker and John Woodward on the reliability of ecclesiastical history: CUL, Add. 7647, nos 26–44.

38 Zachary Grey's manuscript notebook, while a student at Trinity Hall, *c.* 1707–09 (SJCC, Aa3). Grey's notebook is unpaginated. Unless otherwise noted, the references in the next five paragraphs draw from this notebook.

39 Cf. D. Levitin, 'Matthew Tindal's *Rights of the Christian Church* (1706) and the Church-State Relationship', *HJ* 55 (2012), pp. 717–40; A. Barber, '"The Voice of the People, no Voice of God": A Political, Religious and Social History of the Transmission of Ideas in England, 1690–1715' (Ph.D. thesis, University of London, 2010), pp. 43–101.

40 R. Cornwall, 'Charles Leslie (1650–1722)', *ODNB*.

41 [C. Leslie], *Second part of the wolf stript* (1707: T082682), pp. 17–18, 36.

42 Ibid., pp. 2, 5.

43 J. Pocock, 'Enthusiasm: The Antiself of Enlightenment', *HLQ* 60 (1998), pp. 7–28.

44 [Leslie], *Second part*, p. 3.

45 Ibid., p. 10.

46 Ibid., pp. 23, 24, 25.

47 Ibid., pp. 46–7. See also ibid., pp. 73–5.

48 In 'Concerning the Power of the Keys & Absolution', Grey compared Matthew 16:19; Matthew 18:18; and John 20:23.

49 J. Champion, 'Godless Politics: Hobbes and Public Religion', in W. Bulman and R. Ingram (eds), *God in the Enlightenment* (Oxford, 2016), pp. 42–62; J. Collins, *The Allegiance of Thomas Hobbes* (Oxford, 2005).

50 W. Sherlock, *Preservative against popery* (1688: R498230), pp. 80–91; W. Sherlock, *Vindication of ... the preservative against popery* (1688: R21011), pp. 102–5. See also

B. Sirota, *The Christian Monitors: The Church of England and the Age of Benevolence, 1680–1730* (New Haven, 2014), pp. 160–3, 180–3.

51 C. Haydon, *Anti-Catholicism in Eighteenth-Century England, c. 1714–80* (Manchester, 1993).

52 P. Lake, 'Antipopery: The Structure of a Prejudice', in R. Cust and A. Hughes (eds), *Conflict in Early Stuart England* (1989), pp. 72–106; P. Lake, 'Post-Reformation Politics or, on Not Looking for the Long-Term Consequences of the English Civil War', in M. Braddick (ed.), *Oxford Handbook of the English Revolution* (Oxford, 2015), pp. 21–42. G. Glickman, *The English Catholic Community, 1688–1745: Politics, Culture and Ideology* (Woodbridge, 2009), best captures Catholic life in eighteenth-century England.

53 Zachary Grey, *Mahometism and Popery compared*, n.d. [unpublished] (BL, Add. 5960, fols 62–86). Grey wrote *Mahometism and Popery compared* after 1734, since he cites George Sale's English translation of the Qur'an (1734–35). Henry Care's two-volume *History of Popery* also appeared in 1735–36.

54 W. Bulman, *Anglican Enlightenment: Orientalism, Religion and Politics in England and Its Empire, 1648–1715* (Cambridge, 2015) is the essential work on oriental scholarship and clerical polemics. See also A. Hamilton, 'The Study of Islam in Early Modern Europe', *Archiv für Religionsgeschichte* 3 (2001), pp. 169–82.

55 P. Holt, *Studies in the History of the Middle East* (1957), pp. 50–4; G. Toomer, *Eastern Wisdom and Learning: The Study of Arabic in Seventeenth-Century England* (Oxford, 1996), pp. 289–92; J. Champion, 'Legislators, Impostors and the Politic Origins of Religion: English Theories of "Imposture" from Stubbe to Toland', in S. Berti, F. Charles-Daubert and R. Popkin (eds), *Heterodoxy, Spinozism and Free Thought in Early-Eighteenth-Century Europe* (Dordrecht, 1996), pp. 333–56; H. de Quehen, 'Humphrey Prideaux (1648–1724)', *ODNB*.

56 Holt, *Studies*, pp. 3–49.

57 Grey, *Mahometism*, fols 64–7. Cf. F. Donner, 'The Historical Context', in J. McAuliffe (ed.), *Cambridge Companion to the Qur'an* (Cambridge, 2006), pp. 23–39.

58 Grey, *Mahometism*, fols 67, 72.

59 A. Bevilacqua, 'The Qur'an Translations of Marracci and Sale', *JWCI* 73 (2013), pp. 93–110; L. Schwoerer, *The Ingenious Mr. Henry Care* (Baltimore, 2001), pp. 44–75.

60 Grey, *Mahometism*, fols 74–80.

61 A. Marotti, *Religious Ideology and Cultural Fantasy: Catholic and Anti-Catholic Discourse in Early Modern England* (Notre Dame, 2005), pp. 131–201.

62 Zachary Grey, *The Horrid Barbarity of the Spanish Inquisition Exemplify'd*, n.d. [unpublished manuscript] in Zachary Grey's Notebook, *c.* 1738–60 (CUL, Add. 3308, fols 2–32). See also Zachary Grey's commonplace book (CUL, Ee.VI.42, no. 28).

63 A. Geddes, *Miscellaneous Tracts* (1714: T109462), I.

64 Quoted in M. Smolenaars, 'Michael Geddes (c. 1647–1713)', *ODNB*.

65 H. Kamen, *The Spanish Inquisition: An Historical Revision* (New Haven, 1998), pp. 214–29; H. Kamen, *Imagining Spain* (New Haven, 2008), pp. 126–49.

66 Grey, *Horrid Barbarity*, fol. 7.

67 Ibid., fol. 4.

68 Ibid., fol. 11. Kamen, *Spanish Inquisition*, p. 227, puts the number of expelled Moriscos at around three hundred thousand.
69 M. Garnett, 'William Lithgow (b. 1582, d. in or after 1645)', *ODNB*.
70 Grey, *Horrid Barbarity*, fols 15, 23.
71 Ibid., fols 24, 27.

Chapter 11

Factions, seditions and schismatical principles: Puritans and Dissenters

In Daniel Neal's April 1743 funeral sermon, the Dissenting minister David Jennings extolled the 'impartial Regard to Truth' Neal had shown in his *History of the Puritans* (1732–38).[1] Zachary Grey, though, excoriated Neal's historical errors. 'That [Neal] had good Talents for writing of History I readily grant', Grey conceded, 'but pray, Sir, how did he use these good Talents in the Volumes under Consideration? Is not that Accuracy wanting which is requisite to form the Character of an exact Historian? And that Impartiality, which is absolutely necessary to distinguish History from Romance?'[2] Jennings acknowledged that Neal had got some things wrong in his four-volume study of Puritanism. But he chalked up the errors to Neal's 'declining State of Health'. Moreover, he protested that

> [i]t certainly ought not to be cast as a Reproach upon an Historian, who has occasion to relate such a Multitude of Facts, which his own Eyes have never seen, nor his Ears heard, but for which he must intirely depend on the Testimony of others, if a few little Mistakes should have crept into his History. Such Errors are unavoidable; and it is no other imperfection than what, probably, belongs to all mere human Histories of the Past, that ever were wrote.[3]

Grey countered that the real reason errors had crept into Neal's *History of the Puritans* was that he suffered from 'too strong a Bias to Party' and therefore could not merit distinction as 'a First Rate Historian'.[4] Grey, by contrast, routinely styled himself on the title-pages of his numerous works as 'impartial'; 'a lover of truth'; 'a lover of history'; 'a believer'; 'a sincere Protestant'; or 'one who is neither Jacobite, nor Republican, Presbyterian, nor Papist'. In Zachary Grey's mind, these self-descriptions were synonymous.

This chapter anatomizes the dispute between Zachary Grey and Dissenting historians like Daniel Neal who together mined the English past for ammunition in eighteenth-century religious and political fights. It locates these historical debates within efforts during the 1730s to repeal the Test and Corporation Acts. It then charts the development of Grey's take on sixteenth- and seventeenth-century English history. It shows, in the process, that, while the seventeenth-century wars of religion were over, their causes and lessons remained contested. Precisely because the causes and lessons of those wars were not settled, polemical divinity retained practical political value. The chapter also uses Zachary Grey's anti-Dissenting historical scholarship further to consider the economic realities of polemical divinity. While religious works dominated booksellers' catalogues, they had to be pitched and packaged in ways that were marketable. Grey's anti-Neal tracts were hardly profitable. The chapter concludes by examining a work of English historical scholarship that was financially successful: Zachary Grey's scholarly edition of Samuel Butler's *Hudibras*.

Perceived scholarly success in historical debate during the eighteenth century depended much on the quality of one's sources.[5] Presentation mattered, but the key to polemical success, most thought, was to deploy higher-quality sources than one's opponent. In this regard, Zachary Grey's friendship with another member of Thomas Baker's Cambridge circle, Phillip Williams (*c.* 1695–1749), proved critical during the 1730s. Williams was a fellow of St John's College, and later its president; throughout the 1730s, he also served as the university's public orator. Williams gave Grey unfettered access to John Nalson's (1637–86) famous manuscript collection.[6] A graduate of St John's, Nalson wrote for the government during the 1670s against papists, Protestant nonconformists and Whigs. The manuscript materials that went into Nalson's two-volume *Impartial Collection of the Great Affairs of State from the Beginning of the Scotch Rebellion in 1639 to the Murder of King Charles I* (1682–83) proved especially useful to Grey a half-century later. To aid Nalson's researches for the royally supported *Impartial Collection*, the office of Parliament's clerk opened up its collection to him. Nalson transcribed many original manuscripts concerning mid-seventeenth-century English political and religious history: he took with him many which he did not return. Nalson also read in and transcribed portions of the Ormonde papers, which now form the core of the Bodleian's Carte collection.[7] At the time of his death, Nalson willed the collection to his daughter, Elizabeth, who later married in 1690 Philip Williams (d. 1719), rector of Doddington. Some time before 1730, the Nalson manuscripts passed into the possession of his son, the younger Philip Williams (*c.* 1695–1749), who had them organized and bound. Thereafter, Williams allowed his resolutely orthodox friends (those like Francis Peck and Grey) to mine the collection's contents for their work. The Nalson collection, then, was a significant collection of primary materials to which none writing in support of Protestant nonconformity had access.[8] Grey's access to the Nalson cache proved a polemical boon. Peck reprinted some of the Nalson material in his *Desiderata Curiosa* (1735), while Grey deployed material from it most prominently in his ripostes to Daniel Neal.[9]

Daniel Neal's *History of the Puritans*, its author promised, would 'preserve the Memory of those great and good Men among the Reformers, for attempting a further Reformation of its Discipline and Ceremonies; and ... account for the Rise and Progress of that Separation from the National Establishment which subsists to this Day'.[10] Neal had studied in the Netherlands before returning to London in 1703 to become a Dissenting minister.[11] Like Grey, Neal had access to a singularly rich manuscript collection – the papers of Roger Morrice (1628–1702).[12] The *History of the Puritans* formed one half of a diptych. He had first published a two-volume *History of New England* (1720), a work whose central theme was the flight of the Puritans from 'Oppression and Persecution' in England and the establishment in North America of a commonwealth in which flourished 'an Universal Loyalty to the best of Kings, ... a becoming Zeal for the Sacred Truths of the Reformation, and ... an Universal Love, Charity, and Forbearance of each other in your differing Sentiments'.[13] His subsequent *History of the Puritans* formed the diptych's other side, recounting the story of Puritan persecution by the established Church back home in England.

Neal's study was the most influential eighteenth-century history of English Puritanism, and some still commend it for its accuracy.[14] Yet Neal's work was a polemical history with a practical purpose. In particular, Neal wrote within the context of the fiercely anticlerical 1730s and his was one of the most prominent voices in the Dissenting campaign for greater religious liberties. The push for repeal in the early 1730s rode a cresting wave of anticlericalism, with the 1727–34 Parliament taking on something of the character of the Reformation Parliaments of the 1530s. Beginning in 1730, the Church of England faced a series of anticlerical bills in the House of Commons (a body filled with Walpole's supporters) for limiting suits for unpaid tithes; for preventing the translation of bishops; for reforming church courts; and for amending church rates. From the perspective of Edmund Gibson, Walpole lacked the conviction, though not the power, to stop these blatant attacks on the Church's legal privileges.[15]

Coinciding with the 1730s anticlericalism was the Dissenting political campaign to repeal the Test and Corporation Acts. A co-ordinated publishing campaign highlighted the injustice of these acts.[16] That Dissenting print campaign for repeal, of which Neal's *History of the Puritans* was a self-conscious part, had two central strands. Firstly, Dissenting polemicists argued that the established Church of England was 'popish' because its view of religious authority was anathema to 'consistent Protestantism'.[17] Rather than countenance the right of 'private judgment' (a right, Dissenters insisted, both natural and inherent to 'true religion'), orthodox churchmen contended that any civil state worth its name must be capable of establishing a religion and, hence, of trumping some natural rights, like the right of private judgement.[18] Allied to the argument for the right of private judgment was the argument from history. Despite toleration's legal protection since the Glorious Revolution, Dissenters suffered from civil disabilities and petty ignominies.[19]

They also had a vivid collective memory of the abuses under which their religious forebears had suffered at the hands of the established Church during the sixteenth and seventeenth centuries.[20]

That collective Dissenting memory of mistreatment by established churchmen, no less than the antinomies of 'Protestant popery' and 'consistent Protestantism', had been consciously and carefully built. Dissenting clerical historians like Samuel Clarke (1599–1682), Richard Baxter (1615–91) and Edmund Calamy (1671–1732) had written polemical histories which aimed at accuracy, but accuracy in the service of a greater cause.[21] When Calamy famously detailed the nearly one thousand ministers ejected in 1662, for instance, he simultaneously preserved a record of their ejections; rebutted Samuel Parker; *and* constructed a Dissenting identity of 'an embattled minority who were victims of a historical injustice, martyrs for the principles of conscience and religious liberty'.[22] Daniel Neal aimed for similar results.[23] The full title of his work (*The History of Puritans or Protestant Non-conformists*) equated Puritanism and Dissent, giving a false, if appealing, coherence to both and providing a genealogy for eighteenth-century Dissent that was problematic at best.[24] Connecting his four volumes was a narrative spine which recounted the persecution of Puritans and which cast the Puritans as *the* authentic guarantors of Christian liberty. For Neal the persecutory rot had set into the Church of England from the Elizabethan religious settlement: rather than being the queen who had saved England from popery, Elizabeth became, in Neal's hands, the monarch who legally established a crypto-popish ecclesiology and liturgy.

Neal's was no lone Dissenting voice on these issues. His argument about the relatively seamless evolution of sixteenth-century Puritanism into post-revolutionary Dissent mirrored a wider effort among Protestant Dissenters in the early 1730s to paper over their denominational differences and to work together to repeal the Test and Corporation Acts.[25] Just as Neal had emphasized the persecution of Puritans by 'popish Protestants', so too did other Dissenting historians, like Samuel Chandler (1693–1766), similarly hammering home that the Church of Rome (and, by implication, the Church of England) had a long history of persecution.[26] Neal joined with Chandler and others in 1734–35 to deliver a set of lectures at Salters' Hall on popery's iniquity. Neal's contribution to the series addressed the papacy's 'usurpation' of civil and religious authority and concluded with a dig at Archbishop Laud for having undermined the English 'battle' against 'the Devil' and at the 'foreign tyrant' who tempted the English people to abandon their allegiance to the English crown.[27] Neal left it to his readers to draw the lines of connection between Laud and his eighteenth-century clerical successors.

Orthodox churchmen also collectively remembered and coalesced around a history of past abuse at the hands of Puritans. Long after the internecine strife of the seventeenth century had died down, memories of the England's 'troubles' remained raw.[28] Moreover, the traumatic events of the previous century got recollected and given order and meaning by polemical historians like Peter Heylyn (1559–1662), Jeremy Collier (1650–1726), John Strype (1643–1737), Laurence Echard (1672–1730) and John Walker (1674–1747), whose histories told the story of the political and religious anarchy unleashed by seventeenth-century Puritans. These orthodox historians wrote in the service of a greater cause. When Walker published his *Sufferings of the Clergy of the Church of England* (1714), for instance, he did so in an era when many claimed that the Church was 'in danger' and he provided a martyrology to show that the Church of England had *always* been in danger from the very people held up for admiration by Baxter, Calamy and other Dissenting historians.[29] In the mid-eighteenth century, orthodox historians like Francis Peck (1692–1743) and Zachary Grey continued the polemical work of Walker and his like.

No less than the 1730s Dissenting publishing efforts which buttressed the political campaign against the Test and Corporation Acts, the orthodox counter-responses were carefully planned and co-ordinated. William Webster and Edmund Gibson managed the initial orthodox response to Neal's historical project. At the time Neal published the first instalment of his *History of the Puritans* in winter 1732, Webster was launching his hyper-orthodox *Weekly Miscellany*. Webster – one of Daniel Waterland's protégés and one of Conyers Middleton's and William Warburton's antagonists – had long held an interest in sixteenth- and seventeenth-century English history, with his first publication being an introduction to Thomas Skinner's life of George Monck (1608–70).[30] Monck was a hero, someone who pulled down the Puritans' 'beloved Idol of Anarchy and Confusion' and someone about whom eighteenth-century 'Men of rigid Republican Principles' were no less 'violent in their Expressions of Rage and Malice' than had been Edmund Ludlow (1616–92) 'and other hot Republicans' during the mid-seventeenth century.[31] Webster seems to have connected Grey with Edmund Gibson.[32] Gibson, too, reckoned that the 'Fanatic Times' of the mid-seventeenth century evidenced the true intentions of Protestant nonconformists.[33] Having got hold of Grey's anti-Neal research notes through Webster's intervention, Gibson shuttled them along to Isaac Maddox (1697–1759), Queen Caroline's clerk of the closet.[34] Gibson's choice of his protégé Maddox to respond to Neal was astute since Maddox was a former Dissenter who had studied at the University of Edinburgh before conforming to the established Church in the early 1720s. Maddox was one of the two dozen or so Dissenting apostates whom Edmund Calamy lamented losing to the Church of England, noting that they 'were, generally, persons of sobriety and unblemished character'.[35] Maddox, though, had previously published nothing. Nor would he ever demonstrate any scholarly expertise in English history. His apostasy from Dissent may have been useful to Gibson; but his relative ignorance of the historical record was a polemical liability. This is where Zachary Grey stepped in as Maddox's orthodox ghost-researcher: Grey provided the ordnance; Maddox, at least initially, chose where to lob it.

Zachary Grey

Zachary Grey was the logical person to whom Webster and Gibson could turn, as he had built up a reputation during the 1720s as orthodoxy's most vocal and learned historian of sixteenth- and seventeenth-century English religion and politics. His first foray into the polemical arena came in 1720, when he published his two-volume *Vindication of the Church of England* (1720) in response to James Peirce's *Vindication of the Dissenters* (1717). There quickly followed over the next five years a stream of eleven other pamphlets and books attacking prominent Dissenting and anticlerical writers, including Richard Cocks, Benjamin Bennet, John Oldmixon and Edmund Calamy. In these works, Grey honed a form of argument and outlined a historical interpretation upon which he would build for the rest of his career. Grey's historical works almost exclusively were animadversions (line-by-line rebuttals), a literary form still favoured by many at the time but one which became rarer as the century wore on.[36] At its worst, the animadversion was a literary form which could quickly devolve into a list of mistakes. Moreover, it was a literary form which easily lent itself to polemical immoderation, as no error seemed too small nor too insignificant to pass without mention. Authors who wrote narrative history during the mid-eighteenth century aimed for plausibility in the whole: their facts had to be accurate but that accuracy was in the service of a story which itself had to fit together convincingly. Those who wrote animadversions, by contrast, had forthrightly corrosive purposes: they aimed to demolish the reader's confidence in what they deemed to be wrong-headed narratives by identifying and correcting each and every perceived inaccuracy.

Why Grey rose to the bait of James Peirce's *Vindication of the Dissenters* or how he got first published is clear. Peirce's *Vindication of the Dissenters* actually was not new, but merely an English reprint of a Latin work he had written during the height of the Sacheverell crisis. Grey's retort was unequivocal and uncompromising. Peirce (1674–1726), on Grey's view, meant to 'propagate Schism' and his book should have been censored. ''Twere to be wished the Press was under some better Regulation', Grey complained, 'that not only Schism, but Atheism, Profaneness, Irreligion, and the destructive Principles of those, who pride themselves in the Name of Free-thinkers, and Patrons of Liberty (though falsely so called) might be less encouraged, than at present they seem to be'.[37]

The acid tone that characterized nearly all of Grey's polemical works was on display from the very first sentence of his very first publication. '[T]he vile Principles, and evil Practices of the Dissenters, of what Kind or Denomination soever, have been sufficiently, both formerly and of late Years, exposed and laid open by several Members of the Church of England', he opened. '... Yet the Writers on that Side still presuming to rake together all the Party Scandal, frivolous Objections, and groundless Censures and Surmises; which, modestly speaking, have been fully confuted a hundred Times over'.[38] Dissenters in general were duplicitous; James Peirce was purposefully deceitful. For if he 'has given sufficient Testimony of his Learning', so too, Grey contended, 'he has given an unquestionable Proof of Want of Veracity, and has shewn, that there is nothing but he'll endeavor to pervert it to a wrong Sense, in order to do Service to his Party or Cause'.[39] Indeed, Peirce's book was 'one of the most erroneous Pieces that has been published within the Compass of a Century, scarce carrying the least Shadow or Appearance of Truth in any one Page thereof'.[40] Grey also liked to pick at open Dissenting wounds, wondering in print – with the Salters' Hall controversy and Peirce's own Christological heterodoxy in mind – why the Dissenters could not resolve their own internal conflicts before attacking the Church of England.[41]

Two themes ran through Grey's riposte to Peirce's historical defence of Dissent. Firstly, he insisted that the Church of England alone was an 'Orthodox and pure Church'.[42] The whole of the second volume of Grey's *Vindication* was given over to a sixteen-chapter defence of the Church of England's primitivity, from its ecclesiology and public liturgies to its practice of kneeling at the sacrament and bowing at the name of Jesus. Grey especially defended the established Church's episcopal ecclesiology, which he insisted had an unmistakably primitive pedigree: 'if it must be esteemed a Remnant of Popery, the Apostles themselves, and the Fathers of the very first Ages of Christianity, must be accounted papists'.[43] Presbyterians, by contrast, had an ecclesiology that was novel, not primitive.[44] The Church of England alone among the reformed churches had avoided 'the two Extremes of Popish Superstition on the one Hand, and Presbyterian Indecency on the other'.[45]

The second theme pervading Zachary Grey's *Vindication* was the persistence of Puritan violence and intolerance. The Church of England had, it could not be denied, been marred by Henrician Erastianism. Even Thomas Cranmer was guilty of professing an overly Erastian conception of the royal supremacy during Henry's reign.[46] But, Grey continued, from Edward VI's reign onwards, 'our Kings ... have laid Claim to no other Power over the Church, but a supreme Civil Power'.[47] Moreover, in Elizabeth's reign, 'the Church [was] thoroughly purged and reformed from all these Dregs of Corruption and Superstition'.[48] How did the Puritans respond to the purifying Elizabethan Reformation? On Grey's reading, their opposition to the established Church only deepened, as they became increasingly implacable. In response to Peirce's claims that every Elizabethan archbishop of Canterbury had unrelentingly persecuted Puritans, Grey detailed the lives of those Puritans in Elizabeth's reign who were schismatic, seditious or both. Where Peirce held up Elizabethan Puritans like Thomas Cartwright, Edward Dering, Robert Johnson, John Udall, Robert Brown, Henry Barrow, Edmund Coppinger, William Hacket, Henry Atherington and John Penry as victims of religious persecution, Grey cast them as inveterate opponents of episcopal ecclesiology, theological orthodoxy and civil peace. Likewise, against Peirce's objection that only a few anonymous Puritan authors were 'notorious Transgressors of all the Rules of Decency and Order in God's Church', Grey retorted, 'There were more than Two or Three obscure nameless Authors of a Party, a considerable Number of them, and the most leading Men, were guilty of this Crime ... He can't (I believe) name any one of the Party, who was not notoriously guilty of this Fault'.[49] Grey repeatedly drew connections between the past and the present. Of Peirce's depiction of Thomas Cartwright (1534/5–1603), a vocal supporter of the anti-episcopal, pro-Presbyterian *Admonition to Parliament* (1572), for instance, Grey observed that 'had [Peirce] been somewhat more tart in his Expressions against Cartwright, who used his Adversaries commonly with the like Scurrility and Contempt that a certain Dissenting Teacher lately ejected at Exon (who shall be nameless) does his, 'twould have been very justifiable'.[50] That ejected Exeter Dissenting teacher was James Peirce.[51]

That Elizabethan Puritans were heterodox and seditious schismatics was bad enough, but Grey went farther to argue that they had also been unwitting dupes of the papists. Faithful Commin, for instance, 'a Person generally reputed a Zealous Protestant and, and much admired, and followed by the People, for his seeming Piety, and for speaking against Pius V, then Pope', was, as John Strype had supposedly earlier shown, an incognito Dominican friar bent on subverting Protestantism from within.[52] Indeed, Commin was one of those whom Pope Pius V had 'granted [an] Indulgence to several Orders of the Romish Church, to set up Tenets and Principles of Religion; and they themselves, seemingly to be Enemies to that Church, purposely to confound the Protestant Religion, and to hinder for the future all general Assemblies ... lest thereby a better Understanding might be had amongst Protestants; and thence at length, spring a general Union and Agreement amongst all of them'.[53] Moreover, Grey continued, Elizabethan Puritans sometimes even went beyond being papist dupes to being popish imitators. In 1596, for instance, a number of Puritan ministers engaged in demonic exorcism, acting in the process like 'Miracle-Mongers, who performed so many surprising and stupendous Things, by the Force and energy of their extempore Effusion, and devout Fastings'.[54]

The accession of the Stuart family to the English throne after Elizabeth's death intensified tensions between the English church-state and Protestant nonconformists. James I, rather than being the popish persecutor of Puritans that Peirce made him out to be, emerged in the pages of Grey's *Vindication* as something entirely different. His early dealings with Scottish Presbyterians lay behind his admonition in the *Basilikon Doron* to '[t]ake heed ... of such Puritans, very Pests in the Church and Commonweal, whom no Deserts can oblige, nor Oaths, nor Promises bind, breathing nothing but Sedition and Calumnies, aspiring without Measure, Railing without Reason, and making their own Imagination without any Warrant of the Word of God the Square of their Consciences'.[55] By the same token, James's parliamentary speeches, wholly neglected by Peirce, testified eloquently to his unswerving anti-popery.[56] Likewise, Charles I and his archbishop of Canterbury, William Laud, turned out to be the antidotes to the Puritan problem, not tyrants bent on establishing an English popery. Grey's defence of Laud is especially notable. He praised his 'excellent and laudable Qualities', which were out of step with the 'licentious' times; and he noted that Laud had tried to help with the 'dispelling of Ignorance, and Promotion of useful Knowledge' among both the clergy and the laity. By contrast, Puritans like John Bastwick, Henry Burton and William Prynne deserved prosecution because they were 'Indendiaries' who threatened 'the Security of the Government'. Like other Puritan 'Factious Lecturers', they preached 'Factions, Seditions and schismatical Principles'.[57]

Therein lay the Puritans' original sin, from Grey's point of view: they fomented sedition and rebellion. At heart they were anti-monarchical, espousing principles 'that of Consequence tend either to a Republic, or [to] what is ten thousand Times worse, Anarchy and Confusion both in Church and State'.[58] Their own governing record during the 1640s and 1650s proved this without question, for when Puritans actually controlled the levers of government during the mid-seventeenth century they showed their true colours. 'Nay, ... there was more arbitrary Power and illegal Commitments, exorbitant Taxes, Rapine and Plunder, Sequestrations and Sacrilege, with whatever else could be most Unjust and Tyrannical, voted and put in Practice during the 20 Years Usurpation of the several Juntos, than by all the crowned Heads and their Favourites too ... since the Conquest', Grey argued. 'I might add, since the Creation, did our Histories reach so far.'[59] Were Dissenters allowed political power in the eighteenth century, the result would surely be the same: 'the Magistrate's Power would be very precarious, could [Peirce] and the Party resolve the ultimate resort into the Hands of their Darling Mob, and make them the proper Judges of what is to be retained in our churches, and what destroyed for fear or being perverted to wrong Uses'. By way of evidence, Grey argued that it was not Henry Sacheverell who had been 'the Church's Incendiary' but rather that the 'Mobs and Tumults have of late been encouraged ... by those of Mr Peirce's party, in order to make the Church and those of her Communion odious'.[60] Eighteenth-century Dissenters were, in other words, trying to undermine the established Church, just as the popish priests had tried to undermine Elizabethan Protestantism.

Throughout his polemical career, Grey rarely strayed far from the subjects first adduced in *A Vindication of the Church of England*. What he did do during the first half of the 1720s, though, was to develop more fully a few central themes and to hone his polemical style in a series of viperous back-and-forth quarrels with Benjamin Bennet (1674–1726), Richard Cocks (1659–1726), John Oldmixon (1672–1742) and Edmund Calamy. Grey, for instance, increasingly emphasized the dangers posed by the theologically heterodox to the political order, noting, for instance, that 'if once [MPs] fail to be Guardians of our Pure, Unspotted, and Holy Religion, we cannot reasonably expect that our Civil Liberties will be far behind'.[61] Parliament had to guard against heterodoxy because the 'Liberty of the Press' allowed 'every Bold Pretender who has more Conceit than Brains ... to make successful Attacks on the Christian Religion'. Little wonder, Grey continued, 'that the most Heterodox, nay, that the most Irreligious and Abominable Opinions should be Propagated and Patronized'.[62] Press censorship, something Grey had earlier advocated, was therefore essential for security in Church and state. So too was a more vigorous clericalism, which would help, for instance, to settle disputes over religious teaching. If the 'Truth of the Church's Authority in Controversies of Faith were not granted, it would be impossible to determine any Controversies at all of that kind', Grey pointed out. 'For though the Scripture must be allowed to be the Rule of Faith, and the Supreme Judge in all such Controversies; yet as both the Contending Parties, in all Disputes of this kind, generally pretend to deduce their Opinions from Scripture; and as they can't be both Right, so there ought to be some Rule whereby to judge where the Right lies'.[63] For this reason, 'to keep such Pests of Religion (whose chief Business was to Undermine and Sap the very Foundations of the Christian Religion by denying the Author and Founder of it) out of the Pale of the Church' required a strict 'Test of Orthodoxy'.[64] Unofficial coercion also seemed to have been acceptable to Grey, as he even went so far as to condone the anti-Dissenting rioters of the mid-1710s.[65]

Grey's pamphlets of the 1720s provided him the occasion not just to amplify core themes but also to improve his arguments and to develop his polemical style. *A Vindication of the Church of England*, his first publication, for instance, relied almost exclusively on the work of other historians, especially orthodox or even nonjuring, ones like Nalson, Strype, Heylyn, Collier, Walker and Thomas Brett. Increasingly, though, Grey began to bolster his arguments with evidence drawn from sixteenth- and seventeenth-century books, pamphlets, speeches and the like. The fruits of his deepening research into sixteenth- and seventeenth-century printed sources showed up not just in his pamphlets but also in long published collections of quotations around a central theme, such as the 'Seditious and Republican Principles' of the Westminster Assembly divines.[66] Likewise, Grey's early works showed him honing a polemical style, one of whose chief characteristics was its aggressive *ad hominem* attacks. He judged John Oldmixon, for instance, to have been little 'above the Rank and Level of a Common Hackney-Writer', while Richard Cocks was a 'Dirty Baronet' who had 'ingenious Kindred in Bedlam' and who wrote books that were useful to 'Pastry-Cooks, Grocers and Tobacconists'.[67] Grey's early works, then, were amalgams of deeply held principle, substantive research and scurrilous personal insult.

They were also the product of evident self-reflection. Grey kept interleaved copies of much of his own work.[68] Those annotated works reveal someone who revisited his arguments again and again, as the margins and interleaves are covered with notes, references and corrections in different inks and in Grey's evolving hand. Most of the subsequent references corroborated his original interpretations, as when he noted in his copy of the *Vindication of the Church of England*, 'See Mr B: Bennet's Memorial of the Reformation wherein He differs from His Friend Mr Pierce with Relation to the Hampton Court Conference p. 124'. At other points, though, Grey privately recanted a position, such as when he noted having regretted disparaging Richard Mocket's *Disciplina et politia ecclesiae Anglicanae* (1615): 'I am Sorry I have spoken what I have of Dr Mocket's Book' after having received exculpatory evidence of his character from 'My Most Excellent & Worthy Friend Mr Tho. Baker of St. Johns'.[69] The self-annotated copies of Grey's own works, then, show that he crafted, revisited and revised his arguments well after their initial publication. They show, as well, that he paid close attention to what his opponents had to argue.

By the time Daniel Neal's *History of the Puritans* started to roll off the press in 1732, Zachary Grey had built up a reputation as an ardent defender of the established Church of England and as a scourge of Protestant nonconformity. He was someone to whom William Webster and Edmund Gibson might naturally turn for help to rebut Neal's work. Grey gave them his own heavily annotated interleaved copies of Neal's *History of the Puritans*, which survive today in the library at St John's College, Cambridge.[70] To anyone who had read Grey's work from the 1720s, Maddox's *Vindication of the government, doctrine, and worship of the Church of England, established in the reign of Queen Elizabeth* (1733) would have been wholly familiar. Readers of Webster's *Weekly Miscellany* also got a distilled version of Maddox's argument in a front-page story to coincide with Maddox's book's publication.[71] Firstly, Maddox sought to undermine confidence in Neal's work by disparaging his use of sources. Though Neal claimed to have had access to a significant collection of manuscripts in Cambridge, Maddox complained that 'he names no particular Library or College; nor does he acquaint us *when* the Papers themselves were wrote or by whom or who was the Collector of them'.[72] As it turned out, Neal had access to the Roger Morrice manuscripts, though he acknowledged them ambiguously.[73] Secondly, Maddox chipped away at Neal's argument about the connection between Puritanism and liberty. Like Grey, he blamed schism for popery's rise: popery thrived thanks to Protestant disunity, disunity that, Maddox argued, arose from the Dissenters' undue attention on the 'external and disputed Parts of Religion, in Place of true Doctrine and real Goodness'.[74] Maddox's counter-history of the Puritans highlighted Puritan intolerance and the inherent schismatic tendencies of Protestant nonconformists from the Reformation's very beginnings. Elizabeth I had inherited a 'universally Popish' nation and was, from her reign's outset, beset by popish threats at home and from abroad.[75] In crafting her religious settlement, Elizabeth had to lure in papists while the same time creating a Church that would comprehend within it 'the greatest Number of Protestants'.[76] All English Protestant, though, did not support the young queen in the face of the popish menace. The Puritans, especially those who had spent their Marian exile in Geneva, would not relent until the 'Genevan Plan' had been established in England, despite the fact that episcopal ecclesiology had both biblical and primitive precedents and was, in Maddox's words, the 'happy medium between Calvinists and Lutherans'.[77] Maddox went even further to contend that Puritans were persecutory, noting that they even had hounded John Foxe and his son for being insufficiently Protestant.[78] Moreover, Elizabethan Puritans were profoundly insincere, since they dubbed 'everything ... Popery which [they] did not relish'.[79] That insincerity extended to their political theology, for Maddox hammered home the idea that Neal had cherry-picked his evidence regarding Puritan loyalism. ''Twas easier for him to celebrate their Loyalty, when he thus carefully omitted all Instances of the Contrary', Maddox contended. Indeed, he continued, Elizabethan Puritans were actually committed anti-monarchists: 'The State ... was to be reduced to the same Form. Their comitial, provincial, or national Assemblies, the whole frame of their Church Government was perfectly Popular or Republican'.[80] Maddox left it to his readers to draw the lines of connection between the Elizabethan Puritan crypto-republicans and their eighteenth-century Dissenting descendants.

Maddox's rebuttal of Neal primarily took the form of a thematic narrative. To convince his readers that he was treating Neal's argument fairly, he pre-emptively agreed only to cite historians whom Neal approved (Thomas Fuller, for instance) and not to cite evidence from those whom Neal disapproved (Heylyn and Collier, for instance).[81] While the body of Maddox's book proceeded thematically, his 163-page appendix offered a line-by-line rebuttal. That the appendix's tone – biting, sarcastic, ridiculing, unrelenting – differed from the main body is unsurprising since the appendix was little more than a cleaned-up cut-and-paste of the marginalia from Grey's annotated edition of Neal's work.

Maddox's *Vindication* did not convince all of the orthodox, some of whom thought that Neal had the better of the case regarding the destabilizing effects of Laudian anti-Calvinism.[82] But Maddox's book touched a nerve with Neal, who wrote a lengthy response in which he protested unconvincingly that he had intended for his work to have absolutely no present-day application. 'My Design ... was not to defend [the Puritans'] Doctrine or Discipline, but to set their Principles in a fair Light ...', he began. 'This I have done ... without reflecting on the present Times, or giving just Occasion of Offence to moderate Man of any Persuasion.'[83] Yet, Neal's argument in his riposte was unmistakably topical. In particular, he defended the Elizabethan Puritans' anti-establishment rhetoric, noting that, while they might have preached against the religious establishment, they did not *actually* rebel against Elizabeth. He tried to turn sixteenth-century Puritan anti-establishment rhetoric to his favour not by citing evidence from Elizabeth's reign but rather by quoting repeatedly from the managers of Henry Sacheverell's trial regarding Elizabeth's persecution of the Puritans.[84] The path from the persecutory Virgin Queen through Sacheverell to Edmund Gibson and his fellow orthodox churchmen was one that Neal left his readers to trace for themselves.[85]

Gibson became an increasingly polarizing figure during the 1730s, as he strengthened the resolve of the bench of bishops to defend the established Church. The 1734 parliamentary election returned a Commons ready to press forward with anticlerical measures, especially regarding mortmain and tithes for Quakers.[86] Clearly Gibson had too much on his plate to co-ordinate the subsequent orthodox responses to Daniel Neal. This, along with Isaac Maddox's apparent refusal to acknowledge Zachary Grey's research assistance in print, irked William Webster. 'I have not sent your MS to Maddocks', he informed Grey upon the appearance of Neal's third volume of the *History of the Puritans*. 'A Parcel of Scrubs! Why should we help them to Credit, when they will neither return the Civility, nor own it. They did not so much as acknowledge your Assistance.' Instead, urged Webster, 'Your MS, with a Preface, will make a Vol[ume]'.[87] Yet even had Maddox properly thanked Grey for his research, his promotion to the episcopal bench in 1736 likely made him wary of engaging in a print battle with Daniel Neal. Sitting bishops (even seasoned polemical divines like Thomas Sherlock or Benjamin Hoadly) kept their powder dry longer and usually entered into the arena of public debate with weighty works, like Sherlock's *Tryal of the Witnesses* (1729) or Hoadly's *Plain Account*. So, from Gibson's perspective, Daniel Neal was worth seeing off, but not worth Maddox sullying his reputation, especially in the midst the decade's febrile anticlericalism.

Zachary Grey, by contrast, had little to lose, as he clearly would never rise above his comfortable rectorship. To this expendable country cleric fell the orthodox job of refuting Neal's last three volumes of his *History of the Puritans*, with Gibson and Maddox urging him on from the sidelines.[88] Grey's animadversions had, buried within their artless litany of evidence, an argument which would have surprised no one familiar with his anti-Dissenting outpourings from the 1720s. Across his three volumes, the first of which appeared in March 1736 and the last of which appeared in April 1740, he reiterated the themes adduced in Maddox's volume: Daniel Neal, the Puritans he venerated and the Protestant Dissenters who succeeded them were intolerant, schismatic and ruinous to the nation's political health. Grey also used a series of complementary pieces, published between winter 1736 and early 1740, either to direct his fire at Neal or to address points raised by Neal, Samuel Chandler and like-minded historians.

Grey argued that Neal and his historian allies were prejudicially selective with their evidence. 'Though Accuracy and Exactness in History is not every Man's Talent, yet even when that is wanting, we might reasonably expect Truth and fair Dealing from an Author, who more than once, makes such large pretences to Impartiality', Grey argued of Neal; Samuel Chandler was a historian whose work was fundamentally suspect because of his 'Attachment to Party'.[89] The belief that Neal and others had intentionally misled their readers accounts for Grey's ostentatious appendices, with their transcriptions of Nalson manuscripts and the long pastiche of quotations from printed primary sources which he provided in his works. Neal might play hide the ball, but Grey, he signalled to his readers, had nothing to hide. Moreover, Grey insisted that Neal, Chandler and others were nothing more than shills for schismatics and rebels, 'downright Republican[s]', 'Patriots with a Dash of Republicanism'.[90]

Picking up where Maddox had left off in his *Vindication*, Grey opened his first riposte to Neal by robustly defending the early Stuarts. James I, for instance, was almost self-evidently no Puritan before coming to England. 'Is it probable, that this King, after such a Series of barbarous and inhumane usage from his Scottish Subjects of that Persuasion, should ever have been a Favourer of their Church-Government, and Discipline?' Grey wondered. 'Could Treason and Rebellion be proper Methods of reconciling him to a Kirk, the leading members of which had given him too many Proofs of their Inclination to both.'[91] Grey noted that James had been kidnapped by Scottish Presbyterian nobles and had been the subject of assassination attempts. Moreover, James had advised his heir unequivocally in *Basilikon Doron* about the danger of Puritans. Nor did James become a papist after he had assumed the English throne, not least since the Roman Catholic Church had denied his right to the English throne in 1601. James also spoke forthrightly against popery in the 1609 Parliament. If Neal could not accept the manifold evidence that James I had been no papist, Grey jibed, '[w]ith the same Reason, and by the very same Rule, we might conclude Mr. Neal to be a Favourer of Monarchy, and Episcopacy'.[92] As for Neal's insinuation that James I had Prince Henry (1594–1612) murdered, Grey could only note that this had gone a bridge too far even for the Whig historian Paul de Rapin de Thoyras (1661–1725), who had decried the notion as 'only Fruits of the blackest Malice'.[93]

Neal also portrayed Charles I in a way that was, from Grey's perspective, fantastical. 'Friends and Foes, from Churchmen, Presbyterians, and Republicans; the worst of them, [were] much less Enemies to the Royal Martyr, than Mr. Neal, who has represented him all along, as a Favourer of Popery, and Arbitrary Principles; as one who had no regard to his Word, or Promise', Grey protested.[94] Only the most partisan of historians could, for instance, accuse Charles of having picked up 'pernicious Maxims' while in Madrid with Buckingham to court the Infanta Maria.[95] Even worse, the notion that Charles I was behind the 1641 Irish rebellion was a 'horrid Aspersion [that] has been so often confuted, that if I was capable of being surprised at anything Mr Neal could say, … I should much wonder that an Historian making such Pretences to Impartiality and Fair Dealing, could again bring such an exploded Forgery upon the Stage'.[96] Similarly, Neal heaped unfounded abuse upon William Laud. Anti-Stuarts had routinely charged Charles's archbishop with being a crypto-papist – stretching back even to his days as an Oxford student – and even that he had aimed to reunite the churches of Rome and England. His altar policies of the 1630s and his reconsecration of the parish churches of St Katherine Creed and St Giles-in-the-Fields in 1631 were also taken by some to be evidence that he encouraged idolatry.[97]

In Charles I and Laud, Neal and like-minded historians found the chief violators of both orthodoxy and orthopraxis. Grey, by contrast, argued that the king and his archbishop had been upholders of undefiled primitive Christianity. 'The many Virtues and Graces of his Life, prove his Religion to have been what an Apostle styles it, Pure and undefiled before God', Grey suggested of Charles I; Grey also signed a pamphlet on *The schismatics delineated from authentic vouchers* on 10 January, 'the Day that the truly primitive Archbishop Laud was martyred'.[98] Grey blamed the problems of the seventeenth century on Puritan excesses. From Peter Smart to Alexander Leighton, from William Burton to William Prynne, from Henry Sherfield to Richard Baxter, Grey saw schismatics, republicans and 'fanatics' who designed to overturn the religious and political order as established by law during Elizabeth I's reign. Lest his readers think that any of this was immaterial to the eighteenth century, Grey noted, by way of quoting his father-in-law Robert Moss's 30 January 1707 sermon before the House of Commons, that the origins of the current 'Spirit of Infidelity and Atheism' derived directly from the seventeenth-century 'troubles'. 'For this also we are indebted to those pious Times, when Religion was made the Watchword of Rebellion, and a Warrant for Sacrilege and Murder', Moss had assured the Commons. 'And what wonder if the Hypocrisy of those Days, which was but Religion in Disguise, hath in a less demure Age ventured to pluck off the Mask, and appear like itself, no better than bare-faced Profaneness.'[99]

Whatever the merits of Grey's arguments in his dispute with Daniel Neal, his prosecution of them was, quite literally, unprofitable. In the summer of 1738, the nonjuror John Lindsay reported that London booksellers were refusing to print Grey's fourth instalment: 'The truth is, that, after divers meetings and advances made towards the publication of your present work, when I had reason to think there was nothing more to do but to report to you the conclusion of a contract, ... but I found, the taste of the times is such, that the three former parts of the same work did not answer in trade; and therefore I have no hopes of dealing for it, unless you will print it at your own hazard'.[100] Grey's fourth anti-Neal book eventually got printed because Grey rounded up private subscriptions. Within a few months his friends were relaying reports back to him about their efforts to find subscribers for the new work and to peddle unsold volumes of his first two responses.[101] Even still, it could be hard going for Grey's friends to drum up subscribers. William Bedford, for instance, reported from Yelden in Bedfordshire that he regretted being able only to line up seven subscribers, 'but, as few of my neighbourhood have the former parts of the Controversy, I find it on that account only very difficult to engage any more at present'.[102] Perhaps not surprisingly, John Lewis would report in March 1739 that he was having trouble finding a copy of Grey's third refutation, since 'I believe no Bookseller will print them'.[103]

Lewis's explanation for the booksellers' refusal to print turned on clerical habits. 'Our Clergy have something else to do: at Day, to hunt &c; & at night, to meet in Clubs, to drink & game till Midnight', he lamented to Grey, '& they who mind their Studies & their Cures, are treated with Sneer & Neglect, & their Company avoided'.[104] Lewis's explanation, though, falls short of the evidence, for polemical divinity still dominated eighteenth-century booksellers' catalogues. William Cole hit closer to the mark when identifying the weakness of Grey's anti-Neal animadversions. Whereas Isaac Maddox had written he first volume 'in so masterly a manner', Grey's last three volumes were poorly written. His books 'suffer[ed] by coming after the former', particularly because Grey had employed 'so little art to knit his materials together'.[105] Booksellers were furthermore unlikely to print what they could not sell: they were unwilling to flog polemical books in a one-sided fight. Isaac Maddox's *Vindication* (1733) had elicited from an irked Daniel Neal a stand-alone refutation. But Neal wrote no such response to any of Grey's ripostes. Whether that was because Neal's health was declining rapidly or whether he simply decided that ignoring was bliss matters little. Polemical divinity was premised on the idea of duelling polemicists: if one of the duellists did not fight back, the printers and booksellers often stayed away. They, like the polemical divines they sometimes published, had a bottom-line goal. They had nearly to be certain to profit from the works of polemical divinity which they did print.

Zachary Grey's 1744 edition of Samuel Butler's *Hudibras* managed to be commercially successful while also dealing in its often rambling footnotes with precisely the same themes and subject matter covered in his anti-Neal tracts. The story of what it took Grey to get that edition of *Hudibras* into print further illumines the economic realities of polemical divinity. For while the subject matter remained topical, form and artistry also mattered.

Structured like *The Fairie Queene*, modelled on *Don Quixote* and written in doggerel, *Hudibras* (1662–77) recounted the adventures of the paunchy Presbyterian knight Hudibras and his companion, the Independent squire Ralpho.[106] At the start of their journey to stamp out sin, they encountered a group of people dancing and enjoying a bearbaiting, which they aimed to stop. In the ensuing fight, Hudibras captured and put into the stocks a one-legged fiddler before an Amazonian named Trulla turned the tables on the Presbyterian moral reformer and placed him into the stocks. There Hudibras received a visit from a wealthy widow whom he had hoped to marry for her money. She offered to free him from his confinement, but only on the condition that he submit to a whipping. To this he agreed, but, soon after his release, he debated with Ralpho whether he could lawfully break his oath to the widow. After being pelted with rotten eggs by another crowd who came upon them, Hudibras and Ralpho visited an astrologer, Sidrophel, both having agreed beforehand that it is perfectly acceptable for a Christian man on a Christian mission to consult with diviners. Convinced that Sidrophel might be fraudulent and in league with the Devil, Hudibras sent Ralpho to fetch the authorities; instead the squire went straight to the widow and confessed to her that Hudibras intended to break his oath to be whipped. The widow then confronted the Presbyterian knight and the poem's action ends with Hudibras and Ralpho escaping through a window and riding away on their saddleless horses, exposed as inveterate liars and cheats. The moral of the story was neither elusive nor subtle.

What drew Zachary Grey to Butler's 'incomparable Poem' was the skill with which Butler had 'expose[d] the Hypocrisy and Wickedness of those, who began and carried on the Rebellion, under a Pretence of promoting Religion and Godliness; at the same time they acted against all the precepts of Religion'.[107] *Hudibras* portrayed the seventeenth-century 'troubles' in a way almost entirely consonant with Grey's own vision of the period. To both Butler and Grey, it was a time when sectaries had turned the world upside-down. While Grey distinguished carefully between the 'Presbyterian Scheme' and the 'Independent Scheme' of Church government in his edition's preface, he did so merely to guide his eighteenth-century audience through parts of the poem 'which to the generality of Readers may be thought not a little intricate', since the terms *Presbyterians* and *Independents*, he noted, 'are now promiscuously used by others, and they are called indifferently by either of those names'.[108] These two purportedly antithetical versions of anti-episcopal Protestantism had, in other words, become by the mid-eighteenth century what they were essentially: interchangeable sectarianisms bent on undermining the rightly ordered English church-state. To distinguish between an eighteenth-century Presbyterian and an Independent was to make a distinction without a difference.[109]

Hudibras was an enormously popular poem, so much so that a century after its first publication Samuel Johnson could still reckon that it 'is one of those compositions of which a nation may justly boast'.[110] If some like Samuel Pepys thought *Hudibras*'s humour not that humorous, most others seem to have enjoyed it greatly and the poem went through multiple editions, including a 1726 one which featured William Hogarth's illustrations.[111] What particularly distinguished Grey's edition, though, was the depth and thoroughness of its explanatory notes.[112] These were necessary because Butler's references, as even the polymath Johnson noted, would have eluded many in the eighteenth century: they knew 'the sour solemnity, the sullen superstition, the gloomy moroseness, the stubborn scruples of the ancient Puritans' primarily from 'books or from tradition' and therefore 'cannot but by recollection and study understand the lines in which they are satirised'.[113] While some of Grey's contemporaries mocked his copious notes, subsequent Butler editors have acknowledged the usefulness of his labours.[114]

Zachary Grey's primary challenge with an edition of *Hudibras* was actually getting it printed. He was at work on the edition in earnest by 1739.[115] There are suggestions that he might have begun to cast about for publishers as early as late April 1737, when Matthias Symson was visiting London booksellers with an unidentified manuscript of Grey's. The response was lukewarm. 'Mr

Strahan ... will not engage in it unless you take off 100 copies', while James Watson, printer for Isaac Maddox's *Vindication*, was likewise loath to take on the job. Watson 'is a man that wishes well to the true Church party, and has suffered Government punishment for it; but I am afraid it will scarcely take', Symson reported. But Maddox 'has not used him well. [Watson] not only has got a great many copies in sheets from him, but several of them bound, not only in calf, but in Turkey and Morocco leather, finely gilt and bound, for the Royal Family, for which he never got a farthing.'[116] A few years later, in late February 1743, by which time Grey's work on his edition had neared completion, James Tunstall met with similar resistance from London booksellers. After a long conversation with Charles Bathurst about the putative edition of *Hudibras*, Bathurst 'peremptorily rejected [Grey's] proposals in every form'. Grey's initial proposal had insisted 'on 600 copies certain, and half the number of copies subscribed for that exceed 1000, with the "General Historical Dictionary," neatly bound, gilt and lettered; and 13 copies in large paper, bound in red morocco leather, gilt and lettered; and 12 copies in calf-skin, gilt and lettered. You had said, that Mr Bathurst offered you 600 copies, provided there were 1000 subscriptions.' Bathurst's objections and demands were explicit, and his exchange with Tunstall highlights what mattered most to the booksellers selling polemical divinity. Aside from the number of subscribers Grey proposed, Bathurst was 'utterly against any agreement whereby you shall retain any property [of the footnotes] in any future impression, either of the notes separately, or together with the text of Hudibras'. He evidently feared that Grey would try to profit somehow else from the notes, undermining the value of the edition he wanted Bathurst and others to publish for him. Tunstall, in turn, offered a counter-proposal which he hoped would address Bathurst's business concerns.[117] Despite some initial optimism that a deal would be hammered out by late March 1743,[118] negotiations between Grey and the booksellers dragged on into the summer, with particular discussion concerning the number of required subscribers and whether or not the onus of drumming up subscriptions would fall solely to Grey.[119] The final contract incorporated all of Tunstall's counter-proposals to Bathurst along with most of Grey's subsequent demands, including a finely bound copy of Bayle's *General Historical Dictionary* once certain subscription targets had been hit. Grey and the booksellers also agreed that the subscriber's copy of *Hudibras* 'in Octavo on very good paper; and Neat Letters' would cost 12 shillings total, while those who wanted their copy on 'royal paper' would have to pay 1 guinea. For the booksellers to begin publication, Grey had to deliver to them £195 up front from his initial subscription receipts.[120]

With the contract settled, Grey had next to line up the requisite 1500 subscribers. To do so, he tapped into the Cambridge clerical and scholarly networks that he had been enmeshing himself within for nearly two decades.[121] Some owed him a subscription. He had, for instance, subscribed to Conyers Middleton's life of Cicero and had solicited other subscriptions for Middleton's work: Middleton, in turn, got a number of people to subscribe to Grey's *Hudibras* and himself subscribed for a royal paper copy, despite the fact that by the early 1740s he and Grey had wholly different polemical agendas.[122] Grey's friends also worked in their neighbourhoods to solicit subscriptions for him. William Bedford promised him ten from Bedfordshire, while Edmund Law subscribed and promised Grey that he could depend upon his 'communicating the Proposals to the booksellers of Carlisle and Penrith, the first opportunity'.[123] In the end, Grey managed to get nearly 1600 subscribers, well over half of whom were clergy or Oxbridge college fellows, in addition to a number of college and cathedral libraries. Groups like the 'Club of Clergy meeting at Horncastle' and Gentleman's Society of Peterborough, whose membership included old Grey friends, also took up subscriptions.[124] Unlike Conyers Middleton's subscriber list for his life of Cicero, Grey's had fewer prominent literary figures, save for those like Christopher Smart and Horace Walpole; far fewer members of the nobility; and only one episcopal subscriber, Isaac Maddox.[125] In Ireland, by contrast, the two-volume octavo edition of his *Hudibras* had nearly 250 subscribers who were significantly more prestigious than his English subscribers: among the Irish subscribers 24 (10 per cent of the total) were nobility and another five were Church of Ireland bishops, representing just over one-fifth of the Irish bench.[126]

The editorial practices in Grey's editions of *Hudibras* owed much to the work of the eighteenth-century Shakespeareanist Lewis Theobald.[127] Like Theobald's editions of Shakespeare, Grey's *Hudibras* was a massively footnoted volume, which surely came easily to him since the footnote was something of the animadversion's first cousin.[128] On the whole, it seemed to have exceeded the booksellers' expectations. Yet *Hudibras* had not been the only work that Zachary Grey initially had trouble publishing. Around the same time he began thinking about an edition of Samuel Butler's poem, he was also at work on a response to Isaac Newton's posthumous theological works. His work on Newton itself illustrates how polemical divines tried to connect up the errors of early Christianity with the errors of contemporary Protestantism.

NOTES

1 D. Jennings, *Origin of death, and of immortal life, considered* (1743: T091460), p. 32. Parts of this chapter appeared in R. Ingram, 'Representing and Misrepresenting the History of Puritanism in Eighteenth-Century England', *SCH* 49 (2013), pp. 202–15.

2 Z. Grey, *Review of … History of the Puritans* (1744: T113000), pp. 1, 2.

3 Jennings, *Origin of death*, p. 33.

4 Grey, *Review of … History of the Puritans*, p. 2.

5 B. Shapiro, *A Culture of Fact: England, 1550–1720* (Ithaca, NY, 2000), pp. 168–88. Cf. R. Serjeantson, 'Testimony and Proof in Early-Modern England', *Studies in the History and Philosophy of Science* 30 (1999), pp. 195–236.

6 R. Richardson, 'John Nalson (bap. 1637, d. 1686)', *ODNB*; R. Macgillivray, *Restoration Historians and the English Civil War* (The Hague, 1974), pp. 109–19.

7 HMC, *Manuscripts of ... the Duke of Portland* (1891), I, pp. iii–v; William Cole's transcription of Nalson's will and an account of his manuscripts (BL, Add. 5841, fol. 3v–5).

8 See, for instance, the lengths to which Gilbert Burnet had to go to gain access to the Cotton Library after Sir John Cotton (1621–1702) forbade his entry because Burnet was 'no friend to the prerogative of the Crown, nor the constitution of the Church': quoted in J. Champion, *The Pillars of Priestcraft Shaken: The Church of England and Its Enemies, 1660–1730* (Cambridge, 1992), p. 32.

9 Zachary Grey's transcriptions from the Nalson manuscripts (BL Stowe 1058, fols 6–136).

10 D. Neal, *History of the Puritans* (1732–38: T133485), I, p. iii.

11 J. Toulmin, 'Memoirs of ... Daniel Neal' in Daniel Neal, *History of the Puritans* (1793: T096358), I, pp. xvi–xlii; L. Okie, 'Daniel Neal (1678–1743)', *ODNB*. Neal, who served as pastor of a church in Jewin Street, remained neutral in the 1719 Salters' Hall debates about subscription to Trinitarian formulae.

12 M. Goldie, *Roger Morrice and the Puritan Whigs* (Woodbridge, 2007), pp. 299–303; J. Lorimer, *John Knox and the Church of England* (1875), pp. 245–50. It is uncertain to which portion of the Morrice papers Neal had access, but it is clear that he used them in at least the first few volumes of his *History of the Puritans.*

13 D. Neal, *History of New England* (1720: T140578), I, pp. ii, iv.

14 J. Seed, *Dissenting Histories* (Edinburgh, 2008); L. Okie, 'Daniel Neal and the "Puritan Revolution"', *Church History* 55 (1986), p. 456. Cf. T. Claydon, *Europe and the Making of England, 1660–1720* (Cambridge, 2007), pp. 85–8.

15 S. Taylor, 'Whigs, Tories and Anticlericalism: Ecclesiastical Courts Legislation in 1733', *PH* 19 (2000), pp. 329–55; N. Sykes, *Edmund Gibson* (Oxford, 1926), pp. 149–61.

16 London Metropolitan Archives, CLD/171/MS03083/001: Minute Book of Protestant Dissenting Deputies, 1732–67.

17 A. Thompson, 'Popery, Politics and Private Judgment in Early Hanoverian Britain', *HJ* 45 (2002), pp. 333–56; A. Thompson, 'Contesting the Test Acts: Dissent, Parliament and the Public in the 1730s', *PH* 24 (2005), pp. 58–70.

18 E. Gibson, *Dispute adjusted* (Dublin, 1733: T075446), pp. 8–10.

19 D. Wykes, '"So bitterly censur'd and revil'd": Religious Dissent and Relation with the Church of England after the Toleration Act', in R. Bonney and D. Trim (eds), *Persecution and Pluralism* (Oxford, 2006), pp. 294–314.

20 J. Bradley, 'Anti-Catholicism as Anglican Anticlericalism: Nonconformity and the Ideological Origins of Radical Disaffection', in N. Aston and M. Cragoe (eds), *Anticlericalism in Britain, c. 1500–1914* (Stroud, 2000), pp. 67–92.

21 P. Lake, 'Reading Clarke's *Lives* in Political and Polemical Context', in K. Sharpe and S. Zwicker (eds), *Writing Lives* (Oxford, 2008), pp. 293–318; N. Keeble, *'Settling the Peace of the Church': 1662 Revisited* (Oxford, 2014), pp. 209–32.

22 J. Seed, 'History and Narrative Identity: Religious Dissent and the Politics of Memory in Eighteenth-Century England', *JBS* 44 (2005), p. 61. See also D. Wykes, '"To let the memory of these men dye is injurious to posterity": Edmund Calamy's Account of the Ejected Ministers', *SCH* 33 (1997) pp. 379–92.

23 Neal had originally intended to partner with John Evans (1679/80–1730) to write a comprehensive history of English Protestant nonconformity, with Evans covering the period until 1640 and Neal picking up the story from there. Evans's declining health during the late 1720s and his death in 1730, though, led Neal to write the entire thing himself: Toulmin 'Memoirs', pp. xxv–xxvii. More generally, see K. Fincham and S. Taylor, 'The Restoration of the Church of England, 1660–1662: Ordination, Re-Ordination and Conformity', in S. Taylor and G. Tapsell (eds), *The Nature of the English Revolution* (Woodbridge, 2013), pp. 197–232.

24 P. Lake, 'The Historiography of Puritanism', in P. Lim and J. Coffey (eds), *Cambridge Companion to Puritanism* (Cambridge, 2008), pp. 346–71.

25 J. Bradley, 'The Public, Parliament and the Protestant Dissenting Deputies, 1732–1740', *PH* 24 (2005), pp. 71–90; R. Barlow, *Citizenship and Conscience: A Study in the Theory and Practice of Religious Toleration during the Eighteenth Century* (Philadelphia, 1963), pp. 57–97; N. Crowther-Hunt, *Two Political Associations: The Quakers and the Dissenting Deputies in the Age of Sir Robert Walpole* (Oxford, 1961), pp. 113–62.

26 S. Chandler, 'Introduction', in P. van Limborch, *History of the Inquisition* (1731: T090184), pp. 1–125.

27 D. Neal, *Supremacy of St. Peter* (1735: T048959), pp. 39–40. Daniel Waterland complained to Grey that the Salters Hall Dissenter sermons aimed to promote idolatry and to undermine Nicene Christology: 'Neal and Chandler, I observe, are lashing the Establishment of our Church through the sides of the Papists, in their late sermons. Chandler has slandered Athanasius, without the least colour for it': Waterland to Grey, 5 February 1735 (BL, Add. 5831, fol. 172).

28 G. Watson, 'The Augustan Civil War', *Review of English Studies* 36 (1985), pp. 321–37.

29 A. Milton, *Laudian and Royalist Polemic in Seventeenth-Century England* (Manchester, 2007); A. Starkie, 'Contested Histories of the English Church', *HLQ* 68 (2006), pp. 329–45; M. Neufeld, 'The Politics of Anglican Martyrdom: Letters to John Walker, 1704–1705', *JEH* 62 (2011), pp. 491–514; D. Stephan, 'Laurence Echard – Whig Historian', *HJ* 32 (1989), pp. 843–66.

30 Webster translated and introduced Louis Maimbourg's two-volume study of Arianism at Waterland's urging: W. Webster, *History of Arianism* (1728–29): T099367).

31 T. Skinner, *Life of General Monk*, ed. W. Webster (1723: T139787), p. ix.

32 Around the same time, Webster also negotiated a contract on Grey's behalf with London booksellers for Robert Moss's collected sermons: Webster to Grey, 14 December 1732 (BL, Add. 5143, fol. 100). Grey wrote the preface to R. Moss, *Sermons and discourses* (1736: T115539), pp. 1–25.

33 Gibson, *Dispute adjusted*, p. 16.

34 Webster to Grey, 7 September 1732 (BL, Add. 5831, fol. 208); Gibson to Grey, 9 September 1732 (LPL, 2029, fol. 24); Webster to Grey, 14 December 1732 (BL, Add. 5143, fol. 100).

35 E. Calamy, *Historical Account of my own life*, ed. J. Rutt (1830), II, pp. 503–5. Cf. R. Ingram, *Religion, Reform and Modernity in the Eighteenth Century: Thomas Secker and the Church of England* (Woodbridge, 2007), pp. 19–44.

36 K. O'Brien, 'History and the Novel in Eighteenth-Century Britain', *HLQ* 68 (2006), p. 401.
37 [Z. Grey], *Vindication of the Church of England* (1720: T097509), I, preface.
38 Ibid., I, preface.
39 Ibid., II, p. 2.
40 Ibid., I, p. 2.
41 Ibid., I, preface.
42 Ibid., I, p. 218.
43 Ibid., I, p. 142. See also ibid., II, pp. 8–52.
44 Ibid., I, p. 184.
45 Ibid., I, p. 23.
46 Ibid., I, pp. 3–7.
47 Ibid., I, p. 9.
48 Ibid., I, p. 45.
49 Ibid., I,.
50 Ibid., I, p. 50.
51 A committee ejected Peirce from his Exeter living in spring 1719 for refusing to subscribe to the Trinity: D. Wykes, 'James Peirce (1674–1726)', *ODNB*; *Report and Transactions of the Devonshire Association* 28 (1896), pp. 159–62.
52 J. Strype, *Life ... of Matthew Parker* (1711: T100944), p. 244. Peirce rejected Strype's account of Faithful Commin, but Grey countered that Peirce had offered no concrete evidence to support his claim: [Grey], *Vindication*, I, p. 32. D. MacCulloch, *All Things Made New: The Reformation and Its Legacy* (Oxford, 2016), pp. 321–58, points out that the Commin story was a forgery.
53 [Grey], *Vindication*, I, p. 37.
54 Ibid., I, p. 104–5. Zachary Grey, *The Jesuit in Disguise; or, One Popish Method of Dividing Us, exemplified* [unpublished] (CUL, Add. 3308, fols 36–48), dealt with Commin's imposture.
55 [Grey], *Vindication*, I, p. 134.
56 Ibid., I, pp. 140–1.
57 Ibid., I, pp. 134–9, 150.
58 Ibid., I, p. 133.
59 Ibid., I, p. 131.
60 Ibid., I, p. 160.
61 [Z. Grey], *Presbyterian prejudice* (1722: N020437), p. 4.
62 [Z. Grey], *Pair of clean shoes and boots for a dirty baronet* (1722: T101887), p. 3.
63 [Z. Grey], *Caveat against Benjamin Bennet* (1724: T103423), p. 13.
64 [Grey], *Pair of clean shoes*, p. 8. See also [Z. Grey], *Knight of Dumbleton* (1723: T103424), pp. 14–15.
65 [Grey], *Presbyterian prejudice*, p. 84; [Grey], *Pair of clean shoes*, p. 32; Z. Grey, *Letter of thanks to ... Benjamin Bennet* (1723: T103426), pp. 40–1.
66 Grey's *Century of eminent Presbyterian preachers*, title-page. Grey published six other collections like this during his career.
67 [Z. Grey], *Defence of our antient and modern historians* (1725: T114762), preface; [Grey], *Knight of Dumbleton*, pp. 4, 14.
68 BL, shelfmark 112.2.45 (1–6) contains Grey's annotations of his *Ministry of the*

dissenters; *Caveat*; *Letter of thanks*; *Knight of Dumbleton*; and *Century of eminent Presbyterian preachers* (1723: T103422).

69 Grey's annotated *Vindication of the Church of England*, 111, 129 (CUL, shelfmark Adv.d.57.7).

70 Grey's annotations in all four volumes of Neal's *History of the Puritans* may be found at St. John's College, Cambridge: shelfmarks Q.13.5, 7–9, 10. The annotations in the first two volumes are far heavier than in the last two volumes. Gibson described the Grey materials that he forwarded to Maddox as 'Observations upon Mr. Neal's History, and lately, the Book relating to it': Gibson to Grey, [*c.* 9 September 1732] (LPL, 2029, fol. 24). This letter is reproduced in BL, Add. 5831, fol. 157 and *LI*, II, 540: the former dates it 9 September 1734, the latter 9 September 1736. The letter's internal evidence, though, suggests that it must have been written in the autumn of 1732, when Isaac Maddox was preparing a response to Neal.

71 *WM* (26 May 1733), p. 1.

72 I. Maddox, *Vindication of ... the Church of England* (1733: T152358), p. 190.

73 Goldie, *Roger Morrice*, pp. 301–2.

74 Maddox, *Vindication*, p. 4.

75 Ibid., p. 17.

76 Ibid., p. 32.

77 Ibid., p. 105.

78 Ibid., p. 40. Cf. [Grey], *Presbyterian prejudice*, p. 26; [Grey], *Letter of thanks*, p. 16.

79 Ibid., pp. 120, 124.

80 Ibid., p. 210.

81 Ibid., pp. 2, 251.

82 Samuel Knight to [Maddox], 24 March 1734 (BL, Add. 5831, fols 197–8); Knight to Grey, 24 March 1734 (*LI*, IV, p. 326).

83 D. Neal, *Review of the principal facts* (1734: T064429), p. 3.

84 Ibid., pp. 39–40, 46, 49–51.

85 Similarly Neal's treatment of the dangers of popish claims regarding apostolic succession in *Supremacy of St. Peter*, p. 34, had clear contemporary relevance.

86 Sykes, *Edmund Gibson*, pp. 161–82; S. Taylor, 'Sir Robert Walpole, the Church of England and the Quakers Tithe Bill of 1736', *HJ* 28 (1985), pp. 51–77.

87 Webster to Grey, October [1735/6] (BL, Add. 5831, fol. 208). Cf. Webster to Grey, [1736] (BL, Add. 5831, fols 207–8), in which Webster asked for Grey's notes on the Neal's third volume of the *History of the Puritans*, which had first appeared in mid-November 1735. Maddox always acknowledged Grey's support and applauded the 'great Integrity and Judgement, & ... great Compass of Knowledge of English History' that Grey displayed in his responses to Neal: Maddox to unknown, 18 June 1739 (BL, Add. 5831, fols 164–5). See also Maddox to [Grey], 15 April 1740 (ibid., fols 165–6).

88 Gibson to Grey, 24 March 1737; Maddox to Grey, 15 April 1740 (ibid., fols 157, 165–6).

89 Grey, *Impartial examination of the second volume*, p. 4; [Z. Grey], *Examination of Mr. Samuel Chandler's History of Persecution* (1736: N001520), pp. 3–4. See also Z. Grey, *Impartial examination of the third volume of ... Daniel Neal* (1737: T112826) pp. 7, 17, 123; [Z. Grey], *Schismatics delineated from authentic vouchers*

(1739: T130375), p. 12; Z. Grey, *English Presbyterian eloquence* (1736: T066059), preface

90 Grey, *Impartial examination of the second volume*, p. 72; [Z. Grey], *Attempt towards the character of … Charles I* (1738: T070676), p. 54.

91 Grey, *Impartial examination of the second volume*, p. 4.

92 Ibid., p. 15.

93 Ibid., p. 62. Cf. Anonymous, *Defence of English history* (1734: T122501), p. 93.

94 Ibid, p. 418.

95 Ibid, pp. 73–82.

96 Ibid, p. 290. See also Grey, *Review of … Neal's History of the Puritans*, p. 14.

97 Cf. J. Sheehan, 'Sacred and Profane: Idolatry, Antiquarianism and the Polemics of Distinction in the Seventeenth Century', *P&P* 192 (2006), p. 45.

98 [Grey], *Attempt towards the character*, p. 29; [Grey], *Schismatics delineated*, p. 20.

99 Grey, *Impartial examination of the third volume*, p. 137. See also [Grey], *Examination of … Samuel Chandler*, pp. 73–74; R. Moss, *Sermon preach'd … Jan. 30 1706/7* (1707: T049030), p. 14.

100 Lindsay to Grey, 20 July 1738 (*LA*, I, p. 734).

101 Thomas Doughty to Grey, 28 August 1738 (*LI*, IV, 309–10); Waterland to Grey, 12 January 1739 (BL, Add. MS 5831, fol. 175); R. Sher, *The Enlightenment and the Book* (Chicago, 2006), pp. 224–35; W. Speck, 'Politician, Peers and Publication by Subscription, 1700–50', in Rivers (ed.), *Books and Their Readers in Eighteenth-Century England*, pp. 47–68.

102 Bedford to Grey, 9 December 1738 (*LI*, IV, p. 260). When Grey's response to Neal's fourth volume of *History of the Puritans* finally appeared in spring 1739, Bedford apologized to him for having purchased only ten copies of it from the bookseller James Bettenham, explaining 'that much of the greatest share of the number I took of the last volume lies still upon my hands': Bedford to Grey, 28 April 1739 (ibid.).

103 Lewis to Grey, 16 March 1739 (BL, Add. 5831, fols 128–9).

104 Ibid.

105 Cole to Horace Walpole, 29 January 1779 (*WC*, II, pp. 360–1).

106 J. Wilders, 'Textual Introduction', in *Hudibras*, ed. J. Wilders (Oxford, 1967), pp. xliv–lviii; E. Richards, *Hudibras in the Burlesque Tradition* (New York, 1937); B. Parker, *The Triumph of Augustan Poetics* (Cambridge, 1998), pp. 25–60.

107 S. Butler, *Hudibras*, ed. Z. Grey (Cambridge, 1744: T2679), I, pp. iii, iv.

108 S. Butler, *Prose Observations*, ed. H. de Quehen (Oxford, 1979), pp. v, xiv.

109 K. Poole, *Radical Religion from Shakespeare to Milton* (Cambridge, 2002), 182–5.

110 S. Johnson, *Lives of the Poets*, ed. J. Middendorf (New Haven, 2010), I, p. 214.

111 Wilders, 'Textual Introduction', pp. lviii–lxi.

112 Christopher Byron to Grey, 15 June 1742 (HL, 19, no. 17).

113 Johnson, *Lives of the Poets*, pp. 221–2.

114 'Walpole's Memoir of Grey' (*WC*, XLIII, p. 191). Cf. Wilders, 'Textual Introduction', p. lx.

115 William Bedford to Grey, 1739 (*LI*, IV, p. 260): 'When your Hudibras is published, I should be glad if you would order your bookseller to send me ten copies'.

116 Symson to Grey, 26 April 1737 (ibid.). Watson had been subject to a search

warrant in 1728 in relation to 'scandalous and seditious libels' purportedly being printed by him: H. Plomer, *A Dictionary of the Printers and Booksellers who Were at Work in England, Scotland and Ireland from 1726 to 1775* (Oxford, 1968), p. 258.

117 Tunstall to Grey, 22 February 1743 (*LI*, IV, pp. 372–3). Bathurst had been the partner and successor to the 'high-flyer' printer and bookseller Benjamin Motte: Plomer, *A Dictionary ... 1726 to 1775*, p. 20. See also D. McKitterick, *A History of Cambridge University Press* (Cambridge, 1992), II, pp. 158–60.

118 Grey to Andrew Coltee Ducarel, 9 March 1743 (*LI*, IV, p. 285).

119 Thomas Potter to Grey, 27 June and 6 July 1743 (ibid., pp. 339–41).

120 Agreement for publishing Zachary Grey's *Hudibras*, 6 July 1743 (BL, Add. 33554, fol. 245). Even still, at least two of the booksellers later would balk, at least temporarily, at fulfilling certain of their contractual obligations: George Grey to Zachary Grey, 6 and 11 February 1744 (*LI*, IV, pp. 316–17).

121 McKitterick, *History of Cambridge University Press*, II, pp. 154–8.

122 Middleton to Grey, 4 December 1740 (*LA*, II, p. 535).

123 Bedford to Grey, 1739 (*LI*, IV, p. 260); Law to Grey, 31 May 1743 (*LA*, II, p. 535).

124 Thomas Doughty to Grey, 20 September 1743; Robert Smyth to Grey, 15 March 1745 (*LI*, IV, pp. 312, 357). Doughty had also lined up private subscribers for some of Grey's responses to Daniel Neal: Doughty to Grey, 28 August 1738, 16 September 1738 (ibid., pp. 309–10).

125 M. Walsh, 'Literary Scholarship and the Life of Editing', in I. Rivers (ed.), *Books and Their Readers in Eighteenth-Century England: New Essays* (2001), pp. 211–12.

126 S. Butler, *Hudibras* (Dublin, [1744]: N007227). No correspondence remains which documents anything regarding the Irish edition of Grey's work. That there were subscribers suggests that this edition, unlike many Irish offprints of English works, was not pirated.

127 R. Jones, *Lewis Theobald* (New York, 1919), pp. 233–4.

128 Walsh, 'Literary Scholarship', p. 203.

Chapter 12

The religion of the first ages: primitivism and the primitive Church

In September 1735, Matthias Symson visited the London bookseller George Strahan to gauge Strahan's interest in publishing his friend Zachary Grey's response to Isaac Newton's *Observations upon the prophecies of Daniel, and the Apocalypse of St. John* (1733). Strahan, owner of one of London's largest printing houses, had no interest, explaining to Symson that 'he did not care to meddle: it being an abstruse subject, he did not know how it would take': he worried that Grey's retort would leave him with a financial loss.[1] James Roberts, another substantial London trade publisher, eventually produced it. How the book sold, we do not know, but its content illustrates both how the primitive Church was put to polemical use by scholars less able and learned than those like Daniel Waterland or Conyers Middleton and how they all owed a significant debt to seventeenth-century scholarship.

This chapter illustrates why the history of the early Christian Church was not an abstruse subject during the eighteenth century but a topical one. For the primitive church remained the standard for both orthodoxy and orthopraxis well into the eighteenth century. This chapter demonstrates how that was the case by focusing especially on two pieces by Zachary Grey – his *Examination of the fourteenth chapter of Sir Isaac Newton's observations upon the prophecies of Daniel* (1736) and his *Short history of the Donatists* (1741). Neither was a paragon of style or scholarship, but both convey the primitivist appeal during the first half of the eighteenth century. Grey's engagement with Newton's work on prophecy centred on Newton's treatment of saints and of God's nature. In writing about these subjects, Newton had argued that the post-fourth-century Church was infested with theological impurities; Grey rejoinded that the eighteenth-century Church of England understood both the saints and God's nature in a primitively pure way. Grey's treatment of the ancient Donatist heresy similarly related to contemporary concerns. For he tried to show that Methodism was not novel but, instead, a revival of an ancient heretical sect which had rent the fourth-century North African Church.

It is a commonplace that the Anglican tradition especially venerates the early Church. The Church of England, many of its adherents claim, is the *via media* between 'the symmetrical excesses' of Rome and Geneva; it alone retains primitively pure ecclesiology and doctrine.[2] Whether or not this self-conception was or is accurate, scholars have long recognized that the seventeenth and nineteenth centuries were moments of exceptional interest in primitive Christianity. The eighteenth century, by contrast, was supposed to have been a period during which apologists for the established Church mostly ignored it, favouring instead 'a philosophical divinity intended to defend Christian faith against contemporary Deism'. As Gareth Bennett succinctly put it, '[i]n the early eighteenth century, Anglican writers were almost wholly ignorant of patristic scholarship, and the question of the authority of the Early Church was scarcely ever raised'.[3] In fact, primitivism remained the route to truth during the eighteenth century. Reason's chief function was to help inquirers discern what historical claims were or were not true. The Reformation had, from a Protestant perspective, been necessary – the Church had rotted. Scholarly study of the primitive Church helped to identify when the rot had set in.

This is what Isaac Newton sought to do in his study of Daniel's prophecies. A notoriously difficult person who wrote notoriously difficult works, Newton was the paragon of eighteenth-century natural philosophy. At home and abroad, Newton's contemporaries reckoned him a singular person possessed of a singular genius.[4] Despite his pre-eminence, neither his natural philosophical thought nor his posthumous writings on religion went unquestioned. John Hutchinson (1674–1737), for instance, worried about the implications of Newtonian natural philosophy. He reckoned that Newtonianism was a one-way street to Arianism or deism. Hutchinson's *Moses's Principia* (1724) proposed an alternative approach. There he argued that the Hebrew Bible, properly interpreted, both provided an accurate account of the Earth's creation and contained a complete system of natural philosophy.[5] The key to unlocking the Bible's hidden truths was a textual approach that ignored the vowels (on Hutchinson's view, a later, intentional Jewish corruption) and focused instead on the consonantal skeleton which revealed the Bible's true meaning.[6] Historians have found in Hutchinson and his followers slow-moving targets whose 'baroque metaphysics' were preposterous, then and since.[7] Yet there were many others fully within the mainstream of eighteenth-century English theological opinion who also opposed elements in or implications of Newtonian thought. Daniel Waterland and Edmund Law, for instance, diverged on many important theological matters; both came armed with a rival Lockean epistemology and a consequent argument that the *a priori* rationalism of Newtonian natural theology subverted 'true religion'.[8] One need have been neither a Tory nor an opponent of 'a rather cerebral religion' to have found Newtonianism wanting.[9]

Isaac Newton probably prudently kept much about his theology hidden from public view. His private papers reveal a man as interested in religion as in natural philosophy and one who furthermore saw an essential unity to knowledge.[10] He also believed in the necessity of a dual reformation. His was a primitivist belief in the need to cleanse both natural philosophy and religion by recovering the ancient purity of man's knowledge of nature and of nature's God.[11] For there once had been a time, he contended, when both natural philosophy and religion had been unadulterated. Where religion was concerned, Newton reckoned that the Noachian religion had been pure: 'This was the religion of the first ages till they forsook the right worship of the true God & turned aside from the worship of dead men & Idols'.[12] After the Flood man had introduced corruptions, most notably regarding the nature of God, into the original 'true religion'. For Newton, the apotheosis of corruption came at the fourth-century Council of Nicea when, urged on by Athanasius and his followers, the councillors decreed as the Church's official position belief in the triune Christian God in which the Son is held to be consubstantial (*homoousios*) with the Father.[13] Henceforth, Newton held, Christianity had been idolatrous. While the Protestant Reformation had removed much of the idolatrous practices and beliefs which characterized popery, it had nevertheless left unexamined and untouched the most glaring instance of idolatry – Nicene Trinitarianism. Newton was no deist: he believed in a God of dominion, a providential God without whose existence the world would neither exist nor continue to function. But he espoused a Christology which amalgamated elements of Arianism and Socinianism.[14] Christ had been made, not begotten, and was not one in being with the Father.[15] Newton's were heretical views, and publicly expressed Christological heresy, even in the early eighteenth century, was illegal. So, he adopted the stance of a Nicodemite, communicating his anti-Trinitarian views only to those he viewed as fellow adepts, and worked quietly, though concertedly, to undermine the Nicene Christology.[16] In part this required a close exegesis of the Bible, the one text he thought could reveal religious truth to the adept reader. In part it required creating an alternative historical narrative of the early Church to counter the orthodox one which saw in the Nicene Creed the crystallized orthodoxy concerning God's true nature.[17] Newton's alternative historical narrative attracted the attention of Daniel Waterland, Zachary Grey and others beginning in the late 1720s.

Had his contemporaries known about Isaac Newton's closely guarded heretical views, his reputation would have suffered. As it was, even his relatively circumspect public comments about Christian history and theology unnerved many. Hints at his underlying heterodox Christology were on public display as early as 1713, when he added a 'General Scholium' to his *Principia*, in which he characterized God as 'This Being [who] governs all things, not as the soul of the world, but as Lord over all: and on account of his dominion he is wont to be called *Lord God Pantokrator*, or *Universal Ruler* ... The supreme God is a Being eternal, infinite, absolutely perfect;

but a being, however, perfect, without dominion, cannot be said to be Lord God.'[18] Even more disturbing to many of his orthodox contemporaries, though, were Newton's posthumous works on ancient chronology and biblical prophecy. His *Chronology of the ancient kingdoms amended* (1728) sought to correct early modern chronologists.[19] The work reads as a list of dates associated with events. But Newton's prefatory dedication to Queen Caroline hinted at his intent, as he pointedly noted that 'an Abhorrence of Idolatry and Persecution' had been 'one of the earliest Laws of the Divine Legislator, the Morality of the first Ages, and the primitive Religion of both Jews and Christians'. His revised chronology identified when idolatry and persecution had entered into the Christian Church.[20] A few years later Newton's executors published *Observations upon the Prophecies of Daniel, and the Apocalypse of St. John,* in which he unpacked the meanings of two biblical books of prophecy. Many contemporaries thought that both the *Observations* and the *Chronology* had decidedly heterodox implications. Daniel Waterland, in particular, took umbrage with what he read in Newton's work on Daniel, though he and his allies had previously applauded parts of Newton's revised ancient chronology.[21] 'He is a man of such great weight in other matters', but in biblical scholarship, he 'was plainly out of his element' and 'has given too much encouragement to Popery by his large concessions, such as our best Protestant writers, all the time of King James, as well as before, would never make', Waterland complained.[22] And yet Waterland, in the midst of writing against the Newton-inspired *a priorism* of Samuel Clarke and on the cusp of entering into a debate over the Eucharist, had no time to reply to Newton's *Observations.* 'I have scribbled the margin all the way; but I have so many other things to do ... that I cannot ... undertake it myself; I wish somebody else would', he prodded Grey, who would soon take up Waterland's challenge, the results of which appeared in print in March 1736.[23]

Zachary Grey was not the first to have questioned Newton's chronological and prophetical writings.[24] When the avowed Newtonian William Stukeley (1687–1765), synopsised Newton's *Observations* for *The Present State of the Republick of Letters,* he praised Newtonian natural philosophy while withholding encomiums regarding his theological works. 'The Author of this Work has been deservedly admired by the Learned of all Nations, as a consummate Philosopher and Mathematician, and his Works have been esteemed so many Master-pieces in their respective Kinds. We are now to consider him as a Commentator and an Historian', Stukeley opened his review.[25] When he came to parts where he had to acknowledge that Newton 'differs in some of these Points from several eminent Critics and Commentators, and is even singular in others', Stukeley pressed on, refusing to criticize Newton: 'But we shall not presume to engage in a Dispute, which has employed so many able Hands among the Ancients and Moderns', he blithely insisted before entering into his synopsis.[26]

If even ardent Newtonians quietly balked at some of Newton's conclusions, others were more overtly sceptical. Some heterodox polemical divines (Conyers Middleton and William Whiston, for example) distrusted Newton's chronological calculations.[27] The orthodox viewed Newton's religious writings even more sceptically. The anti-Hutchinsonian Arthur Bedford's *Animadversions* (1728), for instance, acknowledged that Newton had been a mathematical genius, one whose astronomical work had improved chronologers' calculations. But Newton's conclusions on the ancient chronology differed 'from all the rest of the learned World, in an Art, which many of them had made their professed Studies'.'[28] Bedford worried most that Newton's chronology undermined confidence in the Bible, so that if his *Chronology* were 'put into the Hands of Youth', it would lead 'to the Rooting out of Religion, and the Bringing in of Infidelity'. While not arguing that Newton's chronology was implicitly anti-Trinitarian, Bedford judged it was unhelpful at a time when '[t]he Prophecies, which relate to Christ, are ridiculed, and his Miracles are treated as Impostures'.[29] After Newton's *Observations* appeared, Arthur Young wrote a two-volume history of 'idolatrous corruptions in religion' in which he specifically challenged Newton's argument regarding the institutionalization of idolatry in the Christian Church during the fourth century. Young countered that Christianity was not, as many claimed, 'the Offspring of Superstition', but rather that during antiquity 'Idolatry, and false Worship, prevailed' before God had 'put an end to the almost infinite Superstitions of the heathen Worship, and all their detestable Rites' by sending 'his only begotten Son into the World to destroy Idolatry, and to deliver Men from the horrible Slavery of worshipping false Gods, and the Miseries of a mistaken Devotion'.[30] The problem, as all Protestants recognized, was that idolatry had somehow crept back into the Church: the crucial question was *when* it had done so. On Newton's reading, idolatrous practices (such as the worship of saints) had been common in the Church before the fourth century. As Young recognized, if this were so, it would be a 'great Prejudice to the Protestant Cause, it being too late to make [saint worship] a Catholic Doctrine'.[31] Young aimed to show that Newton had got his religious history wrong. Not until the sixth century, Young countered, had images made their way into the Church and not until the eighth century was veneration of saints first introduced. Furthermore, Young continued, in England, image worship did not become official doctrine until the early fifteenth century, when the English Church began to persecute Lollards.[32]

In his own riposte to Newton's *Observations*, Zachary Grey focused solely on the book's fourteenth chapter, in which Newton contended that Christian worship of saints had developed organically from pagan practices, further proof of his argument that the post-Noachian religion was idolatrous. Grey opened his *Examination of the fourteenth chapter of Sir Isaac Newton's Observations* (1736) by agreeing with Arthur Young that Newton had inadvertently given ammunition to the papist and deistical causes because such was Newton's standing as a natural philosopher that some readers might mistakenly presume that what he had to say about religious matters was likewise canonical.[33] Grey spent the rest of his book prosecuting a two-pronged argument. Firstly, he argued, Newton's grasp of the primitive Church's history was such that he had completely misunderstood the origins of saints and human communication with them. Newton had posited a three-stage process by which the invocation of saints had entered into Christian worship. In the first stage, early Christians in Decius's reign (r. 249–51) adopted heathen holidays like Bacchanalia, Saturnalia, May-Day and Floralia to encourage heathen conversion to Christianity. The second step towards the veneration of martyrs involved the practice of praying at their tombs, a practice begun during the reign of Diocletian (r. 284–305). In the third and final stage, which took place during the persecutions of Constantius (r. 305–6) and Julian the Apostate (r. 361–63),

> [a]fter the sepulchres of Saints and Martyrs were thus converted into places of worship like the heathen temples, and the Churches into sepulchres, and a certain sort of sanctity attributed to the dead bodies of the Saints and Martyrs buried in them, and annual festivals were kept to them, with sacrifices offered to God in their name; the next step towards the invocation of Saints, was the attributing to their dead bodies, bones and other relics, a power of working miracles by means of the separate souls, who were supposed to know what we do or say, and to be able to do us good or hurt, and to work those miracles.[34]

Thus by the fourth century, an indisputably popish practice (the invocation of saints) had, on Newton's view, been firmly ensconced within Christian belief and practice. Grey rejected this. He countered, for instance, that Christians had held the Sabbath since the days of St Paul and that, during the first century after Christ's death, the primitive Church had celebrated the Lord's Day, Easter and Pentecost.[35] Similarly, Newton had mistaken the origin of saints' days, something which, Grey noted, even his heterodox theological fellow-traveller William Whiston recognized.[36]

Even more damning, Newton had mistaken the whole intent and process of communicating with the saints. Protestantism rejected the cult of the saints, something tied up intimately with the inter-confessional debates about the cessation of miracles. For late medieval Catholics, saints were at once exemplars of Christian behaviour and intermediaries for an immanent God with whom lines of communication ran both ways.[37] For Protestants, venerating and invoking saints were idolatrous and superstitious acts.[38] But what the saints themselves existed to do was a point of unsettled doctrine and unsettling debate. Certainly the Church of England's official doctrine on saints was a fudge. The English Church accepted the Apostles' Creed, which pointedly, if cursorily, affirmed belief in 'the communion of saints'. The twenty-second of its Thirty-Nine Articles forbade only the 'invocation of Saints' as it related to purgatory, but did not forbid belief in saints in themselves: how could it since, as English Protestant catechisms of the late seventeenth and eighteenth centuries noted, there were unambiguous biblical mentions of saints? Yet as for what it meant to be a *saint*, the catechetical answers tended to be cursory and vague.[39] The unquestionably orthodox William Wake, an authority whom Zachary Grey cited, dealt with the issue in his commentary on the catechism. He freighted his discussion with ambiguity. When it came time to discuss Article XXII, Wake had necessarily to define *saints* and when he did so he hedged: 'Though the Word, in our Language, be more Restrain'd; yet in that, in which this Creed was composed, it may indifferently denote either *Holy Persons* or *Holy Things*: And this Article may very well be extended to both of Them'. As to what it meant to be a *holy person*, Wake noted that in the Bible it could refer to 'all Christians in general', but that in this particular case it was 'most properly to understand such as answer the End of their Calling, by a Lively Faith, and a Holy Conversation, in which Two, the Gospel-Saintship does consist'.[40] But what did it mean to communicate with the saints? In so far as the saints' communication with humans was concerned, he admitted, 'How the Saints departed maintain Communion with Us, We cannot tell. Probable it is that they do, in general, pray for Us, as it is certain they wish well to us.' Wake was, though, bluntly clear that Catholic veneration and invocation of the saints 'is not only Vain, and without all Warrant from God's Word; but is indeed Superstitious, and Idolatrous'. For praying 'to any Creature, and He at a vast Distance from Us ... with a Confidence that the Person prayed to, can Hear our Prayers, and Answer our Desires ... cannot be done without the Peril of Idolatry'.[41] Wake, then, was only willing anodynely to acknowledge saints' existence while vigorously reaffirming the Protestant line that invoking them obviously and self-evidently violated 'true religion', for to grapple forthrightly with the issue of how communication of the saints worked was to offer a hostage to polemical fortune.[42]

Zachary Grey's discussion of primitive saints rushed in where Wake had feared to tread. Grey distinguished between honouring and invoking the saints. To invoke the assistance of saints was, Grey acknowledged, wholly errant. To venerate them, however, was perfectly acceptable. Indeed, he contended that primitive Christianity had not been sullied by the veneration of the martyrs, not least because there had been genuine miracles worked at their sepulchres. And those sepulchral miracles had clear biblical precedents – the bones of Elisha (2 Kings 13:21), for instance – and had, as Augustine noted at the time, been worked solely through 'the Power of God'.[43] Indeed, Julian the Apostate had destroyed the temples not because of Christian 'Frauds or Impostures' but, rather, precisely because the miracles worked by God at the Christian temples were 'plain Miracles' which unbelievers 'could not contradict'.[44] Grey concluded that 'it has not been proved, that I know of, that such Veneration of the Relics of Martyrs is superstition. If it be, it is as old at least as the beginning of the 2d Century, as the Martyrdom of Saint Ignatius, and Saint Polycarp'. Grey thought the tombs of martyrs and saints were sites of immanence, places where it had been perfectly fine for early

Christians '[n]ot to pray to them, but to pray with them'.[45] All of this must have sounded like crypto-popery to many at the time.[46]

If so, Zachary Grey's defence of Athanasius (296–373) would have only convinced critics of his unreliable Protestantism, for allied to his argument that Newton had misunderstood the worship of saints was his contention that Newton had distorted the evidence in order to besmirch Athanasius. In encouraging Grey to rebut Newton's fourteenth chapter, Daniel Waterland had particularly latched onto the notion that Newton had 'slyly abuse[d] the Athanasians'. 'That prophetical way of managing this debate on the side of Arianism, is a very silly one, and might be easily retorted', Waterland wrote to Grey in early 1735, adding '[t]hat what Sir Isaac has said is most of it false History'.[47] Waterland's own interest in the Athanasian Creed had been long-standing, and it continued to interest him and the orthodox into the 1730s. Where one stood on Athanasius was a theological litmus test during the eighteenth century. For some, Athanasius and his eponymous creed were the apotheosis of Christological orthodoxy; for others, both were emblematic of crypto-popery with its extra-biblical superstitious doctrines and idolatrous practices.[48] To defend Athanasius and the Athanasian Creed marked off one as unmistakably orthodox. For his part, Zachary Grey had since the early 1720s vigorously defended Athanasius against anticlericals and others of 'the Infidel Scheme' who accused of him of being 'Unchristian' or a 'Creed-making Rascal'. Even at the outset of his polemical career, Grey reckoned that 'the Sin of Heresy was a Damnable Sin, and ... those who would not assent to the Articles of that Creed (which were fairly deducible from Scripture) were to be esteemed (upon the Terms of the Gospel) in a Condition not the most safe'.[49] Nothing had changed in his attitude by the mid-1730s, when he took Newton to task for having taken side-swipes at Athanasius throughout the fourteenth chapter of his *Observations*: 'His applying that Part of his Book to the Athanasians ... shews how far a Man of his great Parts, Learning and Abilities could stretch his Fancy upon Occasion, [and] discovers at the same time no small Inclination to disparage the Orthodox, in a covert way'. Grey, by contrast, would deal 'about Facts only, about the Truth of History'.[50] So, for instance, Athanasius had not related a story about souls appearing after death, nor had he advocated the invocation of saints.[51] Indeed, Grey continued, the charges that Athanasius and his followers had been idolatrous saint-worshippers held no water because even their most bitter contemporary Arian opponents had 'never retorted upon them the Worship or Invocation of Saints, a plain sign that they knew of no such thing, or at least that both were equally concerned in what related to the Honour of Saints, and therefore there is no reason to throw all the Blame (if there was any) upon the Athanasians'. He even went so far as to contend 'that the Athanasians all along charged the Arians with Idolatry and Creature Worship'.[52]

Grey returned to Newton's treatment of saints not in subsequent publications but in the margins of his own copy of his *Examination*.[53] In the published book, he had grounded his argument on two kinds of sources: evidence drawn from the writings of the patristic fathers themselves and the conclusions drawn by prominent seventeenth- and early eighteenth-century English (and sometimes French) scholars. In particular, he had cited favourably the works of William Cave (1637–1713), Joseph Bingham (1668–1723), Edward Wells (1667–1727), Nicholas Clagett (1654–1727), Edward Gee (1657–1730) and William Wake. In the margins of the *Examination*, Grey quoted at length mostly from George Morley's *Two Letters to ... Janus Ulitius* (1707), a work which aimed to show, as its subtitle indicated, 'that neither St. Augustine, nor any one of those Fathers, who flourished in the Ages before him, did, either by their Doctrines or Practice, in any wise countenance the Invocation of Saints'.[54] Choosing Morley (1598–1684) was suggestive, for Morley had originally written the letters in Latin to Ulitius in 1659, when he was in exile with Charles II. A 1706 preface by the nonjuror George Hickes emphasized that Morley had suffered for his faith at the hands of Protestant nonconformists. Moreover, he contended that the Church of England for which Morley had suffered was – or, at least, had been – primitively pure. The Church's doctrines after the Restoration were 'pure, primitive Doctrines, in the Possession of which the Faithful Sons and Daughters of the Church of England are safe, as being thereby embarked in the Ark of the Catholic Church', Hickes insisted.[55] In the letters to which Hickes wrote the preface, Morley tried to show that none of the Greek or Latin fathers before the fourth century had invoked saints.[56] Neither had reasonable papists. Cardinal du Perron (1556–1618), for instance, had assured Isaac Casaubon that he himself had never invoked saints, save for public professions, when, presumably, he had to of necessity.[57] Furthermore, du Perron explained, the primitive fathers mostly spoke cautiously on theological matters, given that their aims were often defensive; and they had 'avoid[ed] and decline[d] all occasion of delivering their thoughts concerning the Invocation of Saints', fearing that the Gentiles might liken it to the honour 'which the Heathens offered to their Imaginary Deity's'.[58]

All of this confirmed Grey's conviction that the Newtonian narrative of a three-stage corruption regarding saints had no evidentiary basis. Indeed, there was much about Isaac Newton's scholarship to which a resolutely orthodox polemicist could object. Yet it was to Newton's historical scholarship, rather than to his natural philosophy, that Zachary Grey and the orthodox dissented. For Newtonian natural philosophy was quite easily amalgamated into the orthodox theological worldview, since Newton's theories allowed (indeed positively required) both God's special and general providence. There was little, by contrast, which the orthodox saw redeeming in the thought of another contemporary religious figure and the movement he helped to lead – George Whitefield and Methodism.

The Methodist movement originated in Oxford during the late 1730s, following Whitefield's 'new birth' in 1735 and John Wesley's conversion at a religious meeting in Fetter Lane in 1738. There, Wesley reported, 'I felt my Heart strangely warmed. I felt I did trust in Christ, Christ alone for Salvation: And an Assurance was given me, That he had taken away *my* sins, even *mine*, and saved *me* from the Law of Sin and Death.'[59] Afterwards, Wesley, Whitefield and others began preaching campaigns, both in Britain and in North America, that drew huge crowds, though perhaps not huge membership: by 1767, there were no more than 24,000 Methodists in England. Nonetheless, Methodism's emergence worried many English.[60]

While the Methodist movement itself was part of a larger, transatlantic Evangelical revival that stretched from Moravia to Massachusetts, the English located Methodism not within its international contexts but within its national ones.[61] In particular, they understood Methodism against the backdrop of the previous century's religio-political troubles. Zachary Grey's own first published response to Methodism tellingly compared Whitefield and the seventeenth-century Quaker leader, George Fox (1624–91). Both, Grey asserted, were 'fond of the same Phrase and Diction; and their Pretences to Inspiration, to every intimate Familiarity with the Deity, and the Power of working Miracles, are of the same Stamp and Authority'.[62] Implicit in Grey's account was that the Quakers had been enthusiastic and schismatistic; that both *enthusiasm* and *schism* had been centripetal forces during the seventeenth century; and that the eighteenth-century Methodists were enthusiastic and schismatistic.[63]

In a later anti-Methodist piece, *A Serious Address to Lay-Methodists* (1745), Grey returned to the theme that Methodists were like sixteenth- and seventeenth-century schismatics and enthusiasts. This time, though, it was to popery, not Protestant nonconformity, that he likened to Methodism, whose preachers, like papist priests, tried to lead the laity 'into the Bogs, or Whirlpools of Error and Delusion'.[64] Indeed, Methodist clergy were 'false Prophets, and false Teachers ... who are set on work by the grand Deceiver of Mankind, to divide Us, with an intention, no doubt, of destroying one of the best constituted Churches, this day in the Christian world'.[65] By way of example, Grey cited the example of Faithful Commin, a disguised Dominican who had posed as a devout Protestant during the late sixteenth century in order to subvert Protestantism from within; Methodists likewise were guilty of imposture and of sowing seeds of division.[66] In the end, though, Grey reckoned that Methodists were not simply crypto-papists but that they also were like ancient heretical sects: they 'resemble the Gnostics of old, an upstart Sect of Heretics, who were mighty Pretenders to Inspiration, proudly arrogant to themselves'.[67]

Grey's anonymous *Short History of the Donatists* (1741) pursued the connections between modern Methodist error and ancient Christian heresy more deeply by way of an examination of the fourth-century North African rigorists – and separatists known as the Donatists.[68] Three parts comprised the work: a preface, a history of Donatism and an appendix which juxtaposed examples of 'the proud and Hypocritical Pharisee and Schismatical Donatist' with George Whitefield. The preface quoted at length from the work of Henry Wharton (1664–95), whose anti-popish *Enthusiasm of the Church of Rome demonstrated* (1689) Grey would in later works mine for evidence.[69] In the preface to *A Short History of the Donatists*, though, he drew from Wharton's *Defence of pluralities* (1692) on anticlericalism; on mendicant religious orders; and on 'popularity', all of which were presumably among Methodism's besetting sins. The issue of 'popularity' in particular would have been meant to link Methodism both with ancient Donatism and with the schismatic and anti-hierarchical puritanism of the late sixteenth and seventeenth centuries. Wharton had pointed to popularity's long lineage. 'This Air of Popularity hath been the great Pest of the Church in all Ages', he had complained. 'When Church-men employ their Designs not so much to preserve to themselves the Honour of Religion, as to acquire to themselves a Name and Interest among the Multitude: When they apply themselves to obtain the Favour of the professed Enemies of the Church, and at the same Time stick not to betray her Constitution, and to be instrumental in her Disgrace.'[70] Early modern defenders of the established Church had also routinely fretted about the destabilizing religious and political effects of appeals to popular sentiment, and Grey was surely gesturing to that when quoting Wharton.[71]

The story of Donatism which comprised the body of Grey's book focused not on antiquity. That ancient story mapped directly on to the contemporary one of Methodism. Donatists had routinely been objects of obloquy in sixteenth- and seventeenth-century anti-separatist polemic, so that Grey in his 1741 work was merely pursuing an older polemical strategy.[72] Donatism, he began, itself had emerged in the wake of Diocletian's persecution of Christians (*c.* 303–5), during which Christians were not permitted to worship together and during which Bibles and other sacred objects were ordered to be surrendered to the state.[73] The Church's leaders opted not to advocate mass martyrdom, choosing instead to do what they could to protect and to hold together the Christian communities until the persecution had passed. This was the strategy adopted by the North African bishop, Mensurius (d. *c.* 311), and his successor Caecilian of Carthage (d. *c.* 343). The Donatists – who took their name from the Numidian bishop, Donatus (d. *c.* 355) – had opposed this sort of tactical conciliation, accusing those who had handed over Bibles and sacred vessels of being *traditores* (simultaneously, surrenderers and traitors). To the Donatists' way of thinking, a *traditor* had betrayed the Church and, thus, was an apostate; the sacraments which he subsequently administered were invalid. Indeed, only those ordained or consecrated by non-*traditores* were legitimate priests. Because Caecilian had been consecrated by a putative *traditor*, Felix of Aptunga, his consecration was deemed invalid. In his stead, a Donatist council, led by seventy Numidian bishops, elected Majorius as bishop. The ensuing schism between the Donatists and the Catholics (the latter so-called because they claimed to be a part of the church universal) lasted in the North African Church for more than a century, throughout which both the bishops of Rome and the Roman emperors consistently supported the Catholic side. So too did the most notable North African church father also condemn Donatism: Augustine of Hippo wrote more against Donatist schismatics than on any other single subject.[74]

Zachary Grey told the story of the Donatist schism in a way that made it implicitly, if unmistakably, about Methodism. The true protectors of the Church during the Diocletian persecution were the very Catholic clergy whom the Donatists had accused of apostasy. Grey noted, for instance, that Bishop Mensurius had protected a deacon named Felix, 'who had, in an Epistle, severely girded the Emperor for his Tyranny; and refused to obey the Commands of the Inquisitors who had commanded him to deliver up the Ornaments of his Church, and the Evangelical Books that were in his keeping'.[75] Indeed, Mensurius secreted away the church's sacred goods for safekeeping before heading to Rome to face the emperor and what he thought would be a martyr's death. He was ultimately acquitted, dying on his way back to Carthage. What faced his successor Caecilian and the bishops thereafter was a determined group of schismatics led by Donatus – a 'turbulent man' filled with 'Pride and Malice' – who gained members by 'Methods of Seduction'.[76]

During his reign, Constantine the Great (r. 306–37) tasked both local bishops and Pope Miltiades with ensuring 'the Establishment of Unity'.[77] When this failed and 'for the sake of Peace and Unity', Constantine called a meeting of Eastern and African bishops: 'But this his good Intention proved no Effect, being defeated by the implacable Spirit of those wretched Sectaries, who had received already but too many Favours at his hand'.[78] Much besides Constantine's death in 337 prevented the Donatists from being brought quickly to heel. Firstly, the rise of the Donatist schism coincided with the rise of 'the Arian Heresy', which itself preoccupied the 'Catholic Bishops'.[79] Secondly, not all of Constantine's successors as emperor supported orthodoxy or the Church. His son Constantius (r. 337–61), for instance, rejected Nicene Christology and when he 'became sole Emperor, ... immediately after professed himself an Arian, and of consequence an Enemy to the Catholic Church: Upon which the Donatists joined with the Arians and other Heretics in order to distress her'.[80] This would not be the last time that the Donatists allied themselves with heretics aiming to undermine the Church. During the reign of the Julian 'the Apostate' (r. 361–63), for example, 'the Donatists were very liberal in their Thanks to Julian, though he distinguished the Christians with the Nick-name of Galileans, and encouraged the Arians, and other Heretics, who denied the Divinity of the second and third Persons in the ever blessed Trinity against the Orthodox'.[81] This sort of intermittent imperial support allowed Donatism to survive throughout the fourth century and to spawn even other sects, including the Luciferians, Salvians,

Maximinianists, and, most destructively, the Circumcellians, 'a mad hare-brain'd Sect of Enthusiasts'.[82] In the end, Grey concluded, so bad were the Donatists that Augustine of Hippo, who 'was a great Enemy to Persecution in every Shape; and thought ... that no one ought to be compelled to Unity, but to be persuaded by sound Reason and good Arguments to Conformity', changed his mind and accepted that the Donatists must 'first [be] awed by Fear, [so] that Truth (which was not to be met with amongst their schismatical Leaders) afterwards convinced them, and made them abhor their former wicked Practices'.[83]

The connections that Zachary Grey made between Donatism and Methodism were clear, if implicit, in his short history of the ancient sect. The Donatists, like the Methodists, were always schismatic and enthusiastic, while Donatus, like George Whitefield, was both enthusiastic and relentlessly obdurate. The Church of England, by contrast, was like the primitively pure Church during its first four centuries. Furthermore, the Donatists, like the Methodists, were either heretical or, at the very least, supportive of heresy: either way, they both were solvents of orthodox Christian doctrine. Lastly, the Donatists, like the Methodists, would, unchecked by state coercion, spawn other schismatical movements and further catalyse disunity. In case any of this implicit message had escaped the reader, Grey made it explicit in an appendix which compared in parallel columns the actions of 'the schismatical Donatist' with those of 'Mr Whitefield'.

One of the ironies of Zachary Grey's use of the primitive Church as a weapon against Methodism was that one of Methodism's founders, John Wesley, himself considered the movement he founded as an attempt to revive the primitive Christian spiritual discipline, liturgy and ethos.[84] He, no less than Grey and the orthodox, reckoned that there had once been a moment of primitive Christian purity, a moment lost but one that could be identified and should be recovered. This, indeed, was a conviction shared by almost all eighteenth-century English Protestants. Their inability to reach a consensus on what precisely constituted primitively pure doctrine, liturgy or ecclesiology only exacerbated intra-Protestant divisions. No amount of scholarly erudition or polemical skill could make it otherwise. Faced with the prospect of unending disagreement over orthodoxy and orthopraxis, many argued for restraint's efficacy. Certainly this was what Zachary Grey consistently advocated to his congregations in rural Bedfordshire and in Cambridge.

NOTES

1 Symson to Grey, 9 September 1735 (*LI*, IV, p. 359).

2 J.-L. Quantin, *The Church of England and Christian Antiquity* (Oxford, 2009), p. 1. For a muted version of this argument, H. Chadwick, 'Tradition, Fathers and Councils', in J. Booty and S. Sykes (eds), *The Study of Anglicanism* (Philadelphia,

1988), pp. 100–15. Cf. D. MacCulloch, 'The Myth of the English Reformation', *JBS* 20 (1991), pp. 1–19.

3 G. Bennett, 'Patristic Authority in the Age of Reason', *Oecumenica* (1971/2), p. 76. See also E. Duffy, 'Primitive Christianity Revived; Religious Renewal in Augustan England', *SCH* 14 (1977), pp. 298–300; H. McAdoo, *The Spirit of Anglicanism* (1965), pp. 316–414; N. Sykes, *From Sheldon to Secker: Aspects of English Church History, 1660–1768* (Cambridge, 1959), pp. 105–39. Cf. Quantin, *Church of England*, pp. 396–411.

4 M. Jacob and L. Stewart, *Practical Matter: Newton's Science in the Service of Industry and Empire, 1687–1851* (Cambridge, MA, 2004); L. Stewart, *The Rise of Public Science: Rhetoric, Technology and Natural Philosophy in Newtonian Britain, 1660–1750* (Cambridge, 1992).

5 C. Wilde, 'Hutchinsonianism, Natural Philosophy and Religious Controversy in Eighteenth Century Britain', *History of Science* 18 (1980), pp. 1–24; G. Cantor, 'Revelation and the Cyclical Cosmos of John Hutchinson', in L. Jordanova and R. Porter (eds), *Images of the Earth* (Chalfont St Giles, 1979), pp. 4–22; D. Katz, 'Hutchinsonians and Hebraic Fundamentalism in Eighteenth-Century England', in D. Katz and J. Israel (eds), *Sceptics, Millenarians and Jews* (Leiden, 1990), pp. 237–55.

6 R. Muller, 'The Debate over the Vowel Points and the Crisis in Orthodox Hermeneutics', *Journal of Medieval and Renaissance Studies* 10 (1980), pp. 53–72.

7 M. Jacob, 'Christianity and the Newtonian Worldview', in D. Lindberg and R. Numbers (eds), *God and Nature* (Berkeley, CA, 1986), p. 253. Cf. J. Friesen, 'Hutchinsonianism and the Newtonian Enlightenment', *Centaurus* 48 (2006), pp. 40–9.

8 B. Young, *Religion and Enlightenment in Eighteenth-Century England* (Oxford, 1998), pp. 83–119; B. Young, 'Newtonianism and the Enthusiasm of Enlightenment', *Studies in History and Philosophy of Science: Part A* 35 (2004).

9 M. Jacob, *Scientific Culture and the Making of the Industrial West* (Oxford, 1997), p. 79. Jacob, *Newtonians* is the *locus classicus* of her influential thesis that Newtonian Christianity ('liberal Christianity') necessarily threatened orthodox Christianity and that opponents to Newtonians were Tories. Cf. G. Holmes, 'Science, Reason and Religion in the Age of Newton', *BJHS* 11 (1978), pp. 164–71; J. Gascoigne, 'From Bentley to the Victorians: The Rise and Fall of British Newtonian Natural Theology', *Science in Context* 2 (1988), pp. 224–5.

10 J. Force, 'Newton's God of Dominion: The Unity of Newton's Theological, Scientific and Political Thought', in J. Force (ed.), *Essays in the Context, Nature and Influence of Isaac Newton's Theology* (Dordrecht, 1990), pp. 75–102; S. Snobelen, 'The Theology of Isaac Newton's *Principia Mathematica*: A Preliminary Survey', *Neue Zeitschrift für Systematische Theologie und Religionsphilosophie* 52 (2010), pp. 377–412. Cf. R. Westfall, *Never at Rest: A Biography of Isaac Newton* (Cambridge, 1980), pp. 139–40.

11 S. Snobelen, '"The true frame of Nature": Isaac Newton, Heresy and the Reformation of Natural Philosophy', in J. Brooke and I. Maclean (eds), *Heterodoxy in Early Modern Science and Religion* (Oxford, 2005), pp. 223–62.

12 Newton, 'A short Schem[e] of the true Religion' (*NP*). See also R. Westfall, 'Isaac

Newton's *Theologiae Gentilis Origines Philosophicae*', in W. Wagar (ed.), *The Secular Mind* (New York, 1982), pp. 15–34.

13 S. Mandelbrote, '"Than this nothing can be plainer": Isaac Newton Reads the Fathers', in G. Frank, T. Leinkauf and M. Wridt (eds), *Die Patristik in der Frühen Neuzeit* (Stuttgart, 2006), pp. 283–4; S. Mandelbrote, '"A duty of the greatest moment": Isaac Newton and the Writing of Biblical Criticism', *BJHS* 26 (1993), p. 287.

14 S. Snobelen, 'Isaac Newton, Socinianism and the "One Supreme God"', in M. Mulsow and J. Rohls (eds), *Socinianism and Cultural Exchange* (Leiden, 2005), pp. 241–93.

15 Isaac Newton, 'Twelve articles on religion' (*NP*).

16 S. Snobelen, 'Isaac Newton, Heretic: The Strategies of a Nicodemite', *BJHS* 32 (1999), pp. 381–419.

17 Mandelbrote, '"Than this nothing could be plainer"'; R. Iliffe, 'Friendly Criticism: Richard Simon, John Locke, Isaac Newton and the *Johannine Comma*', in A. Hessayon and N. Keene (eds), *Scripture and Scholarship in Early Modern England* (Aldershot, 2006), pp. 137–57; R. Iliffe, 'Prosecuting Athanasius: Protestant Forensics and the Mirrors of Persecution', in J. Force and S. Hutton (eds), *Newton and Newtonianism: New Studies* (Dordrecht, 2004), pp. 113–54.

18 I. Newton, *Mathematical principles*, trans. A. Motte (1729: T142590), p. 389. L. Stewart, 'Seeing Through the Scholium: Religion and Reading Newton in the Eighteenth Century', *History of Science* 34 (1996), pp. 123–65; S. Snobelen, '"God of Gods, and Lord of Lords": The Theology of Isaac Newton's General Scholium to the *Principia*', *Osiris* 16 (2001), pp. 169–208.

19 A. Grafton, *Defenders of the Text* (Cambridge, MA, 1991), pp. 104–44; S. Mandelbrote, '"The Doors shall fly open": Chronology and Biblical Interpretation in England, c. 1630–c. 1730', in K. Kileen, H. Smith and R. Willie (eds), *Oxford Handbook of the Bible in Early Modern England, 1530–1700* (Oxford, 2015), pp. 176–95; J. Buchwald and M. Feingold, *Newton and the Origin of Civilization* (Princeton, 2013).

20 I. Newton, *Chronology of ancient kingdoms amended* (1728: N000962), pp. vii–ix. For Grey's mostly anodyne notes on Newton's *Chronology*, Zachary Grey's reading notebook (CUL, Ee.VI.45, fol. 143).

21 [Z. Pearce], *Reply to the Letter to Dr. Waterland* (1731: T044639), pp. 42–50; [Z. Pearce], *Reply to the Defence of the Letter to Dr. Waterland* (1732: T012466), pp. 9–40.

22 Waterland to Pearce, 21 January 1731 (WAM 64087).

23 Waterland to Grey, 5 February 1735 (BL, Add. 5831, fols 172–3). I have been unable to locate this volume with Waterland's marginalia. See also Waterland to Grey, 17 March 1736 (*LI*, IV, p. 389).

24 S. Mandelbrote, 'Newton and Eighteenth-Century Christianity', in I. Cohen (ed.), *Cambridge Companion to Newton* (Cambridge, 2002), pp. 409–30; S. Mandelbrote, 'Eighteenth-Century Reactions to Newton's Anti-Trinitarianism', in J. Force and S. Hutton (eds), *Newton and Newtonianism* (Dordrecht, 2004), pp. 93–111.

25 [W. Stukeley], review of Isaac Newton's *Observations*, *Present State of the Repubick of Letters* 11 (February 1733), pp. 121–2. This review was unsigned, but see David Hartley to Stukeley, 6 January 1735 (Beinecke, Osborn Files Folder 6788), which

praises Stukeley's take on 'Sir Isaac's Chronology as stated in the Republic of Letters'. Synopses of Newton's *Observations* appeared in *Present State of the Republick of Letters* 11 (February and March 1733), pp. 121–41, 165–77. See also Warburton to Stukeley, 10 February 1733 (Bodleian, Eng.lett.d.35, fol. 30). For Stukeley's Newtonianism, D. Haycock, '"The long-lost truth": Sir Isaac Newton and the Newtonian Pursuit of Ancient Knowledge', *Studies in History and Philosophy of Science: Part A* 35 (2004), pp. 605–23.

26 [Stukeley], review of Newton's *Observations*, p. 123.

27 [C. Middleton], *Defence of the letter to Dr. Waterland* (1731: T032264), pp. 69–71; [C. Middleton], *Some remarks on a reply to the defence* (1732: T012468), pp. 6–7; W. Whiston, *Six dissertations* (1736: T025855), pp. 275–346.

28 A. Bedford, *Animadversions* (1728: T144360), p. 2. Bedford, *Scripture chronology* (1730: T128161), pp. ii, iii, argued that Newton's revised ancient chronology 'would destroy the Authority of the Hebrew Text ... by bringing the History too far backward' and that it 'puts the whole Scripture History into Confusion'. See also Buchwald and Feingold, *Newton and the Origin of Civilization*, pp. 381–4, 387–8.

29 Bedford, *Animadversions*, p. 143.

30 A. Young, *Historical dissertation on idolatrous corruptions* (1734: T078093), I, p. iii; II, p. 180.

31 Ibid., II, p. 268.

32 Ibid., II, pp. 272–7, 282.

33 Z. Grey, *Examination of the fourteenth chapter* (1736: T114725), pp. 2–4. Later in the book, Grey argued that Newton had written about saints' relics in much the same way as John Toland, Anthony Collins and Matthew Tindal, heterodox figures all: ibid., p. 70.

34 I. Newton, *Observations* (1733: T041883), pp. 203–7.

35 Grey, *Examination of the ... Observations*, pp. 10–17.

36 Ibid., p. 9. See, for instance, Whiston, *Six dissertations*, p. 319.

37 E. Duffy, *The Stripping of the Altars* (New Haven, 1992), pp. 155–205; H. Parish, *Monks, Miracles, and Magic: Reformation Representations of the Medieval Church* (London, 2005), pp. 71–91.

38 C. Eire, *War Against the Idols: The Reformation of Worship from Erasmus to Calvin* (Cambridge, 1989).

39 J. Williams, *Brief exposition of the church-catechism* ((1689): R26375), p. 23, for instance, defined saints as 'in a large sense to be understood of all those that are visible Members of Christ's Church', while W. Beveridge, *Church-Catechism explained* (1704: T072689), p. 73, was content merely to define saints mere as 'holy Persons'.

40 W. Wake, *Principles of the Christian religion explained* (1720: T146616), pp. 66–7.

41 Ibid., p. 69.

42 Wake's ambivalence regarding saints was similarly evident in sixteenth- and seventeenth-century discussions of angels. See, for instance, A. Walsham, 'Invisible Helpers: Angelic Intervention in Post-Reformation England', *P&P* 208 (2010), pp. 77–130; Walsham, 'Angels and Idols in England's Long Reformation', in P. Marshall and A. Walsham (eds), *Angels in the Early Modern World* (Cambridge, 2006), pp. 134–67.

43 Grey, *Examination of the ... Observations*, pp. 24–5, 50, 51.

44 Ibid., p. 66.
45 Ibid., pp. 70, 94, 95.
46 Cf. O. Hughes, *Veneration of saints and images* (1735: T006587).
47 Waterland to Grey, 5 February 1735 (BL, Add. 5831, fols 172–3).
48 B. Young, *Religion and Enlightenment in Eighteenth-Century England* (Oxford, 1998), pp. 45–80; M. Wiles, *Archetypal Heresy: Arianism Through the Centuries* (Oxford, 1996), pp. 62–163.
49 [Z. Grey], *Knight of Dumbleton* (1723: T103424), pp. 15–16. See also [Z. Grey], *Spirit of infidelity, detected* (1723: T081205), p. 49; [Z. Grey], *Caveat against Mr. Benjamin Bennet* (1724: T103423), p. 3.
50 Grey, *Examination of the ... Observations*, p. 4.
51 Ibid., pp. 35, 82.
52 Ibid., pp. 116, 113.
53 Zachary Grey, annotations of Grey, *Examination of the ... Observations* (CUL, shelfmark 7100.d.46).
54 G. Morley, *Two letters to ... Janus Ulitius* (1707: T098968), title-page.
55 Ibid., preface.
56 Morley, *Two letters*, pp. 57–8; Grey, annotations of *Examination of the ... Observations*, p. 138.
57 Morley, *Two letters*, pp. 26, 60; Grey, annotations of *Examination of the ... Observations*, inside front cover. On Casaubon and du Perron, see W. Patterson, *King James VI and I and the Reunion of Christendom* (Cambridge, 2000), pp. 133–6.
58 Morley, *Two letters*, p. 29; Grey, annotations of *Examination of the ... Observations*, unpaginated front pages.
59 J. Wesley, *An Extract of ... John Wesley's Journal, from February 1, 1737–8* ((1740): T17126), p. 30.
60 C. Field, 'Anti-Methodist Publications of the Eighteenth Century: A Revised Bibliography', *Bulletin of the John Rylands Library* 73 (1991), pp. 159–280; C. Field, 'Anti-Methodist Publications of the Eighteenth Century: A Supplemental Bibliography', *Wesley and Methodist Studies* 6 (2014), pp. 154–86; R. Green, *Anti-Methodist Publications Issued during the Eighteenth Century* (London, 1902), itemize the print responses.
61 G. Ditchfield, *The Evangelical Revival* (1998); J. Walsh, 'The Origins of the Evangelical Revival', in J. Walsh and G. Bennett (eds), *Essays in Modern English Church History* (Oxford, 1966), pp. 132–62.
62 [Z. Grey], *Quaker and Methodist compared* (1740: N21921), preface.
63 Cf. Timothy Cutler to Grey, 24 September 1743; E. Miller to Grey, 6 October 1743 (*LI*, IV, pp. 303–5).
64 [Z. Grey], *Serious address to Lay-Methodists* (1745: T017554), p. 1. More generally, S. Lewis, 'A "Papal Emissary"? George Whitefield and Anti-Methodist Allegations of Popery, c. 1738–c. 1750', *Journal of Religious History, Literature and Culture* 2 (2015), pp. 16–34.
65 [Grey], *Serious address*, p. 2.
66 Ibid., p. 3. Zachary Grey, *Jesuit in Disguise; or, One Popish Method of Dividing Us, exemplified* [unpublished manuscript] (CUL, Add. 3308, fols 36–48), expounded on Commin's imposture and explicitly compared Commin to George Whitefield.

Grey drew his information on Commin from Strype, *Life ... of Matthew Parker*, p. 244, and [J. Nalson and R. Ware], *Foxes and firebrands* (Dublin, 1682: R202238), pp. 14–30. See also J. Nalson, *Impartial collection of the great affairs of state* (1682: R6970), pp. xxxix–xliv. D. MacCulloch, *All Things Made New: The Reformation and Its Legacy* (Oxford, 2016), pp. 321–58, examines Ware's Commin forgery.

67 [Grey], *Serious address*, p. 19.

68 Field, 'Anti-Methodist Publications of the Eighteenth Century: A Revised Bibliography', p. 177, misattributes authorship to J. Trevor, whose affidavit forms part of the work's preface; Green, *Anti-Methodist Publications*, no. 118, does not attribute authorship. Thomas Potter to Grey, 23 April 1741 (*LI*, IV, pp. 337–8), and Timothy Cutler to Grey, 24 September 1743 (*LI*, IV, p. 302), show that the work was, in fact, written by Grey but published anonymously.

69 [Z. Grey], *Popery in its proper colours* (1745: T178347), pp. 22–3.

70 [Z. Grey], *Short history of the Dontatists* (1741: T096899), p. v.

71 P. Lake, 'Post-Reformation Politics or, on Not Looking for the Long-Term Consequences of the English Civil War', in M. Braddick (ed.), *Oxford Handbook of the English Revolution* (Oxford, 2015); P. Lake, 'Puritanism (Monarchical) Republicanism and Monarchy; or John Whitgift, Antipuritanism, and the "Invention" of Popularity', *JMEMS* 40 (2010), pp. 463–95.

72 J. Hoover, '"They bee Full Donatists": The Rhetoric of Donatism in Early Separatist Polemics', *Reformation and Renaissance Review* 14 (2013), pp. 154–76.

73 H. Chadwick, *The Early Church* (1993), pp. 219–25; H. Chadwick, *The Church in Ancient Society* (Oxford, 2001), pp. 382–93; E. Rebillard, 'The West (2): North Africa', in S. Harvey and D. Hunter (eds), *Oxford Handbook of Early Christian Studies* (Oxford, 2008), pp. 309–15.

74 H. Chadwick, *Augustine* (Oxford, 2001), pp. 80–90.

75 [Grey], *Short history of the Donatists*, p. 1.

76 Ibid., pp. 5, 7, 13.

77 Ibid., p. 7.

78 Ibid., p. 11.

79 Ibid., p. 13.

80 Ibid., p. 16.

81 Ibid., p. 17.

82 Ibid., pp. 15, 26–9.

83 Ibid., pp. 23–4. Cf. J.-L. Quantin and S. Mandelbrote, 'Augustine in the Seventeenth and Eighteenth Centuries', in W. Otten (ed.), *Oxford Guide to the Historical Reception of Augustine* (Oxford, 2013), I, pp. 88–9.

84 G. Hammond, *John Wesley in America: Restoring Primitive Christianity* (Oxford, 2014); E. Duffy, 'Primitive Christianity Revived; Religious Renewal in Augustan England', *SCH* 14 (1977), pp. 299–300.

Chapter 13

None of us are born free: self-restraint and salvation

In the wake of two earthquakes – one in London in 1750, another in Lisbon in 1755 – English presses poured out responses, including ones from Zachary Grey.[1] Though the form of Grey's pieces – which he called 'a chronological and historical account' of 'the most memorable earthquakes' in England and abroad – differed from many, their analysis and message were unexceptional. The earthquakes were natural phenomena with natural explanations. Nearly everyone agreed on this during the mid-eighteenth century, though naturalists divided about what caused earthquakes. Some thought them the product of 'subterraneous Fire' and 'Subterraneous Vapours', while others advanced an electrical airquake theory, whereby electrical disturbances 'produce that snap, and that shock, which we call an earthquake; a vibration of the superfices of the earth'.[2] Grey reckoned that Martin Lister's theories regarding 'the inflammable breath of mineral pyrites' were most probably true, not least since the infrequency of earthquakes in the British Isles correlated to the relative absence there of pyrites.[3] Zachary Grey offered nothing but naturalistic explanations for the earthquakes. Like most of his contemporaries, though, he also thought God had caused those naturally explicable earthquakes. This was possible because he distinguished between first and second causes.[4] As Samuel Chandler explained it, 'God is really the proper Agent in these and other like natural Effects, and the Operations of the Laws, which he from the first Origin of Nature fixed, which he by his continued Influence constantly maintains in their Activity'.[5] God was not just immanent, but transcendent, omnipotent and interventionist.[6]

Most during the mid-eighteenth century believed that God intervened in the affairs of his creation to punish and to warn. Two distinct impressions emerge from the period's published and manuscript sources regarding the London and Lisbon earthquakes, for instance. Firstly, those earthquakes deeply unnerved contemporaries. Secondly, most commonly understood them as providential messages.[7] Grey cautioned that England had been spared destruction purely by 'a superintending Providence', not on account of the nation's 'Goodness'. Nor could England count on the 'Protestant Religion' to shield it from God's wrath. 'Can the best Religion in the World sanctify Sin, or afford it any security?', he asked rhetorically. 'No; that is an absurd and ridiculous supposition, suiting only with the opinions of some lamentable Enthusiasts in the time of the Grand Rebellion, and Usurpation'. Indeed, even if it were possible to count on works to protect a nation from God's providential punishments, England surely would not qualify for protection, given that there were some who 'dispute the Being of a God covertly, if not openly'; who 'disown his Revelations'; and who 'have reformed away all reverence for God's Holy Name, and Word, and Sacraments'. There were, Grey lamented, 'too many nominal Protestants among us, who scarce deserve the name of Christians, who hardly believe one article of the Christian Faith; who make a Mock even at God's solemn Institutions, and are zealous of teaching others so to do'.[8] Repentance and reformation offered the only sure remedy. England needed restraint from sin, and, given the nature of the post-revolutionary religious settlement, restraint that was mainly self-imposed. To encourage that self-restraint, clergy needed to encourage widespread belief in a future state of rewards and punishments. They needed also to urge people publicly to censure the sinful behaviour of others.

Eighteenth-century English historians tend to treat providential language as an archaic holdover from a bygone era, a kind of verbal tic that was hard to shake.[9] Belief in providence, though, emerged organically from eighteenth-century conceptions of sin and salvation. This chapter sketches the lineaments of the orthodox soteriological position of the eighteenth-century Church of England. It draws its evidence from Zachary Grey's unpublished manuscript sermons, delivered to his parishioners across the middle third of the century. Through them runs a coherent soteriological argument, one with a stable conception of God; of how God operated in the world; and of how and why humans (God's rational creatures) are damned or saved after death. Through Grey's sermons also runs a coherent argument about how sin and salvation related to natural and human history. God's active providential management of his creation was purposeful and responsive: he punished and warned because people sinned. Restraining sin offered a way to secure civil peace. This chapter explains why the eighteenth-century orthodox thought as much.

The sermon's formative role in the early modern English public sphere is now recognized; but those sermons that made it into print during the eighteenth century were mostly one-off pieces whose subjects reflected the particular occasions for which they were composed.[10] Those occasional published sermons emerged from a variety of particular moments and settings, including the royal court, visitations, consecrations, funerals, feast and fasts and prominent dates on the English Protestant calendar (30 January, 29 May, 5 November, for instance).[11] Almost all reflected purposes of the singular moments which occasioned them. While published sermons are valuable and revealing sources, they are also anomalous works not just because they were bespoke but also because they comprised only a small fraction of the sermons actually delivered in any year.[12] The difficulty has been to discern what sorts of things got discussed each week in the pulpits of the more than ten thousand parish churches in England and Wales. Unpublished manuscript sermons provide one source of evidence. In particular, the extant unpublished sermons from the period suggest that priests concerned themselves with soteriology even more concertedly in their ordinary sermons than they did in their extraordinary ones.[13]

A tight soteriological argument runs through Zachary Grey's extant manuscript sermons. These cover the period between the late 1720s and the late 1750s. This chapter reconstructs how Grey, a not-atypical member of the eighteenth-century orthodox, explained sin and salvation to his parishioners. Grey gave these sermons mainly in the Bedfordshire parishes of Houghton Conquest (where he was rector 1726–67) and of Liddlington (where he held no office but sometimes preached).[14] He delivered other sermons in the Cambridge parishes of St Giles (where he served as vicar 1729–55) and of St Peter's (where he was curate 1751–64).[15] Both Houghton Conquest and Liddlington were rural parishes with between 70 and 110 families; with few to no religious Dissenters; and with religious provision that met or exceeded national norms.[16] These Bedfordshire parishes were not the sorts of churches that would have been packed with theologically sophisticated parishioners.[17] Grey spent his springs and summers in Bedfordshire and his winters in Cambridge, where the parishes of St Giles and St Peter's lay. During the late 1720s, around 540 people lived in the parish of St Giles, while another 270 lived in St Peter's.[18]

The eighteenth-century orthodox soteriological position, which emerges from Grey's sermons was not the same as it had been in England two centuries earlier. The Reformation had begun as a debate about salvation, and the role of human agency in the salvation process had been contested from the Reformation's outset.[19] Protestants accused Roman Catholics of being Pelagians, who thought that salvation could be earned with good works. Protestants, by contrast, contended that man is so scarred by original sin that all deserve damnation and that salvation is thus a gift given by the grace of God. But did this mean that the individual had no say in his or her eternal fate? Over this Protestants divided. The Church of England's official formularies, drawn up during the mid-sixteenth century, suggested not. Man lacked the free will to do good works 'without the grace of God'. While good works please God, they are only 'the fruits of Faith, and follow after Justification, [and] cannot put away our sins'. In fact, 'Works done before the grace of Christ, and the Inspiration of the Spirit, are not pleasant to God' and likely 'have the nature of sin'. We are, instead, 'accounted righteous before God, only for the merit of our Lord and Saviour Jesus Christ, by Faith, and not of our own works or deservings'. Furthermore, some (the elect) were predestined for eternal salvation.[20] These formulations in the Thirty-Nine Articles (1562) reflected John Calvin's theological understanding of salvation and, by the late sixteenth century, a Calvinist consensus regarding soteriology, if not ecclesiology, held in England.[21] That Calvinist consensus, though, got disturbed during the 1630s, when Archbishop William Laud and like-minded clergy propounded an Arminian soteriology, one whose 'essence ... was a belief in God's universal grace and the freewill of all men to obtain salvation'.[22] To many Calvinists, this sounded like popery, both in its rejection of predestination and in its sacramental theology. In the short term, the Calvinists won out, since both Laud and Laudianism were casualties of the English Civil Wars. But by the turn of the eighteenth century, there was, in England, an Arminian soteriological consensus.[23] By the mid-eighteenth century, this Arminian consensus had developed into a soteriology in which salvation could not be earned through works, but neither could it be achieved without them.[24] Consequent from that soteriology was an imperative of self-restraint, a theme clearly on display in Grey's unpublished sermons.

Zachary Grey identified for his parishioners the barriers to their eternal salvation. 'Our lives as Christians are frequently in Scripture compared to a Warfare; and though we are not always engaged by our Enemies, We may be in Constant Danger of Them', he cautioned. 'Temptations from without, Lusts from within, and the wicked Suggestions of the Devil do so often beset us, that we can never be too much upon our Guard.'[25] External temptation stood as the first barrier to salvation, and the chief temptation came from liars. 'Our God is by nature a God of Truth', Grey warned in a sermon on Ephesians 4:25. And the God who made us 'after His own Image and Similitude' also 'commanded us to be Holy, as He is Holy, and Perfect as He is Perfect'.[26] This necessarily entailed a strict fidelity to the truth. For the purposes of this sermon on Ephesians delivered in Houghton Conquest, Grey defined *truth* and *lies* as they related to intent, rather than to content. *Truth* 'must consist in the conformity of the tongue with the sentiments of the mind'. The *lies* referred to in Ephesians were 'the wilful Kind; When a Man speaks otherwise than He thinks in His Heart. Though the Thing spoken should prove to be True.' Lies themselves came in three varieties – the 'Pernicious kind'; the 'Ludicrous & jovial lye'; and the 'Jesting Lie'. Though each had different effects, all 'consist in the Intention of Speaking what is False'.[27] Indeed, there has been 'No Sad Disorder [that] ever befell any Person or People ... That a Lie was first or last the Principal Engine to bring It about'. The fate of liars is 'Eternal Separation from God', as both the Psalms and the Book of Revelation testified.[28]

For Grey, sincerity might be Truth's touchstone, but it was not its measure. Rather, Truth was transcendent; and there were two ways to ascertain it.[29] One was through philosophy ('the Nice Speculation of the Schools') and the other was through 'the Revelations of Scripture'.[30] What made the Bible a better source of truth than philosophy was that it was a work of history. Consider, for instance, Christ's resurrection or any of the other biblical miracles. Grey had none of the qualms about them that plagued some of his contemporaries.[31] Instead, he noted, while 'we who live in these times cannot have the satisfaction of Ocular demonstration' of them, nonetheless 'we have the memory of these things transmitted to us in those undoubted records upon the credit of Eye-Witnesses Themselves whose knowledge of what they report and their Integrity in reporting it must be allowed to be above all suspicion'. Anticipating those who would question the biblical authors' own reliability, Grey retorted that the 'singular proof' of their truthfulness was that 'they sacrificed all their worldly Interest to the cause they undertook, and sealed to the truth of what they delivered with their dearest Blood'.[32] Martyrdom (sincerity's ultimate sign) provided the definitive stamp of authenticity on Truth. Anyone who denied this spread lies.

The quintessential liar was the Devil. He stood as a second barrier between humans and their eternal salvation. The personification of evil, the Devil was God's anti-type. No less than God, he was immanent in the world, serving either as an agent of divine judgement or as a tempter.[33] The Church of England's rites and formularies expressed this view. The Church's baptismal rite, for instance, involved either godparents or the person being baptised formally to renounce 'the Devil and all his works', while the rite of confirmation was designed expressly to fortify the baptised so that 'they may receive strength and defence against all temptations to sin, and the assaults of the world and the devil'.[34] Similarly, the Thirty-Nine Articles cast the Devil as the tempter who led those 'lacking the Spirit of Christ' – and, thus, who were uncertain of their salvation – 'either into desperation, or into wretchlessness [*sic*] of most unclean living, no less perilous than desperation'.[35] While the Devil's presence did not perhaps loom quite as large during the eighteenth century as it had before, the Devil nonetheless remained a present figure of theological importance.[36] In a turn-of-the-century exposition of the Church of England's catechism, William Wake reaffirmed the Devil's historical reality, though he conceived of him as a composite character rather than as a single individual. In his exposition, Wake defined the Devil as 'the common name given to those wicked Spirits, who having rebelled against God, and being thereupon justly cast off from that Glorious State in which they were created by him; do make it their constant Business and Endeavour to draw as many of us as they can into the same Rebellion, and thereby into the same State of Misery as themselves'. The 'Works of the Devil' renounced in baptism include those 'which either more immediately relate to him, or proceed from his Suggestions; such as Pride, Malice, Envy, Revenge, Murder, Lying; and, above all, Witch-craft, and Idolatry'.[37] Even Daniel Defoe's *Political History of the Devil* (1726), a work which rejected many widely held beliefs regarding Satan and demonism, argued unambiguously for the Devil's existence and for his continued interference in human affairs.

Zachary Grey's Devil ('that Grand Adversary of Mankind') was more like Wake's and Defoe's than John Milton's in *Paradise Lost*.[38] Nonetheless, he was, for Grey, an actual historical figure who catalysed the Fall. 'For how came our first parents to sin, & to lose their primitive innocence?' he asked his congregation. 'Why they were deceived, & by the subtlety of the Devil made to believe a lie.' On Grey's reading, the Devil was the instigator of sin, the being who 'first introduced [it] into the World by a Lie (being equally the Base Original of Both). So He still propagates and promotes It by the Same Methods.'[39] He could not make people sin, but he did possess the power to tempt people into sin. Indeed, the Devil 'is constantly employed in the undoing us' and 'walks about seeking whom He may devour'.[40] To do that, he 'may involve as many as He can into the same miserable condition with Him and ... [t]hose apostate spirits, who entered into Rebellion against the great God of Heaven and Earth'.[41] Human life, then, was a perpetual struggle against the Devil's temptations. So where Thomas Hobbes famously identified a world in which traditional Christianity held sway as the 'Kingdom of Darkness', Grey reckoned that the Devil's 'Kingdom is this world and perfectly a Kingdom of Darkness'.[42]

The Devil took advantage of humans' natural susceptibility to the passions. Eighteenth-century moral philosophers from Locke to Shaftesbury to Hutcheson to Smith focused especially on the passions, and they were likewise of central concern to those interested in politeness, a mode of behaviour that was supposed to tame, if not overcome, the passions.[43] What precisely constituted the passions was debated during the eighteenth century; but that the passions, whatever they were, influenced the ways that humans behaved was a commonplace.[44] Certainly the effect of the passions on human behaviour exercised the minds of the clergy, including Zachary Grey.[45] For Grey, the passions included the antimonies of 'our very Sense of Pain and Pleasure, our Love and Hatred, our Joy and Grief, our Hope and Fear'. But what really concerned him was the 'unbridled Lust and Appetite, some misplaced or misgoverned affection, with respect to those temporary things, that ... so easily and so often, led away and enticed' people.[46] Those 'works of the flesh' that especially tempted humans were 'Adultery, Fornication, Uncleanness, Lasciviousness, and such like'.[47] In fact, the root of all sin, he argued, was man's subjection to the flesh. Sinners were those 'that live to the flesh and to the world, whose chief Informers are their senses and whose chief entertainment and delight is in sensual satisfactions, and therefore not seeing him that is invisible through the gross medium of sense, They live on after their own rate, as if they were out of his sight too, or as if there were no God in the world.'[48] Elsewhere, he argued that '[n]one of us are born Free. For Nature Subjects us to a State of Servitude. And the Ungovernable Desires which we bring into the world with us render us Slaves Unavoidably.'[49] Yet Grey was also clear that the passions themselves were not inherently bad: 'God, who made us ... remembereth that we are Dust; nor can it be conceived, that he should furnish us with Senses, and yet command us, to be insensible that he should implant passion in us, and yet require us, to be wholly disproportionate; or impose it for our Task to root out those Passions which he himself hath planted'. Humans needed, instead, 'to check our Senses and Passions, by the Help of Reason, and regulate them, by the Laws of our Holy Religion'.[50]

Like Locke, Grey related reason to the soul.[51] It was the human soul 'which besides the inferior powers of Sensation, Imagination and Memory is endowed with the nobler faculties of understanding and will, whereby it is empowered to actuate, determine and control, all corporeal motions, appetites and passions, whereby it is enabled to make a nice discernment betwixt good and Evil, and freely to choose the one and refuse the Other'.[52] And yet, Grey concluded, reason alone could not enable humans to have a 'true measure of that Indifferency or Moderation towards the things of this world' which the Bible counsels. Even ancient Stoicism proved inadequate to the task, for '[t]he Rants of the Stoic are no Rules for the Christian nor can Stupidity deserve the name of Virtue'. Instead, only 'the Laws of our Holy Religion' stood any chance of helping humans successfully to withstand the temptation to sin.[53] In particular, Grey advised his parishioners to think closely about God's nature and to reason from there about their own past, present and future.

God was 'our great Creator and our Governor ... the Founder and Builder of the Universe'. Among his divine attributes were 'omnipresence' and 'omniscience'.[54] Throughout the Bible, God revealed his all-encompassingness, an attribute which, Grey acknowledged, was incomprehensible. 'The Manner how, is inexplicable by the Wit of Men, but the thing certain from the Word of God, that he who is Infinite, and can't be circumscribed is so present everywhere, that there is no place, nor can any be conceived, where he is not.'[55] So too was God all-knowing. As Grey explained it, 'all things near or far off, past, present or future, even contingent things, Little or Great whether the Works of God, the Effects of Nature, the Necessary Actions of Brutes, the Free Ones of Men, their Words and thoughts, and whatsoever is knowable, they are all, clearly open, at one View, to the Divine Omniscience'.[56] From a due regard for the fact that God was everywhere at once and that he knew all that had been, was, would and could be should flow the realization that each and every person stands constantly in God's all-seeing gaze. That gaze was, Grey insisted, a judging one. 'And can the Christian be fearless the meanwhile of that God whom he believes and knows to be the constant observer of all his thoughts, words and actions in order to proceed to Judgment with Him?', he asked his parishioners. The answer was self-evident: God 'is able to destroy both Body and Soul in Hell where the worm dieth not and the fire is not quenched'.[57]

Heaven and Hell were features, not bugs, of eighteenth-century orthodox soteriology. Yet neither a future state of rewards and punishments nor soteriology more generally have merited much attention from eighteenth-century English historians.[58] The likeliest explanation for this is the common assumption that the age was marked, as Paul Hazard put it, by 'the progressive dulcification of faith and morals': it was a time when the belief in Heaven and Hell waned markedly and, indeed, 'could no longer be cogently defended'.[59] Allied to this dulcification was a rejection of the traditional argument that Christianity, with its built-in belief in a future state of rewards and punishments, necessarily was the only solid foundation of morality. First Bayle, then Shaftesbury, Hume and others showed that morality need not be grounded on the belief in a religion which punishes the errors of the here forever in the hereafter.[60] Put most reductively, most historians reckon that, as the eighteenth-century secularized, God's hold in the imagination of its inhabitants progressively eroded. Yet there is ample evidence not only that the prospect of eternal reward in Heaven or everlasting punishment in Hell survived into the eighteenth century but that it was a mainstream view. This was true not just among Christian clerics, but also among eighteenth-century Anglophone philosophers.[61]

When explaining to his parishioners what would happen after their deaths, Grey explicitly rejected mortalism. A distinctively Protestant heresy, mortalism held that the soul 'slept' between death and body's resurrection.[62] Grey contended, instead, that both reason and revelation showed that 'God is pleased to prolong the Soul's Existence, after Death and provide for it another State', a state that 'will be Unlimited and Endless'.[63] By implication, there would be no respite from God's wrath for disobeying him, nor any break in the everlasting enjoyment to be gained from following his divine laws.

Grey tried to get his parishioners to think about that future state by comparing its scope with the fleetingness of their own earthly lives. '[T]he life of a man is a vapour that soon vanisheth, a shadow that is perpetually flitting and fleeing, 'tis brought suddenly to an end even as a tale that it told or a Dream when one awaketh, and no footsteps of it [are] left', he explained. Furthermore, mortal life's very brevity meant that it 'is confined within such narrow bounds, it's plain that it is not so much as the capable Subject of any lasting enjoyment or very tedious suffering'.[64] The incalculable immensity of the eternity within which humans lived their brief lives provided more sobering stuff for reflection. 'A Drop to the Ocean, an Atom to the Universe do bear a certain Mathematical proportion, which upon an hypothesis may easily be calculated', Grey warned. 'But all that Revolution of Years, Ages which is to pass from the first Creation to the Confirmation of all things is not so much as what we call the twinkling of an Eye or the glance of a thought to Eternity.' And, crucially, in the never-ending hereafter, reward or punishment would be inflicted on individual sinners: for each, it will be a state of 'Eternal Happiness' or one of 'Eternal misery'.[65]

Reason and revelation offered ample proof of the future state. Grey admitted that '[i]n matters of sense ... the information of sense supersedes all other proof'. But he pointed out, as well, that there were some things - 'maxims of abstracted reason and mathematical axioms', for instance – which were themselves incapable 'of sensible proof'.[66] The future state was likewise incapable of being proved by the senses. There were, though, other evidences of it that were 'both proper and sufficient'. To begin with, a future state of rewards and punishments was 'a very just and rational conclusion from the very being and attributes of God'. For if God was 'just and provident ... it seems almost naturally to follow, that there must be a State of Recompense hereafter, wherein justice shall be equally and universally distributed, and Every Man exactly rewarded according to his Works'. Even 'the more discerning Heathens' had recognized this.[67] But Christians had other, more secure, proofs, from revelation: 'we ground the Belief of it upon the infallible Testimony of God Himself'.[68] In particular, both Christ's teachings and his resurrection – itself 'a Gracious condescension to Sense' and 'an indisputable and inimitable Miracle' – made clear that all would be judged after death.[69] Grey reckoned that together reason and revelation should convince anyone of an afterlife. If his parishioners did not accept the fact of a future state, they nonetheless should take a Pascalian bet on its existence. 'If there be an Eternity to come, Happy They that have made a timely provision for It by a virtuous course of living', Grey counselled. 'They will [be] unspeakably Gainers at the foot of the Account'. Indeed, 'prudence' requires that we 'consult our own safety and provide for what may possibly happen'.[70]

Within Grey's cautions to his parishioners about securing their everlasting happiness lay the gist of his soteriology. To be sure, St Paul had made clear in his letters 'the Doctrine of Justification by an operative Faith exclusive of the works of the Ceremonial Law'.[71] Under that law, certain sins – 'sins of Presumption', for example – were 'punished with death, and no atonement was admitted in such cases'. When God had delivered the laws to Moses on Mount Sinai or revealed them to the prophets, he had purposefully incited their fear. 'The Law was ... ushered in with all the Motives of Human Terror such as Thunder and Earthquakes, Fire and Smoak', Grey declared, 'intimating Thereby, That if God should think fit to proceed against Man according to the Strict Rules of Justice, there would be Little Room left for Rational pleasure But Every Creature must languish with Terror under a Sense of God's Wrath and Indignation in a Future State of Trial.'[72] The Jews, though, had squandered the opportunity afforded to them in the old covenant. They had either misunderstood God's revelations to them or, more damagingly, they had possessed a 'gross and carnal Conception [which] had strangely corrupted and perverted ... the genuine Sense and Meaning' of God's instructions and laws.[73] For this reason, God had punished them and had made a new covenant, opening up the prospect of salvation to all mankind. To that end, 'the Son of God was manifested, that he might destroy the works of the Devil' (John 3:8). Practically this meant that Christ had atoned for all mankind's sins by 'purchas[ing] of God for us a Remittance and Discharge from the Punishment of Sin'.[74] In addition, Christ empowered humans to withstand sin. As Grey explained it, Jesus 'has farther destroyed the Works of the Devil in that he hath Enabled us, by the power of his Grace, to resist the Temptations of them and so far to cease from the Commission of them, that henceforth, we should not serve them'.[75] Christ, put simply, gave humans the ability to achieve a 'Reformation of Manners', one which allowed each person to earn his or her own salvation.[76]

The role of works in the salvation process was a subject to which Grey returned again and again. As he succinctly put it in a 1754 sermon in Houghton Conquest, 'On our Conduct here, depends all Our Success hereafter ... In the next Life vice and virtue will each produce, its own Natural Effects, however External Causes may cooperate with them.'[77] Heaven followed from obeying God's law; Hell followed from disobeying it.[78] This ran counter to what Grey and other orthodox churchmen understood as Calvinist antinomianism. Daniel Waterland, for instance, decried the antinomianism that he thought flowed naturally from Calvinist theories of predestination. On Waterland's reading, God foresaw 'how a race of free-agents would behave' and thus created humans so that they could freely contribute to their own salvation or damnation. He called this 'conditional election and reprobation', and he thought it 'wise and just and good' since 'it would not have been reasonable to have debarred thousands or millions the privilege of working out their own salvation, only because equal or greater numbers would have by their own fault incur damnation'.[79] Zachary Grey concurred.

Grey argued that those who will be punished most severely in Hell will not be the 'infidels' but those Christians who persist in sin. '[T]he wicked and impenitent Christian is the vilest of all Rebels and the most perfidious of all Revolters, the most inexcusable in the sight of God, and the most irreclaimable', Grey contended.[80] As such, absent a reformation of manners, 'our condemnation [will be] heavier' than 'if we had been ignorant of, or Infidels, in [God's] attributes'.[81] Yet lest his parishioners take these as counsels of despair, Grey assured them that God did not expect absolute perfection from them: God 'does not exact or require impossibilities of us, but only our best endeavours'. Put another way, sincerity might not have been the touchstone of Truth, but it – along with steady perseverance – was a test of good works. '[T]he Imperfections of our Services provided they are true and sincere, ought to deter and discourage no good men from the hopes of Salvation', Grey explained. '... [I]t is a particular Comfort that God judges it not, or measures our Sincerity and Righteousness by the Seasons of our affections and Inclinations at certain times, but by the constant course of our resolutions and the general method of our lives and actions.'[82] To be both sincere and steady in performing good works, one needed to focus not on the fear of eternal punishment but on the love of God, or what Grey sometimes called having 'religious Joy' or 'a merry Heart': 'He that can take no Pleasure or Delight in Religion; cannot hinder his Soul from seeking after It Elsewhere'.[83]

While the Holy Spirit might bolster a person's resolve, it required a sincere inner reformation to feel the kind of joy without fear that, Grey argued, was the hallmark of those destined for Heaven.

While Heaven and Hell were the sites of eternal rewards and punishments for individual sinners, they had at least two other functions. Firstly, they were the sites of the final, eternal balancing of the good and evil done in this world. Grey acknowledged that 'there is no regular Distribution of Good and Evil in this Life'. But knowing that there will be a time when God will balance the moral ledgers means that 'the unequal, and irregular Distributions of this Life, are easily solved, and readily accounted for'. Indeed, without the prospect of 'Futurity … this present Life becomes, in the Eyes of all Thinking Men, all Darkness, Discomfort, and Perplexity; a Sad Scene of Desperate Disorder, and inextricable Confusion'.[84] Perhaps more importantly, the prospect of a future state in which virtue is rewarded and vice is punished necessarily meant that people should self-restrain in the here and now. And that self-restraint had potential corporate, as well as personal, advantages. After the Glorious Revolution, England abounded with initiatives and formal societies to redress the moral problems of the day. Indeed, the eighteenth century was an 'Age of Projects' that both flowed from and fed into the post-Restoration 'Anglican revival'.[85] The moral ills which plagued English society were many, contemporaries argued, ranging from Sabbath-breaking to lewd and disorderly conduct, from gambling to prostitution, from drunkenness to criminal violence.[86] Hogarth's paired *Beer Street* and *Gin Lane* (1751) nicely capture the sorts of personal and societal ills that the eighteenth-century English thought flowed from moral and immoral behaviour.[87] There were, to be sure, a variety of explanations offered for why England faced such an array of moral challenges. But even as late as the 1750s, there was also a generally held view that 'God had an argument with his chosen nation' and that the English needed 'a national revival', which entailed both 'moral and social reform'.[88] The reason the London and Lisbon earthquakes of the 1750s so spooked contemporaries was that most reckoned them to have been either divine warnings or collective punishments for immorality; so too was the success or failure in war understood providentially. This providential worldview connected up individual sin not just with eternal salvation or damnation in the hereafter but also with national flourishing or disorder in the here and now: that connection gave the issue of moral reform particular urgency.[89]

The problem was how to achieve that moral reform. The various eighteenth-century societies for the reformation of manners had proved themselves unable to extirpate sinful behaviour, nor had moral legislation been much more effective.[90] And the church courts, while not completely out of business, were not thought sufficiently up to the task of stamping out sin.[91] So, moral reform needed to be self-guided, and its individual and group benefits needed to be emphasized. Grey hammered home this theme to his parishioners. '[T]he Right Practise of this duty, of setting God always before us, is the likeliest course to promote our Temporal Security and our Everlasting Salvation', he argued at one point.[92] Elsewhere he stressed that keeping a 'merry heart' would produce 'a clear reputation, a comfortable Fortune, an healthful body, and a quiet mind'.[93] Grey never argued that this sort of good behaviour could be coerced. Instead, only through self-mastery, enabled by God's grace, could people behave morally. Consequently, if the sorts of behaviours that Grey and many of his contemporaries thought threatened to destabilize society and to condemn individual souls to eternal punishment were to be restrained, those behaviours needed to be restrained mostly without the coercive apparatus of church or state. There would need to be self-restraint; and belief in a future state of rewards and punishments might encourage socially and personally beneficial self-denying behaviour.

Another way to encourage self-restraint was through public censure, something about which Grey was evidently torn. On the one hand, he acknowledged that people needed to worry pre-eminently about their own sins, since 'a strict self-examination is a very difficult work and will without doubt take up all our leisure hours which are commonly employed in finding out occasions of censure against our Brethren'. Moreover, we risk eternal damnation by unjustly judging others: 'this crime of Judging and Censuring one another is not a trivial one, but highly criminal, offensive to God and dangerous, extremely dangerous to our own Souls, and that of consequence it stands us instead to avoid it as much as possible'.[94] Nonetheless, Grey pointed out that St. Paul had admonished that sin need to be pointed out publicly and censured roundly. '... [I]f we were negligent of Judging in some cases, we ourselves should be very liable to censure.' In particular, if someone denied God's existence or rejected 'any fundamental Article of the Christian Religion', any 'good man would ... be moved by a zeal for his religion to express his abhorrence of such enormous wickedness'. If done with a 'Regard to the welfare of their Souls', criticizing heretics was entirely just, though Grey tellingly added that 'censuring the actions of our Superiors ... is the most criminal of any'.[95] Maintaining the established social and political order was, by implication, a good work.

What emerged from Zachary Grey's unpublished sermons was a coherent soteriology and an allied understanding of providence. God is providentially interventionist, not a passive observer of his creation. What earned God's providential wrath was sin. God designated two sites - Heaven and Hell – in which to reward and to punish those who sinned. Christ, however, came to atone for human sin; he also gave humans the grace to withstand sin. So armed, they could earn their eternal salvation by obeying God's laws or their eternal damnation by disobeying them. For their own good and for the good of their communities, then, people needed to restrain themselves from sinning. If neither individuals nor the state lacked the will or the means to restrain sin, communities at the very least needed publicly to criticize and shame those who sinned. They censured for the sake of the sinners' souls and of society's well-being. In its outlines, this represented the eighteenth-century orthodox position. It was a position broadly shared by one of the era's most prominent polemical divines, William Warburton.

In 1755, when the Lisbon earthquake struck, Warburton held a preachership at Lincoln's Inn in London. Already a noted polemical divine, he was a natural to be chosen on the public fast day to sermonize on the lessons to be drawn from the recent seismic activity. To an audience in Lincoln's Inn, he explained that that '[i]n man's state and condition here, natural and civil events are the proper instruments of God's moral government'.[96] While cautioning against the 'superstition' of reading *all* natural and civil events as divine warnings, he nonetheless insisted that God 'uphold[s] the world as the moral Ruler of it' and is not merely 'the physical Dispenser only'.[97] In making this argument about God's providential government of his creation through natural causes, Warburton was swimming with the tide. When, though, he wrote about the future state of rewards and punishments, he most decidedly was not.

Unlike Zachary Grey and most of his orthodox contemporaries, Warburton denied that the ancient Jews believed in a future state. And, indeed, this non-belief was, for Warburton, proof itself of Christianity's truth. In the *Divine Legation of Moses* (1738–41), as Warburton explained to Thomas Sherlock, he aimed 'not [to prove] that the doctrine of a future state of rewards and punishments is true; (that I take for granted or leave for others to prove;) but that it is so useful that no lawgiver, without divine assistance, could be able to leave it out of his scheme of government'.[98] On Warburton's view, without the threat of eternal sanctions for misdeeds in the present, ancient lawgivers could not expect people to obey their governments. But, crucially, many eighteenth-century freethinkers reckoned that the ancient rulers themselves did not actually believe in a future state. Hence, religion was a human invention brought into being for purely instrumental reasons by rulers who hoped to control the people by religious lies. Warburton, in a bit of intellectual jiu-jitsu, ceded this freethinking point to undermine the larger freethinking attack on religion. He argued that the ancient Jews had been unique in not believing in a future state of rewards and punishments and that this not-belief proved that God's revelations to the Jews were true and that his governance of them was just. Put another way, Moses, whom God had legated as his lawgiver, did not need to threaten the Jews with eternal damnation for disobedience because God providentially governed them, ensuring that they had all that they needed in the here and now. Warburton's conclusion, then, was perfectly orthodox – Christianity was the only true religion – but he had reached it in a thoroughly unorthodox way. It was a position that he argued tenaciously both privately to friends and publicly in his numerous editions of the *Divine Legation of Moses* and other books and sermons. It was not, though, the only perverse position he held. A survey of the polemical career in which he developed and promulgated those perverse positions itself reveals how England's long Reformation drew to a close.

NOTES

1 Z. Grey, *Chronological and historical account of ... earthquakes* (1750: T082798); Z. Grey, *Farther account of memorable earthquakes* (1756: T082799). See also N. Rogers, *Mayhem: Post-War Crime and Violence in Britain, 1748–53* (New Haven, 2013), pp. 89–107.

2 [E. Montagu], *Dissertation upon earthquakes* (1750: T120672), pp. 23–68; W. Stukeley, *Philosophy of earthquakes* (1750: T146242), pp. 25–40 at p. 23.

3 Grey, *Chronological and historical account*, pp. 1–5.

4 P. Harrison, 'Newtonian Science, Miracles and the Laws of Nature', *JHI* 56 (1995), pp. 531–53; P. Harrison, 'Was Newton a Voluntarist?', in Force and Hutton (eds), *Newton and Newtonianism*, pp. 39–63. See, for instance, W. Nowell, *Sermon preached ... Nov. 1. 1755* (Newcastle, 1755: T047628), p. 7.

5 S. Chandler, *Scripture account of ... earthquakes* (1750: T001306), p. 7.

6 Cf. Rogers, *Mayhem*, p. 107.

7 T. Cahill, 'Porn, Popery, Mahometism and the Rise of the Novel: Responses to the London Earthquakes of 1750', *Religion in the Age of Enlightenment* 2 (2010), pp. 277–302; R. Ingram, '"The trembling earth is God's Herald": earthquakes, religion and public life in Britain during the 1750s', in T. Braun and J. Radner (eds), *The Lisbon Earthquake of 1755* (Oxford, 2005); B. Harris, *Politics and the Nation: Britain in the Mid-Eighteenth Century* (Oxford, 2002), pp. 291–4.

8 [Grey], *Chronological and historical account*, pp. iii, v.

9 But see J. Sheehan and D. Wahrman, *Invisible Hands: Self-Organization and the Eighteenth Century* (Chicago, 2015), pp. 11–46; Harris, *Politics and the Nation*, pp. 278–323.

10 T. Claydon, 'The Sermon, the "Public Sphere" and the Political Culture of Late Seventeenth-Century England', in P. McCullough and L. Ferrell (eds), *The English Sermon Revisited: Religion, Literature and History, 1600–1750* (Manchester, 2000), pp. 208–34; R. Dixon, 'Sermons in Print, 1660–1700', in P. McCullough, H. Adlington and E. Rhatigan (eds), *Oxford Handbook of the Early Modern Sermon* (Oxford, 2011), pp. 460–79; J. Caudle, 'Measures of Allegiance: Sermon Culture and the Creation of a Public Discourse of Obedience and Resistance in Georgian Britain, 1714–1760' (Ph.D. dissertation, Yale University, 1995), I, pp. 58–110.

11 W. Gibson and K. Francis (eds), *Oxford Handbook of the British Sermon, 1689–1901* (Oxford, 2012), pp. 229–74, 305–21; Caudle, 'Measures of Allegiance', I, pp. 192–271.

12 W. Gibson, 'The British Sermon, 1689–1901: Quantities, Performance and Culture', in W. Gibson and K. Francis (eds.), *Oxford Handbook of the British Sermon, 1689–1901* (Oxford, 2012), pp. 3–30.

13 J. Chamberlain, 'Parish Preaching in the Long Eighteenth Century', in W. Gibson and K. Francis (eds), *Oxford Handbook of the British Sermon, 1689–1901* (Oxford, 2012), pp. 47–62; J. Farooq, *Preaching in Eighteenth-Century London* (Woodbridge, 2013), pp. 144–56; M. Smith, 'The Hanoverian Parish: Towards a New Agenda', *P&P* 216 (2012), pp. 79–105.

14 The two volumes of Grey's extant sermons (ZGMSSB; ZGMSSC) preserve a combined eighteen manuscript sermons. Grey served as rector of Houghton Conquest, 1726–67, a living which was in the gift of the dean of Ely: *CCED*. The income from this was estimated at £300 per annum: Dispensation for Zachary Grey, 1729 (LPL, VB 1/7/266).

15 *CCED*.

16 P. Bell, *Episcopal Visitations in Bedfordshire, 1706–1720* (Woodbridge, 2002), pp. 49–50, 58–9, 141, 151.

17 Grey seems to have felt a bit socially out of place, since he lived in the market town of Ampthill, three miles from Houghton Conquest. William Cole suggested that the Greys lived in Ampthill because Houghton 'was too dull for Mr Grey & his Daughters' and because it was where his daughter and stepson also lived: F. Stokes (ed.), *Blecheley Diary ... of William Cole ... 1765–67* (1931), p. 160; Cole to Gough, 29 June 1780 (BL, Add. 5843, fol. 106). For Houghton Conquest, W. Page (ed.), *Victoria History of the County of Bedford* (London, 1912), III, pp. 288–96; John Lea, 'Houghton Conquest, its Church and one-time Rector, Zachary Grey' Bedfordshire Archives, P/11/28/13).

18 Zachary Grey, Transcripts of various documents (BL, Stowe 1058, fol. 249). The St Peter's curacy was linked to the St Giles's vicarage and both were in the gift of the bishop of Ely, at that time Thomas Greene. William Cole noted that Grey 'officiates in the morning at one of these churches and in the afternoon only prayers at the other, and so by turns': W. Palmer *William Cole of Milton* (Cambridge, 1935), p. 144. The St Giles income was estimated at £40 per annum: Dispensation for Zachary Grey, 1729 (LPL, VB 1/7/266). For St Giles and St Peter's, J. Roach (ed.), *A History of the County of Cambridge and the Isle of Ely* (London, 1959), III, pp. 123–32.

19 D. MacCulloch, *Reformation* (London, 2003), pp. 106–15, 118–34.

20 *BCP*, p. 555 [Articles X–XII, XVII]. Article XVII (Of Predestination and Election) was notably silent about whether God had actually predestined some (the reprobate) to eternal damnation.

21 P. Lake, 'Calvinism and the English Church, 1570–1635', *P&P* 114 (1986), pp. 32–76.

22 N. Tyacke, *Aspects of English Protestantism, c. 1530–1700* (Manchester, 2001), p. 132. More generally, N. Tyacke, *Anti-Calvinists: The Rise of English Arminianism, c. 1590–1640* (Oxford, 1987).

23 S. Hampton, *The Anti-Arminians: The Anglican Reformed Tradition from Charles II to George I* (Oxford, 2008); N. Tyacke, 'From Laudians to Latitudinarians: A Shifting Balance of Theological Forces', in G. Tapsell (ed.), *The Later Stuart Church, 1660–1714* (Manchester, 2012), pp. 46–70.

24 N. Yates, *Eighteenth-Century Britain, 1714–1815* (2008), pp. 104–29; G. Scholtz, 'Anglicanism in the Age of Johnson: The Doctrine of Conditional Salvation', *ECS* 22 (1988–89),', pp. 182–207. Cf. D. Greene, 'Augustinianism and Empiricism: A Note on Eighteenth-Century Intellectual History', *ECS* 1 (1967), pp. 33–68; and D. Greene, 'How Degraded Was Eighteenth-Century Anglicanism?' *ECS* 24 (1990), pp. 93–108, which, while iconoclastic, are unpersuasive. For a different reading of sin and salvation from the one on offer here, see M. Kadane, 'Original Sin and the Path to the Enlightenment', *P&P* 235 (2017), pp. 105–40.

25 Sermon on Psalm 2:1, Houghton Conquest, n.d. (ZGMSSC, p. 53).
26 Sermon on Ephesians 4:25, Houghton Conquest, 7 July 1727/April 1729 (ZGMSSC, pp. 4–5).
27 Ibid., pp. 2, 3.
28 Ibid., pp. 8, 11. Cf. S. Shapin, *The Social History of Truth: Civility and Science in Seventeenth-Century England* (Chicago, 1995), pp. 3–41.
29 Cf. M. Knights, 'Occasional Conformity and the Representation of Dissent: Hypocrisy, Sincerity, Moderation and Zeal', *PH* 24 (2005), pp. 41–57; M. Knights, *The Devil in Disguise: Deception, Delusion and Fanaticism in the Early English Enlightenment* (Oxford, 2011), p. 5; D. Thomas, 'Benjamin Hoadly: The Ethics of Sincerity', *Enlightenment and Dissent* 15 (1996), pp. 71–88.
30 Sermon on Psalm 16:8, Houghton and Liddlington, 1741/1742/1751/1757 (ZGMSSB, pp. 41, 42).
31 M. Legaspi, *The Death of Scripture and the Rise of Biblical Studies* (Oxford, 2010), pp. 3–26; J. Sheehan, *The Enlightenment Bible: Translation, Scholarship, Culture* (Princeton, 2005), pp. 27–53.
32 Sermon on II Corinthians 4:18, n.d. (ZGMSSB, p. 173).
33 N. Johnstone, *The Devil and Demonism in Early Modern England* (Cambridge, 2006); S. Clark, *Thinking with Demons: The Idea of Witchcraft in Early Modern Europe* (Oxford, 1997), pp. 80–93, 161–78; K. Thomas, *Religion and the Decline of Magic* (1971), pp. 470–7.
34 *BCP*, pp. 270, 285; B. Cummings (ed.), *The Book of Common Prayer: The Texts of 1549, 1559 and 1772* (Oxford, 2011), p. 58.
35 *BCP* [Article XVII], p. 557.
36 Chamberlain, 'Parish Preaching in the Long Eighteenth Century', pp. 57–8; T. Curtis and W. Speck, 'The Societies for the Reformation of Manners: A Case Study in the Theory and Practice of Moral Reform', *Literature and History* 3 (1976), pp. 46–47. Cf. S. Snobelen, 'Lust, Pride and Ambition: Isaac Newton and the Devil', in J. Force and S. Hutton (eds), *Newton and Newtonianism: New Studies* (Dordrecht, 2004), pp. 155–81; D. Oldridge, *The Devil in Early Modern England* (Stroud, 2000), pp. 195–201.
37 W. Wake, *Principles of the Christian religion explained* (1720: T146616), p. 7. Cf. Sermon on John 3:8, 1751/1753/1758 (ZGMSSB, p. 70).
38 Sermon on Matthew 6:24, Houghton Conquest, August 1728 (ZGMSSC, p. 89).
39 Sermon on Ephesians 4:25 (ZGMSSC, p. 7). See also Sermon on John 3:8 (ZGMSSB, pp. 70–1). Cf. P. Almond, *Adam and Eve in Seventeenth-Century Thought* (Cambridge, 1997), pp. 173–214.
40 Sermon on Matthew 6:24 (ZGMSSC, p. 89).
41 Lectures on the Catechism (ZGMSSC, p. 163).
42 Sermon on Ephesians 4:25 (ZGMSSC, p. 7). Cf. J. Champion, 'Godless Politics: Hobbes and Public Religion', in W. Bulman and R. Ingram (eds), *God in the Enlightenment* (Oxford, 2016), pp. 42–62.
43 A. Schmitter, 'Passions, Affections, Sentiments', in J. Harris (ed.), *Oxford Handbook of British Philosophy in the Eighteenth Century* (Oxford, 2013), pp. 197–225; L. Klein, 'Politeness and the Interpretation of the British Eighteenth Century', *HJ* 45 (2002), pp. 869–98; J. Brewer, *The Pleasures of the Imagination* (London, 1997), pp. 94–107.

44 J. Harris, 'Government of the Passions', in Harris (ed.), *Oxford Handbook of British Philosophy in the Eighteenth Century*, pp. 270–88.
45 A. Brinton, 'The Passions as Subject Matter in Early Eighteenth-Century British Sermons', *Rhetorica* 10 (1992), pp. 51–69.
46 Sermon on I Corinthians 7:20, 30–1, Liddlington and Houghton Conquest, 2/16 November 1740 (ZGMSSB, pp. 15, 16).
47 Lectures on the Catechism (ZGMSSC, p. 169).
48 Sermon on Genesis 3:9, Houghton Conquest, 20 July 1729/22 March 1730 (ZGMSSC, p. 34).
49 Sermon on Matthew 6:24, Houghton Conquest, August 1728 (ZGMSSC, p. 86).
50 Sermon on I Corinthians 7:20, 30–1 (ZGMSSB, pp. 10, 11).
51 J. Locke, *Essay Concerning Human Understanding*, ed. P. Nidditch (Oxford, 1975), pp. 110–17. Cf. J. Wright, 'The Understanding', in J. Harris (ed.), *Oxford Handbook of British Philosophy in the Eighteenth Century* (Oxford, 2013), pp. 149–70; R. Serjeantson, 'The Soul', in D. Clarke and C. Wilson (eds), *Oxford Handbook of Early Modern Philosophy* (Oxford, 2011), pp. 126–34.
52 Sermon on Genesis 3:9 (ZGMSSC, p. 21).
53 Sermon on I Corinthians 7:20, 30–1, Houghton Conquest and Liddlington, 2/16 November 1740 (ZGMSSB, pp. 7, 9).
54 Sermon on Ephesians 4:25 (Grey MS Sermons C, p. 19). Cf. J. Clark, '"God" and "the Enlightenment": The Divine Attributes and the Question of Categories in British Discourse', in W. Bulman and R. Ingram (eds), *God in the Enlightenment* (Oxford, 2016), pp. 215–35.
55 Sermon on Psalm 16:8 (ZGMSSB, p. 45).
56 Ibid., pp. 48–9.
57 Sermon on Genesis 3:9 (ZGMSSC, p. 32).
58 Historians who have treated nonjuring arguments about the role of the priesthood in achieving salvation are the exception. See, for instance, B. Sirota, *The Christian Monitors: The Church of England and the Age of Benevolence, 1680–1730* (New Haven, 2014), pp. 149–86; R. Cornwall, *Visible and Apostolic: The Constitution of the Church in High Church and Non-Juror Thought* (Newark, 1993), pp. 59–72.
59 P. Hazard, *Crisis of the European Mind, 1680–1715* (New York, 2013), p. 419; D. Walker, *The Decline of Hell: Seventeenth-Century Discussions of Eternal Torment* (Chicago, 1964), pp. 3–70; P. Almond, *Heaven and Hell in Enlightenment England* (Cambridge, 1994), pp. 144–61; P. Davies, 'The Debate on Eternal Punishment in Late Seventeenth- and Eighteenth-Century English Literature', *ECS* 4 (1971), pp. 257–76.
60 Hazard, *Crisis*, pp. 284–91; D. Norton and M. Kuehn, 'The Foundations of Morality', in K. Haakonssen (ed.), *Cambridge History of Eighteenth-Century Philosophy* (Cambridge, 2013), I, pp. 941–71; J. Champion, *The Pillars of Priestcraft Shaken: The Church of England and Its Enemies, 1660–1730* (Cambridge, 1992), pp. 196–222, pp. 196–222; J. Champion, 'Bayle in the English Enlightenment', in W. van Bunge and H. Bots (eds), *Pierre Bayle (1647–1706), le philosophe de Rotterdam: Philosophy, Religion and Reception* (Leiden, 2008), pp. 175–96.
61 T. Ahnert, 'Religion and Morality', in J. Harris (ed.), *Oxford Handbook of British Philosophy in the Eighteenth Century* (Oxford, 2013), pp. 638–58.
62 B. Young, '"The Soul-Sleeping System": Politics and Heresy in Eighteenth-

Century England', *JEH* 45 (1994), pp. 64–81, is the best treatment of English mortalism.

63 Sermon on Ecclesiastes 12:7 (ZGMSSB, pp. 109, 110).

64 Sermon on II Corinthians 4:18, n.d. (ZGMSSB, p. 181). See also Sermon on Proverbs 17:22, Houghton Conquest, 27 July 1755 (ZGMSSB, p. 118).

65 Sermon on II Corinthians 4:18, pp. 186–7.

66 Ibid., p. 168. Cf. Serjeantson, 'Testimony, Authority and Proof', pp. 148–84.

67 Ibid., pp. 170–1. Cf. A. Grafton, G. Most and S. Settis (eds), *The Classical Tradition* (Cambridge, MA, 2010), pp. 475–81; C. Eire, *Very Brief History of Eternity* (Princeton, 2009), pp. 38–48.

68 Sermon on II Corinthians 4:18, p. 171.

69 Ibid., pp. 171, 172.

70 Ibid., pp. 187–8, 189.

71 Sermon on Romans 14:10, Houghton Conquest, 1728/1737 (ZGMSSB, p. 59).

72 Sermon on Psalm 2:1 (Grey MS Sermons C, pp. 43–4).

73 Sermon on John 3:8, Houghton Conquest and Liddlington, 1741/1752 (ZGMSSC, pp. 57–).

74 Ibid., p. 54.

75 Sermon on John 3:8, Houghton Conquest, Liddlington and Marston, 1751/1753/1758 (ZGMSSB, p. 72).

76 Ibid., p. 73.

77 Sermon on Ecclesiastes 12:7, Houghton Conquest, 22 December 1754 (ZGMSSB, pp. 111–12).

78 Sermon on John 3:8, 1751/1753/1758 (ZGMSSB, pp. 76–8).

79 Waterland to Thomas Bishop, [*c.* 1731] (MCC/MR); D. Waterland, *Case of the Arian subscription* (1721: T116447), p. 57.

80 Sermon on Genesis 3:9 (ZGMSSC, p. 29).

81 Sermon on Psalm 16:8 (ZGMSSB, p. 50).

82 Sermon on I John 3:10, n.d. (ZGMSSB, pp. 156–7).

83 Sermon on Psalm 2:1 (ZGMSSC, p. 45); Sermon on Proverbs 17:22, Houghton Conquest, 27 July 1755 (ZGMSSC, p. 118).

84 Sermon on Ecclesiastes 12:7 (ZGMSSB, pp. 103, 106, 108).

85 Sirota, *Christian Monitors.*

86 See, for example, R. Shoemaker, 'Reforming the City: The Reformation of Manners Campaign in London, 1690–1738', in L. Davison, T. Hitchcock, T. Keirn and R. Shoemaker (eds), *Stilling the Grumbling Hive: The Response to Social and Economic Problems in England, 1689–1750* (New York, 1992), pp. 99–120; S. Burtt, 'The Societies for the Reformation of Manners: Between John Locke and the Devil in Augustan England', in R. Lund (ed.), *The Margins of Orthodoxy: Heterodox Writing and Cultural Response, 1660–1750* (Cambridge, 1995), pp. 149–69; T. Isaacs, 'The Anglican Hierarchy and the Reformation of Manners, 1688–1738', *JEH* 33 (1982), pp. 391–411; E. Duffy, 'Primitive Christianity Revived; Religious Renewal in Augustan England', *SCH* 14 (1977), pp. 287–330.

87 Cf. Rogers, *Mayhem*, pp. 137–87.

88 Harris, *Politics and the Nation*, pp. 6, 10, 16.

89 Ibid., pp. 278–323.

90 J. Innes, 'Managing the Metropolis: London's Social Problems and Their Control,

c. 1660–1830', in P. Clark and R. Gillespie (eds), *Two Capitals: London and Dublin, 1500–1840* (Oxford, 2001), pp. 53–80; J. Innes, 'Politics and Morals: The Reformation of Manners Movement in Later Eighteenth-Century England', in E. Hellmuth (ed.), *The Transformation of Political Culture* (Oxford, 1990), pp. 72–118.

91 Isaacs, 'The Anglican Hierarchy and the Reformation of Manners'; W. Jacob, *Lay People and Religion in the Early Eighteenth Century* (Cambridge, 1996), pp. 135–54.

92 Sermon on Psalm, 16:8 (ZGMSSB, p. 39).

93 Sermon on Proverbs 17:22 (ZGMSSB, pp. 126–7).

94 Sermon on Romans 14:10 (ZGMSSC, pp. 74, 75).

95 Ibid., pp. 66, 67.

96 W. Warburton, *Natural and civil events* (1756: T009119), p. 4.

97 Ibid., p. 12.

98 Warburton to Sherlock, 27 January 1738 (Kilvert, p. 53).

Part IV

The abuses of fanaticism: William Warburton

Chapter 14

The incendiaries of sedition and confusion

In March 1731, Zachary Pearce received a letter from 'W' praising his 'admirable' pamphlet, which had defended Daniel Waterland's *Scripture Vindicated* against Conyers Middleton.[1] The anonymous letter writer complimented Pearce for 'the temper of candour and integrity which you preserve amidst all the vanity, insult and ill manners of your adversary, so unbecoming the civility of his education, and the gravity of his profession'. More substantively, 'W' criticized the 'argument *ad ignoratiam*' with which Middleton had tried to rebut Waterland. However, he thought that Waterland 'had not ... acquitted himself in [*Scripture Vindicated*] with his usual dexterity'. In particular, 'W' contended that Middleton had essentially parroted 'the unsatisfactory solutions of the Commentators and officers of the objections of the Deists'. While 'W' reckoned that Pearce had 'convincingly proved' the errors of Middleton and his putatively deistic allies, he offered yet another example that Pearce might employ in future exchanges – the rainbow which followed the Noachian flood. 'Deists' insisted that, because a rainbow had appeared before the Flood, it 'could not properly be used as a token of God's covenant' because 'being a common appearance it could give no extraordinary assurance of security'. 'W' countered that 'this objection is founded on the most egregious ignorance of the nature of promises and compacts'. As he explained to Pearce, the 'security of the performance' could be grounded only 'in the evidence of the good faith of the promiser'. Given that God was the 'promiser', it was reasonable for Noah and his children to have interpreted the rainbow as a 'token of the Covenant. That is for a mark to keep up the remembrance of it.' This, 'W' noted, was '[a] method of the utmost universal practice in civil contracts'.

While Conyers Middleton had not dealt with the rainbow when writing about the Flood, he had, like other heterodox figures at the time, historicized Moses in a way that threatened to undermine the ancient legislator's credibility.[2] 'W' especially objected to Middleton's argument that Moses had used fraud to prosecute his divine mission.[3] 'Our modern infidels insist much on

Figure 5 'William Warburton', *c.* 1725–50, by John Lodge, after Thomas Worlidge

this conceit, persuading us they see a perfect semblance between his conduct and the other ancient Legislators', 'W' complained. 'And allowing their premises we must own their conclusion just, that therefore Moses was as great an Imposter as the rest.' 'W' retorted that the ancient 'pagan Legislators' had used 'fraud [as] a pretence to Divine mission', whereas God had genuinely deputed Moses as his messenger. 'W' reckoned that far closer attention needed to be paid to the claims of other ancient legislators in order to 'deduce a demonstration of Moses's divine Mission' that was unanswerable. In particular, only Moses fitted the criteria for a divinely ordained lawgiver, namely 'that a wise Legislator in making laws acts with design and for ends, and not capriciously or at random'.

'W' subsequently revealed himself to Pearce as William Warburton (1698–1779) and his interest in Moses's *bona fines* proved abiding.[4] At the time he wrote to Pearce in 1731, Warburton was a still mostly unknown Church of England parish priest in Lincolnshire, with but two minor publications to his name. By the end of the decade, he had published the first instalment of his *Divine Legation of Moses* (1738–41), which elaborated on the themes in the

1731 Pearce letter. Though Warburton eventually sat on the episcopal bench as the bishop of Gloucester, *The Divine Legation* – widely ranging, powerfully learned and seemingly wilfully perverse – remains the thing for which he is principally known.[5] Literary scholars have also concerned themselves with Warburton's friendship with and published defences of Alexander Pope and with his editions of and polemical quarrels regarding William Shakespeare.[6] This section of the book, however, focuses only tangentially on *The Divine Legation* and on Warburton's works regarding Pope and Shakespeare. Neither does it offer anything like a comprehensive treatment of Warburton's life and polymathic polemical career. Rather, it tries to show how his varied polemical interests were informed by past and present political and ecclesiastical imperatives.

To that end, Part IV of this book concentrates primarily on three of Warburton's works. Together the chapters in this part illumine how so much of Warburton's work were engagements with the previous century's 'troubles'; with the Reformation-spawned problems which had catalysed them; and with the post-revolutionary settlement which had tried to resolve them.[7] Chapter 15 deals with *The Alliance between Church and State* (1736). In that work – subsequently repurposed in the first section of the *Divine Legation of Moses* – Warburton fleshed out his thoughts on the proper relation of Church to state. The margins of his copy of Clarendon's *History of the Rebellion* reveal that he had earlier refined his thoughts on Church–state relations by thinking closely about the breakdown of the seventeenth-century English religious and political order. Chapter 16 turns to consider *Julian* (1751). In this defence of a fourth-century miracle, Warburton engaged with the history of the early Christian Church and attempted to distance himself from a prominent contemporary historian of the subject, his old friend Conyers Middleton. Chapter 17 concludes Part IV by examining *The Doctrine of Grace* (1763). That work tackled the problem of Methodist 'enthusiasm'. Again, the marginalia of one of Warburton's books sheds light on to his thinking. This time it was his detailed notes in Daniel Neal's *History of the Puritans* that catalysed his thinking about the threat that religious enthusiasts posed to the English religio-political order. This introductory chapter (Chapter 14) to Part IV charts Warburton's idiosyncratic path to polemical divinity and the principles which guided his work: it traces his path from the law to the Church. It also considers his first substantive publication, *A Critical and Philosophical Enquiry into the Causes of Prodigies* (1727). That work posited a method to distinguish truth from lies and first broached many of the subjects with which Warburton dealt during his long polemical career.

Late in that career, Warburton praised 'that Heroic Moderation so necessary to allay the violence of public disorders'. But the *moderation* he lauded had nothing to do with temperament.[8] Memorably described by Leslie Stephen as having 'led the life of a terrier in rat-pit, worrying all theological vermin',

Warburton was one of the most visible and vituperative polemical divines of his day.[9] He insisted that '[a] state of authorship is a state of war'. Though he rose to the office of a bishop in the Church of England, he reckoned that that his more important work 'in the service of religion' had been polemical, not pastoral: 'In defending Revelation, and the established church of this land against the rude attacks of ribald writers of all denominations, atheists, deists, libertines, freethinkers, bigots and fanatics; and what is the accumulation of all that is execrable in one – political scribblers of all sides and parties – the trumpeters, the incendiaries of sedition and confusion'.[10] His job as a polemical divine was, by his own estimate, to defend Truth. 'Polemical Divinity is, in the fancy of a Libertine, a squabble for preference between two Falsehoods; in which there is no room enough for ridicule', he explained, 'but on the Principles of a Believer, it is a conflict between Truth and Falsehood; in which, there is nothing to be laughed at, though much to be lamented'.[11] If Warburton was a moderate, then, it was not on account of his stridency; of his zero-sum-game understanding of polemical divinity; or of his absolutist non-relativism. He was but an especially rebarbative member of that notably belligerent species, the eighteenth-century polemical divine: as Neville Figgis put it, '[h]e was a born Ishmaelite'.[12]

Nonetheless Warburton perplexed his contemporaries. An obituarist observed, '[a]t the outset of his life, he was suspected of being inclined to infidelity, and it was not until many years had elapsed, that the orthodoxy of his opinions was generally assented to'.[13] Subsequent historians have likewise struggled to pigeonhole him. Some have highlighted his singularity. Thomas Whitaker long ago contended that 'Warburton was a kind of comet which came athwart a system of the Church of England, at a time when all its movements were proceeding with an uniformity extremely unfavourable to the appearance of such a phaenomenon'.[14] Mark Pattison similarly suggested that Warburton belonged to none of the major parties of the mid-eighteenth century, but, instead, 'came athwart all of them at one period or another in his bellicose career'. Isaac Disraeli likened Warburton to a 'portentous meteor' which 'seemed unconnected with the whole planetary system through which it rolled'.[15] Others, by contrast, cast him as a figure emblematic of his age. Figgis insisted that Warburton's 'writings express for us with a fidelity, of which he was unaware, certain of the most important and characteristic aspects of the eighteenth century'. His early twentieth-century biographer likewise reckoned that in Warburton it was uniquely 'possible to see many of the characteristic features of the time more distinctly or in bolder relief', including what he characterized as its 'didactic and argumentative temper; its rationalizing philosophy; its prudential ethics; its self-confidence; its intellectualist conception of religion; its distrust and dislike of everything that it called "enthusiasm"; its cultivation of the spirit of inquiry; [and] its growing toleration'.[16] More recently, he has been held up as the exemplar of a putative English 'Moderation'.[17] John Pocock ranks the *Divine Legation* with

Gibbon's *Decline and Fall of the Roman Empire* as the two 'principal achievements of the "conservative Enlightenment" in Hanoverian England'.[18] There is, then, no consensus about how to characterize Warburton. Perhaps it might simply be said that that while Warburton's conclusions were almost always orthodox, his proofs were sometimes idiosyncratic, and that. while he eventually became a member of the ecclesiastical establishment, he was in it but not of it.[19] His sometime friend Conyers Middleton put it best, shortly after the *Divine Legation*'s publication. Warburton 'has lived wholly in the Country and writes with the spirit of one, who has been long used to dictate to the Provincial Clergy around him', Middleton explained to Lord Hervey. 'But when he has been exercised awhile in controversy, ... he will make a very considerable writer; for though he is ingenious, lively and learned, yet he often disputes, for want only of conversing with men of sense, or being lashed a little by the hand of a smart adversary.'[20] Warburton was orthodox but bumptious. His contemporaries also regarded his work as unquestionably important.

William Warburton was born on Christmas Eve 1698, the son of a Newark lawyer and town clerk named George Warburton and his wife, Elizabeth, herself the daughter of a Newark alderman. Warburton's paternal grandfather, also named William and also an attorney, had been a Royalist during the English Civil War and had fought against the parliamentary forces in Booth's Rising in 1659; his grandmother had regaled him with stories of the seventeenth-century English history. This all clearly sparked some interest in him, for his protégé Richard Hurd later reported that Warburton used to say that 'there was scarce a pamphlet and memoir published between 1640 and 1660, which he had not read'. 'And thus', Hurd concluded, 'he not only acquired an early insight into that part of our history, but continued through life to be so fond of it, that he had thoughts, at one time, of writing the history of the civil wars'.[21] Though Warburton never wrote that history, the seventeenth-century English experience persistently shaped his views of the present.

Warburton's polemical divinity also bore the mark of his early training in the law. He went first to the school in Newark run by John Twells (the author of five works on oratory, eloquence and grammar) and then to the grammar school in Oakham, Rutland, where he would have learned some Latin and Greek.[22] In 1714, when he was sixteen, he returned home to study under his cousin, also named William Warburton, a fellow of St John's College, Cambridge, who in 1714 became the new master of the Newark grammar school.[23] That same year, though, he was articled to an attorney, John Kirke of East Markham, Nottinghamshire, under whom he apprenticed for five years. In training for a legal career, Warburton followed in the steps of his own attorney father, who had died in 1706, leaving behind his wife, William, another son and two daughters. Given the circumstances, Elizabeth

Warburton's decision to article her oldest son as an apprentice to an attorney would have been prudent: it trained him for a career that was eminently respectable and potentially lucrative.[24]

It is unclear what Warburton did during his five years as a legal clerk. The work of an eighteenth-century law clerk was normally marked by drudgery, but it aimed to prepare the apprentice for the practical and technical problems that regularly confronted attorneys. While Warburton fulfilled the terms of his apprenticeship, legal work seems not to have captured his imagination. Hurd acknowledged that he did his duties 'with no signal assiduity'. Instead, he evidently carved out time to read widely both in the classics and in more contemporary works so that 'by the time his clerkship was out, [he] had laid the foundation, as well as acquired a taste, of general knowledge'.[25] Some contended that he was admitted to one of the inns of court in London after his clerkship ended in 1719, and he seems briefly to have practised law in Newark.[26] What is certain is that he soon abandoned a career in the law for one in the Church. Nevertheless, his legal apprenticeship left its mark on him. Contemporaries, like Robert Lowth, mocked him for his early legal training, highlighting, by implication, that Warburton, unlike most polemical divines, had not gone to university.[27] It hardly seems cod psychology to suggest that Warburton's later ostentatious displays of erudition were some sort of compensation for his lack of formal higher education. More importantly, though, Warburton's relentlessly litigious polemical style was singular, something which many traced to the law's influence upon him. His friend William Stukeley contended that Warburton had 'quite mistook his talent when he entered into holy orders, for had he followed the bar he must needs have advanced himself exceedingly'.[28] Later historians agreed. He was, jibed one biographer, 'the Judge Jeffreys of English theological quarrels'; Leslie Stephen reckoned that he 'brought to theological controversies the habits of mind required in an attorney's office'.[29] The effect often backfired. As Samuel Johnson rightly observed, '[h]is abilities gave him a haughty confidence which he disdained to conceal or mollify, and his impatience of opposition disposed him to treat his adversaries with such contemptuous superiority as made his readers commonly his enemies, and excited against the advocate the wishes of some who favoured the cause'.[30]

By the time Warburton first met Johnson in 1742, he had long ago left the law and had become an ordained clergyman in the established Church of England. Why he switched careers remains elusive. Hurd explained that 'the love of letters growing every day stronger in him, it was found advisable to give way to his inclination of taking Orders: the rather, as the seriousness of his temper and purity of his morals concurred with his unappeasable thirst of knowledge, to give the surest presages of future eminence in that profession'.[31] Warburton had also got a patron, Sir Robert Sutton (1671–1746), an MP and sometime diplomat who promised him ecclesiastical preferment if he took holy orders.[32] Sutton proved a reliable and effective patron and

Warburton, a grateful client.[33] Warburton's uncle, Samuel Rastall, a former Newark mayor, was also instrumental in securing some of his early livings.[34] To prepare for the priesthood, Warburton studied under his cousin, the Newark grammar school master. In December 1723, Archbishop William Dawes ordained him a deacon in York cathedral. Four years later, Edmund Gibson ordained him into the priesthood in London, when Warburton was twenty-eight years old. Once ordained, he became a pluralist, serving as rector of Newton Blossomville, Buckinghamshire, for a year (1726–27); as first preacher and then vicar of Greasely, Nottinghamshire, for four years (1727–30); and as rector of Irby on the Humber for another year (1727–28), before Sutton named him rector of Brant Broughton, Lincolnshire, a living he held from 1728 until his death in 1779.[35]

During his nearly two decades actually living in Brant Broughton ('a good Living, but no society in it') Warburton pursued a programme of reading and writing that marvelled contemporaries.[36] The parish was small, with around fifty families, 10 per cent of whom were religious Dissenters of one sort or another.[37] Though there is no indication that Warburton did not perform his pastoral duties, his intellectual pursuits clearly mattered more to him. 'Impatient of any interruptions, he spent the whole of his time that could be spared from the duties of his parish, in reading and writing', Richard Hurd recorded. '... [A]nd a change of reading, or study, was his only amusement.'[38] The result of this two-decade intensive reading programme was an impressive, if unsystematic, erudition. The Cambridge classicist Richard Bentley remarked after reading *The Divine Legation of Moses* 'that the author had a voracious appetite for knowledge, but he doubted whether he had good digestion'.[39] Samuel Johnson likewise commented disparagingly on Warburton's seemingly indiscriminate learning. 'He was a man of vigorous faculties, a mind fervent and vehement, supplied by incessant and unlimited enquiry, with wonderful extent and variety of knowledge, which yet had not oppressed his imagination nor clouded his perspicacity', Johnson observed. '... But his knowledge was too multifarious to be always exact, and his pursuits too eager to be always conscious'.[40]

Warburton formed important literary connections even before entering into the priesthood. One literary friend was William Stukeley (1687–1765), with whom Warburton 'became acquainted about 1718, and afterwards ... entered into the most intimate friendship, always visiting or writing to one another'.[41] A decade older than Warburton, Stukeley had, like his younger friend, been a law clerk, before studying medicine at Cambridge. Around the time he met Warburton, Stukeley was admitted to fellowship in the Royal Society and had recently helped to re-establish the Society of Antiquaries. Both these brought him into the orbit of London-based authors, including Isaac Newton. Stukeley conceived of his scholarly work, both on natural philosophy and on Druidical circles at Stonehenge and Avebury as part of a Newtonian project to recover 'the long-lost truth'.[42] Stukeley contended, for instance, that the

'British Druids' were Christians *avant la lettre*, a group who had come to the British Isles during Abraham's lifetime and who 'brought along with them the patriarchal religion, which was so extremely like Christianity'. Moreover, they were a group with a purpose and 'had separated from the gross of mankind, to stifle the seeds of idolatry'.[43] Warburton travelled with Stukeley to some of the archaeological sites at which he researched England's ancient religious past. Through Stukeley, Warburton also met others, including the antiquarian Francis Peck, the physician and philosopher David Hartley and a fellow polemical divine, John Towne. Stukeley also brought him into the Spalding Gentleman's Society.[44] To Stukeley Warburton also first confided his designs for *The Divine Legation of Moses*, though putting him 'under great injunction of secrecy, for fear somebody should steal his notion & publish it for their own'. Yet while the two remained in contact throughout their lives, their friendship 'cool[e]d' markedly because Stukeley, like most at the time, doubted Warburton's central premise, contending instead 'that it was impossible any religion should come from God without the sanction of future life'. Stukeley insisted that 'this difference had not the least influence upon my friendship toward him, for I admired him as a true genius'; Warburton, evidently, felt otherwise.[45] After Stukeley's death in 1765, Warburton recollected archly that there was in his friend 'such a mixture of simplicity, drollery, absurdity, ingenuity, superstition, and antiquarianism, ... a compound of things never meant to meet together'.[46]

In addition to Stukeley, Warburton had connections with other literary figures in London, a group Mark Pattison later snidely characterized as 'a coffee-house set of fourth-rate literati'.[47] Among the most significant for Warburton were Matthew Concanen, Lewis Theobald and Sir Thomas Hanmer. Concanen (1701–49), whom Warburton seems first to have met during a visit to London in late 1726, was an Irish pamphleteer and lawyer who defended the Walpolean Whigs during the late 1720s and early 1730s and who publicly aspersed the poet Alexander Pope, aspersions evidently assisted by Warburton himself.[48] Warburton later abjured their friendship. Another in Concanen's circle who assisted him in his anti-Pope publications was Lewis Theobald (1688–1744). Theobald was both an attorney and a literary editor, who made his name as an editor of Shakespeare. During the early 1730s, Theobald turned to Warburton for advice on variant readings of Shakespeare's works. Theobald's edition pointedly aimed to expose 'the many Errors, as well Commented, as Unamended' by Alexander Pope in his 1725 edition of Shakespeare's works. Warburton's expertise derived solely from wide reading: 'I used to make it one good part of my amusement in reading the English Poets, those of them I mean whose vein flows regularly and constantly, as well as clearly, to trace them to their sources; and observe what ore, as well as what slime and gravel they brought down with them'.[49] Shakespeare was among those 'English Poets', and Theobald's extensive correspondence with Warburton testifies to the degree to which the

Lincolnshire rector assisted him in the task of 'restor[ing] the True Reading of Shakespeare'.[50] Yet it too was a collaborative partnership from which Warburton would later distance himself. As Warburton later described it, Theobald 'wanted Money', and so 'I allowed him to print what I gave him for his own Advantage: and he allowed himself the Liberty of taking one Part of his own, and sequestering another for the Benefit, as I supposed, of some future Edition'.[51] The fault, as ever, was not Warburton's. Another Shakespearean editor who benefited from Warburton's assistance was Sir Thomas Hanmer (1677–1746), formerly a Tory MP and speaker of the House of Commons, who eventually produced a quarto edition, published by Oxford University Press in 1744.[52] Again, the collaboration fell apart after an amiable start. Hanmer, Warburton later griped, was 'absolutely ignorant of the Art of Criticism, as well as of the Poetry of that Time, and the Language of his Author'. For that reason, he 'wanted nothing but what he might very well be without, the Reputation of a Critic, [and] I could not so easily forgive him for trafficking with my papers without my Knowledge; and, when the Project failed, for employing a number of my Conjectures against my express Desire not to have the Honour done unto me'.[53] Scholars now generally agree that Hanmer's edition was 'ponderous'. They also rate Theobald's Shakespearean scholarship far superior to that on display in Warburton's own 1747 edition, notwithstanding Warburton's title, *The Works of Shakespear[e] … Restored from the Blunders of the First Editors, and the Interpolations of the Two Last*.[54]

While Warburton devoted much energy to his literary scholarship, it was for his theological work, not his editorial service, that he was and is principally known. The first significant piece he published was *A Critical and Philosophical Enquiry into the Causes of Prodigies and Miracles*, a work he later disavowed and sought to suppress.[55] In a letter to Hurd three decades later, he protested, 'I was very much a boy when I wrote that thing about Prodigies, and I had never the courage to look into it since; so I have forgot all the nonsense that it contains'. He blamed Matthew Concanen for the book having appeared in print at all. 'I met many years ago with an ingenious Irishman at a Coffee-house near Gray's Inn, where I lodged. He studied the law, and was very poor', Warburton protested. 'I had given him money for many a dinner; and, at last, I gave him those papers, which he sold to the booksellers for more money than you would think, much more than they were worth.' Warburton recollected that, after Concanen had sold the manuscript of *A Critical and Philosophical Enquiry* to the press, he met a Walpolean MP named Sir William Yonge (1693–1755), who got him writing in defence of the Walpolean administration. Concanen subsequently got rewarded by being named attorney-general in Jamaica, where he married 'an opulent widow' and returned to England a rich man. He was, Warburton claimed, 'of so scoundrel a temper, that he avoided ever coming into my sight'.[56] The problem with this explanation is that, where it is not patently wrong, it jibes uneasily with the evidence from the late 1720s and early 1730s. Though Warburton's *Critical and Philosophical Enquiry* did not have his name on the title-page, he nonetheless handed out presentation copies. Furthermore, Warburton had not cut off relations with Concanen before the latter shipped off to Jamaica in late 1732; indeed he wrote a positively oleaginous congratulatory letter to him on learning of his appointment the post.[57] What had changed between Concanen's decampment for Jamaica in the early 1730s and Warburton's recollection in the late 1750s was that Warburton had, in the interim, made a name for himself not as Alexander Pope's critic but as a defender so ardent that Pope had named him his literary executor. That early association with the anti-Popish Concanen, then, was later a source of great embarrassment.

It is harder, though, to see what would have mortified Warburton about the *Critical and Philosophical Enquiry*, written when he was twenty-nine and hardly the work of 'a boy'. The work was entirely of a piece with his mature mode of argument and with the principles which guided him in those arguments. It concerned prodigies, miracles and their evidences. Prodigies and miracles had long been understood as tools and as evidence of God's providential management of his Creation. Until recently, historians routinely noted the erosion of this providential worldview during the seventeenth and eighteenth centuries, thanks to Protestantism and natural science, the twin engines of the 'disenchantment of the world': Protestantism rejected Catholic mysteries, including those in nature, while the new natural science explained how nature worked, not what it meant.[58] None of this is quite so obvious now, and, indeed, recent historians have shown how nature remained 'God's great book in folio' long after its putative disenchantment.[59] Perhaps for this reason, eighteenth-century English debates over miracles were mostly about the evidences for the miraculous rather than about the existence of miracles themselves. Certainly this was Warburton's concern in the *Critical and Philosophical Enquiry* and again two decades later in *Julian*. So too did prodigies – divinely instructive events that lay somewhere on the continuum between the miraculous and the unusual – remain live possibilities well into the eighteenth century: at issue were the evidences for prodigious events.[60]

Warburton's *Critical and Philosophical Enquiry* was not, as some have claimed, 'the most definitive statement of the anti-providential view of prodigies' since John Spencer's *Discourse concerning prodigies* (1663).[61] Rather it was a work which enunciated a method for distinguishing between real and unreal miracles and prodigies or, more pointedly, between truth and lies. This was important, Warburton contended, because 'while the other Sciences are daily Purging and refining themselves from the Pollutions of superstitious Error, that have been collecting throughout a long Winter of Ignorance and Barbarism; History ... contracts the more Filth, and retains it in the additional Ordure of every Soil through which it passes'.[62] There were, he asserted, four principal causes of error: superstition; 'weakness of mind'; 'national pride'; and 'the knavery of the writer'. Superstition, the most obvious cause of error, was the one to which Warburton devoted the least space, reckoning as he did that, while it was a besetting sin of 'the whole Mob of monkish Writers', it was not 'so universal a Practice in Men of all Religions, Times and Temperatures'. Nonetheless, he acknowledged superstition's 'Capacity for universal Sway, throughout the large Wastes of History. It runs through every Order of Historians, from the visionary Midnight Monk, to the sharp-sighted, exalted Statesman, long hackneyed in the Ways of Men'.[63]

The rest of Warburton's *Critical and Philosophical Enquiry* focused on what he took to be the other causes of error, which he thought were consistently present in all times and places. 'Weakness' of mind, by which Warburton meant the human mind's inherent and unfixably imperfect nature, topped that list. 'There is a Flaw, which was certainly in the original Formation of the Mind, that all its Reason could never solder', he argued. 'But it will ever be an Inlet, and most hospitable Harbour of Imposture; of which nothing is a more clear and melancholy Proof, than our great Facility in deceiving ourselves, and our Complaisancy and Constancy in the Cheat'.[64] One needed only look to the works of Pliny the Elder (*c.* 23–79) or into Thomas Browne's *Pseudodoxia Epidemica* (1646) to discover 'with what Zeal the sacred Depositum of Error has been transmitted from Age to Age, for Two thousand Years together, through all the Changes and Subversions of Religion, Customs and Civil Government'.[65] The chief things which weaken the mind are 'Admiration' ('one of the most bewitching, enthusiastic passions of the mind') and the conjoined passions from which 'Admiration' itself springs, 'Novelty and Surprize, the inseparable Attendants of Imposture'. As a result, lies have 'no Antitypes in Nature'; they are, instead, 'put together at the pleasure of the Inventor'.[66] For Warburton, then, lies are artificial creations which originate from and are accepted and perpetuated by minds that are enslaved to one or another passion. Truth, by contrast, is a passionless product, the result 'of much cooler Contemplation; as paying its court to the Understanding only, by affording a regular View of its simple univocal Original, with the universal Relation, Dependence and Harmony of its Parts'. As Warburton stressed, '[s]o calm a Prospect often raises no Emotion, or but that of the lowest kind, which we call Approbation'.[67] Taming the passions countervailed 'the disordered Imagination'.[68]

If the human mind's inherent weakness begat error, so too did 'national pride'. Whereas the mind's weakness results from a deficit of a good thing (reason), national pride was the surfeit of good thing ('the noblest Cause in the World, the Love of one's Country').[69] Warburton reckoned that the 'Love of the Species' was something 'implanted in the Mind by Nature' and that happiness consists in seeking it; indeed, 'our Enquiry, at length, discovers that nothing can produce this Happiness, but public Liberty' and that obtaining that happiness is nothing but trying to gratify 'the noblest of [our] innate Passions', something recognized by everyone from 'Moses to William the Third'.[70] As such, Warburton bore special animosity for those he referred to as 'a Sect of Anti Moralists', which included Thomas Hobbes ('the jolly Philosopher of Malmesbury') and François, duc de la Rochefoucauld (1613–80). He hated them because they 'endeavour[ed] to create a Contempt and Horror' of the species, which undermined the conjoined 'ancient Doctrine[s] of the Dignity of human Nature and public Liberty'.[71] Hobbes he especially excoriated for his 'Hypothesis of human Baseness'; Warburton contended that Hobbes could only have developed that hypothesis out of an insufficient acquaintance with antiquity, Hobbes's translations of Thucydides and Homer notwithstanding.[72]

Whereas Hobbes, Rochefoucauld and their like were misguidedly wrong, other historians intentionally misled their readers, so that 'knavery of the writer' was Warburton's fourth main cause of error. The main reason that historians have purposely deceived their readers was to 'catch the applause of the people'.[73] By way of example, Warburton held up René Aubert, Abbé de Vertot (1655–1735), who wrote histories of revolutions in the Roman republic, Portugal and Sweden. In his work on the Roman republic, in particular, Vertot highlighted the inherent instability of republics and the degree to which 'Luxury and Softness' weakened the republic despite the best efforts of its leaders; the durable virtues, by contrast, were those of the aristocrats who populated the Senate.[74] Warburton, by contrast, thought that Vertot's fixation upon revolutions both distorted his reading of history and risked corrupting his readers' minds. To begin with, '[t]he busy, active Catastrophe of Revolutions, gives a tumultuous kind of Pleasure to those vulgar Minds, that remain unaffected with the calm Scenes, that the still and steady Advances of a well balanced State, to secure its Peace, Power and Durability, present before them'. Moreover, revolutions are 'the great Repository of all the Stores for Admiration, whose Power and Fascination on the Fancy, we have at large examined: Whereas the steady Part affords Entertainment only for the Understanding, by its sober Lessons on public Utility'.[75] Playing upon this, 'French Charlatans' like Vertot tried to trick their readers into believing that monarchical regimes were the only durable ones; Warburton (citing Machiavelli's *Discourses on Livy* by way of evidence) insisted that 'those that are the least acquainted with Civil History, must know, that the Equilibrium of Power, so essential to a free State' was made possible by the division of power such as that in the Roman republic and, by implication, in eighteenth-century English constitutional government.[76] Yet, Warburton lamented, modern historians had done a terrible job of demonstrating just that. English historians were especially culpable, with two notable exceptions: Sir Walter Raleigh and Edward Hyde, the earl of Clarendon. Raleigh 'excell[ed] in Grandeur and Majesty of Thought, equal to the Subject he undertook', while Clarendon, 'for his comprehensive Knowledge of Mankind will for ever bear the unrivalled Title of the Chancellor of human Nature'. In Clarendon's *History of the Rebellion*, Warburton contended, 'there are more and far greater Excellencies than in the whole Body of Ancient History. It is, indeed, the only one of English

History we can glory in'. Because Clarendon appreciated human nature for what it was, he, unlike his French counterparts, wrote histories that were deeply true, their epiphenomenal errors notwithstanding. By comparison, the other English histories were a 'mere Hodge-podge of abortive Embryos, and rotten Carcases, kept in an unnatural Ferment (which the Vulgar mistake for real Life) by the Rank Leven of Prodigies and Portents'.[77]

If Warburton's contemporaries would only approach the study of history mindful of the causes of error, they too could produce histories comparable to Raleigh's *History of the World* and Clarendon's *History of the Rebellion*. Those histories, Warburton made clear, might legitimately consider God's providential treatment of one nation as against another. He acknowledged that '[t]he ordinary Dispensations of Providence are dark and perplexing and have ever wore a double Face; from which, with equal Force, may be drawn Conclusions, according to the Humour or Interest of the Contemplator'. Nonetheless, much about providence might be understood by a proper historian, not the least because a historian had credible miracles and prodigies as evidences for God's providential management. The trick was to distinguish the credible from the incredible. Like most of his contemporaries, Warburton thought neither the miraculous nor the prodigious were metaphysically impossible, since '[t]he Interposition of Providence in human Affairs has all the Marks of Truth, that such a Thing is capable of'.[78] To be credible, a miracle or prodigy had to pass two tests. Firstly, it had to have 'Universal Consent in Testimony, and Opinion' – the corrosive effects of 'sceptical and Idle Wits' with their 'sophistical Distinctions and Distinctions' notwithstanding. Secondly, credible miracles or prodigies needed to be 'Interposition[s] in Favour of the common Principles of Morality and Religion', which 'fixes the Features, and leaves no Room for an ambiguous Meaning'.[79] If these two tests were passed, then miracles and prodigies could be included in civil histories as evidence of God's providential management of human affairs. He pursued the subject more deeply two and a half decades later in *Julian*, but he first broached it in the *Critical and Philosophical Enquiry*.

That 1727 book, unlike much of Warburton's later works, did not receive widespread critical comment. *Critical and Philosophical Enquiry*'s beginning and end, though, drew notice. The book closed with a plagiarized bit from John Milton's *Areopagitica* (1644), while it opened with a fawning dedication to Warburton's patron, Sir Robert Sutton ('A True Englishman').[80] The dedication concluded with the lament that Sutton's 'great Name can but lift me up to be the more exposed; while, like young Euryalus in the shining Helmet of the divine Messapus, my bright Defence but makes me the more obnoxious to Danger; safe had I been contented in my native Obscurity'.[81] As it turned out, Sutton, not Warburton, soon faced public punishment. In 1732, he got expelled from the House of Commons, for 'neglect of duty' in his role on a committee managing the Charitable Corporation. An opposition MP, Samuel Sandys, chaired the committee investigating the corporation and hoped those investigations would embarrass Walpole. Disgraced, Sutton left Parliament, only to be re-elected by a venal borough in the 1734 election; but his active political career was over.[82] However, Warburton, who normally showed no compunction before hopping off a losing horse, publicly defended Sutton. In particular, he penned a long *Apology for Sir Robert Sutton* (1733), in which he brought to bear his earlier legal training to rebut the charges against the disgraced MP which had been levelled by 'the Bigots of Mammon or Spleen' whose censures were but 'the Overflowings of Ignorance, Avarice or Prejudice'.[83] The *Apology* was no vacuous encomium to Sutton's supposed virtues but instead was a lengthy, closely argued forensic defence of Sutton's record on the committee.[84] During the early 1740s, Warburton intervened with Alexander Pope on Sutton's behalf. In his *Epistle to Bathurst* and the *Epilogue to the Satires*, Pope had pilloried Sutton. Warburton subsequently pleaded with Pope to remove Sutton's name, noting, 'I have known this Gentleman about 20 years'. Sutton, Warburton acknowledged, had tried to profit from the Charitable Corporation, 'Yet I am sure with a view of an honest profit. For he is very far from an avaricious man' but was instead someone who 'lives up to his fortune, without being guilty of any vice or Luxury' and was 'an extreme good and faithful Husband'; a 'tender and indulgent Father'; and 'a kind master and one of the best Landlords to his Tenants'.[85] The appeal worked, and Pope removed Sutton's name from his texts.[86] By the time Warburton wrote to Pope, he and the poet had become friends, and Warburton had made a name for himself as author of the *Divine Legation of Moses*. But it was his *Alliance between Church and State* (1736) that had first earned him notice as a polemical divine. That work both evinced the influence of his historiographical hero, Clarendon, and offered a novel solution to the problems Clarendon had highlighted in his *History of the Rebellion*.

NOTES

1 [William Warburton] to Pearce, 4 March 1731 (WAM 64779). Unless otherwise noted, all quotations in this and the next paragraph draw from this letter. Cf. Warburton to William Stukeley, 4 February 1732 (Bodleian, Eng.lett.d.35, fol. 22), in which Warburton complained that 'Pierce is a heavy writer', while 'Middleton writes very agreeably', though 'in his vindication of his letter has run into a great absurdity'. See also Warburton's annotations to Matthew Tindal's *Christianity as old as the creation* (HL, R.a.23).

2 [C. Middleton], *Defence of the letter to Dr. Waterland* (1731: T032264), pp. 66–7, deals with the Noachian flood.

3 Cf. J. Champion, *Republican learning: John Toland and the Crisis of Christian Culture, 1696–1722* (Manchester, 2003), pp. 173–85.

4 B. Young, 'William Warburton (1698–1779)', *ODNB*; A. Evans, *Warburton and the Warburtonians* (Oxford, 1932); W. Watson, *The Life of William Warburton*

(1863). B. Young, *Religion and Enlightenment in Eighteenth-Century England* (Oxford, 1998), pp. 167–212, is especially perceptive.

5 J. Assmann, *Moses the Egyptian: The Memory of Egypt in Western Monotheism* (Cambridge, MA, 1998), pp. 96–115; J. Assmann, *Religio Duplex: How the Enlightenment Reinvented Egyptian Religion* (Cambridge, 2014), pp. 61–73; Pocock, *Barbarism and Religion*, V, pp. 230–7; J. Robertson, *The Case for the Enlightenment: Scotland and Naples, 1680–1760* (Cambridge, 2005), pp. 280–3; P. Rossi, *Dark Abyss of Time*, trans. L. Cochrane (Chicago, 1984), pp. 236–45; J. Sheehan, 'Suffering Job: Christianity Beyond Metaphysics', in W. Bulman and R. Ingram (eds), *God in the Enlightenment* (Oxford, 2016), pp. 182–200. D. Levitin, *Ancient Wisdom in the Age of the New Science: Histories of Philosophy in England, c. 1640–1700* (Cambridge, 2015), p. 229, reckons the *Divine Legation* was a 'populist' work. For earlier treatments, J. Stephen, *Horae Sabbaticae* (London, 1892), II, pp. 315–32; L. Stephen, *History of English Thought in the Eighteenth Century* (1902), II, pp. 355–65.

6 B. Young, 'Pope and Ideology', in P. Rogers (ed.), *Cambridge Companion to Alexander Pope* (Cambridge, 2007), pp. 118–33; B. Young, '"See Mystery to Mathematics fly": Pope's *Dunciad* and the Critique of Religious Rationalism', *ECS* 26 (1993), pp. 435–48; M. Walsh, *Shakespeare, Milton and Eighteenth-Century Literary Editing* (Cambridge, 1997), 149–75; S. Jarvis, *Scholars and Gentlemen: Shakespearean Textual Criticism and Representations of Scholarly Labour, 1725–1765* (Oxford, 1995), pp. 107–28, 175–80; P. Seary, *Lewis Theobald and the Editing of Shakespeare* (Oxford, 1990), pp. 102–30.

7 Cf. Stephen, *Horae Sabbaticae*, II, pp. 333–48.

8 W. Warburton, *Divine Legation of Moses* (1765: T214226), dedication.

9 L. Stephen, *Essays on Freethinking and Plainspeaking* (London, 1873), p. 280.

10 W. Warburton, 'Thoughts on Various Subjects', in Kilvert, p. 342; Warburton, 'Speech in the House of Lords on the Prosecution of Mr Wilkes, 15 November 1763', in ibid., pp. 281–2.

11 W. Warburton, *Doctrine of Grace*, in *WWW*, VIII, p. 309.

12 J. Figgis, 'William Warburton', in W. Collins (ed.), *Typical English Churchmen* (1902), p. 245.

13 *Westminster Magazine* (1779), p. 663.

14 *Quarterly Review* (1812), p. 383.

15 M. Pattison, 'Life of Bishop Warburton', in Nettleship (ed.), *Essays by ... Mark Pattison* (Oxford, 1889), p. 120; I. Disraeli, *Quarrels of Authors* (New York, 1814), I, p. 3.

16 Figgis, 'William Warburton', p. 216; Evans, *Warburton and the Warburtonians*, pp. 2–3.

17 D. Sorkin, *The Religious Enlightenment: Protestants, Jews and Catholics from London to Vienna* (Princeton, 2008), pp. 25–65.

18 J. Pocock, *Barbarism and Religion: Volume 5. Religion: The First Triumph* (Cambridge, 2015), p. 230. See also J. Pocock, 'Clergy and Commerce: The Conservative Enlightenment in England', in R. Ajello and F. Venturi (eds), *L'eta dei Lumi* (Naples, 1985), pp. 525–62.

19 Disraeli, *Quarrels*, I, pp. 25–6, argued that Warburton had modelled himself on Pierre Bayle and had imitated Bayle by introducing 'Invention' into his works, 'a

talent, indeed, somewhat dangerous to introduce in researches where Truth, and not Fancy, was to be addressed'.

20 Middleton to Hervey, 9 March 1738 (BL, Add. 32457, fol. 37).

21 R. Hurd, 'A Discourse of a General Preface ...; containing Some Account of the Life, Writings and Character of the Author', in *WWW*, I, p. 73.

22 W. Page (ed.), *A History of the County of Nottingham* (London, 1910), II, p. 211.

23 *AC*, IV, p. 330.

24 R. Robson, *The Attorney in Eighteenth-Century England* (Cambridge, 1959), pp. 52–83; C. Brooks, *Lawyers, Litigation and English Society since 1450* (London, 1994), pp. 149–64. Warburton's premium of £95 was on the high end of premiums during the period (Robson, *Attorney*, p. 55).

25 Hurd, 'Life', p. 4.

26 *Westminster Magazine* (1779), p. 500; *LA*, V, pp. 531–3; Stukeley, *Family Memoirs of ... William Stukeley* (Durham, 1882–87), I, p. 129. There were even rumours that he was, for a time, a wine merchant or a schoolmaster: Watson, *Life*, p. 7.

27 Warburton's first patron, Sir Robert Sutton, got Warburton an M.A. from Cambridge during the king's visit of 1728: William Stukeley to Maurice Johnson, mid/late April 1728 (D. Honeybone and M. Honeybone (eds), *The Correspondence of William Stukeley and Maurice Johnson, 1714–1754* (Woodbridge, 2014), p. 205).

28 Stukeley, *Family Memoirs*, I, p. 129.

29 G. Kitchin, *Seven Sages* (1911), p. 235; Stephen, *Essays on Freethinking*, p. 280.

30 S. Johnson, *Lives of the Poets*, ed. J. Middendorf (New Haven, 2010), IV, p. 41.

31 Hurd, 'Life', p. 5.

32 Johnson, *Lives of the Poets*, ed. Middendorf, I, p. 384.

33 Warburton to Alexander Pope, [1743/1744] (Hurd Library, MS 16, no. 2).

34 Rastall to Newcastle, 4 July 1725; Warburton to Newcastle, 19 July 1735 (BL, Add. 32687, fols 109, 115). See also Warburton to Newcastle, 11 November 1727 (ibid., fol. 233).

35 *CCED*. Greasley was in the gift of George I, who presumably named Warburton vicar at the suggestion of the duke of Newcastle. Newcastle was the patron of both Irby on the Humber and Firsby, Leicestershire, while Sutton was patron of Brant Broughton. While rector of Brant Broughton, Warburton also served as rector of Firsby (1730–56), though he never resided there. *GM* XC (1820), p. 200, defends Warburton's pastoral provision of Firsby, while noting that he was not a good superintendent of its income.

36 Stukeley, *Family Memoirs*, I, p. 128; Johnson, *Lives of the Poets*, ed. Middendorf, p. 128.

37 J. Broad, *Bishop Wake's Summary of visitation Returns from the Diocese of Lincoln, 1706–1715. Part 1: Lincolnshire* (Oxford, 2012), pp. 334–5.

38 Hurd, 'Life', pp. 9–10.

39 J. Monk, *The Life of Richard Bentley* (1833), II, p. 410.

40 Johnson, *Lives of the Poets*, ed. Middendorf, IV, p. 41. See also J. Mitford (ed.), *Correspondence of Thomas Gray and William Mason* (1853), p. 39.

41 Stukeley, *Family Memoirs*, I, p. 127.

42 D. Haycock, *William Stukeley: Science, Religion, and Archaeology in Eighteenth-Century England* (Woodbridge, 2002); P. Monod, *Solomon's Secret Arts: The Occult in the Age of Enlightenment* (New Haven, 2013), pp. 167–79.

43 W. Stukeley, *Stonehenge* ((1740): T146679), I, p. 2.
44 Stukeley to Maurice Johnson, 31 January 1729 (Honeybone (ed.), *Correspondence*, p. 57).
45 Stukeley, *Family Memoirs*, I, p. 127. Cf. Stukeley to Johnson, 5 January 1744 (Honeybone (ed.), *Correspondence*, p. 86).
46 Warburton to Hurd, March 1765 (*LLEP*, p. 358).
47 Pattison, 'Life of Bishop Warburton', p. 123.
48 J. Sambrook, 'Matthew Concanen (1701–1749)', *ODNB*; S. Targett, 'Government and Ideology during the Age of Whig Supremacy: The Political Argument of Sir Robert Walpole's Newspapers Propagandists', *HJ* 37 (1994), pp. 289–317; L. Hanson, *Government and the Press, 1695–1763* (Oxford, 1967), p. 111.
49 Warburton to Concanen, 2 January 1727 (*LI*, II, p. 195).
50 The Warburton–Theobald correspondence is in BL, Egerton 1956; Folger Shakespeare, W.6.74, W.64.75; R. Jones, *Lewis Theobald* (New York, 1919), pp. 258–346. Cf. Warburton to Robert Taylor, 22 November 1729 (HRC, Warburton I, 7–12); Warburton to Hurd, 12 January 1757 (*LLEP*, pp. 224–5). Seary, *Lewis Theobald*, pp. 102–30, assesses Warburton's contributions to Theobald's work; Walsh, *Shakespeare, Milton and Eighteenth-Century Literary Editing*, pp. 126–49, anatomizes Theobald's attacks on Pope.
51 W. Warburton (ed.), *Works of Shakespear[e]* (1747: T138851), I, p. vii.
52 The Warburton–Hanmer correspondence is in BL, Egerton 1957. On Hanmer's edition, see A. Murphy, *Shakespeare in Print: A History and Chronology of Shakespeare Publishing* (Cambridge, 2003), pp. 110–14.
53 Warburton (ed.), *Works of Shakespear[e]*, I, p. viii, ix. Cf. Warburton to Hanmer, 21 May 1739 (Pierpont Morgan Library, Misc Bishops English, MA Unassigned) in which Warburton spelled out what he understood the nature of his relationship with Hanmer to have been.
54 Walsh, *Shakespeare, Milton and Eighteenth-Century Literary Editing*, pp. 149–75. Cf. Stukeley to Johnson, 15 May 1750 (Honeybone (ed.), *Correspondence*, p. 150).
55 During the mid-1740s, the notorious publisher Edmund Curll informed Warburton that he had purchased the rights to the *Critical and Philosophical Enquiry* and that, 'as it had long been out of print, he was going to re-print it; only he desired to know if [Warburton] had any additions or alterations to make'. Warburton noted that '[t]he writer, and the contents of his letter, very much alarmed me', and so he instructed John Knapton to buy back the book, which he did: Warburton to Hurd, 3 January 1757 (*LLEP*, p. 218). Hurd did not include *A Critical and Philosophical Enquiry* in his collected editions of Warburton's works, though Samuel Parr included it in S. Parr (ed.), *Tracts by Warburton and a Warburtonian* ((1789): T132878), pp. 71–144. Warburton's two earlier published works had been anonymous, including his *Miscellaneous translations* (1723: T132384) and, with Samuel Burroughs, *Legal judicature of Chancery stated* (1727: T095693). See also J. Rudolph, *Common Law and Enlightenment in England, 1689–1750* (Woodbridge, 2013), pp. 249–55.
56 Warburton to Hurd, 3 January 1757 (*LLEP*, p. 218).
57 Warburton to Concanen, 16 August 1732 (BL, Egerton, fols 1–2).
58 See, for instance, K. Thomas, *Religion and the Decline of Magic* (London, 1971), pp. 78–112; C. Webster, 'Puritanism, Separatism and Science', in D. Lindberg and

R. Numbers (eds), *God and Nature* (Berkeley, 1986), pp. 192–217. Cf. P. Harrison, 'Religion, Scientific Naturalism and Historical Progress', in D. Yerxa (ed.), *Religion and Innovation: Antagonists or Partners?* (2016), pp. 74–86.

59 See, for instance, A. Walsham, *The Reformation of the Landscape* (Oxford, 2009), pp. 327–94; A. Walsham, 'The Reformation and "the Disenchantment of the World" Reassessed', *HJ* 51 (2008), pp. 497–528; A. Walsham, *Providence in Early Modern England* (Oxford, 1999); P. Harrison, *Territories of Science and Religion* (Chicago, 2015), pp. 21–116; P. Harrison, *The Bible, Protestantism and the Rise of Natural Science* (Cambridge, 2001).

60 See, for instance, Warburton, *Natural and civil events*; Grey, *Chronological and historical account*; Grey, *Farther account of memorable earthquakes*.

61 W. Burns, *An Age of Wonders: Prodigies, Politics and Providence in England, 1657–1727* (Manchester, 2002), pp. 166–70.

62 [W. Warburton], *Critical and philosophical inquiry* (1727: T146881), p. 2. Cf. Bulman, *Anglican Enlightenment*, pp. 73–114.

63 Ibid., p. 66. Cf. A. Walsham, 'Recording Superstition in Early Modern Britain: The Origins of Folklore', *P&P* (2008), pp. 178–206.

64 [Warburton], *Critical and philosophical inquiry*, pp. 4–5.

65 Ibid., p. 5. Cf. R. Barbour, *Sir Thomas Browne* (Oxford, 2013), pp. 296–309.

66 [Warburton], *Critical and philosophical inquiry* pp. 12, 13.

67 Ibid., p. 13. Cf. Locke, *Essay*, ed. Nidditch, pp. 508–23. For early modern theories of error, see M. Ayers, 'Theories of Knowledge and Belief', in D. Garber and M. Ayers (eds), *Cambridge History of Seventeenth-Century Philosophy* (Cambridge, 1998), pp. 1041–9.

68 [Warburton], *Critical and philosophical inquiry* p. 18.

69 Ibid., p. 25.

70 Ibid., p. 28.

71 Ibid., pp. 26, 27, 29–31. Cf. B. Gert, 'Hobbes's Psychology', in T. Sorrell (ed.), *Cambridge Companion to Hobbes* (Cambridge, 1996), pp. 157–74.

72 [Warburton], *Critical and philosophical inquiry* p. 29.

73 Ibid., p. 42.

74 A. Vertot, *History of the revolutions* (1721: T081016).

75 [Warburton], *Critical and philosophical enquiry*, 43–4; I. Cohen, *Revolution in Science* (Cambridge, MA, 1987), pp. 51–76. Cf. S. Pincus, *1688: The First Modern Revolution* (New Haven, 2009), pp. 30–45.

76 [Warburton], *Critical and philosophical inquiry*, pp. 46–53 at p. 53.

77 Ibid., pp. 60–2. Cf. N. Popper, *Walter Ralegh's History of the World and the Historical Culture of the Late Renaissance* (Chicago, 2012), pp. 254–89.

78 Ibid., p. 121.

79 Ibid., p. 122. Cf. R. Serjeantson, 'Testimony and Proof in Early-Modern England', *Studies in the History and Philosophy of Science* 30 (1999), pp. 195–236; R. Serjeantson, 'Testimony: the artless proof', in S. Adamson, G. Alexander and K. Ettenhuber (eds), *Renaissance Figures of Speech* (Cambridge, 2007), pp. 179–94.

80 Stephen, 'Warburton', p. 291.

81 [W. Warburton], *Critical and Philosophical Enquiry* (1727: T146881), pp. xv, xxii.

82 R. Sedgwick (ed.), *House of Commons, 1715–1754* (1970), II, pp. 456–8.

83 [W. Warburton], *Apology for Sir Robert Sutton* (1733: N016622), pp. 3, 4. See also Warburton to Stukeley, 9 May 1732 (Bodleian, Eng.lett.d.35, fols 24–5).
84 Warburton's *Apology* appeared in late May 1733. The House of Commons itself issued a lengthy report on Sutton's case two months later: *Report, with the Appendix from the Committee* (1733: T044770).
85 Warburton to Pope, n.d. (HL, Hurd 16, no. 2).
86 Pope to Warburton, 27 January 1744 (G. Sherburn (ed.), *Correspondence of Alexander Pope* (Oxford, 1956), IV, pp. 495–6).

Chapter 15

Neither a slave nor a tyrant: Church and state reimagined

In May 1736, *The Old Whig*, a London newspaper committed to the Dissenting interest, carried a piece by 'Atticus' criticizing William Warburton's recent *Alliance between Church and State*. Warburton had defended the Church of England's legal establishment 'from the Essence and End of Civil Society, upon the Fundamental Principles of the Law of Nature and Nations'.[1] Atticus, though, complained that the *Alliance*'s defence of religious establishments 'does not even make Pretension to Truth'.[2] A few weeks later, another *Old Whig* editorialist complained similarly that 'the Truth and Goodness of a Religion, and the Civil Utility resulting from an Establishment of it, always coincide, and can't be separated into strict and true Reasoning'. In fact, the editorialist continued, '[t]he true End why any Religion at all is established, is Civil Utility; but the true End why a particular Scheme of Religion is established is, or ought to be, because it is the true Religion, and only because it is the true Religion; since that alone can give it a Preference to others, as a Means more conducive to the Public Good'. In the *Alliance*'s professed agnosticism about the metaphysical truth of any established religion, the *Old Whig* editorialist saw something dark. He thought Warburton aimed to 'mak[e] Religion a Convenient Engine for ambitious and intriguing Politicians to work by; and the Clergy the Tools of Power, and a separate Interest from the Community; a Strain of Sentiments and Language, exactly calculated for despotic and arbitrary Governments, but absolutely inconsistent with the Genius and Spirit of Liberty'.[3] What the *Old Whig* editorialist envisaged was an eighteenth-century justification for the pre-revolutionary English religio-political order. That order, thought many eighteenth-century Dissenters and their allies, had been persecutory.

Initial public support for Warburton's *Alliance* against the *Old Whig*'s criticisms came from an unlikely source: William Webster's stridently orthodox *Weekly Miscellany*. Webster characterized Warburton as a 'mortal Enemy to all Quixotism' and commended him for having 'given the noblest and truest Specimen of that Understanding and Honesty which animates and supports the Cause'.[4] Webster also connected Warburton's argument with the English past; he too fretted about the revival of older dangers to civil peace. Yet whereas the *Old Whig* foresaw a renascence of persecutory clericalism, Webster apprehended a resurgence of enthusiastic schismatics. 'A New Kind of Fanaticism is risen up, and takes strong Root amongst us', Webster warned. 'As the old-fashioned one took its Birth from the mistaken Love of God, so this from its Pretended Love of Mankind: And as they of the old Stamp have been accused to lie for Truth; so these, for the New, will do it on a much more inexcusable Account, even for the Support of Absurdity and Nonsense.' According to Webster, the *Old Whig* and its sympathizers absurdly and unwarrantedly imagined 'a Troop of Black Inchanters perpetually way-laying them; and traversing, and defeating their generous Efforts for the Good of Mankind'.[5] The 'Impartial Reader' had only to read the *Alliance*, Webster insisted, to see that Warburton had not argued for an overbearing clerical order but, instead, simply had proved that the 'State established a Religion, on Account of Civil Utility'. Furthermore, Warburton had shown that if the Church–state alliance's ends were to be achieved, there could not, as the *Old Whig* suggested, be a number of legally established churches. As Webster put it, 'the Alliance can be made only with one Church of one Denomination; and ... the Project of bringing all into it, is the wildest whimsy that ever enter'd the brain-sick Skull of a modern State-Fanatic'.[6]

Neither the *Old Whig* nor the *Weekly Miscellany* thought about William Warburton's *Alliance between Church and State* in terms of the recent English past. Warburton, though, seemed to have avoided any explicit engagement with history in the *Alliance*: in fact, he had structured its argument quite intentionally to avoid the inconclusive wrangling that so often characterized early modern historical scholarship. Yet the *Alliance*, no less than every other eighteenth-century work on English Church–state relations, ruminated on the previous century's internecine religious and political conflicts and proposed solutions to forestall them ever happening again.

This chapter anatomizes Warburton's theory of Church–state relations. It opens by detailing the competing theories of Church–state relations in relation to which he situated his *Alliance between Church and State*. It turns next to consider his marginal notes in Clarendon's *History of the Rebellion*, a work which detailed the breakdown of the religious and political order in mid-seventeenth-century England. The chapter concludes by considering Warburton's *Alliance*, highlighting the ways he thought his conception of Church and state might prevent a recurrence of the previous century's religio-political breakdown.

The Glorious Revolution had forced a fundamental rethinking of Church–state relations. Some of the most important works of polemical divinity during the first third of the eighteenth century concerned the established Church's standing *vis-à-vis* the English state.[7] The seventeenth century had been brutal for the Church of England. The institution had nearly been destroyed in the 1650s, during England's stretch of 'unkingship' and religious disestablishment. Even after the monarchy's restoration and the Church's re-establishment in 1660, the memory of those years reminded churchmen what might happen if religious Dissenters got their way. The Test and Corporation Acts (1661, 1673), which disbarred Protestant Dissenters from public office, aimed to prevent a return of the religious and political anarchy of the mid-century.[8] The Glorious Revolution ushered in a new kind of religious settlement, one which had at its core the Toleration Act (1689), a piece of legislation that allowed the Church to retain its establishment status while at the same time depriving the institution of its functional monopoly on public worship.[9] The Occasional Conformity and Schism Acts (1711, 1714) tried to undo some of the post-revolutionary settlement. But their repeal in 1719, along with routine indemnity acts – which softened the Test Act's effects on Dissenters – at once confirmed and condoned England's religious pluralism.[10] It was a *modus vivendi* which pleased few and which fuelled yet more vitriolic public debate about the proper relation of Church to state.

Mainstream early eighteenth-century English Protestant thought on the post-revolutionary religio-political order was bounded by positions outside which Hobbesian Erastianism sat.[11] Near to one end of the spectrum stood Charles Leslie, the high churchman whose incendiary pamphlets fuelled the 'Church in Danger' controversy of the eighteenth century's first decade.[12] In the run-up to the Occasional Conformity Act's passage and as the counter-revolutionary Convocation of 1710–11 was collapsing, Leslie published *The Mitre and the Crown*, a pamphlet which detailed the differences and delineated the boundaries between Church and state.[13] The central questions concerning the Church's relationship to the state turned on the sources of authority. Did Christ grant to clergy or to civil magistrates 'the Keys of the Kingdom of Heaven, that is, the Key of Doctrine, by which God's Mercies and Judgments are Authoritatively declared and denounced; and the Key of Discipline, by which all Persons are Authoritatively and Ministerially either admitted to, or rejected from the Privileges of Church-Communion, and their Sins are bound or loosed'? Did Christ invest the civil magistrate with the power 'juridicially to remit or retain Sins, Authoritatively to dispense the Word, Sacraments, or Censures of the Church, or any one of them?' Did Christ give to the civil magistrate 'the Keys, which consists in governing the Spiritual Household by Discipline, as well as feeding the same by Doctrine?' Or, instead, did he allot those powers to 'the Apostles and their Successors'?[14] Leslie reckoned that Christ had granted all of these powers to the clergy rather than to the civil magistrate.[15]

Indeed, Leslie insisted, 'God [had] separated the Sacerdotal and Regal Offices'. The Bible made explicit 'that not Christian Kings, as such, but Christian Bishops, and Priests as such, have, and are without Let or impediment to execute, the Power of the Keys, the Power of Spiritual Censures'.[16]

Reason and history confirmed this arrangement. Firstly, there were no Christian magistrates before the early fourth century; neither did the Bible enjoin transferring the spiritual authority and functions from the clergy to the civil magistrates, even if the magistrates were professing Christians. Moreover, if the civil magistrate had a *jure divino* claim to spiritual authority, that would have meant that the Roman Catholic James II ('whom all of us reckoned our Rightful Prince before the Revolution') would have wielded spiritual authority over England's Protestant established Church. 'Will Protestants affirm, that a Popish Prince had Power to make what Constitutions he thought fit for the Church of England?' Leslie wondered.[17] The Glorious Revolution, consequently, had been fought to prevent James II from asserting his authority over the Protestant national church: those who later encouraged the English monarchs to control the Church were nothing more than 'Church-Empsons and Dudleys' who wanted to make English monarchs like 'Popes to the Church, Devourers of her inherent Spiritual Rights'.[18] Leslie thought that England's spiritually independent, clerically guided and legally established church was a branch of the 'Catholic Church'.

Those nearer to the other end of the clerical spectrum rejected Leslie's argument. Benjamin Hoadly's satirical *Dedication to Pope Clement XI*, for instance, mocked Lesliean sacerdotalism as crypto-popery. Prefixed to Richard Steele's *Account of the state of the Roman-Catholic religion throughout the world* (1715), Hoadly's dedication assured the pontiff that England's Protestant churches were daily becoming like the Roman Catholic Church, with its 'Privileges and Perfections, which you boast of, as peculiar to your own'.[19] Given time the established Church of England would soon become that which it putatively rejected. 'I believe in time no man of sense will be able to see any difference between your Popery and that of many amongst us, but that ours is Protestant popery and yours is Popish popery', Hoadly boasted.[20]

Hoadly's 1717 sermon at the royal court which sparked the Bangorian controversy more fully described the true church. Hoadly would have said that his vision was anti-sacerdotal; his opponents would have added that it was Erastian.[21] Like Leslie, Hoadly turned for authoritative guidance to the primitive source of Christian teaching, the Bible, since truth resided there. He took as his text John 18:36 ('Jesus answered, My Kingdom is not of this World'). Recovering the Bible's original intent was difficult, though. During the apostolic age, for instance, *religion* had meant 'Virtue and Integrity, as to ourselves, and Charity and Beneficence to others'. In Hoadly's day, it meant 'the Performance of everything almost, except Virtue and Charity; and particularly, a punctual Exactness in Regard to particular Times, Places, Forms and Modes'. The clergy who had instituted rigorist forms of worship had overstepped their remit from Christ.[22] Similarly, the clergy had corrupted the apostolic meaning of the *Church of Christ*. As Hoadly explained it, to understand the true Church of Christ one had to recognize that Christ is 'King' in his kingdom and that 'He is himself the sole Law-giver to his

Subjects, and himself the sole Judge of their Behaviour, in the affairs of Conscience and Eternal Salvation'.[23] No man could claim to act as Christ's regent on earth. Moreover, because Christ's kingdom is not of this world, any rewards or punishments for transgressing divine law were to be meted out in the afterlife. Thus, the application of force regarding religious matters was impious: 'to apply Force or Flattery, Worldly pleasure or pain; is to act contrary to the Interests of True Religion'.[24] From this it followed furthermore that members of Christ's true church were members by choice, not coercion. 'The Church of Christ, is the Number of Persons who are Sincerely, and Willingly, Subjects to Him, as lawgiver and Judge in all matters truly relating to Conscience, or Eternal Salvation', Hoadly insisted.[25] Truth was not something to be determined by another; only the individual believer could discern truth. For Hoadly, truth seemed subjective, not objective.

While making divergent arguments about the English Church, Charles Leslie and Benjamin Hoadly nevertheless shared a mode of argument. They grounded their claims not in abstractions but in the documented Christian and English pasts. Yet they arrived at irreconcilable conclusions. Coming at the problem of English Church–state relations during the 1730s, William Warburton attempted an ahistorical mode of reasoning. But that mode of argument nonetheless sat atop a deep consideration of England's seventeenth-century 'troubles'.

Three decades after the *Alliance*'s publication, Warburton explained that he had written it with the post-revolutionary religious settlement in mind.[26] He took it as a commonplace that 'Religion hath lost its hold on the minds' of the English people. He blamed both liberty-loving Whigs and the irreligious for that. In the Glorious Revolution's aftermath, the Whigs (who 'loved their Country; but were too eagerly intent on one part only of their Object, the security of its Civil Liberty') pursued policies which unintentionally emasculated the established Church of England. In particular, the 'Church in Danger' days of the eighteenth century's first decade had intensified Whig anticlericalism.[27] After the Hanoverian succession in 1714, 'some warm Friends of the Accession, newly gotten into power, had too hastily perhaps suspected that the Church (or at least that party of Church-men which had usurped the name) was become inauspicious to the sacred Era from whence we were to date the establishment of our civil happiness'. They reckoned that it was 'good policy to lessen the credit of a body of men, who had been long in high reverence with the People, and who had so lately and so scandalously abused their influence in the opprobrious affair of Sacheverell'. To this end, the Whigs encouraged pro-Hanoverian clergy to write polemics against Jacobite clergy. Alas, they 'did it so effectually, that under the professed design of confuting and decrying the usurpation of a popish Hierarchy, they virtually deprived the Church of every power and privilege, which, as a simple Society, she had claim to' and 'delivered her up gagged and bound, as the rebel-Creature of the State'. It did not help the Church of England that the

Tory clergy 'who opposed these Erastian notions, so destructive to the very being of a Church, reasoned and disputed against the Innovators on the principles' which had as their foundation 'the authority of a Papal or (if they like it better) of Puritanical usurpations'. The Whigs, then, unintentionally brought the established Church 'into general contempt', while the Tories offered no effective theoretical defence of the institution. Seeing the institution hobbled, 'Enemies of obnoxious Churchmen found much assistance in the forward carriage of the Enemies of Religion itself'. These enemies of religion piggybacked their campaign against divine revelation on to the Whig anticlerical campaign.

Warburton understood himself to have been writing under these circumstances when he penned the *Alliance*. It was, he acknowledged, 'a ticklish subject'.[28] 'My purpose, I am not ashamed to own, was to repel the cruel inroads made upon [the Church's] Rights and Privileges' and to prevent 'the mischiefs done to Society by Fanaticism, or Religion run mad'. He claimed that he had pursued his case with 'honester principles than those which had been employed to prop up, with Gothic buttresses, a Jacobite or High-Church Hierarchy'. Contemporary reception was mixed. 'But as I made the Church neither a Slave nor a Tyrant ...,' he lamented, '*The Alliance between Church and State*, though formed upon a Model actually existing before our eyes, was considered as an Utopian refinement'. Many admired the *Alliance* for its ingenuity and, while it earned Warburton considerable notice, it did not garner unqualified assent. As Warburton recollected, the *Alliance* earned the equivocal praise both of low church Erastians (like Benjamin Hoadly) and of orthodox stalwarts (like Thomas Sherlock): Hoadly 'allowed my principles', while Sherlock 'espoused my conclusion; which however amounted only to this, that the One was for Liberty however they would choose to employ it; and the Other for Power, however they could come at it'.[29] Other contemporaries also wrestled with the *Alliance*. Even after the Hanoverian succession and the Jacobite rising in 1715, the high church view that the Church was an independent spiritual body with a sacerdotal clergy remained normative, even among Whigs.[30] Warburton's *Alliance* rejected these propositions. In addition, Warburton's seeming rejection of historical argumentation struck contemporaries as odd. They thought it a novel work, one which owed much to the contractarian theory of John Locke, whom Warburton later called 'the true philosopher' and 'the Glory of this Age, and the Blessing of Futurity'.[31] Yet Warburton, like Locke, obsessed about how to prevent a recurrence of the seventeenth-century civil disorder. In Warburton's case, it was thinking carefully through Clarendon's celebrated *History of the Rebellion and Civil Wars in England* that guided his early thinking about the nature and causes of the previous century's wars.

Clarendon was 'that best of Men, of Patriots, and of Writers', Warburton insisted.[32] Warburton's detailed annotations of Clarendon were printed in nineteenth-century editions of the *History* and drew from the marginalia in volumes now housed in the Hurd Library at Hartlebury Castle. Warburton had read Clarendon by the mid-1730s. The original annotations, in Warburton's own handwriting, are in a 1732 octavo edition of the *History*; some time after 1794, Richard Hurd's nephew copied those annotations into a 1704 folio volume of the *History*.[33] While Warburton had lavishly praised Clarendon in his *Critical and Philosophical Enquiry* (1727), he could have penned the marginalia no earlier than 1732. Both penmanship and content indicate that he annotated this edition of Clarendon in the 1740s and again in the 1760s.[34] Nonetheless, a note in the back pages of the 1732 edition of the *History* points toward the original annotations being written during the 1730s. There Warburton scribbled out a long paragraph which he claimed to have drawn from Clarendon's personal manuscripts but that was not printed in the *History* itself. He referred to this paragraph in letters to Thomas Birch in October 1737 and again in March 1738.[35] It is not unreasonable, then, to hold that Warburton had worked his way through Clarendon carefully some time before 1737 and most likely before or while writing up the first edition of *The Alliance*.[36] At the very least, it may confidently be held that Warburton had read Clarendon's *History* by the time he wrote the *Alliance*; that his annotations give insight into what he thought about Clarendon's *History*; that his readings of Clarendon were reflected in the subsequent expanded editions of the *Alliance* in 1741, 1748 and 1766; and that those expanded editions merely amplified the basic argument laid out in the *Alliance*'s original 1736 edition.

Warburton put Clarendon's *History of the Rebellion* on par with Thucydides's *History of the Peloponnesian War*.[37] Clarendon's power of explanation especially distinguished him. He, unlike so many historians, did not unquestioningly accept past explanations for the civil war's eruption but instead provided his own, more sophisticated take on the cataclysm's origins. The resulting *History* explained 'all the concurrent causes of the Rebellion, not only sufficient to overturn a kingdom, but a world'.[38] Warburton broadly agreed with Clarendon's judgments, save for Clarendon's 'greatest imperfection', which was 'looking with too much veneration on [royal] courts'.[39] Unlike Clarendon, Warburton reckoned that Charles I's government bore most responsibility for the breakdown in relations between crown and Parliament before 1642. Charles, for instance, chose to listen to 'evil counsellors' like Buckingham ('the most debauched, the most unable, and the most tyrannical that ever was') and Thomas Wentworth, earl of Strafford (who 'laboured to make the king arbitrary').[40] Their policies led the English people to question 'whether [Charles] had their happiness in view, since he prosecuted that pretence by means very unjustifiable, namely, encroachments on the people's rights'.[41] Throughout the margins of Clarendon's *History*, Warburton complained of 'the arbitrary proceedings of the court'; of 'a tyrannical invasion of [the people's] rights'; of Charles's 'arbitrary government'; of the government's 'acts of tyranny and injustice exercised over all'; and the like.[42] Warburton thought it self-evident that Charles had ruled arbitrarily and unlawfully during the 1630s.

If Charles I had not acquitted himself well, neither had Archbishop William Laud. Warburton contended that Laudian religious policies fomented popular resentment at 'the injustice of ruling churchmen and arbitrary ministers'. This, in turn, catalysed civil strife.[43] Warburton blamed Laud for his 'ecclesiastical innovations', where Clarendon had been prepared to look more favourably upon the archbishop's efforts. Clarendon, for instance, had insisted that John Williams (1582–1650), author of the anti-Laudian *Holy Table: Name and Thing* (1636), had been Laud's implacable enemy, one who had attacked the archbishop in Parliament 'with all the malice and bitterness imaginable'. Warburton countered that '[i]t must be remembered that [Williams] had been cruelly and unjustly persecuted by Laud' and that Williams's *Holy Table* did not espouse views that were 'against the church itself' but merely ones that rejected 'the innovations brought in by Laud'.[44] Likewise, where Clarendon criticized those who complained about Laudian ceremonies ('which had been in constant practice since the reformation, as well as before'), Warburton reckoned them to have been 'taken from the popish superstitions'.[45] That the leader of the established Church of England espoused a particular doctrine or policy did not make that doctrine orthodox nor that policy prudent. For Warburton, religious innovation was both wrong and politically destabilizing.

Laud's flaws did not end there. Warburton reckoned that the archbishop had been soft on popery, though not actually a crypto-papist. Laud, Warburton concluded, 'was an enemy indeed to a pope at Rome, but not to a pope at Lambeth'.[46] For instance, if 'Laud was so intent on suppressing puritanism, why did he not curb these insolencies of the papists?' The lure of 'temporal grandeur' was surely the answer, for he 'turned minister of state; and we see the papists were the ready instruments of the most odious and grievous of the court projects'.[47] Yet Warburton would not have advised actively persecuting Roman Catholics, since he also held that persecution both radicalized religious minorities and fertilized their growth: 'It is persecution only that can increase an old sect'.[48] Persecution was both impolitic and imprudent, if not inherently wrong. Laud's innovative ecclesiastical policies combined with his persecution of some religious minorities had done nothing to stop the nation's descent into war and, more probably, had caused the crisis. Indeed, Warburton compared Laud unfavourably to Cardinal Richelieu, to whom he 'was as inferior in politics ... as he was superior in theology'.[49]

If Warburton could not accept Laud's innocence, neither did he accept arguments that episcopal ecclesiology was the only legitimate ecclesiology. Richard Hooker's views on the subject especially appealed to him, since 'Hooker had demonstrated, that no form of church government was *jure divino*, but all were *jure humano*'.[50] This meant that 'episcopacy, even admitting it to be of divine right, might lawfully be changed to another form of government' and that the Church of Scotland's members were not 'schismatics from the church of England' but members themselves of a lawfully established church.[51] By implication, the established Churches of England and Scotland had equally legitimate forms of Church government, but ones whose legitimacy held only within England and within Scotland.

With all of this said, Warburton blamed the cataclysmic civil wars and interregnum on the post-1642 anti-royalists. Warburton did not fault Parliament for having initially opposed Charles's arbitrary measures, since '[l]ong experience had shewn the oppressed people, that an arbitrary governor never redresses the grievances out of conscience, but necessity'. Yet it was 'remarkable' that 'the deputies of the people ... having got all the public credit, as they advanced in power, most horribly abused it'.[52] The English revered Parliament, Warburton argued, because 'parliaments [had] been their only protection against despotism'.[53] By 1642, though, the Parliament had fully restored the rights deprived by the crown. As Warburton put it, '[t]he labyrinth in which the king had involved himself was of his own and his father's making, and the late extricating himself from it, which indeed he had done, was by restoring the nation's rights by a number of salutary laws'.[54] Having resecured the rights of the English, Parliament unjustifiably pressed further, aiming to destroy the monarchy itself. In August 1642, for instance, it rejected Charles's submission to parliamentary demands regarding religious and civil liberties. 'There cannot be a stronger proof given that the parliament was now become a faction, and a faction of the most destructive nature', Warburton judged. 'This declaration being the infallible means, and obvious to foresee, of attaching the far greater part of the nobility and gentry to the king's interest more firmly than ever. As they could not but foresee this, it is plain their quarrel was now with the monarchy itself.'[55] Because the post-1642 parliamentarians were opposed to the very idea of a monarchy, they rebuffed Charles's concessions and levelled spurious charges against him: 'To hide their factious views, which would not suffer them to acquiesce to the satisfaction the king had given them by his consent to several salutary laws, which were a secure barrier against the return of his arbitrary measures, they were forced to have recourse to popery and Irelandish massacres; neither of which he could be justly charged with'.[56] Aiding and abetting them were the 'presbyterian clergy [who] became the instruments of the overthrow of the constitution'.[57] Warburton saw hardly any difference between Presbyterians and the Independents: 'All the difference between them ... being only this, that [the Presbyterians] were indeed for having a pageant of a king, but the other went to the abolition of the very name'.[58] In the end, he reckoned that while both the king and his parliamentary opponents had made mistakes, the monarchy's opponents had been more wrong than right. Clarendon had wrongly contended that 'all resistance to royal authority was rebellion'. Nevertheless, he had correctly recognized that '*this* resistance or war of the parliament on the king was unreasonable and unjust'.[59] Charles I, his 'evil counsellors' and his ecclesiastical minister (Laud) bore responsibility for having catalysed conflict. But the anti-royalist parliamentarians and their Presbyterian and Independent clerical allies shouldered the blame for the civil war, the regicide, the unkingship and the religious free-for-all of the 1650s.

The post-1689 revolution settlement had legally restrained the crown's ability again to cause the sort of mischief done during the 1630s: the system got rejiggered to preclude the possibility of another Buckingham or Laud or even Charles I. But that post-revolution settlement had not fully removed the Church's potential to destabilize. While the Church–Whig alliance engineered by Robert Walpole and Edmund Gibson had aimed to domesticate the bishops, the virulent anticlericalism of the 1730s showed this insufficient to forestall public religious dissension. Warburton's *Alliance* offered a theoretical justification for the established Church's alliance with the English state that proved the alliance's necessity while circumscribing the Church's claims to temporal authority. Warburton made that justification on grounds other than the high church sacerdotalism of Charles Leslie or the bald Erastianism of Benjamin Hoadly.

Knowing Warburton's take on Clarendon's *History of the Rebellion* puts the *Alliance*'s arguments into a clearer light. Clarendon had explained how the mid-seventeenth-century English world had been turned upside-down; Warburton reconceived the alliance between Church and state in a way that would prevent a return to that sort of anarchy. That reconception, though, included at its core an avowed and explicit defence of the post-Restoration Test Acts, which banned non-members of the established Church of England from full political liberties. It grounded that defence not on scripture and tradition, as Jeremy Taylor had mostly done in his *Liberty of Prophesying in Defence of Religious Toleration* (1647), but on the 'abstract Principle of Right'.[60] Taylor's mode of argument, Warburton contended, befit an age characterized by '[t]hat narrow, sour, ignorant Spirit of Bigotry ... [which] is no more'. Warburton's mode, by contrast, befit the eighteenth century, which was 'attentive to disengage itself from Prejudices, enlarge its Views, and Follow Truth and Nature withersoever they lead'.[61] Notably, 'Truth and Nature' led Warburton precisely to where scripture and tradition had led Taylor – to the necessity of an established church and religious tests, both of which he acknowledged were 'solecisms' in his own day.[62]

Warburton's argument for the necessity of an established church and test acts flowed from his Locke-informed understanding of civil society's origins and purposes. In the state of nature, humans were driven by the 'Appetite of Self-Preservation'; yet to gratify that appetite 'Man ... soon ran into violent excesses'.[63] Religion, though, prevented people wholly from destroying each other. It was 'the restraining Principle of Religion that kept men from running altogether in the Confusion necessarily consequent on the Principle of inordinate self-love'. Yet religion without the force to defend its tenets and to enforce its mores proved inadequate sufficiently to forestall violence. Therefore, Warburton explained, '[t]he restraining Principle of Religion ... found it necessary to call in a Civil Magistrate, as an Alley to turn the Balance. Thus was Society invented for a Remedy against Injustice.'[64]

Crucially, however, if religion without the coercive powers of society proved 'an ineffectual Remedy to moral Disorders', the state without religion proved 'equally insufficient'. Civil laws addressed only 'open Violation[s] of Right', not private wrongs, which 'equally tend[] to the public Prejudice'. Moreover, civil laws only dealt with what Warburton called 'Duties of Perfect Obligation'. By contrast, the 'Duties of Imperfect Obligation' remained unaddressed, mostly because 'they were supposed not so immediately and vitally to affect the Being of Society'. However, these 'Duties of Imperfect Obligation' – things like 'Gratitude, Hospitality, Charity, &c' – were crucial to a well-ordered, peaceful society. Most importantly, though, civil society's very existence created new problems. As Warburton explained it, 'Society ... increased and inflamed, to an infinite Degree, those inordinate Appetites for whose Correction, it was invented and introduced ... Our phantastic Wants are infinitely numerous, to be brought under no certain Measure or Standard, and increase exactly in proportion to our Improvements in the Arts of Life. But the Arts of Life owe their Original to Civil Society.'[65] Warburton saw managing the passions as crucial to maintaining civil order.

The most effective way to manage the passions was for the state formally to ally itself with religion. Most strictly understood, *religion* 'is a Commerce and Intercourse with the Supreme Cause of all Things'. Yet while religion thus conceived necessarily involved 'Contemplation on [God's] Nature, and on the Relations we stand in towards him', it was more than simply 'a kind of divine Philosophy in the Mind'.[66] Instead, religion required action. One simply could not think one thing privately and act publicly in a contrariwise way, unless, of course, one were a papist, a Muslim or an atheist. But these, Warburton would have argued, were not real religions. Part of the requirement to act on real religious belief entailed an 'open Profession ... so as to be seen by others'. That, in turn, meant that there needed to be clearly defined articles of faith and a set liturgy. '[A] Religion as is suitable to the Nature of Man, here, must have the Mediation on the divine Nature drawn out into Articles of Faith', Warburton contended, 'and the Mediation on our several Relations to him, into suitable and correspondent Acts of Religious Worship; and both of them to be professed and performed in common'. Articles of faith and a common liturgy, then, were bound up together. Unambiguous articles preserve 'pure and incorrupt' conceptions of the divine, since the way in which one conceived of the divine 'entirely influence[s] all Religious Practice'; a shared liturgy ensured that the divine was worshipped properly.[67] Safeguarding both religious articles and the liturgy should be a dedicated priestly office. The priest's job was 'to preside in, direct and superintend the

Acts and Offices of Religion, lest anything childish, profane, or superstitious (as it certainly would, if left to ever ones Fancy) obtrude themselves into them'.[68] Unlike many, Warburton thought it possible for priests to safeguard public peace.

Priests certainly promoted civil order and tranquillity when teaching that there existed a future state of rewards and punishments in which the ledger of things done and undone in this world would be balanced permanently and eternally. While notionally agnostic about religion's precise content, Warburton had clear ideas about what constituted legitimate religion. In the *Alliance*, he summarized the three 'fundamental Principles of natural Religion', which he took to include 'the Being of a God'; 'his Providence over human Affairs'; and 'the natural essential Difference of Moral Good and Evil'.[69] This was as far as he went in the *Alliance*, but in the *Divine Legation of Moses*, whose first book carefully recapitulated the *Alliance*'s argument, he expounded at greater length on these points. There he focused especially on the doctrine of a future state of rewards and punishments. Law, he contended, had two 'great Sanctions': 'Rewards for Observance, and Punishments for Transgression'.[70] Yet while civil society could easily punish those who broke civil laws, it could not adequately reward those who obeyed them. One needed to know motives to reward, but such knowledge was unnecessary to punish transgressors. More importantly, though, civil society does not possess the sorts of rewards that might impel people to obey its laws. Religion, by contrast, 'can supply the Sanction of Rewards, which Society wants, and has not'. For this reason, it 'is absolutely necessary to Civil Government'.[71] As Warburton explained it,

> To supply these Defects, in Civil Laws, some other coactive Power must be added, that hath its Influence on the Mind of Man; to keep Society from running back into Confusion. But there is no other than the Power of Religion; which teaching an over-ruling Providence, the Rewarder of good Men and the Punisher of ill, can oblige to the Duties of imperfect Obligation, which human Laws overlook; and teaching, also, that this Providence is omniscience, that it sees the most secrete Actions and Intentions of Men, and hath given Laws for the perfecting their Nature, will oblige to those Duties of perfect Obligation, which human Laws cannot reach, or sufficiently inforce.[72]

Religion, rightly understood, teaches that God providentially superintends his creation and that he metes out rewards and punishments. Crucially, because it is evident that providential rewards and punishments are not evenly distributed in this mortal life, there must be an eternal afterlife. 'And therefore human Affairs not being dispensed, at present, agreeably to that Superintendence, he must conclude, that Man shall exist after Death, to be brought to a future Reckoning in another Life, where all Accounts will be set even, and all the present Obscurities and Perplexities in the Ways of Providence unfolded and explained', Warburton contended. 'From hence Religion acquires irresistible Force and Splendour; and rises on a solid and unshaken Basis.'[73] For Warburton, an afterlife of rewards and punishments was simultaneously an essential mark of any legitimate religion *and* the primary benefit which religion had to offer the state in its chief mission, 'the Conservation of Body and Goods'.[74]

But why would the state need to enter into a formal alliance with the Church to receive these benefits? Warburton offered three reasons. By allying formally with the Church, the state can 'preserve the Essence and Purity of Religion', which would, in turn, help the Church most efficiently and durably benefit the state. 'For if Truth and public Utility coincide, the nearer any Religion approaches to the Truth of Things the fitter that Religion is for serving Civil Society', Warburton argued.[75] A church unallied with the state will drift away from its original purity. The second reason the state should unite with the Church is that an alliance best harnesses the Church's aid. Allied churches, in particular, excel at 'bestowing additional Reverence and Veneration on the Person of the Civil Magistrate; and on the Laws of the State', not least because people are more likely to heed the Church's enjoinders if the civil magistrate is also the Church's head. Finally, the state benefits from an alliance with the Church because it 'prevent[s] the Mischiefs that, in [the Church's] natural independent State, it might occasion to Civil Society'.[76] The potential dangers of an unallied church had so 'terrified' Thomas Hobbes that he had insisted upon 'the Magistrate's natural Right of Dominion and Supremacy over the Church, its Servant and Creature'.[77] While Warburton stopped short of Hobbes, he discerned the potential threats of independent churches. Indeed, he argued that a Church–state alliance along the terms he proposed would reduce the dangers of religious pluralism. The postmodern shibboleth that strength comes from diversity would have baffled Warburton. Religious diversity needed to be managed, not embraced. During the late seventeenth century, the proposed Hobbesian solution to disallow freedom of non-state-approved religious action lost out to the Lockean solution of qualified freedom of religious action. But even so – and even after the Toleration Act's passage in 1689 – religious difference remained a problem to be managed.[78] Warburton reckoned that his proposed Church–state alliance offered the best way to manage potentially destabilizing religious differences. 'Another Mischief there is still more certain and fatal, whenever above one Religion is found in a State; which an Alliance only can prevent', he contended. 'For every Sect, or Church, thinking it self alone the true, or at least the most perfect, is naturally pushed to the advancing its own Scheme on the Ruin of all the Rest.'[79] By signalling to the nation that a particular church was the lone legally established one, the state could stifle the divisive passions that necessarily attended religious pluralism.

While Warburton favoured a formal alliance between Church and state, he was unequivocal that the Church needed to be the state's junior partner. Here the lessons he drew from Clarendon's *History* were germane. During the 1630s and early 1640s, Archbishop Laud and his supporters had unnecessarily roiled the political waters. Even if the anti-royalists bore ultimate responsibility for civil war and regicide, the too-powerful leaders of England's established Church had catalysed the crisis. Warburton's *Alliance* claimed to reconceive of the Church–state relationship in a way that forestalled this possibility.

Warburton asserted that his theory of Church–state relations was the moderate one positioned between two fundamentally erroneous theories. At one extreme lay the 'Systems ... of the high-Church clergy'. These lobbied 'for the absolute Independency of the Church with all the Prerogatives and Powers it is found to stand possessed of under an Establishment'.[80] High churchmanship, though, was but popery 'little disguised' and even more 'irrational' than the perverted system it aped. At the other extreme from high church crypto-popery lay Hobbesian Erastianism of the sort propounded by Matthew Tindal and Thomas Gordon. They sought to make all churches 'the Creatures of the Civil Magistrates'.[81] This too Warburton rejected in favour of an alliance in which two 'Sovereign and Independent' bodies joined together by 'Free Convention and Mutual Compact'.[82] In that alliance, the 'Fundamental Article' will be 'that the Church shall apply all its influence in the Service of the State; and that the State Shall support and Protect the Church'. Under the terms of Warburton's alliance, the state has to ensure 'a settled Maintenance for the Clergy, and an Ecclesiastical Jurisdiction with coactive powers'.[83] Financial maintenance of the clergy has to be legally obligatory, while the church courts exist purely for 'the Reformation of Manners' and have only excommunication as their punishment.[84] In addition, the established Church gets representation in the legislature, though its representatives sit there by the state's grace rather than by right: in no way do the clergy constitute a distinct third estate.[85] Together these three things – tithes, church courts and parliamentary representation – ensure 'the Dependency of the Clergy on the State'. In turn, from 'the State's Obligation to support and protect the Church; proceeds the State's Supremacy in the Church'.[86] To guarantee that the Church remains the subordinate partner, the 'Civil Magistrate' also serves as the 'Supreme Head of the Church; without whose Approbation and Allowance, she can now decree or determine nothing'.[87]

The question still remained, though, with which church should the state ally itself. 'Truth', Warburton explicitly argued, bore no consideration for the state in choosing its ecclesiastical partner: it was wrong to insist 'that Religion was to be Established and protected as it was the True Religion; not for the sake of Civil Utility; which is the great Principle whereby we erect an Established Religion'.[88] Given that 'Civil Utility' was the litmus test, Warburton advised that 'the Alliance is made by the State with the largest of the Religious Societies'. In the context of England, this meant that the state should ally itself with the episcopal Church of England; and in Scotland it should ally with the Presbyterian Church of Scotland. Each alliance needed to be 'perpetual, not irrevocable, i.e., it subsists so long as the Church, thereby

Established, maintains its superiority of Extent': the alliance is 'dissolved' when the Church's hold on the populace 'loses to any considerable Degree'.[89] The English Church–state alliance, in particular, perfectly conformed to 'the universal Law of Reason'.[90] Ireland, of course, presented a particular difficulty, since Roman Catholics accounted for the bulk of the populace. Nonetheless, Warburton would have responded that the Church of Rome disqualified itself from such an alliance by being interminably bent on seeking temporal power by 'exalt[ing] the Chair Apostolic far above the Thrones of earthly Potentates, of whom she has required and received Homage'.[91] Roman Catholicism was not a real religion.

Where the state allied itself with a real religion, test laws were necessary. In part, this was because the nature of the Church–state alliance requires that the state protect the established Church. 'As Man, when he entered into Civil Society, necessarily parted with some of his natural Rights, so the Church when it entered into Union with the State did the same', Warburton reasoned. 'The Right, she parted with, was her Independency, which she transferred to the Civil Sovereign.'[92] Yet, Warburton continued, even if the state had never promised the established Church its protection, test laws were prudent ways to manage the problems of religious pluralism. He contended that 'wherever there is a diversity of Religion, each Sect, believing its own the truest, strives to advance it self on the Ruins of the Rest'. If a sect cannot triumph over others through 'the force of Argument', it turns its attention to 'introducing a Party into the public Administration' so that it can employ 'the coercive Power of the State'. The results for civil society are predictably bad: 'What Persecutions, Rebellions, Revolutions, loss of Civil and Religious Liberty, these intestine Struggles between Sectaries have produced, in every Age, is well known to those acquainted with the History of Mankind'.[93] So great a threat was sectarian competition to civil peace that Warburton forthrightly justified 'Restraint' and 'Punishment'. The two most dangerous groups were atheists and papists. 'The Atheist' threatens the civil order because he is 'incapable of giving Security for his Behaviour in Community' and holds principles which 'directly overthrow the very Foundation on which it is built'. Without question, he 'should certainly be banished [from] all Civil Society'. The 'English Papist' was only slightly less dangerous, for he 'owns an Ecclesiastical Power superior to all temporal Dominion, [and] should not be tolerated in any Sovereign State'. Other religious sects – Anabaptists and Quakers, for instance – should be restrained only in proportion to their threat to 'Civil Peace'.[94]

Toleration was something that Warburton conceived of as a form of restraint, not as a punishment. Tolerating non-established sects who were neither atheists nor papists was the surest way to guarantee the peace. As he explained it, 'once grant a Toleration, as the Law of Nature and Nations require, with the Establishment of one, and an Exclusion of all the rest from the public Administration, and the Evil vanishes, and many Religions become as harmless as one'.[95] Toleration, on this view, was not a softening of legal restrictions on religion that followed from a recognition of religion's waning hold on human minds in the modern world. Rather, it was a legal acknowledgement of religion's lasting hold on human minds and, as John Dunn has rightly argued, 'a peremptory barrier to the very best of intentions exerted in the wrong place'.[96]

In the end, Warburton's *Alliance between Church and State* endorsed the English religio-political *status quo*. Warburton reckoned that it had been appropriate for the post-revolutionary English state to confirm its alliance with the Church of England; to maintain the Test and Corporation Acts; and to grant limited religious toleration only to some who dissented from England's legally established national church. He defended all of this for reasons not normally offered up by mid-eighteenth-century orthodox apologists, who continued to conceive of the Church of England as a spiritually independent body superintended by a sacerdotal clergy. Nonetheless, contemporaries recognized it as the work of 'a Gentleman whose Capacity, Judgment, and Learning, deserve some eminent Dignity in the Church'; and leading orthodox clerics took up Warburton's cause after the *Alliance*'s publication.[97] Francis Hare, bishop of Chichester, in particular, did what he could to promote Warburton's career. Not least Hare recommended Warburton to Queen Caroline's attention.[98] Nonetheless, Warburton rose no higher than rector of Brant Broughton, Lincolnshire, for another decade and a half, when he got named to prebends in Gloucester (1753) and Durham (1755) in quick succession. By 1757, he was dean of Bristol cathedral and in 1760, he was tapped to be the bishop of Gloucester, a post he held until his death in 1779. For someone with evident intellectual talents and with active episcopal support, the lag in preferment was odd. In part, it could be put down to untimely deaths of both Queen Caroline (1737) and Hare (1740). After their deaths, though, he found other patrons, Ralph Allen (*c*. 1693–1764) most prominent among them. Indeed, it was not solely a lack of patronage which retarded his career.[99] Rather, Warburton's tepid praise for Conyers Middleton in the first volume of the *Divine Legation of Moses* (1738) helped to account for his slow initial career advancement. By the late 1730s, praising Middleton, even equivocally, was an unforgivable sin amongst the orthodox, one for which Warburton and his clerical allies evidently thought he needed to make public propitiation.

NOTES

1 [W. Warburton], *Alliance between church and state* (1766: T21264), p. 3. The *Alliance* first appeared in print in 1736. Subsequent, and increasingly heavily amended, editions followed in 1741, 1748 and 1766.

2 *OW* (13 May 1736), p. 1. See also A. Thompson, 'Popery, Politics and Private Judgment in Early Hanoverian Britain', *HJ* 45 (2002), pp. 333–56. : C. Gerrard

The Patriot Opposition to Walpole: Politics, Poetry and National Myth, 1725–1742 (Oxford, 1994), pp. 31–3; M. Harris, *London Newspapers in the Age of Walpole* (London, 1987), p. 183; S. Taylor, 'Church and State in the Mid-Eighteenth Century: the Newcastle Years, 1742–62' (Ph.D. thesis, University of Cambridge, 1987), pp. 42–3.

3 *OW* (27 May 1736), p. 1.

4 *WM* (19 June 1736), p. 1.

5 Ibid.

6 Ibid., p. 2.

7 M. Goldie, 'The English System of Liberty', in M. Goldie and R. Wokler (eds), *Cambridge History of Eighteenth-Century Political Thought* (Cambridge, 2006), pp. 50–4; J. Clark, 'Great Britain and Ireland', in S. Brown and T. Tackett (eds), *Enlightenment, Reawakening and Revolution, 1660–1815* (Cambridge, 2006), pp. 54–71; J. Gascoigne, 'The Unity of Church and State Challenged: Responses to Hooker from the Restoration to the Nineteenth-Century Age of Reform', *Journal of Religious History* 27 (1997), pp. 60–79; Taylor, 'Church and State', pp. 41–66; N. Sykes, *Church and State in England in the XVIIIth Century* (Cambridge, 1934), pp. 284–331.

8 J. Spurr, *The Restoration Church of England, 1646–1689* (New Haven, 1991), pp. 29–104; W. Bulman, 'Enlightenment and Religious Politics in Restoration England', *History Compass* 10 (2012), pp. 752–64. Cf. G. Tapsell, 'Introduction: The Later Stuart Church in Context', in G. Tapsell (ed.), *The Later Stuart Church, 1660–1714* (Manchester, 2012), pp. 1–19.

9 G. Bennett, *The Tory Crisis in Church and State, 1688–1730: The Career of Francis Atterbury Bishop of Rochester* (Oxford, 1975), pp. 3–22; B. Sirota, 'Occasional Conformity Controversy, Moderation and the Anglican Critique of Modernity, 1700–1714', *HJ* 57 (2014), pp. 81–105; A. Barber, 'Censorship, Salvation and the Preaching of Francis Higgins: A Reconsideration of High Church Politics and Theology in the Early 18th Century', *PH* 33 (2014), pp. 114–139'. On the Glorious Revolution's contested legacies, see G. Glickman, 'Political Conflict and the Memory of the Revolution, 1689–1745', in S. Taylor and T. Harris (eds), *The Final Crisis of the Stuart Monarchy* (Woodbridge, 2013), pp. 243–72; J. Kenyon, *Revolution Principles: The Politics of Party, 1689–1720* (Cambridge, 1977).

10 K. Short, 'English Indemnity Acts, 1726–1867', *Church History* 42 (1973), pp. 366–76; J. Bradley, *Religion, Revolution, and English Radicalism: Nonconformity in Eighteenth-Century Politics and Society* (Cambridge, 1990), pp. 49–90.

11 J. Champion, 'Godless Politics: Hobbes and Public Religion', in W. Bulman and R. Ingram (eds), *God in the Enlightenment* (Oxford, 2016), pp. 42–62.

12 B. Sirota, *The Christian Monitors: The Church of England and the Age of Benevolence, 1680–1730* (New Haven, 2014), pp. 149–86.

13 [C. Leslie], *Mitre and the crown* (1711: T079079) appeared in print on 7 June 1711; Convocation was prorogued on 12 June 1711: A. Barber, '"The Voice of the People, no Voice of God": A Political, Religious and Social History of the Transmission of Ideas in England, 1690–1715' (Ph.D. thesis, University of London, 2010), p. 309; G. Bennett, 'The Convocation of 1710: An Anglican Attempt at Counter-Revolution', *SCH* 7 (1971), pp. 311–19. ESTC attributes *Mitre and crown* to Francis Atterbury; Bennett, *Tory Crisis*, does not. In his manuscript notes on ecclesiastical

history, now housed in the British Library, White Kennett attributes the pamphlet to Leslie. At the least, it may be said that pamphlet conveys a high churchman's view of Church-state relations during Queen Anne's reign. I thank Brent Sirota for the information regarding Kennett's attribution.
14 [Leslie], *Mitre*, pp. 5–6.
15 Ibid., pp. 9–10, 11.
16 Ibid., pp. 12, 13.
17 Ibid., pp. 15–16.
18 Ibid., pp. 21, 26.
19 B. Hoadly, 'Dedication to Pope Clement XI', in J. Hoadly (ed.), *Works of Benjamin Hoadly* ((1773): T018831), I, p. 535.
20 Ibid., p. 544.
21 Cf. Clark, 'Great Britain and Ireland', pp. 60–1; W. Gibson, *Enlightenment Prelate: Benjamin Hoadly, 1676–1761* (Cambridge, 2004), pp. 147–98; A. Starkie, *The Church of England and the Bangorian Controversy, 1716–1721* (Woodbridge, 2007.
22 Hoadly, *Nature of the Kingdom, or church, of Christ* (1717: T170750), p. 5. Cf. P. Harrison, *Territories of Science and Religion* (Chicago, 2015).
23 Ibid., p. 11.
24 Ibid., p. 20.
25 Ibid., pp. 25–6.
26 Warburton, *Divine Legation of Moses ... Volume III* (1765: T214226), dedication. Unless otherwise noted, all quotations in this paragraph and the next are drawn from this unpaginated dedication.
27 Cf. J. Champion, '"Religion's Safe, with Priestcraft is the War": Augustan Anticlericalism and the Legacy of the English Revolution, 1660–1720', *European Legacy* 5 (2000), pp. 547–61; G. Holmes, *Religion and Party in Late Stuart England* (London, 1975).
28 Warburton to Stukeley, 1735 (Bodleian, Eng.lett.d.35, fol. 36).
29 W. Warburton, *Divine Legation of Moses* (1765: T214226), dedication.
30 J. Gascoigne, 'The Unity of Church and State Challenged: Responses to Hooker from the Restoration to the Nineteenth-Century Age of Reform' *Journal of Religious History* 27 (1997), pp. 63–6; S. Taylor, 'William Warburton and the Alliance of Church and State', *JEH* 43 (1992), pp. 271–86. Cf. R.W. Greaves, 'Working of an Alliance: A Comment on Warburton', in G. Bennett and J. Walsh (eds), *Essays in Modern English Church History* (Oxford, 1966), pp. 163–80; Clark, 'Great Britain and Ireland', p. 61.
31 [W. Warburton], *View of Lord Bolingbroke's Philosophy* (1754: T113197), p. 107; W. Warburton, *Divine legation of Moses* (1738: T133104), I, p. xxiv.
32 Warburton, *Divine legation* (1738), I, p. 17. On Clarendon's *History*, see Paul Seaward, 'Introduction', in Edward Hyde, *The History of the Rebellion: A New Selection*, ed. Paul Seward (Oxford, 2009), pp. vii–xvi; B. Worden, *God's Instruments: Political Conduct in the England of Oliver Cromwell* (Oxford, 2012), pp. 373–400.
33 The Hurd Library requests that shelfmarks of its books not be listed in publications. While citations to Warburton's marginalia here are sourced to the 1849 printed edition of Clarendon's *History* (in which Warburton's notes were reproduced), the references have been confirmed in the original volumes in the Hurd

Library. I thank Chris Penney and Nigel Sharp for their help with Warburton's Clarendon marginalia in the Hurd Library.

34 At various points in the margins of his copy of Clarendon's *History of the Rebellion*, Warburton cited evidence from John Thurloe's state papers, published in 1742, and from Clarendon's state papers, published in 1767.

35 Warburton to Birch, 24 October 1737, 23 March 1738 (BL, Add. 4320, fols 110–11, 114–15).

36 The *Alliance* first appeared in print in late January 1736.

37 W. Warburton, 'Fragments', in Kilvert, pp. 287, 298.

38 Ibid., p. 307.

39 Ibid., p. 300.

40 WNC, pp. 478, 498.

41 Ibid., p. 475.

42 Ibid., pp. 475, 476, 492, 510, 526, 529.

43 Ibid., p. 530. Cf. N. Tyacke, *Anti-Calvinists: The Rise of English Arminianism, c. 1590–1640* (Oxford, 1987).

44 WNC, p. 508. Cf. K. Fincham and N. Tyacke, *Altars Restored: The Changing Face of English Religious Worship, 1547–c. 1700* (Oxford, 2008), pp. 162–4, 176–81, 196–8.

45 WNC, p. 497

46 Ibid., p. 505

47 Ibid., pp. 485, 492.

48 Ibid., p. 492.

49 Ibid., p. 486.

50 Ibid., p. 561. See also Warburton to Hurd, 1 September 1750 (*LLEP*, pp. 57–8). Cf. MacCulloch, *All Things Made New*, pp. 279–320; P. Lake, 'Business as Usual? The Immediate Reception of Hooker's *Ecclesiastical Polity*', *JEH* 52 (2001), pp. 456–86.

51 Ibid., pp. 484, 580.

52 Ibid., p. 490.

53 Ibid., p. 516.

54 Ibid., p. 520.

55 Ibid.

56 Ibid., p. 521.

57 Ibid., p. 540.

58 Ibid., p. 569.

59 Ibid., p. 580.

60 [Warburton], *Alliance* (1736), p. 6.

61 Ibid., pp. iv, v.

62 Ibid., p. 1.

63 Ibid., p. 7.

64 Ibid., p. 8.

65 Ibid., pp. 10–12.

66 Ibid., p. 35.

67 Ibid., pp. 37, 38.

68 Ibid., p. 39.

69 Ibid., p. 24.

70 Warburton, *Divine Legation* (1738), p. 14.

71 Ibid., p. 20.
72 Ibid., p. 21.
73 Ibid., p. 23.
74 [W. Warburton], *Alliance between church and state* (1736: T021261), p. 24.
75 Ibid., pp. 55, 56.
76 Ibid., p. 61.
77 Ibid., p. 62.
78 Champion, 'Godless Politics'; J. Dunn, 'The Claim to Freedom of Conscience: Freedom of Speech, Freedom of Thought, Freedom of Worship?', in O. Grell, J. Israel, N. Tyacke (eds), *From Persecution to Toleration: The Glorious Revolution and Religion in England* (Oxford, 1991), pp. 171–195.
79 [Warburton], *Alliance* (1736), p. 63.
80 Ibid., p. 48.
81 Ibid., p. 49. Cf. William Warburton's annotations of Matthew Tindal's *Christianity as old as the creation* (HL, Hurd MSS).
82 Ibid., p. 53.
83 Ibid., p. 68.
84 Ibid., pp. 69–73, 76.
85 Ibid., pp. 73–6. Cf. William Warburton's speech to Parliament [draft], March 1762 (HL, 16, no. 7) in which Warburton examined whether bishops are peers in the House of Lords.
86 Ibid., pp. 68–9.
87 Ibid., p. 83.
88 Ibid., p. 149.
89 Ibid.
90 Ibid., p. 108.
91 Ibid., p. 42. Cf. D. Hayton, 'Early Hanoverain Ireland, 1690–1750', in A. Jackson (ed.), *The Oxford Handbook of Modern Irish History* (Oxford, 2014), pp. 404–8.
92 [Warburton], *Alliance* (1736), p. 115.
93 Ibid., p. 116.
94 Ibid., pp. 119–27.
95 Ibid., p. 134.
96 J. Dunn, 'The Grounds of Toleration and a Capacity of Tolerate', in J. Parkin and T. Stanton (eds), *Natural Law and Toleration in the Early Enlightenment* (Oxford, 2013), p. 209.
97 *Present State of the Republic of Letters* XVII (June 1736), p. 471.
98 *LA*, V, p. 544.
99 B. Buchanan, 'Ralph Allen (bap. 1693, d. 1764)', *ODNB*; B. Young, 'William Warburton (1698–1779)', *ODNB*. Warburton met Allen through Alexander Pope and married Allen's niece, Gertrude Tucker, in 1745. Others also tried to help Warburton. The earl of Chesterfield who offered to make him chaplain to the Irish lord lieutenant in 1745 (Philip Dormer Stanhope to Warburton, 4 June 1745 (BL, Egerton 1955, fol. 5)). In 1746, Charles Yorke and William Murray (later Lord Mansfield) helped to get him elected a preacher at Lincoln's Inn.

Chapter 16

The triumph of Christ over Julian: prodigies, miracles and providence

'I have been a little diverted upon an important Subject. A Discourse to prove the miraculous interposition of Providence in defeating Julian's attempt to rebuild the Temple', William Warburton confided to Philip Doddridge in June 1749. Three sections were to comprise that discourse: the first, 'to establish the truth by human testimony, and the nature of the fact'; the second, 'An Answer to Objections'; and a final part, to enquire 'into the nature of that evidence which is sufficient to claim a rational assent to the miraculous fact'.[1] Warburton's *Julian* appeared in March 1750 and interrogated the circumstances surrounding the failed rebuilding of the temple of Jerusalem in the mid-fourth century AD. The Roman emperor Julian (the Apostate) had encouraged Jerusalem's Jews to rebuild the Temple in 363. But the project was abandoned after an earthquake at the temple site killed a number of builders and after the emperor died in June of that year.[2] Warburton's *Julian* aimed to prove that God had directly wrought the earthquake which brought the construction to a close.

On the face of it, Warburton's *Julian* was but another contribution to mid-eighteenth-century discussions about God's providential interventions in his creation. Providence is the longstanding Christian doctrine regarding God's sovereignty. It is premised on the notion that the omnipotent, omniscient and eternal God who created and sustains the universe for supremely good purposes has a plan for mankind. In the very way he designed and ordered the universe, he ensured that many of those good purposes can be achieved: this is his *general providence*. At other times, though, God intervenes directly in natural and human events to secure his divine designs. These interventions come through miracles, prodigies and other non-miraculous acts: this is his *particular providence*.

Eighteenth-century discussions about providence differed from the sixteenth- and seventeenth-century discussions.[3] In the sixteenth and seventeenth centuries, few found God's general and particular providences contradictory. During the eighteenth century, some questioned how to reconcile the watchmaker God who had created the seemingly immutable laws that guide nature with the Bible's interventionist God who worked miracles and fulfilled prophecies.[4] Orthodox Christians believed that God was specially provident and the eighteenth-century orthodox apologists tried to explain why and how God specially governed his creation. Most focused on *why* God intervened and interpreted the meaning of his various interventions. In *Julian* and other pieces of the 1740s and 1750s, William Warburton demonstrated not just *why* God had intervened providentially but *how* he had intervened.

Yet Warburton wrote *Julian* not just to explain God's general and particular providences. This chapter examines *Julian*'s origins, illuminating once again how the orthodox tried to manage and marginalize not just the heterodox but even those who expressed mild support for the heterodox. Warburton's study of the fourth-century failed rebuild of the Temple was part of a sustained attempt to demonstrate his orthodox *bona fides* after his *Divine Legation of Moses*: he wrote *Julian* publicly to distance himself from his old friend Conyers Middleton. This chapter opens with an examination of the *Weekly Miscellany*'s attack on Warburton during the late 1730s for having insufficiently criticized Middleton in the *Divine Legation*. Afterwards, Warburton's orthodox episcopal allies advised him publicly to distance himself from Middleton, which led to their friendship unravelling. The chapter turns next to anatomize *Julian*'s arguments. It concludes by illuminating how Warburton distinguished between miracles (like the destruction of the Jerusalem Temple rebuilding project in 363 AD) and prodigies (like the London and Lisbon earthquakes of the 1750s), while seeing both as tools of God's providential management of his creation. Warburton, then, contributed to a public discussion of providence for reasons that were also deeply personal. In that discussion, he employed Newtonian natural philosophy to interpret both natural and human history. Warburton employed it for orthodox ends, but in sometimes deeply idiosyncratic ways.

Warburton's problems with the orthodox began in late February 1738, when the *Weekly Miscellany* ran a letter from William Webster which complained about Warburton's approval of Conyers Middleton.[5] In a throwaway line in the *Divine Legation*, Warburton had praised Middleton's attacks on Matthew Tindal, characterizing Middleton as '[a]n excellent Person, and one of [Tindal's] most formidable Adversaries'.[6] Webster pounced on this. His front-page letter in the *Weekly Miscellany* robustly defended clericalism. 'We are Stewards of the Mysterious Doctrines and Institutions of our Religion', he insisted. 'We are listed, not only at our Baptism, but at our Ordination, into our Christian Warfare, under the Great Captain of our Salvation. We must study the Arts of it and assume a firm Resolution to fight the Good Fight of Faith.' Webster got irked that Warburton, whom he seems not to have met, had criticized orthodox polemical divines and had praised Conyers

Middleton. In the *Divine Legation*, Warburton had been 'very severe upon All Clergymen who take the Liberty of censuring the Conduct of any of their Brethren', while, Webster groused, '[h]e is a warmer Advocate for Dr ——— who denies the Divine Inspiration of the Scriptures, than for the Scriptures themselves'. None of the *Weekly Miscellany*'s readers would have mistaken whom Webster was excoriating. It was not the first time that the newspaper had criticized Middleton. Earlier, Richard Venn had likened Middleton to an 'apostate Priest'; Webster pressed that particular theme in his 1738 piece, as well.[7] 'If a Clergyman writes, under a pretence of defending Revelation, in the very same manner that an artful Infidel might naturally be supposed to use in Writing against it, such a Writer must excuse me if I suspect his Faith', Webster insisted. This was especially the case if the writer was, like Middleton, a clergyman. For Webster, Middleton's protestations that he had defended Christianity in a way that might persuade rationalist doubters beggared belief: 'I hear, the Infidels have already sounded the Praises of this Book, and I will do them the Justice to own, they generally know what they commend. This I am very sure of; the Author must be a subtle Enemy of Religion, or a very indiscreet Friend.' In not condemning Middleton in the *Divine Legation*, Warburton had tacitly supported someone whom the orthodox establishment had fingered as an enemy of true religion. Webster thought it a black-and-white issue; Warburton judged it decidedly more complicated.[8]

The Warburton–Middleton friendship began in early 1736, when, unbidden, Warburton sent Middleton a copy of his *Alliance between Church and State*. 'You will not be displeased I dare say at a project for securing Moses not only from the misrepresentations of his Enemies', he wrote to Middleton, 'but from the impertinencies of some of his friends, whose manner of defending him, I entirely agree with you, to be destructive of reason and consequently of true Religion'.[9] While this was not what Warburton had always thought, he quickly befriended Middleton, who admired the *Alliance*.[10]

The substantive part of their early correspondence concerned whether the ancients, particularly Cicero, had believed in a future state of rewards and punishments. Their debates turned on how to read historical sources.[11] Warburton, then working on the first volume of the *Divine Legation*, reckoned that Cicero (an 'Academic' philosopher) did not believe in life after death. Furthermore, he argued that Cicero's private letters – where Cicero spoke 'his real sentiments [that] there is not the least room for doubt' – revealed that he did not believe that the dead were either rewarded or punished after death.[12] Middleton, by contrast, rejected Warburton's contention that the ancients had a 'double Doctrine; the external, and the internal; the one for the Vulgar, the other for the Adept'.[13] On Middleton's reading, there was a fundamental coherence to Cicero's thought. To ascertain it one needed not to look for esoteric meanings but merely to read his works contextually. 'I find in him but one general, consistent, glorious character', Middleton retorted, 'of a great and good Man, acting and speaking on all Occasions, what the greatest

Prudence with the greatest Virtue would suggest'.[14] Middleton also rejected Warburton's characterization of Cicero's philosophical disposition. Where Warburton understood Cicero to have been 'perfectly sceptical', Middleton judged him to have been a probabilist. To be sure, the 'Philosophy of the Academy' to which Cicero had adhered had 'disclaimed all Certainty': but that did not mean that its adherents had rejected the possibility of ascertaining truth. Instead, '[t]hey imagined Truth and Falsehood to be so mixed and blended by Nature, that it was extremely difficult, if not impossible, to separate them entirely; that Probability was the utmost, that human Wit could arrive at'.[15] Recognizing this and reading Cicero's various works in their proper contexts, it became clear that Cicero had indeed believed in a future state. 'The whole Turn of his Writings, and the Tenor of his Life shew it', Middleton claimed. 'He lived expecting it, and always, so as to deserve it; and declares it to be his favourite Opinion; which, though possibly an Error, he was resolved to indulge.'[16] On this issue, Middleton and Warburton uncharacteristically (and, is turned out, only temporarily) agreed to disagree. Middleton chalked up their disagreement to their differing philosophical presuppositions: 'while my academic Complexion leaves me grovelling perhaps in the mire of Doubt, or turning the faint Track of Probability, your more sanguine Spirits, like the greater Mysteries, make you at once an Autoptes, and admit you to the joyous Regions of clear Day and Intuition'.[17] Nonetheless, their friendship began to deteriorate following the *Weekly Miscellany*'s attacks on Warburton.

Middleton first alerted Warburton to the *Weekly Miscellany*'s critical letter. He reckoned that Webster had written the piece with Richard Venn and that it 'breathes the genuine spirit of that insolent but impotent malice which animates them both'. He predicted that the newspaper's criticism would have no effect: 'it will be your comfort to find that the Paper is as stupid as it is spiteful. It is detested by all in this place, even those, who were disposed to be severe, as well as those, who justly applaud you.'[18] Middleton badly misread the situation, for Warburton's powerful clerical allies frowned on his public approbation of Middleton. Zachary Pearce, for instance, reminded Warburton of the 1731 letter in which Warburton (writing as 'W') had expressed 'a very ill opinion' of Middleton and had lamented Middleton's 'Insults, & ill-manners, unbecoming the civility of his Education & the gravity of his profession'.[19] Warburton pled that he had written to Pearce in 1731 having only read Middleton's first two anti-Waterland tracts, '[t]he great freedom of sentiment in which, much shocked me, & more, the air of insult that runs through them'. But, he continued, as he got to know Middleton, he became convinced that he had initially misjudged him: 'I find him humane, candid, generous, & always professing belief in Revelation'.[20]

Some on the episcopal bench also warned Warburton of the threat posed to his career prospects by the *Weekly Miscellany*'s criticism. Thomas Sherlock and Francis Hare, bishops of London and Chichester, had advised Warburton on edits to the final drafts of the *Divine Legation*. They counselled him, in particular, to soften his criticism of William Wollaston's work on natural religion.[21] Wollaston, Sherlock admonished, was 'a sober serious writer and scholar, and of exceeding good character in private life'.[22] Warburton heeded their advice, though he denied the widespread rumour that Sherlock and Hare 'had revised [his] sheets, as they came from the Press'.[23] However, he evidently showed neither Sherlock nor Hare the long dedication in which he applauded Middleton's anti-Tindal apologetical efforts. In hindsight, he erred. Sherlock, one of Middleton's *bêtes noires*, objected to Warburton's insistence in the *Divine Legation* that Middleton had been a 'formidable' opponent of freethinking, since many clergy thought that Middleton had reduced Moses to being 'a mere politician' and had defended 'the Christian religion as useful only for the present circumstances of life'. Even a qualified endorsement sullied Warburton's public reputation. 'I do not vouch for these conclusions', Sherlock explained, 'but those who are assured they are just, take your declaration to be approving the method, and to be a key to your own sentiments'.[24] When crafting his response, then, Warburton had to pitch his case not at Webster and Venn but at others 'who may possibly be desirous to see all ground of suspicion removed. In drawing the answer, you should consider such persons, much more than your angry adversary.' In particular, Sherlock advised, '[t]he case of Dr. M[iddleton] (which is the *hinc illae lachrymae* of the whole complaint) will require your last consideration'.[25]

Warburton came into Sherlock's orbit by way of Francis Hare, the person who also brought Warburton to Queen Caroline's attention.[26] Like Sherlock, Hare advised Warburton to respond to the *Weekly Miscellany*'s aspersions, which he initially attributed to Daniel Waterland.[27] Rather more than Sherlock, though, Hare spelled out for Warburton precisely why his casual approbation of Middleton had offended and how difficult it would be to undo the damage. 'The great difficulty is what to say with respect to Dr. Mid[dleton]', Hare acknowledged. 'If you say nothing of him, you might as well not write at all; since it is certainly that which gives the great offence.' Though surprised that Warburton had befriended Middleton *after* the publication of his *Letter to Dr. Waterland*, Hare professed to bear Middleton no personal ill will. Nonetheless, he unambiguously defended his earlier efforts to block Middleton's ascent of the ecclesiastical ladder of preferment. Lest Warburton not want to be 'marked for heterodoxy or infidelity', then, he needed publicly to distance himself from Middleton. The best way to do this, Hare and Sherlock counselled, was for Warburton to write a vindication of himself in which he should note that his 'commendation of [Middleton], as an *able adversary*, should be put upon the ability with which he has argued against the Freethinkers *upon their own principles*'.[28]

Within three weeks of receiving Sherlock's and Hare's admonishments, Warburton published a *Vindication of the author of the Divine Legation of Moses*.[29] This time, Hare and Sherlock vetted the whole text before publication.

Warburton opened the *Vindication* defending Middleton, arguing that his friend had shown far greater 'Candour, Sincerity, Benevolence and Charity' than William Webster.[30] Thereafter, Warburton gently distanced himself from Middleton. 'I differ widely from him in the Matter of Inspiration, and as widely in some others', he protested. In particular, he parted company with Middleton over one of the *Letter to Dr. Waterland*'s more provocative claims: Warburton claimed that his *Divine Legation* had shown that lying 'for the Public Good in Matters of Religion ... had no Place in the Propagation or Genius of the Jewish and Christian Religion'. In the end, Warburton claimed implausibly that his earlier public praise for Middleton was meant, in part, merely to 'engag[e] him to a further and more complete Vindication of our Holy Faith'.[31]

Though Webster inveighed against *The Divine Legation* for two more years, Warburton's episcopal supporters thought that his *Vindication* had been effective.[32] 'The part that relates to Dr Mid[dleton] the bishops think extremely well done', Hare assured Warburton. 'It was the only difficult part; and it cannot but please every candid writer, to see you do justice to yourself, and yet not to do it at his expense.'[33] Yet even still, months later Hare admitted that not all the damage had been undone: 'I have been told the Miscellanies have had an influence on many of the inferior clergy, and raised a spirit against your book'.[34] More importantly, the *Weekly Miscellany*'s criticism had given other orthodox polemical divines a handle in their subsequent attacks on the *Divine Legation*.[35] When orthodox criticism came, Warburton knew that he had only himself to blame. Middleton acknowledged the difficulty his friend faced. 'I can easily imagine, that you have suffered in the Opinion of [the archbishop of Canterbury] & many others of the same stamp, for your charitable Opinion of me', he wrote to Warburton, though he added that 'the free manner with which you treat certain characters & opinions, which pass for sacred with all such, is your fundamental and unpardonable crime'.[36]

For Middleton, Warburton's unpardonable crime was challenging the *Letter from Rome*'s thesis. Where Middleton held that many early Jewish and Christian practices had their origins in ancient pagan ones, Warburton's second volume of the *Divine Legation of Moses* countered that it was 'utterly wrong' to think that 'the Catholic borrowed from the Heathens' or that 'a great Part of the Jewish Ritual was composed in Reference to the Superstitions of Egypt'. To argue otherwise, Warburton contended, 'betrays the grossest Ignorance of human Nature, and the History of Mankind'.[37] Middleton took this as a direct slight and used an appendix to the 1741 edition of his *Letter from Rome* to target Warburton specifically.[38] Rather than descend into a public tit-for-tat, Warburton, prodded by his friend George Lyttleton, tried to make peace with Middleton.[39] Middleton accepted the olive branch.[40] And yet Warburton's muted praise for Middleton in the first volume of the *Divine Legation* continued to hurt his career prospects, or so he thought. In late 1742, Warburton fretted to Zachary Pearce that Archbishop Potter 'was disgusted at something I wrote'. In particular, Potter, Francis Hare told him, 'did appear to be offended with me, and that it as for commending Dr Middleton'.[41] Though Pearce reassured Warburton that Potter did not, in fact, think this, Warburton took the occasion in 1744 to publish a defence of the *Divine Legation* which singled out Middleton for criticism. With that pamphlet, their friendship – and, Warburton surely hoped, his association with Middleton's heterodoxy – was over.[42]

At around the same time during the early 1740s that the Warburton–Middleton unravelled, English interest in providence intensified. The Anglo-Spanish war of 1739, the 1745 Jacobite rebellion and earthquakes in London and Lisbon led many to offer providential explanations, as the tumult of the times got interpreted as God's warnings, punishments or rewards. Warburton began to think concertedly about providence within this context. *Julian* was his most sustained treatment of the subject. He also wrote about it in a variety of occasional sermons which bookended *Julian*.

David Hume was one of Warburton's targets in *Julian*. Warburton loathed Hume. 'He is an atheistical Jacobite, a monster as rare with us as a hippogriff', he inveighed upon the publication of Hume's *History of England* (1754–63).[43] None could dissuade him from these views. 'You have often told me of this man's moral virtues', he wrote to Andrew Millar, Hume's publisher. 'He may have many, for aught I know; but let me observe to you, there are vices of the mind as well as the body: and I think a wickeder mind, and a more obstinately bent on public mischief, I never knew.'[44] Warburton eventually got Hume's 'Of Suicide' and 'Of the Immortality of the Soul' banned, and his opposition compelled Hume to tone down *The Natural History of Religion* (1757).[45] When writing *Julian*, Warburton had in mind Hume's *Enquiry concerning Human Understanding* (1748), in which Hume had assaulted the very foundations of religious belief and in which he attacked the miraculous in particular. But Warburton was unsure whether the Scot was worth challenging explicitly. He confided, 'I am strongly tempted to take a stroke at Hume in parting. He is the author of a little book called Philosophical Essays. In one part of which he argues against the Being of God, and in another (very needlessly you will say) against the possibility of miracles.' Warburton wanted 'to do justice on his argument against miracles, which ... might be done in a very few words'. But he worried this might actually gain Hume a wider readership: 'But does he deserve notice? Is he known amongst you? Pray answer me these questions. For if his own weight keeps him down, I should be sorry to contribute to his advancement to any place but the pillory.'[46] In the end, *Julian* made only passing reference to Hume, though some of Warburton's friends encouraged him to target Hume more directly.[47]

Julian's chief target, instead, was Conyers Middleton, whose *Free Inquiry into the miraculous powers* (1748), had challenged the reliability of miracles from the patristic age, though not miracles generally nor biblical ones in particular.[48] When Warburton started writing *Julian*, he envisioned a 'sober and well weighted discourse' and had Middleton's *Free Inquiry* in his sights.[49] When drafting *Julian*, though, Warburton admitted that he still respected Middleton and that he tried to craft the argument so as not to offend him. 'I esteem Dr Middleton to be an honest man', he explained to Richard Hurd. '... This, and my acquaintance with him, and my dislike of his adversaries' scheme, make me begin the discourse in a manner he ought not to dislike, and conclude it in a manner, I am sure, they will not approve.'[50]

Warburton tried to explain why miracles happened. God involved himself in the world through acts of particular providence, such as miracles, because he directed the universe's natural and moral government. God, 'the moral Governor of the universe, whose essential character it is, not to leave himself without a witness, doth frequently employ the physical and civil operations of the natural system, to support and reform the moral', Warburton argued. It followed that, if God really were to govern the moral universe, 'he must manifest his dominion in whatever world he is pleased to station and to exercise his accountable and probationary creatures. In man's state and condition here, natural and civil events are the proper instruments of moral government.'[51]

'Deists' refused to make God 'the moral, that is, the close, the minute and immediate inspector of human actions' because they thought this role both degraded the universe's creator and defied reason.[52] Warburton rejected this, countering that reasonableness is not the appropriate criterion to judge God's actions.[53] Rather, necessity was the appropriate touchstone of the miraculous. A miracle was 'of so high importance as to be even necessary to Revelation, and to the religious Dispensation to which it belongs'.[54] Elsewhere he explained that when a miracle is 'performed by the immediate power of God, without the intervention of his servants', it must meet one of two criteria: 'either that an inspired servant of God predicted it, and declared its purpose beforehand ... or that it be seen to interpose so seasonably and critically as to cover and secure God's moral government from inevitable dishonour'.[55] The fiery eruption that halted Julian's Temple reconstruction in 363 was 'necessary to secure God's moral government from inevitable dishonour': thus it was a miracle. For in the Bible, God had providentially linked the Temple's destruction with Christianity's rise. '[T]he truth of Christianity must stand or fall with the ruin or restoration of the temple at Jerusalem', Warburton explained, 'for if that temple should be rebuilt for the purpose of Jewish worship, Christianity could not support its pretensions; nor the Prophets, nor Jesus, the truth of their predictions'.[56]

Having shown why God could not allow the Temple to be reconstructed, Warburton explained how he had stopped the construction through a miracle. He acknowledged that God's operations often surpassed human comprehension. 'The ordinary Dispensations of Providence are dark and perplexing, and have ever wore a double Face', he acknowledged, 'from which, with equal

Force, may be drawn contrary Conclusions, according to the Humour or Interest of the Contemplator'.[57] Nonetheless, he thought it possible at times to discern the mechanisms of divine action.

In the tenth section ('Of Miracles') of his *Enquiry*, Hume defined a miracle as 'a violation of the laws of nature' and as 'a transgression of a law of nature by a particular volition of the Deity, or by the interposition of some invisible agent'. By this definition miracles were impossible: 'as a firm and unalterable experience has established these laws, the proof against a miracle, from the very nature of its fact, is as entire as any argument from experience can possibly be imagined'.[58] Warburton disagreed comprehensively with Hume's definition. Miracles, he argued as far back as 1727, did not violate nature's immutable laws. Rather, a miracle 'is the giving new laws to those Portions of Matter wherein the Sphere of the Miracle, which carry with them the equal Marks of stupendous Wisdom and Power'.[59] Later he held that '[t]he agency of a superior Being on any part of the visible creation lying within the reach of our senses, whereby it acquires properties and directions different from what we hold it capable of receiving from the established laws of matter and motion, we call a Miracle'.[60] Miracles came in three varieties. First are those 'where the laws of nature are suspended or reversed' (e.g., Jesus raising Lazarus from the dead). Second are 'those which only give a new direction to its Laws' (e.g., water pouring forth from stone). Third are those which 'compounded of the two, where the laws of nature are in part arrested and suspended; and, in part only, differently directed' (e.g., the Biblical flood).[61] Either God immediately effected these miracles himself or he worked through his messengers, such as the Apostles.

Warburton's understanding of divine action and the miraculous evidenced his debt to contemporary natural philosophy. Bacon, Boyle, Locke and Pascal were among 'the great Masters of science' who held a 'warm attachment to Revelation'.[62] The nascent field of geology, in particular, spoke to Christianity's truth. 'In natural Philosophy', Warburton explained, 'more exact enquiries have been made into the contents of the superior covering of the terraqueous Globe; the peculiarities of whose arrangements give the strongest evidence of the Mosaic account of the Deluge'.[63] Similar fossils, he noted, had been found across the earth and in varying types of soils: 'Had these adventitious fossils not been found in every quarter of the Globe, we would not conclude the Deluge to have been universal.' However, he continued, 'when we see them spread over every climate, and yet only in such soils as are proper for the preservation of foreign bodies, we rightly conclude them to be the deposit of a Deluge of waters which covered the whole face of the Earth'.[64]

The star that shone brightest in the natural philosophical firmament for Warburton was Isaac Newton. Admittedly Warburton read Newton's biblical scholarship with a wary eye. Of Newton's *Observations upon the Prophecies of Daniel, and the Apocalypse of St John* (1732), he reckoned that 'tho' [Newton] was a prodigy in His way, yet I never expected great things of this kind (which requires a perfect knowledge of ancient literature, History and Mankind) from a man who spent all his days in looking through a Telescope'.[65] Warburton approved more fully of Newton's natural philosophical writings, which informed his understanding of divine action in the natural world.[66] 'And the immortal Theory of Newton absolutely demonstrates that intimate relation which Moses speaks of, between the Creator and his work', Warburton argued.[67] The portion of Newton's 'immortal Theory' he found especially useful concerned the distinction between matter and activity. Newton theorized that matter was wholly inert and had activity imposed upon it by a God who was immanent in the world.[68] Likewise, Newton distinguished between causes, so that physical laws governing nature were but second causes created and put in place by God, the first cause. He also held that God ruled the world providentially, not just through the general mechanical laws of nature that governed his creation but also through particular voluntary actions.[69] The early Boyle lectures often popularized and more explicitly Christianized Newton's natural philosophy.[70] Warburton was parroting the early Boyle lecturers when he drew the connections for his audiences at Lincoln's Inn between Newtonian natural philosophy and God's governance of the universe. When we examine the universe 'on the unerring experience of Newtonian physics', Warburton explained, it is evident 'that God is intimately present to every particle of Matter, at every point of Space, and in every instance of a Being':

> For *vis inertiae*, or resistance to the change of its present state, being an essential quality of Matter, and inconsistent with any motive force, or power in that Substance, all those effects commonly ascribed to a certain essence residing in it, such as gravity, or attraction, elasticity, repulsion, or whatever other tendencies to Motion are observed in Matter, are not powers naturally belonging to it, or what can possibly be made inherent in it. So that these qualities without which, Matter would be utterly unfit for use, must needs be produced by the immediate influence of the first Cause, incessantly performing, by his almighty finger, the minutest Office in the Material Economy; working still near us, round us, within us, and in every part of us.[71]

The distinction between matter and activity and between first and second causes provided the intellectual foundation of Warburton's explanations of God's providential interventions in the natural world. Nowhere is this more evident than in *Julian*.

A series of extraordinary natural occurrences in 363 halted construction on the Jerusalem Temple. They all, Warburton argued, could be traced directly to God's hand. Collating, examining and comparing the patristic testimony regarding the abandoned Temple reconstruction, Warburton identified the natural events that led authorities to abandon the Temple reconstruction. 'The first signs the Almighty gave of his approaching judgment, were the storms, tempests and whirlwinds', he explained. 'These instruments of vengeance performed their office, in the dispersion of loose materials.'[72]

Shortly thereafter, lightning struck. 'The effects of this produced were, first, destroying the more solid materials, and melting down the iron instruments: and secondly, impressing that prodigious mark on the bodies and garments of the assistants.' The lightning was prelude to an earthquake which 'cast out the stones of the old foundations ... it shook the earth into the new-dug foundation ... and it overthrew the adjoining buildings and porticos'. Then followed a 'fiery eruption, which destroyed and maimed so many of the workmen and assistants; and at length forced the undertakers to give over the attempt as desperate'. Finally, there appeared 'a lucid cross in the heavens, circumscribed within a luminous circle'. This, Warburton noted, was a fittingly symbolic end to the chain of events: 'Nature, put so suddenly into commotion by its Creator, was, on the despair and dispersion of its enemies, as suddenly calmed and composed ... And what could be conceived so proper to close this tremendous scene, or to celebrate this decisive victory, as the Cross triumphant, incircled within the Heroic symbol of conquest?'

Warburton explained a number of these phenomena naturalistically. The encircled cross in the sky, for instance, 'was neither more nor less than one of those meteoric lights, in a still and clouded sky, which are not unfrequently seen in solar or lunar haloes'.[73] The crosses were also phosphorific: 'They shown at night, and were dark, and smoky-coloured by day ... the very property ... of Phosphori'.[74] Likewise, the lightning that attended the fiery eruption was subject to naturalistic explanation. Air 'put into a violent motion, always produces lightning, when it abounds with matter susceptible of inflammation', he reckoned. 'And those columns of air, which lie over places that labour with convulsive throws to cast out an inkindled matter from its entrails, must needs be impregnated with vast quantities of sulphurous particles, which the earth ... exudes from its pores, and which the solar heat draws upwards'.[75]

Natural philosophy and orthodox theology converged in Warburton's explanation of what had set these natural events in motion. Having examined the evidence, Warburton concluded 'that the mineral and metallic substances (which by their accidental fermentation, are wont to take fire and burst into flames) ... would have slept, and still continued in the quiet innoxious state in which they have so long remained had not the breath of the Lord awoke and kindled them'. Having 'miraculously interposed to stir up the rage of these fiery elements, and yet to restrain their fury to the objects of vengeance, he then again suffered them to do their ordinary office'. For, Warburton noted, 'Nature thus directed would, by the exertion of its own laws, answer all the ends of the moral designation'. The effects which attended the fiery eruption in 363, then, 'would be the same with those attending mere natural eruptions'. Warburton concluded that

> the specific qualities of the fermented elements, which occasioned the frightful appearances, though they were natural or enflamed matter under certain circum-

> stances, were yet, by the peculiar pleasure of Providence, given on this occasion; and not left merely to the conjunction of mechanic causes, or the fortuitous concourse of matter and motion, to produce. And my reason is, because these frightful appearances, namely the cross in the heavens, and on the garments, were admirably fitted, as Moral Emblems, to proclaim the triumph of Christ over Julian.[76]

Newtonian matter theory helped explain *how* God had intervened in fourth-century Jerusalem, while necessity proved *why* God had no choice but to effect the miraculous fiery eruption that brought the Temple's reconstruction to an end.

Warburton wrote *Julian* in 1749 to defend orthodox understandings of miracles and to display publicly the theological distance between him and Conyers Middleton. The book's publication in late spring 1750 was inadvertently timed for maximum impact, since it followed a series of earthquakes that had shaken London. A minor earthquake struck London on 8 February 1750. When a more violent tremor rumbled under London exactly a month later, the concerns of February turned to widespread panic, especially when a mad soldier predicted that God would destroy London a month later on 8 April with a third earthquake.[77] Many fled London, hoping that distance from the capital would save them when the next earthquake hit. 'This frantic terror prevails so much, that within these three days 730 coaches have been counted passing Hyde Park Corner, with whole parties removing into the country', Horace Walpole reported in early April.[78] The third earthquake never materialized, but the seismic activity of that winter and early spring unnerved many. Most people believed that the London earthquakes were divinely caused. But were they miracles? Warburton thought not. Instead, the London earthquakes – and the calamitous earthquake that struck Lisbon on 1 November 1755 – were prodigies, what Samuel Johnson characterized as 'Anything out of the ordinary process of nature from which omens are drawn'.[79]

Warburton sought to explain both *why* God had produced these prodigies and *how* he had effected them. The London and Lisbon earthquakes were not miraculous, he argued, because they met neither of the 'two necessary occasions' for miracles: firstly, 'to attest and support the truth of a new Religion coming from God' or, secondly, 'to administer a Theocratic government'.[80] God intended them nonetheless as warnings to a sinful nation, a belief expressed in eight out of ten publications in England occasioned by the London and Lisbon earthquakes.[81] Providentialism likewise informed the government's decision, in the wake of the earthquake, to call for a day of public fast and humiliation on 6 February 1756. 'Whereas the manifold Sins and Wickedness of these Kingdoms, have most justly deserved heavy and severe Punishments from the Hand of Heaven', read the English proclamation, '... [we] send up our Prayers and Supplications to the Divine Majesty, to avert all those Judgments which We most justly have deserved'.[82] Only a national reformation of manners, Warburton preached in his fast sermon, could avert

England's imminent punishment at God's hands: 'A Sincere, a speedy and a thorough reformation will not fail to avert the anger of the Lord, now gone out against the sinful inhabitants of the earth.' Party politics, luxury and greed had corrupted the nation, which God now punished for that corruption. The only solution was 'a reformation of the general manners, where each of us ... may concur to heal the breaches made in our excellent constitution by our party-follies; to oppose the enormous progress of avarice and corruption; to check the wasting rage for displeasure and amusement; to shake off those unmanly luxuries crept in to domestic life, some for the gratification of our appetites, but more for the display of our vanities'.[83]

Warburton adopted this line of argument because he believed that God punished nations corporately for their sins.[84] 'The temporal punishments which God inflicts upon iniquity, have three objects. Particulars; a People; and a State or Government', he explained. 'The punishments of the first two Objects, I hold to be for the Crimes of Men; the latter only for the Crimes of the State.'[85] God punished nations collectively instead of their inhabitants individually because states were moral agents: societies 'as well as private Men, [have] all those essential Qualities, which constitute a moral Agent; the Discernment of Good and Evil, a Will to choose, and a Power to put their Choice into Execution. In one word, artificial Men.' For that reason, 'the Hand of Heaven distributes Good and Evil to Societies, according to their Merit or Demerit'.[86] During the middle third of the eighteenth century, wars abroad and unrest at home gave Warburton, the English and their government ample reason to think that God was punishing the nation. Despite these internal and external threats to the nation's security, England somehow survived. Warburton, like many of his contemporaries, discerned a clear message from that deliverance: this 'Preservation of them, at every important Crisis, when Human Power and Policy ... seemed combined to our Destruction' indicated God's 'Election of us for the Instruments of his Glory'. But elected to do what? 'Tis possible we may be chosen by Providence ... to preserve the Memory of Civil Liberty amongst the degenerate Sons of Man', Warburton speculated, 'as the House of Israel was formerly, to keep alive True Religion amidst a Universal Apostasy'.[87]

Having explained the reasons for prodigies, Warburton turned to explain how they occurred. He was clear that prodigies were not miracles and, thus, were not the result of God suspending, reversing, redirecting or compounding the mechanical laws of nature. Prodigies did, however, have 'natural effects; whose causes we being ignorant of, we have made them ideal creatures of distinct species, but rank with all other natural effects'.[88] Prodigies were not, in other words, part of God's particular providence, but were, instead, part of his general providence. They were the 'pre-established direction of natural events' where 'the stated laws of physics while they are promoting their own purpose, are, at the same time ... contrived as to support, invigorate and inforce the sanctions of religion'.[89] God had preordained 'the circumstances of the natural and moral systems, so to make the events of the former serve the regulation of the latter'.[90]

Prodigies were instruments of warning or punishment that required God to preset the operation or confluence of nature's immutable laws in a certain way, at a certain time and in a certain matter. This belief jibed easily with the natural philosophical distinction between first and second causes. For Warburton to explain how divine action shaped human historical causation, however, required him to leave behind natural philosophy and to venture into territory few of his orthodox contemporaries wished to visit. His arguments on providence and human action highlight the explanatory limits of Newtonian natural philosophy for orthodox Christians during the mid-eighteenth century.

Warburton agreed with most orthodox that God interposed directly in human events, just as he did in the natural world. 'Indeed, all who believe the moral Government of God, how much soever they may differ concerning his mode of administering it among Particular, and how obscure soever his ways may appear in the tracts of private life, yet concur to acknowledge and to revere his visible interposition in the revolutions of States and Empires', he explained.[91] These interpositions enabled God to govern the moral universe. 'Civil commotions have the same use, and do the same service in the political world, that stormy and tempestuous seasons do in the physical', he contended. 'In the stagnation of a continued calm, the whole system would sicken and decay; but these periodic agitations stifle corruption in the seed, give fresh vigour to the vital parts, and enable all the active principles to perform their destined operations.'[92]

The tricky issue, as the orthodox saw it, was not *whether* God intervened in human events but *how* he intervened. In their jeremiads, few eighteenth-century polemical divines discussed the means of God's interposition in human affairs.[93] Warburton offered conflicting explanations of divine action upon human societies. In a 30 January 1760 sermon to the House of Lords commemorating Charles I's death, he argued that God does not actually control human affairs. 'The System of Nature has the Providence of God to curb the blind violence of stubborn matter, which else, in the impetuosity of its course, would soon reduce itself to its former Chaos', he told the assembled nobles. The 'Political System', though, has only the 'Providence of Government to sustain it against its own fury, from falling into Anarchy'. Because the 'Providence of Government is weak and bounded' it requires 'all the assistance of good subjects to strengthen its hands, and enforce obedience to its insulted Authority'. Regicide and republicanism resulted from the failure of the English in 'this salutary duty' during the 1640s.[94] Where politics were concerned, then, there was no check on free will.

Elsewhere, though, Warburton contended that God does actually directly shape human actions. In the *annus mirabilis* of 1759, he preached that God fought 'our battles', proving that England was the 'sole remaining Trustee of Civil Freedom, and so of the great Bulwark of Gospel Truth'.[95] How had God fought and won them on England's behalf? God 'governs the material world, has immediate access to the minds of men, and manages and turns them as rivulets of water'. Consider, for instance, 'what multitude of thoughts shall come uncalled and unforeseen' into your mind, and 'how suddenly without design and even against our will, they shall dart from object to object'. Sometimes only a 'trifling incident' will set in motion 'a train of ideas with which are connected events of the last consequence to our own comfort, and the happiness of those around us. Can we fail to conclude that God is within over-ruling the mind?', Warburton asked. 'And in what instance does this influence and direction more remarkably appear than in the thoughts that guide and give efficacy to the conduct and events of war? the rise, the rebuke or revolution of great enterprises?' God, then, tinkers with our very thoughts when he finds it necessary to do so. The 'noblest genius, and the most sanguine expectations of princes' are no match for God when he chooses to take control of men's minds.[96] It is easy to see why some might have been loath to make such an argument, robbing man, as it does, of free will and the unimpeded use of his rational faculties.[97]

William Warburton lived in a world whose unfolding history was shaped and governed directly by God. Indeed, he could barely contemplate a world in which God's fingerprints on events were not evidently visible. When Conyers Middleton died, he wondered why Middleton rejoiced in confidence that 'he had given the Miracles of the early ages such a blow as they would not easily recover'. He failed to 'see how the mere discovery of Truth affords such pleasure':

> If this Truth be, that the Providence of God governs the moral as well as the natural world; and that, in compassion to human distresses, he has revealed his will to mankind, by which we are enabled to get the better of them, by a restoration of his favour, I can easily conceive the pleasure that, at any period of life, must accompany such a discovery. But, if the Truth discovered be that we have no farther share in God than as we partake of his natural government of the Universe; or that all there is in his moral government is only the natural necessary effects of Virtue and Vice upon human agents here, and that all the pretended Revelations of an hereafter were begot by fools, and hurried up by knaves; if this, I say, be our boasted discovery, it must, I think, prove a very uncomfortable contemplation, especially in our last hours.[98]

When something horrible, like the Lisbon earthquake, occurred, Warburton found comfort in the belief that it was God's doing. 'It is indeed a dreadful thing to suppose these disasters the vengeance of our offended Master', he wrote to Joseph Atwell, 'but it is ten times more terrible to believe we have our precarious being in a forlorn and fatherless world. In the first case, we have it in our power to avert our destruction by the amendment of our manners; in the latter, we are exposed without hopes of refuge to the free range of matters and motion in a ferment'.[99]

In arguing this, Warburton was well within the mainstream of contemporary thought. One contemporary who broadly agreed with him regarding God's providence was John Wesley, a Church of England clergyman and one of Methodism's founders. In 1755, Wesley published some *Serious thoughts occasioned by the earthquake at Lisbon*. He argued that eighteenth-century man was 'not more virtuous than the ancient Heathens' and that God disapproved of this.[100] The Portuguese, in particular, had earned God's wrath for having supported the Inquisition. '[I]s it not surprising that He should begin there, where so much Blood has been poured on the Ground like Water', Wesley wondered, 'where so many brave man have been murdered; in the most base and cowardly, as well as barbarous Manner, almost every Day, as well as Night, whilst none regarded or laid it to Heart'?[101] The Lisbon earthquake, then, was providentially explicable. England, though, had also sinned serially, if less egregiously. Like Warburton, Wesley was interested not just in why God intervened providentially but how God had employed nature in those interventions. For instance, Wesley explained the natural causes of a recent spate of seismic events in England, subscribing in particular to the theory that 'imprisoned Air' suddenly released had caused the seismic activity. But he was explicit that these natural causes were the direct result of God's providential hand: God is active, not a 'lazy, indolent, Epicurean deity', he insisted.[102] That actively providential God warns and punishes both individuals and nations.

For Wesley, though, avoiding those punishments demanded a certain kind of behaviour. In particular, to 'secure the Favour of this great God' required 'worshipping Him in Spirit and in Truth'.[103] This entailed a reformation of the heart, not espousing particular doctrines or worshipping in a particular way. 'Surely you did not imagine that Christianity was no more than such a System of Opinions (as is vulgarly called Faith?) or a strict and regular Attendance on any kind of external Worship?' Wesley asked rhetorically. To his Methodist followers, this was a call to a spiritual rebirth and renewal. To many orthodox churchmen, including William Warburton, it sounded like the antinominan ravings of seventeenth-century religious radicals. He made this case in a series of works during the mid-eighteenth century culminating in *The Doctrine of Grace* (1763), a work directed against both John Wesley and Conyers Middleton.

NOTES

1 Warburton to Doddridge, 10 June 1749 (Beinecke, Osborn File Folder 15703). See also Warburton to Hurd, 6 August 1749 (*LLEP*, pp. 6–8). Parts of this chapter appeared in R. Ingram, 'William Warburton, Divine Action and Enlightened Christianity', in W. Gibson and R. Ingram (eds), *Religious Identities in Britain, 1660–1832* (Aldershot, 2005), pp. 97–119.

2 G. Bowersock, *Julian the Apostate* (Cambridge, MA, 1978), pp. 88–90.
3 A. Walsham, *Providence in Early Modern England* (Oxford, 1999); J. Sheehan and D. Wahrman, *Invisible Hands: Self-Organization and the Eighteenth Century* (Chicago, 2015), pp. 11–46.
4 J. Israel, *Radical Enlightenment: Philosophy and the Making of Modernity, 1650–1750* (Oxford, 2001), pp. 218–29; J. Wigelsworth, '"God always acts suitable to his character, as a wise and good being": Thomas Chubb and Thomas Morgan on Miracles and Providence', in W. Hudson, D. Lucci and J. Wigelsworth (eds), *Atheism and Deism Revalued: Religious Identities in Britain, 1650–1800* (Aldershot, 2014), pp. 139–56.
5 *WM* (24 February 1738), pp. 1–2. Webster used his common pseudonym, 'A Country Clergyman'. Unless otherwise noted, all quotations in this paragraph are drawn from this letter.
6 W. Warburton, *Divine Legation of Moses* (1738: T133104), I, p. xviii.
7 *WM* (15 February 1735). Cf. Middleton to Venn, 23 February 1735 (BL, Add. 32457, fols 112–13); *Independent London Journal* (19 July 1735), p. 1.
8 It should be remembered that Webster was a Daniel Waterland protégé, who had translated and introduced Louis Maimbourg's *History of Arianism* during the late 1720s at Waterland's encouragement: Webster, *History of Arianism*, preface. Warburton himself did not think highly of Waterland: Warburton to Robert Taylor, 1740 (HRC, Warburton I, pp. 103–4); Warburton to Middleton, 8 February 1741, [1741] (BL, Egerton 1953, fols 48, 49).
9 Warburton to Middleton, 19 January 1736 (BL, Egerton 1953, fol. 1).
10 Middleton to Warburton, 10 February 1736 (BL, Add. 32457, fol. 114). Cf. Warburton to Zachary Pearce, 4 March 1731 (WAM 64779); Warburton to Stukeley, 4 February 1733 (*LI*, II, 19–20).
11 'You remember we had some discourse concerning Tully's real sentiments of a future state of rewards and punishments': Warburton to Middleton, 15 May 1736 (BL, Egerton 1953, fol. 4).
12 Ibid., fol. 5.
13 Middleton to Warburton, 11 September 1736 (*MWCM*, II, p. 460).
14 Ibid., p. 474.
15 Ibid., p. 461.
16 Ibid., p. 465. Cf. Warburton to Middleton, 5 October 1736 (BL, Egerton 1953, fols 6–13).
17 Middleton to Warburton, 23 February 1738 (BL, Add 32457, fols 126–7).
18 Middleton to Warburton, 28 February 1738 (ibid., fol. 128).
19 Pearce to Warburton, 30 March 1738 (WAM 64780). See also [Warburton] to Pearce, 4 March 1731 (WAM 64739).
20 Warburton to Pearce, 3 April 1738 (WAM 64781).
21 Warburton to Sherlock, 27 January 1737; Hare to Warburton, 11 November 1737; Sherlock to Warburton, 29 November 1737 (Kilvert, pp. 50–3, 56, 110–11).
22 Sherlock to Warburton, 18 October 1737 (Kilvert, p. 55). See also Hare to Warburton, 11 November 1737 (Folger Shakespeare Library, V.b.268, after p. 364). Cf. D. Lucci, 'William Wollaston's Religion of Nature', in W. Hudson, D. Lucci and J. Wigelsworth (eds), *Atheism and Deism Revalued: Religious Identities in Britain, 1650–1800* (Aldershot, 2014), pp. 119–38.

23 Middleton to Warburton, 14 March 1738 (BL, Add. 32457, fol. 116); Warburton to Middleton, 18 March 1738 (BL, Egerton 1953, fol. 28).

24 Sherlock to Warburton, 2 March 1738 (Kilvert, p. 62).

25 Sherlock to Warburton, 9 March 1738 (ibid., pp. 63–4).

26 Hare to Warburton, 29 January 1736 (ibid., pp. 94–5); Warburton to Pierre Maizeaux, 22 May 1736 (BL, Add. 4288, fol. 235); Pattison, 'Life'.

27 Hare to Warburton, 28 February 1738, 8 June 1738 (Kilvert, pp. 100, 115–16). Middleton doubted that Waterland had penned the *Weekly Miscellany* piece, but agreed that Waterland had offered Webster the intellectual ammunition to attack him: Middleton to Warburton, 5 August 1738 (BL, Add. MS 32457, fol. 132). Cf. Warburton to Middleton, 12 August 1738 (BL, Egerton 1953, fols 35–6).

28 Hare to Warburton, 9 March 1738 (Kilvert, pp. 101–2). Emphasis in the original.

29 Warburton to Doddridge, 27 May 1738 (Folger Shakespeare Library, MS Y.c.1451 (2)).

30 W. Warburton, *Vindication of the author* (1738: T050839), p. 11.

31 Ibid., pp. 13, 14.

32 [W. Webster], *Remarks on The divine legation of Moses* (1739: T046804); [W. Webster], *Letter to a bishop* (1741: T133062).

33 Hare to Warburton, 23 March 1738 (Kilvert, p. 104).

34 Hare to Warburton, 8 June 1738 (ibid., p. 116).

35 Hare to Warburton, 20 January 1730 (Folger Shakespeare Library, W.b.74).

36 Middleton to Warburton, 4 September 1739 (Beinecke, Osborn Files Folder 10185).

37 W. Warburton, *Divine Legation of Moses* (1741: T133104), II, pp. 362, 363.

38 C. Middleton, *Letter from Rome* (1741: T087410), pp. 225–48.

39 Lyttleton to Warburton, 7, 27 October 1741 (Kilvert, pp. 197–200; Pierpont Morgan Library, Misc. English, MA Unassigned); Warburton to Middleton, 16 September, 26 October 1741 (BL, Egerton 1953, fols 52, 53).

40 Middleton to Warburton, 22 October 1741 (*MWCM*, II, pp. 488–90).

41 Warburton to Pearce, 1742 (WAM 64787). Pearce noted in a postscript that Potter did not recall having spoken with Hare about Warburton and asked Pearce to reassure Warburton that Hare must have misremembered.

42 Their correspondence broke off in late 1741, after Warburton privately spelled out to Middleton the nature of their disagreement over whether the ceremonies of the Church of Rome originated in paganism: Warburton to Middleton, 26 October 1741 (BL, Egerton 1953, fol. 53).

43 Warburton to Joseph Atwell, 8 January 1755 (Kilvert, p. 257).

44 Warburton to Millar, 7 February 1757 (ibid., pp. 309–10).

45 B. Young, *Religion and Enlightenment in Eighteenth-Century England* (Oxford, 1998), pp. 210–11.

46 Warburton to Hurd, 28 September 1749 (*LLEP*, pp. 10–11).

47 Warburton to Doddridge, 15 June 1750 (Huntington, HM 20438).

48 But see C. Middleton, 'Reflections on the Variations, or Inconsistencies, which are found among the Four Evangelists in their different Accounts of the Same Facts', *MWCM*, II, pp. 23–75; W. Heberden, 'A short account of some manuscripts of Dr. Middleton's', n.d. (BL, Add. 32459, fols 155–6).

49 Warburton to Nathaniel Forster, 28 February 1749 (BL, Add. 11275, fol. 187).

50 Warburton to Hurd, 6 August 1749 (*LLEP*, 7). See also Warburton to Forster, 3 April 1750 (BL, Add. 11275, fol. 198); Warburton to Hurd, 10 February 1750 (*LLEP*, pp. 28–30).

51 W. Warburton, *Natural and civil events the instruments of God's moral government* (1756: T009119), p. 4.

52 W. Warburton, 'God's Moral Government', *WWW*, IX, p. 36.

53 W. Warburton, 'On the Resurrection', *WWW*, IX, p. 215.

54 Ibid., p. 208.

55 Warburton, *Julian*, in *WWW*, VIII, p. 214.

56 Ibid., p. 48. See also Warburton to Nathaniel Forster, 28 February 1749 (BL Add. 11275, fol. 187); Warburton to Hurd (*LLEP*, pp. 20–2).

57 W. Warburton, *Critical and Philosophical Enquiry* (1727: T146881), p. 122.

58 D. Hume, *An Enquiry Concerning Human Understanding: A Critical Edition*, ed. T. Beauchamp (Oxford, 2000), p. 173. M. Levine, 'Hume on Miracles: It's Part 2 That Matters', in P. Russell (ed.), *Oxford Handbook of Hume* (Oxford, 2016), pp. 591–606, surveys the philosophical literature. See also J. Harris, *Hume: An Intellectual Biography* (Oxford, 2015), pp. 228–30; B. Gregory, *The Unintended Reformation* (Cambridge, MA, 2012), pp. 61–2.

59 Warburton, *Critical and Philosophical enquiry*, p. 127.

60 Warburton, *Julian*, p. 202.

61 Ibid., pp. 203–5.

62 Warburton, 'The Influence of Learning on Revelation', *WWW*, IX, p. 260.

63 Ibid., pp. 258–9.

64 Ibid., p. 259. See also R. Rappaport, 'The Earth Sciences', in R. Porter (ed.), *Eighteenth-Century Science* (Cambridge, 2003), pp. 417–35.

65 Warburton to Stukeley, 10 February 1733 (Bodleian, Eng.lett.d.35, fol. 28).

66 Warburton to Robert Taylor, 23 December 1729 (HRC, Warburton I, Letter 4) found Warburton asking Taylor to buy him a copy of Henry Pemberton's *View of Sir Isaac Newton's Philosophy* (1728). It was clear that Warburton knew large parts of Newton's natural philosophical work, for Thomas Birch published Warburton's thoughts on Newton's theories of the solar system and of colours in his *Life of Newton*: Warburton to Birch, 17 June 1738 (BL, Add. 4320, fol. 124). Warburton also approved of Andrew Baxter's attempt in *Matho* (1738) to detail 'the true system of the Universe, and its close and immediate dependence on its Creator; in which he endeavours to bring the Newtonian principles to the capacity of a boy of 12': Warburton to Birch, 16 September 1738 (BL, Add. 4320, fol. 143).

67 Warburton, 'The Influence of Learning', p. 259.

68 See, for instance, P. Heimann and J. McGuire, 'Newtonian Forces and Lockean Powers', in R. McCormmach (ed.), *Historical Studies in the Physical Sciences* (Philadelphia, 1971), pp. 233–306; P. Heimann, 'Voluntarism and Immanence: Conceptions of Nature in Eighteenth-Century Thought', *JHI* 39 (1978), pp. 271–83; S. Schaffer, 'Natural Philosophy', in G. Rousseau and R. Porter (eds), *The Ferment of Knowledge* (Cambridge, 1980), pp. 58–71; C. Wilde, 'Matter and Spirit as Natural Symbols in Eighteenth-Century British Natural Philosophy', *BJHS* 15 (1982), pp. 99–131; J. Yolton, *Thinking Matter: Materialism in Eighteenth-Century Britain* (Minneapolis, 1983). Cf. D. Levitin, 'Newton and Scholastic Philosophy', *BJHS* 49 (2016), pp. 53–77.

69 D. Kubrin, 'Newton and the Cyclical Cosmos: Providence and the Mechanical Philosophy', *JHI* 28 (1967), pp. 325–46; A. Ramati, 'The Hidden Truth of Creation: Newton's Method of Fluxions', *BJHS* 24 (2001), pp. 417–38.
70 M. Jacob, *The Newtonians and the English Revolution, 1689–1720* (Ithaca, NY, 1976), pp. 162–200; J. Gascoigne, 'From Bentley to the Victorians: The Rise and Fall of British Newtonian Natural Theology', *Science in Context* 2 (1988), pp. 222–6. Cf. R. Ingram, 'Nature, History and the Search for Order: The Boyle Lectures, 1730–1785', *SCH* 46 (2010), pp. 276–92.
71 Warburton, 'God's Moral Government', pp. 40.
72 Unless otherwise noted, all quotations that follow in this paragraph are drawn from Warburton, *Julian*, pp. 136–8.
73 Ibid., p. 116.
74 Ibid., p. 120.
75 Ibid., p. 118.
76 Ibid., p. 206.
77 See, for instance, Catherine Talbot to Elizabeth Carter, 3 April 1750 (*A series of letters between Mrs. Elizabeth Carter and Miss Catherine Talbot from ... 1741 to 1770* [1809], I, p. 332); A. Savile (ed.), *Secret Comment: The Diaries of Gertrude Savile, 1721–1757* (Devon, 1997), p. 291.
78 Walpole to Horace Mann, 2 April 1750 (*WC*, XX, pp. 136–7).
79 Johnson, *Dictionary*, II, unpaginated.
80 Warburton, *Natural and civil events*, p. 9.
81 R. Ingram, '"The trembling earth is God's Herald": Earthquakes, Religion and Public Life in Britain during the 1750s', in T. Braun and J. Radner (eds), *The Lisbon Earthquake of 1755* (Oxford, 2005), p. 101.
82 *Proclamation for a General Fast* [6 February 1756], p. 1.
83 Warburton, *Natural and civil events*, p. 14. Cf. W. Burns, *An Age of Wonders: Prodigies, Politics and Providence in England, 1657–1727* (Manchester, 2002), p. 187.
84 D. Napthine and W. Speck, 'Clergymen and Conflict, 1660–1763', *SCH* 19 (1983), pp. 231–2.
85 Warburton 'A Defence of the preceding Discourse' (1746), *WWW*, IX, p. 308.
86 W. Warburton, *Nature of the national offences* (1745: T039702), pp. 19, 20.
87 W. Warburton, *Sermon preached ... for the suppression of the late unnatural rebellion* (1746: T004534), pp. 28–9.
88 Warburton to Hurd, [1752] (*LLEP*, pp. 80–1).
89 Warburton, *Natural and civil events*, pp. 9, 10.
90 Ibid., p. 6.
91 W. Warburton, 'Sermon preached ... January 30, 1760', *WWW*, X, p. 19.
92 Ibid., p. 38.
93 Napthine and Speck, 'Clergymen and Conflict'.
94 Warburton, 'Sermon preached ... January 30, 1760', p. 38.
95 W. Warburton, 'Sermon preached at Bristol, November 29th, 1759', *WWW*, X, p. 128.
96 Warburton, *A people's prayer for peace* (1761: N026094), pp. 21–2.
97 S. Greenberg, 'Liberty and Necessity', in J. Harris (ed.), *Oxford Handbook of British Philosophy in the Eighteenth Century* (Oxford, 2013), pp. 248–69.

98 Warburton John Jortin, 30 July 1750 (*LI*, II, pp. 179–81).
99 Warburton to Atwell, 9 December 1755 (Kilvert, pp. 257–8). See also Warburton to Hurd, [December 1755] (*LLEP*, p. 149).
100 J. Wesley, *Serious thoughts* (1756: N022199), p. 3.
101 Ibid., p. 4.
102 Ibid, p. 17.
103 Ibid., p. 18.

Chapter 17

A due degree of zeal: enthusiasm and Methodism

William Warburton hated *Credulity, Superstition and Fanaticism*, William Hogarth's 1762 print. 'It is a horrid composition of lewd obscenity & blasphemous profaneness for which I detest the artist & have lost all esteem for the man', Warburton groused.[1] Hogarth's print satirized Methodists in general and George Whitefield (1714–70) and John Wesley (1703–91) in particular. At the print's foot lay the admonition, 'Believe not every Spirit; but try the Spirits whether they are of God: because many false Prophets are gone out into the World' (1 John 1:4). Atop it loomed a cross-eyed preacher, meant to be Whitefield. He was a disguised Jesuit whose wig covered a tonsured head and whose cassock hid a harlequin's costume. He dangled a witch from one hand and a devil from the other, while raving to the congregation, which he whipped into paroxysms of religious fervour. Some of his congregants had been driven mad; others had been driven to immorality. All were disordered in one way or another, with emotions, as the spiritual thermometer showed, fluctuating between madness and madness. Above them all hung a 'Globe of Hell' to which a preacher (meant to be Wesley) pointed and at which a wild-eyed congregant gaped in horror.

Credulity, Superstition and Fanaticism was a revised version of an earlier unpublished print called *Enthusiasm Delineated*. In that 1759 original, Hogarth had given what he described as 'a lineal representation of the strange Effects of Literal and low conceptions of Sacred Beings as also of the Idolatrous Tendency of Pictures in Churches and prints in Religious books &c.' In particular, he satirized Roman Catholic Eucharistic doctrine, depicting most of the congregants either holding or eating Christ. In *Credulity, Superstition and Fanaticism*, Hogarth removed the anti-transubstantiation images from *Enthusiasm Delineated*, tweaked other parts and lampooned Methodism instead of popery, suggesting how interchangeable they were to him.[2]

Hogarth's identification of Methodism with popery was not novel: it had been a central theme of anti-Methodist polemic from the start.[3] His contemporaries objected to Methodism for other reasons too, including its 'novelty',

Figure 6 William Hogarth, *Credulity, Superstition and Fanaticism*, 1762

its clandestine nature, its emphasis on the 'new birth', its crypto-Jacobitism, its supposed social subversiveness and so forth.[4] The average English man or woman found much worrying about the new religious movement. But underlying most anti-Methodism was an often unspoken fear – fear of relapse into civil war – and it was related directly to the most common complaint about Methodists, that they were *enthusiasts* who lacked all *moderation*.[5] William Warburton's concerns with Hogarth's *Credulity, Superstition and Fanaticism* certainly had much to do with his worry that Methodists were less crypto-papists than they were latter-day Puritans, ones whose enthusiasm threatened to breed the credulity, superstition and fanaticism which had beset England during the bad old days of the late sixteenth and seventeenth centuries. He worried that Methodists were schismatics who threatened the post-revolutionary religious settlement. Around the time that Warburton was railing against Hogarth's prints, he was writing his two-volume *Doctrine of Grace*. That anti-Methodist tract, which drew responses from both Wesley and Whitefield, emerged from a sustained engagement with the English past.

This chapter details how William Warburton reached his way to the *Doctrine of Grace*'s conclusions. Firstly, it reveals how Warburton's engagement with George Whitefield's *Journals*; with John Byrom's work on enthusiasm; and with Daniel Neal's *History of the Puritans* shaped and sharpened his thinking about Methodism. Secondly, it anatomizes the argument of a long anti-Methodist manuscript – *The True Methodist* – that Warburton wrote during the mid-1750s, yet never published. Finally, it shows how Warburton reworked the *True Methodist*'s anti-Methodist arguments in his *Doctrine of Grace*. Running through all of Warburton's thinking on Methodism, from Methodism's emergence in the late 1730s until the end of his life, was a fear of enthusiasm. Precisely what constituted *enthusiasm* was up for debate during the eighteenth century.[6] Edmund Gibson defined it as 'a strong Persuasion of the Mind, that as they are guided in an extraordinary Manner, by immediate Impulses and Impressions of the Spirit of God. And this is owing chiefly to the Want of distinguishing aright between the ordinary and extraordinary Operations of the Holy Spirit'. Such enthusiasm, however well-intentioned, had 'mischievous Consequences.'[7] Shaftesbury was more pointed, relating enthusiasm to the passions and characterizing it as a kind of 'Panic, when the Rage of the People, as we have sometimes known, has put them beyond themselves; especially where Religion has had to do'.[8] Shaftesbury's contemporaries would not have missed his meaning, for while *enthusiasm* was a labile term during the eighteenth century, it was almost always associated with the disordered religious and political life of sixteenth- and seventeenth-century England. This chapter shows how and why contemporaries made that association.

During William Warburton's lifetime, Methodism was an intra-Anglican reform movement led by John Wesley and George Whitefield.[9] Its founders aimed to revitalize the Church of England's religious devotion, which they thought had become ossified, and to evangelize more broadly. 'What a dead and barren time has it now been, for a great while, with all the churches of the Reformation', the Calvinist evangelical William Cooper worried in 1741. 'The golden showers have been restrained; the influences of the Spirit suspended; and the consequence has been that the Gospel has not had any eminent success: conversions have been rare and dubious ... and the hearts of Christians not so quickened, warmed and refreshed under the ordinances, as they might have been.'[10] Evangelicals (of whom Methodists were a subset) sought to revive the spirit of the Reformation and of the early Christian

Church.[11] To spread 'heart religion', Wesley and Whitefield broke free from traditional parish structures – 'the world is my parish', Wesley famously proclaimed – and used voluntary religious societies, field preaching, love feasts and the like to evangelize, all the while remaining within the established Church of England.[12] In this way might the ethos of primitive Christianity be revived.[13] Not until later did Methodists break away from the Church of England. Nonetheless, many during the mid-eighteenth century thought of Methodists as Dissenters. Even so, Warburton's lasting opposition to the Methodists had little to do with their real or imagined schism. He was, after all, good friends with nonconformist divines like Philip Doddridge (1702–51), approving strongly of Doddridge's work on regeneration, a theme central to eighteenth-century debates over Methodism.[14] Instead, the Methodists worried Warburton primarily because feared a revival of seventeenth-century-like enthusiasm.

Warburton's first written take on Methodism came during the late 1730s, when he drafted a tract on Wesley, Whitefield and the Methodists. Warburton had read George Whitefield's *Journals* (1738), which exhibited some of the problems highlighted in Henry More's *Enthusiasm Triumphant* (1656).[15] Warburton's first instinct was to liken Whitefield, Wesley and their followers to sixteenth- and seventeenth-century English religious Dissenters. It was a common move. In 1739, the Oxford high churchman Joseph Trapp linked Methodist 'field-conventicles' to the previous century's religious nonconformity. 'We have ... had something of this nature in England, as practised by Brownists, Anabaptists, Quakers, Ranters and such like', he complained. 'But for a clergyman of the Church of England to pray and preach in the fields, in the country, or in the streets in the city, is perfectly new.'[16] Historians since have teased out the connections between seventeenth-century religious nonconformity and eighteenth-century Methodism.[17] So too did contemporaries. Whitefield, Warburton reckoned, was 'as mad as ever George Fox the Quaker was'. Nor did he think highly of John Wesley, whom he mocked for aping native habits during his Georgian missions and whom he imagined would 'return thither and then will cast off his English dress with a dried skin like the Savages better to ingratiate himself with them'. It would be best for English 'virtue and religion' if 'our overheated Bigots' would go to America 'to cool themselves in the Indian Marshes'.[18] Barring that, 'the best way of exposing these idle Fanatics [was] the printing out of Geo[rge] Fox's Journal, and Ign[atius] Loyola, and Whitefield's Journals in parallel columns. Their conformity of folly is amazing.'[19] In a 1740 letter, he fleshed out his thinking more fully. 'I have been lately reading the Trials and last Behaviour of the Regicides', he explained to a friend. 'They were mostly, you know, Enthusiasts; but, what surprized me, of the same kind of the Methodists; and bottomed all on their grand principle, Regeneration.'[20] The issue of regeneration — what Daniel Waterland characterised as 'but another Word for the new Birth of a Christian' – lay at the heart of earliest anti-Methodist writings during the

1730s and 1740s. In 1740, Waterland explained that 'Scripture-Inspiration' had been the predominant sort of inspiration in Christian history, 'and all the other, so far as they have been considered as such, have passed off as Dreams'. However, England had a bad experience with enthusiasm during the seventeenth century. 'That Vanity seems to have commenced first herein England (since the Reformation, I mean) or however to have first made some Figure, about 100 Years ago, set up by persons who have neither Commission, nor Talents, nor Furniture proper for the Ministry.'[21] Those seventeenth-century ministers, in turn, had fomented rebellion and regicide. Both the regicides and the Methodists suffered from what William Warburton called a 'natural Enthusiasm'. Yet, Warburton warned that clamping down on the Methodists would radicalize them and destabilize politics since '[f]anaticism rises from oppression ever'. The object lesson for him was the 1630s and 1640s, when Laudian clergy sharply treated religious Dissenters. A century later, during the 1730s, 'the Clergy are right in giving no encouragement to this spirit, [as] appears from the dismal effects it produced amongst the Fanatics in Charles the First's time, who began with the same meekness and humility with these'.[22]

Nothing survives of Warburton's first attempt during the late 1730s to write an anti-Methodist tract.[23] But he returned again to the subject in the 1750s. Two things catalysed his later thinking on the subject. The first was John Byrom's poetry; the second was Daniel Neal's *History of the Puritans*. In late 1751, John Byrom (1692–1763) published *Enthusiasm: a Poetical Essay*. Byrom was a fellow of Trinity College, Cambridge, during the late 1710s, when he had sided with Richard Bentley against Conyers Middleton and the other fellows. A high churchman with Jacobite sympathies, he resigned his fellowship because he refused to take holy orders. He was friend both to the nonjuring mystic William Law and to John and Charles Wesley, so that, when he penned *Enthusiasm*, it was unsurprising that he chose not to make a blanket condemnation of his poem's subject.[24] In a prefatory letter, he observed that 'Enthusiasm is grown into a fashionable Term of Reproach' but that the 'indiscriminate Use of the Word has evidently a bad Effect: It pushes the general Indifferency to Matters of the highest Concern into downright Aversion'.[25] Rather than lump together all kinds of enthusiasm, it was best to distinguish a bad kind (which 'reigns and rages unsuspected') from another 'juster kind, the genuine Effect of a true Life and spirit, arising from what is lovely, harmonious, and substantial'.[26] Byrom expounded on this theme in the poem *Enthusiasm*, part of which dealt directly with Warburton's *Divine Legation of Moses*. Byrom claimed that Warburton had a 'heated Brain' whose 'Erudition so unblest' in the *Divine Legation* had rendered 'Christians, a brainsick, visionary Crew' instead of simply *sola scriptura* Protestants who 'read the Bible with a Bible view, / And thro' the Letter humbly hope to trace / The living Word, the Spirit, and the Grace'.[27]

After reading *Enthusiasm*, Warburton remarked to a friend that Byrom is 'plunged deep into the rankest fanaticism', but that 'I forgive him heartily, for he is not malevolent, but mad'.[28] Nonetheless, he disabused Byrom of his arguments, writing a letter to him in which he objected to Byrom's 'insinuations of my being an unbeliever, and an Enemy to Christianity'.[29] Rather than doubting revelation, Warburton protested that he had written books defending it. But, he noted, he and Byrom offered distinctly different proofs of revelation's truth: 'You would convince men of the truth of the Gospel by inward feelings; I, by outward facts and evidence'. Moreover, the two differed on what constituted *enthusiasm*. 'You suppose enthusiasm consists in the mind's being carried with eagerness and violence towards its object', Warburton charged. 'I imagine this alone does not constitute the passion; and that, justly to charge the mind with this weakness, you should add that, in it's progress, for the establishment of the supposed truth which it makes its object, the conviction of its conclusions exceed the evidence of its principles'. If one suffers from this sort of enthusiasm, 'truth begins to be betrayed', to religion's detriment. In a subsequent exchange of letters, Byrom tried to mollify Warburton, while Warburton tried to clarify his thoughts regarding enthusiasm. In particular, Warburton distinguished between 'innocent' and 'hurtful' forms of enthusiasm, 'the first of which is chiefly employed in drawing pictures from the imagination; the other, in advancing opinions as the result of the judgment'.[30] Neither man convinced the other, but their disagreement did not metastasize into full-on polemical war either. This itself was unusual for Warburton.

Warburton's consideration of Daniel Neal's *History of the Puritans* (1732–38) formed a second stimulus to his thinking about Methodism. In March 1755, he was appointed a prebend of Durham cathedral. In the cathedral's library, he found a copy of Neal's *History* 'but not one answer. This disgusted him; and provoked him to make ... lively remarks' in the margins. At some point, John Price (1735–1813), the Bodleian librarian, got a copy of Warburton's copious annotations.[31] It is unclear exactly when Warburton read and annotated the Neal volumes, which remain in the cathedral library. There is no internal evidence from the volumes themselves. Warburton first visited Durham in May 1755.[32] The first reference to the annotations is in a 1765 letter, in which Warburton recounted a dinner-table conversation with Archbishop Thomas Secker. By this time Warburton had been bishop of Gloucester for nearly five years. The discussion at Lambeth Palace turned to Gloucester Ridley's forthcoming answer to Thomas Phillips's life of Cardinal Reginald Pole (1500–58). Warburton noted to Secker that 'during one of my residences I took [Neal's *History*] home to my house, and, at breakfast-time, filled the margins quite through; which I think to be full confutation of all his false facts and partial representations'.[33] The marginalia, then, could have been made no earlier than early 1755 and likely no later than mid-1760, the last time we have evidence of Warburton visiting Durham.[34]

Like Zachary Grey, who had also annotated Neal's *History of the Puritans*,

William Warburton thought that Neal had misrepresented Puritans and Puritanism. Firstly, Puritans had always been enthusiasts and fanatics. For instance, Warburton inveighed against Neal's treatment of Puritan responses to William Barrett's anti-predestinarian sermon in Cambridge and of Archbishop Whitgift's subsequent Lambeth Articles (1595). He observed of Neal's treatment,

> See the feverish State of a puritanical Conscience. These men could set Church and State in a flame for square caps, surplices, and the cross in Baptism, while they swallowed, and even contended for these, honourable Decrees: the frightful and disordered Dreams of a crude, sour tempered, peasanting Bigot: who counterworks his Creature and makes God after man's image and chooses the worst model he could find, himself.[35]

Later, he concluded that 'fanaticism was called Religion by Oliver [Cromwell], just as cant is called Religion by [Neal]'.[36] That Puritan 'fanaticism' compensated for profound ignorance: to make up for 'want of acquired knowledge', Puritan ministers 'abounded in inspired' knowledge.[37] These were the people Warburton ultimately blamed for the seventeenth-century English 'troubles'; and he reckoned that the spirit of enthusiasm had survived into the mid-eighteenth century. 'A mad fanatic ... will always draw the people after him', he concluded of the Dedham lecturer John Rogers (*c.* 1570–1636), before adding, 'We have at present of these bull-finches without number, and their wild notes are as awakening as ever'.[38] The 'bull-finches' of Warburton's day were the Methodists.

In addition to being fanatical enthusiasts, Puritans always had been rebellious and persecutory because they sought to overturn the English church-state arrangements and to punish those who opposed their schemes. Even during the 1580s, Puritans had not wanted just the 'relief' of a 'toleration', but had aimed secretly for 'an establishment'. Their goal, Warburton believed, 'was to bring in their discipline by degrees; first to quarrel with surplices and square caps; then to cavil with the common prayer; and lastly to condemn episcopacy'.[39] As the decades wore on, Puritan goals remained constant. Neal had bragged that it was 'the Honour of the present Generation of those commonly called Presbyterians' that they had abandoned their desire of the 1640s to enforce 'an absolute Uniformity, which can never be maintained but upon the Ruins of a good Conscience' and had instead defended the 'Civil and Religious Liberties of Mankind upon the most solid and generous Principles'. Warburton countered that 'it is no wonder that a tolerated sect could espouse these principles of Christian Liberty, which support their toleration'. However, when Presbyterians (a term he used interchangeably with *Puritans*) led the established Church during the mid-seventeenth century, they adhered 'to the old principle of intolerance'. Indeed, 'the use of force in religious matters' was one of 'their two darling points' which had led them to foment civil war.[40] To restrain innately rebellious and persecutory religious minorities like the Puritans, England needed an established church: it was simultaneously a guarantor of truth and a prophylaxis against revolution. Yet, echoing points he had made years earlier in the margins of Clarendon's *History of the Rebellion*, Warburton insisted that no church government was divinely instituted. In particular, Richard Hooker's *Laws of the Ecclesiastical Polity* (1593–97, 1648, 1661) had been an 'unanswerable confutation of the Puritan principles, which, by the way, claimed their Presbytery as of divine right'.[41] Charles I and the Laudians had also misread Hooker when they cited him in support of episcopacy's divine warrant. For Warburton, then, all debates on forms of church government were unnecessarily divisive debates.

While Warburton highlighted Puritanism's corrosive and fissiparous effects, he also noted the divisive effects of Elizabethan anti-Puritan polemical divinity. When Daniel Neal came to the Babbington Plot in his *History*, he recounted the testimony of one of the plotters, the Roman Catholic priest George Ballard (d. 1586). Under interrogation, Ballard reportedly argued that the works of Archbishop John Whitgift (1530–1604) rebutting Thomas Cartwright (1534–1603) had unwittingly done much 'to prove [Ballard's] Doctrine of Popery'. In the margins of Neal's *History*, Warburton observed that Whitgift's anti-Puritan works had suffered from traits that had been 'the general fault of Controversial Divines ... in every age since the Apostolic times. In combatting one extreme they fall into another; and while they are opposing their Enemies on the right hand, give advantages to those on their left'. Many polemical divines fought 'only for their Party, their reputation and advancement' and acted 'like mere Engineers, who never inquire whose ground it is they stand upon, while they are erecting a Batter against their Enemies'. Many others were like Whitgift, 'who are combatting honestly for what they think the truth': yet even they, Warburton concluded, often fell into the trap of immoderation, despite their caution.[42] Undoubtedly religious enthusiasts like the Puritans posed the greatest threat to the civil order, but their orthodox opponents were not immune from fault either.

Around the time he read Daniel Neal's *History of the Puritans*, Warburton wrote an anti-Methodist treatise which he called *The True Methodist, or Christian in Earnest*.[43] He prepared the work for publication in July 1755, but never actually published it. Warburton aimed in this long treatise to contrast the 'true Methodist' with the 'modern Enthusiastics' who had led people into 'False Methodism'. *The True Methodist* was a slightly indirect work, never mentioning either Wesley or Whitefield by name. Nonetheless, they were the unmistakable anti-types of Warburton's 'true Methodist'.[44] A few salient themes stand out in this otherwise slightly disjointed manuscript. Firstly, the primitive Church remained the touchstone of doctrinal and liturgical orthodoxy. Primitive Christians were 'the standing Example to all Christians, in all succeeding ages of the Church both of the Practicality of those precepts, which Christ enjoined, and of the certainty of the truth he revealed'.[45] Yet the lengths to which primitive Christians had gone in their 'voluntary mortifications' of the flesh and in their 'rigorous self Denials' were inappropriate during the eighteenth century. Early Christians had faced unrelenting persecution and, understandably, had used their sufferings as missionary tools. 'Their life then was properly and indeed a warfare', Warburton reckoned. 'They had Principalities and powers in High places to contend with, and no other weapons but the word of God, the sword of the spirit, wherewith to conquer the enemy, or defend themselves'.[46] The eighteenth-century Church of England, by contrast, enjoyed the state's support. That state support rendered the primitive austerities unnecessary, especially because they smacked of the 'severities' which the Church of Rome had copied from early monastics and had later endorsed 'in all her Dreams of Image Worship, Purgatory, Merits, Indulgences, and even of Transubstantiation'. None of this meant that the primitive example should be jettisoned: Warburton insisted that '[w]e have the same Enemies to combat as they had'. However, eighteenth-century English Christians needed to recognize that 'the Disposition of the Battle, and the posture of the Enemy, be changed'.[47] Not least among these changes, the English Church was legally established.

The second theme running through Warburton's manuscript was that the 'true Methodist' recognizes the Church of England's perfections. '[H]is Church is truly Christian, truly Orthodox, without spot or wrinkle or any such thing', Warburton boasted.[48] The English Church's only 'Imperfections' had to do with the nature of 'our Establishment', especially with the sacramental tests which Warburton thought religious dissenters might easily evade and, thus, profane. Nevertheless, the more that the 'true Methodist' 'examines the Constitution of our Church, and the further he tries it by the Scriptures, or the Original Model of the purest Ages of Primitive Christianity; the more consonant and agreeable to both he discovers it to be'.[49] In particular, the Thirty-Nine Articles and the catechism, which together contained the Church of England's doctrinal essence, jibed perfectly with the Scriptures. On the two thorny issues of Christology and predestination, the articles of religion especially stood out for praise. Regarding God's nature, the articles left 'no room to doubt as to her Judgment'; regarding predestination, the articles were 'cautiously worded, with a pious Design to avoid the two Extremes of limiting Divine Prescience on one hand, and man's free Will on the other'.[50] The established English Church, then, was not one from which anyone who valued either scriptural or primitive precedent would want or need to separate.

The third theme which ran through Warburton's manuscript was that the 'true Methodist' tries to control his sinful nature through prudent, non-zealous means. He realizes that 'the Flesh, the world, and the Devil' tempt him, but he develops a method that does not itself involve 'usurping the authority of God, making new Laws for him and his People'.[51] In particular, he follows the guidance of the Cambridge Platonist Henry More (1614–87) – 'the most spiritual Man and truest Methodist of the last age' – who carefully distinguished between 'what is Good and what is Evil and what is indifferent'.[52] In so doing, he takes care to have a 'due regulation of the Limits and Bounds of Christian Liberty' and be 'careful to observe the Golden mean'.[53] Warburton's genuine Methodist was someone who self-moderated his zeal. The Church of England's rubrics offered ways to help with that self-moderation, so that fidelity to them was a mark of the 'true Methodist'. As Warburton explained it, the genuine Methodist must 'live up to her Rules, and ... be a regular and exact Conformist to all her Orders and Institutions, ... to observe all her Fasts and Days of Abstinence; to keep all her Festivals Holy, especially her Sabbaths, and to reverence her Sanctuary; yea, every day, as far as he possibly can, to frequent the public Worship both Morning and Evening'.[54]

Within Warburton's analysis of self-moderation lay the gist of his soteriology. Like many of his contemporaries, Warburton believed in the Devil's active presence in the world. Satan is 'the grand Adversary of his soul', and the 'true Methodist' neither can know who Satan is and what he desires nor withstand Satan's temptation on his own. 'His Reason is no match at all to cope with the subtlety of the old serpent, the wiles and devices of Satan', Warburton insisted, 'and his Experience serves only to convince him, that he is no way equal to the Combat'.[55] Instead, he requires the support of God, whose 'Power [is] superior to his Enemy's strength'. After a close study of Satan's actions as recorded in the Bible, the 'true Methodist', furthermore, understands that Satan aims to 'affect the inner man, and defile the Soul or Spirit; particularly Pride and Envy, Malice and Revenge, Deceit and Guilt, Hatred of God and Goodness'.[56] Armed with this knowledge of Satan's strategy and with God's bolstering aid, the 'true Methodist' can work to constrain his passions and to withstand sin. God, of course does not expect humans to be exactly like Christ – 'to be Perfect instantaneously and at once; as some affectedly pretend to' – but he expects sincere efforts. Two things are required for this: repentance and reformation. 'He begins with the Business of Repentance', Warburton noted of the genuine Methodist. 'He considers himself as a sinner; yea, born in sin; his very birth tainted with it'.[57] Then, the genuine Methodist formulates a plan to help him control his passions: he 'lays down a scheme, and enters upon a proper method of restraining, yea of mortifying all the sinful Inclinations of corrupt Nature'.[58] When one did inevitably lapse into sin, the Church was there to help. In particular, Warburton argued, priestly absolution was a necessary part of the salvific process. Confession of sins must be made directly to God in 'private Devotions' but 'an authentic Pardon' required the priesthood: absolution comes 'from the mouth of God's appointed Minister; even from him, to whom is committed the Ministry of Reconciliation; one who is vested with Authority by Christ himself, to loose and to bind to remit or to retain Sins'.[59] The Church provided the tools to help with self-moderation and the means assuredly to secure forgiveness from God for failures of self-moderation.

A final theme running through Warburton's *True Methodist* dealt with political moderation. On Warburton's accounting, the 'true Methodist' did not take party stances either in politics or in religion. In his politics, he was 'neither Whig nor Tory; much less Republican or Jacobite: No, not Whig in State, and Tory in Church'.[60] Similarly, in his religion, he avoided 'basely complying with the Party Interest' but instead guarded 'against Extremes; with the Low he is High, with the High he is Low: with the violent he is moderate; with the Moderate he stirs up a due degree of Zeal'.[61] In all things the genuine Methodist avoids inciting or joining in conflict. Warburton characterized this simply as being a 'Christian; and from the Genius and Spirit, which animates His Religion, he forms all his Principles and Conduct with relation to Government'.[62] Being a 'true Methodist', then, necessarily entailed religious conformity, not schism.

Warburton never published *The True Methodist*, but some of its arguments made their way into his three-part *Doctrine of Grace*, which appeared in print in late 1762.[63] Less oblique in its criticism of Methodism than *The True Methodist*, *The Doctrine of Grace* mined John Wesley's published journals for material to link him and the religious movement he led to sixteenth- and seventeenth-century Puritans. Warburton seems to have begun the writing the *Doctrine of Grace* in late 1760 or early 1761, conceiving of it originally as a 'Discourse on the Holy Spirit'. His protégé Richard Hurd advised him early on to excise the last part of the work which focused on Wesley and the Methodists since 'the Methodists would say your Lordship had written against them; an honour, which, for their own sakes, one would not wish them'.[64] Warburton ignored Hurd's advice because he saw in Methodism something particularly insidious and something which the established Church's leaders had insufficiently addressed. 'The insolences of the Papists are rightly belaboured; but why does the madness of the Methodists escape Scot-free? Is superstition more fatal either to religion or government than fanaticism?', he wondered to Charles Yorke in November 1761. 'The attacks of Popery indeed, like those of the scorpion, are silent and insidious; those of Methodism, like the rattle-snake, give notice of its approach. But this makes no difference amongst those who are ignorant of the nature of these deadly pests of society.'[65] The next month, Warburton acknowledged to Hurd that '[m]y Discourse on the Holy Spirit grows upon me, especially the latter part about the Methodists, which is the part I could have wished have grown the least. But a wen grows faster than sound flesh.'[66] By late 1762, Warburton tellingly described it as 'my discourse on the subject of fanaticism', with John Wesley as 'the picture of fanaticism in a living example'.[67] There could be no doubt that the piece was primarily about the dangers Warburton saw in Methodism. Shortly after publication in early November 1762, Warburton even sent a copy of the *Doctrine of Grace* to Wesley asking for corrections.[68]

The product of a couple of decades of thinking about Methodism and enthusiasm, the two-volume *Doctrine of Grace* has generally been considered one of Warburton's less effective works.[69] Yet it was emblematic of polemical divinity during the first two-thirds of the eighteenth century. Firstly, it read eighteenth-century challenges in the light of England's sixteenth- and seventeenth-century upheavals. Secondly, it saw the source of contemporary religious challenges lying farther back, in the history of the early Christian church. Finally, the ways it tried to resolve those ancient disputes pointed up their ultimate irreconcilableness.

The Doctrine of Grace opened with a defence of the divine gift of tongues to the Apostles. Here Warburton countered Conyers Middleton's posthumous arguments in 'An Essay on the Gift of Tongues' (1752).[70] The Middleton–Warburton disagreement turned on biblical hermeneutics. In his essay, Middleton fleshed out an argument he had made in passing in his *Free Inquiry into the Miraculous Powers.* He argued that the gift of tongues to the Apostles referenced in Acts 2:1–13 was not permanent and was not even that important to their evangelism. The gift of tongues went only to the very first disciples and was intended as a sign of the Apostles' divine mission. 'It is evident ... from the facts and testimonies ... that the chief, or sole end of this gift of tongues, was, to serve as a sensible sign in that infirm state of the first Christians, that those, to whom it was vouchsafed, were under a divine influence, and acting on a divine commission', Middleton reckoned.[71] Moreover, the gift of tongues was not one that had 'a stable or permanent nature', but was, instead, 'adapted to peculiar occasions, and then withdrawn again, as soon as it had served the particular purpose'. Middleton, then, rejected outright the notion 'that from the first communication of it to the Apostles, it adhered to them constantly as long as they lived, so as to inable them to preach the Gospel to every nation, through which they travelled, in its own proper tongue'.[72] To have argued this much would have irked the orthodox, but Middleton's next step in his argument – in which he contended that the Bible's literary style proved that the gift of tongues was not permanent – especially bothered them.

Every reputable scholar, from the patristic fathers to Erasmus, had acknowledged that the New Testament lacked the beautiful style of the best classical literature and had, instead, 'particular imperfections' and 'barbarisms' throughout.[73] The Gospels and Pauline epistles especially suffered from literary infelicities. Matthew was reported to have written his Gospel 'in the Hebrew tongue, for the proper benefit of his countrymen. But we may probably suppose, that the reason of his chusing to write in that language, was his ignorance, or imperfect knowledge of Greek'. Neither were Mark, Luke or John more accomplished in Greek. John, in particular, 'as both the ancients and the moderns with one voice declare, was, of all the Apostles, the most barbarous in his language, and ignorant of letters'. Even Paul, 'the most eloquent of all the Apostles', was judged by many primitive fathers to have been 'either wholly ignorant, or but very moderately skilled in the Greek'.[74]

Instead of being granted Greek by the Holy Spirit, the Apostles had to learn it and then only because 'the necessities of their Apostolic function, and the task of preaching the Gospel, might induce them to apply them to themselves to the acquisition of it, even in their advanced life'.[75]

Warburton rejected Middleton's arguments regarding the gift of tongues, countering that the Apostles had received the gift lastingly and to help them in their evangelism.[76] Moreover, a few of the New Testament books were written 'by persons who acquired the knowledge of the Greek tongue by miraculous infusion, as at the say of Pentecost'.[77] The reason the duration and purpose mattered became clear when Warburton addressed the issue of biblical style. The Apostles had two evangelical missions: '1. The temporary and occasional instructions of those Christians whom they had brought to the knowledge of, and faith in, Jesus, the Messiah: 2. and the care of composing a Written Rule for the direction of the Church throughout all the ages'.[78] The implications of Middleton's arguments regarding Christianity's 'Written Rule' especially bothered Warburton. For in noting that the New Testament's style was coarse and unlettered, Middleton had implied that the Bible itself was not fully divinely inspired, that it was the product of ignorant and intellectually unsophisticated disciples. In the *Doctrine of Grace*'s first half, Warburton grappled with this issue. To begin with, even if the New Testament 'is utterly rude and barbarous, and abounding with every fault that can possibly deform a language', that did not prove 'such language not divinely inspired'.[79] Warburton also rejected the notion that the New Testament resulted from 'organic inspiration': the inconsistencies amongst the Gospel books themselves militated against the idea that 'the language of the Scripture was dictated by the Holy Spirit'. Moreover, to hold that the Gospel authors had directly transcribed the Holy Spirit's words would have been to fall into the precisely the same error as 'the Mahometans', who 'represented their Scriptures as sent them down from Heaven ready written'.[80] Warburton instead posited that the New Testament authors had benefited from 'partial inspiration', which is to say 'by watching over them incessantly; but with so suspended a hand, as permitted the use, and left them to the guidance, of their own faculties, while they kept clear of error; and then only interposing when, without this divine assistance, they would have been in danger of falling'.[81] In this way, God had ensured that the New Testament authors had produced 'an Unerring Rule of Faith and Manners' while at the same time 'obviat[ing] all those objections to inspiration which arise from the too high notion of it: such as trifling errors in circumstances of small importance'.[82] Warburton's Newtonian-inspired mechanistic explanation of God's providential superintendence of the natural world in miracles and prodigies applied to his explanation of human actions like evangelising and writing, as well.

The Doctrine of Grace targeted Conyers Middleton in its first half; John Wesley served as the target for its second half. Wesley's Methodists were but 'modern Fanatics' and like their fellow fanatics since antiquity had falsely claimed for themselves the Holy Spirit's influence. To catch out imposters, Warburton advised applying the 'Apostle's Rule' from James 3:17, which stipulated that 'The Wisdom that is from above is first pure; then peaceable, gentle and easy to be intreated, full of mercy and good fruits, without partiality, and without hypocrisy'. By all these measures, Wesley and the Methodists failed.

To begin with, they taught an impure faith. Wesley was a 'Knight-Errant', possessed of '[a] bravado that would have suited Ignatius Loyola in his first slippery ecstasies in the mire'.[83] Elsewhere Warburton argued that the non-juring mystic William Law (1686–1761) had 'begot Methodism and Count Zinzendorf rocked the cradle'.[84] In the process of making this argument, Warburton posited that doctrine and orthodoxy had always helped to counteract enthusiasm and fanaticism. Wesley had mistakenly rejected 'orthodoxy or Right Opinion' as 'but a very slender part of Religion, if any part of it at all'.[85] Warburton, by contrast, pointed to St Paul's insistence in Ephesians that 'Truth' (which 'consists in Orthodoxy or right Opinion') formed 'a full third of, at least of Religion'.[86] Moreover, early Protestant reformers had valued orthodoxy as an antidote to 'Popery': indeed, they 'for the sake of right opinion, occasioned so many revolutions in Civil as well in spiritual Systems'.[87] Those who adhered to orthodoxy, then, followed primitive and reformed precedent; those who rejected it succumbed to enthusiasm.

Not only did Methodists reject orthodoxy, they did so in a way similar to sixteenth- and seventeenth-century Protestant religious Dissenters. 'They, who now go under the name Methodists were, in the days of our Forefathers, called Precisians'.[88] Under Elizabeth I's 'firm administration', the Precisians 'barely disguised [their] native ferocity, in a feigned submission'. By Charles I's reign, though, the 'Precisians' had renamed themselves first as 'Puritans' and then as 'Independents' and had shown their true schismatical colours.[89] Methodists, on this reading, were heirs of the very same religious dissenters who had thrown the nation into civil war during the mid-seventeenth century and who had killed the king at that war's conclusion. And lest one question this 'Pedigree, which makes Methodism of the younger House of Independency', one could simply compare the spiritual accounts of the seventeenth-century English regicides with Wesley's and Whitefield's journals. In both, one would find 'so exact a conformity in the frenzy of sentiment, and even in the cant of expression, upon the subjects of Faith, Grace, Redemption, Regeneration, Justification &c as may fully satisfy him, that they are both of the same stock'.[90]

Confronted with schismatics in their midst, the eighteenth-century English Church and state had to formulate a response. Warburton again cautioned against 'persecution', not least because Methodists, in common with all other enthusiasts, actively hoped to be persecuted: 'Sectaries must either kick or be kicked. They must either persecute, or they must provoke persecution'.[91] Moreover, the English Church and state needed to tolerate Methodists because the 'Law of Toleration' was of the 'Divine Original'.[92] Toleration, though, was not without limits, either for religious Dissenters or for the established Church. On the one hand, Methodists and religious Dissenters could reasonably expect toleration from the English church-state but not the removal of religious tests for full civil liberties, since a religious test 'is a restrictive, and not a penal Law'.[93] On the other hand, echoing a theme he had worked out in *The True Methodist*, Warburton argued that it would benefit the established Church of England to live within legal restraints. It was, he contended, 'a certain Maxim, that an Established Religion, under a Toleration and a Test, will always go on enlarging its bounds; since the restraint this latter Law imposes, is so light, that it is considered rather as a small inconvenience than an injury'.[94] Give the Church of England security and it would draw in more and more adherents, Warburton reckoned. While the Church of England remained the nation's legally established church, Methodism grew to become the largest nonconformist denomination by the mid-nineteenth century. By then Methodists had become what Warburton and so many of his contemporaries thought they were – not-Anglican religious competitors who fuelled the religious cell-division of English religious life begun at the Reformation. By the mid-nineteenth century, though, the English Reformation was over and the hyper-pluralism instigated by the Reformation seemed less destabilizing than it had a century earlier when Warburton wrote his anti-Methodist tracts.

NOTES

1 Warburton to Thomas Newton, 17 April 1762 (D. Nichol, *Pope's Literary Legacy* (Oxford, 1992), pp. 147–8); B. Krysmanski, 'We See a Ghost: Hogarth's Satire on Methodists and Connoisseurs', *Art Bulletin* 80 (1998), pp. 292–310.

2 Part of the reason Hogarth revised *Enthusiasm Delineated* was that 'some friend suggested that the satire would be mistaken, and that there might be those who supposed [its] arrows were aimed at religion, though every shaft is pointed at the preposterous masquerade habit in which it has been frequently disguised': J. Ireland, *Supplement to Hogarth* (1798: T002313), pp. 233–50, at p. 248.

3 G. Lavington *Enthusiasm of Methodists and papists compared*, 2 vols (1754: T014048); Haydon, *Anti-Catholicism*, pp. 63–6; C. Haydon, 'Bishop George Lavington of Exeter (1684–1762) and *The Enthusiasm of Methodists and Papists, Compar'd*', *Southern History* 37 (2015), pp. 60–85.

4 M. Snape, 'Anti-Methodism in Eighteenth-Century England: The Pendle Forest Riots of 1748', *JEH* 49 (1998), pp. 257–81; J. Walsh, 'Methodism and the Mob', *SCH* 8 (1972), pp. 213–27; A. Lyles, *Methodism Mocked* (London, 1960).

5 Lyles, *Methodism Mocked*, pp. 32–43; M. Anderson, *Imagining Methodism in Eighteenth-Century Britain: Enthusiasm, Belief and the Borders of the Self* (Baltimore, 2012). Field, 'Anti-Methodist Publications of the Eighteenth Century: A Revised Bibliography', and Field, 'Anti-Methodist Publications of the Eighteenth Century:

A Supplemental Bibliography', provide a near-comprehensive list of anti-Methodist publications.

6 L. Laborie, *Enlightening Enthusiasm: Prophecy and Religious Experience in Early Eighteenth-Century England* (Manchester, 2015); J. Gregory, 'Articulating Anglicanism: The Church of England and the Language of "the Other" during the Long Eighteenth Century', in N. Green and M. Chatterjee (eds), *Religion, Language, Power* (London, 2008), pp. 148–55; J. Pocock, 'Enthusiasm: The Antiself of Enlightenment', *HLQ* 60 (1998), pp. 7–28.

7 E. Gibson, *Bishop of London's pastoral letter ... against lukewarmness ... and enthusiasm* (1739: T22834), pp. 19, 51.

8 A. Cooper, *Characteristics of Men, Manners, Opinions, Times* (Indianapolis, 2001), pp. 10–11.

9 J. Gregory, 'Religion in the Age of Enlightenment: Putting John Wesley in Context', *Religion in the Age of Enlightenment* 2 (2010), pp. 19–53, and J. Gregory, 'The Long Eighteenth Century', in R. Maddox and J. Vickers (eds), *Cambridge Companion to John Wesley* (Cambridge, 2010), pp. 13–43, survey the historiography of eighteenth-century Methodism.

10 Quoted in J. Walsh, '"Methodism" and the Origins of English-Speaking Evangelicalism', in M. Noll, D. Bebbington and G. Rawlyk (eds), *Evangelicalism* (Oxford, 1994), p. 20.

11 J. Walsh, 'The Anglican Evangelicals in the Eighteenth Century', in *Aspects de L'Anglicanisme* (Paris, 1974), pp. 87–102; J. Walsh, 'The Origins of the Evangelical Revival', in G. Bennett and J. Walsh (eds), *Essays in Modern English Church History* (Oxford, 1966), pp. 132–62.

12 P. Mack, *Heart Religion in the British Enlightenment: Gender and Emotion in Early Methodism* (Cambridge, 2008); J. Walsh, 'Religious Societies: Methodist and Evangelical, 1738–1800', *SCH* 23 (1986), pp. 279–302.

13 G. Hammond, *John Wesley in America: Restoring Primitive Christianity* (Oxford, 2014); E. Duffy, 'Primitive Christianity Revived; Religious Renewal in Augustan England', *SCH* 14 (1977).

14 Warburton to Doddridge, 5 August 1741 (T. Steadman (ed.) *Letters to and from the Rev. Philip Doddridge* (Shrewsbury, 1790: T095447)), pp. 197–8.

15 Warburton to Middleton, 12 August 1738 (BL, Egerton 1953, fol. 35).

16 Quoted in J. Walsh, *John Wesley, 1703–1791: A Bicentennial Tribute* (1993), p. 4.

17 J. Walsh, 'Elie Halévy and the Birth of Methodism', *TRHS* 25 (1975), pp. 1–20; J. Newton, *Methodism and the Puritans* (1964).

18 Warburton to Pierre Maizeaux, 16 September 1738 (BL, Add. 4288, fol. 240)

19 Warburton to Thomas Birch, 10 September 1739 (BL, Add. 4320, fols 156–7). Cf. Grey, *Quaker and the Methodist compared*; W. Gibson, 'Whitefield and the Church of England', in G. Hammond and D. Jones (eds), *George Whitefield: Life, Context and Legacy* (Oxford, 2016), pp. 46–62.

20 Warburton to Birch, 31 March 1740 (BL, Add. 4320, fols 165–6).

21 D. Waterland, *Regeneration stated and explained* (1740: T046654), p. 37.

22 Warburton to Birch, 31 March 1740 (BL, Add. 4320, fols 165–6).

23 Nor does the '29½ small quarto' letter from Warburton to Whitefield, 6 December 1737, appear to be extant: W. Warburton, *True Methodist; or, Christian in Earnest* (JRULM, 253B), front matter; 'The True Methodist; or, Christian in Earnest',

Notes & Queries 10 (27 February 1905), p. 167; F. Jackson, 'A Rare Tract by Bishop Warburton', *Proceedings of the Wesley Historical Society* 5 (1905–6), pp. 139–41. This letter is listed as being housed in the Gloucestershire Archives (shelfmark SB24.18GS), as part of its large Local Studies collection. However, after an exhaustive search in August 2015, the archivists determined that the letter is lost and had been noted as missing in 2014.

24 J. Watson, 'John Byrom (1692–1763)', *ODNB*.

25 J. Byrom, *Enthusiasm* (1752: N002281), p. v.

26 Ibid., p. vii.

27 Ibid., pp. 14, 15.

28 Warburton to Hurd, 2 January 1752 (*LLEP*, pp. 97, 98).

29 Warburton to Byrom, 12 December 1751 (Chetham's Library, Mun.A.6.87, no. 1). All quotations in this paragraph are drawn from this letter.

30 Warburton to Byrom, 3 April 1752 (Chetham's Library, Mun.A.6.87, no. 2). See also Byrom to Warburton, 22 February, 10 April 1752 (Dr Williams's Library, 186.2 [3i, iii]); William Law to Byrom, [1752] (Chetham's Library, Mun.A.6.87, no. 17).

31 J. Nichols, *Biographical and Literary Anecdotes of William Bowyer* (1782: T058716), p. 356; Warburton to Hurd, 21 March 1755 (*LLEP*, p. 187). Warburton's annotations, in volumes still housed in Durham Cathedral Library, were reprinted in W. Warburton, *Supplemental volume* (1788: T127849), pp. 455–511.

32 Warburton to Charles Yorke, 27 May 1755 (*LWCY*, p. 17).

33 Warburton to Hurd, 26 February 1765 (*LLEP*, pp. 356–7).

34 Warburton to David Garrick, 26 June 1760 (National Art Library, London, F8 F 40/Vol. XXXVI).

35 WNDN, I, p. 581. Cf. P. Lake, *Moderate Puritans and the Elizabethan Church* (Cambridge, 1982), pp. 201–26.

36 WNDN, II, p. 598.

37 Ibid., p. 597.

38 Ibid., p. 290.

39 WNDN, I, p. 483.

40 WNDN, III, pp. 408, 549–50. Cf. J. Gascoigne, 'The Unity of Church and State Challenged: Responses to Hooker from the Restoration to the Nineteenth-Century Age of Reform' *Journal of Religious History* 27 (1997); D. MacCulloch, *All Things Made New: The Reformation and Its Legacy* (Oxford, 2016), pp. 279–320; P. Lake, 'Business as Usual? The Immediate Reception of Hooker's *Ecclesiastical Polity*', *JEH* 52 (2001), pp. 456–86.

41 WNDN, I, p. 498.

42 Ibid., p. 482.

43 Warburton drafted the 205-folio *True Methodist* some time before mid-summer 1755 and revised it for press on 6 July 1755 after reading James Hervey's *Dialogue of Theron and Aspasio*, 'which savours strongly of Methodism': Jackson, 'A Rare Tract by Bishop Warburton'.

44 Warburton, *True Methodist*, fol. 50.

45 Ibid., fol. 176.

46 Ibid., fol. 178.

47 Ibid., fol. 184.

48 Ibid., fol. 119.
49 Ibid., fol. 116.
50 Ibid., fol. 117.
51 Ibid., fols 6, 13.
52 Ibid., fols 14, 15.
53 Ibid., fols 15, 16.
54 Ibid., fol. 119.
55 Ibid., fol. 22.
56 Ibid., fols 24–5.
57 Ibid., fol. 4.
58 Ibid., fol. 7.
59 Ibid., fol. 136.
60 Ibid., fol. 108.
61 Ibid., fol. 112.
62 Ibid., fol. 109.
63 Warburton to Hurd, 27 December 1761 (*LLEP*, p. 335); Warburton to Yorke, 11 September 1762 (*LWCY*, pp. 51–2).
64 Hurd to Warburton, 18 March 1761 (*LLEP*, pp. 321–2).
65 Warburton to Yorke, 29 November 1761 (*LWCY*, p. 44).
66 Warburton to Hurd, 27 December 1761 (*LLEP*, p. 335).
67 Warburton to Yorke, 11 September 1762 (*LWCY*, p. 51).
68 Wesley to Warburton, 26 November 1762 (J. Telford (ed.), *The Letters of the Rev. John* Wesley (1931), pp. 338–84).
69 J. Stephen, *Horae Sabbaticae* (London, 1892), pp. 346–8; C. Abbey, *The English Church and Its Bishops, 1700–1800* (1887), II, pp. 229–30.
70 C. Middleton, 'An Essay on the Gift of Tongues', in *MWCM*, pp. 79–103
71 Ibid., p. 87.
72 Ibid., p. 89.
73 Ibid., p. 91.
74 Ibid., pp. 95, 96.
75 Ibid., p. 102.
76 W. Warburton, *Doctrine of Grace*, in *WWW*, VIII, p. 261.
77 Ibid., p. 280.
78 Ibid., p. 266.
79 Ibid., p. 281.
80 Ibid., pp. 273–5.
81 Ibid., p. 276.
82 Ibid., p. 278.
83 Ibid., pp. 329, 332. Cf. Warburton to Thomas Secker, 5 March 1757 (LPL, Secker Papers 3, fols 232–3).
84 Ibid., pp. 324–43. Cf. Warburton to Doddridge, 12 February 1739, 1 July 1740 (Steadman (ed.), *Letters*, pp. 160–6, 172–6); Warburton to Birch, 31 March 1740 (*LI*, II, pp. 118–22).
85 Warburton, *Doctrine of Grace*, p. 345. This runs counter the putative Warburtonian aphorism that 'Orthodoxy is my doxy, and heterodoxy is another man's doxy': Watson, *Life of Bishop Warburton*, p. 636.
86 Warburton, *Doctrine of Grace*, pp. 346, 347.

87 Ibid., p. 347.
88 Ibid., pp. 362–3.
89 Ibid., p. 363.
90 Ibid., pp. 363–4.
91 Ibid., 362. Cf. J. Gregory, '"In the Church I will live and die": John Wesley, the Church of England, and Methodism', in Gibson and Ingram (eds), *Religious Identities*, pp. 147–78.
92 Ibid., p. 407.
93 Ibid., p. 416.
94 Ibid., p. 409.

Conclusion

This book has argued for thinking about eighteenth-century English history as a late chapter in England's long Reformation. The eighteenth century was an era in which the English still had to grapple with the theological, ecclesiological, liturgical and political difficulties unleashed by the Reformation. For this reason, eighteenth-century English print culture abounded with religious argument, much as sixteenth- and seventeenth-century English print culture had abounded with religious argument. But eighteenth-century debates over Reformation-generated questions about the nature of truth; the nature of the Church; and relation of Church and state got held in the aftermath of two seventeenth-century revolutions. So, while eighteenth-century English history might have been a late chapter in England's long Reformation, it was also a post-revolutionary chapter.

What did it mean for those Reformation debates to be held in post-revolutionary England? The primary idiom of eighteenth-century debates over Reformation questions was historical, which hardly surprises since from its very outset, the Reformation was historically minded. Confessionalization spurred interest in Christianity's history, just as confessional allegiances since the sixteenth century have often informed historical takes on the Reformation.[1] When eighteenth-century polemical divines like Daniel Waterland, Conyers Middleton, Zachary Grey and William Warburton combed through the historical record trying to locate when the primitively pure religion had been corrupted, they were thinking like Reformation figures, ones making polemical arguments about the Church of England and its confessional competitors and opponents. In the eighteenth century, though, they had more potential readers; more opportunities (and, at times, freedom) to make their arguments publicly; and less legal recourse to the state's coercive powers to prosecute (or to persecute) religious dissidents. These new opportunities and restrictions emerged from the seventeenth-century revolutions.

If the English Reformation ran longer than most normally have reckoned, the moment of its death, like that of its birth, came suddenly. By the late eighteenth century, the world in which Waterland, Middleton, Grey and Warburton had lived and argued seemed almost unrecognizable. A little more than a century after William Warburton died in the Gloucester bishop's palace, Mark Pattison (1813–84) reflected that '[h]e had been forgotten by the world long before his decease; and when he actually passed to the tomb, it was without more notice than a few lines in the Gentleman's Magazine'.[2] Pattison echoed the judgement of Warburton's contemporaries. In October 1779, the *Westminster Magazine* opened its review of Warburton's life acknowledging that his recent passing had marked an era's end. 'The Annals of Literature do not furnish an example of a more striking change in the manners of a People, than the alteration which has happened in the course of a few years in the public sentiments concerning some Writers who, though formerly esteemed the first ornaments of their Country, are now quite neglected and almost forgotten', the obituary opened. Warburton was one such writer. 'Tho' the object of fulsome adulation while his faculties were unimpaired, he lived several years longer than his fame; ... [and] he sunk silently into the grave, unnoticed and unlamented.'[3] There is a temptation to push back, to insist that Warburton and his fellow eighteenth-century polemical divines had lasting influence beyond their era. They were indeed consequential figures in their own day, ones whose works suffused the era's print culture. But the truth is that they also had faded in importance unmistakably by the last quarter of the eighteenth century. Warburton's works got collected together and reprinted in 1788, thanks to his dutiful acolyte Richard Hurd, but they sold poorly. Middleton was seen as an idiosyncratic figure. Zachary Grey was almost completely forgotten. Waterland had the longest afterlife because he got cast by the Oxford Movement as a Tractarian forerunner. But mostly he and his fellow polemical divines got remembered by name, not by argument.[4]

So, why were their arguments forgotten? Why, to put it slightly differently, did the English Reformation end? The 'disenchantment of the world' is one possibility. The most caffeinated versions of this supercessionist argument hold that the Scientific Revolution evolved into a secular and secularizing Enlightenment which together produced 'the Fatherless World', one which had 'wiped the slate clean of the very possibility that the natural world, and humanity's place within it, might be intelligible through revelation or any other species of religious experience'.[5] Less robust versions of the disenchantment thesis do not deny religion's importance in the modern world nor do they preclude the possibility that religious explanations might actually be correct explanations. Nonetheless they too hold that a congeries of seventeenth- and eighteenth-century things – 'Cartesian foundationalism', the 'post-Galilean natural science', 'the modern idea of moral order' and the Enlightenment not least among them – created a (perhaps artificial) distinction between *religion* and *reason*. Thereafter *reason* increasingly became the language with which people could debate things in the public sphere, while *religion* increasingly got confined to the private sphere and had no probative value in public debates. The 'enchanted' world was one 'in which Revelation, or religion in general, counted as a source of insight about human affairs'; we live now in a 'disenchanted' world, one in which human affairs are 'understood in purely this-worldly or human terms'.[6] Before the Enlightenment was 'the world we have lost'.[7]

And yet the figures who populate this book did not know that a world had been lost. Instead, they remained all too aware of their connections to that putatively lost world – they thought, indeed, that they lived in it. For this reason, other things likely account for the English Reformation's end. Three stand out in particular. Firstly, by the last quarter of the eighteenth century enough time had passed to make the seventeenth-century wars of religion less threatening than they had seemed earlier in the century. The Church–Whig alliance forged during the Walpolean regime had been meant to forestall the return of religious violence; but it had also bought time for the wounds of war, if not to heal, then at least to be encased in increasingly thick scar tissue.[8] The problems opened up by the Reformation had not been resolved, but the dangers attending their irresolution seemed slightly less threatening, though not wholly innocuous.

Secondly, the issues with which eighteenth-century English polemical divinity had been most concerned got supplanted by other, more urgent ones. Some of those centred on England's empire. Religious and imperial imperatives were not mutually exclusive, but, after the Seven Years War, maintaining the post-revolutionary religio-political order proved harder as the imperatives of Church and a geographically expanding state often rubbed up uneasily against one another.[9] Other practical issues concerned changing English religious demographics and different realities regarding religion and politics. Beginning in 1828, the English Parliament successively repealed the Test and Corporation Acts; emancipated Roman Catholics from civil penalties; and set up the Ecclesiastical Commission thoroughly to reform the Church. A century's worth of indemnity acts and a growing number of Protestant nonconformists made the Test and Corporation Acts seem like an awkward holdover from an earlier age: rather than justify those acts, the state jettisoned them. Roman Catholics got the vote after County Clare returned Daniel O'Connell as a member for Parliament in 1828: rather than justify civil disabilities against Catholics, the state jettisoned them. Faced with a Church whose medieval organization, finances and governance seemed inadequate to the demographic realities of the nineteenth century, Parliament tried to reform away the inadequacies.[10] Together these parliamentary moves signalled that England was a nation with a disestablished established Church which answered to the state. Moreover, it signalled that the truth of a religion mattered not where matters of Church and state were concerned. Absent the French Revolutionary and Napoleonic Wars, during which the Church of England vocally and actively demonstrated its loyalty to the English state, such reforming measures would likely have been enacted a generation earlier.[11]

Finally, the English Reformation ended because it failed. It did not fail pastorally, though perhaps it took a bit longer to Protestantize England than historians once thought.[12] Evidence abounds of Protestants being Protestant by the mid-sixteenth century; and by the eighteenth century being Protestant was a central feature of English and British national identities.[13] But the English Reformation did fail intellectually. And much of the fault for that lies with the polemical divines who have been the subject of this book.

Neville Figgis (1866–1919), a gimlet-eyed scholar of Church and state, glimpsed the failure more than a century ago.[14] In 1905, Figgis argued that '[t]here are two great tasks before the Church. Both are predominantly intellectual. Yet without them practical work must first become hollow and then disappear.' The first task was 'apologetics proper'; and he insisted that '[w]e need to convince the individual that the Christian faith is not an excusable survival among the vulgar, not an emotional eccentricity of the cultivated, but is at once the condition and consequence of personal and intellectual development, when it is complete'.[15] Figgis greatly admired William Warburton, but he did not think much of eighteenth-century polemical divinity. When fretting about the 'intellectual crisis' facing the early twentieth-century Church of England, for instance, Figgis advocated that 'Religion must be presented so as to be interesting. Much of the evil lies in a survival of the eighteenth-century spirit'.[16] That spirit, he reckoned, had reduced Christianity to 'a mere decorated natural religion' when what was needed was 'a redemptive, supernatural, electric force, a new life'.[17] He also noted that the historicization of Christianity had led to a surge in 'comparative religion' which itself encouraged 'men [to] suspect all that is unique in the claims of Christianity'.[18] The reduction of Christianity to natural religion was, on his reading, a consequence of its historicization in the early modern period.

While Figgis's analysis of the eighteenth century's theological legacy surely owed something to his Victorian Anglo-Catholicism, his analysis was also spot on. Eighteenth-century English polemical divines had undoubtedly produced works which were intellectually effective during their own time, but which were also intellectually unpalatable in the long run. Some during the eighteenth century and most everyone during the nineteenth century complained that that the eighteenth century's polemical divinity was arid and tendentious.[19] Georgian England's polemical divines thought they were fighting a theological and political war. The past was the terrain upon which the 'warfare upon earth' got fought; historical scholarship was the chief weapon deployed in that war; and reason was the litmus test for an historical interpretation's truth. What they did was not a game to them but a fight over truth that had practical consequences. That fight's very seriousness surely contributed to its uncompromising character. Yet perhaps there was also something in eighteenth-century polemical divinity's method in fighting that war that was self-defeating? Perhaps, put another way, eighteenth-century polemical divines barrelled to the end of an intellectual cul-de-sac? For historical scholarship did not solve the epistemological and theological problems raised by the Reformation. Instead, it opened up only more and more topics – including Christianity's claim to being the only 'true religion' – to scrutiny.[20]

The inability of eighteenth-century polemical divines to resolve the Reformation-spawned theological problems related to the second of Figgis's 'great tasks before the Church': 'investigating the place of the self-conscious Church in the modern State'. The task, as he conceived it, was 'to show that the Church may claim a due independence, because it is a life not a contrivance; an organism not an organisation'.[21] As Figgis acknowledged, this was not a theological task but a political one. The question to be answered did not concern the Church's divine nature or authority but, instead, 'What rights has the religious society which the State is bound to acknowledge on pain of being false to itself?'[22] Figgis reckoned that during the eighteenth century William Warburton had thought especially insightfully about this subject: he had seen 'further than many of his contemporaries into the real meaning and purpose of an Established Church, of the correlative rights and duties it implied, and had a clearer view than his fellows of the effects of such a system in acting as a safeguard against bigotry'.[23] Not long afterwards, Norman Sykes, an admirer of Figgis, insisted that Warburton had offered the best 'enunciation of the doctrine of the inherent sovereignty and independence of the Church within its proper sphere' and that the *Alliance between Church and State*'s 'exposition of the relations of church and state possess a closer correspondence with the modern situation of their alliance than most rival theories'.[24] Both Figgis and Sykes thought that the seventeenth-century Laudians and their nineteenth-century Tractarian admirers had focused inappropriately on the ancient questions of divine right and authority rather than on the nature of the post-sixteenth-century Church and its relation to the 'modern State'.[25] The problem was that the modern state had not lived according to the terms of the Warburtonian alliance. It had not let the Church be the state's subordinate partner in return for recognition that it was an independent, voluntary society and one that earned the state's protection through its support for the state. Figgis understood that the Reformation had altered the balance of power between Church and state, indeed had created the very distinction of Church *and* state.[26] One consequence of the Reformation was the creation of the concept of what he called 'the Great Leviathan'. The Peace of Augsburg (1555) formalized the *cujus region ejus religio* principle ('the notion of Henry VIII') that 'one elector could say quite readily that his people's conscience belonged to him'. Subsequently Jean Bodin and Thomas Hobbes formulated 'a complete theory of the State' which 'denied every kind of right not derived from the sovereign'.[27] In the late seventeenth century, the English monarch embodied the state, while, in the eighteenth century, Parliament established itself as England's Leviathan. In between, the British Isles got torn apart by wars. But what had caused those wars?

Eighteenth-century polemical divines would have explained that the wars of the seventeenth century were religious wars which themselves had emerged from the Reformation.[28] The work of eighteenth-century polemical divinity was grappling with the Reformation's unresolved and destructive theological and political legacies. To do so, polemical divines relitigated the ancient and English pasts, thinking that this relitigation could establish which Christian doctrines were true and which were not. It failed in the first of Figgis's two tasks (apologetics) because historical scholarship proved inconclusive, not definitive. That historical relitigation also failed in Figgis's second task (defending the Church's independence) because it failed to diagnose the Reformation's most important legacy, the state's sacralisation. As Figgis recognized, during the early modern period, 'the religion of the State ... replaced the religion of the Church'.[29] The modern state was not created in response to seventeenth-century religious wars: its creation was the very cause of those wars.[30] Most eighteenth-century English polemical divines either did not recognize or could not admit that the modern state had subjugated the Church, that Leviathan had won. They thought that historical scholarship could reveal the pure Christian truths and that a supportive state could enforce those truths. Instead, the state, not history, became truth's arbiter. Heresy eventually became that which threatened the civil order, not that which wilfully contravened Truth; and non-state institutions like churches which made truth claims independent of the state's authority were increasingly viewed as suspect at best, anathema at worst. For this reason, Figgis saw rightly, '[m]ore and more it is clear that the mere individual's freedom against an omnipotent State may be no better than slavery; more and more it is evident that the real question of freedom in our day is the freedom of smaller unions to live within the whole'.[31] The history of post-Reformation England has shown that the 'omnipotent State' has been willing to tolerate the Church of England only so long as it has served the state's interests, which is to say only so long as the Church makes truth-claims and enjoins behaviours which the state deems non-threatening. When the state's imperatives and those of its established Church part, the English Church inevitably bends to the state's will rather than getting 'dragged ... under the Juggernaut car of reason of State'.[32] The 'Great Leviathan' answers only to itself.

NOTES

1 P. Lake, '"Puritans" and "Anglicans" in the History of the Post-Reformation English Church', in A. Milton (ed.), *Oxford History of Anglicanism Volume II* (Oxford, 2017), pp. 352–79; E. Duffy, *Reformation Divided: Catholics, Protestants and the Conversion of England* (2017), pp. 1–15; D. MacCulloch, *All Things Made New: The Reformation and Its Legacy* (Oxford, 2016), pp. 239–55; A. Walsham,

'History, Memory and the English Reformation', *HJ* 55 (2012), pp. 899–938; B. Gregory, 'The Other Confessional History: On Secular Bias in the Study of Religion', *History and Theory* 45 (2005), pp. 132–49; J. Kirby, *Historians and the Church of England: Religion and Historical Scholarship, 1870–1920* (Oxford, 2016), pp. 165–88.

2 M. Pattison, 'Life of Bishop Warburton', in Nettleship (ed.), *Essays by...Mark Pattison* (Oxford, 1889), p. 154.

3 'Anecdotes of Dr. William Warburton', *Westminster Magazine* (October 1779), pp. 499, 500.

4 J. Stephen, *Horae Sabbaticae* (London, 1892), pp. 349–50.

5 A. Pagden, *The Enlightenment* (2013), pp. 79–124. See also J. Israel, 'J.G.A. Pocock and the "Language of Enlightenment" in His *Barbarism and Religion*', *JHI* 77 (2016), pp. 107–27; J. Israel, '"Radical Enlightenment" – Peripheral, Substantial, or the Main Face of the Trans-Atlantic Enlightenment (1650–1850)', *Diametros* 40 (2014), pp. 73–98. If we take the most muscular supercessionist account of the Enlightenment seriously, the sorts of theological, ecclesiological, liturgical and political issues which consumed the attentions of eighteenth-century English polemical divines are almost self-evidently irrelevant. Yet the argument for an areligious Enlightenment that (decisively) exposed religion's intellectual baselessness now finds increasingly dwindling scholarly support: W. Bulman, 'The Enlightenment for the Culture Wars', in W. Bulman and R. Ingram (eds), *God in the Enlightenment* (Oxford, 2012), pp. 1–41; D. Van Kley, 'The Varieties of Enlightened Experience', in ibid., pp. 278–316; I. Hunter, 'Secularization: The Birth of a Modern Combat Concept', *Modern Intellectual History* 12 (2015), pp. 1–32; B. Young, 'Enlightenment Political Thought and the Cambridge School', *HJ* 52 (2009), pp. 235–51; B. Young, 'Religious History and the Eighteenth-Century Historian', *HJ* 43 (2000), pp. 849–68. More generally, see B. Gregory, 'No Room for God? History, Science, Metaphysics and the Study of Religion', *History and Theory* 47 (2008), pp. 495–519.

6 C. Taylor, *Dilemmas and Connections* (Cambridge, MA, 2011), pp. 167–379, develops themes and responds to arguments made about C. Taylor, *The Secular Age* (Cambridge, MA, 2007).

7 Cf. J. Sheehan, 'When Was Disenchantment? History and the Secular Age', in M. Warner and J. VanAntwerpen (eds), *Varieties of Secularism in a Secular Age* (Cambridge, MA, 2010), pp. 217–42.

8 E. Nelson, *The Royalist Revolution: Monarchy and the American Founding* (Cambridge, MA, 2014), pp. 29–107, and C. Robbins, *The Eighteenth-Century Commonwealthman* (Cambridge, 1959), illuminate the ways in which the seventeenth-century revolutions got remembered differently in British North America.

9 J. Bell, *A War of Religion: Dissenters, Anglicans and the American Revolution* (2008); P. Langford, 'The English Clergy and the American Revolution', in E. Hellmuth (ed.), *The Transformation of Political Culture* (Oxford, 1990), pp. 275–308; P. Lawson, *Imperial Challenge: Quebec and Britain in the Age of the American Revolution* (Montreal, 1989), esp. pp. 126–46.

10 R. Strong, 'Anglicanism and the State in the Nineteenth Century', in R. Strong (ed.), *The Oxford History of Anglicanism. Volume III* (Oxford, 2017), pp. 92–115.

11 J. Innes, 'Parliament and Church Reform: Off and On the Agenda', in G. Pentland

and M. Davis (eds), *Liberty, Property and Popular Politics: England and Scotland, 1688–1815* (Oxford, 2016), pp. 39–57; R. Hole, *Pulpits, Politics and Public Order in England, 1760–1832* (Cambridge, 1989); H. Dickinson, 'Popular Loyalism in Britain in the 1790s', in E. Hellmuth (ed.), *The Transformation of Political Culture* (Oxford, 1990), pp. 503–34.

12 E. Duffy, 'The Long Reformation: Catholicism, Protestantism and the multitude', in N. Tyacke (ed.), *England's Long Reformation, 1500–1800* (1998), pp. 30–70; J. Gregory, 'The Eighteenth-Century Reformation: The Pastoral Task of the Anglican Clergy after 1689', in S. Taylor, J. Walsh and C. Haydon (eds), *The Church of England, c. 1689–c. 1833: From Toleration to Tractarianism* (Cambridge, 1993), pp. 67–85.

13 A. Ryrie, *Being Protestant in Reformation England* (Oxford, 2013); S. Hampton, 'Confessional Identity', in A. Milton (ed.), *Oxford History of Anglicanism Volume II* (Oxford, 2017), pp. 218–27; J. Martin, 'Early Modern English Piety', in ibid., pp. 395–411; L. Colley, *Britons: Forging the Nation, 1707–1837* (New Haven, 1992).

14 M. Goldie, 'J.N. Figgis and the History of Political Thought in Cambridge', in R. Mason (ed.), *Cambridge Minds* (Cambridge, 1994), pp. 177–92; D. Nicholls, *The Pluralist State: The Political Ideas of J.N. Figgis and His Contemporaries* (1994).

15 J. Figgis, 'The Church and the Secular Theory of the State', *The Official Report of the ... Annual Meeting of the Church Congress* (1905), p. 189.

16 J. Figgis, *Religion and English Society* (London, 1911), p. 10.

17 Ibid., pp. 19–20.

18 Ibid., p. 17. Cf. W. Bulman, *Anglican Enlightenment: Orientalism, Religion and Politics in England and Its Empire, 1648–1715* (Cambridge, 2015).

19 J. Overton and F. Relton, *The English Church from the Accession of George I to the End of the Eighteenth Century (1714–1800)* (1906), p. 1.

20 R. Serjeantson, 'David Hume's *Natural History of Religion* and the End of Modern Eusebianism', in J. Mortimer and S. Robertson (eds), *Intellectual Consequences of Religious Heterodoxy, 1600–1750* (Leiden, 2012), pp. 267–95. Cf. G. McCarren, 'Development of Doctrine', in I. Ker and T. Merrigan (eds), *The Cambridge Companion to John Henry Newman* (Cambridge, 2009), pp. 118–36; B. Daley, 'The Church Fathers', in ibid., pp. 29–46.

21 Figgis, 'The Church and the Secular Theory of the State', p. 189.

22 Ibid., p. 191.

23 J. Figgis, 'William Warburton', in W. Collins (ed.), *Typical English Churchmen* (London, 1902), p. 253.

24 N. Sykes, 'The Ideal of a National Church', in G. Harvey (ed.), *The Church in the Twentieth Century* (1936), p. 21; N. Sykes, *Church and State in England in the XVIIIth Century* (Cambridge, 1934), p. 324.

25 J. Figgis, *Churches in the Modern State* (1913), p. 187.

26 Ibid., pp. 81–2; J. Figgis, *Antichrist, and Other Sermons* (1913), pp. 257–66.

27 Figgis, *Churches in the Modern State*, p. 82.

28 Voltaire, *Letters on the English* (London, 2005), p. 67, made an analogous point: 'It is not Montaigne, nor Locke, nor Bayle, nor Spinoza, nor Hobbes, nor Lord Shaftesbury, nor Mr Collins, nor Mr Toland, etc, who have carried the torch of discord into their countries; it is in the main the theologians who, having begun by aiming at being heads of a sect, soon aimed at being heads of a party'.

29 J. Figgis, *Studies of Political Thought from Gerson to Grotius, 1414–1625* (Cambridge, 1907), p. 110.
30 W. Cavanaugh, *The Myth of Religious Violence: Secular Ideology and the Roots of Modern Conflict* (Oxford, 2009).
31 Figgis, *Churches in the Modern State*, pp. 51–2.
32 J. Figgis, *The Divine Right of Kings* (Cambridge, 1922), p. 332; M. Chapman, 'Church and State in England: A Fragile Establishment', in L. Lefebure (ed.), *Religion, Authority and the State: From Constantine to the Contemporary World* (2016), pp. 199–214. But cf. J. Morris, 'Anglicanism in Britain and Ireland', in J. Morris (ed.), *Oxford History of Anglicanism. Volume IV* (Oxford, 2017), pp. 397–435.

Index

CPSIA information can be obtained
at www.ICGtesting.com
Printed in the USA
BVHW051136021019
560008BV00006B/196/P

9 781526 143570